ROUTLEDGE HANDBOOK OF COMPLEMENTARY AND ALTERNATIVE MEDICINE

The provision and use of complementary and alternative medicine (CAM) has been growing globally over the last 40 years. As CAM develops alongside – and sometimes integrates with – conventional medicine, this handbook provides the first major overview of its regulation and professionalization from social science and legal perspectives.

The *Routledge Handbook of Complementary and Alternative Medicine* draws on historical and international comparative research to provide a rigorous and thematic examination of the field. It argues that many popular and policy debates are stuck in a polarized and largely asocial discourse, and that interdisciplinary social science perspectives, theorizing diversity in the field, provide a much more robust evidence base for policy and practice. Divided into four sections, the handbook covers:

- multi-disciplinary frameworks for analysis
- power, professions and health spaces
- risk and regulation
- critical perspectives on knowledge in CAM.

This volume will interest social science and legal scholars researching complementary and alternative medicine, professional identity and health care regulation, as well as historians and health policymakers and regulators.

Nicola K. Gale is a health sociologist based at the Health Services Management Centre at the University of Birmingham, UK. She started her career at the University of Warwick, where her PhD was a comparative ethnographic study of training colleges for homeopaths and osteopaths in the UK. Since then, she has developed a portfolio of research in the fields of health services research, public health, primary care, community-led health care and complementary and alternative health care. She is committed to theoretically informed empirical work that helps better understand, involve and meet the needs of a diverse population. Methodologically, she specializes in place-based and embodied qualitative methods, user involvement in health care and research, and public engagement in social sciences. Her research has been published in journals such as *Sociology of Health and Illness*, *Health and Place*, *Implementation Science*, *Medical Research Methodology*, *Family Practice* and *Complementary Therapies in Medicine*.

Jean V. McHale is Professor of Healthcare Law and Director of the Centre for Health Law Science and Policy at Birmingham Law School, University of Birmingham, UK. Her books include *Medical Confidentiality and Legal Privilege* (1993), *Health Law and the European Union* (2004, with Hervey) and *Health Care Law Text and Materials* (2nd edn, 2007, with Fox); edited collections include *Principles of Medical Law* (2010, with Grubb and Laing). Her new monograph, *European Health Law*, with Tamara Hervey, will be published in 2015.

ROUTLEDGE HANDBOOK OF COMPLEMENTARY AND ALTERNATIVE MEDICINE

Perspectives from social science and law

Edited by Nicola K. Gale and Jean V. McHale

Routledge
Taylor & Francis Group

LONDON AND NEW YORK

First published 2015
by Routledge
2 Park Square, Milton Park, Abingdon, Oxon OX14 4RN

and by Routledge
711 Third Avenue, New York, NY 10017

First issued in paperback 2017

Routledge is an imprint of the Taylor & Francis Group, an informa business

British Library Cataloguing-in-Publication Data
A catalogue record for this book is available from the British Library

Library of Congress Cataloging in Publication Data
Routledge handbook of complementary and alternative medicine: perspectives from social science and law / edited by Nicola Gale and Jean McHale.
p. ; cm.
Handbook of complementary and alternative medicine
Includes bibliographical references and index.
I. Gale, Nicola, editor. II. McHale, Jean V. (Jean Vanessa), 1965- , editor. III. Title: Handbook of complementary and alternative medicine.
[DNLM: 1. Complementary Therapies. 2. Delivery of Health Care. 3. Internationality. 4. Medicine, Traditional. 5. Risk Management. WB 890]
R733
615.5–dc23
2014035996

ISBN 13: 978–1–138–50343–4 (pbk)
ISBN 13: 978–0–415–81894–0 (hbk)

Typeset in Bembo
by Wearset Ltd, Boldon, Tyne and Wear

CONTENTS

FIGURES

TABLES

CONTRIBUTORS

Editors

Nicola K. Gale, MA, PhD, is a health sociologist based at the Health Services Management Centre at the University of Birmingham, UK. She started her career at the University of Warwick, where her PhD was a comparative ethnographic study of training colleges for homeopaths and osteopaths in the UK. Since then, she has developed a portfolio of research in the fields of health services research, public health, primary care, community-led health care and complementary and alternative health care. She is committed to theoretically informed empirical work that helps better understand, involve and meet the needs of a diverse population. Methodologically, she specializes in place-based and embodied qualitative methods, user involvement in health care and research, and public engagement in social sciences. Her research has been published in journals such as *Sociology of Health and Illness*, *Health and Place*, *Implementation Science*, *Medical Research Methodology*, *Family Practice* and *Complementary Therapies in Medicine*.

Jean V. McHale is Professor of Healthcare Law and Director of the Centre for Health Law Science and Policy at Birmingham Law School, University of Birmingham, UK. Her books include *Medical Confidentiality and Legal Privilege* (Routledge, 1993), *Health Law and the European Union* (CUP, 2004, with Hervey) and *Health Care Law Text and Materials* (Sweet and Maxwell, 2nd edn 2007, with Fox); edited collections include *Principles of Medical Law* (OUP, 2010, with Grubb and Laing). Her new monograph, *European Health Law*, for CUP with Tamara Hervey, will be published in 2015.

Authors

Jane Adams is an associate member of the Centre for the History of Medicine at the University of Warwick, UK where she completed her PhD and post-doctoral research. She has published on spas and hydropathy in Britain and on medical services in Herefordshire. A monograph entitled *Healing with Water: English Spas and the Water Cure, 1840–1960* will be published by Manchester University Press in 2015. Her current research focuses on holistic healing practices in nineteenth- and twentieth-century Britain and includes naturopathy, herbal medicine and spiritual healing.

Alexander Alich is the Director of FoxFire Institute of Shamanic Studies, which he founded in 1988. He opened his private practice in integrative medicine and shamanic practice in 1991. Alexander lectures internationally on shamanism and Native American medicine to the general public, health care practitioners and shamanic practitioners and has been published in a variety of specialty magazines, including *Sacred Hoop*, *Healing Today*, *CoMed* and *Shaman's Drum Journal*. Today he lectures and practises in Berlin, specializing in training shamanic practitioners, and maintains a special interest in ethical practice, professionalism and patient safety in the field of shamanism.

Ruth Barcan is Associate Professor in the Department of Gender and Cultural Studies at the University of Sydney, Australia. Her research explores the body in contemporary culture, with particular interests in nudity, nudism and complementary and alternative medicine. She is the author of *Nudity: A Cultural Anatomy* (Berg, 2004), *Complementary and Alternative Medicine: Bodies, Therapies, Senses* (Berg, 2011) and *Academic Life and Labour in the New University: Hope and Other Choices* (Ashgate, 2013).

Felicity L. Bishop is Lecturer in Health Psychology at the Centre for Applications of Health Psychology, University of Southampton, UK. She has an interdisciplinary programme of mixed methods research around contextual effects in health care, encompassing topics including: ethical, scientific and lay perspectives on use of placebos in clinical practice and research; uptake and adherence to treatments for back pain; applications and elaborations of the common-sense model of illness perception; utilization of complementary and alternative medicines and psychosocial mediators of their effectiveness; and mixing qualitative and quantitative methods.

Roberta Bivins is Associate Professor in the History of Medicine at the University of Warwick, UK. She is currently completing a monograph exploring the impacts of postcolonial immigration on medical research and health policy in post-war Britain. Her case studies include rickets, smallpox, tuberculosis and the genetic haemoglobinopathies, sickle cell anaemia and thalassaemia. Previous and ongoing work examines the cross-cultural transmission of medical expertise, particularly as exemplified by the transmission of acupuncture to the West (*Acupuncture, Expertise and Cross-Cultural Medicine*, 2000) and in interchanges between medical cultures, both orthodox and heterodox (*Alternative Medicine? A History*, 2007).

Heather Boon is a Professor and the Dean of the Leslie Dan Faculty of Pharmacy, University of Toronto, Canada. She completed her BScPhm at the University of Toronto in 1991 and her PhD in 1996. She is one of the founding Directors of the Canadian Interdisciplinary Network for Complementary and Alternative Medicine research and is the current President of the International Society of Complementary Medicine. Her primary research interests are the safety and efficacy of natural health products as well as complementary/alternative medicine regulation and policy issues. She is the author of a textbook on natural health products and over 130 academic publications.

Sarah Cant is a Principal Lecturer in Sociology at Canterbury Christ Church University, New Zealand. She has written extensively in the area of the sociology of complementary and alternative medicine, producing books, edited books, chapters and journal articles. Her co-authored book *A New Medical Pluralism? Alternative Medicine, Doctors, Patients and the State* (Routledge, 1999, with Sharma) made a significant contribution to the field. She has concentrated her studies on professionalization, professionalism and power within CAM and has recently extended her research to examine the use of complementary therapies by nurses and midwives in the NHS.

Jérôme Debons is a PhD student in sociology at the University of Geneva, Switzerland. He is working on carrier narratives of homeopathic doctors in the field of general practice. His books in the field of medical pluralism include *Les soins populaires en Valais. Rebouteux et faiseurs de secrets* (Sierre, Monographic, 2009) and *Le soin et la politique. Cinq médecines non conventionnelles et la LaMal* (with Hélène Martin, Lausanne, Les Cahiers de l'EESP, 2014).

Michael Dodson is the Associate Dean of the Melbourne Clinical School for the University of Notre Dame Australia, and is a current member of the Australian Government's Advisory Committee on Non-Prescription Medicine. He previously occupied a number of senior clinical and executive positions at the Therapeutic Goods Administration, including Head of the Office of Non-Prescription Medicines and Senior Clinical Advisor to the Office of Complementary Medicines.

John Harrington LL.B. (Dublin), BCL (Oxon) is Professor of Global Health Law at Cardiff University, UK. He has been a research fellow at the British Institute in Eastern Africa, the African Population and Health Research Centre (both Nairobi) and the European University Institute (Florence). He has written widely on health and the law in the UK, East Africa and at a global level. Publications include *Global Health and Human Rights: Legal and Philosophical Perspectives* (edited, Routledge, 2010), *Global Governance of HIV/AIDS: Intellectual Property and Access to Essential Medicines* (edited, Elgar, 2013) and *Towards a Rhetoric of Medical Law* (Glasshouse/Routledge, forthcoming 2015).

Morag Heirs studied psychology at the University of Glasgow (MA (Hons) Soc Sci) and the University of Strathclyde (Msc Research Methods), UK while also taking a range of courses in bodywork and therapeutic massage. On graduation Morag established a successful Glasgow-based clinic and worked as a research assistant for Glasgow Homeopathic Hospital. Morag moved to the University of York after winning one of the prestigious Researcher Development Awards in complementary medicine from the National Institutes of Health Research. While working as a postgraduate research fellow, Morag completed her PhD in Health Services Research, focusing on homeopathy in the treatment of ADHD in children. Morag worked for the Centre of Reviews and Dissemination as a Research Fellow in Systematic Reviews from 2008–2014 on projects across a range of health technologies using quantitative and qualitative synthesis techniques. Morag is currently focusing on her business as a companion animal behaviourist (Well Connected Canine), and as a tutor and MSc supervisor for the Northern College of Acupuncture.

Irehobhude O. Iyioha (Ireh Iyioha) (LLB (Hons), BL, LLM, PhD) is a Policy Consultant and Assistant Adjunct Professor of Health Law, Ethics and Policy at the John Dossetor Health Ethics Centre, Faculty of Medicine and Dentistry, University of Alberta, Canada. She has served as Senior Policy Analyst (Legislation and Regulation) with Alberta's Health Ministry (Alberta Health, Canada) and as Policy Resercher on a special project with the Ontario Ministry of Health and Long Term Care. She joined the University of Alberta as a Visiting Academic from the University of Western Ontario where she was Assistant Professor at the Faculty of Law and holder of an Ontario Ministry of Research and Innovation Postdoctoral Research Award. She obtained a Master of Laws degree from the University of Toronto, where she was a Fellow of the Canadian Institutes of Health Research, and a PhD in law from the University of British Columbia, Canada. Dr Iyioha is the recipient of numerous prestigous academic awards, including the World Congress on Medical Law Award – a worldwide honour for best student research and presentation – received in the final year of her PhD studies, and the First Atlantic Bank Prize for Contribution to Peace and Academic Development at the University of Benin, Nigeria. Dr Iyioha's research focuses primarily on health systems governance, health professions regulation, medical negligence and medical pluralism. Some of her publications explore the boundaries of health law and other fields such as immigration, patents and biotechnology, and social and legal theory. Her work has appeared in Canadian and international journals and has been cited in a Submission before the Joint Standing Committee on Migration (Inquiry into the Treatment of Disability) in Australia. She is co-editor of *Comparative Health Law and Policy: Critical Perspectives on Nigerian and Global Health Law* (Ashgate, 2015).

Marie-Andrée Jacob is Professor in Law at Keele University, UK. So far her research has focused on areas pertaining to law medicine and society: organ transplantation, research ethics, and research integrity and misconduct. Her book *Matching Organs with Donors: Legality and Kinship in Transplants* was published in 2012 as part of the Contemporary Ethnography series at the University of Pennsylvania Press. She is currently researching legal and regulatory responses to research misconduct. Marie's work has been supported by various funding bodies, including an Arts and Humanities Research Council (AHRC) Fellowship in the Science and Culture programme. She is a member of the Expert Working Group on Public Issues of the European Platform on Ethical, Legal and Psychosocial Aspects of Organ Transplantation of the European Society of Transplantation (ESOT).

Monique Lewis is a sociologist and teaches Media Studies and Communication at Griffith University and Southern Cross University, Australia. Her research has focused on media representations of complementary medicine, with a fascination in the discourse of risk and risk communication. She has published articles in the *Journal of Evidence-Based Complementary and Alternative Medicine* and *Health Sociology Review* and has presented her findings nationally and internationally. In addition to her academic work, Monique has worked in a media advisory role with the complementary medicine research departments of both Southern Cross University and the University of Western Sydney.

Elodie Marandet is a researcher at the Centre for Human Geography, Brunel University London, UK where she completed her PhD in 2013. She has worked on a number of research projects focusing on gender, care, training and education. Her work has been published in the *British Educational Research Journal* and *Space and Polity* and she recently assisted in editing a Routledge Major Works reader on Gender and the Environment. She is currently working on a project exploring the new landscapes of training for work, focusing on the expanded role of housing associations.

Hélène Martin is Professor of Sociology at the University of Applied Sciences and Arts, EESP, Lausanne Western Switzerland. Among her last publications are: *Le soin et la politique. Cinq médecines non conventionnelles et la LaMal* (with Jérôme Debons, Les Cahiers de l'EESP, 2014); *Les cadres sexués du travail émotionnel dans la relation thérapeutique en physiothérapie*, revue Travailler 32 (with Céline Perrin and Pascale Damidot) and "Le beau sexe. Quelques piste de reflexions sur les Chirugies sexuelles Cosmetiques" (*Genre Sexuality and Society* 12 (2004)).

Jo-Anne Rayner is Senior Research Fellow at the Faculty for Health Sciences, School of Nursing and Midwifery, La Trobe University, Melbourne, Australia. She is a qualitative researcher with a focus on the use of complementary and alternative medicines as health care options.

Mike Saks is Research Professor at University Campus Suffolk (UCS), UK and Visiting Professor in the Institute of Health Policy, Management and Evaluation at the University of Toronto, Canada and in the School of Social and Political Science at the University of Lincoln, UK. He was formerly Provost at UCS, Deputy Vice Chancellor at the University of Lincoln and Dean of Faculty of Health and Community Studies at De Montfort University. He has conducted several funded international research projects and published over a dozen books on professions, health and complementary and alternative medicine – as well as being a member/chair of many NHS committees and advising governments and professional bodies on the regulation of health and social care. He has also recently been the President of the International Sociological Association Research Committee on Professional Groups and Chair of the Research Council for Complementary Medicine.

Romila Santosh has a Master's degree in Ayurvedic Medicine and completed her PhD thesis in December 2013. Romila is currently a visiting Research Fellow at the Centre for Arts as Well-being, University of Winchester. Her current research interests are in understanding holistic approaches to health and well-being, health promotion, and the impact of Ayurveda, yoga, arts and spirituality on health and well-being. Romila is a qualified yoga instructor and has taught yoga since 2010. She is interested in combining her knowledge of research and experience of teaching yoga with establishing a yoga research team in the UK and collaborating with other CAM and yoga practitioners to develop community projects.

Julie Stone is an academic healthcare lawyer and ethicist with a long-standing interest in legal, ethical and regulatory aspects of complementary and alternative medicine. As Deputy Director of the Council for Healthcare Regulatory Excellence (now Professional Standards Authority), Julie helped shape the post-Shipman regulatory environment. Her work also helped create a framework for credible voluntary regulation of the CAM sector. She has lectured nationally and internationally on CAM regulation. Her books in this field include *Complementary Medicine and the Law* (Oxford University Press, 1996), with Joan Matthews, and *An Ethical Framework for Complementary and Alternative Therapists* (Routledge, 2002).

Ayo Wahlberg is Associate Professor at the Department of Anthropology, University of Copenhagen, Denmark. His comparative research has focused on the different ways in which herbal medicine (in Vietnam and the United Kingdom), and more recently reproductive medicine (in China and Denmark), have been mobilized, normalized and routinized in the past few decades. He is co-editor of *Southern Medicine for Southern People: Vietnamese Medicine in the Making* (2012) and has published numerous journal articles on the social study of both herbal medicine and reproductive medicine.

Emma Wainwright is Senior Lecturer and Co-Director of the Centre for Human Geography at Brunel University, London, UK. Her research has been funded by the ESRC and British Academy and focuses on geographies of family/care, education/welfare-to-work, bodies/emotions (with emphasis on gender and urbanism). Recent work has been published in the *Sociology of Health and Illness*, *British Journal of the Sociology of Education*, *Geoforum* and an edited collection of papers on "Women, work–life balance and quality of life" in *Gender, Place and Culture*. Her current research project explores new landscapes of training for work, focusing on the expanded role of housing associations.

Peter Watts is a Senior Lecturer in Sociology at Canterbury Christ Church University, New Zealand. Following research on HIV and Aids he has more recently developed a research interest in CAM. He has published a number of articles and book chapters in collaboration with Sarah Cant.

Sandy Welsh is Professor of Sociology and Vice-Dean, Graduate Education and Program Reviews in Faculty of Arts and Science at the University of Toronto, Canada. She studies work and occupations, complementary and alternative medicine, gender, and social policy. Linking these research streams is her interest in the relationship between the regulation, legal, organizations and employee behaviours. Previous and ongoing research collaborations and publications focus on how the regulation of Homeopaths, Naturopaths and Traditional Chinese Medicine/Acupuncturists in Ontario is changing these occupational groups. Professor Welsh also is a leading expert on workplace and sexual harassment in Canada, with numerous publications and appearances as an expert witness in this area.

Jane Wilkinson is Director of Health Academix, a social enterprise that brings together multidisciplinary associate teams of academics and advisors. The company focuses on projects that relate to innovation and professionalization in the health and wellbeing sector. Formerly Jane was the Director of an R&D unit at the University of Westminster in relation to policy, standards and clinical governance for complementary and alternative medicines in NHS primary care. Other work relating to CAM includes formative evaluations of integrated NHS services, evaluations of CAM interventions provided within NHS and third sector settings, the web-based Mindfulness Centre of Excellence, practitioner surveys and research consultancy in professional development. Prior to this, Jane worked for 15 years as a qualitative researcher in the field of Patient and Public Involvement and Experience for a range of academic institutions and organizations, including the King's Fund, the National Primary Care Research and Development Centre, the Medical Research Council and the Policy Studies Institute.

Karen Willis is Associate Dean (Learning and Teaching) at the Australian Catholic University, Melbourne, Australia. She is a health sociologist and qualitative researcher. Her research focuses on the social and policy shaping of health behaviour and, in particular, how people make choices in healthcare. In addition to research on fertility enhancement and CAM, she has undertaken research exploring why people use St John's Wort, the reasons that people take out private health insurance and community actions for health in farming and fishing communities.

ACKNOWLEDGEMENTS

We would like to express our sincere appreciation to the Wellcome Trust, whose funding for our conference "Regulation and professionalisation in complementary medicine: historical perspectives and contemporary concerns" led to the development of this edited collection (Wellcome Trust Grant No 094097/Z/10/Z). We would also like to sincerely thank for their help and support Professor Jonathan Reinarz, Birmingham Law School and the Economic and Social Research Council (ERSC Grant No ES/J002828/1). Always critical to the development of a book such as this is the editorial support and production team. Our particular thanks for excellent support go to Louisa Vahtrick and Routledge, our copy editor, Kate Short and to Allie Hargreaves at Wearset.

INTRODUCTION

Understanding CAM in the twenty-first century – the importance and challenge of multi-disciplinary perspectives

Nicola K. Gale and Jean V. McHale

I Background and concepts

The search by individuals and communities for ways to improve or maintain health and well-being is a fundamentally social process, shaped by history and values. The availability of different medicines or healing practices and the choices made by individuals to access them have varied over time and space and continue to do so. The Western biomedical model of health and disease has come to have a worldwide influence on health systems. Its dominance is illustrated by the use of terms such as 'traditional', 'complementary' and 'alternative' to describe 'other' healing systems, practices and products. However, the boundaries between all of these are far from clear and we will return to the question of definitions below. To date, much of the popular and policy debate on traditional medicine (TM) and complementary and alternative medicine (CAM) has focused on issues of efficacy and effectiveness, in line with biomedical research priorities, rather than on historical, social and legal aspects of practice. However, there is now a significant body of social and legal research that analyses the phenomenon of TM and CAM. We contend that health policy should be informed by the best quality research and this should include evidence from social science, not just medical science. The primary argument of the book is that the current popular and policy debates are concentrated in what is very much a polarized and largely asocial discourse (e.g. Ernst and Singh 2008) and that a multi-disciplinary social science (law, sociology, geography, history, ethics) perspective seeking to introduce nuance and theorize diversity in the field will provide a much more robust and context-sensitive evidence base for policy and practice in the field.

There are many limitations to the terminology that we have to describe and categorize healing practices. However, there are a number of terms that are used in practice and it is useful to explore them. Box I.1 shows the World Health Organization's definitions of traditional medicine and complementary medicine.

Box I.1 WHO definitions (WHO 2013)

Traditional medicine (TM)

Traditional medicine has a long history. It is the sum total of the knowledge, skill and practices based on the theories, beliefs and experiences indigenous to different cultures, whether explicable or not, used in the maintenance of health as well as in the prevention, diagnosis, improvement or treatment of physical and mental illness.

Complementary medicine (CM)

The terms 'complementary medicine' or 'alternative medicine' refer to a broad set of health care practices that are not part of that country's own tradition or conventional medicine and are not fully integrated into the dominant health care system. They are used interchangeably with traditional medicine in some countries.

Source: www.who.int/medicines/areas/traditional/definitions/en/

The Cochrane Collaboration developed the following definition, which is particularly useful because it highlights the socio-political nature and historically dependent way in which CAM is defined:

> Complementary and alternative medicine (CAM) is a broad domain of healing resources that encompasses all health systems, modalities, and practices and their accompanying theories and beliefs, *other than those intrinsic to the politically dominant health system of a particular society or culture in a given historical period*. CAM includes all such practices and ideas self-defined by their users as preventing or treating illness or promoting health and well-being. Boundaries within CAM and between the CAM domain and that of the dominant system are not always sharp or fixed.
>
> *(Zollman and Vickers 1999, emphasis added)*

In the US, the National Center for Complementary and Alternative Medicine has changed its definitions over the years, but tends now to refer to 'complementary health practices' and distinguishes between natural products, such as herbal medicines and dietary supplements; mind–body practices, which refer to 'a large and diverse group of procedures or techniques administered or taught by a trained practitioner or teacher'; and 'other' complementary health approaches, such as traditional healers or medical systems, homeopathy and naturopathy.[1]

In Europe, the following definition was adopted by CAMbrella, a European research network on CAM:

> Complementary and Alternative Medicine (CAM) utilised by European citizens represents a variety of different medical systems and therapies based on the knowledge, skills and practices derived from theories, philosophies and experiences used to maintain and improve health, as well as to prevent, diagnose, relieve or treat physical and

mental illness. CAM has been mainly used outside conventional healthcare, but in some countries certain treatments are being adopted or adapted by conventional healthcare.

(Falkenberg et al. *2012)*

While these kinds of theoretical definitions can be useful, they do not always help decipher whether a particular type of treatment is CAM or not because its social position can vary by country. Therefore, the Cochrane Collaboration developed an operational definition to help inform the development of the evidence base of CAM; this operational definition details whether a particular intervention is 'CAM' in a particular country and stresses that it will change over time (Wieland *et al.* 2011).

The need for such an operational definition is an indicator of the social basis of the distinction between conventional and complementary. There are many historical antecedents of the 'biomedical' and 'other' split, such as the distinction between the approaches towards health of the Goddesses Hygiea and Panacea in Greek mythology. The former was seen to focus on cleanliness, sanitation and the environment, while the latter represented the universal remedy and lent her name to the concept of the 'panacea', or 'magic bullet' today. However, the two approaches are not mutually exclusive. As Adams points out in this volume, in Scotland in 1910 it was noted that 'the distinction between "medicine and surgery" and "hygiene" was vague and constantly shifting' (HSMO 1910). We must be both critical and cautious of the language we use. Definitions are important and powerful. They have a productive effect in terms of knowledge generation and they frame discussions about what is possible and desirable. From a legal perspective, definitions are vital for framing the boundaries of law and regulation. As well as geographical and historical variation in definitions, we must also be aware that the same practices can have different meanings in different contexts – for instance, the blurring between pleasure and cure in practices such as massage or reflexology (Wolkowitz 2002; also see Wainwright and Marandet, and Adams, this volume), or the boundaries between religion and medicine (see Alich, this volume). Much of the language used in this field is dualistic in character (Gale 2014), which carries with it associated asymmetries of power and value.

TM and CAM are not always coherently applied terms, but they do have political salience because they are widely used both in the academic literature and in public debates. For the purposes of this volume, therefore, we have chosen to use the terms TM and CAM but we have aimed, through the selection of chapters, to be critical of what we think we know about them and to capture some of the diversity within these groupings.

II Why does it matter?

One obvious reason why this topic is important is because of the sheer number of people using TM and CAM across the world to manage their health. In some places, TM is the primary form of health care, particularly in some rural areas in developing countries or amongst poorer sections of the population (WHO 2013), but often, especially in developed nations, CAM is seen as a supplementary form of care, usually accessed by the wealthier, better educated parts of the population. There are a number of legal, ethical and policy issues associated with this, which we explore in the volume.

There has been a major growth in the academic study of TM and CAM since the turn of the century (Gale 2014), and this volume builds on this considerable body of literature, including previous edited collections (Cooter 1988; Lee-Treweek *et al.* 2005; Adams *et al.* 2012), to bring together in one place a range of different disciplinary perspectives. We developed the concept for the book following a Wellcome Trust-funded conference in 2011 and chapters were selected through a combination of invited contributions and an open call. The book is in four parts. Part 1 sets out the disciplinary frameworks of law, sociology and history. Part 2 explores the CAM professions across different health spaces and different countries. Part 3 examines risk and regulation of CAM; the language of risk has underpinned so much of the discourse of health care provision across jurisdictions and its implications for CAM and the movement to regulation of people, practices and premises. Part 4 takes a critical perspective on the knowledge base of CAM. It explores the knowledge that underpins development, delivery and provision. The chapters explore knowledge from the perspectives of patients, professionals and the community. Finally, the book concludes by examining the themes which have emerged from the chapters and considers where CAM research may go in the future.

III Part 1: the disciplinary frameworks

Part 1 explores the academic disciplines that we have used to frame this book and focuses upon history, law and sociology. The lessons of history are particularly pertinent to inform our later examination of regulatory structures and approaches. In the opening chapter, Roberta Bivins provides a historical lens from which to view CAM in her essay 'Limits and liberties: CAM, regulation and the medical consumer in historical perspective'. She explains the transition in practice from 'quackery' to what is now regarded as 'alternative medicine' and the moving paradigms and perceptions which warranted this evolution in language and in approach, in practice not simply a question of professional power but here a strong narrative of consumer choice informing professional development. A fascinating issue is the extent to which some characteristics of the development of professions in the nineteenth century are now being echoed in the turf wars concerning CAM today.

From the lens of history to the lens of society, Mike Saks explores the influential sociological debates around the professionalization of CAM. He charts the marginalization of CAM practice during the 1800s alongside the rise and rise of conventional medicine. Saks examines how CAM itself moved towards professionalization and indeed some statutory legitimacy. He suggests that there is a need for further debate as to the nature and boundaries of professionalization in CAM from the standpoint of consumers rather than simply of professions and of power structures. Finally in this part, Jean V. McHale, a lawyer, explores the existing legal frameworks for CAM in the UK and the extent to which these are truly distinct and different in relation to CAM as compared with conventional medicine. The historical and sociological debates concerning the boundaries of professionalization here are reflected in a regulatory spectrum from detailed distinct statutory structures, and the establishment of statutorily recognized voluntary registers through the work of the Complementary and Natural Healthcare Council (CNHC), through to areas that remain effectively unregulated as far as professional structures are concerned. Yet a myriad of legal constraints exist separately through common law and statute law applicable to actors and products in both CAM and conventional medicine. The patient as consumer may challenge not only the development of a profession, as we saw in Bivins' chapter, but also ultimately professional responsibility through challenging behaviour in the courtroom. McHale also considers the broader international context, noting the impact of EU regulation in framing CAM choices now and in the future. The international and European aspects of CAM regulation and their challenges for framing professions, actors and places are returned to later in the volume.

IV Part 2: power, professions and health spaces

Having examined the importance of historical, social and legal perspectives on the practice of complementary and alternative medicine in the previous part of the book, Part 2 provides evidence for the diversity of complementary and alternative medicine, paying particular attention to differences across time and space. As well as the substantial variation between different CAM modalities, practice within modalities is neither static nor uniform. When CAM is practised in different geographical locations, health care settings and time periods, the cultural and political organization of these different spaces affects the way that power plays out and the professions or practitioners are organized. There are important implications for issues of the regulation and organization of those practising and using the medicines. Critical questions include: Who is 'allowed' in different spaces (patients and practitioners)? Who polices access to different spaces (ethics, equity)? What types of 'body' or 'knowledge' are valued in different spaces? How do 'devalued' bodies or knowledges negotiate creating a legitimate space for practice where biomedical discourses are dominant? What happens when specific practices move across different cultural contexts?

It is useful to think of seven (overlapping) dimensions through which we can make sense of the diversity of practice, although there may be others as well: culture, health spaces, legal structures, practitioners, patients, purpose of treatment and time. The first is variation within and between cultures. Culture is a notoriously slippery concept and we do not intend to attempt to define it definitively here, but we argue that culture, whether at a global, national, institutional, professional or local level, can provide an enabling or disabling context for different practices. When medical practices move from one geographical space to another, such as the growth of 'Eastern' medicine in the West, or 'Western' medicine in the East, the receiving culture shapes and alters both the practice itself and the discourses and language through which social actors make sense of it. The second and closely linked variation is as practice moves between different types of health spaces, including formal health care spaces such as acute hospitals, or informal community spaces, such as those from indigenous communities.

The third is variation because of legal structures or constraints. Looking even across Europe, which is relatively culturally homogenous compared to global variation, there is huge diversity of practice. In France, for instance, the historical allegiance between pharmacists and homeopaths, has provided a system where homeopathy is available in almost every pharmacy in the country, which is very different from elsewhere in Europe. Laws around, for instance, protection of title and restrictions on claims that practitioners can make about the effectiveness of their treatment all influence practice.

The fourth and fifth relate to the social actors involved: the practitioner and the patient. For instance, biomedically trained doctors or allied health professionals have sometimes undertaken supplementary training in a CAM modality, whereas in other cases people with no medical background have decided to undertake professional training in CAM specifically. These types of practitioners can offer very different clinical treatments even if they have the same name. Acupuncture, for instance, when practised in a 'Western' way, tends to be more topical and anatomically local to the pain, whereas Chinese acupuncture focuses on the movement of *qi* (energy) in the body. Different patients, with different conditions or different worldviews, for example, may be looking for different types of treatment and practitioners may have to be flexible within their practice to meet the needs and expectations their patients have.

The sixth is that the purpose of the treatment might vary (linked to the perspectives and beliefs of the practitioner and patient). Treatment may be considered complementary in order to support the patient during conventional medical treatment, or it may be focused on prevention. Some treatments may focus on 'health', while others may primarily purport to be focused on 'wellbeing', 'beauty' or 'performance', such as in competitive sports.

The final variation is that of time. The historical development of a profession or the biographical changes in an individual's illness career can have a profound effect on the everyday practices of social actors. History is created through the tension between drives for continuity and change, and while some change (and continuity) is driven strategically, other change is a reaction or response to environmental and social changes. It is with history that this part of the book begins. Jane Adams provides a historical perspective on the development of the profession of naturopathy, perhaps highlighting for today's reader how many parallels and continuities there are with contemporary professional struggles and strategies in the CAM sector. We then move onto two stories of cultural translations, both rare contributions written by practitioner-researchers and providing rich insights into the impact of dramatic geographical movement on the everyday practices of shamanic and Ayurvedic practitioners. Informed by her own practice, Romila Santosh has observed that the written analyses of how Ayurvedic practice has changed as it moves from East to West have often been idealized and infused with colonial assumptions. On the basis of in-depth, qualitative empirical research with both UK and Indian-trained practitioners working in the UK, she developed a comprehensive typology of the types of clinical changes that happen as a traditional practice moves into a different cultural and legal setting. Alexander Alich's contribution, by contrast, focuses on issues of patient safety. Based on twenty years of experience working as a shaman and being a guest at various shamanic communities throughout the world, Alich has taken the courageous step to write publically from within the profession about the risks of shamanic practice as it is practised in a modern, Western context and provides an exploratory analysis of what the roots of the safety challenges are. His contribution represents the first, tentative steps towards a more comprehensive safety culture in shamanic practice. In the subsequent chapter, Sarah Cant and Peter Watts examine nurses' and midwives' use of CAM in their practices within the English National Health Service. Specific CAM techniques and interventions have a very different social meaning when used by qualified conventional health care practitioners in conventional health care spaces compared to trained lay people in community settings. Their chapter eloquently describes the political and value-based strategies that underpinned nurses' and midwives' use of CAM, which were around recapturing aspects of 'care' that they felt they had lost in their work. The chapter also shows how the system within which they were working, dominated by doctors and biomedical knowledge, served to constrain their practice and limit their success. Finally, the chapter by Jo-Anne Rayner and Karen Willis explores the use of CAM in relation to fertility. Certain CAM treatments can be seen to be targeted towards, not the recovery from illness, but the achievement of a social ideal of a family with children. The authors show how CAM's use in this way is contingent on and produced by wider medicalization of infertility.

V Part 3: risk and regulation

The safety and quality of the practice of complementary and alternative medicine remains a source of heated debate in the public and policy sphere. Part 3 of the book considers issues of risk and regulation. External considerations and safety concerns may drive regulation but equally regulation itself may be driven by the professional group or the state using regulation to legitimatize a practice. Key issues here concern the role of professions and the state in relation to regulation. What models of regulation are appropriate and are there agreed approaches to regulation across jurisdictions? How can legal frameworks direct change and evolution in professional practice? Are some forms of CAM, by their very nature, inevitably excluded from comprehensive formal regulation because an area of practice is so far away from accepted regulatory paradigms? Does the very existence of risk translate through subsequent regulation to legitimacy and status being given to a practice? Is evolution inevitable in regulatory structures and who and what drives such evolution?

Part 3 begins with Ayo Wahlberg's chapter, 'Making CAM auditable: technologies of assurance in CAM practice today'. Wahlberg suggests that the evolution of CAM regulation is demonstrated by a 'problematic of governance' with the evolution of the role of the Council, rather than the arena of competing interests. What is interesting is that, while this may indeed be the case in relation to some forms of CAM practice, others are still to take such an approach. Ireh Iyioha examines the extent to which freedom to practice can be in effect constrained through the operation of malpractice laws in North America. She examines the operation of freedom to practice legislation and the extent to which such legislative amendments can be utilized to give freedom to CAM practitioners to innovate in their practice. Monique Lewis undertakes an innovative sociological analysis of media representations of herbal medicine, examining the impact of such media portrayals on perceptions of risk. The relationship between traditional medicine and legal regulation in Kenya is explored by John Harrington in his chapter. What constitutes 'alternative' in medicine can of course be very much a construct of time and jurisdiction and this is highlighted by the evolution of the law in Kenya. The various forms of legal regulation are juxtaposed from practice and professional regulation to the impact of regulation in relation to the global dimension of health care delivery through the use of intellectual property law. Drawing upon the work of Rose and Miller, Harrington explores the problematization of traditional medicine.

Michael Dodson, in his essay on the regulation of complementary medicines in Australia, discusses the relationship between state, industry and consumers in framing complementary medicines regulation. Whether mainstreaming of complementary and alternative medicine is inevitable or whether the very nature of the practice itself renders regulatory and legal structures incomprehensible is explored by Ruth Barcan in relation to the use of spiritual healing in her chapter, 'Intuitive spiritual medicine: negotiating incommensurability'. She discusses the issues of epistemology, incompatibility and consequent medical and ethical difficulties. Major questions such as the prospect of relationships, ethical codes and integration remain, while transparency and real cooperation pose risks for both healers and conventional medical groups. She suggests that any cooperative strategies may be 'limited, cautious and highly circumscribed'. Whether the state can and should have a broader role in framing regulation, and the implications if the state does step in, forms the backdrop to the next chapter by Sandy Welsh and Heather Boon, 'Traditional Chinese medicine and acupuncture practitioners and the Canadian health care system: the role of the state in creating the necessary vacancies'. The chapter examines what happens if the state grants self-regulatory status to a profession which is still in the nascent stage of development. As they highlight, finding regulatory space for a professional group by no means resolves many fundamental issues concerning the internal and external characterization and acceptance of such groups. A paradigm of regulating for risk can obscure the broader complexities which can underpin effective regulatory structures. Finally in this part, UK lawyer Julie Stone, in her chapter 'Aspirations, integration and the politics of regulation in the UK, past and future', explores the dimensions of regulation in the UK context. As with Welsh and Boon, this chapter makes clear that the dynamics of regulation go well beyond a simple question of risk; instead, it is rather complex, involving a myriad of factors. Moreover, regulation needs to itself evolve over time. Effective regulation requires re-evaluation and the ability and willingness to reconceptualize.

VI Part 4: critical perspectives on knowledge

Having focused in the previous part of the volume on risk and regulation, this part will draw together various themes hinted at earlier concerning the question of the 'knowledge base' on which CAM practices are based, including its relationship to the recent historical rise of the idea of 'evidence-based medicine'. It is around the knowledge base of CAM that the biggest public and (medical) scientific controversies lie. Science is, of course, not value-free. With a simple social science analysis, it is possible to see that knowledge is socially produced in many places, such as the research process, the experiences of social actors and the pedagogies in formal and informal learning spaces (Gale 2014). This final part of the book covers issues of the production, consumption and governance of knowledge.

Knowledge about CAM is found in multiple places and from multiple perspectives. CAM practitioners learn their skills through formal training courses, such as public sector university degree courses or shorter private sector courses, or through less formal arrangements, such as apprenticeships or initiation rituals. Patients learn about CAM through their personal social networks, and sometimes through other health professionals or marketing materials. Other health care professionals, such as doctors, nurses, allied health professionals and public health professionals, may learn about CAM through their undergraduate education or informally during practice as their patients expose them to other approaches that they have taken. Knowledge about CAM can be produced through experience (of practitioners and patients) or through research, and all forms of knowledge production are profoundly social in character, from the networks used by patients to identify therapies or practitioners they might like to try, to the highly institutionalized forms of knowledge production in university-based research.

Key questions include: How do different environments value different types of knowledge? How do people make sense of and reconcile conflicting sources of knowledge? Is knowledge something 'out there' – rational, abstract and codifiable – or is knowledge of the body in health and illness also sometimes intimate, embodied and contextual? How can we govern the production and use of different types of knowledge? How can we value diversity of knowledge and different perspectives, while also working towards high quality and safe practice?

The opening two chapters of Part 4 focus on patients' knowledge, choices and practices. Hélène Martin and Jérôme Debons explore the decisions of Swiss health care users to use CAM. They explore the extent to which insurance systems affect these decisions and find that financial and legal frameworks around health care insurance have little impact on whether or not people choose CAM. On the contrary, values about health and health care have a much more profound impact. Felicity L. Bishop, drawing on a number of previous studies she has conducted, provides an insight into the way that, once a person has decided to try a particular CAM modality, they go about selecting a practitioner.

The next two chapters focus on practitioners' experiences and practices. Emma Wainwright and Elodie Marandet consider the impact on the experience of training in CAM on the identities of the practitioners. They critically investigate how the 'classroom-salon' provides a space in which embodied and gendered norms are challenged or reproduced in the learning of professionalism. Morag Heirs considers how homeopaths engage with the idea of 'evidence-based' practice and how they understand, use and deploy knowledge in their everyday practice.

There are still many uncertainties in the knowledge base of many CAM approaches and the last two chapters in this part of the book focus on issues of the governance of clinical and research knowledge in CAM. There is scope for CAM to engage with other ways of acquiring and managing knowledge. Jane Wilkinson and Nicola Gale consider the potential contribution of clinical governance processes to CAM. They recognize that clinical governance has tended to be implemented in large, well-developed health care organizations. They challenge the resistance of many CAM practitioners to forms of governance, arguing that the principles of clinical governance could be adapted to fit CAM professions, independently from clinical research activities, with potentially positive effects on the quality and safety of care. Marie-Andrée Jacob offers a much more radical reading of the potential for governance, this time within the research rather than the clinical setting, arguing that current research on CAM tends to reproduce biomedical norms and values. She challenges the sector to think about whether, if they are attempting to offer an alternative form of medicine, they should also be translating those values into the way they govern research practice. She offers an inspiring example from particle physics of alternative research governance arrangements.

VII Concluding thoughts

Despite the number of chapters contained in this volume, given the vast nature of this subject, it is necessarily limited in its scope. The chapters which follow raise pertinent issues and provide illustrative examples but cannot provide a totally comprehensive account. In the concluding chapter of this book, we consider the cross-cutting themes which can be said to underpin the chapters and suggest some further avenues for future academic and policy engagement and research in this area in the future.

Note

1 NCCAM website: http://nccam.nih.gov/health/whatiscam (accessed 8 May 2014).

References

Adams, J., G. J. Andrews, J. Barnes, A. Broom and P. Magin, Eds. (2012). *Traditional, Complementary and Integrative Medicine: An International Reader*. Basingstoke, Palgrave Macmillan.

Cooter, R., Ed. (1988). *Studies in the History of Alternative Medicine*. St Antony's/Macmillan Series. London, Macmillan.

Ernst, E. and S. Singh (2008). *Trick or Treatment: The Undeniable Facts About Alternative Medicine*. London, W. W. Norton & Company.

Falkenberg, T., G. Lewith, P. Roberto di Sarsina, K. von Ammon, K. Santos-Rey, J. Hök, M. Frei-Erb, J. Vas, R. Saller and B. Uehleke (2012). 'Towards a pan-European definition of complementary and alternative medicine – a realistic ambition?', *Forschende Komplementärmedizin/Research in Complementary Medicine* 19(Suppl. 2): 6–8.

Gale, N. (2014). 'The sociology of traditional, complementary and alternative medicine', *Sociology Compass* 8(6): 805–822.

HSMO (1910). 'Report as to the practice of medicine and surgery by unqualified persons in the United Kingdom presented to both Houses of Parliament by Command of his Majesty'. London, HSMO.

Lee-Treweek, G., T. Heller, J. Stone, H. MacQueen and J. Katz, Eds. (2005). *Perspectives on Complementary and Alternative Medicine: A Reader*. London, Routledge.

WHO (2013). *WHO Traditional Medicine Strategy 2014–2023*. Geneva, World Health Organization.

Wieland, L. S., E. Manheimer and B. M. Berman (2011). 'Development and classification of an operational definition of complementary and alternative medicine for the Cochrane collaboration', *Alternative Therapies in Health and Medicine* 17(2): 50–59.

Wolkowitz, C. (2002). 'The social relations of body work', *Work, Employment and Society* 16(3): 497–510.

Zollman, C. and A. Vickers (1999). 'What is complementary medicine?', *BMJ* 319(7211): 693–696.

PART 1

Disciplinary frameworks, law, sociology and history

1

LIMITS AND LIBERTIES

CAM, regulation and the medical consumer in historical perspective

Roberta Bivins

I Introduction

It is the devil's own science, this medical science.... It matters little which sect we follow. We are marked men and cannot escape. If cold water don't do for us – warm will – or mercury will – or homeopathy will – or a family physician will – or the common druggist will.... Keep from them as long as you can, and thank God when you get rid of them.

(The Penny Satirist 1842: 1)

In 1813, a well-known British satirist published an image that, for many of his peers, all too accurately represented the medicine of his age. Titled 'Doctors Differ or Dame Nature against the College', it is a scene of mayhem: four bewigged physicians in frock coats are attacking each other with their gold-topped canes, contesting the correct treatment for a wealthy patient (see Figure 1.1). Each offers a prescription more violent than the last, including emetics, blood-letting, sweating and blistering. All contenders are offering prescriptions drawn from the established medical canon of the early nineteenth century: there was no single or even dominant orthodox view of how to diagnose or treat a case. Chuckling in the background, the patient gleefully watches the fray – he has already chosen his healer: 'Dame Nature'. Cured by nature while the physicians fought amongst themselves, he prepares to escape his would-be doctors, saving 'both my money and my Life' (Williams 1813).[1]

Already a familiar phrase by the seventeenth century, the assertion that 'doctors differ' achieved proverbial status in the nineteenth century as an expanding medical marketplace in Europe and North America heightened professional competition for status, clients and authority. As in this image, heated and very public debates broke out amongst those claiming the status of professional healer and, with it, the exclusive right to diagnose and treat ill health. Here, I will offer a historical sketch of the nineteenth-century debates which laid the enduring foundations for contemporary understandings of 'alternative' and 'complementary' medicine in Britain and the United States. While the battle between 'allopathy' and 'homeopathy' (and other alternative systems) is well known, I will draw out its most persistent tropes and discuss the ways in which they informed late nineteenth- and early twentieth-century responses to alternative medicine in

13

Figure 1.1 'The Cold Water Cure', *The Penny Satirist* (London, England), Issue 267 (Saturday, 28 May 1842).

the US and UK (Bynum and Porter 1987; Cooter 1988; Gevitz 1988; Haller Jnr 2005; Kaufman 1971; Martyr 2002; Nichols 1988). The right of consumers to select therapeutic systems, regimens and individual interventions according to their own preferences and beliefs has been crucial to the survival and diffusion of the practices which have become 'CAM'. Yet the ability of consumers to do so intelligently and safely has long been questioned, particularly by members of the orthodox medical profession (today, biomedical professionals), seeking restriction of the medical marketplace.

Many have interpreted the willingness of consumers to 'experiment' with novel or alternative approaches to self-care or healing as an indication of long-term discontent with either the explanatory system or the standard of care provided by established medical professionals and institutions. I will argue that the relationship between CAM use and use of orthodox medicine has, historically, been more complicated; consumer choices have been affected not simply by desperation, discontent or ignorance, but by strong economic and cultural drivers – and indeed, rich traditions of empiricism and self-sufficiency – only some of which have been explored or acknowledged in detail. In other words, while some consumers may have been driven to the use of heterodox medicine by the failures and limitations of the medical establishment, others have actively and positively sought care and cures from beyond its boundaries. For some, such choices have been founded in beliefs inimical to orthodox practices or biomedicine's insistence on materialism – whether rooted in religion, morality or the enduring appeal of now-discarded medical theories like vitalism. For others, the practicalities of cost and access have been crucial. Finally, some consumers' preferences have been informed by personal and familial experiences of care and cure outside the surgery, clinic or hospital; or by preferences for domestic self-care and direct control of the medical encounter.

II From quackery to 'alternative medicine': the rise of the nineteenth-century systems

With the late medieval and renaissance universities and the retranslation of Greek and Roman medical texts preserved, systematised and improved by Islamic scholar-practitioners, a discernible medical establishment emerged in Europe (and was later replicated to a greater or lesser degree in European colonies and settlements around the world). Spreading from the cosmopolitan Mediterranean basin, this new secular and humanistic medicine – as much a reinvention as a re-discovery of classical learning – rejuvenated learned medicine and its institutions: curricula of instruction; guilds, colleges and faculties of credentialed healers; and some degree of self- and state regulation. (Porter 1997; Siraisi 1990). However, even among the tiny university-educated elite, marked differences in training and epistemology ensured heterogeneity in medical beliefs and practices. Beyond this loose circle, alternative understandings of disease, health and the body persisted (rooted in religion, folk practices, alchemy and astronomy, among others), and a dizzying variety of practitioners provided the vast majority of medical care (Rutten 2011). The sixteenth-century Scientific Revolution introduced new debates and divisions alongside novel experimental and mathematical methodologies, and the seventeenth century saw ever-greater European awareness of the diverse medical systems of China, Japan and the Indian subcontinent (Bivins 2007; Cook 2007; Webster 1975). In part, interest in the latter was a popular response to enduring dissatisfaction with the failures of established medicine: despite their increasing knowledge of anatomy and physiology, doctors remained largely unable to cure even the most mundane of illnesses.

With so many competing sources of medical authority and so few reliable therapies, it is perhaps unsurprising that scholars have described the eighteenth century as the 'golden age of quackery' (Gentilcore 2006; Porter 1989). Under regulations dating back to the late-medieval and early modern trade guilds, physicians in many European nations may have been legally entitled to monopolise diagnosis and prescription. In practice, however, their claims were rarely enforced and – with only a minority of patients able to access their services – were perhaps unenforceable (Pelling 2003; Wallis 2008). Even clients who could afford such care often mocked medical obfuscation and bookish theorising. As diplomat and gout-sufferer Sir William Temple wrote of the elite profession in the late seventeenth century, 'I had ever quarreled [*sic*] with their studying art more than nature, and applying themselves to methods, rather than to remedies' (1680: 207).

In contrast, their 'bastard brethren', from itinerant nostrum-vendors hawking their potions and pills alongside other market-traders to gentlemanly mountebanks proffering specialist skills to genteel families and courtly elites, offered remedies in plenty. Moreover, while condemning such healers, even some 'regulars' admitted that the charlatans proffered their cures with no more deception than was used by their more respectable medical competitors. Kindred in practice, if not equal under the law, both depended on 'the gullibility of mankind' (Beddoes 1808: 107, 105). 'Quackery' – that is, the commercial promotion, marketing and provision of products, services or treatments hyperbolically claimed (but not proven) to cure illness or engender health – is an abiding presence on the global medical stage. 'Kwakzalvers' cried their wares across northern Europe in the sixteenth century, and 'quacks' were well-ensconced in the English language by the 1730s. Then as now, however, most quacks did not challenge the medical orthodoxies of their day, but hijacked them in support of their own cures. They operated by subverting or sidestepping the nominal controls on practice optimistically instituted by a growing and increasingly confident, if not yet fully organised, medical establishment. With limited state intervention, and in a marketplace where paying patients still held medicine's purse-strings, little action could be taken against such profit-seeking ventures. Moreover, only in the second half of the nineteenth century did the established medical profession begin to act against the lucrative practices of nostrum-selling and panacea-patenting among its own ranks. They would thrive, within the profession and without, until the twentieth century.

In the late eighteenth and early nineteenth centuries, however, a new breed of challengers to established medicine emerged: these upstarts sought to replace, rather than to ride the coattails of conventional medical understandings and practices. This was an era marked by explorations of a wide range of invisible forces and substances including magnetism, caloric (1783), oxygen (1774) and galvanism (1791). With so many novel 'ethereal fluids' attracting attention and redefining popular and scientific understandings of the natural world, it is perhaps unsurprising that systems explicitly challenging the underlying epistemology of orthodox or 'regular' medicine swiftly followed. Between 1775 and 1810, the groundwork was laid for two such systems: mesmerism and homeopathy. Founded by charismatic individuals – respectively, Franz Anton Mesmer (1734–1815) and Samuel Hahnemann (1755–1843) – both systems incorporated the latest scientific understandings of the natural world as full of powerful, if intangible, Newtonian fluids capable of acting on the human body just as oxygen and electricity manifestly did. Thus Mesmer (1784) described his system as rooted in 'the property which bodies have of being susceptible to the actions of a universally distributed fluid ... which serves to maintain the equilibrium of all the vital functions' and thus to maintain health. This fluid, he believed, was possessed by all living beings, but in unequal measures; those richly endowed with 'animal magnetism' could learn to augment and then to use their reserves to stimulate or replenish the defective or depleted stores of the infirm through his methods.

Both systems, too, relied on up-to-date notions of experimental evidence as a source of authority and objective knowledge, and criticised the medical establishment for clinging to unproven theories and practices (including, for example, bloodletting and heroic dosing with mercury and arsenic). Mesmer himself would swiftly fall foul of the experimental system in which he so firmly believed. In what has often – if somewhat anachronistically – been described as a precursor to the randomised controlled trial, Mesmer's 'magnetic fluid' and his practices of 'magnetising' were tested in 1784 by a royally appointed Académie de Médecine commission of the scientific great and good (Antoine Lavoisier and Benjamin Franklin both served). When Mesmer's patients were unable to distinguish between actual and sham 'magnetism', he was publicly discredited, and his Parisian practice disintegrated.

Yet the practice of mesmerism persisted despite its founder's disgrace, spreading to London in the 1820s and 1830s, and from there to North America and the British Empire. In part, mesmerism's durability derived from its adaptability, and in particular from a new use developed for the trance-like state produced by mesmerism among those susceptible to it. In the absence of reliable anaesthetics and pain-relievers, this new 'mesmeric anaesthesia' seemingly allowed surgery (or labour) without pain. While it was largely superseded by the discovery of ether in 1846 and then ferociously purged from 'regular' practice, mesmerism continued to be applied in private homes and in theatrical displays, often under the untainted name of 'hypnotism'. Under that name and stripped of its claims to a material basis, it has since been partially integrated into biomedicine.[2] Mesmerism models one trajectory commonly followed by medical 'alternatives', over the course of which a given practice emerges, provokes controversy, investigation, experimentation and limitation, and is then absorbed, in part or entirely, into normative medicine.

In contrast, homeopathy blazed a very different trail, one in which the challenging system resists integration and retains a separate identity as an alternative to established medical knowledge and practice. Like Mesmer, Hahnemann did not initially position himself as a medical iconoclast; a university-trained physician and translator of medical texts, he expected to reform medicine from within. Thus, Hahnemann at first simply declared his discovery of two new medical 'laws'. The first – called 'the law of similars' after Hahnemann's famous phrase 'similia similibus curantur' (like treats like) – was, he asserted, based on careful observation of nature and deliberate self-experimentation. Hahnemann reported that those substances which *caused* the symptoms of a particular disease in a healthy person would *relieve* those symptoms in their sufferers. He had become convinced of this 'law' through an experiment initially constructed to explore the workings of an established medicine: in 1790, Hahnemann deliberately ingested cinchona bark – rich in quinine – and experienced in consequence symptoms of the malarial fevers which that drug famously cured.

Hahnemann's second principle (much derided both in the nineteenth century and today) was the 'law of infinitesimals'. Unlike the law of similars, the law of infinitesimals was rooted as much in theoretical reasoning on the metaphysical nature and origins of disease as in observation or experiment (though Hahnemann and subsequent homeopathists did experimentally test the theory). Essentially, Hahnemann believed that disease sprang not from a simple breakdown in the bodily mechanism (which might demand similarly mechanical treatment: for example, purges to vent impurities, or emetics to remove blockages) but from disturbances of the body's ethereal vital force. Thus treatments needed to act on the metaphysical, rather than the corporeal level. Hahnemann argued that the therapeutic potency of a medicine in this metaphysical realm grew as the physical medicinal substance itself was mixed, diluted and refined (Nichols 1988; Devrient and Stratten 1833). Homeopathists from Hahnemann onwards would later claim inoculation as further evidence supporting both of their new laws (see Hahnemann 1962: section 46, note 47, cited in Nichols 1988: 12).

Hahnemann claimed to have derived his laws and the therapeutic system built around them through *reasoned* experiment, rather than through either scholarly theory-building or empiricism alone. In this, his 'new science' was attuned to on-going debates in the medical community. Most importantly, Hahnemann's system incorporated the growing faith, shared by medical professionals and consumers alike, in the *vis medicatrix naturae* – the very healing power of nature that so appealed to the gleeful patient with which this chapter began. Similarly, he accepted and built upon emerging models of disease as 'self-limiting'. These models proposed that diseases had a natural course through which they would inevitably progress, ending in a 'crisis' during which the patient's 'dynamis' or vital force would either be exhausted or be restored to a state of healthy balance.[3] In combination, these two ideas suggested that the most effective therapeutic strategy was to strengthen the body for its inevitable ordeal and to assist nature in reaching the 'crisis' before the body had been exhausted (a doctrine that would subsequently underpin the mid-nineteenth century orthodox reformers' turn towards therapeutic nihilism). Hahnemann had no doubt that his method of treating like with like would surpass and supersede orthodox methods, which he denigrated as 'allopathy' (treatment with opposites) and derided for opposing nature's own healing process and thus depleting the body. Looking back at the heroic treatments of the early nineteenth century – bloodletting to syncope, mercury dosing to salivation, puking, purging, blistering and leeching – his critique, at least, still resonates.

Hahnemann's new medical system focused on individuals and their collection of symptoms, rather than on any presumed disease entities. Indeed, in his view, the symptoms *were* the disease: 'Illness is the sum of its symptoms' (translation from Hamlyn 1981: 19). Given this assumption, it was imperative that homeopathic practitioners elicit from their patients a complete and detailed description of their entire disease experience. Like his mild medicines, Hahnemann's emphasis on patient testimony presented a sharp contrast to trends in orthodox practice, where doctors were increasingly interested in uncoupling diagnosis from the 'subjective' experience of illness (see Fissell 1991; Jewson 1976; Porter 1997: 309–311). Where regular medicine was striving to declare its independence from the patient, homeopathy instead reinforced the role of the patient as a (junior) partner in the diagnostic process. Hahnemann explicitly notes that the patient's 'own account of his sensations is most to be trusted' adding only the parenthetical caveat '(unless he is feigning illness)' (Hahnemann 1913).

With its gentle methods and careful attention to each patient's individual experience of ill health, homeopathy proved enormously attractive to a public grown weary of the harsh methods and sometimes dismissive manners of regular practitioners. Moreover, despite almost a century of remarkable growth in medical and anatomical knowledge about the body's structures and function, the medical establishment could claim no new cures; even Jenner's celebrated vaccine for smallpox was simply a safer method of preventing rather than treating the deadly disease. The limitations of their therapeutic arsenal, however, did not dissuade the established medical profession from organising itself and stridently asserting its own right to a monopoly of practice and expertise. Without a stronger foundation in therapeutic success, such claims prompted accusations of arrogance, elitism and even conspiracy in the US and UK. (In revolutionary Paris, they had already produced outright rebellion when radicals wrenched control of medicine from the hands of the Church and established medical elites.) Medical regulars and the medical establishment came under intense pressure.

In the US, public faith in organised medicine reached new lows just as popular impatience with elitism of all types soared. By 1830, thirteen states had enshrined in law the rights of local medical societies to license medical practitioners. Such tentative first steps towards an established orthodoxy, however, confronted and affronted a wider cultural trend towards scepticism of elitism, exclusivity and monopoly. With abundant faith in the power of self education and common-sense empiricism, the American public believed that 'medicine like every useful science should be thrown open to the observation and study of all'. They sought to 'explode the whole machinery of mystification and concealment – wigs, gold canes, and the gibberish of prescription – which serves but as a cloak to ignorance and legalized murder'.[4] Moreover, other medical systems, from Thomsonianism and Eclectic Medicine, to hydropathy and chiropractic, continued to proliferate over the course of the nineteenth century. Many were better suited – by their willingness to allow greater autonomy to patients, and to provide for self-medication – to the American context of a largely rural and scattered population. A burgeoning industry in medical certification further clouded the picture and tainted popular views of orthodox medicine: legal equivalency between medical diplomas and professional society licenses prompted a glut in proprietary medical schools – 'diploma mills' – admitting virtually all comers, and providing them with little more than the certificates required to practise medicine legally. Between 1830 and 1840 in the United States, 6,800 new doctors graduated from such schools, to the disgust of their better-trained colleagues and medical consumers alike. Medicine had become the 'ONE unfailing city of refuge' for those incapable of entering other, more discriminating professions (*Medical Record* 1869). In response, by 1850, only two states retained laws restricting medical practice to regular practitioners. Although the US was extreme in so thoroughly stripping away the profession's legal protections, states across Europe had likewise refused to legislate against individual consumers' rights to make their own choices in a thriving medical marketplace. 'Regular' medical professionals, exhausted by their internal disagreements and threatened from without, finally turned their hands to collective organisation and self-regulation.

III From 'regular' to 'orthodox' to 'scientific': competition, regulation and reform

Contemporary medical consumers and providers often draw a strict division between orthodox medicine – in the West, typically high-tech, hospital-based, officially sanctioned and steeped in science – and 'alternative', 'complementary' or 'quack' therapies. But this distinction is fluid and contingent: the boundary between 'orthodox' and 'heterodox' must be actively policed by both lay and professional authorities if it is to remain stable and impermeable. This boundary was originally defined and has subsequently been maintained through a complex network of regulatory interventions and processes. From a historian's perspective, it is possible to identify three separate regulatory strands which have consistently played a role since the mid-nineteenth century: these include the internal pressures of self-regulation applied within a given healing profession; the external regulatory powers acquired by or transferred to the state; and the mixed economy of informal regulation imposed by economic actors (e.g. in the US, the insurance industry; more generally, medical consumers themselves[5]) and fluctuations in the value and authority – the cultural capital – ascribed to particular elements of a given therapeutic or knowledge system.

In the US and Britain, it is relatively easy to trace both the first and the second strands of modern regulation, and to identify their origins in the competitive, contentious and, above all, highly public medical marketplace of the early and mid-nineteenth century. While professional organisation – essential to any self-regulatory processes – and state regulation began earlier, these scattered efforts could not by themselves contain vibrant pluralism or draw a firm boundary between heterodoxy and orthodoxy (Corfield 2009; Porter 1987, 1997, 2000; Bivins 2007). Not until the established medical professions had accrued sufficient cultural capital could they begin to apply effective restrictions on their would-be members, or call upon the state for legal protection and exclusive rights. Such standing only gradually emerged, in part through the laborious production of professional consensus about the human body, and what constituted 'good medicine'.[6] Improved standing came too from medicine's ever-closer association with the production of accurate knowledge about the natural world (for example, through anatomical dissection, and professional and amateur participation in natural history, the physical sciences and clinical experimentation).[7] By the late nineteenth century, these created what Paul Starr has called 'legitimate complexity' and made credible the medical profession's renewed and revivified claims to exclusive knowledge, and with it an entitlement to regulatory protection (Starr 1982). Rising public confidence in the sciences encouraged the active – but at the time much contested – efforts of medical reformers to define medicine as a 'science' and not an 'art' (see, for example, Warner 1991).

In medicine, as in many other arenas, consensus and shared identity developed faster in the face of an external threat. Homeopathy and the myriad other alternative systems of the nineteenth century provided the established profession with exactly the stimulus required to drive such self-regulation and reform forward, and motivated far stronger calls for state regulatory interventions. Britain's self-declared 'regulars' – physicians, surgeons and apothecaries – had spent the years between 1704 (when apothecaries won the legal right to prescribe medicines) and 1832 (when the Provincial Medical and Surgical Association, the forerunner to the British Medical Association, was founded) fighting each other for status and trade. However, facing mounting enthusiasm for alternatives ranging from homeopathy to hydropathy to mesmerism, the profession's university-educated elites finally joined forces with its less-polished medical masses (today's general practitioners) to campaign for regulation enabling 'Persons requiring Medical Aid ... to distinguish qualified from unqualified Practitioners'. In 1858, Britain passed the Medical Act, establishing both the General Medical Council (GMC) and the Medical Register, and banning anyone not on the Medical Register from practising as a qualified medical doctor. Since the GMC was constituted in law almost entirely from the orthodox elite, and an orthodox medical qualification was required for inclusion on the Register, the 1858 Act in theory privileged the 'regulars'.

To their disappointment, however, the Act explicitly denied the orthodox profession a monopoly on the right to heal, to provide or even to sell diagnostic and therapeutic services; even the right of qualifying bodies – that is, universities and medical colleges – to mandate that their candidates select a single medical system was contingent and could be revoked by the Privy Council. Nor could qualified members be struck off the Medical Register for professing a particular system of medicine. Indeed, at first glance, it seemed that the medical profession's prize consisted merely of the exclusive right to claim to be a 'legally qualified' practitioner of medicine, surgery or pharmacy, along with the right to recover their fees via the courts. But the Act also stipulated that only registered practitioners could be appointed to fill posts in the army, navy, merchant fleet,

> or in any [state-supported] Hospital, Infirmary, Dispensary, or Lying-in Hospital … or in any Lunatic Asylum, Gaol, Penitentiary, House of Correction, House of Industry, Parochial or Union Workhouse or Poorhouse, Parish Union, or other public Establishment, Body, or Institution, or to any Friendly or other Society for affording mutual Relief in Sickness, Infirmity, or old Age, or as a Medical Officer of Health…[8]

Thus, although the 1858 Act (and regulations like it, passed across the United States from the mid-century) did not offer an exclusive mandate to any particular system of medicine, it nonetheless at least potentially provided the medical establishment with considerable leverage: from its enactment, while no one could be prevented from practising homeopathy or any other system, would-be healers were required either to be educated and qualified under the tenets of orthodoxy or to relinquish their claim to the title of 'doctor' and the remunerative posts that would henceforth fall only to registered practitioners.[9] To the great perturbation of many civilians in the United States, the US (Union) Army Medical Corps operated similar restrictions on would-be Army medics in the US Civil War, in effect excluding homeopaths and other 'irregulars' from the opportunities offered by that devastating conflict to enhance their skills and authority (and forcing soldiers to adopt allopathic practice regardless of their own preferred system).[10]

The text of Britain's 1858 Act, and the parliamentary and public debates which accompanied its passage, clearly demonstrate that there was no appetite in British politics for medical monopoly; homeopathy was popular particularly among the middle and upper classes, while the poor relied on self-dosing with patent and domestic remedies, as well as irregular healers (Roberts 2009: 46). In the United States, there remained considerable antipathy to the idea. Consequently, while the American Medical Association (AMA), founded in 1847, was explicitly dedicated to combating the 'irregulars' who had flourished in the deregulated US market, it had to look also to self-reform. Therefore the AMA simultaneously committed itself to the challenge of eliminating from its own ranks the 'regulars' who practised 'medicine as a trade instead of a profession, and [studied] the science of patient-getting to the neglect of the science of patient curing' (Hooker, 1849: ix). In short, the AMA sought to restore the credibility of the 'regular' profession, both by defeating its external rivals and by ending the internecine battles, low standards and commensurately low fees provoked by competition between orthodox practitioners. To these ends, it introduced and enforced minimum fees among its members and banned them from puffery and advertising, as well as from consulting with irregulars (and thus lending them the appearance of professional acceptability).

Despite increasing levels of organisation and self-regulation, orthodox medicine in both nations faced an uphill battle against 'irregular' competitors. Homeopaths were often 'regularly' educated and better qualified, and their cures were far more palatable; as one US journalist versified in 1848: 'The homeopathic system, sir, just suits me to a tittle/It proves of physic, anyhow, you cannot take too little' (*United States Magazine and Democratic Review* 1848, quoted in Kaufman 1971: 30). Moreover, they were rapidly establishing parallel structures of medical associations, colleges and journals, mimicking the regulars' professionalising strategies, and benefiting from commensurate improvements in their standing. The British Homeopathy Society, for example, was founded in 1843, just a decade after the orthodox profession organised (and before the Provincial Medical and Surgical Association rebranded itself as the 'British Medical Association'). Other competing systems drew on cultural resources unavailable to 'allopathy'. Thus, hydropaths tapped into established and attractive spa cultures and rising interest in civic and domestic hygiene, as well as a growing Romantic fascination with the therapeutic benefits of nature and natural cures (and like homeopathy, boasted of their numerous regularly trained 'converts') (Bradley and Dupree 2001, 2003; Marland and Adams 2009). And while orthodox medicine was struggling to remove the taint of trade by barring – with only mixed success – its members from advertising, heterodox healers flourished economically and expanded the market for their systems through advertising products intended for home use: for instance, mail-order homeopathic medicine chests, or hydropathic bathing apparatus (Marland and Adams 2009). These institutions and businesses alike persisted well into the twentieth century, despite major challenges both from the orthodox profession and from the rising power and authority of a 'scientific medicine' that did not hesitate to pillage the 'alternatives' and 'allopathy' alike for their successes while condemning both as dogmatic. As Abraham Flexner, the great reformer of medical education, wrote in his 1910 report, 'Modern medicine ... wants not dogma but facts ... Science once embraced, will conquer the whole' (Flexner 1910). Prefiguring many modern commentators who argue against 'integrative medicine', he added, 'everything of proved value in homeopathy belongs of right to scientific medicine ... nothing else has any footing at all, whether it be of allopathic or homeopathic lineage' (Flexner 1910: 161–162).[11]

IV 'No analogy with business': trade restriction or consumer protection in the medical marketplace

Perhaps it was the very success with which the medical alternatives appealed directly to the public that provoked the orthodox profession to bitterly condemn their clientele. Certainly, direct attacks on medical consumers were among the most persistent tropes of the nineteenth-century medical response to the new systems. The *Lancet* and the *British Medical Journal* inveighed bitterly against the faddish, ignorant, deluded, self-indulgent, hysterical and hypochondriacal patients who so enthusiastically flocked to their competitors. They spoke of 'volatile' and 'indolent' victims of 'modern charlatanism', desperately in need of rescue by the regular profession (*Association Medical Journal* 1853); and grumbled about 'the peculiar proneness in the English nobility to run after quackery ... in defiance of what is due to science and to decency' (*Lancet* 1835). 'Hypochondriac men and nervous women', they argued, were drawn to the 'mystery' of alternative systems and practices in defiance of reason and their own senses (Dick 1850). US critics concurred, dismissively, that in relation to medicine, 'even ... the intelligent and judicious, may readily be misled', while popular opinion was too easily swayed by 'exaggerated statements of the interested and the enthusiastic' (Palmer 1882). Patients in particular, 'weak-ened and discouraged by exhausting diseases' were deemed susceptible to delusion:

> Many unfortunates, afflicted with incurable or tedious chronic diseases, grasp at anything that offers a hope of relief, whether it be a remedy recommended by a sympathizing friend or a cure advertised in the secular press. Unhappily, the demand for panaceas and for the services of those who claim to cure by extraordinary means is not confined to those who are deficient in intelligence.... So long as the love of the marvellous exists, so long will there be a certain demand for quackery, and the supply will not entirely fail.
>
> *(Flint 1889: 492)*

Crucially, almost all of these criticisms suggested that consumers who opted to use heterodox treatments were *unable* to make intelligent and informed choices, whether through ignorance, desperation or mental weakness.

Patients and consumers, meanwhile, viewed these all-too public debates with dismay. For many, all contenders were equally untrustworthy. An early British critic complained, 'How a poor invalid is tossed about by these medicine mongers, and bothered out of his wits and his wealth as well as his health to know what to do with their conflicting counsel!' He likened 'medical science' to theology: 'its sects are innumerable and each sect calls its rival a murderer' (*The Penny Satirist* 1842: 1). For others, common sense and experience remained the gold standard of proof, and self-experimentation the therapeutic norm. Far from credulous, these consumers were entrenched in scepticism. They sampled a wide range of remedies and sought aid from an equally varied cast of practitioners without committing wholeheartedly to any single system. Some, like London businessman R. B., read the medical press, adapted its latest innova-tions and even submitted their own accounts to the medical journals (see Bivins 2007: 1–3). Moreover, while professional elites on both sides of the orthodox divide battled over dogma and epistemology, a sizeable proportion of practitioners followed their clients into mixed practice, prescribing homeopathic and allopathic remedies, hydropathic cures and patent medicines with equal enthusiasm. While homeopathy fragmented between the 'Pures' and those who modified Hahnemannian strictures (and in particular, the law of infinitesimals), copious professional endorsements and testimonials in the advertising ephemera of the latter half of the nineteenth century bear witness to fractures in 'regular' medicine.[12]

Nonetheless, in presenting the purchasers and users of medical 'alternatives' as gullible victims, the nineteenth-century medical establishment presaged a commonplace of con-temporary debates over medical regulation and the commodification of medical goods and services: the idea that the medical marketplace was uniquely asymmetrical in relation to informa-tion and therefore to power, with the consumer very much in a position of weakness. In turn, the presumed inability of consumers to make rational and fully informed choices in the booming medical marketplace justified strong calls for increased regulation of medicines and the providers of medical treatment. 'Regular' practitioners urgently pressed the British and US governments to introduce regulation on two fronts: first, to control the supply of medical practitioners by setting higher standards for medical licensing (and thus education); and second, to regulate at least the marketing of medical products themselves (Eggleston 1889; Flint 1889).

Simultaneously, the commercial and therapeutic successes of the alternatives forced major changes in orthodox medical practice. Speaking of homeopathy in 1858, respected 'regular' John Forbes admitted that such competition, driven by patient demand, was 'the means of less-ening, in a considerable degree, the monstrous polypharmacy which has always been the dis-grace of our Art' (Forbes 1858: 162–163). Determined efforts to enforce self-regulation also increasingly marginalised the grubbier commercial practices that had tarred orthodox practice with the same quackish brush as its rivals (though the *BMJ* continued to carry advertisements for dubious commercial preparations well into the 1960s, despite sharp criticism from its membership, Parliament and the American Medical Association) (Bartrip 1995; Loeb 2001). In the US, the forces of self-regulation and a well-funded campaign of public education – in the form of Abraham Flexner's swingeing 1910 critique of medical education, published and widely disseminated by the Carnegie Foundation – likewise effected major reforms and drastically elevated professional standards (albeit at the cost of reducing professional diversity and availability). An added benefit of the Flexner Report from the orthodox perspective was its condemnation of the vast majority of alternative medical institutions as little more than diploma mills. Most were out of business only years later (Bonner 2000).

The alternative systems did not go quietly. If the broadsides of the regular profession – that 'irregulars' were either self-deluded mystics or outright quacks, and that their patients were variously credulous, ignorant, irrational, hysterical or desperate – sound familiar, so too will those of their opponents. Accusing the medical establishment of seeking a profitable monopoly at the expense of their patients' health, advocates of the medical alternatives vaunted their own approaches as hewing to the dictates of nature, rather than the dangerous – even poisonous – artifices of 'allopathy'. Their treatments were 'safe' or at least 'harmless', and rooted in empirical facts not scholarly theories; their approach focused on the individual, and not the disease; and they practised from a sense of duty, rather than a love of gain (Gevitz 1988; Haller Jr 1998, 1999; Gisjwijt-Hofstra *et al.* 1997; Jütte *et al.* 2001) They differed too in their greater willingness to welcome women and others excluded from an almost monolithically white and male medical establishment (Taylor-Kirschman 1999; Rogers 1998). Both sides claimed the authority of science and the methodology of experiment – but as medical 'science' moved away from the individual case study and towards sophisticated statistical methods and later the clinical trial, the alternative systems lost their hold (Hardy and Magnello 2002).

V Alternative medicine in the 'golden age' and its aftermath

Despite entering the twentieth century in good order, supported by a broad consumer base and a range of professional institutions, and largely unfettered by legal constraint, the major alternative systems declined dramatically in visibility until the last third of the twentieth century. Much of their diminution is attributable to a corresponding increase in both the therapeutic and the institutional power of the new 'scientific medicine', and to its enormous popularity. Empowered to cure (and thus freed from therapeutic nihilism) by the early years of the twentieth century, and exalted by the burgeoning field of medical journalism, orthodox practitioners and especially the new medical scientists became hero figures (Hansen 1998; Tomes 1998; Rogers 1998). Their new status, and the increased public faith in medicine, made it easier for the profession to argue for legal protection in the marketplace. In particular, they were able at last to insist that medical consumers should be protected from the adulteration of medicines (and foods) and from certain kinds of medical products and claims. In 1875, Britain introduced controls on the content and purity – but not the efficacy or safety – of medicinal substances through the Sale of Food and Drugs Act. Similar US legislation followed, in the 1902 Biologics Control Act (to regulate the new sera, vaccines and anti-toxins that represented the acme of medical science) and 1906 Food and Drug Act. Through these acts, the medical professions in both nations moved to attack quackery and patent-medicine panaceas, albeit with limited success. In Britain, only the thalidomide disaster of the early 1960s prompted further regulation (and then not initially in law) via the 1964 establishment of the Committee on the Safety of Drugs. Not until

1968 was the Medicines Division of the Department of Health established as Britain's licensing authority in law. But in the US, the advent of the Food and Drugs Administration in1938 gave the regulators of medicines considerably sharper teeth, and the remit of ensuring drug safety as well as purity (Abraham and Davis 2006).

Efforts to eliminate heterodox medical practices were less successful. Neither in the US nor in the UK would the state regulate against alternative medical systems – though as with the 1858 Medical Act and its successors, the increasing role played by the state in the funding and provision of medical care (from Britain's 1911 National Insurance Act to the 1965 establishment of the Medicare and Medicaid programmes) continued to privilege the now-established practices and practitioners of biomedicine. In the US, no federally funded programme pays for care under any other medical system (although recently some states have approved the limited incorporation of CAM treatments via discounted or subsidised cost for Medicare recipients). Nor, until very recently, would private insurers reimburse such charges (Tillman 2002). In the UK, homeopathy and the remaining homeopathic hospitals were, contentiously and painfully, incorporated in the National Health Service in 1948, on the grounds that 'patients should have the free and unfettered right to attend the practitioner of their own choice'.[13] However, the constraints placed on homeopathic practice in the NHS satisfied no one: while biomedical practitioners resented homeopathy's inclusion as an official legitimation of what they saw as an unproven and unscientific system, homeopaths were bitterly divided about whether true homeopathy could survive integration. Their practices, too, suffered financially from structures designed to suit the majority system. The British Medical Association (through its postgraduate offshoot) ensured that homeopathy was excluded from publicly funded medical training and, by the late 1950s, homeopathy persisted largely in private practice (Bivins 2007).

Only in the 1970s and 1980s would medical alternatives and heterodox epistemologies again play a significant role in British and American medicine. Many scholars have linked their resurgence to the end of medicine's 'Golden Age' in a welter of ethical scandals (notably including the Tuskegee Syphilis Study) and iatrogenic disasters (from waves of deadly nosocomial infections which threatened the hospital's standing as a machine for healing, to the thalidomide disaster and other failures in drug safety). As in Jacksonian America, which was characterised by growing scepticism of elites and enthusiasm for individual democratic empowerment, the rise of a distrustful, anti-authoritarian 'counter culture' has likewise been credited with raising the profile of home-grown and exotic alternative systems. Moreover, the rise of chronic illnesses, and later new conditions like HIV/AIDS and multidrug-resistant tuberculosis, struck at the heart of biomedicine's claims to therapeutic predominance, while creating a mass of determined, dissatisfied and even desperate medical consumers actively seeking to protect or restore their health with or without licensed medical assistance. In 1977, the US medical profession took a body-blow when the American Medical Association was successfully prosecuted by the Federal Trade Commission (FTC) for monopolistic practices. The AMA had argued that medicine should be exempt from free market competition on the grounds that:

> Possibilities for deception are particularly serious in the area of medicine because most consumers lack the training to evaluate medical claims and because many are vulnerable to superficially appealing promises or suggestions of cures. And the consequences of deception can be more horrible than in perhaps any other area.[14]

This claim, and the vision of hapless medical consumers which had so long been the mainstay of the orthodox profession's anti-quackery and anti-alternative medicine rhetoric, was rejected. In a statement prepared for (but never presented to) Congress, FTC Chair Michael Pertschuk instead asserted that the 'striking degree of physician self-regulation' and 'relative lack of participation by representatives of groups with at least potentially different interests – including, most notably, consumers' had created a nearly 'medieval' system in which 'neither government regulation nor competition was permitted to impede the efforts of the tradesman or artisan to achieve professional success and economic prosperity'.[15] It is unlikely that the FTC foresaw or desired the marketplace free-for-all which its legal victory facilitated. Nonetheless, it captured a crucial shift in attitudes away from regulatory paternalism and the reification of medical judgement and back towards laissez-faire health consumerism. In the UK, by 1991 a new GP Fundholding scheme gave general practitioners (family doctors) more discretion to determine at the local level which services they commissioned for their patients. From this point, complementary therapies from acupuncture to aromatherapy were available on the NHS from willing general practitioners. In the same year, the US Congress imposed an Office of Alternative Medicine on the National Institutes of Health, and demanded the scientific investigation of heterodox practices and medical substances. Thus, as the pendulum swung again towards deregulation in the US context and neoliberal reform in the NHS in Britain, alternative and complementary medicine gained new footing and new opportunities to thrive. The degree to which such opportunities may stimulate changes in biomedicine and the provision of healthcare remains to be seen: history suggests that challenges at the boundary between heterodoxy and orthodoxy in medicine are likely to have profound impacts on both. Certainly, these changes have provoked a resurgence of the polarised and highly polemical debates between CAM practitioners and their biomedical counterparts which bewildered and frustrated nineteenth-century medical consumers. Yet the nineteenth-century hardening of positions by professional bodies on both sides of the orthodox/heterodox divide failed either to reflect practice on the ground – health consumers and their care providers simply adopted therapies and commodities from across the therapeutic spectrum – or to produce regulatory victory for either side. Regulatory initiatives, whether driven by or responsive to changes in the medical sciences or strategies of professionalisation and commodification, have been similarly unable to produce an overall consensus on the meaning of 'good' medicine or a monopoly for any single system of practice. Perhaps, therefore, it is time to adopt strategies of exploration, interpretation and practice that look beyond familiar disciplinary boundaries and professional categories to understand complementary, alternative, integrative and indeed 'orthodox' medicine in new ways.

Notes

1 Williams produced a number of images and caricatures satirising the medical profession and its claims, illustrating their popularity with early nineteenth-century audiences. In 'The Guide to Health: or Bonnell Thornton's Consultation of Physicians' (which represents the profession as a trio of wigs on wooden stands), for example, he reiterated his points about the healing powers of nature and the grasping avarice of medical professionals: 'Nature is the best physician and she works with very few medicines, the assistance she wants I shall give and save my fees and my life.' His scorn was not limited to the orthodox profession; another image caricatured the contemporary fad for 'Perkins' Metallic Tractors'.

2 For more on the history of mesmerism, see Bivins (2007: 80–89, 147–152) and Winter (1998). For examples of its use in contemporary medicine, see Landolt and Milling (2011); Lang *et al.* (2000); Berger *et al.* (2010); Pulver and Smith (1961).

3 For example, the flu might be said to progress through headaches, to swollen glands and body aches, to fever and nausea, to the breaking of the fever, to recuperation.

4 *New York Evening Star*, 1833, quoted in Starr (1982: 56).

5 For a study of these effects in contemporary USA, see Tillman (2002).

6 On consensus, see Corfield (2009). On the professions in general, see Corfield (1995) and Digby (1994).

7 For a summary of medicine's gradual adoption of observations, quantitative and experimental method-ologies, see Porter (1997: 304–347) and Weatherall (1996).
8 All quotations above are from *Medical Act 1858*, accessed at www.legislation.gov.uk/ukpga/Vict/21-22/90/section/XXXVII/enacted on 20 February 2013.
9 Weatherall (1996: 176–177) describes some of the Act's limitations.
10 Library of Congress, Abraham Lincoln Papers, Series 1. General Correspondence, 1833–1916. 'Mrs. Charles P. Bunting to Abraham Lincoln, Thursday, September 1, 1864' (Homeopathic treatment for soldiers), accessed at 'American Memory' (http://memory.loc.gov) on 10 March 2013.
11 On contemporary opposition to 'integrative medicine', see, for example, Cassidy (2011) and the numerous online 'Rapid response' commentaries, or compare with the words of former *New England Journal of Medicine* editor-in-chief Arnold Relman, who wrote in 1998:

> There are not two kinds of medicine, one conventional and the other unconventional, that can be practiced jointly in a new kind of 'integrative medicine.' Nor ... are there two kinds of thinking, or two ways to find out which treatments work and which do not. In the best kind of medical practice, all proposed treatments must be tested objectively. In the end, there will only be treatments that pass that test and those that do not, those that are proven worth-while and those that are not.
>
> (Relman, 14 December 1998)

12 See for an example encompassing many of these schisms among the regulars, 'MATTEI', *The Woman's Herald* 10 (27 April 1893), 157. An interview with Britain's first female homeopathic physician illus-trates the growing impact of debates over dosage within homeopathy: 'Interview. Emily Hill', *The Woman's Signal* 137 (13 August 1896), 1–2. See also Rogers (1998).
13 See the 'Clause 33' debates in the House of Commons 'Clause 33. –(Arrangements for general medical services.)', *House of Commons Official Report (Hansard)*, 23 July 1946, cols 1888–1917; the Letters column of the *British Medical Journal* also offers a flavour of these debates, e.g. Winnicott (14 February 1948); Benjamin (20 March 1948); Spoor (28 February 1948). See also Nichols (1988: 220–221).
14 'Trial Brief of Respondent American Medical Association, Docket No. 9064 (filed 19 August 1977)', 54, quoted in Ameringer (2000: 460).
15 Congress, Senate, Judiciary Committee, *Hearing before the Subcommittee on Antitrust and Monopoly* (state-ment of Michael Pertschuk), 10 October 1977, quoted in Ameringer (2000: 465).

Bibliography

Abraham, J. and Davis, C. (2006) 'Testing Times: The Emergence of the Practolol Disaster and its Chal-lenge to British Drug Regulation in the Modern Period', *Social History of Medicine* 19:1, 127–147.
Ameringer, C. F. (2000) 'Organized Medicine on Trial: The Federal Trade Commission vs. the American Medical Association', *Journal of Policy History* 12:4, 445–472.
Association Medical Journal (1853) 'Review: Homeopathy: Its Globules Analyzed', 1:9 (4 March).
Bartrip, P. (1995) 'Secret Remedies, Medical Ethics, and the Finances of the *British Medical Journal*', in Robert Baker, ed., *The Codification of Medical Morality: Historical and Philosophical Studies of the Formaliza-tion of Western Medical Morality in the Eighteenth and Nineteenth Centuries. Volume Two: Anglo-American Medical Ethics and Medical Jurisprudence in the Nineteenth Century* (Boston, MA: Kluwer Academic), 191–204.
Beddoes, T. (1808) *A Letter to the Right Honourable Sir Joseph Banks, Bart. P. R. S.: On the Causes and Removal of the Prevailing Discontents, Imperfections, and Abuses in Medicine* (London: Richard Philips).
Benjamin, A. (1948) 'Homoeopathy', *British Medical Journal, BMJ* 20 March, 571–572.
Berger, M. M., Davadant, M., Marin, C., Wasserfallen, J.-B., Pinget, C., Maravic, P., Koch, N., Raffoul, W. and Chiolero, R. L. (2010) 'Impact of a Pain Protocol Including Hypnosis in Major Burns', *Burns* 36:5, 639–646.
Bivins, R. (2007) *Alternative Medicine? A History* (Oxford: Oxford University Press).
Bonner, T. (2000) *Becoming a Physician, Medical Education in Britain, France, Germany, and the United States, 1750–1945* (Baltimore: Johns Hopkins University Press).
Bradley, J. and Dupree, M. (2001) 'Opportunity on the Edge of Orthodoxy: Medically Qualified Hydrop-athists in the Era of Reform, 1840–60', *Social History of Medicine* 14, 417–437
Bradley, J. and Dupree, M. (2003) 'A Shadow of Orthodoxy? An Epistemology of British Hydropathy, 1840–1858', *Medical History* 47, 173–194.

Bynum, W. F. and Porter, R. (1987) *Medical Fringe and Medical Orthodoxy 1750–1850* (London: Croom Helm).

Cassidy, J. (2011) 'The College of Medicine', *BMJ* 342: d3712.

Cook, H. (2007) *Matters of Exchange: Commerce, Medicine and Science in the Dutch Golden Age* (New Haven: Yale University Press).

Cooter, R., ed. (1988) *Studies in the History of Alternative Medicine* (Basingstoke: Macmillan Press).

Cooter, R. (2001) *Historical Aspects of Unconventional Medicine: Approaches, Concepts, Case Studies* (Sheffield: European Association for the History of Medicine and Health).

Corfield, P. J. (1995) *Power and the Professions in Britain, 1700–1850* (London: Routledge).

Corfield, P. J. (2009) 'From Poison Peddlers to Civic Worthies: The Reputation of the Apothecaries in Georgian England', *Social History of Medicine* 22:1, 1–21.

Devrient, C. and Stratten, S. (1833) *The Homeopathic Medical Doctrine or, 'Organon of the Healing Art'; A New System of Physic Translated from the German of S. Hahnemann* (Dublin: W. F. Wakeman).

Dick, R. (1850) 'On the Practice of Homeopathy', *The Lancet* 55:1396 (June), 659–660.

Digby, A. (1994) *Making a Medical Living: Doctors and Patients in the English Market for Medicine, 1720–1911* (Cambridge: Cambridge University Press).

Eggleston, W. G. (1889) 'The Open Door of Quackery', *The North American Review* 149:395 (October), 483–491.

Fissell, M. E. (1991) 'The Disappearance of the Patient's Narrative and the Invention of Hospital Medicine', in Roger French and Andrew Wear, eds, *British Medicine in the Age of Reform* (London: Routledge), 92–109.

Flexner, A. (1910) *Medical Education in the United States and Canada Bulletin Number Four* (New York City: The Carnegie Foundation for the Advancement of Teaching).

Flint, A. (1889) 'The Open Door of Quackery', *The North American Review*, 149:395 (October), 491–496.

Forbes, J. (1858) *Of Nature and Art in the Cure of Disease*, 2nd edition (London: John Churchill).

Gentilcore, D. (2006) 'The "Golden Age of Quackery" or "Medical Enlightenment"? Licensed Charlatanism in Eighteenth-Century Italy', *Cultural and Social History* 3:3, 250–263.

Gevitz, N., ed. (1988) *Other Healers: Unorthodox Medicine in America* (Baltimore: Johns Hopkins University Press).

Gisjwijt-Hofstra, M., Marland, H. and de Waardt, H., eds (1997) *Illness and Healing Alternatives in Western Europe* (London: Routledge).

Hahnemann, S. (1962) *The Organon of Medicine*, 6th edition (Calcutta: Roysingh and Co.).

Hamlyn, E. (1981) *The Healing Art of Homeopathy* (Chicago: Keats Publishing).

Haller, J. S. Jr (1998) *Kindly Medicine: Physio-Medicalism in America 1836–1911* (Kent, OH: Kent State University Press).

Haller, J. S. Jr. (1999) *A Profile in Alternative Medicine: The Eclectic Medical College of Cincinnati, 1845–1942* (Kent, OH: Kent State University Press).

Haller, J. S. Jr (2005) *The History of American Homeopathy: The Academic Years 1820–1935* (New York: Pharmaceutical Products Press).

Hansen, B. (1998) 'America's First Medical Breakthrough: How Popular Excitement about a French Rabies Cure in 1885 Raised New Expectations for Medical Progress', *The American Historical Review* 103, 373–418.

Hardy A. and Magnello, M. E. (2002) 'Statistical Methods in Epidemiology: Karl Pearson, Ronald Ross, Major Greenwood and Austin Bradford Hill, 1900–1945', *Social-und Präventivmedizin/Social and Preventive Medicine* 47:2, 80–89.

Hooker, W. (1849) *Physician and Patient, or A Practical View of the Mutual Duties, Relations and Interests of the Medical Profession and the Community* (New York: Baker and Scribner).

Jewson, N. D. (1976) 'The Disappearance of the Sick-Man from Medical Cosmology, 1770–1870', *Sociology* 10 (May), 225–244.

Jütte, R., Eklöf, M. and Nelson, M. C. (2001) *Historical Aspects of Unconventional Medicine: Approaches, Concepts, Case Studies* (Sheffield: European Association for the History of Medicine and Health).

Kaufman, M. (1971) *Homeopathy in America: The Rise and Fall of an American Heresy* (Baltimore: Johns Hopkins University Press).

The Lancet (1835) 'Editorial', 23:604 (28 March), 931–934.

Landolt, A. S. and Milling, L. S. (2011) 'The Efficacy of Hypnosis as an Intervention for Labor and Delivery Pain: A Comprehensive Methodological Review', *Clinical Psychology Review* 31:6 (August), 1022–1031.

Lang, E. V., Benotsch, E. G., Fick, L. J., Lutgendorf, S., Berbaum, M. L., Berbaum, K. S., Logan, H. and Spiegel, D. (2000) 'Adjunctive Non-Pharmacological Analgesia for Invasive Medical Procedures: A Randomised Trial', *The Lancet* 355:9214 (29 April), 1486–1490.

Loeb, L. (2001) 'Doctors and Patent Medicines in Modern Britain: Professionalism and Consumerism', *Albion: A Quarterly Journal Concerned with British Studies* 33:3 (Autumn), 404–425.

Marland, H. (1987) *Medicine and Society in Wakefield and Huddersfield, 1780–1870* (Cambridge: Cambridge University Press).

Marland, H. and Adams, J. (2009) 'Hydropathy at Home: The Water Cure and Domestic Healing in Mid-Nineteenth-Century Britain', *Bulletin of the History of Medicine*, 83, 499–529..

Martin, S. C. (1994) '"The Only Truly Scientific Method of Healing": Chiropractic and American Science, 1895–1990', *Isis* 85 (June), viii, 207–227.

Martyr, P. (2002) *Paradise of Quacks: An Alternative History of Medicine in Australia* (Sydney: Macleay Press).

Medical Record (1869) 'American vs. European Medical Science Again', 4:183.

Mesmer, F. A. (1784) 'Catechism on Animal Magnetism', in G. J. Bloch, ed. and trans., *Mesmerism: A Translation of Original Medical and Scientific Writings of F. A. Mesmer, M. D.* (Los Altos, CA: William Kaufmann, Inc., 1980), 81–86.

Nichols, P. A. (1988) *Homeopathy and the Medical Profession* (London: Croom Helm).

Palmer, A. B. (1882) 'Fallacies of Homeopathy', *The North American Review* 134:304 (March), 293–315.

Pelling, M. (2003) *Medical Conflicts in Early Modern London: Patronage, Physicians, and Irregular Practitioners, 1550–1640* (Oxford: Oxford University Press).

The Penny Satirist (1842) 'The Cold Water Cure', Issue 267 (Saturday 28 May), London, England.

Porter, R. (1987) '"I Think ye both Quacks": The Controversy between Dr Theodor Myersbach and Dr John Coakley Lettsom', in W. F. Bynum and Roy Porter, eds, *Medical Fringe and Medical Orthodoxy, 1750–1850* (London: Croom Helm), 56–78.

Porter, R. (1989) *Health for Sale: Quackery in England 1660–1850* (Manchester: Manchester University Press).

Porter, R. (1997) *The Greatest Benefit to Mankind: A Medical History of Humanity* (London: HarperCollins).

Porter, R. (2000) *Quacks: Fakers and Charlatans in English Medicine* (Stroud: Tempus).

Pulver, S. E. and Smith, L. H. (1961) 'Teaching Medical Hypnosis: A Pilot Course at a University Medical School', *Comprehensive Psychiatry* 2:3 (June), 157–162.

Relman, A. S. (1998) 'A Trip to Stonesville: Some Notes on Andrew Weil', *The New Republic*, 14 December.

Roberts, M. D. J. (2009) 'The Politics of Professionalization: MPs, Medical Men, and the 1858 Medical Act', *Medical History* 53:1, 37–56.

Rogers, N. (1990) 'Women and Sectarian Medicine', in Rima D. Apple, ed., *Women, Health, and Medicine in America: A Historical Handbook* (New York: Garland), 281–310.

Rogers, N. (1998) *An Alternative Path: The Making and Remaking of Hahnemann Medical College and Hospital of Philadelphia* (New Brunswick: Rutgers University Press).

Rogers, R. (2008) '"Silence Has Its Own Stories": Elizabeth Kenny, Polio and the Culture of Medicine', *Social History of Medicine* 21:1 (Spring), 145–161.

Rutten, T. (2011) 'Early Modern Medicine', in Mark Jackson, ed., *The Oxford Handbook of the History of Medicine* (Oxford: Oxford University Press), 60–81.

Siraisi, N. (1990) *Medieval and Renaissance Medicine* (Chicago: Chicago University Press).

Spoor, W. H. (1948) 'Free Choice of Doctor', *BMJ*, 28 February, 412.

Starr, P. (1982) *The Social Transformation of American Medicine: The Rise of a Sovereign Profession and the Making of a Vast Industry* (New York: Basic Books).

Taylor-Kirschmann, A. (1999) 'Adding Women to the Ranks, 1860–1890: A New View with a Homeopathic Lens', *Bulletin of the History of Medicine* 73:3, 429–446.

Temple, W. (1680) *Miscellanea. By a Person of Honour* (London: Edward Gellibrand, 1680).

Tillman, R. (2002) 'Paying for Alternative Medicine: The Role of Health Insurers', *Annals of the American Academy of Political and Social Science* 583, 64–75.

Tomes, N. (1998) *The Gospel of Germs: Men, Women, and the Microbe in American Life* (Cambridge, MA: Harvard University Press).

Wallis, P. (2008) 'Consumption, Retailing, and Medicine in Early-Modern London', *Economic History Review* 61:1, 26–53.

Warner, J. H. (1991) 'Ideals of Science and their Discontents in Late Nineteenth-Century American Medicine', *Isis* 82:3 (September), 454–478.

Weatherall, M. (1996) 'Making Medicine Scientific: Empiricism, Rationality, and Quackery in Mid-Victorian Britain', *Social History of Medicine* 9, 175–194.

Webster, C. (1975) *The Great Instauration: Science, Medicine and Reform, 1626–1660* (London: Duckworth, reissued by Peter Lang, 2002).

Williams, C. (1813) 'Doctors Differ or Dame Nature against the College', London: S. W. Fores, British Museum ID Number 1935, and 0522.8.139.

Winnicott, D. W. (1948) 'Pathies in a State Service', *British Medical Journal*, 14 February, 313–314.

Winter, A. (1998) *Mesmerized: Powers of Mind in Victorian Britain* (Chicago: University of Chicago Press).

2

POWER AND PROFESSIONALISATION IN CAM

A sociological approach

Mike Saks

I Defining CAM: the centrality of power

This chapter will set out a sociological approach to complementary and alternative medicine (CAM) in Western societies in general and Britain in particular, with a focus on power and professionalisation in CAM. Too often, this latter concept is seen statically in terms of a group of specific therapies, which are frequently viewed as either traditionally or holistically based. Aside from the fact that only some CAM therapies have long historical roots or take a whole-person approach philosophically and in their practical orientation to the client (see, for example, Coward 1989), developing a definition based on a fixed cluster of therapies does not capture the dynamic nature of CAM in the West. This is best conceptualised as fluidly related to orthodox medicine – the boundaries of both of which are interlinked and change over time (Saks 2003). CAM is therefore defined here in terms of its subordinated position in relation to orthodox health care, centred on the marginality of CAM practitioners in relation to power in the occupational division of labour.

In this sense, orthodox medicine is viewed sociologically as health care underwritten by the state, which is at present based on biomedical dominance and focused heavily on drugs and surgery (as highlighted by Le Fanu 2011). CAM conversely is viewed as those therapies usually not supported by the state and currently largely subordinated to biomedicine (see, for example, Saks 1992a). As such, in Western societies, CAM covers a great range of approaches, from acupuncture and aromatherapy through herbalism and homoeopathy to naturopathy and reflexology. The diverse therapies contained under the umbrella of CAM, moreover, do not necessarily form in any sense a coherent set of practices, except in so far as they are marginalised; the line between medical orthodoxy and the nature of CAM may therefore vary not only historically (Saks 2005a), but also between specific societies and different parts of the world – from Western societies like Britain and the United States to Eastern countries such as China and India (see, for instance, Adams *et al.* 2012).

The interpretation of CAM in this sense is inevitably shaped by theoretical perspectives. My own neo-Weberian approach is based on the concept of exclusionary social closure in the market giving rise to professionalisation (Saks 2010). On this approach, CAM is viewed as a marginal area in terms of the associated creation of bodies of insiders and outsiders through legally enshrined social closure in which medicine and the allied health professions have generally captured the higher political ground. In this respect, CAM is defined in terms of its subordination in the politics of health – and is not simply held to be those therapies that lack available scientific evidence as regards efficacy and effectiveness compared to orthodox medicine (see, for example, Wallis and Morley 1976). This latter view is contentious and can be seen as a part of the dominant ideology of the medical profession in a fluid political game underpinned by group interests involving critical debates about what orthodox medicine has achieved in practice and what is to count as evidence in this discussion (Richardson and Saks 2013).

The essence of the definition of CAM subscribed to in this sociological approach, therefore, is that its constituent therapies are not based on homogeneous intrinsic characteristics, but rather on their politically marginalised position (Saks 2008). Depending on the balance of power, therefore, the orthodoxy of one period can become the unorthodoxy of another, and vice versa. As the title suggests, while CAM can be used in a complementary, more politically acceptable way, to orthodox medicine, it can also be used in a more challenging manner in providing alternative patterns of health care to orthodoxy. This can be illustrated by the complementary use of osteopathy to treat the mechanical aspects of musculo-skeletal problems for which prescribed medicine like analgesics and anti-inflammatory drugs are being given. This contrasts with using alternative therapies like herbalism in place of orthodox medication for conditions such as allergies and asthma (Stone and Katz 2005). However, in all such guises, CAM represents different shades of marginal practice. Central to the process of marginalisation is the crucial notion of professionalisation based on legally bounded exclusionary social closure in the marketplace of occupations which – in elevating the standing of orthodox medicine – underwrites the lack of power of CAM practitioners and their position as outsiders (Saks 2002).

This neo-Weberian view of professionalisation based on the operation of power and interests in the market provides a stronger framework for the analysis of CAM than many other theoretical perspectives since it is centred on a relatively non-assumptive model about the core differentiating characteristics of professional and non-professional groups in simply recognising the legally underpinned existence of professions linked to exclusionary social closure (Saks 2010). This contrasts with the longer standing trait and functionalist approaches to professions which, as part of their very definitions of these groups, reflexively see 'top dog' professions like medicine as rather flatteringly centred on their distinctiveness in terms of such features as high-level expertise, rationality and altruism (see, for instance, Greenwood 1957 and Goode 1960) – while those outside such professions, including semi-professions like nursing, are not thought to have such fully developed characteristics in these areas and this is held to account for their lower position in the pecking order (Etzioni 1969).

More critical approaches to professionalisation linked to the 1960s/70s counter culture and beyond – such as interactionism, Marxism and Foucauldianism – also have their virtues in providing a challenge to the previously dominant orthodoxy. Nonetheless, unlike the neo-Weberian perspective based on seeing professions as a form of market control, they fall foul of the criticism of making rather too many constraining assumptions, albeit in a negative rather than a positive direction. The interactionists typically base their analysis at a micro-level on the largely non-substantiated premise that there is no real difference between professionals and non-professionals – and that being a member of a profession means little more than possessing an honorific symbol (see, for example, Becker 1962 and Hughes 1963). Marxists, meanwhile, tend reflexively and somewhat tautologically to see the operation and role of professions as serving the interests of the capitalist state (as illustrated by Esland 1980), while Foucauldians debunk the ideology of progress associated with professions by employing a concept of governmentality that is very difficult to operationalise (Johnson 1995) and playing fast and loose with the evidence (Foucault 1989).

However, it is argued here that the neo-Weberian approach provides a more productive framework for analysing professionalisation, not least in the context of the position of CAM, and adds to a greater extent to our understanding of its historical dynamics in a wider socio-political environment. Without claiming that the neo-Weberian approach is always applied appropriately (Saks 2010), its particular strength is that it allows us to grasp in an evidential manner the role of power and group interests in the development of health care and other related professionalised fields, including their representation in the contemporary occupational division of labour. Pleasingly, the approach has also been applied in a manner designed to enable the understanding of gender in the politics of professionalisation (Witz 1992) – a dimension that, as will be seen in this and other chapters in this volume, is also important in understanding the marginality of CAM. All of this is highly applicable to examining the interface between orthodox medicine and CAM within a neo-Weberian framework to which we now turn from a historical viewpoint, with particular reference to the political marginalisation of CAM in Britain.

II The political marginalisation of CAM

Here it is crucial to understand that pre-industrial health care in Britain up to the mid-nineteenth century was historically characterised by a comparatively undifferentiated field, with the absence of a nationally enforceable legal monopoly of medicine in neo-Weberian terms (Saks 2005a). In this environment, in which women were traditionally important players both as healers and in their health care role in the home (see, for instance, Oakley 1992), it was very difficult to differentiate practitioners involved in the delivery of health care. While those involved used a broad plethora of practices, which ranged from patent medicine with secret formulae to heroic medicine like bleeding and cupping, their training was often based on apprenticeships and they made parallel use of medical theories and language. Practitioners were also largely indistinguishable in terms of repute. Indeed, at this time there was no central reference point from which to judge best practice – with serious caveats about the knowledge, integrity and modus operandi of even some of those groups that were later to become professionalised. As such, in the first half of the nineteenth century in Britain, groups like apothecaries and surgeons, who became part of the new medical orthodoxy, co-existed with competitors such as herbalists and homeopaths in a mainly open field in which participants hawked their wares in the market for practitioners and self-help remedies (Porter 1995).

This relatively open pluralistic health care field was to be superseded, however, with the creation of a medical profession in Britain through the 1858 Medical Registration Act and subsequent reforming legislation which formalised the power relationship between health groups, including the marginality of CAM. This initial legislation came about as a result of the lobby for a unified profession by the previously fragmented body of apothecaries, surgeons and high-status physicians, led by the Provincial Medical and Surgical Association that later became the British Medical Association – as science came to the fore with the Enlightenment and the demand for health care rose from the middle classes with the industrial revolution (Waddington 1984). The successful campaign to professionalise medicine was thereafter increasingly sustained by state underwriting through first the 1911 National Health Insurance Act and then the 1946 National Health Service Act – facilitated by the so-called 'medical-Ministry alliance', based on collusion between the medical profession and the Department of Health. This informal, but embedded, structural arrangement ensured that, amongst other things, the scope of CAM practice was limited to certain conditions through legislation enacted in the period leading up to the Second World War – with areas like diabetes, epilepsy and glaucoma excluded from claims to treatment by its practitioners (Larkin 1995).

The run-up, and aftermath, to the 1858 Medical Registration Act led to attacks by what was initially an emerging all-male medical profession on rival health groups as incompetent 'quacks' who were a threat to the public, through the media – including mainstream medical organs such as the *Provincial Medical and Surgical Journal* and the *Lancet* (Saks 1995). Such increasingly marginalised practitioners, many of whom were to become CAM practitioners, could still practise under the Common Law outside the publicly funded sector – albeit without the state sanctioned titles of medicine and/or that of the increasing range of other orthodox professions. However, largely as a result of being under siege from the medical profession, the numbers of CAM therapists in operation were significantly driven down in the predominant private domain in which they practised. Medical dominance, even with greater gender differentiation in the profession (Witz 1992), was further reinforced from a neo-Weberian perspective with its ever wider state market shelter, growing orthodox paradigmatic unity around biomedicine, the development of a range of predominantly female subordinated orthodox health professions like nursing and midwifery and the establishment of the even more privileged profession of medicine in terms of income, status and power (Saks 2003).

The position of doctors at the pinnacle of the health pecking order in Britain was also underlined by scientific developments in medicine, such as the discovery of penicillin and the development of more advanced surgical procedures in the first half of the twentieth century (Le Fanu 2011). However, the formal process of differentiation that began in the mid-nineteenth century in Britain appears to have been primarily political rather than justifiable scientifically at that time. This was because, amongst other things, medicine in this period was mainly oriented towards the classification of diseases as opposed to their treatment; aseptic and antiseptic techniques had not been introduced into medicine at this point; anaesthesia was not typically used in surgical operations, with all the associated hazards this brought; and hospitals were still popularly seen as gateways to death (Saks 2003). It is not surprising, therefore, that it proved so difficult to pass the necessary legislation in the mid-nineteenth century establishing the British medical profession, which took seventeen bills and much Parliamentary debate to bring to fruition (Waddington 1984).

It is instructive in this light that medicine did not become professionalised until the early twentieth century in the United States. Whatever the rationale for this differential position, the growing marginality of CAM followed the rise of orthodox medicine, as in the United States. As noted earlier, in Britain – unlike the United States where there was specific state licensing – CAM practitioners retained the right to practise under the Common Law, but otherwise had no real state legitimacy. In this sense, CAM therapists worked within the framework of a *de facto* medical monopoly rather than the *de jure* monopoly by physicians that existed in the United States in neo-Weberian terms (Berlant 1975). In addition, medical ethics in both countries continued to restrict collaboration between medical and CAM practitioners, which only took place under the potential threat of orthodox doctors being struck off as a result of such relationships. There were also intensified attacks in medical journals like the *British Medical Journal* on deviant CAM practitioners in the profession and informal medical colleague controls such as career blockages of medical practitioners using CAM, as well as the stifling of incipient efforts of specific CAM groups of therapists to professionalise – not least the osteopaths in the 1930s (Larkin 1995). This action against competitors who threatened the increasingly powerful leaders of the medical profession helped to bring about a fall in the use of CAM in Britain – even on a self-help basis – by the mid-twentieth century (Saks 2005a). This, however, was a prelude to the growing professionalisation of CAM that was to follow.

III The professionalisation of CAM

Despite this low point of usage in its comparatively short history, there was growing public demand for CAM from the late 1960s and early 1970s in Britain, as well as in the United States. This was inspired by the development of a counter culture on both sides of the Atlantic, which was associated with the search for alternative lifestyles, including through fashion, mysticism and hallucinogenic drugs (Roszak 1970). The specifically medical counter culture was based on, amongst other things, increasing awareness of the limits to medicine linked to its sometimes restricted efficacy and effectiveness; the focus on technocratic solutions to medical problems; the not always helpful extension through medicine of sick life; the increasing availability of a wide range of attractive medical alternatives; a desire to go beyond medical depersonalisation and disempowerment; and a drive by consumers to exercise greater control over their own health care (Saks 2000a). The development of this counter culture provided a spur to the resurgence of interest in CAM in Britain as highlighted by its ever increasing self-help use. More than this, by the beginning of the new millennium, some one-seventh of the population were visiting CAM practitioners each year, more than 60,000 CAM practitioners were in existence and CAM was increasingly employed in the National Health Service by medical and non-medical practitioners alike (Saks 2003).

These trends are an important background to the professionalisation of CAM in Britain in neo-Weberian terms. The increased professionalisation of CAM was prompted by the changing balance of power between orthodox medicine and CAM in this country – paralleling similar shifts in the United States. For the first time, there were strong political pressures for doctors and other orthodox health practitioners to incorporate CAM from a professional interest viewpoint, with the increasing popularity of CAM and rising disaffection with orthodox medicine. Indeed, by the 1980s more than three-quarters of the population wanted more established forms of CAM to be available in the National Health Service – and with the reduction in stigma associated with CAM, many orthodox practitioners, from general practitioners to physiotherapists, began to take up private practice outside the National Health Service (Saks 1992a). The General Medical Council also relaxed its prescriptive ethical codes on referrals to CAM practitioners around this time. This shift was fuelled by the greater receptivity of government to the professionalisation of CAM – driven in part by increased political lobbying for CAM, not least through influential figures such as Prince Charles and the All-Party Parliamentary Group for Complementary and Alternative Medicine (Saks 2005a).

This is not to say that medical opposition to CAM was dropped at this time. There were still accusations in the medical journals condemning CAM for its irrationality and lack of safety (Saks 1995) – as well as its comparative lack of efficacy, particularly in the context of developments in orthodox medicine by the turn of the twenty-first century in such areas as cataract surgery and hip replacements (Le Fanu 2011). The negative approach by orthodox medicine towards CAM was most fully exemplified by the report on alternative therapy by the British Medical Association (1986). This lauded the march of scientific medical progress, before linking CAM therapies with superstition and witchcraft. However, signs of the changing climate towards CAM were epitomised by the more favourable report on this area by the British Medical Association (1993) in which the discussion focused less on the 'alternative' therapies that threatened the interests of many of its members and more on 'complementary' therapies, calling for a more medicalised CAM curriculum including anatomy and physiology. One of the fundamental obstacles to progress in terms of the exercise of power, though, remained that of the extremely low state medical research funding of CAM and its marginality in the undergraduate medical curriculum. This began to change, however, with the publication of the field breaking report of the House of Lords Select Committee on Science and Technology (2000) on CAM, which took a positive stance on increasing research and practice in selected CAM therapies, particularly where there was sufficient evidence for their operation and robust self-regulatory mechanisms – a position now underpinned by a General Medical Council requirement to teach undergraduate medical students about CAM.

Largely as a consequence of this shifting political context, there has been a growing move to professionalise CAM in Britain. Certainly, as discussed further in this volume, CAM practitioners have increasingly based their work on a greater amount of formal education and training to enhance their expertise, along with the development of stringent ethical frameworks for practice. In line with this, ever more groups of CAM therapists have introduced voluntary self-regulation with its associated professionalising accoutrements (Saks 2003). Groups of non-medical acupuncturists and homoeopaths are illustrative cases in point. The former overcame the many previous organisational splits in acupuncture by founding in 1980 the British Acupuncture Council as a voluntary registration body, followed later by the British Acupuncture Accreditation Board, which together set minimum educational and ethical standards. Similarly, while homoeopathy has not been as unified in the contemporary context as acupuncture, the Society of Homoeopaths was established in 1981 with a voluntary register, a code of ethics, a degree-level educational programme and related accreditation arrangements – thereby progressing professionalisation in this parallel CAM field.

The osteopaths and chiropractors, moreover, went one step further in moving beyond some of their own internal divisions by putting in place more developed legally based mechanisms of exclusionary closure in Britain through private member's bills (Saks 1999). More specifically, in 1993, the Osteopaths Act established the General Osteopathic Council, with the main function of upholding a statutory register underpinned by educational and ethical standards and providing legal protection of title. In 1994, the Chiropractors Act laid the foundation for the introduction of the General Chiropractic Council based on statutory regulation with its own standards of education and practice. It is interesting that, of all the CAM therapies, these professionalised groups are the most male dominated in a CAM environment where women are in the large majority. It should be noted, though, that there are restrictions on their legal monopolies – not least because state underwriting does not provide the privileged access for osteopaths and chiropractors to National Health Service practice that it does for more orthodox health professions. Against this, as noted previously, some qualified health professionals have themselves been delivering certain types of CAM because of the attractions it offers from a professional interest perspective at particular stages in the career ladder – in providing additional opportunities to engage in both state and private practice (Saks 2003).

Nonetheless, until recently, CAM therapists in Britain have generally been very reluctant to professionalise as they move from the cottage stage of their development based on apprenticeships and other informal means of skill acquisition (Cant and Sharma 1999). This is highlighted by the considerable delay that has occurred in Britain in forming voluntary and statutory regulatory organisations in CAM in modern times, not least compared to the United States (Saks 2000b). There also remain many outlying individual CAM therapists who do not wish to join professional bodies, even in currently rapidly professionalising CAM areas. In addition, some CAM practitioners continue to resist consolidated professionalisation in their specific fields, such as aromatherapists and crystal therapists. This is partly explained by the value placed on independence by CAM practitioners who often variously work in private practice, operate outside the National Health Service, dislike bureaucracy and hierarchy, regard individualism as sacrosanct, see a free spirit as essential to practice, hold egalitarian philosophies and do not tend to collaborate either within or across disciplines (see, for example, Saks 1997).

The term 'herding cats' has sometimes been applied to CAM therapists as their individualistic approach – together with factional divisions within their ranks – has served to undermine their unity and collective power in the politics of professionalisation. However, the main reason for the limits to CAM professionalisation from a neo-Weberian approach is the impact of wider systems of power. This includes the negative response to the resurgence of CAM from orthodox health practitioner groups based on professional self-interests because of the challenge that it poses through competing philosophies and practices to their income, status and power (Saks 2006). This is well illustrated by acupuncture, which in its traditional form as a panacea involves needling points on meridians to regulate the flow of yin and yang – thereby philosophically existing completely outside the realm of orthodox biomedicine (Saks 1992b). The limitations also relate to the initial rejection by government of specific CAM therapy interest in gaining professional standing without a unified approach across all the diverse CAM approaches, which was never likely to happen (Sharma 1995). Finally, the pressures bought by other interest groups against the acceptance of CAM cannot be ignored – most notably, by the pharmaceutical industry, with which there are clear interest-based CAM conflicts (Goldacre 2013), notwithstanding the increasing provision of mass-produced over-the-counter CAM remedies. This discussion leads neatly on to the consideration of the question of the future of CAM professionalisation in Britain.

IV The future of the professionalisation of CAM

In assessing the future of CAM professionalisation in Britain, it is very important to understand not just power relationships, but the benefits and costs of such a development to the public and practitioners alike. In gauging these, the position is not entirely straightforward because, as has been seen, there are different forms of professionalisation of CAM, such as voluntary and statutory regulation, which may be differentially regarded in terms of both the interests of practitioners and the public good. The view that is taken here also depends on the theoretical approach of the enquirer. This was explored earlier in the chapter in outlining the different sociological theories of professions which can run in opposite directions in relation to the professionalisation of CAM as they start out from positive or negative views of the professions. In addition, what is of benefit or cost to the CAM groups concerned may not always serve the interests of their clients and/or the wider public – although it should not be assumed that professional interests and the public interest necessarily conflict, as there is also the potential for them to coalesce (Saks 1995).

Having said this, the benefits to the public and practitioners of the professionalisation of CAM in Britain may variously include, for example, the possession of a stronger educational base, centred on certified knowledge and expertise; a greater commitment to evidence-based practice; the existence of codes of ethics protecting the public; the improved security of the position of those engaged in practising CAM therapies; and the enhanced income, status and power of CAM practitioners. There are also potential downsides in terms of the costs of CAM professionalisation, like increased social distancing from the client; constraints on the scope of practice in an era of specialisation; closed shop self-regulation giving rise to the operation of self-interested professional tribalism; silo-based professional barriers to multi-disciplinary and integrated working; and more limited client accountability and responsiveness (Saks 2003). Overall, though, the benefits may outweigh the costs for at least some CAM therapies – depending on the hazards to clients that exist in particular CAM fields.

In this light, it is perhaps not surprising that, although in the past there have been obstacles to the professionalisation of CAM, this is now becoming more of a direction in Britain. This may seem perverse given recent media attacks on health and social care professions, including orthodox medical practitioners, in the wake of scandals involving those found guilty of abusive behaviour towards patients – from the case of Dr Harold Shipman, the serial-killing general practitioner who was convicted through the courts of disposing of over 200 of his patients (Allsop and Saks 2002), to the more recent case of the staff at the Mid Staffordshire NHS Foundation Trust who neglected the most basic elements of patient care (Francis Inquiry 2013). However, these dilemmas related to the health professions have increasingly been addressed at a wider level by government – not least through the White Paper on *Trust, Assurance and Safety – The Regulation of Health Professionals in the 21st Century* (Department of Health 2007). The reforms highlighted here covered such areas as assuring the independence of regulatory bodies; ensuring continuous fitness to practise; and addressing new roles and emerging professions. Pleasingly, they have now largely been implemented and considerably enhance the protection of the public – even if there is clearly some way to go in policing health and social care provision at a professional and institutional level (Law Commission, Scottish Law Commission and Northern Ireland Law Commission 2012 and 2014 – see further McHale, this volume).

There were proposals in the White Paper on *Trust, Assurance and Safety* specifically relating to CAM as a professionalising area. These were primarily aimed at ensuring a system of regulation proportionate to the risks and benefits involved and providing statutory regulation for certain groups such as psychotherapists and counsellors (Department of Health 2007). In this respect, the White Paper also led to a CAM Steering Group being established to explore the regulation of acupuncture, herbal medicine and traditional Chinese medicine. This reported to ministers in 2008 on the statutory regulation of these groups – and prompted a consultation with key stakeholders, the results of which were fed back in 2011. This showed that most respondents preferred statutory to voluntary regulation to protect the public in these fields and to enhance practice quality. The future prospects for the further professionalisation of CAM in Britain, though, are not strong. Even acupuncture, for which statutory regulation has long been lobbied and which has one of the strongest systems of voluntary regulation (Saks 2005b), does not look like it will be allowed to have statutory regulation at present as it is not seen as such a great threat to the health of the public (Hansard 2011).

V Conclusion

The situation in relation to the professionalisation of CAM in Britain has been restricted by recently renewed attacks on CAM as non-scientific and the reluctance of some orthodox scientists to give such therapies political legitimacy – when what may be required is a more flexible, but no less rigorous, methodological approach going beyond the longstanding biomedical gold standard of the randomised controlled trial in appraising different therapeutic approaches in a pluralist society (Callahan 2002). This, however, has not prevented CAM from gaining professional standing in neo-Weberian terms in Britain and elsewhere in the Western world – even if the Anglo-American self-regulatory professional model is not so prevalent in continental Europe (Collins 1990). In countries in the latter area, a model more closely aligned to the growth of the state and state bureaucracies based on government regulated training and examination tends to prevail (Svensson and Evetts 2010). However, the trends are still unmistakeable – even if the form that the professionalisation of CAM takes necessarily varies widely. In the United States, for example, there has been state-by-state licensure of therapies like osteopathy and chiropractic, which in these specific cases interestingly preceded their statutory regulation as professions in Britain. In France, meanwhile, certain CAM therapies like acupuncture and homoeopathy have long been absorbed exclusively into the practice of the medical profession, backed with the force of law against other orthodox health professionals and non-orthodox CAM practitioners (Saks 2003).

A key question that therefore arises in conclusion is what the most appropriate form of professional regulation may be in particular societies and in relation to which specific CAM therapies – given, as was seen at the outset of this chapter, the great diversity of the constituent elements of CAM. What should, for instance, be the balance between voluntary and statutory regulation of CAM? What rights relative to orthodox medicine should exist for CAM practitioners in relation to these modes of regulation? Should all CAM therapies be so professionalised – and where should any limits be drawn? How far should the practice of CAM be restricted to orthodox medical or allied health professionals? And how much discretion should be given to the public in terms of safety to engage with CAM through self-help rather than practitioner delivery? These issues all require further debate politically from the standpoint of consumers, both in Britain and internationally. However, from a sociological viewpoint, the form that CAM takes in the future seems likely to continue to be based on the prevalent configurations of power and interests discussed. Nonetheless, sociological knowledge of the operation of these power structures by groups such as users, CAM practitioners and orthodox health professionals may usefully feed into the debate – along with the contributions of disciplines other than sociology, from public health specialists to health economists. This will help to promote a positive resolution of the issues raised in the public interest in terms of future policy on professionalisation in CAM in Britain and beyond.

References

Adams, J., Andrews, G. J., Barnes, J., Broom, A. and Magin, P. (eds) (2012) *Traditional, Complementary and Integrative Medicine: An International Reader*, Houndmills: Palgrave Macmillan.

Allsop, J. and Saks, M. (eds) (2002) *Regulating the Health Professions*, London: Sage.

Becker, H. (1962) 'The nature of a profession'. In: National Society for the Study of Education (eds) *Education for the Professions*, Chicago: University of Chicago Press.

Berlant, J. L. (1975) *Profession and Monopoly: A Study of Medicine in the United States and Great Britain*, Berkeley: University of California Press.

British Medical Association (1986) *Report of the Board of Science and Education on Alternative Therapy*, London: BMA.

British Medical Association (1993) *Complementary Medicine: New Approaches to Good Practice*, London: BMA.

Callahan, D. (ed.) (2002) *The Role of Complementary and Alternative Medicine: Accommodating Pluralism*, Washington D.C.: Georgetown University Press.

Cant, S. and Sharma, U. (1999) *A New Medical Pluralism? Alternative Medicine, Doctors, Patients and the State*, London: UCL Press.

Collins, R. (1990) 'Market closure and the conflict theory of the professions'. In: Burrage, M. and Torstendahl, R. (eds) *Professions in Theory and History: Rethinking the Study of the Professions*, London: Sage.

Coward, R. (1989) *The Whole Truth: The Myth of Alternative Medicine*, London: Faber and Faber.

Department of Health (2007) *Trust, Assurance and Safety – The Regulation of Health Professionals in the 21st Century*, London: The Stationery Office.

Esland, G. (1980) 'Diagnosis and therapy'. In: Esland, G. and Salaman, G. (eds) *The Politics of Work and Occupations*, Milton Keynes: Open University Press.

Etzioni, A. (ed.) (1969) *The Semi-professions and their Organization: Teachers, Nurses and Social Workers*, New York: Free Press.

Foucault, M. (1989) *Madness and Civilization: A History of Insanity in the Age of Reason*, London: Routledge.

Francis Inquiry (2013) *Report of the Mid Staffordshire NHS Foundation Trust Public Inquiry*, London: The Stationery Office.

Goldacre, B. (2013) *Bad Pharma: How Drug Companies Mislead Doctors and Harm Patients*, London: Faber and Faber.

Goode, W. (1960) 'Encroachment, charlatanism and the emerging profession: Psychology, sociology and medicine', *American Sociological Review* 25: 902–14.

Greenwood, E. (1957) 'Attributes of a profession', *Social Work* 2(3): 45–55.

Hansard (2011) 'Written ministerial statements: Acupuncture, herbal medicine and traditional Chinese medicine', *Hansard*, 16 February.

House of Lords Select Committee on Science and Technology (2000) *Report on Complementary and Alternative Medicine*, London: The Stationery Office.

Hughes, E. (1963) 'Professions', *Daedalus* 92: 655–68.

Johnson, T. (1995) 'Governmentality and the institutionalization of expertise'. In: Johnson, T., Larkin. G. and Saks, M. (eds) *Health Professions and the State in Europe*, London: Routledge.

Larkin, G. (1995) 'State control and the health professions in the United Kingdom: Historical perspectives'. In: Johnson, T., Larkin. G. and Saks, M. (eds) *Health Professions and the State in Europe*, London: Routledge.

Law Commission, Scottish Law Commission and Northern Ireland Law Commission (2012) *Regulation of Healthcare Professionals/Regulation of Social Work Professionals in England: A Joint Consultation Paper*. See: http://lawcommission.justice.gov.uk/areas/Healthcare_professions.htm.

Law Commission (2014) *Regulation of Health Care Professionals: Regulation of Social Care Professionals* (England, Scotland, Northern Ireland) Law Comm No 345 London.

Le Fanu, J. (2011) *The Rise and Fall of Modern Medicine*, London: Abacus, 2nd edition.

Oakley, A. (1992) 'The wisewoman and the doctor'. In: Saks, M. (ed.) *Alternative Medicine in Britain*, Oxford: Clarendon Press.

Porter, R. (1995) *Disease, Medicine and Society, 1550–1860*, Cambridge: Cambridge University Press, 2nd edition.

Richardson, J. and Saks, M. (2013) 'Researching orthodox and complementary and alternative medicine'. In: Saks, M. and Allsop, J. (eds) *Researching Health: Qualitative, Quantitative and Mixed Methods*, London: Sage, 2nd edition.

Roszak, T. (1970) *The Making of a Counter Culture*, London: Faber and Faber.

Saks, M. (1992a) 'Introduction'. In: Saks, M. (ed.) *Alternative Medicine in Britain*, Oxford: Clarendon Press.

Saks, M. (1992b) 'The paradox of incorporation: Acupuncture and the medical profession in modern Britain'. In: Saks, M. (ed.) *Alternative Medicine in Britain*, Oxford: Clarendon Press.

Saks, M. (1995) *Professions and the Public Interest: Medical Power, Altruism and Alternative Medicine*, London: Routledge.

Saks, M. (1997) 'Alternative therapies: Are they holistic?', *Complementary Therapies in Nursing and Midwifery* 3: 4–8.

Saks, M. (1999) 'The wheel turns? Professionalisation and alternative medicine in Britain', *Journal of Interprofessional Care* 13: 129–38.

Saks, M. (2000a) 'Medicine and the counter culture'. In: Cooter, R. and Pickstone, J. (eds) *Medicine in the Twentieth Century*, Amsterdam: Harwood Academic Publishers.

Saks, M. (2000b) 'Professionalization, politics and CAM'. In: Kelner, M., Wellman, B., Pescosolido, B. and Saks, M. (eds) *Complementary and Alternative Medicine: Challenge and Change*, Amsterdam: Harwood Academic Publishers.

Saks, M. (2002) 'Professionalization, regulation and alternative medicine'. In: Allsop, J. and Saks, M. (eds) *Regulating the Health Professions*, London: Sage.

Saks, M. (2003) *Orthodox and Alternative Medicine: Politics, Professionalization and Health Care*, London: Sage.

Saks, M. (2005a) 'Political and historical perspectives'. In: Heller, T., Lee-Treweek, G., Katz, J., Stone, J. and Spurr, S. (eds) *Perspectives on Complementary and Alternative Medicine*, London: Routledge.

Saks, M. (2005b) 'Regulating complementary and alternative medicine: The case of acupuncture'. In: Lee-Treweek, G., Heller, T., Spurr, S., McQueen, H. and Katz, J. (eds) *Perspectives on Complementary and Alternative Medicine: A Reader*, London: Routledge.

Saks, M. (2006) 'The alternatives to medicine'. In: Gabe, J., Kelleher, D. and Williams, G. (eds) *Challenging Medicine*, London: Routledge, 2nd edition.

Saks, M. (2008) 'Policy dynamics: Marginal groups in the healthcare division of labour in the UK'. In: Kuhlmann, E. and Saks, M. (eds) *Rethinking Professional Governance*, Bristol: Policy Press.

Saks, M. (2010) 'Analyzing the professions: The case for the neo-Weberian approach', *Comparative Sociology* 9(6): 887–915.

Sharma, U. (1995) *Complementary Medicine Today: Practitioners and Patients*, London: Routledge, revised edition.

Stone, J. and Katz, J. (2005) 'Can complementary and alternative medicine be classified?' In: Heller, T., Lee-Treweek, G., Katz, J., Stone, J. and Spurr, S. (eds) *Perspectives on Complementary and Alternative Medicine*, London: Routledge.

Svensson, L. G. and Evetts, J. (2010) 'Introduction'. In: Svensson, L. G. and Evetts, J. (eds) *Sociology of Professions: Continental and Anglo-Saxon Traditions*, Gothenburg: Daidalos.

Waddington, I. (1984) *The Medical Profession in the Industrial Revolution*, London: Gill and Macmillan.

Wallis, R. and Morley, P. (1976) 'Introduction'. In: Wallis, R. and Morley, P. (eds) *Marginal Medicine*, London: Peter Owen.

Witz, A. (1992) *Professions and Patriarchy*, London: Routledge.

3

LEGAL FRAMEWORKS, PROFESSIONAL REGULATION AND CAM PRACTICE IN ENGLAND

Is CAM "the special one"?

Jean V. McHale

I Introduction

The development of CAM practice in England and internationally over the last thirty years has led to what in many respects can be viewed as a polarized debate. It has been suggested that some forms of CAM are untested and have the potential to place patients at risk of considerable harm (Singh and Ernst, 2009). In contrast, others have identified the dangers of seeing CAM in such uncomplicated terms, not least because alternative medical practices are utilized in main-stream medical practice by clinicians and nurses (Saks, 2002, chapter 4). CAM can be better seen as a spectrum of practices involving widely different types of practice, and consequently different risks and different challenges. Thus while "CAM" may prove a useful "umbrella" term, in other respects it can be misleading as it brings together such different bedfellows. At one extreme, CAM practice involves the prescription of pharmaceuticals in the form of herbal medicine, something which is regulated as part of the general EU regime for the regulation of pharmaceuticals. At the other end of the spectrum are practices such as shaman healing (see Alich, this volume), which fall considerably outside standard Western medical models.

This spectrum is mirrored in a range of different professional regulatory responses in England. Certain parts of CAM regulation can be seen as very much akin to the regulation of conventional medical practice. So, for example, in the case of two specific groups, chiropractors and osteopaths, as discussed below the regulation is rooted in a statutory basis. Indeed in many respects the regulatory system here is similar to professional statutory regulatory structures which apply to doctors and to nurses. In relation to another group, there is voluntary self-regulation for example, through the Complementary and Natural Healthcare Council, which is in turn underpinned by statute through the role of the Professional Standards Authority. There has been notable resistance in some parts of the community to regulate CAM, which may be seen as analogous with the turf wars in relation to conventional medicine and the battles to stop regulation being vested from the control of the medical profession itself and entrusted to a more independent body (Stacey, 1992; Davies, 2007). Nonetheless, while some CAM practitioners are not subject to formal professional regulatory processes, as we shall see, that does not at all mean that they are excluded from broader legal regulation.

What is interesting is that, despite the differences between areas of CAM and conventional medical practice in relation to law and regulation, the discourses, policy questions and challenges have similar themes. As various commentators have noted with any area of medicine, CAM may give rise to safety risks. These could include errors in clinical practice, problems with the relationship between CAM medication and other medication clinically prescribed, incorrect dosage of drugs or incorrect preparation (Robinson *et al.*, 2011; see also Wilkinson and Gale, this volume). As Robinson *et al.* note, there are also risks from "lack of quality control, licensing, regulation and misrepresentation" or indeed when used as an alternative to conventional medicine (Robinson *et al.*, 2011: 50). The precise safety risks will inevitably vary according to the area of CAM practice – but they are very real. That does not mean of course that all forms of conventional medical practice are necessarily safe or necessarily of high quality. Whether hospitals, for example, can be regarded as "safe" places has been placed under the public spotlight following major scandals from the 1990s onwards (Bristol Royal Infirmary Inquiry, 2001; Francis Inquiry, 2013). The deficiencies in professional regulatory structures in relation to safeguarding patients from bad practices by clinicians have been subject to criticisms for many years (Stacey, 1992; Davies, 2007) and were acutely highlighted in the Shipman Inquiry (Shipman Inquiry, 2004). In addition, some forms of "conventional" health care practitioners are not subject to statutory regulation, such as health care assistants, of whom there is widespread use today across the NHS. While neither areas of patient care can thus be seen as totally free of controversy and areas of bad practice, what is clearly the case is that there is not as much systematic regulation of practice across CAM as a whole. In contrast, in relation to conventional medicine, the last few years have seen growth in practices such as audit and inspection – through the role of bodies such as the Care Quality Commission, see Gale and Wilkinson in this volume. What appears to be the case is that the evidence in relation to various aspects of the safety of CAM practice remains somewhat problematic. This is due to the fact that there are no standardized data available across the sector and, moreover, there are challenges in relation to recording adverse safety events, not least because there has been some professional resistance to the introduction of such audit practices in the past (Robinson *et al.*, 2011).

Should CAM be regarded as "special" or "different" for the purposes of legal and regulatory structures or is it the case that we can learn from the lessons of conventional medical practice when considering how regulatory structures and processes can operate in relation to professional frameworks and operational issues in practice? This chapter explores the legal and regulatory structures which operate in relation to CAM practitioners. First, the "professional" regulation of CAM practice is considered. The role of the professional regulatory body is examined and its effectiveness and appropriateness as a regulatory tool is explored. It compares and contrasts systems for statutory and voluntary regulation. Recent proposals advanced by the Law Commission for reforming the structure of professional regulation of health and social care professionals are explored in this context. It is suggested that, while both may have their place at certain times, if CAM practitioners wish truly to take on the mantle of "health care" professionals, such regulatory accountability will become not only desirable but necessary. Second, while law may create professional regulatory structures, this is only one part of professional practice regulation. Other legal frameworks inform and at times constrain the boundaries of professional practice. General principles of health law in England are considered and how these specifically apply in the context of CAM practice. This highlights the fact that the nature of legal responsibilities of CAM practitioners is no different than that of their medical counterparts and that there is a danger in assuming that practitioners will not ultimately be subject to the scrutiny of the courts. Third, the growing role of the EU in relation to regulation of CAM practice through its engagement with the regulation of products and practitioners and how this is also framing the legitimacy of regulation is examined. Finally, the chapter concludes by asking whether further alignment of conventional and CAM regulatory practice in this area is inevitable in the future. It suggests that there may be a case for practitioners engaging with reflexive, responsible regulatory practice in terms of both professional structures in general and issues of day-to-day operational concern, rather than these being foisted upon them ultimately through external pressures.

II Regulating CAM "professionals"

The evolution of CAM professions and professionals has a long history (see Bivins, Adams and Stone, this volume). Whether someone is a "professional" remains a major source of debate (see, further, Saks, this volume). Historically, the term professional centred on certain specific groups of practitioners. Today the word professional is used in a wide range of different contexts: at one extreme, a profession subject to formal statutory regulatory processes, a regulatory body and detailed ethical code; at the other, the term "professional" is used to indicate that an individual has a specific level of competence in a designated activity. Currently there is considerable variation in the amount of professional regulation which exists in relation to complementary and alternative medicine. The House of Lords Science and Technology Select Committee in their Sixth Report (2000) divided CAM therapies and disciplines into three broad categories. The first group they termed "principle disciplines". They included osteopaths and chiropractors. This group also included acupuncture, herbal medicines and homeopathy. In their second group were those therapies seen as "complementary" – included in this category were the Alexander technique, aromatherapy, Bach and other flower remedies. Their third category included "alternative disciplines", described as "long established and traditional systems of health care", such as athroposophical medicine and Chinese herbal medicine, and also what they called "other alternative disciplines", such as crystal therapy and iridology. Well over a decade on, it remains the case that the formal regulation of such practitioners and or practices in the UK can be seen in terms of these three groups, though with less engagement by formal statutory regulatory structures than might have been thought to be the case. Osteopaths and chiropractors remain the sole recipients of a formal statutory regulatory structure. While, as we will see, voluntary regulation does also apply in relation to a widening group of other practitioners, the scope of such regulation remains far from universal.

The regulation of CAM professionals is an area of heated debate. There are a number of reasons why a specific professional body may be the subject of regulation. One reason may be that of safeguarding the professional autonomy of the profession, of maintaining power, of controlling access. Individuals may seek professional identification to reinforce professional status. Another reason may be that of safeguarding the interests of the public. This rationale was well expressed in *Gupte v General Medical Council*. Here the court stated that, "The public must be able to approach doctors, lawyers and other professionals with complete faith that they are both honest and competent. Without that faith the problems that would arise are too obvious to state."[1] Professions need trust to operate; without it, the profession itself would simply collapse. There is a major concern and indeed public interest to ensure that professional practice is safe, as we have seen. However, there is also a further rationale, that of maintaining professional standards of behaviour. Professionals are seen as needing to behave "professionally" and "ethically" – being beholden to standards of conduct – be honest, act in good faith and uphold high standards of decency. This has been reflected, as we shall see below, in the increased use of professional codes of practice. Yet the drive towards professional uniformity, with the constraints that such uniformity would impose, would not be welcome in many areas of CAM practice. (For further, see Saks and Stone in this volume.)

The legal regulation of complementary and alternative medical practitioners in England and Wales is divided up in relation to, first, those areas where there is specific statutory regulation which governs their operation and, second, those areas in which, while there may be no specific statutory provision targeted at a specific activity undertaken by those professions, their day-to-day activities are governed by the operation of applicable provisions of criminal and civil law, which may be determined by statute or by common law.[2] Thus, while certain areas of CAM activity may on first glance not be subject to legal regulation, in fact this is very far from being the case. Here we consider those CAM areas which are currently subject to statutory and to non-statutory regulation.

III Statutorily regulated CAM professionals: osteopaths and chiropractors

1 The regulatory framework

Both osteopaths and chiropractors became subject to statutory regulation in the 1990s (Stone and Matthews, 1995). Osteopaths are regulated under the Osteopaths Act 1993 and chiropractors under the Chiropractors Act 1994. As both pieces of legislation follow what is substantially the same structure, they will be considered together in this chapter. While there is not a statutory definition of osteopath and chiropractor contained in the respective pieces of legislation, some further guidance is provided in the codes and statements of proficiency produced by their regulatory bodies. So in the case of the chiropractic profession, the code states the following definition:

> A health profession concerned with the diagnosis, treatment and prevention of mechanical disorders or the musculoskeletal system and the effects of those disorders on the functions of the nervous system and general health. There is an emphasis on manual treatments including spinal adjustment and other soft-joint and tissue manipulation.
>
> *(WFC Dictionary Definition, World Federation of Chiropractic, 2001)*

Both the Acts establish a general regulatory body. In the case of osteopaths, the General Osteopathic Council has the role of developing, promoting and regulating the profession.[3] As of June 2014, there were 4,795 osteopaths registered on the Osteopaths Register. In the case of chiropractors, the professional regulatory body is the General Chiropractic Council.[4] The establishment of these statutory bodies follows the approach of existing professional regulatory bodies, such as the General Medical Council or the Nursing and Midwifery Council. Professional competence which is afforded by proper professional education and training is a theme which underpins both statutes. The respective councils are required to establish Education Committees,[5] which have general duties of promoting high standards of professional education and training in their respective areas.[6] The Acts also provide that the Committee can appoint "Visitors" to visit[7] and report back upon places providing education or training as regulated under the legislation.[8]

The title of a profession has consequences which resonate across time and space. It affords professional status and is a badge of identity. Once assumed, it also highlights the responsibilities and obligations that flow from professional practice. In relation to the medical profession, both the Osteopaths Act and the Chiropractors Act safeguard the professional title itself. In order to use the title of osteopath in the UK, an individual must be registered with the General Osteopathic Council and similarly, in relation to the title chiropractor, they must be registered with the General Chiropractic Council. Failure to do this constitutes a criminal offence under both pieces of legislation.[9]

Professional oversight is provided by a registrar, who is also required to establish a register of the relevant professionals.[10] The general council of either body may recognize a qualification which has been provided by a UK institution or which is proposed to be recognized by a UK institution.[11] Likewise, power is given to the council to withdraw recognition.[12] In addition, provision is given for rules in relation to the continuing professional development of practitioners.[13] Further scrutiny powers are given in relation to education institutions – the general council can look at what the requirements are for the course, the financial position of that institution and, interestingly, the "efficiency of the institutions management".[14]

In order to be registered in their respective professional registers, the legislation provides that both chiropractors and osteopaths must be of "good character" and established to be in good health.[15] They must also have paid the fee required and have a recognized qualification.[16] Specific provision is also made for conditional registration in cases where practitioners without such a qualification can demonstrate at least four years in "lawful, safe and competent practice" and, if required to do so, pass a test of competence.[17] Provision also exists under section 5A of both the Osteopaths and the Chiropractors Acts for the temporary registration of a visiting practitioner from a "relevant European state".

Transparency and accountability of osteopaths and chiropractors is also facilitated through the register being made available to the public at all reasonable times.[18] Powers are also given to the registrar to examine registrations which may have been procured frequently.[19] Under section 29 of the Osteopaths Act 1993 and the Chiropractors Act 1994, appeals lie against the refusal of the respective registrar to register an individual, their issuance of only a provisional or conditional registration, or their removal of the name of a chiropractor/osteopath from the relevant register.[20]

2 *Professional conduct and health matters*

As with the medical and nursing professions, professional conduct forms a major part of the statutory regulatory structure. Both the Osteopaths Act and the Chiropractors Act establish committees which consider aspects of professional regulation: first, the Investigating Committee, which investigates complaints made against practitioners;[21] second, the Professional Conduct Committee, which has regulatory powers in relation to professional standards;[22] and finally, the Health Committee, which addresses issues of health and their impact upon professional practice.[23] The registrar has power to suspend the registration of a practitioner.[24] In some situations, practitioners who have been struck off the register may be reinstated; however, in such situations the registrar must refer this question of reinstatement to the Professional Conduct Committee of the relevant council. Professional conduct and fitness to practice proceedings may be brought against chiropractors and osteopaths under section 20(1) of both the Osteopaths and Chiropractors Act where an allegation has been made against them relating to the following:

a   he has been guilty of conduct which falls short of the standard required of a registered osteopath [or chiropractor];
b   he has been guilty of professional incompetence;
c   he has been convicted (at any time) in the United Kingdom of a criminal offence; or
d   his ability to practice as an osteopath [or chiropractor] is seriously impaired because of his physical or mental condition.

The legislation provides that "unacceptable professional conduct" is conduct falling short of the standard expected of the relevant professional.[25] The case would be initially examined by the Investigating Committee. If they found that there was a case to answer, then the matter would be referred either to the Professional Conduct Committee or to the Health Committee, depending on the issue raised.[26] A number of specific powers are given to the Professional Conduct Committee as disposal powers if the allegations are proved. These are to admonish the practitioner, make an order imposing conditions which must be complied with while practising, and order suspension of registration for a specified period or removal from the register.[27] If the Health Committee is satisfied that the allegations are well founded, then it can make an order imposing conditions which they should comply with or order suspension from the register for a specified period.[28] Where satisfied that it is necessary to do so "in order to protect members of the public", both the Professional Conduct Committee and Health Committees have interim powers while an investigation is ongoing and can order the registrar to suspend registration.[29] The committees are also required to appoint legal and medical assessors to provide specialist advice.[30] The powers under both these pieces of legislation were clearly modelled upon those adopted in relation to medical and analogous professions, to provide a clear, formal structure, with expertise and independent checks and balances as part of the process.

3 Codes of practice

One of the standard features of professional regulatory structures across professions today is the publication of codes of practice – guidance to facilitate day-to-day conduct alongside the bare bones of a statute. Both the General Osteopathic Council and the General Chiropractic Council are required by statute to publish a code of practice[31] and also to produce a standard of efficiency.[32] It is not surprising that there is some engagement in these codes with questions of ethics. As Stone has highlighted, there are a myriad of different ethical issues which arise in relation to CAM practice (Stone, 2002). The codes contain many of the issues to be found in codes of practice produced by bodies such as the General Medical Council, such as provisions concerning patient confidentiality and informed consent (General Osteopathic Council, 2012). So, for example, the code of the General Osteopathic Council begins with a section which focuses upon "Communication and Patient Partnership", addressing questions such as informed consent. In addition to general statements, there are also related publications providing specific ethical guidance – for example, the General Osteopathic Council guidance document "Obtaining Consent", which is again analogous with the approach taken by the General Medical Council. The style of the codes varies. The chiropractic code is more detailed than the osteopathic code. It is underpinned by six principles. First, practitioners must respect the dignity, individuality and privacy of patients. Second, they must respect the rights of patients to be involved in decisions concerning their healthcare. Third, practitioners are exhorted to "justify public trust and confidence by being honest and trustworthy". Fourth, they are expected to provide "a good standard of practice and care". In addition, they are told that they must safeguard both patients and colleagues from risk of harm. Furthermore, they should cooperate with "colleagues from their own and other professions". The advantage of ethical codes is that they can effectively facilitate reflective practice and better communication and trust between practitioner and patient. In order to do so, they need to be embedded not only in initial education but also in subsequent professional training and practice. However, this assumes a good knowledge of such codes and highlights the need for continuing professional development and training to ensure that there is awareness of changes in codes and how these may evolve. Levels of detailed awareness of codes can be a major problem in relation to practice areas dominated by sole practitioners, working in the community and subjected to less day-to-day scrutiny.

IV Voluntary registration and the Complementary and Natural Healthcare Council

The Complementary and Natural Healthcare Council (CNHC) was established in 2008 with financial support from the UK government (CNHC, 2013). The background to the CNHC was given in a Select Committee Report. Initially, the aim was to have registers for each therapy, and the Prince's Foundation for Integrated Health (PFIH) worked with professional bodies to take this forward (PFIH, 2008). However, in 2006, the influential Stone report proposed that a federal (multi-registering) regulatory body would be the most effective model (Stone, 2005) and this approach was supported after a consultation (Jack, 2006). This led to the establishment of a Federal Working Group chaired by Dame Professor Joan Higgins, which reported in February 2008. This led to the establishment of a federal regulatory body, which led to the CNHC. The perceived advantages of such a body were that this was one point of contact for the public, could reduce regulatory costs and could facilitate the rationalization of standards. The functions of the CNHC are those of:

- keeping a register of practitioners who meet national standards of practice in their work
- setting the standards that practitioners need to meet to get onto and then stay on the register
- requiring CNHC registered practitioners to keep to our strict code of conduct, performance and ethics
- investigating complaints about alleged breaches of the code
- imposing disciplinary procedures and sanctions that mirror those of the statutory healthcare regulators.

The Council consciously decided not be use the word "alternative". They argued that this implied an approach that is used *instead of* conventional healthcare and, therefore, described a substantially different health paradigm (CNHC, 2013: 6).

The CNHC now operates a national voluntary register for complementary therapies. It is approved as an accredited voluntary register by the Professional Standards Authority for Health and Social Care. The registered therapies include Alexander technique teaching, aromatherapy, Bowen therapy, Craniosacral therapy, healing, hypnotherapy, massage therapy, microsystems acupuncture, naturopathy, nutritional therapy, reflexology, reiki, shiatsu, sports therapy and yoga therapy. While voluntary, the registration system is clearly modelled, at least to some extent, on the approach taken by statutory regulatory bodies as highlighted above. In order to be registered on the database, therapists must have undertaken an education and training programme. This must include, as a minimum, what is known as the National Occupational Standards and core curriculum for the relevant therapy. Alternatively, they must be able to establish that they have obtained competency up to the level of the National Occupational Standards for three years by relevant experience and training and there has been an assessment that they have reached these standards. In addition, applicants must confirm either that they do not have a criminal record or that they have informed the CNHC of this fact prior to acceptance. There must be no health "issues" impacting upon ability to practice. In addition, there must be no disciplinary or civil issues in relation to their practice or they must have informed the CNHC in relation to this before their entry onto the register. They must have professional indemnity insurance and no successful claims made against this. Those who register with the Council can use the Council's quality mark on their websites and publicity materials.

The mechanisms for professional scrutiny very much reflect those of the "statutory" professions. The CNHC now operates a Professional Committee, which addresses issues of professional standards, competence and conduct. The Professional Committee is formed of relevant experts. Investigation Committees, Conduct and Competence Panels or Health Panels are drawn from this committee. The Professional Committee also provides advice to the CNHC board on professional and training issues. The CNHC may in turn provide a stepping stone towards a specific statutory regulatory structure, encouraging participation and effective regulation. Such developments though remain the subject of heated debate in CAM as we have seen elsewhere in this book (see Saks, Stone and Wallberg, this volume). Some groups such as homeopaths undertake their own organization outside such structures (this is particularly interesting given that legislation facilitated the recognition of homeopathy through the Faculty of Homeopathy Act 1950 which set out educative functions for the Faculty (Bivins, 2008)). More formal statutory regulatory structures may be viewed as cumbersome and inhibitory to effective regulation. However, it is suggested that this is not necessarily the case at all and that rather effective statutory structures can prove responsive, as we see when we consider recent proposals for reform of statutes concerning regulation of CAM below.

V Statute, regulation and the future

The English Law Commission, in conjunction with the Law Commissions of the devolved jurisdictions, produced a report in spring 2014 which set out proposals for reforming the framework of health and social care professional regulatory bodies (Law Commission, 2014). These proposals present an opportunity for existing CAM professionals and regulatory bodies to reflect upon their status and how they wish their professional regulatory structures to be framed in the future. This report scrutinized the existing regulatory bodies and how their roles should develop in the future. Currently, nine bodies regulate thirty-two health and social care professions. They emphasized that: "The primary purpose of professional's regulation ... is to ensure public safety..." (Law Commission, 2014, para. 1.1) and yet, despite this, and "[g]iven the importance of health and social care professional regulation, it is a matter of some concern that its UK legal framework is fragmented, inconsistent and poorly understood" (Law Commission, 2014, para. 1.2). The Law Commission's initial consultation paper was published in 2012 and this was then followed by a public consultation exercise, with the final report published in April 2014.

The Law Commission have proposed a new piece of legislation which would combine the current statutory regulatory structures for all health professionals, from registered medical practitioners and nurses to chiropractors and osteopaths. This would have the advantage of streamlining the system and leading to consistency in approach (Law Commission, 2014, para. 2.3). While reform of the system was seen as being advantageous, there were potential difficulties in relation to the idea of imposition of consistency at the expense of specific circumstances and resources (Law Commission, 2014, para. 2.7 but more consistent approach in relation to certain areas such as fitness to practice would clearly be in the public interest (Law Commission, 2014, para. 2.12). This "consistent" approach was supported by a range of different stakeholders. Some existing regulators were happy with such alignment as they regarded a single statute as better able to give them flexibility within which to adapt the existing regulatory framework. In addition, patient groups and lawyers welcomed such an approach as they suggested that fitness-to-practice rules should be the same regardless of which disciplinary body was addressing this issue (Law Commission, 2014, para.

1.19). A single statute was also seen by the Law Commission as enabling an overhaul of the regulatory rules and facilitating joint working between the professions (Law Commission, 2014, para. 2.15). The reform would facilitate consistency between the regulators but at the same time it was recognized that there was a tension here and that there was some advantage to adaptability. As a consequence, the Law Commission have recommended, controversially, that the regulators themselves should be given formal rule-making powers without the need for parliamentary approval (Law Commission, 2014, para. 2.24). The rationale for this is the delays and complexity associated with formal legal Privy Council and parliamentary approval of rule amendment, something which can be seen as a problem, particularly in the context of CAM professions if they wish to try and gain space and time in the parliamentary schedule to enable amendments to existing statutory powers (Law Commission, 2014, paras 2.13–14). Set against this is the advantage of external scrutiny of rule-making practices. Currently, such rule-making needed the approval of the Privy Council. The Law Commission proposed the removal of its role (Law Commission, 2014, paras 2.56, 2.70) They saw its current role as not substantial, and in fact it could conceal who the real "actors" were behind the initiatives to change and develop rules in this area (Law Commission, 2014, para. 2.53). Nonetheless, it is not envisaged that total control should be given to regulators; in fact, government should retain the power to make regulations in relation to decisions to establish new regulators, professions or protected titles (Law Commission, 2014, para. 2.70). Moreover, the government was to have ultimate "back-stop" powers whereby they could both "notify and then give directions" to the Professional Standards Authority and the Regulator where there was failure or likely failure of the statutory functions (Law Commission, 2014, para. 2.79).

In relation to statutory regulators, there is also the further prospect of accountability through the scrutiny of Parliamentary Select Committees. Currently scrutiny may be undertaken by the Health Committee. However, it was suggested that, given the breadth of its remit, it would be difficult for it to call all regulators to account (Law Commission, 2014, para. 2.86). It was thus proposed that consideration should be given by parliament to establish a specific joint committee to address all the health and social care professional regulation. As an alternative, it was suggested that the Health Committee should examine the possibility of establishing an annual hearing with regulators (Law Commission, 2014, para. 2.85). Such parliamentary scrutiny over the work of CAM practice in relation to statutory regulators would, it is suggested, be an excellent way both of facilitating accountability and of increasing public awareness and acceptability of the legitimacy of such practices.

Further tensions in professional regulation concern what the role should ultimately be of such professional bodies: public safety and/or upholding values of professional behaviour. Here lies an interesting issue as to the dividing line between professional conduct and the "personal" realm of behaviour of a practitioner and the extent to which these two issues can be regarded as being separate and distinct. The statute would align the regulatory approaches across all these professions while retaining the distinctiveness of each profession. In terms of the rationale for regulation, the proposals are that, first, the main regulatory objective of regulators and the Professional Standards Authority is that of public safety and public interest, "to protect, promote and maintain the health, safety and wellbeing of the public". In addition, there are "general objectives", which are stated as being "to promote and maintain public confidence in the profession and to promote and maintain proper professional standards and the conduct for individual registrants" (Law Commission, 2014, para. 3.23). The Law Commission proposed that regulatory bodies should become more board-like in operation, with delegation of functions (Law Commission, 2014, para. 4.8).

Establishing regulators is only one part of the process. What is critical for effective regulation is openness, transparency and accountability as to how the regulators themselves operate. The government accepted that the process of appointments to the regulatory bodies – which had moved from initial election by members of the profession to appointment by the Privy Council but with an election overseen by the regulatory body – should essentially continue in the same form. However, the role of the Privy Council, consistent with the recommendations elsewhere in the document, would be taken by the government (Law Commission, 2014, para. 4.19). The Law Commission also highlighted that the definition of lay registrants was something which differed across the regulatory bodies. The report set out definitions of both lay and registrant members.

> A registrant member of a regulatory body should be defined as someone who is or has been registered with any of the professional's regulators, including predecessor organisations or is eligible to be registered. A lay member should mean a member who is not a registrant when appointed.
>
> *(Law Commission, 2014, para. 4.32)*

One concern in relation to membership of such bodies is that some people served simultaneously on a range of different regulatory bodies, leading to concerns of an "old boy network" (Law Commission, 2014, para. 4.33). The Law Commission expressed concerns in relation to this practice and proposed that concurrent membership of regulatory bodies be prohibited (Law Commission, 2014, para. 4.35). In relation to the composition, the Law Commission followed the approach taken by the General Medical Council: that issues such as the constitution of the regulator should be left to the government (Law Commission, 2014, para. 4.15). A further important issue was in relation to the balance between lay and registrant members on the professional body. The Law Commission determined that the registrant members should not constitute a majority on the body (Law Commission, 2014, para. 4.19).

There was general support for continuation of the practice of maintaining professional registers, such as the Chiropractors and Osteopaths Register. While there was some case for professional bodies having discretion to determine how this was done in practice (Law Commission, 2014, para. 5.8), ultimately what the government felt was that, in relation to issues such as the appointment of a registrar, it was important to maintain consistency between the regulatory bodies (Law Commission, 2014, para. 5.10). There was also a need to be able to evolve registration through professional development, and thus the government should also have the power to alter the structure of registers (Law Commission, 2014, para. 5.14).

Student registration has been highlighted as an important issue. Currently, of the various different statutory bodies across health and social care regulation, this is only undertaken by the General Ophthalmic Council. While there were no plans across other regulators to introduce student registers, it can be argued that this should be an issue for the future, particularly where practitioners are working outside a clinic setting. As a consequence, the Law Commission recommended that, in any Act, there should be provision for the government to introduce compulsory student registration in the future (Law Commission, 2014, para. 5.24). There was considerable debate and discussion, as a result of the consultation, over whether voluntary registers such as the CNHC should be retained. Some argued that such registers could provide an effective delineation of professional boundaries, that these could reinforce public confidence, make complaints processes more effective and, moreover, be a stepping stone to broader statutory regulation (Law Commission, 2014, para. 5.27). In contrast, others, including some registers, saw that the continuation of compulsory and voluntary registers (e.g. operated by the same body) may lead to confidence being undermined through the risk of mixed messages in relation to the protection of the public should different approaches be taken (Law Commission, 2014, para. 5.28). The Law Commission supported these concerns and proposed that professional bodies' power to maintain voluntary registers should be removed, with the power to establish and operate such voluntary registers given solely to the Professional Standards Authority (Law Commission, 2014, para. 5.32). Thus if the government takes these proposals forward, a body such as the CNHC, if it continues to be formally recognized, would remain in operation, but any other voluntary registers in relation to CAM such as the General Regulatory Council for Complementary Therapists may be placed in a difficult position.

What do not appear to be currently used in relation to CAM are non-practising registers – registers which, as the name suggests, state those individuals who are professionals but who choose not to practice. The Law Commission noted the dangers of such registers, such as these being seen as a "badge of honour" (Law Commission, 2014, para. 5.39). However, the Law Commission did accept that there could be some public safety benefits in continued, albeit limited, use of such registers where those non-practising professionals undertook roles which could impact upon patient care (Law Commission, 2014, para. 5.40). The Law Commission proposed that "all registrants should intend to practice the profession in order to be registered", however regulation making powers should exist which would enable the Government to require a supplementary register of non-practising professionals" (Law Commission, 2014, para. 5.44).

One issue which should be considered in relation to registration is that of the introduction of "barring schemes". These are lists of those who are prohibited to practice. In such situations, it is normally a criminal offence to continue to work in the area (Law Commission, 2014, para. 5.45). Examples of current schemes apply in relation to social work students operated by the Health and Care Professionals Council. (Law Commission, 2014, para. 5.46). This could operate in relation to CAM to attempt to reduce the prospect of unsafe practitioners, a half-way house in relation to formalization of regulatory scrutiny. While there was some concern that there might be confusion if barring schemes operated alongside professional self-registration schemes, the Law Commission nonetheless proposed that the government should be able to introduce such schemes (Law Commission, 2014, para. 5.50). It suggested criteria that could apply in relation to such barring schemes, including:

1 a breach of a code (where one has been issued)
2 an order is necessary for the protection of the public or otherwise in the public interest and/or
3 certain convictions, cautions or banning decisions.

(Law Commission, 2014, para. 5.51)

It was proposed that the government should have the power to make regulations to create such schemes where needed to protect the public, which regulators would then operate (Law Commission, 2014, para. 5.54).

An integral part of the work of regulators should be setting standards for continuing professional development (Law Commission, 2014, para. 6.50). It is suggested that this is extremely important and should be an integral part of professional practice. So, for example, the CNHC has produced a document entitled "Continuing Professional Development Standards" (CNHC, 2011). It is suggested that such an approach should be mirrored across the CAM community. The Law Commission also considered professional revalidation. It recognized that, while the latter may be beneficial, equally it may prove unduly costly and thus, while regulatory powers should be available to facilitate this, it has not been made mandatory at this stage (Law Commission, 2014, para. 6.51). Education oversight roles would be maintained by regulators in relation to approving education, training and experience, oversight and publication of lists of approved institutions (Law Commission, 2014, paras 6.15, 6.25, recommendations 46–51).

The Law Commission also examined the fitness-to-practice grounds. It proposed that the category of misconduct needed to be reformed to provide greater clarity. They proposed that misconduct in the sense of deficient professional performance should be categorized differently from misconduct which otherwise brings disgrace on the practitioner and can harm the reputation of the profession (Law Commission, 2014, para. 7.15.) They proposed that a new ground for impaired fitness be introduced relating to "insufficient knowledge of the English language" (Law Commission, 2014, para. 7.17). Other grounds they proposed included inclusion of a person in a barred list, adverse physical or mental health and a conviction or caution for a criminal offence in Great Britain or an offence committed in another jurisdiction which would constitute a criminal offence (Law Commission, 2014, para. 7.22, recommendation 55). In relation to investigations, these should be brought if there is a "reasonable prospect" that the panel should be able to establish the criteria and it is in the public interest (Law Commission, 2014, para. 8.54). They also propose that there should be a review of decisions not to refer a case for investigation (Law Commission, 2014, para. 8.84). Fitness-to-practice panels should continue to be undertaken by panels of at least three members with at least one lay member, and regulatory body members should not be able to sit on such bodies (Law Commission, 2014, para. 9.39). The standard of proof should also be that utilized at present, namely the civil standard of the balance of probabilities (Law Commission, 2014, paras 9.60–2). Hearings should be in public "unless the particular circumstances of the case outweigh the public interest in holding the hearing in public" (Law Commission, 2014, para. 9.69). The right to appeal to the High Court in England and Wales should remain.[33]

One important issue for healthcare regulation is the need for effective cooperation between diverse bodies performing what are distinct but related functions. As the Law Commission noted in their report, "Health and social care regulation does not exist in a vacuum" (Law Commission, 2014, para. 10.2). Joint working between professional bodies can of course be problematic. There needs to be understanding of working practices, communication and data-sharing powers and, as the Law Commission rightly highlighted, there were concerns of compromising independence and moreover barriers of "defensive professional posturing" (Law Commission, 2014, para. 10.10). They recommended that the existing oversight body, the Professional Standards Authority, have a general function to promote cooperation and that two or more regulators should be able to arrange for respective functions to be jointly exercised (Law Commission, 2014, para. 10.14). In relation to cooperation, regulators should be required to cooperate not only amongst themselves but in addition with the Professional Standards Authority and other relevant authorities (Law Commission, 2014, recommendation 96). In many respects, if this proposal were to be adopted, it can be seen as yet further symbolic recognition of the legitimacy of two CAM professional bodies, osteopaths and chiropractors, while at the same time noting the differences here with other professional bodies.

VI Responsibility, accountability and the courts

In both areas, regardless of specific statutory regulatory structures, legal regulation of course operates. All practitioners – whether CAM or conventional medicine – are subject to the standard provisions of criminal and of civil law. If patients suffer harm or if their human rights are not respected, then the practitioner may find themselves in the dock of a criminal court or facing an expensive civil law action for compensation. If a patient dies through the negligent action of a CAM practitioner, then this could lead to a prosecution for manslaughter (Sanders and Griffiths, 2013). In such a situation, this would very likely be an action for gross negligence manslaughter, where death is caused through a breach of duty of care to the deceased. Such an action should be negligent and the death reasonably foreseeable.[34] Negligent treatment by a CAM practitioner may give rise to liability in the tort of negligence. The test in negligence was set out in the leading case of *Bolam v Friern Hospital Management Committee* by Judge McNair in 1957.

> The test is the standard of the ordinary skilled man exercising and professing to have that special skill. A man need not possess the highest expert skill; it is well established law that it is sufficient if he exercises the ordinary skill of an ordinary competent man exercising that particular art. [35]

Initially the courts were prepared to accept evidence from a professional body that a specific type of conduct would come within the ambit of responsible body of professional practice. Today the courts have indicated that such practice must be "logical" and defensible and rooted in evidence-based practice; moreover, in some, albeit limited, cases the courts would be prepared to disagree with a body of professionals' opinions evidenced by the defence.[36] There are few cases concerning CAM practitioners and one of the challenges here was in ascertaining which approach the court would take to what constituted a standard of responsible practice. This issue arose in the case of *Shakoor v Situ* in 2001.[37] Mr Shakoor had visited a Chinese herbalist in Nottingham trading as "the Eternal Health Company", run by Mr Situ. Situ had trained for five years as a herbalist in China and had obtained qualifications and been rated as excellent. He did not have any UK qualifications. He prescribed Chinese herbal remedies for Mr Shakoor, who was suffering from a benign lipomata, a skin condition producing fatty tissue under the skin. The condition does not have any adverse health outcomes and in the UK the only treatment proposed is skin removal. Shakoor was given a mixture of herbs in ten packets to be taken on alternate days after food. After nine doses, he became ill, he suffered heart burn and his eyes went yellow. He also suffered abdominal pain. He went to hospital and was found to be likely suffering from hepatitis A. His liver failed and he suffered from hepatic neurosis, and despite an operation, he died. A postmortem was undertaken and the liver was found to contain the product Bai Xian Pi (dictamnus dasycarpus), which it has been suggested can be hepatotoxic. At trial, His Honour Livesey QC held that this was "idiosyncratic" to the mix of herbs. He stated that:

> unlike some alternative therapies TCHM has a long and distinguished history; it has an oral tradition extending back some 2,000 years. It is practised alongside modern medicine in China and accordingly I am told a larger proportion of the world's population is treated by it than is treated by modern or by Western medicine. However I learned little during the course of this trial as to the extent of current teaching, research, monitoring and verification of its practices in China or elsewhere.

In relation to the standard of care to be imposed upon the herbalist, he said that the standard should be different than in the case of a normal registered medical practitioner.

> The Chinese herbalist, for example, does not hold himself out as a practitioner of orthodox medicine. More particularly the patient has usually had the choice of going to an orthodox practitioner but has rejected him in favour of the alternative practitioner or reasons person and best known to himself and almost certainly at some personal financial cost. Those reasons may include a passionate belief in the superiority of the alternative therapy or a fear of surgery or of reliance (perhaps dependence) on orthodox chemical medications which may have known undesirable side effects either short- or long term.

He emphasized that, as long as the practitioner acted in accordance with a responsible body of practice in his area and kept informed as to relevant information in conventional medical journals, he would be held to the standard of a reasonable herbalist practising TCHM. What is notable is that, first, there is effectively strong judicial recognition of TCHM being a legitimate profession. Second, the court was prepared to allow the practitioner to be judged by reference to the norms of his professional peers. It should be noted that this is a decision at first instance and it remains to be seen how this translates in relation to subsequent judicial scrutiny of such practices and whether all CAM therapies will be afforded such judicial recognition. The CAM professional who has a civil action brought in negligence would, in the same way as medical practitioners, have to adduce evidence from professional colleagues supporting the action taken.

Should treatment be undertaken without proper consent and harm results then liability may arise in criminal law through the crime of battery, in civil law through the related tort of battery, or in relation to the failure to disclose risks of treatment in negligence.[38] There do not appear to date to be any reported informed consent cases in England concerning CAM practitioners, although such actions have been brought in other jurisdictions, such as the United States of America (Ernst and Cohen, 2001). Failure to respect patient confidences – whether or not the practitioner has signed up to the tenets of the Hippocratic code or the confidentiality requirements of any other ethical code – may also give rise to an action in the courts for the equitable remedy of breach of confidence, underpinned by the right to privacy.[39] Patients are becoming increasingly litigious – whether treated inside or outside the NHS. But this is not simply an "ambulance chasing" issue. Rather there is a public interest in safe clinical practice, which in some situations militates in favour of criminal law being used to prosecute others. If patients die as a result of treatment, then this may lead to a prosecution for murder or for manslaughter. In other instances, poor standards of care may lead to prosecutions under health and safety legislation.

One major concern for health professions in recent years has been the rise in claims of negligence being brought against them. While actually establishing such a successful claim can be problematic, not least because there is a need to establish causation, something which in relation to health can be particularly difficult, the lead-up to litigation can involve substantial costs due to instructing lawyers etc. The Law Commission proposed that there was a need to have rules in place to determine whether specific indemnity provisions were in existence for health professionals (Law Commission, 2014, para. 5.77). This approach is already adopted, for example, in relation to the CNHC, and it is suggested that all practitioners should avail themselves of this (Scott, 2010; CNHC, 2014). Indemnity cover following the approach already taken by registered medical practitioners will inevitably be expensive and attempts to make this compulsory are likely to be heavily resisted. However, given the changing nature of the professional environment, this is likely to be inevitable.

VII EU regulation: products, people and CAM practice

The European Union has increasingly impacted upon the provision and delivery of healthcare across member states (Hervey and McHale, 2004) and thus it was unsurprising that this also extended to CAM practice. In 1997 the Lannoye Report called for the recognition of complementary practitioners through harmonization of qualifications at the highest level and regulation of medicinal products used by such practitioners through amendment to existing pharmaceutical regulation. (Lannoye, 1997). Not quite two decades on while there is indeed some regulation in relation to products used in this area the regulation of practitioners remains undeveloped. Today, the EU does not provide any form of comprehensive regulation of CAM practice itself. This is unsurprising given the wide variety of approaches to CAM regulation across member states

(CAMDOC Alliance, 2011; Weisener *et al.*, 2012). The EU has long had in place an extensive system of pharmaceutical regulation. This was triggered by events such as the Thalidomide scandal (Goldberg, 2013). There is an overarching scheme for the approval of trials concerning pharmaceutical products intended for human subjects in the form of the EU Clinical Trials Directive.[40] Further provision concerning pharmaceutical regulation is contained in Directive 2001/83/EC of the Community Code relating to medicinal products for human use (as amended).[41] An oversight and regulatory EU body, the European Medicines Evaluation Agency (EMEA) began operating in February 1995.[42] The particular challenges of regulating herbal medicine have been recognized by the EMEA, which now includes a specific Committee for Herbal Medicinal Products (HMPC), established in 2004, which replaced an earlier Working Party on Herbal Medicinal Products.[43] The committee members are drawn from twenty-eight EU member states and also members from Iceland and Norway. Members can be co-opted with additional expertise in areas such as clinical pharmacology, experimental pharmacology, toxicology, paediatric medicine and general and family medicine. It has the role of facilitating the harmonization of those provisions concerning herbal medicinal products across the EU and integration within the regulatory framework of the EU. One of the tasks of the HMPC is the creation of community monographs for traditional herbal medicinal products. In addition, they are charged with the preparation of a draft list of herbal substances in medicinal use for what is regarded as being a "sufficiently long time". Such substances will then be regarded as not being harmful under normal conditions.

The EU Directive on Traditional Herbal Medicinal Products did impact upon CAM practice in the UK.[44] Prior to this, regulation operated at member state level. The EU was concerned after an incident in the early 1990s, the Aristolochia case, in which Aristolochia had been prescribed to patients as part of a slimming programme, after which some 135 suffered kidney damage (Littoz-Monnet, 2014). This led to the European Medicines Agency examining the issue and it being placed upon the EU's reform agenda. Now all herbal medicinal products must be subject to market authorization. The directive applies to products placed on the market after 20 April 2004. Medicines available prior to that date could be marketed up to 30 April 2011 but would require authorization after that date. This has been incorporated into English law now under the Human Medicines Regulations 2012, para 7, SI 2012 No 1916 (as amended). Herbal medicine is a "medicinal product whose only active ingredients are herbal substances or herbal preparations" or both. Herbal preparation concerns "preparation obtained by subjecting herbal substances to processes such as extraction, distillation, expression, fractionation, purification, concentration or fermentation". Included are comminuted or powdered herbal substance, a tincture, an extract, an essential oil, an expressed juice or a processed exudate. Herbal substances refers to "a plant or part of a plant, alga, fungus or lichen" (Directive 2004/24/EU, Article 1.1). They also include unprocessed exudate of plants defined by the plant part used. The directive only extends to medicines administered orally, externally or by inhalation (Directive 2004/24/EC, Article 1.1). It does not extend to anything which would have to be administered intravenously. It applies only to those medical products which will not be used under the supervision of a registered medical practitioner to diagnose the condition for which it is to be used to treat, to prescribe it or to monitor its use. The criteria to be considered when deciding whether a product will be authorized are its traditional history and pharmacological properties. So the licensing authorities – in the case of the UK, the Medicines and Healthcare Products Regulatory Agency – may authorize it if it has been in continuous medicinal use for thirty years and has been in continuous medicinal use in the EU for fifteen years. Moreover, there must be sufficient information to establish that the traditional use is not harmful and the product's pharmacological effects/efficacy are plausible in the light of the longstanding experience of the products. This excludes certain substances.[45] There are also set out specific requirements in relation to the labelling of such products, namely that these are traditional herbal medicines, that they may be used for certain specific purposes due to longstanding use and that if symptoms persist or if adverse effects arise that are not mentioned on the package or leaflet, the patient should consult a doctor or other healthcare professional.[46] The directive caused controversy and consternation when initially enacted but it is submitted that this should not be seen as an attack on alternative medical practices. In fact, the content and the approach taken in the directive is entirely consistent with the EU's cautious approach in relation to the regulation and licensing of pharmaceutical products more generally, driven by concerns in relation to risk and of patient safety. CAM practice has not been singled out for punishment and constraints, rather it is entirely consistent with what has happened in other areas. In fact in many respects, this regulation, with the establishment of a specific CAM committee, may be seen as confirming legitimacy and recognition of herbal medicine.

The manner in which CAM provision of medicines is regulated at EU and consequently at domestic level remains the subject of criticism (Jackson, 2012). In relation to homeopathic medicines, these initially could have been subject to automatic recognition through what was known as product licences as of right when the Medicines Act 1968 came into force.[47] Today, application can be made under a simplified registration scheme initially introduced under EU Directive 92/97/EC, which applies to medicines for oral or external use where sufficiently dilute for safety to be guaranteed. Alternatively, under the Medicines for Human Use (Homeopathic) Regulations 2006, (SI 2006, No 1952) homeopathic products can be marketed for these are minor conditions and thus can be relieved/treated without a doctor's involvement. Safety, quality and efficacy must be established but evidence of standard clinical trials is not needed; rather, study reports must be provided concerning the literature or "scientific provings". This absence of alignment with the regulatory processes which operate in relation to other medicinal products has been subject to heavy criticism (Singh and Ernst, 2009: Jackson, 2012). At the same time it should be noted that homeopathic medicine is subject to oversight through the Medicines and Health Care Products Regulatory Agency. Clearly in relation to any medicinal products, issues of safety and efficacy are crucial. Public policy arguments militate in favour of aligning regulation of products as well as of people in terms of the regulation of CAM professions in the future. The question remains as to whether standard clinical trials models provide the most appropriate approach. Any truly effective regulation here needs transparency and openness and receptiveness to questions of efficacy, safety and audit by those CAM practitioners using medicinal products and also by the conventional medicine community.

A further issue relates to that of the mobility of CAM professionals across borders. The EU internal market has long recognized the importance of mutual recognition of qualifications to facilitate movement of workers across the EU. There are tensions here, which the EU recognizes, regarding the need to ensure public safety while at the same time facilitating mobility. There does not at present appear to be widespread cross-border movement into the UK of CAM practitioners. This may not be surprising given the fact that, even in relation to established professions such as osteopaths and chiropractors, many EU member states do not formally recognize these as being professions in law at all and that there may be differences both in terminology and approaches in practice. One further development is that of mobility of patients across the EU. For a number of years, patients have been asserting their rights under EU law, under the principles of free movement of persons to seek treatment in another EU member state, where they have suffered undue delay in receiving state-funded treatment in their home member state and then claimed reimbursement from the home state on their return (McHale, 2007).[48] This area is now governed by the EU Patients' Rights Directive, which enables states to impose limitations upon access to treatment in situations such as hospital care or expensive experimental care.[49] The directive provides that such prior authorization can operate where it concerns "treatment presenting a particular risk to the patient or the population".[50] States can refuse authorization in a situation in which the health provider in another member state is one which raises serious concerns regarding the quality and safety of their care.[51] Generally speaking, CAM services are not available as part of a standard NHS package of care (for further, see Stone, this volume), although given changes to NHS purchasing arrangements under the Health and Social Care Act 2012 through the development of GP consortia and more localized prescribing may in fact be the case in certain parts of the country longer term. The directive may become more relevant in this context in the future (Sheppard, 2013). One interesting point to note, however, is that the directive does mandate member states to publish details of the therapies. The directive provides that there must be national contact points for cross-border care,[52] which has to give patients information on request in relation to, for example, the quality and safety of healthcare for which providers are subject to such standards. Furthermore, obligations are placed on "healthcare providers [to] provide relevant information to help individual patients to make an informed choice, including on treatment options, on the availability, quality and safety of the healthcare they provide in the Member State of treatment".[53] This may ultimately enhance transparency to patients across the EU as to the range of approaches taken across member states, which may fundamentally change perceptions as to what constitutes "standard" treatments in the future. This in turn may drive acceptance of and/or perceptions of CAM practice across the EU.

VIII Conclusion

As CAM practice has grown and developed, it was inevitable that there should be greater focus and concern as to the interface with law in this area. Law, as we have seen, can be viewed as a vehicle to confer professional legitimacy and status. Law too can be seen as a constraint – a means of safeguarding the public and reducing risks of practice. But likewise that very constraint, that very real concern with risk, can be welcomed as an opportunity. Hand in hand with professional status, whether that arises in the context of formal professional roles or professionalization in relation to high-quality practice, comes professional responsibility and professional accountability. Safe and competent practice is key, whether this be conventional medicine or complementary and alternative medicine. Furthermore, as we have seen, regardless of the debates around formalization of professional regulation, the practitioner will be accountable in civil and criminal law should harm to an individual patient arise. The practitioner will be judged by the standard of the responsible body of practitioners in their area – which means of course that, for this to happen, there has to be an acceptable standard of professional practice. It is not a question simply of avoiding harm but also of respecting patient rights and entitlements as they arise in the context of practice. Recent developments in this area, as in relation to other areas of healthcare practice, have highlighted the cross-jurisdictional nature of factors impacting on healthcare regulation. The EU is already having and is likely to have in the future an increasing impact on practice through its effect on domestic legal regulation.

Ultimately there are challenges in relation to accommodating professional regulation within a formal structure. In the case of an emerging "profession", this simply may not be appropriate. Practitioners need to cohere sufficiently to facilitate such a professional identity. Forcing that via a statutory framework would be highly problematic. In the case of many areas of complementary and alternative medicine it can be argued however that there is already considerable degrees of coherence, if not necessarily always agreement in relation to the formation of such a professional role. What needs to be borne in mind is that even regardless of such a formal structure, the law does delineate the actions of such "professionals" and that different expectations and professional standards will be expected of persons performing such a role. The unregulated practitioner is not simply invisible moreover, they are not going to be treated as a lay person – and enhanced responsibilities will result, regardless, from this role.

What is important for CAM practitioners, while recognizing the differences in many areas of CAM practice as compared with conventional therapies, is also to recognize that, in many other respects, CAM practice is not "special"; it necessarily involves legal issues such as consent to treatment and professional negligence, which apply across different areas of health care practice. Moreover, the models of professional regulation for those areas of CAM practice where formal structures have been adopted are drawn from existing regulatory structures – for example, from medicine and nursing.

It is the case that legal frameworks and regulatory paradigms can provide an opportunity for practitioners to critically reflect upon their own practice, both similarities and differences, to frame regulation in the future. There may be an opportunity for CAM practitioners to engage with professional regulation working alongside other health care professionals if the Law Commission proposals are taken forward by the government. Moreover, if existing professional regulatory models are inadequate – if, rather than being led by a conventional medicine model, other paradigms are appropriate and there is a need perhaps to reframe conventional medical approaches to regulation – then the scope for this needs to be explored. If there is a case for special new frameworks which may be better suited to the diversity of CAM practice, such reform proposals provide such an opportunity for further dialogue and indeed for innovation in regulatory approaches from the CAM health practitioners themselves (see Marie-Andrée Jacob, this volume). In that respect, law can perhaps be better seen as a facilitator rather than as an inhibiter of good practice – a means of promoting effective and responsible regulation in CAM in the future.

Notes

1 [2002] 1 WLR 1691.
2 This refers to law which has evolved through case law development via precedent.
3 Section 1(1) Osteopaths Act 1993.
4 Section 1 Chiropractors Act 1994.
5 Section 1(5)(a) of the Osteopaths Act 1993, s 1(5)(a) Chiropractors Act 1994.
6 Section 11(1) Osteopaths Act 1993, section 11(1) Chiropractors Act 1994.
7 Section 12 Osteopaths Act 1993, section 12 Chiropractors Act 1994.
8 Section 11(5) Osteopaths Act 1993, section 12(5) Chiropractors Act 1994.
9 Section 32 Osteopaths Act 1993, section 32 Chiropractors Act 1994.
10 Section 2 Osteopaths Act 1993, section 2 Chiropractors Act 1994.
11 Section 14(2)(a)(b) Osteopaths Act 1993, s 14(2)(b) Chiropractors Act 1994.
12 Section 16 Osteopaths Act 1993, section 16 Chiropractors Act 1994.
13 Section 17 Osteopaths Act 1993, s 17 Chiropractors Act 1994.
14 Section 18(4) Osteopaths Act 1993, Chiropractors Act 1994.
15 Section 3(2)(b)(c) Osteopaths Act 1993, section 3(2)(b)(c) Osteopaths Act 1994.
16 Section 3(a)(d) Osteopaths Act 1993, section 3(a)(d) Chiropractors Act 1994.
17 Section 4(2)(d)(e) Osteopaths Act 1993, section 4(2)(d) Chiropractors Act 1994.
18 Section 9 Osteopaths Act 1993, section 9 Chiropractors Act 1994.
19 Section 10 Osteopaths Act 1993, section 10 Chiropractors Act 1994.
20 Section 29 Osteopaths Act 1993, section 29 Chiropractors Act 1994.
21 Section 1(5)(b) Osteopaths Act 1993, section 1(5)(b) Chiropractors Act 1994.
22 Section 1(5)(c) Osteopaths Act 1993, section 1(5)(c) Chiropractors Act 1994.
23 Section 1(5)(d) Osteopaths Act 1993, section 1(5)(d) Chiropractors Act 1994.
24 Section 7 Osteopaths Act 1993, section 7 Chiropractors Act 1994.
25 Section 20(2) Osteopaths Act 1993, section 20(2) Chiropractors Act 1994.
26 Section 20(12) Osteopaths Act 1993, section 20(12) Chiropractors Act 1994.
27 Section 22(4) Osteopaths Act 1993, section 22(4) Chiropractors Act 1994.
28 Section 23(2) Osteopaths Act 1993, section 23(2) Chiropractors Act 1994.

29 Section 24(2) Osteopaths Act 1993, section 24(1) Chiropractors Act 1994.

30 Sections 27 and 28 Osteopaths Act 1993, sections 27 and 28 Chiropractors Act 1994.

31 Section 19 Osteopaths Act 1993, section 19 Chiropractors Act 1994.

32 General Chiropractic Council Code of Practice and Standard of Proficiency, General Chiropractic Council, London (2010).

33 And to the Court of Session in Scotland and High Court in Northern Ireland.

34 *R v Adomako* [1995] 1 AC 171, *R v Misra* [2005] 1 Cr App Rep 21.

35 [1957] 2 All ER 118.

36 *Bolitho* [1997] 4 All ER, 771.

37 [2001] 1 WLR 410.

38 *Sidaway v Royal Bethlem Hospital* [1985] 1 All ER 643 (HL); *Pearce v United Bristol NHS Trust* ([1999] PIQR) P53; (CA) *Chester v Afshar* [2005] 1 AC 134.

39 See further *Campbell v MGN* [2004] UKHL 22.

40 Directive 2001/20/EC on the approximation of the laws, regulations and administrative provisions of the member states relating to the implementation of good clinical practice in the conduct of clinical trials on medicinal products for human use, OJ 2001 L 121/34.

41 OJ 2001 L 311/67.

42 It was established by Regulation 2309/93/EC; see now Regulation (EC) No 728/2004 of the European Parliament and of the Council of 31 March 2004 laying down community procedures for the authorization and supervision of medicinal products for human and veterinary use and establishing a European Medicines Agency.

43 Established by Article 16h of Directive 2001/83/EC of the European Parliament and of the Council of 6 November 2001 on the Community Code Relating to Medicinal Products for Human Use.

44 Directive 2004/24/EU of the European Parliament and of the Council of 31st March 2004 as amending as regards traditional herbal medicinal products Directive 2001/83/EC on the Community Code relating to medicinal products for human use.

45 As set out in Part 1 of Schedule 20.

46 Human Medicines Regulations 2012, SI No 1916. Regulations, Ref 265(1) and Schedule 29.

47 SI 2006, 252.

48 *Kohll* [1998] *ECR*-I-1935; *Geraets-Smits v Stichting Ziekenfonds VGZ* and *Peerbooms v Stichting CZ Groep Zorgverzekerigen* [2001] *ECR* I-5473; ECJ, Case C-368/98 *Abdon Vanbraekel and others v Alliance nationale des mutualities chretiennes* [2001] *ECR*-I-5363; ECJ, Case C-385/99, *Müller-Fauré and van Riet* [2003] *ECR* I-4509; ECJ, Case C-56/01, *Inizan v Caisse primarie d' Assurance Maladie des Hauts de Seine* [2003] *ECR*-I; ECJ, Case C-372/04 *R (on the application of Watts) v Bedford Primary Care Trust, Secretary of State for Health* [2006] ECR I-4325.

49 Directive 2011/24/EU of the European Parliament and of the Council of 9 March 2011 on the application of patients' rights in cross-border healthcare.

50 Ibid., Article 8(6)(a)(b).

51 Ibid., Article 8(6)(c).

52 Article 6(2).

53 Ibid., Article 4(2)(b).

References

Bivins, R.(2008) *Alternative Medicine: A History* Oxford: OUP.

Bristol Royal Infirmary Inquiry (2001) *The Report of the Public Inquiry into Children's Heart Surgery at the Bristol Royal Infirmary 1984–1995: Learning from Bristol*, Cond. 5207 (I) 2001.

CAMDOC Alliance (2011) *The Regulatory Status of Complementary and Alternative Medicine for Medical Doctors in Europe*, Brussels and Strasbourg: ECH, ECPM, ICMART, IVAA.

Complementary and Natural Healthcare Council (2011) *Continuing Professional Development Standards: A Guide for CNHC Registered Practitioners*, London: The Complementary and Natural Healthcare Council.

Complementary and Natural Healthcare Council (2013) *The First Five Years*, London: The Complementary and Natural Healthcare Council.

Complementary and Natural Healthcare Council (2014) *Policy in Respect of Requirement to Provide Copies of Insurance Certificates and CPD Log*, London: The Complementary and Natural Healthcare Council.

Davies, M. (2007) *Medical Self-Regulation: Crisis and Change*, Aldershot: Ashgate.

Ernst, E. and Cohen, M. H. (2001) "Informed Consent in Complementary and Alternative Medicine", *Archives of Internal Medicine* 161(9): 2288–2292.

Francis Inquiry (2013) *Report of the Mid Staffordshire NHS Foundation Trust Public Inquiry*, London: The Stationery Office.

General Osteopathic Council (2012) *Practice Standards*, London: General Osteopathic Council.

General Osteopathic Council (2014) *Governance Handbook*, London: General Osteopathic Council.

Goldberg, R. (2013) *Medicinal Product Liability Regulation*, Oxford: Hart.

Hervey, T. K. and McHale, J. V. (2004) *Health Law and the EU*, Cambridge: Cambridge University Press.

House of Lords Science and Technology Select Committee Report (2000) *Sixth Report: Complementary and Alternative Medicine*, HL 123.

Jack, P. (2006) *Exploring a Federal Approach to Voluntary Self-Regulation of Complementary Healthcare: Consultation Document*, London: PFIH.

Jackson, E. (2012) Law and the Regulation of Medicines, Oxford: Hart.

Lannoye, P. (1997) Report of the 6th March 1997 on Non-Conventional Medicine, Committee on the Environment, Public Health and Human Protection, Brussels.

Law Commission (2014) *Regulation of Health Care Professionals: Regulation of Social Care Professionals* (England, Scotland, Northern Ireland), Law Comm No 345, London.

Littoz-Monnet, A. (2014) "The Role of Independent Regulators in Policy Making: Venue-Shopping and Framing Strategies in the EU Regulation of Old Wives Cures", *European Journal of Political Research* 53(1): 1–17.

McHale, J. (2007) "Framing a Right to Treatment in English Law. Watts in Retrospective", *Maastricht Journal of European and Comparative Law* 14(3): 263–287.

Robinson, R., Lorenc, A. and Lewith, G. (2011) "Complementary and Alternative Medicine Professional Practice and Safety: A Consensus Building Workshop", *European Journal of Integrative Medicine* 3(2): 49–53.

Saks, M. (2002) *Orthodox and Alternative Medicine: Politics, Professionalisation and Health Care*, London: Continuum.

Sanders A. and Griffiths D. (eds) (2013) *Bioethics, Medicine and the Criminal Law: Medicine, Crime and Society*, Cambridge: Cambridge University Press.

Scott, F. (2010) *Independent Review of the Requirement to have Insurance or Indemnity as a Condition of Registration as a Healthcare Professional*, London: Department of Health.

Sheppard, M. (2013) "Treatments of Low Priority and the Patients Mobility Directive 2011: An End to Legal Uncertainty for the English NHS?", *European Journal of Health Law* 20(3): 295–314.

Shipman Inquiry, Fifth Report (2004) *Safeguarding Patients: Lessons from the Past, Proposals for the Future*, 9 December, Cm 6394.

Singh, S. and Ernst, E. (2009) *Trick or Treatment? Alternative Medicine On Trial*, London: Corgi Books.

Stacey, M. (1992) *Regulating the General Medical Council*, Chichester: John Wiley.

Stone, J. (2002) *An Ethical Framework for Complementary and Alternative Therapists*, London: Routledge.

Stone, J. (2005) *Development of Proposals for a Future Voluntary Regulatory Structure for Complementary Healthcare Professions*, London: PFIH.

Stone, J. and Matthews, J. (1995) *Complementary Medicine and the Law*, Oxford: OUP.

The Prince's Foundation for Integrated Health (2008) *A Federal Approach to Professionally-Led Voluntary Regulation for Complementary Healthcare*, London: PFIH.

Wiesener, S., Falkenberg, T., Hegyi, G., Hok, J., Roberti di Sarsina, P. and Fonnebo, V. (2012) "Legal Status and Regulation of Complementary and Alternative Medicine in Europe" *Forsch Komplementmed* 19(Suppl. 2): 29–36.

PART 2

Power, professions and health spaces

4

DEVELOPING NATUROPATHY IN INTERWAR BRITAIN

Jane Adams

I Introduction

This chapter traces the development of naturopathy in Britain in the interwar years, a period associated with increased involvement by the central state in the funding of services through National Health Insurance (NHI) and planning for the National Health Service (NHS). The failure of efforts by osteopaths to gain state recognition in the 1930s has been seen as evidence of further consolidation of the relationship between the state and the orthodox medical profession with a concomitant weakening of the position of unorthodox healers (Cooter, 1988; Larkin, 1992; Saks, 1992). Research findings presented here demonstrate that, despite these far-reaching changes to the market for health services, naturopaths achieved significant improvements in their profile and established viable practices offering distinctive therapies in this period. Despite low numbers – only a few hundred practitioners in the 1930s – British naturopaths were able to take steps to forge an identity separate from other unqualified healers and differentiate themselves from the orthodox profession. One of the methods they used to achieve this was the publication of books and periodicals aimed at the general public which explained the philosophy of nature cure and its basic therapeutic practices. A number of associations were established to strengthen links between individual practitioners and particular consideration was given to the need to improve and standardise training. Naturopaths endorsed the principle of self-regulation and opposed the attempts of osteopaths to secure a system of state registration on the basis that this might restrict their own practice. They were also active in the British Health Freedom Society (BHFS), which lobbied to safeguard the right of patients to freedom of choice of practitioner and sought to ensure that unorthodox healers were not disadvantaged by the expansion of a state-funded system of health care. Although this campaign was only partially successful, the crucial principle of freedom to choose and receive treatment from unqualified healers was safeguarded under legislation introducing the NHS. This principle was fundamental in shaping the market conditions that allowed naturopaths to continue to practice their distinctive approach. The gains made by naturopaths in the interwar period demonstrate that the growth of state-funded health services did not necessarily lead to a decline in unorthodox practice.

II The status of naturopathy in early twentieth-century Britain

At the beginning of the twentieth century, the British market for health services was character-ised by a variety of orthodox and unorthodox practitioners. While the 1858 Medical Act had introduced a register of qualified medical practitioners, the right to provide therapeutic services was not limited to this group. In 1909, concerns about the prevalence of 'quackery' led to a review of unqualified healers to assess the extent of unorthodox practice 'and the potential detri-mental effect this might have on public health' (*Unqualified persons*, 1910). Information compiled from reports by local medical officers recorded chemists and medical herbalists as the most numerous practitioners with both groups considered to be flourishing. Other healers identified in the report were bonesetters, dentists, electricians, faith healers, 'wise women' and hydro-pathic establishments. There was no reference to naturopaths, osteopaths or chiropractors. A Scottish correspondent commented on several difficulties inherent in the task of assessing unqualified practice. Distinguishing between orthodox and unorthodox methods or categoris-ing individual practitioners was, as always, problematic because the boundary between 'medi-cine and surgery' and 'hygiene' was vague and constantly shifting. Classification of healers was further complicated as some unqualified practitioners worked under medical supervision, a problem compounded by 'the frequent acceptance by the medical profession of ideas and methods first elaborated by unorthodox healers'. 'Diet specialists' and 'massage establishment practitioners' were examples of therapists who sometimes practised independently and some-times acted in collaboration with a qualified medical practitioner. The chief threats to public health identified in the report were the excessive use of drugs and delays in referring cases of serious illness such as tuberculosis, venereal disease or cancer. Proprietary medicines (commer-cially produced products branded by the manufacturer) were widely available by post as well as from chemists and other retail outlets, a situation which facilitated the misuse of drugs not pre-scribed by orthodox practitioners. Concerns were also expressed about inappropriate treatment by unorthodox healers. In addition to wasting significant amounts of money on ineffective rem-edies, the public were deemed to be at risk of delays in receiving orthodox therapy, which could have serious consequences for their health as well as that of the wider community. Sales of abortificants were another worry, as was the continuing practice of unqualified midwives, despite recent moves to professionalise this area of practice. The issue of the efficacy and poten-tial dangers of proprietary medicines was taken up by the *British Medical Journal*, which published analyses of various patent medicines from 1909. Although most were assessed as being harmless, even if ineffective, a few were identified as posing a threat to health. In 1912, greater awareness of these issues led to the appointment of a Select Committee to investigate patent medicines and foods. Its recommendations, delayed due to the outbreak of war in August 1914, included estab-lishing a register of licensed manufacturers of patent medicines (Vaughan, 1992).

An influential strand of medical holism which valued the 'vis mediatrix naturae' or healing power of nature persisted among some orthodox practitioners into the interwar years (Lawrence and Weisz, 1998). This period was also marked by a culture of positive health, and belief in the importance of hygiene attracted broad support (Zweiniger-Bargielowska, 2010). The prophy-lactic benefits of a healthy lifestyle were promoted by George Newman, the first Chief Medical Officer, who urged the need to address the burden of illness affecting all social classes through preventive as well as curative medicine. Better health for the nation was promoted by individual organisations too – for example, the New Health Society, run by Sir Arbuthnot Lane, who, after a career in surgery, had turned to promoting health principally through management of diet (Zweiniger-Bargielowska, 2007). Naturopathy was well placed to appeal to the diverse groups already persuaded of the importance of a healthy lifestyle in improving and maintaining health. Several of the 'natural' methods they promoted were also used by orthodox practitioners. Unqualified hydropathists and those interested in lifestyle reform movements had contributed to the development of several physical therapies, including baths and douches, the use of hot air, steam and mud, massage and physical exercise systems after 1840. These methods were consolidated into orthodox medical practice through the specialty of balneology and hydrotherapeutics (the therapeutic use of water in baths and other applications) that developed from spa practice in the last decades of the nineteenth century. The specialty later developed into physical medicine encompassing a wider range of treatments, including electrical applications and heat and light therapy. Interest in these approaches had increased during World War I due to their use in the rehabilitation of wounded servicemen (Adams, forthcoming 2015). Despite rapid growth in medical knowledge, relatively few effective therapies had been developed by the 1920s. Although salvarsan, vaccine therapy and insulin had had some impact, many diseases, including common ailments such as constipation and catarrh, remained difficult to treat (Hardy, 2000). Action to encourage the body's natural tendency to heal and the use of diet, massage and physical treatments were promoted by practitioners from both orthodox and unorthodox groups. For example, fresh air, nourishing food and exercise and rest played an important part in the treatment of tuberculosis.

Issues of self-drugging, the safety of foodstuffs and medicines and the overlap in therapeutic methods adopted by qualified and unqualified practitioners were all relevant to the strategies adopted by naturopaths to develop their profile. A key slogan employed by the group was 'drugless healing' and pharmaceutical preparations were eschewed in favour of active measures used to promote the body's natural healing propensities. These included fasting, vegetarian foods, hydropathic baths, sunbathing, exercise, massage and herbs as well as new manipulative techniques introduced by chiropractic and osteopathy. The British Association for Nature Cure, founded in 1906 by Watson Macgregor Reid, recognised diverse influences from radical healing traditions as well as more mainstream physical culture and mind cure (Brown, 1988, pp. 187, 193). The *Nature Cure Annual and Health and Pleasure Guide* for 1907/08 reported on a gathering organised to celebrate the centenary of the birth of Vincent Preissnitz, lauded as the founder of hydropathy in the 1840s. The volume included advertisements for publications authored by the established Scottish hydropathists Archibald and Annie Hunter, as well as a health home run by the well-known physical culturist Bernarr Macfadden at Orchard Leigh. Here, the regime was based on 'Nature Cure methods of treatment; Hydropathy, Massage, Sun Baths, Open-air Gymnasia, Open-air Sleeping Châlets, Individual Dieting, Graduated Exercises and Open-air Games' (p. xxxvi, inside front cover, p. 113 and p. xix).

Despite cultural trends supporting their vision, British naturopaths perceived they were in a weaker position than their colleagues in America or Germany, who were presented as being at the forefront of a growing international movement. The foundations of nature cure were traced back to the work of Preissnitz in Silesia around 1830 and his influence, along with others, including Johannes Schroth in Austria and Father Sebastian Kniepp, led to a strong natural healing tradition becoming established in Germany. James Whorton notes that emigrants to the USA were an important conduit for the transmission of these practices and, from the 1890s onwards, a distinctively North American approach developed (Whorton, 2002). Benedict Lust founded the Naturopathic Society of America in 1901 and from 1900 published the *Kniepp Water Cure Monthly*, later renamed *The Naturopath and Herald of Health*. Like the founders of many unorthodox practices, Lust had been converted to naturopathy by personal experience. Following his own successful treatment for tuberculosis by Sebastian Kniepp in the early 1890s, he returned to the US to 'go into the new World and spread the Gospel of the Water Cure' (Whorton, 2002, p. 192). The connection between Germany and the US was further reinforced by Henry Lindlahr, who set up a school of Natural Therapeutics in Chicago. Harry Benjamin, author of the most popular British treatise on nature cure, asserted that naturopathy's 'great home today is America' (Benjamin, 1936, p. 8). The importance of this flourishing international movement is apparent in the personal experience of several of those who emerged as leaders of the British movement in the interwar period.

III Developing naturopathy: scope, publicity and training

The parents of Stanley Lief, one of the acknowledged champions of British naturopathy, had emigrated to South Africa from Latvia when he was a child, partly due to their son's poor health. As an adolescent, he began to follow the dietary and exercise advice in *Physical Culture* magazine published in the US by Bernarr Macfadden. Heartened by a dramatic improvement in his health and strength, Lief became an ardent convert to nature cure and later travelled to the US to study at Macfadden's college, where he was exposed to the innovative approaches of naturopathy, chiropractic and osteopathy. Lief came to Britain around 1914 and worked at Macfadden's health homes in Brighton and the Chilterns (*British Naturopathic Journal and Osteopathic Review*, 1963, p. 252). James Thomson also trained in America, working with Henry Lindlahr in Chicago before setting up a successful practice in Edinburgh around 1919 (Thomson, 1960). Other practitioners gained their knowledge and experience in the European tradition of nature cure. Andrew Pitcairn-Knowles, who opened the Riposo Health Hydro in Hastings in 1913, had lived much of his life in Europe and his institution was inspired by German nature cure methods. He later specialised in the cure developed by Johannes Schroth, which was based on hot moist packs and a dry diet (Pitcairn-Knowles, 2012, pp. 81–92).

Despite sharing some similarities with established therapeutic methods, this generation of naturopaths was eager to publicly assert the fundamental differences between their philosophy of health and disease and that of orthodox medicine. James Thomson defined nature cure as 'a system of man-building in harmony with the constructive principle in nature on the mental, moral and physical planes of being' (Thomson, 1920, p. 10). The task of the naturopath was to help the body restore itself by harnessing the close interaction between physical, mental and spiritual factors. Benjamin discussed the differences between orthodox medicine and naturopathy, arguing that the former saw disease as caused by external agents such as micro-organisms. He criticised orthodox treatment for its focus on suppressing the symptoms of disease by 'poisonous drugs and vaccines, and the very drastic employment of the surgeon's knife' rather than by tackling their fundamental causes. In contrast, naturopaths viewed disease as a natural process arising from within the body 'as a result of the accumulation of toxins and impurities generated therein through years of wrong habits of living'. For many acute cases, the therapeutic approach was bed rest and fasting, while chronic disease was tackled through education in healthy living, including advice on diet, exercise, rest and relaxation, thought and habits (Benjamin, 1941, pp. 1–6). The future success of naturopathy was recognised to be dependent on improving knowledge about this system among the British public. This would be vital to safeguard livelihoods through attracting individual patients and to build support for a system which opposed the tenets of orthodox medicine. The fundamental task was to per-suade the public of the 'underlying futility of orthodox methods of treatment', in particular its focus on symptoms rather than the treatment of underlying causes of disease. This was not necessarily easy as 'Medical Science with its attitude that disease is something that "happens to one" more or less by chance, is appealing to most people'. In contrast, nature cure emphas-ised the need for self-control and self-directed effort that required dedication and persistence (Benjamin, 1951, p. 23).

Nature cure magazines were important vehicles for the popularisation of the system with the public. The most influential of these, launched in 1927, was *Health for All*, edited by Stanley Lief and John Wood. This venture built on established demand for popular health and lifestyle magazines apparent from the nineteenth century. Examples of earlier publications with a strong lifestyle reform message include the *Herald of Health*, published by Mary Gove and Thomas Low Nichols from 1875, which continued under different owners into the twentieth century, and *Sandow's Magazine*, published by Eugene Sandow, founder of the Institute for Physical Culture in London in the 1890s. Bernarr Macfadden, Lief's mentor, also started a UK-based publishing house to distribute his works on physical culture and health. *Health for All* adopted a tried-and-tested format which aimed to provide its readers with information and inspiration as well as all the accoutrements needed for a healthy lifestyle. This model proved to be successful, with *Health for All* continuing in press into the 1960s when it was taken over by *Here's Health*. The magazine was produced by a London-based group of naturopaths and achieved a wide circulation. A number of other publishing ventures were developed by naturopaths, including *The Healthy Life* and *Health and Life*, edited by London-based Edgar J. Saxon, *Light on Health*, produced by B. St John Doherty from Manchester, and *The Kingston Chronicle*, published by James Thomson in Edinburgh.

An indication of the growing popularity of nature cure is shown in *The Health and Nature Cure Handbook (H&NCH)*, first published in 1931. This was planned as the first in a series of annual directories and was followed by two further editions in 1932 and 1934, after which it lapsed. These volumes included a variety of articles on nature cure theory and practice by well-known names in the field, including Lief, Saxon and Thomson, as well as lists of recognised nature cure associations and qualified practitioners. They were designed to appeal to a range of people interested in naturopathy, both practitioners and potential patients, and provided opportunities for advertisements for businesses and products. The 1934 edition listed around 150 practitioners, forty of whom were in London, eighty distributed throughout the rest of England, seventeen in Scotland, eleven in Wales and two in Northern Ireland (*H&NCH*, 1934, pp. 222–226). Although London and the surrounding southern counties were the best served region, there was limited access to naturopathy across the country, with most practitioners based in sizeable towns. Manchester, Birmingham, Bristol, Liverpool, Newcastle and Nottingham all had more than one listed practitioner, as did Cardiff, Belfast, Glasgow and Edinburgh. Twenty-seven women were included in the list, just under a fifth of the total. Several of these women were married to practising naturopaths, including Stella Lief, Mrs St John Doherty, Jessie Thomson and Mrs Milton Powell. Jessie Thomson and Stella Lief worked at the same established nature cure institutions as their husbands, the Kingston Clinic in Edinburgh and Champneys in Tring, Hertfordshire, respectively. Although Margaret Pitcairn-Knowles was not listed as a qualified naturopath, she was nevertheless recognised as a specialist on diet and cookery, authoring an article in the handbook for 1934 in which she was described as 'joint-principal' of the Riposo Nature cure and dietetic establishment near Hastings (Pitcairn-Knowles, 1934).

A number of associations were developed to represent naturopaths and foster their interests. The creation of occupational associations was accepted as an effective vehicle for developing a separate and distinct identity, a first step towards developing consistent training, self-regulation and a register of approved practitioners. However, while these strategies were widely recognised to be crucial in challenging allegations of quackery, the diversity of approaches among naturopaths proved to be a stumbling block to unity. Milton Powell is credited as an early advocate of the benefits of a voluntary association. An article in *Healthy Life* in 1919 inspired a conference held in Northampton the following year, which led to the creation of The Nature Cure Association of Great Britain and Ireland (NCA). Established in 1925, it aimed to provide a register of qualified practitioners, approve training schools and act to promote naturopathy. Membership was open to those with a recognised qualification or five years' experience in practice and successful completion of written and practical tests set by the NCA. The first cohort of members included individuals with American qualifications, such as James Thomson and Stanley Lief. Others, including Andrew Pitcairn-Knowles, had developed knowledge and skills through informal methods and practical experience. There was an urgent need to establish reputable training schools in Britain if naturopathy was to survive and prosper independent of other national associations. By the 1920s, two schools linked to the NCA had been established, the Edinburgh School of Natural Therapeutics run by James Thomson, which offered a full-time course, and the London School of Natural Therapeutics, offering a part-time course. A separate school offering part-time study was set up to train those wishing to join the British Association of Naturopaths (BAN) (Chambers, *c*.1996, pp. 6–8). Another option available for those wishing to gain professional recognition was home study based on a correspondence course run by J. Allen Pattreiouex of the Manchester School of Natural Therapeutics (*H&NCH*, 1931, p. 121).

Curriculum content and study methods proved to be contentious (Power, 1984, pp. 37–40). In 1927, Thomson and colleagues broke away from the NCA to form the Society of British Naturopaths, renamed the Incorporated Society of Registered Naturopaths (ISRN) in 1934. Although the curriculum at the London School of Natural Therapeutics was revised in 1934 to offer a four-year, full-time course with a requirement that entrants be educated to matriculation level, these divisions were not resolved (*H&NCH*, 1934, p. 181). Thirty-six practitioners listed in the *H&NCH* for 1934 claimed qualification through membership of the NCA of Great Britain and Ireland and forty-three as members of the BAN. Thirty were listed as qualified osteopaths and twenty-one as chiropractors. A handful were recorded as holding a qualification from a small college near Newcastle run by Victor Davidson, a graduate of Lindlahr's American school. Several practitioners listed more than one qualification, for example, as osteopath and naturopath, or one of a variety of other titles less easy to link to a specific association. While this variety of qualifications demonstrates the importance attributed to being able to distinguish qualified from unqualified practitioners, it also highlights continuing debates over the scope of naturopathy and its relationship with other unorthodox healers.

The boundary between osteopathy and naturopathy proved especially contentious in this period, highlighted by the campaign by osteopaths to secure a system of state registration. While regulation, whether voluntary or supported by statute, was seen as a way to improve protection of the public from unregistered practitioners, it could also serve the self-interest of an occupational group by securing or improving their market share (Stone and Matthews, 1996, p. 55). The benefits of state registration for orthodox practitioners had increased from the mid-nineteenth century as the growing opportunities for state-sponsored employment in developing public health services were restricted to orthodox practitioners (see Bivins's chapter). This policy acted to further enhance the prestige of this group and its dominance over other unorthodox practitioners in the market for health services. Other occupational groups which took up the option of state regulation, notably midwives in 1902 and nurses in 1919, remained subordinate to medical practitioners and practised within the framework of orthodox medicine (Larkin, 1992). In contrast, unorthodox healers such as medical herbalists and osteopaths claimed independence from the orthodox medical profession and challenged aspects of its underlying theory and practice. Claims that osteopathy was a separate system of medicine were at the heart of opposition by the British Medical Association (BMA) to proposals for state registration for osteopaths. Following the defeat of earlier attempts, a third bill proposing the registration and regulation of osteopaths led to a Select Committee of Enquiry of the House of Lords in 1935. The Select Committee report commented that three important conditions had been satisfied for all groups that had achieved statutory registration but were not yet in place for osteopaths. 'The sphere of territory within which the vocation operates has been clearly defined. The vocation has already long been in general use. There has already been in existence a well-established and efficient system of voluntary examination and registration.' The report recommended any further assessment of registration should be deferred 'until the sphere of osteopathy has been defined, and a system of education in the principles and practice of osteopathy has been developed in this country in one or more well equipped and properly conducted institutions' (Osteopaths' Bill, 1935). Following the bill's defeat, British osteopaths changed their strategy and began to work towards voluntary regulation and improved provision for training (*Osteopathic Blue Book*, 1953, p. 64). These aims were similar to those of naturopaths.

Naturopaths were among those who opposed the bill for state registration of osteopaths, arguing that it would restrict the 'traditional freedom of practice and choice and will be the basis for endless agitation for separate legislation by the different schools of medical thought'. If the bill were approved, naturopaths claimed they would be restricted from using manipulation in their own practice and this would 'adversely affect the Nature Cure Movement' as these techniques had 'always formed a part of the equipment of the Nature Cure Practitioner' (Nature Cure Association, 1935). Chiropractors opposed the bill for similar reasons. The scope of methods suitable for inclusion in the naturopathic armoury was another source of tension between the ISRN and the NCA. Thomson's followers endorsed 'strict nature cure', and the ISRN byelaws noted 'No member of the Register shall prescribe "remedies", e.g., Biochemicals, Tissue Salts, Hormones, Vitamin Concentrates, Pharmaceutical, Homeopathic or Herbal Preparations'. In contrast, the NCA took a more eclectic approach, arguing that providing the principles of nature cure lay at the heart of healing it was acceptable to use auxiliary treatments in particular cases (Benjamin, 1951, p. 35). The manifesto of the British Naturopathic Association (BNA), formed in 1945 from the merger of the NCA and the BAN, endorsed the freedom to use a wide range of treatments, including dietetics, fasting, light, water, exercise, psychological and structural adjustment and included the freedom to select from osteopathic and chiropractic methods if so desired (Manifesto, BNA, 1945).

IV Freedom to use unqualified practitioners

Naturopaths actively participated in coordinated action with other unorthodox practitioners to protect their established freedom to practise and to minimise financial penalties incurred when patients chose to use them. John Wood, co-founder of *Health for All* magazine, became chairman of the British Health Freedom Society (BHFS), formed to raise public awareness and ensure an effective parliamentary lobby to influence legislation framing NHI and state-funded health services. A strategy meeting of the society held in March 1946 was attended by representatives of naturopaths, osteopaths, chiropractors, medical herbalists and other practitioners (TNA, MH 77/112, BHFS, 27 March 1946). The groups represented were listed as the NCA, ISRN, General Council and Register of Osteopaths, Osteopathic Association of Great Britain, Natural Therapeutics Association, British Chiropractors Association, National Association of Medical Herbalists, Healers Association, Institute of Botanic Medicine and unaffiliated practitioners. This action had been prompted by initial drafts of the National Insurance (Industrial Injuries) Act 1946, which 'declared that an injured workman should follow the treatment decided by his medical practitioner under penalty of possible forfeiture of his weekly benefits and also a penalty of up to £10 a day' (BHFS letter to MPs, April 1946).

In 1946, the society wrote to all MPs alerting them of the campaign to maintain current freedoms and requesting support for amendments to the proposed bill to 'preserve existing rights' under Clause 38 of the NHI Act, 1936. This allowed an individual to 'make his own arrangements for advice and treatment outside the ordinary general practitioner provisions' (BHFS circular, May 1946). Representatives of medical herbalists had already emphasised the importance of establishing funding arrangements for unorthodox treatment within the state schemes in order to support the principle of free choice. The current situation was 'not only an injustice but a financial burden (especially to the skilled and unskilled worker) to have to pay this [national health insurance] and find, in addition, the fee for the treatment obtained from the medical herbalist'. Although Section 38 did make provision for an insured person to recover the cost of treatment by an unorthodox practitioner from his local insurance committee, this had 'been a dead letter as far as the patient of the medical herbalist is concerned', as any reimbursement was discretionary and 'permission is very rarely granted'. Without access to funds prior to a consultation, the freedom of the less well-off to choose an unorthodox practitioner was severely compromised. An improved reimbursement scheme was needed as 'the economic position of the industrial worker does not permit of two payments being made by him in return for one medical service' (MH 77/110 BHFS, Deputation re herbal medicine, 1946). The BHFS campaign was successful in ensuring passage of an amendment to the 1946 Act whereby

> the £10 penalty against freedom of choice was withdrawn, and subject to the approval of the local insurance officer and following that, if necessary, the local tribunal, the right of the patient to attend the practitioner of his own choice was maintained.
>
> *(BHFS letter to MPs, April 1946)*

Thus, the principle of choice was preserved under the NHS, although access to funding for unorthodox care was not provided for in the scheme.

The BHFS brought together lay supporters and unorthodox practitioners who worked through local branches to raise public awareness of the issues at stake. It is estimated that there were some 2,000–3,000 active supporters coordinated through fifty branches (Collins, 2005, p. 205). A nationwide campaign was launched 'to secure testimony from people who have benefited from treatment by unregistered practitioners'. Individuals were invited to complete pre-printed forms that included details of their case and the name and address of patient and practitioner and to send these to the Ministry of Health (MH). Surviving forms and letters show that individuals raised a number of points relating to freedom of choice and financial considerations, made a case for the superior results achieved by unorthodox therapies and demanded that provision of free treatment be included in the proposed health service. A. G. Sellan noted his own successful treatment by osteopath G. R. Curzon Barrow and at Lief's nature cure resort at Champneys and requested that legislation 'is worded so as to allow Insured persons freedom to choose their own practitioner whether he be an osteopath, naturopath or orthodox medical man' (MH 77/110 BHFS, 22 January 1946). Mary Stimson was one of several correspondents who highlighted the financial burden of having to pay twice should unqualified practitioners not be covered by the scheme (MH 77/110 BHFS, 18 January 1946). L. Spence, signing herself 'one of the common people', went further and protested 'vigorously against any part of my earnings going to strengthen the Maxi-cult of Allopathy' and demanded the right to withhold her funds from any service based on orthodox medicine as she wanted to allocate them to her chosen practitioner based at Hyde's Herbal Clinic, Leicester (MH 77/110 BHFS, 20 January 1946). Janet Falconer used the example of her own family to make the case that access to naturopathic methods made sound financial sense with the potential to release savings from reduced drug bills and absenteeism. Falconer claimed she had spent 'some small fortune in drugs and ointments' and her husband had endured prolonged absence from work before gaining better health through advice and treatment from James Thomson in Edinburgh (MH 77/111 BHFS, 21 February 1946). In addition to supporting this postal campaign, local societies raised public debate through meetings and newspaper publicity in which they were able to strike a more strident note than that adopted by the parliamentary campaign. A flyer for the Bristol branch called on all lovers 'of freedom and justice' to resist the attempts by the state and the BMA to assert their authority and drew parallels with earlier calls for religious freedom: 'All sane human beings should be masters of their own bodies, just as they are of their own souls' and claiming 'the freedom to seek advice *wherever it pleases us* for the treatment of our bodies in illness, without fear of persecution and penalties' (MH 77/110, BHFS, undated).

A similar approach was taken by the Bath branch, which passed a resolution that:

> the same freedom which our forefathers won in matters of religion shall be retained by each individual in relation to personal health, and therefore insists that the National Health Bill shall contain a proviso to safeguard the individual from compulsion either to seek advice or to receive treatment from any one source.
> *(MH 77/112, BHFS, Bath and Wiltshire Chronicle and Herald, 18 February 1946, p. 4)*

The standard response letter developed by the MH reiterated government policy that 'it is not the intention to restrict the rights of individuals to continue to make their own arrangements for particular forms of advice on health and treatment', although 'the new Service itself must clearly be based on practitioners whose status has been recognised by Parliament' (MH 77/112 BHFS, draft letter, January 1946). The campaign by the BHFS was therefore only partially successful; while patients retained the right to choose their practitioner, funding for unorthodox treatment was not available under the new state-funded service. The potential benefits of longer term coordinated action were recognised and, in March 1946, George House from the BHFS proposed the establishment of a Federation of Independent Associations to represent the interests of groups of all alternative practitioners on issues including legislation, training and education (MH 77/112, BHFS, 27 March 1946.) At a further meeting in July, the BNA, the Natural Therapeutics Association and the National Association of Medical Herbalists all agreed to join the Federation of Natural Therapists (MH 77/112, BHFS, 26 July 1946). This was renamed The General Council of Natural Therapeutics in 1952 (Chambers, *c.*1996, p. 10).

V Conclusion

This chapter has explored the strategies and actions adopted by British naturopaths in the first half of the twentieth century to build a distinctive identity and mitigate the effects of fundamental change in the structure of the British market for health care. Efforts to promote natural methods of healing were helped by concerns over excessive self-drugging and contaminated food stuffs, as well as the prevalence of a broader culture of positive health that endorsed the importance of lifestyle and health maintenance. In order to build a community of like-minded practitioners able and willing to challenge the theoretical basis of orthodox medical practice, naturopaths drew on business skills and commercial awareness, as well as dedication to nature cure principles. Thus, advertisement and public education through magazines such as *Health for All* were pursued alongside strategies to introduce better standards of training and develop professional associations. Although the 1909 report on unqualified practice did not recognise naturopaths as a distinct group of healers, within twenty years there were several hundred qualified practitioners across the country. In the interwar period, increased central funding of health services introduced through the implementation of NHI acted to consolidate the close relationship between the state and orthodox medicine as reimbursement was limited to treatment provided by designated practitioners. The case of British naturopaths demonstrates that this increased state involvement did not simply lead to a decline in unorthodox practice. Naturopaths were successful in improving their profile and developing a distinctive practice in these years. In the 1940s, naturopaths played an important and active role in the campaign run by the BHFS to challenge proposals that sought to restrict patient choice and impose financial penalties on those choosing unorthodox healers. Although this campaign was unsuccessful in achieving state funding for services provided by unorthodox healers, the action taken helped to ensure continuation of the right of patients to select their own practitioner and thereby preserved the opportunities for unorthodox practice after the introduction of the NHS.

Archives

The National Archives (TNA)

Ministry of Health (MH) 77/110 BHFS, Bristol Branch of the BHFS, printed flyer, undated.

MH 77/110, British Health Freedom Society (BHFS), 'The case for presentation by the deputation of associations representing herbal medicine to the Minister of Health', 1946.

MH 77/110, BHFS, letter from Mary Stimson, 18 January 1946.

MH 77/110, BHFS, letter from L. Spence, 20 January 1946.

MH 77/110, BHFS, letter from A. D. Sellan, 22 January 1946.

MH 77/111, BHFS, letter from Janet Falconer, 21 February 1946.

MH 77/111, BHFS, circular to MPs, May 1946.

MH 77/112, BHFS, draft letter, January 1946.

MH 77/112, BHFS, newspaper cutting 'Health contribution injustice: free choice of treatment demanded at Bath', *Bath and Wiltshire Chronicle and Herald*, 18 February 1946, p. 4.

MH 77/112, BHFS, minutes of 'Meeting of joint committee of unorthodox practitioners', 27 March 1946.

MH 77/112, BHFS, circular to MPs, May 1946.

MH 77/112, BHFS, minutes of 'Meeting of joint committee of unorthodox practitioners', 26 July 1946.

National Osteopathic Archive (NOA)

BHFS, circular letter to MPs, April 1946, with brochure 'Nature healing in the House of Commons'.

Byelaws of the Incorporated Society of Registered Naturopaths.

Manifesto of the British Naturopathic Association limited by guarantee,1945.

Memorandum by the legislative committee of the Nature Cure Association of Great Britain and Ireland (limited by guarantee) on the Bill for the Registration and Regulation of Osteopaths (1935).

References

Unpublished sources

Power, R. (1984), 'A natural profession? – issues in the professionalisation of British nature cure, 1930–1950', unpublished MSc dissertation, Polytechnic of the South Bank.

Printed sources

Adams, J. M. (forthcoming 2015), *Healing with water: English spas and the water cure, 1840–1960* (Manchester: Manchester University Press).

Anon. (1931), *The health and nature cure handbook: a complete and independent guide to nature cure and healthy living (H&NCH)*, Vol. I (London: Nature Cure Educational Association); Vol. II (1932) (London: Nature Cure Educational Association); Vol. III (1934) (London: James Clarke).

Benjamin, H. (1936), *Everybody's guide to nature cure, 1st edition* (London: Health for All Publishing Co.).

Benjamin, H. (1941), *Everybody's guide to nature cure, 4th edition* (London: Health for All Publishing Co.).

Benjamin, H. (1951), *Unorthodox medicine versus medical science* (London: Health for All Publishing Co.).

British Naturopathic Journal and Osteopathic Review (Spring, 1963).

Brown, P. S. (1988), 'Nineteenth-century American health reformers and the early nature cure movement in Britain', *Medical History*, 32, 174–194.

Chambers, M. (n. d. but *c*.1996), *The British Naturopathic Association: the first fifty years* (London: BNA).

Collins, M. (2005), *Osteopathy in Britain: the first hundred years* (privately published).

Cooter, R. (1988), *Studies in the history of alternative medicine* (Basingstoke: Macmillan).

Hardy, A. (2000), *Health and medicine in Britain since 1860* (Basingstoke: Palgrave Macmillan).

Larkin, G. (1992), 'Orthodox and osteopathic medicine in the inter-war years' in Mike Saks (ed.), *Alternative medicine in Britain* (Oxford: Clarendon Press), pp. 112–123.

Lawrence, C. and Weisz, G. (1998), *Greater than the parts: holism in biomedicine, 1920–1950* (New York and Oxford: Oxford University Press).

Nature Cure Annual and Health and Pleasure Guide (1907/08).

Osteopathic Blue Book (1953).

Pitcairn-Knowles, Mrs A. (1934), 'Diet and cookery for the sickroom', *Health and Nature Cure Handbook*, pp. 88–97.

Pitcairn-Knowles, R. (2012), *Riposo Health Hydro 1912–1962* (St Leonards on Sea: Impression IT for the author).

Report as to the practice of medicine and surgery by unqualified persons in the United Kingdom presented to both Houses of Parliament by Command of his Majesty (1910) (London: HMSO).

Report from the Select Committee of the House of Lords appointed to consider the registration and regulation of Osteopaths Bill (House of Lords) together with the proceedings of the committee and minutes of evidence (1935) (London: HMSO).

Saks, M. (1992), 'Introduction' in M. Saks (ed.), *Alternative medicine in Britain* (Oxford: Clarendon Press), 1–21.

Stone, J. and Matthews, J. (1996), *Complementary medicine and the law* (Oxford: Oxford University Press).

Thomson, C. L. (1960), *James C. Thomson, pioneer naturopath* (Edinburgh: Kingston Clinic).

Thomson, J. C. (1920), *An introduction to nature cure*, 2nd edn (London: C. W. Daniel); 1st edn 1916.

Vaughan, P. (1992), '"Secret remedies" in the late nineteenth and early twentieth centuries', in M. Saks (ed.), *Alternative medicine in Britain* (Oxford: Clarendon Press), 101–111.

Whorton, J. C. (2002), *Nature cures: the history of alternative medicine in America* (Oxford: Oxford University Press).

Zweiniger-Bargielowska, I. (2007), 'Raising a nation of "good animals": the New Health Society and health education campaigns in interwar Britain', *Social History of Medicine*, 20, 73–89.

Zweiniger-Bargielowska, I. (2010), *Managing the body: beauty, health and fitness in Britain, 1880–1939* (Oxford: Oxford University Press).

5

PRACTISING AYURVEDA IN THE UK

Simplification, modification, hyphenation and hybridisation

Romila Santosh

I Introduction

Ayurveda, a system of healing from India,[1] has gained popularity in recent years in the West as a holistic approach to health and well-being because it claims to address the body, mind and soul. Deepak Chopra,[2] David Frawley,[3] Vasant Lad[4] and Robert Svoboda[5] are prominent among those who have written books describing the basic principles of Ayurveda for a non-medical Western audience and presented it in a spiritualised form to the West (Wujastyk and Smith, 2008: 18). According to Warrier (2009: 1–2), Ayurveda in the UK has become part of the holistic health milieu, where practitioners trained in a range of complementary and alternative medical (CAM)[6] traditions offer healing and treatments that are deemed to be holistic, i.e. address the mind, body and spirit of their clients.

I trained as an Ayurveda practitioner and became fascinated by how a spiritualised holistic approach to health might look in an Ayurvedic consultation and how practitioners are adapting the traditional practice to the UK environment. As there is little research on Ayurveda in the UK, I employed a qualitative approach to explore how Ayurveda practice is changing. I found that Ayurveda practitioners have found creative and novel ways to adapt and contemporise the traditional system of Ayurvedic healing. The four processes I identified were simplification, modification, hyphenation and hybridisation, which are described in this chapter.

II Background

Ayurveda in India has been shaped through history by various foreign influences, including Unani medicine from the Middle East in the thirteenth century and first encounters with Western medicine which began in the sixteenth century. Major changes in the revival of Ayurveda occurred in the nineteenth century (Meulenbeld, 1995: 9; Leslie, 1976: 356; Das 1993: 68), leading to 'Modern Ayurveda'. This term was coined by Wujastyk and Smith (2008: 2), meaning Ayurveda as contained within the geographical boundaries of the Indian sub-continent from the nineteenth century onwards, when colonial pressures[7] forced professional-isation and institutionalisation.

Broom *et al.* (2012: 116) suggest that Ayurveda in India is 'deeply embedded in local cultural sensibilities and religious ideologies, producing a complex interplay of medicine, culture and identity'. Tirodkar's (2008: 227–241) study of Ayurvedic practice in an urban city in India describes how a contemporary practitioner can draw upon various elements from Ayurveda, including those that could be described as spiritual.[8]

1 UK Ayurveda[9]

In recent decades, Ayurveda has crossed national boundaries and been 'transplanted' outside South Asia (Reddy, 2002: 98), undergoing further changes in its new environments (Zysk, 2001: 10; Zimmerman, 1992: 209; Warrier, 2009: 1). Wujastyk and Smith (2008: 2)[10] use the term 'Global Ayurveda' to refer to Ayurvedic knowledge that has been transmitted to a wide geographical area outside India. Newcombe (2008: 252–275) gives a helpful historical overview of Ayurveda in Britain, which shows that Ayurveda's practical use of traditional home remedies, diet and lifestyle is part of the South Asian culture which came with Indian migrants to the UK.

The academic literature on Global Ayurveda describes two distinct processes of simplification and spiritualisation as significant in shaping Ayurveda practice in the West. Some scholars suggest the process of spiritualisation is a key influence in the West (Zysk, 2001: 11; Reddy, 2002: 99; Warrier, 2009: 1; Zimmerman, 1992: 221), whereas practitioner researchers point to the restricted range of remedies and treatments available in the West, resulting in a more simplified practice compared to that in South East Asia (Svoboda, 2008: 127; Welch, 2008: 137; Pole, 2008: 216; Bruwer, 2009: 24–26). Alter (2005: 122) suggests that state restrictions are also likely to be driving the changes for the simplification of practice.

2 The state influence

In the UK, the state is paramount in shaping the healthcare market as the National Health Service (NHS) is part of the public sector and funded by the taxpayer. Nonetheless, a considerable amount of care is available through the private sector, and an increasing number of consumers seek care from the private and CAM sectors which do not get state funding.

According to Sharma (1995: 113), CAM professionals practice in a 'curious context' in the UK because they have widespread public support and a small degree of medical acceptance, but they do not have full state support. In India, Ayurveda is one of the six systems of medicine officially recognised by the Indian government (Murthy, 2010: 16). In the past, the protected title of '*vaidya*' was given to practitioners who had completed a long apprenticeship (Langford, 2002: 101). It continues to be awarded to successful graduates from institutions that teach a Bachelor of Ayurvedic Medicine and Surgery (BAMS) degree.

With regards to herbal remedies, the Medicines and Healthcare products Regulatory Agency (MHRA)[11] is the government agency responsible for ensuring that medicines and medical devices are safe. The MHRA is an executive agency of the Department of Health. The European Union (EU) herb law, the Traditional Herbal Medicinal Products Directive (THMPD) 2004/24/EC),[12] came into force on 1 May 2011 (see further discussion in McHale, this volume, p 55). Since then, it has been illegal to manufacture therapeutic herbal products that do not have a traditional herbal registration (THR), although shops in the UK were permitted to sell their remaining stocks of unlicensed herbal medicines. The purpose of the THMPD was to stop the sales of poor-quality or unsafe herbal products.

It is inevitable that any regulation of natural medicines will have a profound effect on the practice of those forms of CAM that are based on the administration of substances to the patient.

Any kind of restriction to supply or prescribe such remedies will restrict the freedom of many therapists to practise at all (Sharma, 1995: 105). The impact of the EU Directive is described below.

In summary, the literature on Ayurveda outlines a dynamic history of changes in the practice, which have been occurring as a result of contact with foreign healing traditions arriving in India. The postcolonial period appears to have brought about the most dramatic changes to the identity of the Ayurvedic profession and in particular the biomedicalisation of the practice in education, research and production of Ayurvedic products,[13] which continues to date. Globalisation is producing further new versions of Ayurveda in the social and political environments of the West. The impact of social trends such as the New Age movement[14] and postmodernism has produced holistic and spiritualised versions.

In this chapter, I provide a practitioner perspective on what happens to a healing tradition when it moves across geographical boundaries into new spaces and focus upon the processes underlying the changes in practice of UK Ayurveda.

In the research that forms the basis for this chapter, I took an interpretive approach using qualitative methods to examine the processes influencing change in UK Ayurveda (Santosh, 2013). Between 2009 and 2012, I collected and analysed data consisting of unstructured interviews with twenty practitioners and observation of practitioner CPD events organised by the Ayurveda Practitioners Association and the British Association of Accredited Ayurvedic Practitioners and other meetings (from 2009 to 2013). I identified four groups of Ayurveda practitioners: practitioners who had qualified with a BAMS degree from India and were now settled and practising in the UK, practitioners with a non-medical background who had graduated in the UK, practitioners with a medical background who had subsequently studied Ayurveda (that I termed 'medical converts') and practitioners from India who were offering consultations during their visits to the UK.

The data analysis involved initial coding of interview transcripts into categories and themes. The second phase of focused coding identified and developed categories of interest. Data labelled with the same code from the different transcripts were drawn together and further analysed to explain the ways in which Ayurveda practitioners are changing their practice.

Given the various influences on practice described in the academic literature, I examined whether practitioners in the UK embrace a spiritualised version of Ayurveda or another one. The findings of my study show that the processes of simplification, modification, hyphenation and hybridisation are shaping the practice of UK Ayurveda. Simplification of practice is occurring both in quantitative and qualitative ways, the process of modification includes substitution, and hyphenation and hybridisation involves mixing Ayurveda with other healing practices.

III Simplification and modification of Ayurveda practice – working within the Ayurevdic tradition

Simplification is occurring both in the number of remedies and treatments prescribed and in their composition. It is also occurring in the range of medical conditions that are treated and at a conceptual level. Modification is occurring as practitioners are adapting their practice through finding substitutes for Ayurvedic remedies and treatments from within the Ayurvedic tradition.

1 Simplification of Ayurveda practice

The first simplification issue concerns that of the prescription. Although the EU Directive 2004 appeared to be a positive step towards ensuring public health, a number of problems were perceived. As a consequence, practitioners could no longer sell ready-made herbal remedies to their clients. Practitioners who use herbs as part of their treatments can prepare their own remedies using single herbs. The findings show that this has forced practitioners to simplify their prescription. For example, practitioners in this study described resorting to using remedies which have a reduced number of herbal components – for example, changing from multi herb remedies to single herb remedies. Dr Dhani described her predicament:

> The motto I have, because of all the things going on around here – you cannot prescribe this herb, or you cannot prescribe that herb, you keep on going and checking it and I just have decided that I give more of the simple herbs....
>
> *(Dr Dhani, South Asian graduate)*

Practitioners perceive this as 'going back to basics' and buying single herbs and making up their own formulae rather than relying on ready-made combinations. For example, one practitioner commented at a meeting: '[We] will need to go back to the old way of combining herbs' (APA multi-track event, 14 May 2011). Practitioners were optimistic and described working creatively to find ways around the restrictions in order to continue their practice.

It is worth noting that this simplification is also having an impact on manufacturing in India because of a globalised market. Pordié (2012) examined the formulation regime at Himalaya, a large Ayurvedic pharmaceutical company based in India, and found that simplification was also occurring in developing herbal products for the global market. Fewer or single herbs were used instead of the classical multi herb formulae.

Practitioners also gave examples of simplification taking place in the treatments. Ayurvedic *panchakarma* treatment is a key method of treating health conditions involving a series of processes lasting from several days to weeks which aim to cleanse the mind–body system at a very deep tissue level. In the UK, few practitioners have clinics with facilities to carry out the long, complex procedures. Practitioners described employing simplified methods based on principles of detoxification in an attempt to achieve similar outcomes. For example, Dr Neha explained how she uses a modified technique to achieve a detoxing effect:

> Q: Are there any alternatives people can try without the *panchakarma* here?
> A: Yeah, like the detox plan that I always give to the people. Two or three days of just ginger water fasting then five days of *moong* soup fasting only, then another ten days of *moong* and vegetables only, then slowly slowly coming back to normal diet...
>
> *(Dr Neha, South Asian visiting practitioner)*

Practitioners described changing from a comprehensive clinical practice treating a wide range of health issues to a focused clinical practice treating a limited range of health issues. Dr Dhani described her predicament of being restricted in the choice of treatments and herbs and as a consequence focusing on what she believes to be the key aspects of health, such as ensuring good digestion: 'The motto I have, because of all the things going on around here ... we go only on the digestive system as much as possible...' (Dr Dhani, South Asian graduate). In addition to the quantitative and qualitative simplification of remedies, treatments and practice, practitioners described simplification of Ayurveda at a conceptual level. For example, they said that instead of giving complex explanations of Ayurveda theory to their clients they offer simplified versions. For example, Bruwer (2009: 24) examined how Ayurvedic practitioners use Ayurvedic dietary principles in their consultations in the West. Most practitioners recommend basics like '*ghee*' (clarified butter) and '*khichari*' (rice and lentils cooked together), while only a few went as far as explaining the 'six tastes' of Ayurveda, suggesting simplification both at clinical and theoretical levels. The Swedish practitioners in Stahle's (2010: 253) study reported working in a similar manner, making small changes that could have a significant impact in the long term. Svoboda (2008: 127) describes the practice of Ayurveda in the United States as becoming a simplified version of the practice in India. He illustrates this process by describing the focus on the three *doshas* (humours) in the West as a conceptual oversimplification.

2 Modification of Ayurveda practice

There are several forms of modification of practice which can be identified. First, that of modification through substituting treatments. Practitioners in this study gave examples of how they change the nature of their treatments, from complex procedures to simpler, easier alternatives that achieve similar outcomes. For example, Aarti explained how she substitutes shorter more accessible cleansing techniques from the yoga tradition for the longer and more complex Ayurvedic detoxing techniques.

> I tell my Ayurvedic patients what yoga exercise they can do. Like I do not practise *vamana* but I do use yogic technique of kunjal, it's a substitute, what you call in Ayurveda *'sadhya vamana'*, 'easy'. Is a yogic *kriya*. But in yoga, you don't do the massage and the *snehana* and the *swedana*, before the *kunjal*, but I find with the *snehana* and the *swedana* and then the *kunjal*, it works much better. So I combine it.
>
> *(Aarti, UK graduate)*

Pritesh described how he prescribed a simple laxative to achieve the effect of the *virechana* procedure, a form of purgation.

> Q: So really to have an authentic practice you need to be able to offer *panchakarma*?
> A: I think so, but then sometimes when I look at it, I think we don't need to do all of it. Sometimes I've found, like my son had very bad acne, so I said why don't you just take a laxative, one laxative every two weeks, and I said to myself that's like virechana. So you could sort of compromise and do it that way.
>
> *(Pritesh, medical convert)*

In this way, practitioners are compromising the traditional treatments in order to achieve viable outcomes.

Other practitioners are forced to find alternatives to traditional remedies produced in India that are banned in the UK because they do not meet the quality and safety requirements of the European Union (Pole, 2008: 217) or because they are endangered and therefore unavailable for use as medicines (Pole, 2008: 216). A full Ayurvedic pharmacopoeia is neither available nor approved for use by the regulations in the UK, which automatically limits the clinical recommendations that can be made and may affect the efficacy of the treatment. This is contrary to Zimmerman's (1992: 211) argument that Ayurveda pharmaceutical process has been intentionally simplified to make it appealing to the West. Pole (2008: 222) suggests that practitioners need to use more simple forms of medicine such as *churnas* (powder) and *kshayas* (decoctions) or even try new forms such as tinctures.

The second form of modification here is that of avoiding herbal treatments. Practitioners described how they adapted their practice by shifting focus from the use of Ayurvedic herbal remedies as the key treatment. As Ayurveda has several treatment modalities, diet, lifestyle, counselling, yoga, etc., practitioners were able to find ways around the restrictions on the use of herbs by using another modality or a combination of these.

The onus was on each practitioner to be creative and decide how to use the different aspects of Ayurveda to develop their practice. One practitioner commented at an event: 'Ayurveda is so broad, so many healing techniques, we will have to get creative and use other ways to help people' (APA multi-track event, 14 May 2011). This happens in a number of different ways: in terms of the recommendations they make, the focus of their practice and the incorporation of other Ayurvedic or CAM modalities. Dr Ben described how other modalities could be employed.

> Q: . . . Can Ayurveda be practised without herbal medicine?
> A: Absolutely. When you are thinking of lifestyle routine, diet and digestion, the mental aspects, the emotional aspects, spiritual aspects, yoga and range of therapies in panchakarma. So many, it will continue. Herbs are only one aspect, but we want Ayurveda to be holistic.
>
> *(Dr Ben, medical convert)*

Most Ayurvedic practitioners considered yoga and Ayurveda as interrelated and many said they include yoga as part of their recommendations. Yoga is taught on BAMS courses in South Asia and is also included in UK Ayurveda training courses. 'Yoga is a part of Ayurveda – so we should sharpen our skills in these other areas and have a wider eclectic practice' (APA multi-track event, 14 May 2011). This appears to be common to Global Ayurveda, as Murthy (2010: 26) found in his study of Ayurvedic practitioners in New Zealand and Stahle (2010: 247) in his study of Ayurvedic counsellors in Sweden where recommendations may include the practice of certain yogic exercises, or breathing techniques.

Yoga has played a significant role in introducing Ayurveda to a wider group, beyond the Indian migrant community. Yoga, as popularised in the West has been a way of introducing Europeans to an Eastern tradition and philosophy, Sanskrit vocabulary and an alternative method of well-being (Newcombe, 2008). They have become familiar with a different paradigm and vocabulary, which has facilitated the understanding and acceptance of Ayurveda.

IV The processes of hyphenation and hybridisation – with treatments outside of the Ayurvedic tradition

With reference to the inclusion of other healing modalities in Ayurvedic practice, I use the term hyphenation to describe how practitioners prescribe two distinct treatments or remedies from different healing systems in combination. This is perhaps the first step in mixing and matching treatments. The second step is hybridisation, when a meshing of the different systems occurs at a theoretical level to produce a hybrid treatment or remedy.

1 Hyphenation – incorporation of other CAM practices into Ayurveda

Ayurveda describes the changes of practice according to time, place and environment. Accordingly, some practitioners are taking advantage of herbs that are common to both the Western and the Ayurvedic pharmacopeia. Dr Priya described how she brings together Ayurvedic and Western herbal remedies.

> And that's why my practice probably is slightly different from many people here because I use Ayurvedic herbs as Western herbs. I mean, their preparation is Western. I use many

tinctures. I don't use Ayurvedic classical formally apart from *triphala*. I don't stock any of those, so I don't give any of these classical medicine. I've never used them. I use *guggul* a lot but I use it as a tincture.

(Dr Priya, South Asian graduate)

UK graduate Hannah described a similar approach as she integrates Ayurvedic and local Western herbs in her practice:

So I mix that – you know, my Western stuff – with the Ayurvedic stuff, so she's very high *pitta*. She's even got – she's got freckles; she's really small; she's got ginger hair; got a pretty hot temper. So she's getting the anti-pitta regimen, but then I've married it up with herbs that I can use here. So it's horse chestnut.... So all those things come together really, so I'm not a pure Ayurveda really. But then, I think I am possibly, because Ayurveda – I think it is semi-permeable. It's like the English language. It can allow for the other things to come in it.

(Hannah, UK graduate)

In addition to combining Ayurvedic and Western herbs, Hannah brought together Ayurveda and her training in modern nutrition:

The difficulty there has been in having access to the medicines and knowing that you're using an alternative that's only, like, one sixteenth of the possibilities. So it's had to be more about, you know, dietary counselling which fits in with my degree in nutrition, so that's how I've really managed without a lot of medicines.

(Hannah, UK graduate)

The examples illustrate how consultations are becoming more individualised; that is, treating patients according to their individual constitution with practitioners selecting treatment modalities according to their personal inclination. For example, Dr Kishore described his practice, which includes biomedicine, Ayurveda, Chinese medicine and yoga.

If somebody books an appointment, then I have the room and then I call the client over there and the first appointment is about one hour, and detailed history-taking and making the primary diagnosis, and all other treatments are subsequent to that primary diagnosis, which could vary from herbal massage to herbal therapy, including a few of the.... *Panchaka*rma treatment and – plus yoga therapy,... so I combine together Chinese medicine, Ayurvedic medicine as well as – on the back of modern medicine stuff is there, so I know where the client is coming from so, given all those dimensions, equally respected, then I likewise go for the healing part for a particular person on the individualised basis.

(Dr Kishore, medical convert)

Thus Ayurveda practitioners are open to different systems of healing and adopting the process of hyphenation, as a consequence of the restrictions in the UK environment. It was unclear to what extent Ayurveda was different to the systems it hyphenates with and to what extent it was similar. This is an area for further research (Alter, 2005: 6).

Robinson *et al.* (2012: 604) reported numerous differences in practice, training and regulation between East and West. They noted that European acupuncturists were more likely to use other CAM practices with acupuncture, although this was likely to vary between EU countries (ibid.: 610). These findings highlighted how acupuncture, like Ayurveda, can be practised as part of a pluralistic medical practice, integrated either with Western medicine, as in China, or with other CAM, as generally seen in Europe.

2 Hybridisation[15] – combining different CAM practices at a theoretical level

A few practitioners have been making use of local Western herbs in their practice. As one practitioner commented at a CPD event: 'Ayurvedic practitioners are herbalists, though we use yoga etc., we are surrounded by herbs, growing all around us. Therefore get to know all these local herbs' (APA multi-track event, 14 May 2011). A good example is Dr Hans Rhyner,[16] an Ayurvedic practitioner who runs a clinic in Austria and grows local herbs in the surrounding gardens. He prepares fresh decoctions for his patients as required. Similarly, Anne McIntyre, a Western herbalist and Ayurveda practitioner in the UK, has written a book, *Dispensing with Tradition. A Practitioner's Guide to Using Indian and Western Herbs the Ayurvedic Way*, applying the principles of Ayurveda to local herbs – an example of a hybrid practice.[17]

Pordié's (2012) research shows that hybridisation is occurring in India, as illustrated by his findings from the Himalaya Company, which employs both Ayurvedic and biomedical processes to develop new Ayurvedic remedies. The reformulation process involved developing remedies using the descriptions of plant properties from the Ayurvedic texts and then reformulating them to create new Ayurvedic remedies for biomedically defined ailments. The new formulations are stabilised, then given a trademark and labelled as Ayurvedic medicine. These products appear to be closer to hybrids, rather than hyphenated products, as the Ayurvedic and biomedical processes are difficult to separate.

Whether hybridity is a positive or negative social trend is disputed. Pordié (2012) found that some scholars feel that the Himalaya reformulation regime is a corruption of the tradition, leading to questions about what is authentic Ayurveda. However, Bhabha (1994: 54–56) suggests that claims to the inherent purity and originality of cultures are not viable. The notion of an international culture is based on cultural hybridity rather than exoticism or multi-culturalism. The binary understanding of culture is replaced by the hybridised nature of cultures. Hybridity in the Global Ayurvedic context needs further examination for a detailed understanding. The findings here suggest that, while hybridity is partly a product of limitation and restriction to practice, at the same time it denotes creativity and pragmatism in UK Ayurveda practice.

Heelas describes this 'pick and mix' approach in other contexts – for example, in how people select tropes in their spiritual lives mixing shamanism and Christianity, or religious and non-religious ideas and practices (Heelas *et al.*, 1998: 5). Heelas suggests that hybridity is a popular term among postmodern theorists – for example, 'Zennis' is a hybrid of Zen meditation/yoga and tennis. Thus some of the findings in this study, namely the processes of hyphenation and hybridisation can be seen to fit into broader patterns resulting from globalisation and changing social trends. However, as mentioned above, such assimilation and amalgamation has been evident throughout history – for example, Ayurveda and Unani tradition from the thirteenth century onwards, or Ayurveda and Western medicine from the sixteenth century onwards.

V Conclusions

To summarise, I have shown that many practitioners have accepted that they need to change their treatment protocols in order to survive in their new geographical space. They find ways to deal with medical conditions using a limited range of single herbs or other weaker alternatives.

Some practitioners have changed the range of conditions they deal with; others are seeking out herbs that are available locally and including them in their personal *materia medica* to increase their choice of remedies, while others have sought out new approved suppliers. The use of simple herbs and learning how to combine them to make effective remedies is transporting practitioners back to the days before the large-scale, ready-made herbal products had become available. They are re-learning the skills that the traditional practitioners had prior to the phar-maceuticalisation of Ayurveda (Banerjee, 2008).

The paradox that has emerged from this study is that these processes, which have the effect of simplifying the traditional practice of Ayurveda, are causing an increasingly complex range of practice in UK Ayurveda – for example, from focusing more on adjusting a patient's diet and lifestyle, to incorporating Western herbs or advising on yoga techniques instead of complicated Ayurveda procedures. The practice is increasing in diversity as each practitioner develops their practice according to a preferred interest or skill. For example, a patient may go to one practi-tioner whose focus may be on nutritional advice, while another may emphasise the practice of yoga. With such diversity, a patient's satisfaction with their Ayurvedic encounter will depend on whether they have consulted with a practitioner who shares the same focus of treatment as the patient.

The findings also show that herbal regulations are not preventing practitioners from practis-ing Ayurveda in the UK. Rather, they are re-shaping the practice, through the processes of simplification, modification, hyphenation and hybridisation and providing the context by which Ayurvedic practitioners on the ground are diversifying and producing multiple variations of the tradition. Ayurveda continues to be the fluid tradition that it has been in the past.

Robinson *et al.* (2012: 605) have shown parallel findings for traditional Chinese medicine (TCM) whereby concurrent use of acupuncture and herbal medicine is more likely in China, with herbs being the main therapeutic TCM modality. In China, both acupuncture and herbal medicine are taught during TCM training, with specialisation occurring later. In the West, they found only around one-third of acupuncturists use herbs. Although the authors did not report on the reason for this difference in practice, one of the reasons may be perceived safety concerns and the influence of EU regulation on herbal medicines in a similar way to the Ayurvedic prac-titioners in this study.

Although beyond the scope of this study, some Ayurvedic practitioners have been adopting another strategy to overcome the lack of facilities and treatments available in the UK. They recommend patients with complex problems to go to India for *panchakarma* treatments (though the frequency of these recommendations is not known and may be rare). Reed's (2003: 126) findings show that her interviewees of Asian origin gave accounts of travelling between UK and India for health treatments. She suggested that people access plural healthcare in plural contexts enabling them to carry out, what she terms, 'syncretic' practices in a plurality of locations.

Thus UK Ayurveda is multifaceted, combining several techniques (Warrier, 2009: 14). Stahle (2010: 248) reports similar changes in Sweden where various Ayurvedic techniques such as massage, diet and lifestyle are combined with other methods of personal and spiritual develop-ment and for maintaining fitness and well-being. Warrier (2014) describes the immense diver-sity of socio-cultural traditions, national backgrounds, holistic therapies and networks that make up the British Ayurvedic community. Practitioners feed their ideas from their own cultures into different versions of Ayurveda. It is therefore necessary to look at the diversity of the individuals who practise Ayurveda to understand the influences shaping UK Ayurveda.

The findings from my research suggest that Ayurveda practitioners in the UK adopt this open and inclusive ethos in order to compensate for not having the full range of Ayurvedic remedies and treatments. I argue that one of the key drivers for the new eclectic versions of Ayurveda is the regulatory restrictions on herbal medicines, which leave practitioners with restricted opportunities for practice, and is not simply a celebration of globalisation. Without the restrictions, Ayurveda could be practised in its full form as in South Asia, and the hyphenation and hybridisation of different systems of healing may not have occurred to the same extent.

According to Alter (2005: 6), when medical knowledge moves across boundaries, it does necessarily lose some of its character and uniqueness to a particular region or state. In the case of Ayurveda, scholars such as Meulenbeld (1995: 1) have outlined the changes in Ayurveda through history, and Warrier (2011b: 2) specifically points to the exchanges that had begun during colonial times suggesting that the version of Ayurveda that came to the UK had already undergone change.

In the West, there are a number of factors that have led to simplification of practice. Svoboda (2008: 127) writes that this is due to the commodification of Ayurveda:

> Ayurveda is only likely to develop within a commercial framework; and commercial activity provides one avenue for the NAMA (the National Ayurvedic Medical Association) and other Ayurvedic organisations to communicate meaningfully with the general public. Difficulties arise, however, when fidelity to the subject being studied collides with the drive to simplify and commodify.

Cant and Sharma (1999: 105) point to the impact of the state restrictions which inevitably impact on the practice, while Welch suggests that the changes are due to the lack of education in the West as well as access to the remedies:

> At present, Ayurveda must be an adjunct practice, as no full five or six year courses of study are available (or even possible) in the West, licensing is practically non-existent, and the full pharmacopoeia is neither available or approved for use by drug-regulating agencies in the West. Thus for the moment at least, what we have in the West is an altered form of Ayurveda.
>
> *(Welch, 2008: 137)*

There are variations in the way Ayurveda is practised across India, with different schools of Ayurvedic practice and different regional traditions (Warrier, 2011a: 83). Further variations arise from practitioners holding different ideological positions, ranging from *sudha* (pure Ayurveda) to *mishra* (Ayurveda integrated with biomedicine).

The findings of this study show that practitioners are able to adapt Ayurveda in order to practise in the UK environment, through the processes of simplification, modification, hyphenation and hybridisation, thus showing the fluidity and flexibility of this healing system. UK Ayurveda is continuing to change in response to external influences and practitioners' personal preferences.

Research on acupuncturists in Europe has shown similar changes in practice as they tend to specialise in certain areas – for example, treating children or gynaecological issues (Robinson *et al.*, 2012: 610). Other research shows that acupuncture practice in Europe is skewed towards musculoskeletal pain and away from the more serious internal problems. This indicates a tendency for CAM practitioners of Eastern traditions in Europe to develop specialised practices, which is ironic considering that a holistic approach is a key feature of CAM.

In parallel, research on changes in TCM practice found that individual practitioners work very differently in Europe compared to China and use diverse practices, which may include: herbal medicine, acupuncture, cupping, moxibustion, tuina, qigong and dietary therapy (Robinson *et al.*, 2012: 604).

This chapter has identified in detail the ways in which Ayurveda practice is changing in the UK. The processes of simplification, modification, hyphenation and hybridisation describe the ways in which UK Ayurveda practice is changing. These processes of change provide insight into the ways in which Ayurveda practitioners are creatively adapting an ancient healing system to a new environment and the fluidity of Ayurveda as a system of healing.

Both Reddy (2002: 129) and Warrier (2009: 1) suggested, as a result of their empirical field-work, that Global Ayurveda is shaped by the New Age movement, in the US and UK, respectively. The findings of this study indicate that, although the holistic health milieu and the New Age may have enabled the positive reception of Ayurveda in the UK, the processes of simplification, modification, hyphenation and hybridisation are shaping the clinical practice of UK Ayurveda.

This is reflected in the perspectives of the academic community and practitioners. For example, scholars such as Zimmerman (1992), Zysk (2001), Reddy (2002) and Warrier (2009, 2011b) emphasise Global Ayurveda as being the result of processes of spiritualisation and the influence of the New Age, whereas practitioners like Murthy (2010), Pole (2008), Bruwer (2009) and myself are emphasising the regulatory frameworks and restrictions on clinical practice as the foundation for the changes in practice.

The implications of this research are that a bottom-up, patient-centred approach is required to shape the education and training for Ayurveda in the UK, as practice needs to be in line with the changes taking place in clinical practice, rather than an approach based solely on the Indian curriculum or the classical texts. A considered approach is required for research as the practice in the UK is less standardised and more individualised, compared to the practice in India. Therefore, research methods that are sensitive to the diversity of Ayurveda practice need to be employed.

Acknowledgements

I would like to thank the University of Winchester for awarding me a three-year, full-time PhD studentship for the research which forms the basis of this chapter.

Notes

1 According to Alter (2005: 1), the idea that Ayurveda originated in India needs to be considered cautiously as current India is a political entity and the notion of a country and its borders is questionable in terms of meaning and significance. This is appropriately illustrated with the example of Ayurveda, which is currently accepted as a medical system of India, though the history of its development took place in parts of what is now India, Pakistan, Afghanistan, Nepal and Bangladesh through an exchange of ideas across all these borders.
2 Chopra, D., The Chopra Center [online]. Available at: www.chopra.com/aboutdeepak (accessed 10 April 2013).
3 Frawley, D., American Institute of Vedic Studies [online]. Available at: www.vedanet.com/about/about-acharya-david-frawley-pandit-vamadeva-shastri (accessed 10 April 2013).
4 Lad, V., The Ayurvedic Institute [online]. Available at: www.ayurveda.com (accessed 10 April 2013).
5 Svoboda, R., drsvoboda.com [online]. Available at: http://drsvoboda.com (accessed 10 April 2013).
6 See 'The Road Map for CAM European Research', (no date) [online]. Available at: www.cambrella.eu/home.php? (accessed 10 April 2013).
7 The *vaidyas* were compelled to professionalise and establish institutions, associations, colleges and pharmaceutical companies in order to compete with biomedicine or face extinction (Banerjee, 2008: 201; Kumar, 2001: 29).
8 I explored the extent to which spirituality plays a role in an Ayurvedic clinical consultation in the UK in my PhD thesis (Santosh, 2013).

9 I refer to Ayurveda in the UK as 'UK Ayurveda'.

10 Wujastyk and Smith (2008: 11) describe four paradigms of Global Ayurveda: New Age Ayurveda, Ayurveda as mind–body medicine, Maharishi Ayurveda and Traditional Ayurveda in an urban world. These are useful at looking at different practices.

11 MHRA (2013) [online]. Available at: www.mhra.gov.uk/#page=DynamicListMedicines (accessed 29 December 2012).

12 MHRA (2013) [online]. Available at: www.mhra.gov.uk/Howweregulate/Medicines/Herbalmedicinesregulation/index.htm (accessed 29 December 2012).

13 Banerjee (2008) examined the changes in terms of the pharmaceuticalisation of Ayurveda. The manufacturing processes of Ayurvedic remedies were also influenced by competition from mass-produced biomedical medicines and the continuous output of biomedical research information, particularly in relation to the efficacy of new medicines. She gives an excellent account of the practical challenges that Ayurveda practitioners and manufacturers faced in order to compete with biomedicine.

14 Partridge (2004: 2) reports that scholars have used the term 'New Age' to define a particular network of ideas and beliefs, but he also suggests that the New Age is a slippery word (2004: 71), encompassing a broad range of spiritualities and therapies that are broadly mystical and directly influenced by Eastern and Western esotericism. According to Bruce (2002), the New Age resonates with the culture in the contemporary West. He outlines six key themes of the New Age: the self is divine; epistemological individualism (there is no higher authority than the self); epistemological individualism leads to eclecticism; New Age spirituality emphasises holism, rejecting the reductionism of modern scientific worldviews; epistemological individualism and eclecticism lead to relativism (no path is better than another); the goal of New Age spirituality is health and happiness (rather than health and happiness being a by-product of the religious life).

15 Hybridity is a disputed term in postcolonial studies. Hybridisation takes many forms, including cultural, political and linguistic. Though the word hybrid has biological and botanical origins, Young (1995: 18) writes that the hybridity is being used to characterise contemporary culture. Hybridity can imply a range of different meanings: contrafusion and disjunction as well as fusion and assimilation. Young (1995: 5) writes that historically there has been little attention to the mechanics of the process of cultural contact. Postcolonial writing has focused on the hybridised nature of postcolonial culture as strength rather than a weakness. It is not a case of the oppressor obliterating the oppressed or the coloniser silencing the colonised. In practice, it stresses the mutuality of the process.

16 Ayurveda Rhyner [online]. Available at: www.ayurveda-rhyner.com (accessed 9 January 2013).

17 McIntyre, A., annemcintyre.com [online]. Available at: http://annemcintyre.com/books (accessed 26 April 2013).

References

Alter, J. S., Ed. (2005). *Asian Medicine and Globalisation. Encounters with Asia*. Philadelphia, University of Pennsylvania.

Banerjee, M. (2008). 'Ayurveda in Modern India: Standardisation and Pharmaceuticalisation', in *Modern and Global Ayurveda. Pluralism and Paradigms*. D. Wujastyk and F. Smith, Eds, New York, State University of New York.

Bhabha, H. (1994). *The Location of Culture*. London and New York, Routledge.

Broom, A., A. Doron and P. Tovey (2012). 'The Inequalities of Medical Pluralism: Hierarchies of Health, Politics of Tradition and the Economies of Care in Indian Oncology', in *Traditional, Complementary and Integrative Medicine. An International Reader*. J. Adams, G. Andrews, J. Barnes, A. Broom and P. Magin, Eds, Basingstoke, Palgrave Macmillan.

Bruce, S. (2002). *God is Dead: Secularisation in the West*. Oxford, Blackwell.

Bruwer, C. (2009). 'Lighting Candles: The Ayurvedic Diet in Contemporary Western Society: Voices from Practitioners'. Roehampton University, MSc.

Cant, S. and U. Sharma (1999). *A New Medical Pluralism? Alternative Medicine, Doctors, Patients and the State*. London, UCL Press.

Das, R. P. (1993). 'On the Nature and Development of Traditional and Indian Medicine'. *Journal of European Ayurvedic Society* 3: 56–71.

Heelas, P., D. Martin and P. Morris, Eds. (1998). *Religion, Modernity and Postmodernity*. Oxford, Blackwell Publisher Ltd.

Kumar, A. (2001). 'The Indian Drug Industry Under the Raj 1820–1920', in *Health, Medicine and Empire. Perspectives on Colonial India*. B. Pati and M. Harrison, Hyderabad, Orient Longman.

Langford, J. (2002). *Fluent Bodies: Ayurvedic Remedies for Postcolonial Imbalance*. Durham, NC, Duke University Press.

Leslie, C. (1976). 'The Ambiguities of Medical Revivalism in Modern India', in *Asian Medical Systems: A Comparative Study*. C. Leslie, Delhi, Motilal Banarsidas.

Meulenbeld, G. J. (1995). 'The Many Faces of Ayurveda'. *Journal of the European Ayurvedic Society* 4: 1–10.

Murthy, V. S. (2010). 'Positionality of Ayurveda in the New Zealand Healthcare System'. Public Health, The University of Auckland, MSc.

Newcombe, S. (2008). 'A Social History of Yoga and Ayurveda in Britain, 1950–1995'. Faculty of History, University of Cambridge, PhD.

Partridge, C. (2004). *The Re-Enchantment of the West*. London, T&T Clark International.

Pole, S. (2008). 'Practicing Ayurveda in the United Kingdom: A Time of Challenges and Opportunities', in *Modern and Global Ayurveda. Pluralsim and Paradigms*. D. Wujastyk and F. Smith, New York, State University of New York.

Pordié, L. (2012). 'Seminar title: When Big Pharma Turns Green. Drug Discovery, Ayurveda and Global Markets', in *Seminar Series: Circulation and Prescription of Medicines: World Regions Connected and Compared*. EAST Medicine Research Centre, School of Life Sciences, University of Westminster, 29 October.

Reddy, S. (2002). 'Asian Medicine in America: The Ayurvedic Case'. *The Annals of the American of Political and Social Sciences* 583(97): 97–121.

Reed, K. (2003). *Worlds of Health. Exploring the Health Choices of British Mothers*. Westport, US, Praeger Publishers.

Robinson, N., A. Lorenca, W. Ding, J. Jia, M. Bovey and X. M. Wang (2012). 'Exploring practice characteristics and research priorities of practitioners of traditional acupuncture in China and the EU – A survey'. *Journal of Ethnopharmacology* 140: 604–613.

Santosh, R. (2013). 'The Practice of Ayurveda in the UK and the Role of Spirituality. A Practitioner Perspective'. Faculty of Humanities and Social Sciences, University of Winchester, PhD.

Sharma, U. (1995). *Complementary Medicine Today. Practitioners and Patients*. London, Routledge.

Stahle, G. V. (2010). 'Coaching a Healthy Lifestyle: Positioning Ayurveda in a Late Modern Context'. *International Journal for the Study of New Religions* 1(2): 243–260.

Svoboda, R. E. (2008). 'The Ayurvedic Diaspora: A Personal Account', in *Modern and Global Ayurveda. Pluralism and Paradigms*. D. Wujastyk and F. Smith, New York, State University of New York.

Tirodkar, M. (2008). 'Cultural Loss and Remembrance in Contemporary Ayurvedic Medical Practice', in *Modern and Global Ayurveda. Pluralisms and Paradigms*. D. Wujastyk and F. Smith, New York, State University of New York.

Warrier, M. (2009). 'Seekership, Spirituality and Self Discovery: Ayurveda Trainees in Britain'. *Asian Medicine* 4(2): 423–451.

Warrier, M. (2011a). 'Modern Ayurveda in Transnational Context'. *Religion Compass* 5(3): 80–93.

Warrier, M. (2011b). 'Revisiting the Easternisation Thesis: The Spiritualisation of Ayurveda in Modern Britain', in *'Autonomous' Spiritualities beyond Religious Traditions*. P. Heelas, London and New York, Routledge.

Warrier, M. (2014) 'The Professionalisation of Ayurveda in Britain: The Twin Imperatives of Biomedicalisation and Spiritualisation', in *Asymmetrical Conversations: Contestations, Circumventions and the Blurring of Therapeutic Boundaries* (Epistemologies of Healing). H. Naraindas, J. Quack and W. Sax, Eds, Oxford and New York: Berghahn.

Welch, C. (2008). 'An Overview of the Education and the Practice of Global Ayurveda', in *Modern and Global Ayurveda. Pluralism and Paradigm*. D. Wujastyk and F. Smith, New York, State University of New York.

Wujastyk, D. and F. Smith, Eds. (2008). *Modern and Global Ayurveda: Pluralisms and Paradigms*. New York, State University of New York Press.

Young, R. (1995). *Colonial Desire. Hybridity in Theory, Culture and Race*. London and New York, Routledge.

Zimmerman, F. (1992). 'Gentle Purge: The Flower Power of Ayurveda', in *Paths to Asian Medical Knowledge: Comparative Studies of Health Systems and Medical Care*. C. Leslie and A. Young, Berkeley, University of California.

Zysk, K. G. (2001). 'New Age Ayurveda or What Happens to Indian Medicine When It Comes to America'. *Traditional South Asian Medicine* 6: 10–26.

6

SHAMANISM AND SAFETY

Ancient practices and modern issues

Alexander Alich

I Introduction

Shamanism is a field of work that spans the archaic to traditional tribal settings and pluralistic Westernized societies. It is simultaneously ancient and yet, from a Western perspective, in its infancy. As it has changed over time and crossed national borders, it has enhanced and challenged individuals and cultures through art, music, dance and medicine – but it is not without controversy. As it has made its way into contemporary Western culture, it has run into professional and ethical hurdles and, more recently, safety issues, which are the subject of this chapter.

I begin with a brief overview of the shamanic worldview in historical context followed by an explanation of what shamanic practice is and why it was possibly developed and used. I will then explain my background and how I have developed relationships with shamanic communities over the world and my own practice. I will then present the methods and perspective used for this investigation of safety, as well as who is involved in Western shamanic work and their reasons for pursuing this information and experience.

I then look at how shamanism is viewed by some First Nations communities that still hold it as part of their worldview (as not all do) and explain how they have identified a place in their society for a shamanic practitioner and that practitioner's specific role. I will continue by examining how those communities might identify, train and oversee a practitioner as well as the expectations that are placed upon that person.

Finally, I will examine the issue of shamanic practice in modern pluralistic societies by first introducing three vignettes that raise safety, ethical and professional concerns and then exploring some of the challenges in moving from First Nations to a modern Western frame, including safety and professional issues, regulations and training.

II Background

1 The shamanic worldview

To begin to understand shamanism, shamanic experience and practice, it is important to first examine the complex shamanic worldview. Most commonly, the shamanic view divides the world into three or more intricate and interdependent categories or worlds that are organized in a cyclical pattern: (1) the Earth and environment, which includes plants, animals and stones; (2) the human world; and (3) the divine or cosmic world.

Each of these worlds has its own spirit component. It is through the spirit that communication and negotiation are achieved between the worlds and thus the spirit serves as the base for shamanic practice. The worldview is highly dependent on the environment and experiences of the population, which means that, as you travel to different regions, you will see a shift in creation stories and organization of the culture. In some instances, more categories are recognized, such as in some of the Scandinavian shamanic traditions where nine such worlds are acknowledged, that include the four elements (ice, wind, fire and earth), which are seen as living beings that can be spoken to and influenced under some circumstances (Lennerhagen 1991). Communication can be achieved through trance states which could be attained through dance, percussion, chanting or, in some instances, the use of trance-inducing plants (Eliade 1964) that are harvested from the local area.

In the shamanic worldview, we can see what might be the roots of many of today's First Nations culture and customs. As an example, the premise that everything is alive (plants, animals, stones, places, etc.) and has a spirit component, informs people's relationship to their environment or that, "Humans have [the] responsibility for maintaining a harmonious relationship with the natural world" (Barnhardt 2007).

From the Saami shamans of Northern Scandinavia and the Aboriginals of Australia to the Hopi of the American Southwest, shamanism often developed in environments that were precarious for human survival. While the practices of these peoples and others today have become complex with many social components, we can speculate that the ancient shaman's concerns were focused on the survival of their community. For the Matses in the Peruvian Amazon, survival in their potentially deadly environment from disease, poisonous animals and exposure is still a concern today. Not only does the shaman of their community oversee spirit communication, each community member's daily communication with the plants, animals and the earth ensures their well-being (Gorman 1990).

2 The shaman

A person (who could be male or female) having been acknowledged by their community as having special attributes that enable them to attain these states would be trained to master trance states and, through time and experience, to maneuver through the spirit component of these worlds. Their role within the community would be a service position and their life's work would include keeping communication open between the human and other worlds as well as negotiating with the spirits through troubled times to restore balance to a person, place or community.

A shaman therefore was both trained and acknowledged by his or her community. While I will use the word shaman with this meaning in this chapter, it is important to point out that shaman is a modern word with an unclear origin. The Oxford English Dictionary traces the word back to the late seventeenth-century Russian word *šaman* or to the German *Schamane* (*Oxford English Dictionary* 2013). Today's First Nations people will each have a word from their own language to identify this person, if indeed they still have this position and need of this function within their community.

While each shaman is seen to be unique in his or her gifts, relationships and abilities, a few commonalities can be identified. Many have their first experiences of the spirit world in their childhood through illness, profound dreams or visions and many report the experience of their world getting bigger. They must then undergo intensive training, testing (in the human and spirit worlds) and initiation into their role.

During one of his final interviews, anthropologist Joseph Campbell shared this story about a boy who would grow up to be a holy man of the Lakota Nation:

> Black Elk was a young Sioux boy around nine years old. [...] The boy became sick, psychologically sick. His family tells the typical shaman story. The child begins to tremble and is immobilized. The family is terribly concerned about it, and they send for a shaman who has had the experience in his own youth, to come as a kind of psychoanalyst and pull the youngster out of it. But instead of relieving the boy of the deities, the shaman is adapting him to the deities and the deities to himself. [...] Here, the deities who have been encountered − powers, let's call them − are retained. The connection is maintained, not broken. And these men then become the spiritual advisers and gift-givers to their people. Well, what happened with this young boy was that he had a prophetic vision of the terrible future of his tribe.
>
> *(Campbell and Moyers, 1988)*

Trance was, and is today, the most important tool of the shaman's work. While in this state their job was to locate information that would be useful to their community and to bring it back. The next step would be to find an expression for this information that the community could work with and eventually integrate. This expression may take the form of art, music, storytelling or teaching. No matter what the form or expression was, the intention was to momentarily communicate with the divine in order to solve a problem and to eventually move the community forward.

The shaman was and is a rare individual and yet not a superior one. They historically have lived on the edge of the community, both physically and metaphorically, in order to see their community clearly and what may be out of balance. In Joseph Campbell's comparative mythological research, he suggests that today's contemporary shamanic counterpart would be today's artist who both reflects and influences his or her culture (Campbell and Moyers 1988).

While it is common to find the words shaman and priest used interchangeably in mainstream conversation, it might be interesting to note why shamanism has not developed into a formal religion, though it does have some threads of religious thought. Besides there being no formal organization, each practitioner is dependent on their own relationships to the spirit worlds and what they develop for their work. When a practitioner dies, those relationships will most likely end and not be passed on directly to another practitioner. It is the job of the community's new practitioner to develop and maintain his or her own relationships. These relationships vary depending upon the need of the community, time of the practice and individual gifts of the practitioner.

3 My background

I have participated in shamanic work since 1979, training with Native American traditional teachers from the Hopi, Navajo, Southern Cheyenne and the Native American Church for 12 years. At first I learned for my own development and was later drawn into community service work, eventually moving into a professional role in 1991. To this day I continue to travel and maintain working relationships with traditional practitioners in the US Southwest, Scandinavia and Western Europe.

My academic education is in both arts and science. My studies in science were in premedicine, emergency medicine and public health, while my education in the arts was in television and writing. I worked in a hospital setting in San Francisco for seven years.

Since 1988, I have been the ceremonial leader for a Western community in the US and Europe. In 1991, I opened a private practice integrating aspects of Western medicine with shamanic practice and in 1993 began to teach shamanism and self-development classes. Today I am a School Director and teach individuals and health care practitioners who want to integrate shamanic practice into their lives and work and the rare individual who will go into service work for a community.

III Methods and epistemic perspective

I did not conduct my research as a scientific study. With time and experience, I noticed problems emerge as I worked, traveled and met with both First Nations and contemporary Western practitioners. I conducted extensive interviews in the American Southwest, Scandinavia and Western Europe from the late 1980s to date with a special interest in outcomes of students, practitioners and clients of shamanic work.

As I gained professional awareness, I also gained sensitivity toward questions that were relevant to shamanic practice. The set of questions that first helped direct my work were: What is meant by "healing" in a traditional setting? How does this compare with a hospital setting? Can traditional healing practices be brought into a clinical setting? What is the necessary framework to support such a transition? What would be integrated and what would be lost?

Working with these questions, I became especially interested in the area of professionalism, ethics and safety and what happens as shamanism changes from traditional to contemporary practice. The information became grounded as I started to train Western practitioners with a focus on how to improve their practice. Shamanism's move from the archaic to traditional tribal setting to modern Western settings is filled with ethical and professional challenges. Creating a culture of safety has been especially problematic. While there are always inherent risks to all activities, recent injuries and deaths have brought this topic into the public awareness in both the US and Germany.

To date there has been no systematic scholarly examination of the safety issues in shamanism, to my knowledge. In this chapter, I aim to provide an exploratory analysis of issues of safety in shamanism as the practice moves from traditional tribal setting to modern Western settings.

IV Who is interested in shamanism in the West?

Through interviews and observation, I have identified the following four populations of people who are interested in shamanic information, experience and training:

1   Individuals who are seeking something for themselves in order to explain and frame their non-ordinary experiences. These people might also be looking for personal healing and for self-help techniques. They see shamanism as natural, gentle, fast to work and something that still holds old roots and values.
2   Health practitioners trained in other fields (psychology, nursing, CAM practitioners) that want to integrate some shamanic techniques into their practice. They are normally looking for a larger model of the world or of health that can explain their personal and professional experiences that do not typically fit into the models that they learned in their education (e.g., experience of the human spirit). They also want to be able to offer more techniques to their clients and patients.

3   Individuals who feel called by spirit to work for a community or are in some cases asked by a Western community to fulfill the role of a shaman. These people typically have had the "shamanic awakening experience" (discussed above) of being launched into their work, but they most likely have not had the family or community support available in a culture that still holds onto its shamanic roots.

4   Individuals with possible mental health problems such as substance use disorder or psychosis that see shamanism as a way to explain and justify their behaviors or symptoms (e.g. drug taking, explaining delusions and dissociative states as spiritual experience).

V The climate of shamanism today in some US First Nations communities

As of May 2013, there were 566 federally recognized tribes in the United States (USA.gov 2013). Each tribe has its own origin story, culture, customs and language. Some tribes are Christianized, while others are not. Some have roots into their shamanic past that they keep alive through ceremonial and ritual work, while others seemed to have never developed this way to work. Tribes such as the Navajo (the largest in the US), living in the Southwest desert, have only an estimated 25 percent of their members following their traditional ways (Wolf 2007). While the Hopi still perform their Kachina dances to "help keep the world in balance," this is slowly changing as fewer young people are interested in training into positions in these traditional dances (Hopi Elder 1995).

Traditional Native American culture values the individual expression of each person's unique gift and it is hard to know where the culture ends and the medicine begins. There are no offices to regulate practitioners but instead the people rely on tribal elders to oversee and guide tribal members. People who are seen as going "off center" are thought to be dealt with by Great Spirit, an ultimate higher authority.

Keeping this in mind, it is difficult to generalize about training of shamans. My interviews with individuals from Native American tribes as well as Scandinavian practitioners have found the following commonalities which can be viewed as a pathway to shamanic training:

- Foremost there must be a need of the community to have the role of a shaman.
- The elders of the community will typically ask for help from the spirit world to send someone who can fulfill that role with the gifts appropriate to the time and setting.
- Around the time of birth (could be from before birth to early childhood), the person is identified by their talent. It is important to note that there may be many people born with a potential for this role. It may take time for candidates to accept what is being asked of them and to have one of them come forward.
- Next the person is trained into the time, setting and need of the community. The person who currently has the role usually conducts this training.
- The young practitioner will go through a process of "mapping" their work and area of future expertise. This is important because their work will rely on the relationships they build during this phase (for example, having trance experiences in which they become familiar with the different worlds and spirits).
- The person will then go through a time of testing from both the human and the spirit worlds (e.g., having their commitment, knowledge and ethics tested). If they are able to pass these tests, they will still need to make the choice to go into this service position and will need to offer their commitment to their community.
- Finally, they will begin their work and hopefully be able to fulfill their role. They will also be expected to watch out for and eventually train the person who will take their role in the future.

- While it is difficult to estimate the amount of time training takes, it is safe to say that this position is a lifelong one. The learning of additional rites and ceremonies entails more training and time. An example of a generally agreed upon training time for learning the North American sweat lodge ceremony is six to eight years.
- Beyond their training, a person in this role is expected to maintain his or her own health as well as reflective practice. While there are no established offices or laws that oversee shamanic practice within First Nations communities, practitioners are responsible to their community and typically overseen by the community elders.

There are a few controversies that do need to be mentioned. The first is the debate about whether shamans should only come from specific bloodlines or whether "being called by spirit" is sufficient. This has become problematic with tribes that have not been able to maintain their customs and culture through the last century and has fueled many arguments in the current political and social unrest in the indigenous population in the Americas and Australia.

The other controversy has to do with compensation for work. This is a thoroughly modern problem. While historically a community materially provided for their shaman, the transition into modern times has proven problematic. Practitioners that ask for or accept fees are typically viewed with mistrust, yet they may not have another way of maintaining their daily life as we have moved into a monetary-based world.

VI Shamanism enters contemporary Western culture

To explore some of the challenges facing the field of shamanism today, I have chosen three vignettes that illustrate important professional, ethical and safety issues. The first is from my practice and shows potential hazards that can affect clients on a personal level. The second, also from my practice, illustrates the broader impact on an individual and local community. The third is taken from press and court documents and demonstrates how these issues can affect the public at large and potentially society's view of the work of shamanic practitioners.

1 A grey cloud

A German woman in her mid-30s consulted my practice seeking guidance for a difficult encounter she had had with a shamanic practitioner. A few years previously she had sought spiritual guidance in order to help her resolve a history of childhood abuse. While reading a local esoteric magazine that promoted spiritual classes and teachers, she found a man who used the title of shaman and said he could help people retrieve their soul from traumatic situations. She made an appointment to visit him. After asking her a few questions, he announced that he could see a grey cloud over her head and if she did not sign up for his one-year training she would certainly have a brain tumor within a year. She left the meeting in a state of shock and did not return. She became highly suspicious of all shamans and yet developed a fear that she would contract a brain tumor. My meeting with her five years later showed this had not occurred.

2 A drug habit

A German man in his late 20s with a history of major drug dependency consulted my practice seeking guidance for his spiritual way. He said he was very interested in shamanism and told me about a friend who had recently returned from a spiritual journey to Peru. In Peru, his friend had attended a traditional tribal ceremony and had ingested ayahuasca, a local hallucinogenic plant used in a complex healing ritual. Upon returning from Peru his friend, having received no training, began offering the public the "shamanic experience" of ingesting ayahuasca.

The client asked if I thought that using ayahuasca could be a good way for him to learn about shamanism. I told him that I did not think so. I told him that there were many ways of learning about shamanism and most did not involve ingesting substances. He would be taking a big risk by working with an untrained practitioner operating outside of his cultural understanding (not to mention the legality of this situation). Since the client also had a history of drug dependency, I explained that he could have a difficult time discerning potential hallucinations from actual work as well as relapsing into his former addiction.

He consulted his friend after our meeting and raised my concerns. The friend told him he should participate in the ceremony and just "trust the plant," a sentence he had heard in Peru (which is correct within that cultural context).

The client attended an ayahuasca ceremony the following week (which is something that a tribal person might do once in their lifetime – if they are very sick). Shortly thereafter he started attending a ceremony each month and by the end of the year he was self-administering ayahuasca every week. During the next six months, he suffered from extreme physical and psychological stress and symptoms commonly induced by trauma. His behavior became erratic and aggressive and he eventually isolated himself from his friends and family.

When confronted by a concerned friend, he reported that he was becoming very spiritual. By the end of the year, he went on a one-week binge of hallucinogenic plants. When he re-emerged, he said he was now a shaman. While some of his friends and family had become frightened of him, others said they were not sure if he was a shaman but thought his odd behavior could be a sign of advanced spirituality. He went on to advertise himself as a shaman and open a practice working as a healer, teacher and sweat lodge leader.

3 Death in a ceremony

In October 2009, James Arthur Ray led 56 people into a sweat lodge at the conclusion of his five-day "Spiritual Warrior" retreat in the desert of Sedona, Arizona. Traditionally a sweat lodge is a wooden dome-shaped structure covered in blankets or animal skins that is heated from the inside by stones. It is performed so that participants can purify themselves physically as well as spiritually and so that they may also seek guidance from the spirit realm. Up to eight participants might attend an ordinary sweat lodge.

Each participant had paid approximately $10,000 and signed a waiver explaining that they were undertaking events that could lead to their death. They also were told that the leader of the events, James Arthur Ray, was a highly accomplished shaman serving four different communities and that while "you might feel like you are dying no physical harm can happen" (Joy 2010).

By the end of the event, two people were dead inside the lodge. A third died from heat stroke complications ten days later. Approximately 20 other participants claim they are still suffering from neurological damage. Criminal charges were brought against James Ray that led to his conviction on three counts of negligent homicide for which he served a two-year prison term (Duncan 2013).

Legal and criminal investigations into Ray's background would show that he had lied about being trained as a shaman and he did not have the business degrees listed on his website or the job experience he claimed. On the point of shamanic training, he had promoted himself in a way that the public (under current circumstances) could not understand or check. As of June 2014. Mr Ray has been released from prison and is again leading workshops.

VII Challenges in changing settings

Until quite recently, a person from Western Europe would have needed to travel to a different part of the world (e.g., Australia, Siberia, Korea or Peru) to be in contact with a culture that has shamanic roots and practices. It was not until the late seventeenth century that the word shaman first appeared in an English text in reference to the Tonguese culture (*Oxford English Dictionary* 2013). By 1900, minor references could be found in mainstream literature, such as a Harpers Magazine's reference to primitive cultures (*Oxford English Dictionary* 2013) or the 1910 Catholic Dictionary's reference to shamanism as savage magic (*New Catholic Dictionary* 1910). Since then the term shaman and the concepts derived from the shamanic worldview have been studied and documented primarily in the fields of archeology and anthropology with occasional references in the field of psychiatric literature.

In 1951, Romanian religious historian Mircea Eliade published his seminal volume *Shamanism: Archaic Techniques of Ecstasy* and thus helped to introduce shamanism as a minor field of study unto itself. His observations continue to influence how the sciences view shamanism today. Then in 1964, UCLA anthropology postgraduate student Carlos Castaneda published his Master's thesis in which he introduced his version of shamanism – supposedly imparted to him by an indigenous teacher named Don Juan – to the mainstream public. Though discredited in 1973 in a Time Magazine exposé (Burton 1973) for having fabricated his experiences, his books are still in print and his ideas of shamanism as a way to *personal power* in opposition to a path of service for a community continue to influence the field of shamanic work and new generations of students.

Finally in the summer of 1989, *Shaman's Drum Journal* published a full- page ad for American author Lynn Andrew's weekend workshop, *Into the Crystal Dreamtime: A Shamanic Initiation* (Shaman's Drum 1989). During this weekend, which was held in five major cities in the United States, Andrews offered to initiate participants into shamanic working for the fee of US$325 in a venue that would hold up to 1,000 people. This began the era of mass consumption and commercialization of shamanic work culminating today in the approximately 3,000+ books on the subject available in English and an uncountable number of workshops and trainings available internationally.

Rooted in 1960s counter-culture, the idea of an indigenous teacher who would take you by the hand, answer all your questions and introduce you to a larger world quickly became popular. It is an idea, or ideal, that is still popular today within the New Age movement and with some spiritual seekers.

Western practitioners were quick to use the title of shaman (which is not well defined or protected) as something that would both describe and validate their work. Popular books about Western people's experiences in exotic places or with extraordinary teachers added fuel to this situation and book titles such as the German *Auch du bist ein Schamane* (translation: "Everyone is a shaman" or, literally, "You are a shaman too") (Fenkart 2010) have added to the confusion.

Western practitioners also encountered the problem of using or adding shamanic trance techniques to their lives and work. By adopting these practices that, by their nature, add insight to a situation, practitioners were faced with new ethical challenges that they were not ready for. Lacking guidance of what information to share and what not to share with a client (or friend) is a topic that is still discussed today.

VIII Current policies for Western shamanic practitioners

There is currently no consistency of legal status for Western shamanic practitioners. In the United States, practitioners who work in spiritual healing are not registered or regulated nor do they carry professional insurance. Some practitioners will align themselves with a church in order to fall under the United States constitutional right of freedom of religion in order to practice. There is currently no federal oversight.

In Germany, practitioners are allowed to work as spiritual healers or to lead ritual healing based on German Basic Law (Article 12: Section 1), which gives each person the right to pick their profession, their place of work and their place of education. In a test case put before the Federal Constitutional Court in 2004 (BvR 784/03 from 2 March 2004), the court decided that ritual healing or spiritual healing were so different from what the public could expect from a medical doctor or Heilpraktiker (licensed CAM practitioner) that it did not need to be regulated as a medical profession and was exempt from national licensing processes such as the Heilpraktiker examination that tests basic medical knowledge.

The United Kingdom is moving toward government-supported voluntary registration of the different CAM modalities with the Complementary and Natural Healthcare Council. Currently registration is voluntary and being promoted in the public interest to make sure practitioners meet a certain level of education, accountability and financial liability. Shamanism is not currently listed as a discipline and it is not clear if it would ever be.

IX Training and education in the West and special considerations in shamanism

For many Western students, the draw of shamanism is motivated by self-development and improvement. For some who go further, there seems to be a natural extension to move from working with oneself to helping others either privately or in a community setting. The challenge is the step of professionalization, or the point where a practitioner takes responsibility for other people's health and well-being and promotes themselves to the general public.

Currently there is a wide range of education or training. I could find the following pathways used by practitioners in practice:

- No training
- Self-training from books
- Trained by "the spirits" with no human input or guidance
- Trained during informal weekend courses
- A five-year certification course, which includes continuing supervision and an ongoing peer evaluation circle.

Missing from most of the pathways above was a screening process to see if the student is fit to learn and eventually practice. Moving in and out of different states of consciousness requires skill and a certain level of psychological and physical stability. Also, the study of ethics, professionalism and safety was rarely considered. These topics only seemed to emerge when there was a professional breach and I found it was at this point that a student or practitioner was likely to quit their work or studies.

Most shamanic practitioners I interviewed are not trained in psychology or in basic health sciences (e.g., anatomy, disease processes) and can find themselves in a vulnerable position (as can their client) when they mistake their client's psychosis or physical illness for shamanic experience.

A common problematic issue for students was not knowing when their training was complete and when they could use the title of shaman. One young woman shared her frustrating experience from a weekend workshop on trance technique: "We were told if you could journey you were a shaman. After the weekend we asked the teacher if we were shamans and he said he didn't know" (Shira 2003).

Another important consideration for the public is not knowing what a solid education is or should look like. This range of educational possibilities has led to public confusion since there is normally a general assumption that title use has uniformity of education, training and treatment (e.g., general practitioners, chiropractors).

Finally, a special consideration in shamanism is that clients may find themselves in a particularly difficult position by not being able to verify what they have been told by a practitioner, which can cause a lot of confusion (and possibly fear) for the client. This can be detrimental when the shaman offers a horror diagnosis, as we saw in the first vignette.

X Conclusion

Moving toward a culture of safety in shamanic practice in the West has many hurdles ahead of it. If we look at Morath and Turnbull's model of safety cultures in medical practice (see Wilkinson and Gale, this volume), they might describe our current state as a "pathological" culture of safety. In this first phase of their model, practitioners and educators do not want to know about or address safety concerns, failures are concealed and new ideas are actively discouraged (Morath and Turnbull 2005). Many practitioners within the contemporary shamanic community consider it "un-shamanic" to consider self-regulation or government intervention. They are offended by the idea of transparency in regards to their training, background and work or to creating educational standards. This has left the general public on its own when it comes to finding a qualified practitioner and trustworthy information. Some safety concerns in shamanism are summarized in Table 6.1. These are my early observations of a field of work that is struggling to integrate into the West. We certainly have many problems and an ethical obligation to work toward public protection and safe practice. At the very least, further research needed.

Table 6.1 Professional and safety issues in the practice of shamanism in pluralistic Western societies

Education	Current lack of training standards and practitioner education transparency
Professionalization	Current lack of professional bodies, open title use, lack of record keeping, lack of interface with other health professions, lack of place for incidence reporting for clients or practitioners, lack of consistent, safe working environments
Advertising	Current lack of advertising standards, sales v. health information
Ethics	Current lack of ethical standards
Oversight	Need for peer circles and supervision
Power	Need for a better sharing of power in the healing setting
Regulation	Lack of regulation
Substance use	Unregulated use of hallucinogenic substances
Risk seeking	Public desire for extreme experiences
Knowledge	Unrestricted access to knowledge that was once taught with cultural and ethical framework

References

Barnhardt, R. (2007) "Education Indigenous to Place: Western Science Meets Native Reality," Alaska Native Knowledge Network.

Burton, S. (1973) "Don Juan and the Sorcerer's Apprentice," *Time Magazine*, 5 March [Online]. Available at www.time.com/time/magazine/article/0,9171,903890,00.html (accessed 8 August 2012).

Campbell, J. and Moyers, B. (1988) *The Power of Myth*, New York, Random House.

Duncan, M. (2013) "James Ray Withdraws Appeal of Negligent Homicide Conviction," *The Daily Courier*, 5 September [Online]. Available at www.dcourier.com/main.asp?SectionID=1&SubsectionID=1&ArticleID=122937 (accessed 29 August 2013).

Eliade, M. (1964) *Shamanism, Archaic Techniques of Ecstasy*, Princeton, Princeton University Press.

Fenkart, K. (2010) *Auch du bist ein Schamane*, Munich, Ansata.

Gorman, P. (1990) "People of the Jaguar: Shamanic Hunting Practices of the Matses," *Shaman's Drum*, no. 21, pp. 40–49.

Hopi Elder (1995) Unpublished interview conducted by Alexander Alich.

Joy, C. (2010) *Tragedy in Sedona, My Life in James Arthur Ray's Inner Circle*, Bloomington, Indiana, Transformation Media Books.

Lennerhagen, M. (1991) Unpublished interview conducted by Alexander Alich.

Morath, J. and Turnbull, J. (2005) *To Do No Harm: Ensuring Patient Safety in Healthcare Organizations*, San Francisco, Jossey-Bass.

New Catholic Dictionary (1910) *Shamanism* [Online]. Available at http://saints.sqpn.com/ncd07790.htm (accessed 10 August 2012).

Oxford English Dictionary (2013) *Shaman* [Online]. Available at www.oed.com.libezproxy.open.ac.uk/view/Entry/177388?redirectedFrom=shaman#eid (accessed 10 August 2012).

Shaman's Drum (1989) *Shaman's Drum, a journal of experiential shamanism*, No. 17, inside front cover.

Shira (2003) Unpublished interview conducted by Alexander Alich, March.

USA.gov (2013) *Tribal Governments, Official Information and Services from the US Government* [Online]. Available at www.usa.gov/Government/Tribal-Sites/index.shtml (accessed 8 February 2014).

Wolf, S. (2007) Unpublished interview conducted by Alexander Alich, August.

7

THE 'KNOWLEDGEABLE DOER'

Nurse and midwife integration of complementary and alternative medicine in NHS hospitals

Sarah Cant and Peter Watts

I Introduction

The study of power and professional practices within health care has been of longstanding interest to medical sociologists (Parsons 1954; Freidson 1970; Witz 1992; Elston 2009). Such analyses have revealed that the medical division of labour and associated organisational hierarchies cannot be solely explained in terms of the technical knowledge and capacities of the practitioners. Rather, the distribution of power in the health care arena has been shaped by a complex intersection of historical, social, cultural and economic factors, central to which are gender relations. This intersection has been understood by sociologists in terms of 'professional projects', whereby health care occupations have sought to secure a distinctive market position for themselves (Abbott 1988). Such studies reveal a historical interplay between 'professionalism' and 'professionalisation'. Professionalism refers to a distinctive ethic of conduct: an altruistic disposition combined with claims to expertise. Professionalisation, on the other hand, is characterised by the attainment of extensive occupational autonomy, grounded in a state-endorsed monopoly of practice. This chapter draws on insights from the sociology of the medical professions, and on a recent empirical study (Cant *et al.* 2011), to explore and explain efforts by nurses and midwives to integrate complementary and alternative medicine (CAM) into hospital practice within the United Kingdom.

Since the late 1980s, CAM has been implicated in attempts by nurses and midwives to enhance their occupational jurisdiction, professional power and quality of work experience. This reflects a historical contingency: a dramatically expanding market for CAM services occurred simultaneously with a coordinated drive by nurses and midwives to augment their legitimacy, credibility and autonomy of practice. Central to such attempts was the positioning of nurses and midwives as 'knowledgeable doers'; autonomous professionals, with a unique, holistic, caring orientation, able to determine their own parameters of practice and judge their own competency. In practice, though, their professionalisation strategy emphasised university credentials and focused on the technical, procedural and bureaucratic elements of nursing and midwifery practice. A consequence was that many practitioners felt that the caring, *feminine*[1] aspects of their work had been devalued. CAM appeared to provide a territory in which aspirations for both professional autonomy and person-centred practice could be realised, leading to a groundswell of interest by nurses and midwives (Mitchell *et al.* 2006; Rankin-Box 2004; RCN 2003).

This chapter explores the opportunities that CAM afforded for nurses and midwives to enhance their professional autonomy and working practices within a historical context of changing regulatory demands and the hegemony of masculine biomedicine. However, CAM provision in the NHS has tended to be both piecemeal and ad hoc, driven by local initiatives rather than national policy. Overall, we will argue that attempts to integrate CAM into nursing and midwifery have achieved only modest gains for practitioners. The occupational strategies have centred on professionalism rather than professionalisation; a reflection of the marginal status of CAM more generally, the epistemological dominance of biomedicine, regulatory constraints and the prevailing gendered power relations within health care.

II The research study

This chapter will draw extensively on a detailed empirical account of how NHS hospital-based nurses and midwives managed and presented their CAM services to secure a space to practice (Cant *et al.* 2011). The study investigated the nature and extent of CAM use by these practitioners, and specifically the role it played in the extension and/or enhancement of their occupational role and standing. Data were collected in two stages. First, as there is no central database or register recording CAM practice by hospital nurses and midwives, we used a snowball sampling technique, beginning with contacts from the National Nursing and Midwifery Complementary Medicine Forum. This yielded eighteen respondents across England with whom in-depth telephone interviews were undertaken. Second, we adopted a case study approach (Yin 1994), concentrating on NHS midwifery and birthing centres and hospital wards in three district general hospitals within a county in the southeast of England. Nine nurse/midwife CAM practitioners were identified and face-to-face, semi-structured interviews were conducted by the authors with each of them. All but one of the respondents were women and all were aged between their mid-forties and approaching retirement.

All interviews were audio recorded and covered the following themes: the scope, funding and institutional status of CAM practice in the NHS setting; experiences of integrating CAM with conventional practice; perceptions of the role of CAM both therapeutically and in terms of professional development and occupational role; issues of training, competency and risk. Each interview was transcribed verbatim and the data was thematically analysed. Strong congruence between the case study and telephone interview data strengthened the reliability of the findings. Quotations from the research are identified by practitioner type and anonymous numbering. Before looking at this data in detail, however, it is important to contextualise the findings through a review of the professionalisation literature.

III Professionalisation in nursing and midwifery: historical lessons

Attempts by nurses and midwives to integrate CAM into their practice need to be understood within the context of the historically marginalised position they have occupied in relation to medicine. Through the nineteenth century, medicine engaged in its own professional project in order to secure power, autonomy and authority. This involved strategies of social closure, the acquisition of state support, the establishment of expertise underpinned by claims to scientific knowledge and the assertion of occupational jurisdiction over competing health providers (Freidson 1970; Larkin 1983). In particular, medical dominance was premised on the subordination of nursing and the limitation of midwifery (Witz 1992).

However, this should not be construed as a static relationship – the history of relations between medicine and other health care occupations has been characterised by myriad jurisdictional battles

(Abbott 1988). These battles have involved attempts to credentialise practice, to extend occupational remits and to secure state support through registration. For example, midwives employed 'dual closure strategies' to carve out their own occupational field of 'normal births' and achieved an independent existence sanctioned by the state. In contrast, nurses, while being subordinated in the medical division of labour, managed to secure some status and autonomy by employing a variety of strategies to demarcate boundaries within the nursing profession rather than by trying to emulate the medical profession or strive for parity (Witz 1994). The early twentieth century history of both nursing and midwifery was characterised then by attempts to improve their status and market share through two key strategies: strengthening occupational boundaries through exclusion and demarcation; extending occupational remit through inclusionary strategies and the location of new occupational territory (Macdonald 1995).

Notwithstanding these developments, neither nursing nor midwifery achieved full professionalisation in the classic sense, in that they did not accrue full autonomy and authority in practice nor the state-sanctioned right to define and control the production, transmission and use of their own body of socially valuable knowledge (Freidson 1970; Turner 1995). This positioning is revealed in the facts that nurses and midwives are subject to stringent scrutiny by, and are accountable to, not only NHS managers and their own professional bodies, but also the medical profession. As such the scope of their occupational practice is determined and delegated by medicine and accordingly opportunities to exercise discretionary judgement are limited.

The right to make discretionary judgements based on the interpretation of knowledge in practice is central though to the professionalisation project. This is because, according to Jamous and Peloille (1970), occupational knowledges such as biomedicine are characterised by a tension between indeterminacy and technicality. On the one hand, the power and privilege of the medical profession rest on the esoteric nature of biomedical knowledge. On the other, the authority of medical knowledge is grounded in scientific rationalism, which makes it amenable to codification and routinisation, and hence to bureaucratic control. To maintain their position, medics have had to negotiate this tension by strategically colonising the more indeterminate aspects of biomedicine, while delegating the more routine and rationalised elements to auxiliary occupations, of which nursing and midwifery were critical.

During the late 1980s/early 1990s, both nurses and midwives engaged in collective strategies to resist this positioning. Central to this response was the articulation of the practitioner role as being that of the 'knowledgeable doer' (UKCC 1987, 1992): a conscious eschewing of the assumption that nurses and midwives merely execute delegated, formulaic tasks. Instead the practitioners were presented as both autonomous and competent to make judgements without medical endorsement and oversight. This was achieved through initiatives such as: shifting nursing and midwifery training into the university sector; changes in the law regarding prescription of drugs by non-medics; the establishment of midwife-led birth centres; the development of the nurse practitioner/consultant role. According to Witz, this vision presented

> an increasing emphasis on a patient-centred, care-driven model of nurse practice, underpinned by a holistic model of health and elaborated by means of a discursive reworking of the centrality of caring activity as a skilled and indeterminate, theoretically informed activity…
>
> *(1994: 24)*

The new nurse 'would be actively involved in and trusted with patient care, not merely supervising its delivery on terms dictated by medicine' (Witz and Annandale 2006: 27).

While such strategies involved imbuing nursing and midwifery practice with the visible markers of professionalism, it is debatable whether for many practitioners this is equivalent to true professionalisation. In practice, the reconfiguration of nursing and midwifery since the 1990s has still, to a large extent, continued to involve the delegation by medicine of certain routinised, technical tasks. This has effectively ensured that the remit of nursing and midwifery has remained defined and legitimated by medicine and medical knowledge. This was partly due to nurses themselves not taking the opportunity to extend their practice, resultant from a 'culture of uncertainty' (Williams and Sibbald 1999). Also significant, though, was the combination of state policy (and state funding), the organisation of hospital-based health services and the persistence of gendered power relations in health care, which together meant that the acquisition of new responsibilities devalued the traditional, tacit, intuitive, caring, 'female' aspects of nursing and midwifery. In this light, attempts to professionalise the nursing role in the UK are better understood as occupational strategies, in that they tend to extend rather than enhance the remit of practice, and do not afford full occupational self-determination (McDonald *et al.* 2009; Witz 1994; Witz and Annandale 2006).

Moreover, many nurses and midwives found that the qualitative experience of practice was compromised by these developments. The practical realisation of the 'knowledgeable doer' became associated with the task-orientated, technical aspects of practice in contrast to the vocational desire to care that had motivated many nurses and midwives to join the occupations (Lawler 1991). For instance, in Holland's (1999: 232) study, one student nurse commented that: 'A nurse can be knowledgeable doer without being a knowledgeable carer by knowing her subject and procedure without looking at the whole person, how the individual is affected by it, considering his/her feelings and without taking the individuals' suggestions.'

IV An affinity between CAM, women, nursing and midwifery?

In this context, CAM became perceived as a territory where the interpersonal, affective, *feminine* dimensions of nursing and midwifery might be recovered (McDonald *et al.* 2009). Certainly CAM has a strong association with women as its resurgence in the 1980s was driven by female users and practitioners. All consumer studies establish that users are more likely to be women (Eisenberg *et al.* 1998; Harris and Rees 2000; Barnes *et al.* 2008), suggesting that CAM has a resonance with gender-specific needs and experiences and the potential to create spaces for gender-sensitive health care (Cant and Watts 2012; Sointu 2006). This is corroborated by the fact that CAM use amongst women is often associated with gender-specific conditions such as breast cancer, pregnancy, menopause and infertility (DiGianni *et al.* 2002; Samuels *et al.* 2010; Kang *et al.* 2002; Rayner *et al.* 2009).

The majority of CAM practitioners are also women, although chiropractic and osteopathy stand as notable exceptions. A number of writers have speculated as to why this might be the case. For instance, it has been argued that CAM's characteristic focus on holistic, person-centred, subjective, spiritual, egalitarian, care-orientated provision particularly appeals to women. Moreover, women may also be drawn to work environments where men do not dominate (Flesch 2010; Scott 1998; Taylor 2010).

This view was corroborated by our own research study of NHS hospital-based nurses and midwives in England (Cant *et al.* 2011). The research established that CAM provided the respondents with the opportunity to qualitatively improve their working practices in a variety of ways. The respondents in the study lamented the fact that nursing and midwifery had become dominated by technology and bureaucracy. For instance, as one nurse commented:

In 1991, I started working on an oncology ward for children and young people ... so quite a high dependency ward ... and after about five years I just felt like a technician. I was just doing chemotherapy, just giving out drugs all the time, and the parents on more than one occasion did say that they were doing the nursing care and we just give out the drugs, which was absolutely true. And to say that to a nurse, it was like a knife.

(N22)

CAM was seen as providing an opportunity to restate the value of a holistic, feminine approach to practice:

If you're going to have a top, top new hospital, with all the technology ... and if the midwifery care is awful, then you're no better off – in fact you're probably worse off than if you're giving birth in a very run down unit, but with loving, tender midwives working in it.... It [aromatherapy] is a holistic method – when I use the oils I see the woman as whole person, I use the oils to encourage the whole of her, not just seeing her mechanically, and it all goes back to whether you see childbirth as a sort of science or you see it as an art.

(M05)

Similarly, one nurse argued that her motivation to introduce a reflexology service was because in hospitals:

we dissect them ... you go into a clinic, and if you've got something wrong with the pelvis, that's it, you're only that part and if you mention something else you get 'oh I don't deal with that'. You know, so I felt complementary therapy you can address someone as a whole person, every part.... If you can have an hour with a patient you pick up more and they start to literally unburden themselves ... you're actually addressing the whole body, the spiritual, the emotion, the whole lot.

(N23)

Indeed the practitioners expressed considerable nostalgia for the empathetic, holistic and personalised relationships with clients that were once associated with nursing and midwifery. Integrating CAM into their therapeutic repertoire afforded them the opportunity to reclaim this dimension:

If only they could realise how much money it [CAM] saves. You know, it would be amazing – but they say it's taking up a nurse's time: well, nursing *is* time, that's what it is – it's not filling in forms and running around, it's time with the patient. When I first trained we had a system where if the sister sat by the bed, took her apron off, and sat by the end of the bed that meant you did not disturb her while she was with the patient.... In fact, nursing *is* a complementary therapy.

(N04)

CAM was described as empowering and permissive, not least by allowing practitioners the capacity to touch and connect with their patients,

I would say, it's simply, if you like, an extension of nursing practice ... it's like reconnecting nurses if you like with the use of touch which was always there previously, but in this technological age touch seems to have taken a back seat.

(N03)

Overall, CAM practice was described in powerfully positive terms, not necessarily in terms of the efficacy of the modality, but in terms of the opportunities it afforded to develop personal, caring relationships. Specifically, those nurses nostalgic for intimacy and closeness with their patients saw CAM as a legitimate space where these aspects might be emphasised.

V CAM, 'knowledgeable doers' and professionalism

Nurses and midwives were also attracted to CAM as it afforded opportunities for the development of autonomous practice (Adams 2006), supported by an initially favourable policy context. The professional guidelines on the integration of CAM into nursing and midwifery practice (RCN 2003; NMC 2008) handed the responsibility and competency to practice to the practitioners themselves, making no specific stipulations about training or credentials. Moreover, formal regulation through clinical governance[2] was very limited at this time. Taken together, these factors seemed to provide a potential opportunity to realise the nurse and midwife as a 'knowledgeable doer'. However, in practice the true extent of this opportunity was limited by the nature of CAM and the tightening of clinical governance.

The historical positioning of CAM within health care provision in the UK was significant. Despite increases in demand for services, CAM is best understood as occupying a position of 'mainstream marginality' (Cant 2009), reflecting its limited authority and state endorsement. There are a number of factors that underpin this positioning: CAM comprises a heterogeneous range of modalities with varying levels of proven efficacy and scientific credibility. Many CAM modalities tend to rely on experiential rather than experimental evidence to support their therapeutic claims (Barry 2006). Moreover, the professional aspirations of CAM which emerged in the 1980s and were pursued more forcibly during the 1990s achieved inconsistent and limited results. To date, CAM practitioners have not secured state endorsement in the main and instead have had to establish their right to practice through self-regulation and an emphasis upon their professionalism (Evetts 2006; Fournier 1999; Wahlberg 2007). Here professional standing is located: in the practitioner's ability to apply tacit knowledge in practice, rather than in their possession of a state-sanctioned, abstract and theoretical knowledge base; in the self-regulation of their conduct, rather than in having been admitted into a distinctive occupational territory; in a practitioner–client relationship involving the ongoing negotiation of trust, rather than one in which trust is assumed by the professional (Elston 2009; Noordegraaf 2007). It is also the case that the majority of CAM practice has been delivered within the private sector. Moreover, where CAM has been successful in integrating with state health provision, biomedicine has retained both epistemological and jurisdictional superiority (Hollenberg 2006; Shuval 2006). This has resulted in CAM in hospitals being confined to fields such as palliative care and pain management, rather than being afforded any diagnostic or curative role (Mizrachi *et al.* 2005). As such, CAM provided an uncertain territory for the realisation of professional goals for nurses and midwives. Moreover, whilst the 'knowledgeable doer' strategy initially yielded some successes, it ultimately was not sufficiently robust to confer lasting autonomy.

Data from our study established that during the 1980s and 1990s the integration of CAM services within the NHS was often premised on the claim by the nurse and midwife practitioners to be uniquely placed to negotiate between epistemologically diverse therapeutic modalities and biomedicine. Their own biomedical training meant that they could present themselves as guardians of patients' safety (safer than non-medically qualified practitioners) and as competent to make sound clinical judgements about appropriate types and levels of CAM intervention.

This saw the establishment of a range of services, premised on self-regulation and facilitated by a permissive NHS culture: 'I got permission from my manager to use the therapies, I mean in those days we didn't have to, you know, we didn't have to write loads of policies...' (M11). However, such freedoms were associated with vulnerability; the absence of formal advice or pre-requisites to practice put the responsibility for governance on the individual practitioner. The practitioners were responsible for: writing their own policies and guidelines about appropriate forms and levels of intervention; identifying training courses and professional associations; taking out their own indemnity cover. In practice then services were always modest, limited to those situations where biomedical interventions had limited efficacy or there was a lack of resistance or interest from doctors, where there was existing autonomous practice, or the risks associated with CAM interventions were considered to be low (e.g. normal births).

One nurse described how she identified areas for CAM intervention:

> Basically where the therapy is providing something that cannot be provided by conventional medicine, so, you know, for example, chronic pain, pain relief from chronic back pain or eczema or some of the chronic illnesses where you have got treatments but the side-effects are almost worse than the illness itself, or where it's not very effective. What we can do as a therapist is provide a service that you cannot get through conventional medicine ... we are providing something that adds to the patient's care, their well-being, their quality of life, whatever it might be.
>
> *(N05)*

The setting up of CAM services was particularly successful in the midwife-led units, explained in practical terms, relating to both the absence of doctors in the day-to-day running of the service and their general lack of interest in CAM. For instance, one respondent who offered an aromatherapy service noted that midwives:

> are more autonomous than nurses and I think that nurses have probably had a harder time bringing it [CAM] in because patients are the responsibility of doctors, whereas if everything is normal for us then the midwives are responsible for the care.... Well, some of them [consultants] have been more interested than others, but for most of them it's what midwives do – they do their thing and it smells in the corridor.
>
> *(M01)*

The 'knowledgeable doer' strategy in this context was then an individual rather than collective enterprise, and resulted in a patchwork of provision, dependent on the efforts of energetic individuals who often lacked organisational support. Funding for services was localised and uncertain and often relied on unofficial contributions. The modest, individual successes of the 1990s thus failed to mature into properly embedded services and lacked the resilience to withstand the more demanding clinical governance context which emerged in the first decade of the twenty-first century.

Specifically, we found that some CAM services closed when the individual practitioner who had initiated the practice left the NHS or retired. More significantly, financial accountability and increased bureaucratic demands and regulation saw services atrophy. For example, one nurse reported that following a decade of running a successful CAM service: 'I got a letter saying that the hospital had a 60 million pound over-spend, and thanks so much but we don't require your services anymore' (N22). Moreover, hospital trusts no longer supported ad hoc service provision and instead demanded robust guidelines and strict adherence to polices. The processes involved in seeking to fulfil these requirements proved to be arduous and often impossible to meet for individuals lacking institutional support. One midwife described how the documentation she was required to produce had to:

cover everything from what aromatherapy, what the definition [was] the … UKCC rules and regulations defining practice … quality control, stock control, criteria for use and criteria for … contra-indications and cautions, and then how we were going to use it … basically how many drops and things like that and what oils I was going to use, the properties of those oils.

(M19)

While another abandoned her CAM service when faced with such demands:

the biggest barrier is getting it past the Trust and I just became fed up with the hassle … I am disappointed and disillusioned because … I paid for all my training and I do not have the support … and the other thing is that CAM does not have the research evidence, which again, is another big barrier.

(M11)

This example highlights another vulnerability factor: the experiential evidence base character-istic of CAM was deemed insufficient to support the development of services. This proved to be hugely problematic – building status and autonomy on the basis of being a 'knowledgeable doer' assumes either that there is a credible knowledge base that one is competent to judge or that one's competency can be proven. The disallowance of experiential evidence undermined this capacity and jeopardised the practitioners' unique position as mediators between biomedi-cine and CAM knowledges.

VI Gendered professional projects

The interpretation of the 'knowledgeable doer' discourse by nurses and midwives to justify the integration of CAM into practice occurred simultaneously with attempts by non-medically quali-fied CAM practitioners to professionalise their practice (Cant and Sharma 1999; Clarke *et al.* 2004; Kelner *et al.* 2006). Interestingly, both shared characteristics that are associated with strategies of professionalism rather than of professionalisation. That is, both aimed to enhance status and occu-pational opportunities through presenting themselves as exemplars of a distinctive professional identity: self-regulatory; trustworthy; ethical; and competent. This is in contrast to the classic pro-fessionalisation route that seeks to secure legal autonomy and state endorsement.

While the lack of a scientifically acceptable evidence base of CAM goes some way to explain this approach, the established position of the male-dominated medical profession is also highly significant. The ideology of professionalisation is both historically and conceptually male (Witz 1992; Wrede 2012). Medical professionalisation in the nineteenth century can be understood as an attempt by middle-class men to secure status and prestige (Davis 2002), central to which was the positioning of nursing as subordinate, midwifery as limited and CAM as 'quackery'. This was enabled by the patriarchal hegemony that informed the medical division of labour when it was first established, the male doctor standing as the father, the nurse as the obedient wife and the patient as the dutiful child (Gamarnikow 1978). This capacity rested on the successful asser-tion of the primacy of knowledges grounded in masculine modes of thought (Cant and Watts 2012) which: emphasise the distinction between the 'knower' and the 'known'; celebrate 'objectivity'; and devalue forms of understanding derived from subjective and intuitive experi-ence. Bordo (1986) characterises this as a 'flight from the feminine'.

In effect, to professionalise is to masculinise and this produces a fundamental contradiction for any project seeking to improve the status and prestige of an occupation grounded in 'feminine' practices. Attempts to use CAM to professionalise are an exemplar of this. While the practitioners were attracted to CAM because of a nostalgia for holistic, individualised, caring and arguably feminised relations, these very features compromise the potential to professionalise. As Flesch observes:

> the very qualities of CAM that make it an alternative to conventional medicine are, paradoxically, the same qualities that lock women into caring roles, devalued by society, and by the medical profession, and which render them glorified auxiliaries to their biomedical physician counterparts.
>
> *(2010: 170)*

More than this, using the 'knowledgeable doer' strategy was fundamentally problematic because the parameters of *'knowledgeability'* remained defined by medical epistemology. In our study, the practitioners were acutely aware of the need to adhere to boundaries set by biomedicine if they wanted to secure practice within the NHS. For instance, despite being interested in homeopathy, none of the participants had attempted to develop services because of the vehemence of medical opposition. Instead they were attracted to those therapies that had already a degree of acceptance within biomedicine, such as acupuncture, or those that were deemed to play a supportive or palliative role. As such, aromatherapy and reflexology were the most popular, followed by massage and acupuncture. Some use was also reported of yoga, hypnosis, moxibustion, Bach flower remedies and diet therapy.

Indeed, therapies were often presented in such a way as to emphasise that they complemented rather than challenged biomedicine:

> I presented the idea at a directorate meeting where all the consultants were there and my boss and midwifery colleagues and there wasn't a single person who was against the idea. I think because I presented it pretty much hand in hand with conventional Western medicine, saying you know, the idea is just to have something different to offer alongside what we do already, rather than replace what's already going on.
>
> *(M05)*

Similarly a midwife, seeking to introduce an aromatherapy service, explained that she:

> wrote to the consultants to tell them what I was intending to do with the stance that it would be a tool to aid coping with childbirth, you know, for relaxation and helping with the contractions … and just to say that I intend to do that, and that whilst I obviously wouldn't be encroaching on [the] medical arena without their permission.
>
> *(M13)*

Moreover, the ultimate dominance of the biomedical paradigm was revealed in situations when the nurses and midwives found their biomedical and CAM perspectives to be in contradiction. For instance, one midwife acupuncturist reported that in such circumstances she always defaulted to a biomedical stance: 'If I have a concern or if someone has high blood pressure, I'm not going to fiddle around with needles, I'm just not interested in doing that. It's not a time for playing around' (M15).

These examples all serve to illustrate the continuing deference to biomedical authority and knowledge by nurses and midwives, and the defining role that medicine continues to play in establishing the parameters of autonomy for 'knowledgeable doers'.

VII Conclusion

Drawing on the sociology of the professions and empirical findings, this chapter has established there was a strong congruence between the philosophies and practices of CAM and the professional and affective aspirations of nurses and midwives. This congruence perhaps also reflects a shared cultural and political positioning in relation to biomedicine. Beyond this affinity, CAM also provided a practical space in which the practitioners could attempt to extend and enhance their occupational remit and professional jurisdiction. The case study revealed though that these professional projects were in actuality modest: shaped by the status of *feminised* health care practice and CAM knowledge. Both nurses and midwives were drawn to qualitatively different ways of working that enhanced both their relationship with patients and their job satisfaction. However, the opportunities to carve out an autonomous, high-status and sustainable territory were limited by the very characteristics that had attracted the practitioners in the first place. Whilst caring, intimate and holistic relationships are necessarily difficult to quantify and codify and thus are indeterminate, their historical association with femininity simultaneously cast them as subordinate. As such, they did not form a firm ground for professionalisation. Moreover, the fact that CAM relies on an experiential rather than experimental knowledge base further compromised the claims for professional standing. This vulnerability was increasingly revealed as the NHS regulatory demands became more formal and stringent. Ultimately though it was the historical and contemporary gendered power relations characteristic of health care that fundamentally bounded these CAM-based, female-enacted, professional projects. It is the case that nurses, midwives and non-medically qualified CAM practitioners have all had to negotiate their own professional projects in a context where the power of the male biomedical profession is almost omnipotent and unassailable. Accordingly, the opportunities for professional occupational development have been limited, characterised by claims to professionalism rather than strategies of professionalisation.

Notes

1 We italicise 'feminine' deliberately as this is a contested and socially constructed term drawn upon in multiple ways within social theory and by the respondents in this study.
2 Clinical governance in the UK refers to the statutory obligation to continuously monitor and improve the quality of services through increased regulation and an emphasis on evidence-based practice.

Bibliography

Abbott, A. (1988) *The System of Professions: An Essay on the Division Expert Labor*, Chicago: University of Chicago Press.

Adams, J. (2006) 'An exploratory study of complementary and alternative medicine in hospital midwifery: models of care and professional struggle', *Complementary Therapies in Clinical Practice*, 12, 40–47.

Barnes, P. M., Bloom, B. and Nahin, R. (2008) *Complementary and Alternative Medicine Use Among Adults and Children, United States, 2007*, CDC National Health Statistics Report 12.

Barry, C. (2006) 'The role of evidence in alternative medicine: contrasting biomedical and anthropological approaches', *Social Science and Medicine*, 62(11), 2646–2657.

Bordo, S. (1986) 'The Cartesian masculinzation of thought and the seventeenth-century flight from the feminine', in L. Cahoone (ed.) (2nd edn, 2003) *From Modernism to Postmodernism: An Anthology*, Oxford: Routledge.

Cant, S. L. (2009) 'Mainstream marginality: "non-orthodox" medicine in an orthodox health service', in J. Gabe and M. Calnan (eds) *The New Sociology of the Health Service*, London: Routledge.

Cant, S. L. and Sharma, U. (1999) *A New Medical Pluralism? Alternative Medicine, Doctors, Patients and the State*, London: UCL Press.

Cant, S., Watts, P. and Ruston, A. (2011) 'Negotiating competency, professionalism and risk: the integration of complementary and alternative medicine by nurses and midwives in NHS hospitals', *Social Science and Medicine*, 72, 529–536.

Cant. S. and Watts, P. (2012) 'Complementary and alternative medicine: gender and marginality', in E. Kuhlmann and E. Annandale (eds) *The Palgrave Handbook of Gender and Healthcare*, Basingstoke: Palgrave.

Clarke, D., Doel, M. A. and Segrott, J. (2004) 'No alternative? The regulation and professionalisation of complementary and alternative medicine in the United Kingdom', *Health and Place*, 10(4), 329–338.

Davis, C. (2002) 'What about the girl next door? Gender and the politics of professional self-regulation', in G. Bendelow, M. Carpenter, C. Vautier and S. Williams (eds) *Gender Health and Healing: The Public/Private Divide*, London: Routledge.

DiGianni, J., Garber, E. and Winer, E. P. (2002) 'Complementary and alternative medicine use among women with breast cancer', *Journal of Clinical Oncology*, 20(18), 34–38.

Eisenberg, D. M., Davis, R. B., Ettner, S. A., Wilkey, S., Rompay, M. and Kessler, R. (1998) 'Trends in alternative medicine use in the United States 1990–1997: results of a follow-up national survey', *Journal of the American Medical Association*, 280, 1569–1575.

Elston, M. (2009) 'Remaking a trustworthy medical profession in the 21st century', in J. Gabe and M. Calnan (eds.) *The New Sociology of the Health Service*, London: Routledge.

Evetts, J. (2006) 'Short note: the sociology of professional groups', *Current Sociology*, 54(1), 133–143.

Flesch, H. (2010) 'Balancing act: women and the study of complementary and alternative medicine', *Complementary Therapies in Clinical Practice*, 16(1), 20–25.

Fournier, V. (1999) 'The appeal to professionalism as a disciplinary mechanism', *The Sociological Review*, 47, 280–307.

Freidson, E. (1970) *The Profession of Medicine*, New York: Dodd Mead & Co.

Freidson, E. (1994) *Professionalism Reborn. Theory, Prophecy and Policy*, Cambridge: Polity Press.

Gamarnikow, E. (1978) 'Sexual division of labour: the case of nursing', in A. Kuhn and A. Wolpe (eds) *Feminism and Materialism*, London: Routledge.

Harris, P. and Rees, R. (2000) 'The prevalence in complementary and alternative medicine use amongst the general population: a systematic review of the literature', *Complementary Therapies in Medicine*, 8, 88–96.

Holland, K. (1999) 'The journey to becoming: the student nurse in transition', *Journal of Advanced Nursing*, 29(1), 229–236.

Hollenberg, D. (2006) 'Uncharted ground: patterns of professional interaction among complementary/alternative and biomedical practitioners in integrative health care settings', *Social Science and Medicine*, 62(3), 731–744.

Jamous, H. and Peloille, B. (1970) 'Changes in the French university hospital system', in J. A. Jackson (ed.) *Professions and Professionalisation*, Cambridge: Cambridge University Press.

Kang, H. J., Ansbacher, R. and Hammoud, M. M. (2002) 'Use of alternative and complementary medicine in menopause', *International Journal of Gynaecology and Obstetrics*, 79, 195–207.

Kelner, M., Wellman, H., Welsh, S. and Boon, H. (2006) 'How far can complementary medicine go? The case of chiropractic and homeopathy', *Social Science and Medicine*, 63, 2617–2627.

Larkin, G. (1983) *Occupational Monopoly and Modern Medicine*, London: Tavistock.

Lawler, J. (1991) *Behind the Screens: Nursing, Somology, and the Problem of the Body*, Edinburgh: Churchill Livingstone.

Macdonald, K. (1995) *The Sociology of the Professions*, London: Sage.

McDonald, R., Campbell, S. and Lester, H. (2009) 'Practice nurses and the effects of the new general practitioner contract in the English National Health Service: the extension of a professional project?', *Social Science and Medicine*, 68(7), 1206–1212.

Mitchell, M., Williams, J., Hobbs, E. and Pollard, K. (2006) 'The use of complementary therapies in maternity services. A survey', *British Journal of Midwifery*, 14(10), 576–582.

Mizrachi, N., Shuval, J. T. and Gross, S. (2005) 'Boundary at work: alternative medicine in biomedical settings', *Sociology of Health and Illness*, 27(1), 20–43.

NMC (Nursing and Midwifery Council) (2008) *Complementary Alternative Therapies and Homeopathy*, London: NMC.

Noordegraaf, M. (2007) 'From pure to hybrid professionalism: present-day professionalism in ambiguous public domains', *Administration and Society*, 39(6), 761–785.

Parsons, T. (1954) *Essays in Sociological Theory*, New York: The Free Press.

Rankin-Box, D. (2004) 'The last decade – complementary therapies in nursing and midwifery. The first decade – complementary therapies in clinical practice', *Complementary Therapies in Nursing and Midwifery*, 10(4), 205–208.

Rayner, J., McLachlan, H. L., Forster, D. A. and Cramer, R. (2009) 'Australian women's use of complementary and alternative medicines to enhance fertility: exploring the experiences of women and practitioners', *BMC Complementary and Alternative Medicine*, 9(52).

RCN (Royal College of Nursing) (2003) *Complementary Therapies in Nursing, Midwifery and Health Visiting Practice: RCN Guidance on Integrating Complementary Therapies Into Clinical Care*, London: RCN.

Samuels, N., Zisk-Rony, R. Y., Singer, S. R., Dullitzky, M., Mankuta, D., Shuval, J. T. and Oberbaum, M. (2010) 'Use of and attitudes towards complementary and alternative medicine among nurse-midwives in Israel', *American Journal of Obstetrics and Gynaecology*, 203(341), 1–7.

Scott, A. (1998) 'Homeopathy as a feminist form of medicine', *Sociology of Health and Illness*, 20(2), 191–214.

Shuval, J. (2006) 'Nurses in alternative health care: integrating medical paradigms', *Social Science and Medicine*, 63(7), 1784–1795.

Sointu, E. (2006) 'The search for wellbeing in alternative and complementary health practices', *Sociology of Health and Illness*, 28(3), 330–349.

Taylor, S. (2010) 'Gendering the holistic milieu: a critical realist analysis of homeopathic work', *Gender, Work and Organization*, 17(4), 454–474.

Turner, B. (1995) *Medical Power and Social Knowledge*, London: Sage.

UKCC (1987) *Project 2000: The Final Proposals*, London: UKCC.

UKCC (1992) *The Scope of Professional Practice*, London: UKCC.

Wahlberg, A. (2007) 'A quackery with a difference: new medical pluralism and the problem of dangerous practitioners in the UK', *Social Science and Medicine*, 65, 2307–2316.

Williams, A. and Sibbald, B. (1999) 'Changing roles and identities in primary health care: exploring a culture of uncertainty', *Journal of Advanced Nursing*, 9(3), 737–745.

Witz, A. (1992) *Professions and Patriarchy*, London: Routledge.

Witz, A. (1994) 'The challenge of nursing', in J. Gabe, D. Kelleher and G. Williams (eds) *Challenging Medicine*, London: Routledge.

Witz, A. and Annandale, E. (2006) 'The challenge of nursing', in J. Gabe, D. Kelleher and G. Williams (eds) *Challenging Medicine* (2nd edn), London: Routledge.

Wrede, S. (2012) 'Nursing: globalization of a female gendered profession', in E. Kuhlmann and E. Annandale (eds) *The Palgrave Handbook of Gender and Healthcare*, Basingstoke: Palgrave.

Yin, R. (1994) *Case Study Research Design and Methods*, London: Sage.

8

THE NEXUS BETWEEN THE SOCIAL AND THE MEDICAL

How can we understand the proliferation of complementary and alternative medicine for enhancing fertility and treating infertility?

Karen Willis and Jo-Anne Rayner

I Background

Social norms powerfully shape what is viewed as acceptable throughout various life-stages and the transition to parenthood has long been a powerful collective cultural symbol, providing a gendered identity and normalcy status central to adult roles (McQuillan *et al.*, 2012; Dykstra & Hagestad, 2007). In contemporary Australia, where the socio-political milieu encourages fertility and promotes the family (Rich, Taket, Graham & Shelley, 2011; Gray, Qu & Weston, 2008), achieving parenthood is a social norm expected of both men and women. For women in particular, gender identity is linked to becoming a mother (Loftus & Androit, 2012; Thompson, 2005; Letherby, 2002). Female gender identity is defined and performed through socially pre-scribed concepts of femininity that govern bodily attributes and behaviours, which include expectations of motherhood (Van Den Wijngaard, 1997; Moi, 1989). The desire to have children remains high among the majority of Australian men and women across all ages (Holton, Fisher & Rowe, 2011; Thompson & Lee, 2011; Holden *et al.*, 2005; Weston, Qu, Parker & Alexander, 2004) despite the growing tendency to delay childbearing.

Survey research consistently indicates that most Australians want to have children and that many have fewer children than they would like (Holton *et al.*, 2011). Longitudinal studies reveal that fertility expectations are dynamic and attribute relationship status as a major factor in future expectations about childbearing (Mitchell & Gray, 2007). While relationship factors appear to be the most important, other considerations such as economic security and career path planning are also important, particularly in decisions about when to have children. Over the past 20–30 years, men and women are spending an ever longer part of their young adult years in their parental home and education and are delaying their entry into the labour market, union forma-tion and thus parenthood (Weston *et al.*, 2004). This trend is found in other industrialised coun-tries (Beaujot, 2004). There is also an expectation that, because there is now the capacity to decide when *not* to have children using contraception (Keogh, 2006), the decision to have (and when to have) children is also able to be controlled. However, the intersection between age and

110

fertility remains an important one and, while the desire to have children remains high, the capacity to have children is compromised by choosing to do so at an older age.

This increasing trend to shift childbearing to later age among Australians (Macaldowie, Wang, Chambers & Sullivan, 2012) has resulted in increased use of infertility treatments to achieve parenthood. The proliferation of assisted reproductive technologies (ART) to diagnose and treat infertility has transformed childlessness from a social process into a medical problem, shifting normative expectations of the reproductive body and entrenching social norms and expectations (Loftus, 2009; Franklin, 1997; Greil, 1991). International evidence suggests the experience of infertility is also gendered (Thompson, 2005; Carmeli & Birenbaum-Carmeli, 1994; Nachtigall, Becker & Wozny, 1992) and that the burden of treatment falls to women irrespective of reason for infertility (Loftus, 2009; Schmidt, 2006).

Such is the powerful status associated with parenthood, and motherhood in particular, that failure to attain this social norm can still invoke stigma and blame, for example, for past behaviours that may have contributed to infertility, or by not persevering sufficiently with all the options available, generally meaning ART (Allen & Wiles, 2013; Rich *et al.*, 2011). In fact, it has been argued that the proliferation of medical infertility interventions may have contributed to the strength of the social norms about parenting; where previously ambivalence towards motherhood may have been more socially acceptable (Greil, Slauson-Blevin & McQuillan, 2011).

II Biomedical and alternative therapeutic paradigms responses to parenting imperatives

Infertility is medically defined as the failure to conceive a clinical pregnancy after 12 months or more of regular unprotected sexual intercourse (Zegers-Hochschild *et al.*, 2009); and it is estimated that 9 per cent of couples at any given time worldwide experience infertility (Boivin, Bunting, Collins & Nygren, 2007). In 2006, one in six Australian women of reproductive age who tried to conceive or had been pregnant reported infertility (Herbert, Lucke & Dobson, 2009) and of these, 72 per cent sought medical advice and 50 per cent used ART. Conventional medical infertility treatments are accompanied by a number of physical, emotional and financial pressures and despite medical advances many women remain childless (Kessler, Craig, Plosker, Reed & Quinn, 2013; Verhaak, Smeenk, van Minnen, Kremer & Kraaimaat, 2005).

Despite differences in funding arrangements, there is increased demand for fertility treatments in Australia (Chambers, Illingworth & Sullivan, 2011) and internationally (Sunderam *et al.*, 2009). In Australia since 1990, ART have been reimbursed through the national universal health care scheme – Medicare – and associated drug therapies are funded under the National Pharmaceutical Benefits Scheme, although the out-of-pocket expenses remain high. The use of ART in Australia grew steadily until 2009 (Macaldowie *et al.*, 2012) and it is now mainstream therapy for infertility in Australia (Chambers *et al.*, 2011) with the number of initiated treatments increasing by over 10 per cent per year between 2002 and 2008. The most recent estimates suggest that 3.6 per cent of all women giving birth in Australia in 2009 used some form of ART (Li, McNally, Hilder & Sullivan, 2011). In 2010, Australia recorded a decline in the use of ART for the first time in three decades, attributed to a reduction in government subsidies for fertility treatments through Medicare (Macaldowie *et al.*, 2012). This resulted in an increase in the average out-of-pocket expenses, leading to decreased utilisation of ART (Chambers, Hoang, Zhu & Illingworth, 2012). The rate of live births following the use of ART continues to remain at less than 25 per cent and the majority occur in women aged 26–35 years, with the rate among older women still low (Macaldowie *et al.*, 2012). The majority of Australian ART clinics are situated in more populated and affluent metropolitan areas, which anecdotally also appears to be the case for CAM practices specialising in fertility enhancement (Rayner, Willis & Dennis, 2012).

Women are more likely to adopt help-seeking behaviour or seek support for their infertility problems and this increasingly includes CAM as either a substitute for, or a supplement to, the different types of conventional ART. The use of CAM for fertility enhancement or infertility by Australians reflects a trend in CAM use in industrialised countries more generally, which is explained by factors including: dissatisfaction or poor outcomes associated with conventional medicine; a need for more control in decisions; the perceived naturalness of CAM; and the personalised nature of the interaction with CAM practitioners, coupled with the use of individually tailored interventions (Rayner, McLachlan, Forster & Cramer, 2009). Therefore, it is not unexpected that this is the case for infertility. Lower success rates of ART associated with increased age, coupled with the reported negative experiences of ART which are associated with discontinuation of these regimes (Verberg *et al.*, 2008), may provide some understanding of women's increasing use of CAM for fertility enhancement (Rayner *et al.*, 2009) as a supplement to, or substitute for, conventional medical regimes. This is despite much debate about whether there is evidence of effectiveness – one recently published study reported a 30 per cent lower pregnancy and live birth rate among concurrent users of CAM and ART compared to non-users of CAM (Boivin & Schmidt, 2009). Acupuncture receives greater legitimacy and acceptance within a medical approach to infertility. There are two possible reasons for this. First, 'the intervention can be standardized and delivered over a very short timescale' (Bovey, Lorenc & Robinson, 2010). Second, the 'tools' of acupuncture are not dissimilar to those of conventional medicine (i.e. needles), which is also likely to symbolically align it with medicine in a way that other CAM therapies may not.

While much is known about the increased use of CAM among Australian women during pregnancy (Adams *et al.*, 2009; Skouteris, Wertheim, Rallis & Paxton, 2008), less is known about their use of CAM for fertility enhancement as no population-based studies have been undertaken. Among 100 women attending a fertility clinic in South Australia, 66 per cent used CAM, including over-the-counter supplements (78 per cent) and herbal medicines (29 per cent) and their average annual expenditure on consultations with CAM practitioners exceeded AUD$500 (Stankiewicz, Smith, Alvino & Norman, 2007).

As is evident from the brief review above, the social context in which both infertility treatments in general, and use of CAM in particular, are experienced, is therefore important. As discussed in the background, the experience of infertility is gendered and the burden of treatment falls to women. Powerful social ideals about motherhood provide the conditions under which women experience the transition to motherhood. The proliferation of social and 'health' advice to would-be parents (mothers) means that these ideals are inculcated well before conception. Not only women are under self-surveillance and the medical gaze, but the ideas about providing the best conditions under which to become a mother can be argued to provide a 'soft entry point' for CAM through taking of vitamins and supplements, preconception diet advice, etc. Would-be parents bear an early responsibility for their as yet 'unconceived' offspring.

Within the medical literature, there is evidence that lifestyle factors are implicated in infertility (Anderson, Nisenblat & Norman, 2010). Therefore, optimising the conditions under which a pregnancy occurs becomes the responsibility of women and includes factors such as ensuring a nutritious diet with no or limited alcohol, as well an additional intake of vitamins and minerals. The 'naturalness' with which some vitamins and mineral supplements become part of such responsible pre-parenting (some of which are supported by medical authorities) provides a foreground for continuing such treatments into pregnancy, and in instances where pregnancy is difficult to achieve. Locating infertility within the realm of lifestyle also means that many CAM solutions can be seen as a good fit with the problem of failing to conceive. The CAM approach to fertility enhancement involves a continuum approach. Preconception issues which may have an impact on the ability to conceive are addressed initially, such as hormonal imbalances, nutritional deficiencies, stresses and other lifestyle factors, before specific interventions, including herbs, vitamins, homeopathy, naturopathy, stress reduction and acupuncture, with or without ART, are used to facilitate conception.

III Methods

Five studies exploring issues related to women's use of CAM to enhance their fertility are used in this exploration of CAM use for fertility enhancement. These studies are part of a broader programme of research. For ease, the studies will be numerically labelled and the aims and methods of each study described.

Study 1: A review of the literature on women's use of CAM for fertility enhancement was undertaken as little was known about this area, especially the prevalence of use, women's motivations for using CAM for fertility enhancement or how their information about CAM was sourced (Rayner, Willis & Burgess, 2011). This study involved a systematic investigation of the peer-reviewed articles in English between 1990 and 2010 reporting the use of CAM for fertility enhancement using five topics: the prevalence of use; user profile; motivation for use; expectations and satisfaction with use; and referral and information sources. We excluded letters to the editor, case-study reports, clinical studies and randomised controlled trials reporting specific therapeutic treatments or regimes from the review, and found only eight articles published between 1999 and 2010. There were no population-based studies with representative samples, no commonly accepted definitions of CAM and few studies described women's motivations for, and experiences of, CAM for fertility enhancement.

Study 2: A retrospective audit of all new clients attending a CAM practice in Melbourne, Australia during September 2008 (Rayner *et al.*, 2012). This practice specialised in fertility enhancement and offered an array of modalities. The audit aimed to describe new clients seeking fertility advice and therapeutic treatments, and to test the feasibility of recruiting research participants in this environment. Anonymous data abstracted from the client records by a CAM practice administrative staff member included limited demographic information, reason for attending, the modality of the practitioner consulted and use of assisted reproductive technologies. Seventy-seven new clients attended the practice; two-thirds for reasons related to fertility, 43 women and 11 men, and of these 61 per cent were also using ART. This group also included six couples consulting a naturopath for fertility enhancement.

Study 3: Focus groups were conducted in Melbourne, Australia in 2007, two with seven women using CAM to enhance their fertility and one with eight CAM practitioners (Rayner *et al.*, 2009). Both women and practitioners were recruited from five metropolitan CAM practices that specialised in women's health. Women were asked about their views and experiences of both CAM and ART, and practitioners were asked why they perceived women consulted them for fertility enhancement. The median age of the women participating was 40 years (range 34 to 44), three had a medical diagnosis of infertility, six were concurrently using ART and CAM and only one had achieved a pregnancy. The CAM practitioners were all women with a mean time in practice of ten years and most had multiple CAM qualifications, including naturopathy, acupuncture, Western herbal medicine, traditional Chinese medicine (TCM) and psychology.

Study 4: Fertility specialists listed with the Victorian Infertility Treatment Authority were surveyed about women's use of CAM for fertility enhancements in 2008 (Rayner, Forster, McLachlan, Kealy & Pirotta, 2010). This anonymous survey sought their opinions of the safety, usefulness and effectiveness of CAM for fertility enhancement. This study was limited by the poor response rate (18 per cent), believed to be because medical practitioners are generally known to be poor responders (Cummings, Savitz & Konrad, 2001). The respondents were aged between 37 and 69 years, four were female and five were male, and all had undertaken their medical education in Australia. All practised in metropolitan Melbourne and had been in clinical practice for between 12 and 46 years.

Study 5: To explore how individuals spoke to each other informally about their experiences of infertility, their use of conventional medical care such as ART and their use of CAM, if any, for fertility enhancement, we followed a thread on a public blog site for three months in 2010. The 14 participants were women aged between 26 and 40 years of age from geographically disparate locations in Australia. The women listed diverse reproductive histories, two had living children (one conceived naturally) and all were using a form of ART, most for two to three years and in a few instances CAM (acupuncture) to assist them in conceiving. These women also used a combination of conventional and CAM therapies to alleviate the symptoms of pregnancy (Rayner, Willis & Thorpe, unpublished).

IV Findings

1 Defining CAM use for fertility enhancement

Set within a context where there is an intertwining of medical and social imperatives, our research has identified some key issues that must be addressed if we are to fully understand the place of CAM within fertility enhancement. The first of these relates to definitional issues. Defining what is CAM is an issue often raised, with some arguing that we define it in terms of what it isn't, rather than the intrinsic qualities that it brings to health and healing. Study 3 revealed that women use multiple and diverse CAM for fertility enhancement, including practitioner-based therapies, self-medication with over-the-counter and internet-purchased supplements and herbs, in conjunction with ART (Rayner *et al.*, 2009). Thus, what is included in CAM is contested, as also revealed in Study 1 (Rayner, Willis & Burgess, 2011). This raises the question of what should be included as CAM in reproductive health research to further our knowledge in this area. Should a definition of CAM in reproductive health research be limited to the ingestion of biological substances or the use of modalities that can potentially harm women or their foetus and for which a strong biomedical evidence base is needed? Accepting a wider definition, which includes all practices and modalities irrespective of potential harm, could serve different research purposes, such as developing an understanding of women's desperation to achieve parenthood or the impact of relaxation, reassurance and attention on achieving and maintaining a pregnancy. Study 1 identified a diversity of modalities and practices utilised and no clear or common definition of CAM. Various types of CAM were reported, including nutritional advice and the use of vitamins and minerals (either over-the-counter and prescribed), herbal products, acupuncture, reflexology, TCM and traditional faith healers, spiritual healings and religious interventions, meditation, hypnosis, yoga, exercise, naturopathy, kinesiology, mind–body techniques, counselling and/or support groups, and chiropractic.

Stress and depression are well recognised as coexisting with infertility (Smith, Ussher, Perz, Carmady & de Lacey, 2011; Psaros, Kagan, Auba, Alert & Park, 2012); and therefore mind–body therapies may be appropriately included within the definition of CAM therapies for this purpose. Thus while mind–body therapies may not cure infertility, they are drawn on to 'develop resilience in the context of infertility' (Psaros *et al.*, 2012), and as such they provide part of a suite of 'treatments' for the experience of infertility. Acupuncture has also been suggested as an adjuvant treatment modality to increase women's resilience to the psychosocial stress associated with infertility and the use of ART (de Lacey, Smith & Paterson, 2009). Studies of the use of acupuncture as an adjuvant therapy to reduce the stress associated with other chronic conditions have been reported (MacPherson, Thorpe & Thomas, 2006; Paterson & Britten, 2004; Gould & MacPherson, 2001).

2 Seeking CAM for fertility enhancement and infertility

The context within which CAM healing often occurs provides a marked difference from how CAM users report the experience of ART. This is encapsulated by a participant in Alfred and Ried's study of users of TCM who said: 'I felt more of a person with the TCM practitioner … whereas at the IVF clinic you're just another client' (2011, 720). An essential part of the context is the vulnerability and desperation of this group. The pressure to conceive against a backdrop of declining fertility, together with the decreased potential of orthodox medical interventions, means that some women become 'desperate' to try anything to achieve parenthood. The desperation of women was well illustrated in Studies 3 and 5 and can be encapsulated by these quotes:

> I also have a view that I'll try anything no matter how kind of crazy it seems. Sometimes my husband just rolls his eyes when I say 'I'm going to see a hypnotherapist or kinesiologist' or 'I've snuck a couple of crystals into my handbag' or something like that. If someone suggested that I should sit in my back garden and howl at the moon I would do it.
>
> *(Study 3: 42 years, using ART unsuccessfully for many years and, more recently, CAM)*

> Hi Everyone, I'm still finding it hard to believe I'm actually pregnant, as it is only 5 weeks today. I've just had my 2nd BT (blood test) so I hope my HCG (hormones) keeps rising and progesterone is where it should be so I can stop feeling quite so anxious. It felt a bit like FN (fertility nurse) was preparing me for the worst, but I know I'm a bit paranoid and she was just doing her job. My FS (fertility specialist) is going on holidays so I won't have a viability scan until about the 23rd and I'm not sure how I'll go. I really just want to hear a heartbeat as I've never made it that far. Can anyone give me some tips in how to relax.
>
> *(Study 5: 28 years, two previous miscarriages, trying to conceive 2–3 years, pregnant with fresh embryo conceived with IVF[1] and ICSI[2])*

The demographics (particularly age) of women using CAM are indicative of the intense desperation for a solution to infertility. Women participating in Study 3 and Study 5 had an average age of 40 years and 33 years (range 26 to 40), respectively, and in Study 2 (CAM practice audit) the majority (71 per cent) were women aged over 30 years of age, with 44 per cent aged over 36 years.

CAM practitioners in Study 3 suggested their clientele consisted of four different groups of women who are seeking to include CAM as part of their fertility enhancement/infertility treatment. These included: (1) women who want a 'natural' experience and use CAM as part of their pre-conception care; (2) those who use ART but are worried about the side effects, so draw on CAM to maintain their health and well-being; (3) women who have had two or three unsuccessful cycles of ART and want to maximise their success in future cycles; and (4) increasingly the most common group – women who are generally *older* with complex reproductive histories, have had numerous unsuccessful cycles of ART and who are exploring other options. As one CAM practitioner in Study 3 stated:

> I think the women come in [to see CAM practitioner] for various reasons. Some want to get fit and healthy before they get pregnant. Some have already got fertility problems and some have had, they think they've got fertility problems of just a few months, other ones have been trying for over ten years.
>
> *(Naturopath)*

This latter group of women, aware that their 'biological clock' is taking from them the chance to achieve parenthood (Friese, Becker & Nachtigall, 2006), turn to possibilities that will help them achieve their 'last chance babies' (Modell, 1989). It may be that there is variation between practices due to the reported benefits of different modalities. For example, one acupuncturist in Study 3 reported seeing more women who were older and undergoing ART, rather than women wanting acupuncture at the preconception stage: 'I suppose 70 to 80 per cent of the people I see are probably women seeking assistance with fertility and I think increasingly so using ART. I think more of the older age group and more complicated histories' (Acupuncturist). This may be due to the reported benefits of acupuncture as an adjunct to ART in the medical literature (Cheong, Hung Yu Ng and Ledger, 2008; Manheimer *et al.*, 2008) prompting fertility specialists to refer women; and in the media, so women seek this with or without the knowledge of their conventional fertility specialists (Dunn, 2011; Goodyer, 2009; McLean, 2008). Acupuncture featured as an adjuvant therapy for conception with at least one of the women in Study 5:

> I have been having acupuncture the whole time. I do think it helped me get a BFP (big fat positive) the first time round but I read that acupuncture cannot stop a miscarriage. It is predetermined right from the beginning if the embryo will last or not. I am not going back on the pill and I am having a fully natural FET (frozen embryo transfer).
>
> *(34 years, trying to conceive since 2002, pregnant after acupuncture and ICSI)*

Other women participating in the online chat also reported using acupuncture and suggesting it to others as a remedy for morning sickness and nausea associated with the early months of pregnancy.

3 The experience of care

Our research has also pointed to the experience of care that is provided by CAM practitioners (Rayner *et al.*, 2009). In Study 3, two of the three themes explaining why women used CAM related to experience. The first is that the experience of using ART is often a negative one, and this relates as much to the invasive processes as well as interactions with medical specialists. In explaining why women are likely to seek CAM, one practitioner in our study said: 'Perhaps, we're more approachable and there's more time with us, and they don't feel they can ask their specialist because he's so busy' (Naturopath). Further, medical practitioners are seen as being less experienced with, or amenable to, the choices made by women who wish to have a different approach. Indicative of the need for difference in care is this quote by a CAM practitioner in Study 3:

> But that's often a thing that people come for, that they want to come because they want someone who they perceive to have a handle on the whole thing – the natural

therapies, the doctor's side of it, and in fact everybody else's for that matter, but they would never expect their doctor to have any understanding of what we're doing.

(Herbalist)

The second theme that emerges strongly from data is that, in contrast to ART (and as indicated above), women have a positive experience when they use CAM. This highlights the importance of relationships in the health care setting, with CAM seeming to provide something that is not provided by conventional medicine – regardless of the outcome of care. The following quote by this participant in Study 3 using CAM points out the difference in care, even to the different use of language, positively talking about 'when you get pregnant':

> The difference between going from that experience [ART] to going to the naturopath and sitting down and chatting with a lovely woman who talks about when I'm pregnant, that is a radical shift in the way you perceive what you're doing and how you relate to your body and oh there's so much that stems and flows from that, profoundly different to me and that's yeah that was a huge benefit of the alternative therapies, without a doubt, because my experience of the hospital system was just cold hard facts and stats that I'd received so it was very different and a blessing for me.
>
> *(39 years, same-sex relationship, preconception care)*

Similarly, another participant in Study 3 discussed the 'system constraints' within medicine, which are different to CAM:

> I think it's the system to an extent, and perhaps complementary therapies are slightly outside that system and don't have those constraints and they let you give them the opportunity to develop relationships a little bit more but it's a lot about the person and your gelling with the person as well.
>
> *(40 years of age, ART unsuccessful for many years)*

Within such a relational approach, women also talk about 'taking back some control' at a time when they have little control. Another example from a participant in Study 3:

> I find it really empowering cooking up my herbs and I always choose to have raw herbs because I'm actually seeing what's going in and the changes according to what I'm dealing with. I do find it a bit stressful trying to juggle everything but at the same token, I find it empowering because I feel like I'm actually doing something as opposed to doctors just doing things to me and me having to wait, it's that waiting thing that they don't offer any solutions or support to you.
>
> *(44 years of age, used ART for many years unsuccessfully)*

This is not dissimilar to findings from Alfred and Ried's (2011) study of women using TCM where they had responsibilities for monitoring body temperatures, recording menstrual quality and making changes to their diet. They reported that this was an empowering experience, again best understood in the context of a lack of control over their fertility and over the processes associated with ART.

These exampled indicate the importance of having a care relationship in a time of uncertainty. There has now been substantial work on the importance of trust in health care (Calnan & Rowe, 2006). However, what is indicated here is that there is an additional dimension to the trust relationship – rather than women 'trusting' that they will get the outcome that they need, what appears to be important is the trust that they will be cared for during the process of care (Rayner et al., 2009).

In Study 4, we surveyed medical fertility specialists in Melbourne, Australia about the women consulting them for infertility treatment and whether or not women also used CAM (Rayner et al., 2010). Respondents reported that a considerable proportion of women who consult them used CAM (range 25 to 80 per cent) concurrently with ART. However, few medical practitioners reported that they routinely asked women about their use of CAM and some reported that they would sometimes counsel women against using CAM with conventional medicine. Respondents considered that acupuncture, meditation, massage and yoga were 'safe' CAM modalities to use for fertility enhancement, but most felt there was no evidence of effectiveness and they raised concerns about the safety and efficacy of CAM for fertility enhancement overall. While only small numbers of medical practitioners responded to this study, the findings were consistent with the findings from Study 3, which reported that conventional medical practitioners were often dismissive of women's choice to use CAM to enhance their fertility, and this was one of the reasons' women chose not to disclose this to their medical practitioners (Rayner et al., 2009).

4 Social support

The need for social support for women undergoing fertility treatment was also evident in Study 5 of blogs about infertility (Rayner et al., unpublished). Their common experiences of infertility and ART provided a framework for their 'friendship' despite their differences in age, social background and geographic distance apart. The familiarity and candidness in their online chatter, the continual nature of their correspondence at all times of the day and night and in many different circumstances (at work and while waiting in medical rooms for blood tests and scans) are indicative of the support these online relationships provide for women. Even when the women had close family supports, including partners and mothers to console them when pregnancy loss occurred, they still used the blog to seek support from their 'friends' online. These shared experiences enable an unspoken connectedness and support network between the women, which even those closest to them could not provide. The women also shared all early pregnancy symptoms and how they dealt with these, often using CAM, such as morning sickness treated with herbal tea and or acupuncture, and constipation with a healthy diet. There was also an emphasis on having a healthy diet that included the use of vitamins. Indicative of their use of CAM is the following: 'Psyllium husks are also good (natural) and you can sprinkle these onto cereal if you have that and they do the same thing. I haven't had as many issues so far this time' (39 years, pregnant after ART). These women also shared information about consulting CAM practitioners in addition to over-the-counter vitamins and minerals:

> I have had no morning sickness either. In fact since I have been treated for nausea with acupuncture my nausea has gone!! Woo Hoo!
>
> *(28 years, pregnant after second IVF cycle)*

> Glad acupuncture is working for your morning sickness! Might have to give it a try if mine gets bad.
>
> *(26 years, pregnant with twins after six ART cycles)*

V Discussion: commodification of health care and the growth of CAM for fertility enhancement

From a political economy perspective, the linking of social/medical priorities with uncertain outcomes provides a space for healers and other suppliers of goods to enter the market. The proliferation of the CAM market for fertility enhancement has occurred, partly because of the uncertainties surrounding fertility enhancement and infertility, and the desperation to 'try anything'. This raises issues about a marketised approach to health and whether there needs to be greater regulation of both medical and non-medical providers. That geographic location is important for these services suggests that it is a market response with most specialised CAM fertility clinics located in inner-city or wealthier suburbs, where there is greater capacity to pay.

The definitional difficulties about CAM for fertility enhancement therefore fit well with the definitional difficulty of infertility itself. Not an illness per se, but a lack of capacity to achieve parenthood, there are a myriad of ways in which we can think about and act on infertility, including its definition as a medical problem. 'The presence of infertility is signaled, not by the presence of pathological symptoms, but by the absence of desired state' (Greil *et al.*, 2011, 142). Within the context of providing a solution to the problem of infertility, medicine has claimed a space previously occupied by social beliefs and values.

Along with trends related to age, the increase in treatments can also be attributed to the increased availability of diagnostic and treatment modalities. However, the medicalisation of infertility enables not only a medical solution, but a legitimated market response by both conventional and CAM providers. The growth of such markets occurs in a context that Franklin (1997) describes as an 'enterprise culture' where there is broad political support for a 'choice-based' health care market that may be subsidised, partially subsidised or supported by the political regime. While both ART and CAM remain expensive for consumers, in Australia, the push to encourage people to purchase private health insurance means that the expenses of choosing outside the medical mainstream may be partially offset by private insurers, along with the subsidies that such insurance attracts from government (Natalier & Willis, 2008).

Like medical practice, CAM is moving into areas where the boundary between health and illness (and, in the case of CAM, 'wellness') is blurred. The medicalisation thesis is now well established – i.e. the taking of 'non sick' or social arenas of life and making them into diseases and disorders for which there is a medical solution. While there is critique of the medicalisation of social life (Conrad, 1992), and of liberal individualism inherent in the 'healthism' movement (Crawford, 1980, 2006), the critique levelled at medicine is not viewed as the same for CAM. The professional intervention into non-sick areas of life does raise the question – are CAM and conventional medicine more similar than dissimilar? Lowenberg and Davis (1994) illustrated the ways the 'holistic health movement', which includes alternative treatments, simultaneously represents both medicalisation and demedicalisation in both ideology and practice. While, as Conrad and Leiter (2004) point out, the 'medicalisation of infertility' (and hence legitimacy in terms of insuring for treatment) has not been easy due to debates about whether it is a disease in need of treatment, the 'private market for in vitro fertilisation' appears to be here to stay; correspondingly, there is a growth in the market for fertility enhancement provided by CAM practitioners.

Debates about the relationships between conventional medical care and CAM are now well rehearsed. Most often they refer to ideas about 'treatment at the margins', notions of evidence and accountability and regulation (Dwyer, 2011). For example, the growth of integrative medicine where both CAM and conventional medicine are incorporated within medical practice is a contested area (Rayner, Willis & Pirotta, 2011), but one where there is accepted practice based more on 'who' is practising, rather than 'what' is practised. Integrative medical practitioners still do not routinely refer to CAM practitioners; rather they express more faith in medically trained practitioners who utilise some CAM modalities, usually acupuncture (Rayner, Willis & Pirotta, 2011). Research suggests that integrative medical practitioners see their clinical practice as 'different' to their biomedical peers – their philosophical approach includes holism, vitalism and empowerment, and they focus on helping patients to become individually responsible and actively engaged in their health, in particular, in lifestyle change (Willis & Rayner, 2013a). These practitioners are also sceptical about the dominance of the evidence-based medicine movement. They acknowledge that an understanding of clinical benefit may not be scientifically evidenced and utilise discourses of experience and safety in discussing their clinical practice (Willis & Rayner, 2013b).

It may be difficult to discern between CAM, as well as medicine, as accepted and as 'fringe' practices. While there are moves towards putting in place regulatory systems for both CAM practitioners and products, the context of infertility means that this group is most vulnerable to claims made by those who are offering services, and a market-based approach using, in particular, web-based advertising can prey on the vulnerability of this group. The following example of a clinic located in a capital city in Australia is illustrative. While not providing evidence of benefit, testimonials from satisfied clients are provided, with this web advertisement reading: 'IT'S NEVER TOO LATE!', and proceeding with: 'At [name] Naturopathic Clinic, more than 60 women aged 48 and more than a few 50-year-old women have given birth for the first time after being given little to no chance of natural conception.'

For those CAM modalities with a higher level of acceptance from within conventional medicine, there has been some work gathering evidence relating to fertility enhancement. The main example is the use of acupuncture. It is claimed that acupuncture is part of mainstream medical care (Xue, Zhang, Yang, Zhang & Story, 2009) achieving legitimacy through the provision of health insurance rebates, inclusion in higher education programmes and regulation through legislative authorities. Research on whether acupuncture is effective has centred on its use alongside in vitro fertilisation, in particular, whether it increases pregnancy rates if administered at the same time as embryo transfer. Randomised controlled trials have been undertaken, the results of which suggest that there may be benefit, but the results were not statistically significant (Moy *et al.*, 2011; Smith, Coyle & Norman, 2006).

There is also increasing anecdotal evidence of the acceptance of acupuncture as a co-joint therapy with ART by many medical fertility specialists. Our research provides evidence for this in metropolitan Melbourne, Australia. There has been growth in the number of acupuncturists working alongside medical fertility specialists in some fertility clinics and of CAM practices increasing their share in this market. Whether this is led by consumer demand, pragmatism, altruism or the market is hard to tell. Researchers have also suggested that the effects of acupuncture may be in stress reduction and general well-being; and have linked this to improved outcomes for people with infertility. The psychosocial benefits of acupuncture are suggested to be reduction in anxiety, 'infertility self-efficacy' and infertility-related stress (Smith *et al.*, 2011). Smith and colleagues (2011) also discuss the 'engagement with the practitioner', which they argue is integral to acupuncture practice, suggesting again the therapeutic relationship or interaction may also be an important part of the benefits of CAM for this group.

However, there has been much less work taking a political economy perspective to the use of CAM – that the proliferation of CAM and ART occurs where there is a market that is capable of sustaining these. Collyer's (2004) work is an exception. She points out that, not dissimilar to orthodox medicine, CAM was practised originally as a cottage industry, with little government regulation or intervention. However, more recently, CAM has become a business, evident in larger practices, sometimes co-located within orthodox medicine, and with many devices, therapeutic products and equipment now produced and distributed by large, multinational companies (Collyer, 2004). Thus, she argues that increasingly CAM has become 'big business' and mainstreaming of CAM is part of a market strategy. In this way, CAM and conventional medicine have a synergistic relationship. The availability, and proliferation of, services is dependent upon the market. Our observational work undertaken through internet desktop searches of telephone directories in two Australian states (Victoria and Tasmania), along with mapping the location of services when interviewing integrative medical practitioners (Rayner, Willis & Pirotta, 2011), reveals that most multi-practitioner services are located either within or close to the Central Business Districts (CBD) of capital cities, or in the wealthier suburbs, suggesting that practices are strategically located according to the market for services. This positioning of specialist CAM practices is in line with the geographic location of ART clinics/services. Study 3, with women who use CAM and the CAM practitioners they consult, revealed a high level of private health insurance, which in Australia is a good proxy of higher socio-economic status (Rayner *et al.*, 2009).

Thus, while the social values around parenting remain high, and are drivers of the market, there are also groups who are excluded from using CAM (and ART) as an option, due to the cost. For example, cost is important, even to participants who are able to access both ART and CAM, and this was discussed in Study 3:

> I do find IVF is, parts of it are covered and you get a lot of money back and whatever, and that's like expected, but the costs of the alternative therapies do add up, and if you're seeing these different practitioners regularly it really does add up.
>
> *(Female, 40 years of age, used ART for many years unsuccessfully)*

Thus, as Bell (2009) argues, poor women are excluded from 'medicalised infertility'. And some commentators would argue that, while cost is a barrier, there is also a moral dimension to such exclusion, with medicine being in a powerful position to exclude groups that are not seen as 'suitable' to pursue parenthood. In the past, such groups have included single and gay women (Smith, 2003). There has been little discussion of financial barriers acting as exclusionary barriers, but there is considerable literature about the inability of low-income groups, including 'welfare mothers', to achieve the 'good mother ideal' (Bell, 2009; Johnston & Swanson, 2006; Smith, 2003) and cost is one way that such exclusionary practices can be put into effect. This is an effect of a market-based approach to healing that includes both medical and CAM services.

VI Conclusion

Fertility enhancement occurs on a continuum from trying to optimise the conditions to achieve pregnancy to a desperate attempt to achieve and maintain pregnancy when all other options are failing. It is this continuum that needs to be more fully understood, and which is likely to provide patterns of CAM use not seen in the general literature. In this chapter, we have provided examples of the issues that need greater understanding if we are to fully understand the use of CAM for fertility enhancement. While definitional debates are evident across the spectrum of CAM use, the case of fertility enhancement has some particular elements that may be less obvious than for other conditions for which CAM use is sought. First, infertility is a condition that is specifically linked to social aspirations and social norms. It is therefore difficult to define as an illness per se. Second, the growth of CAM use for fertility enhancement is inextricably linked with the medical approach, to the extent that CAM and ART, in particular, can be said to have a synergistic relationship. Third, such is the experience of the medical approach that much of the attraction of CAM is to alleviate the conditions under which ART is experienced. Finally, bringing together all of the above, issues of regulation, accountability and the provision of evidence are particularly relevant due to the vulnerability of a group, primarily composed of women, who are desperately seeking not a 'cure for their illness', but a solution to their problem.

Notes

1 In vitro fertilisation.
2 Intracytoplasmic sperm injection.

References

Adams, J., Lui, C. W., Sibbritt, D., Broom, A., Wardle, J., Homer, C. & Beck, S. (2009). Women's use of complementary and alternative medicines during pregnancy: a critical review of the literature. *Birth*, 36(3), 237–245.

Alfred, A., & Ried, K. (2011). Traditional Chinese medicine: women's experiences in the treatment of infertility. *Australian Family Physician*, 40(9), 718–722.

Allen, R., & Wiles, J. (2013). How older people position their late-life childlessness: a qualitative study. *Journal of Marriage & Family*, 75, 206–220.

Anderson, K., Nisenblat, V. & Norman, R. (2010). Lifestyle factors in people seeking infertility treatment: a review. *Australian & New Zealand Journal of Obstetrics & Gynaecology*, 50(1), 8–20.

Beaujot, R. (2004). *Delayed life transitions: trends and implications*. Contemporary Family Trends. Ontario, Canada: Vanier Institute of the Family.

Bell, A. (2009). 'It's way out of my league': low income women's experiences of medicalized infertility. *Gender & Society*, 23(5), 688–709.

Boivin, J., Bunting, L., Collins, J. A. & Nygren, K. G. (2007). International estimates of infertility prevalence and treatment-seeking: potential need and demand for infertility medical care. *Human Reproduction*, 22, 1506–1512.

Boivin, J., & Schmidt, L. (2009). Use of complementary and alternative medicines associated with a 30% lower ongoing pregnancy/live birth rate during 12 months of fertility treatment. *Human Reproduction*, 24, 1626–1631.

Bovey, M., Lorenc, A. & Robinson, N. (2010). Extent of acupuncture practice for infertility in the United Kingdom: experiences and perceptions of the practitioners. *Fertility & Sterility*, 94(7), 2569–2573.

Calnan, M., & Rowe, R. (2006). Researching trust relations in health care: conceptual and methodological challenges – an introduction. *Journal of Health Organization & Management*, 20(5), 349–358.

Carmeli, Y. & Birenbaum-Carmeli, D. (1994). The predicament of masculinity: towards understanding the male's experience of infertility treatments. *Sex Roles*, 30(9–10), 663–677.

Chambers, G. M., Hoang, V. P., Zhu, R. & Illingworth, P. J. (2012). A reduction in public funding for fertility treatment – an econometric analysis of access to treatment and savings to government. *BMC Health Services Research*, 12, 142.

Chambers, G. M., Illingworth, P. J. & Sullivan, E. A. (2011). Assisted reproductive technology: public funding and the voluntary shift to single embryo transfer in Australia. *Medical Journal of Australia*, 195(10), 594–598.

Cheong, Y. C., Hung Yu Ng, E. & Ledger, W. L. (2008). Acupuncture and assisted conception. *Cochrane Database of Systematic Reviews*, 4, Art. No.: CD006920.

Collyer, F. (2004). The corporatization and commercialization of CAM. In P. Tovey, G. Easthope & J. Adams (Eds) *The mainstreaming of complementary and alternative medicine: studies in social context*. London: Routledge, pp. 81–99.

Conrad, P. (1992). Medicalisation and social control. *Annual Review of Sociology*, 18, 209–232.

Conrad, P., & Leiter, V. (2004). Medicalization, markets and consumers. *Journal of Health & Social Behavior*, 45, 158–176.

Crawford, R. (1980). Healthism and the medicalization of everyday life. *International Journal of Health Services*, 10(3), 365–388.

Crawford, R. (2006). Health as a meaningful social practice. *Health: An Interdisciplinary Journal for the Social Study of Health, Illness & Medicine*, 10(4), 401–420.

Cummings, S. M., Savitz, L. A. & Konrad, T. R. (2001). Reported response rates to mailed physician questionnaires. *Health Services Research*, 35, 1347–1355.

de Lacey, S., Smith, C. A. & Paterson, C. (2009). Building resilience: a preliminary exploration of women's perceptions of the use of acupuncture as an adjunct to in vitro fertilisation. *BMC Complementary & Alternative Medicine*, 9, 50.

Dunn, E. (2011). How to boost your fertility. *The Age Newspaper*, Melbourne, Australia, 20 November.

Dwyer, J. (2011). Is it ethical for medical practitioners to prescribe alternative and complementary treatments that may lack an evidence base? – No. *Medical Journal of Australia*, 195(2), 79.

Dykstra, P. A., & Hagestad, G. O. (2007). Childlessness and parenthood in two centuries: different roads – different maps? *Journal of Family Issues*, 28, 1518–1532.

Franklin, S. (1997). *Embodied progress: a cultural account of assisted conception*. London: Routledge.

Friese, C., Becker, G. & Nachtigall, R. (2006). Rethinking the biological clock: eleventh hour moms, miracle moms and meanings of age-related infertility. *Social Science & Medicine*, 63, 1550–1560.

Goodyer, P. (2009). If you can't get pregnant IVF is the next point of call – but there are alternatives. *The Age Newspaper*, Melbourne, Australia, 12 December.

Gould, A., & MacPherson, H. (2001). Patient perspectives on outcomes after treatment with acupuncture, *The Journal of Alternative and Complementary Medicine*, 7(3), 261–268.

Gray, M., Qu, L. & Weston, R. (2008). *Fertility and family policy in Australia*. Research Paper No. 41. Melbourne, Australia: Australian Institute of Family Studies.

Greil, A. L. (1991). *Not yet pregnant: infertile couples in contemporary America*. New Brunswick, NJ: Rutgers University Press.

Greil, A. L., Slauson-Blevin, K. & McQuillan, J. (2011). The experience of infertility: a review of the recent literature. *Sociology of Health & Illness*, 32(1), 140–162.

Herbert, D., Lucke, J. & Dobson, A. (2009). Infertility, medical advice and treatment with fertility hormones and/or in vitro fertilization: a population perspective from the Australian Longitudinal Study on Women's Health. *Australian & New Zealand Journal of Public Health*, 33, 358–364.

Holden, C. A., McLachlan, R .I., Cumming, R, Wittert, G., Handelsman D. J., de Kretser, D. M. & Pitts, M. (2005). Sexual activity, fertility and contraceptive use in middle-aged and older men: Men in Australia, Telephone Survey (MATeS). *Human Reproduction*, 20, 3429–3434.

Holton, S., Fisher, J. & Rowe, H. (2011). To have or not to have? Australian women's childbearing desires, expectations and outcomes. *Journal of Population Research*, 28, 353–379.

Johnston, D. D., & Swanson, D. H. (2006). Constructing the 'good mother': the experience of mothering ideologies by work status. *Sex Roles*, 54, 509–519.

Keogh, L. A. (2006). Women's contraceptive decision-making: juggling the needs of the sexual body and the fertile body. *Women & Health*, 42(4), 83–103.

Kessler, L. M., Craig, B. M., Plosker, S. M., Reed, D. R. & Quinn, G. P. (2013). Infertility evaluation and treatment among women in the United States. *Fertility & Sterility*, 100(4), 1025–1032.

Letherby, G. (2002). Challenging dominant discourses: identity and change and the experience of 'infertility' and 'involuntary childlessness'. *Journal of Gender Studies*, 11, 277–288.

Li, Z., McNally, L., Hilder, L. & Sullivan, E. A. (2011). *Australia's mothers and babies 2009*. Perinatal statistics series no. 25. Cat. no. PER 52. Canberra: AIHW.

Loftus, J. (2009). 'Oh no, I'm not infertile': culture, support-groups and the infertility identity. *Sociological Focus*; 42(4), 394–416.

Loftus, J., & Andriot, A. L. (2012). 'That's what makes a woman': infertility and coping with a failed life course transition. *Sociological Focus*; 32(31), 226–243.

Lowenberg, J. S., & Davis, F. (1994). Beyond medicalization-demedicalisation: the case for holistic health. *Sociology of Health & Illness*, 16(5), 579–599.

Macaldowie, A., Wang, Y. A., Chambers, G. M. & Sullivan, E. A. (2012). Assisted reproductive technology in Australia and New Zealand 2010. Assisted reproduction technology series no. 16. Cat. no. PER 55. Canberra: AIHW.

MacPherson, H., Thorpe, L. & Thomas, K. (2006). Beyond needling – the therapeutic process in acupuncture care: a qualitative study nested within a low-back pain trial. *The Journal of Alternative & Complementary Medicine*, 12(9), 873–880.

Manheimer, E., Zhang, G., Udoff, L., Haramati, A., Langenberg, P., Berman, B. M. & Boulter, L. M.

(2008). Effects of acupuncture on rates of pregnancy and live birth among women undergoing in vitro fertilisation: systematic review and meta-analysis. *British Medical Journal*, 336, 545.

McLean, T. (2008). Acupuncture aids IVF conception: study. *The Age Newspaper*, Melbourne, Australia, 22 October.

McQuillan, J., Greil, A., Shreffler, K., Wonch-Hill, P., Gentzler, K. & Hathcoat, J. (2012). Does the reason matter? Variations in childlessness concerns among US women. *Journal of Marriage & Family*, 74, 1166–1181.

Mitchell, D., & Gray, E. (2007). Declining fertility: intentions, attitudes and aspirations. *Journal of Sociology*, 43(1), 23–44.

Modell, J. (1989). Last chance babies: interpretations of parenthood in an in vitro fertilization program. *Medical Anthropology Quarterly*, 3(2), 124–138.

Moi, T. (1989). Feminist, female, feminine. In C. Belsey & J. Moore (Eds) *The feminist reader: essays in gender and the politics of literary criticism*. London: Macmillan Education Ltd., pp. 1–23.

Moy, I., Milad, M., Barnes, R., Confino, E., Kazer, R. & Zhang, X. (2011). Randomized controlled trial: effects of acupuncture on pregnancy rates in women undergoing in vitro fertilization. *Fertility & Sterility*, 95(2), 583–587.

Nachtigall, R. D., Becker, G. & Wozny, M. (1992). The effects of gender-specific diagnosis on men's and women's response to infertility. *Fertility & Sterility*, 54, 113–121.

Natalier, K., & Willis, K. (2008). Taking responsibility or averting risk: a socio-cultural approach to risk and trust in private health insurance decision. *Health, Risk and Society*, 10(4), 399–411.

Paterson, C., & Britten, N. (2004). Acupuncture as a complex intervention: a holistic model. *The Journal of Alternative and Complementary Medicine*, 10(5), 791–801.

Psaros, C., Kagan, L., Auba, E., Alert, M. & Park, E. (2012). A brief report of depressive symptoms and health promoting behaviors among women with infertility attending a clinical mind-body program. *Journal of Psychosomatic Obstetrics & Gynaecology*, 33(1), 32–36.

Rayner, J., Forster, D., McLachlan, H. L., Kealy, M. & Pirotta, M. (2010) Women's use of complementary medicine to enhance fertility: the views of fertility specialists in Victoria, Australia. *Australian & New Zealand Journal of Obstetrics & Gynaecology*, 50, 305.

Rayner, J., McLachlan, H., Forster, D. & Cramer, R. (2009). Australian women's use of complementary and alternative medicines to enhance fertility: exploring the experiences of women and practitioners. *BMC Complementary & Alternative Medicine*, 9, 52.

Rayner, J., Willis, K. & Burgess, R. (2011). Women's use of complementary and alternative medicine for fertility enhancement: a review of the literature. *The Journal of Alternative & Complementary Medicine*, 17(8), 685–690.

Rayner, J., Willis, K. & Dennis, C. (2012). Older Australian women use complementary fertility care: a practice audit. *The Journal of Alternative & Complementary Medicine*, 18(1), 6–7.

Rayner, J., Willis, K. & Pirotta, M. (2011). What's in a name: integrative medicine or simply good medical practice? *Family Practice*, 28, 655–660.

Rayner, J., Willis, K. & Thorpe, R. (unpublished data) Women's use of online social networking to keep informed about the use of complementary medicines for fertility enhancement. A study conducted in 2011 with funding from Faculty of Health Sciences, LaTrobe University.

Rich, S., Taket, A., Graham, M. & Shelley, J. (2011). 'Unnatural', 'unwomanly', 'uncreditable' and 'undervalued': the significance of being a childless woman in Australian society. *Gender Issues*, 28, 226–247.

Schmidt, L. (2006). Psychosocial burden of infertility and assisted reproduction. *Lancet*, 367(9508), 378–380.

Skouteris, H., Wertheim, E., Rallis, S. & Paxton, S. (2008). Use of complementary and alternative medicines by a sample of Australian women during pregnancy. *Australian & New Zealand Journal of Obstetrics & Gynaecology*, 48, 384–390.

Smith, C., Coyle, M. & Norman, R. (2006). Influence of acupuncture stimulation on pregnancy rates for women undergoing embryo transfer. *Fertility & Sterility*, 85(5), 1352–1358.

Smith, C., Ussher, J., Perz, J., Carmady, B. & de Lacey, S. (2011). The effect of acupuncture on psychosocial outcomes for women experiencing infertility: a pilot randomized controlled trial. *The Journal of Alternative & Complementary Medicine*, 17(10), 923–930.

Smith, J. L. (2003). 'Suitable mothers': lesbian and single women and the 'unborn' in Australian parliamentary discourse. *Critical Social Policy*, 23(1), 63–88.

Stankiewicz, M., Smith, C., Alvino, H. & Norman, R. (2007). The use of complementary medicine and therapies by patients attending a reproductive medicine unit in South Australia: a prospective survey. *Australian & New Zealand Journal of Obstetrics & Gynaecology*, 47, 145–149.

Sunderam, S., Chang, J., Flowers, L., Kulkarni, A., Sentelle, G., Jeng, G. & Macaluso, M. (2009). *Assisted Reproductive Technology Surveillance 2006. Centers for Disease Control and Prevention, Surveillance Summaries*, Vol. 58. Atlanta, GA: Centers for Disease Control and Preventions.

Thompson, C. (2005). *Making parents: the ontological choreography of reproductive technologies*. Cambridge, MA: The MIT Press.

Thompson, R., & Lee, C. (2011). Sooner or later? Young Australian men's perspectives on timing of parenthood. *Journal of Health Psychology*, 16, 807–818.

Van Den Wijngaard, M. (1997). *Reinventing the sexes: the biomedical construction of femininity and masculinity*. Bloomington, Indiana: Indiana University Press.

Verberg, M., Eijkemans, M., Heijnen, E., Broekmans, F. J., de Klerk, C., Fauser, B. C. J. M. & Mackon, N. S. (2008). Why do couples drop-out from IVF treatment? A prospective cohort study. *Human Reproduction*, 23, 2050–2055.

Verhaak, C. M., Smeenk, J. M. J., van Minnen, A., Kremer, J. A. M. & Kraaimaat, F. W. (2005). A longitudinal, prospective study on emotional adjustment before, during and after consecutive fertility treatment cycles. *Human Reproduction*, 20(8), 2253–2260.

Weston, R., Qu, L., Parker, R. & Alexander, M. (2004). *'It's not for lack of wanting kids': a report on the Fertility Decision Making Project*. Research Report No. 11. Melbourne: Australian Institute of Family Studies.

Willis, K. F., & Rayner, J. (2013a). Integrative medical doctors – public health practitioners or lifestyle coaches? *European Journal of Integrative Medicine*, 5(1), 8–14.

Willis, K. F., & Rayner, J. (2013b). Integrative medical practitioners and the use of evidence. *European Journal of Integrative Medicine*, 5(5), 410–417.

Xue, C., Zhang, A., Yang, A., Zhang, C. & Story, D. (2009). Recent developments of acupuncture in Australia and the way forward. *BMC Chinese Medicine*, 4, 7.

Zegers-Hochschild, F., Adamson, G. D., de Mouzon, J., Ishihara, O., Mansour, R., Nygren, K., Sullivan, E. & van der Poel, S., on behalf of ICMART and WHO. (2009). The International Committee Monitoring Assisted Reproductive Technologies (ICMART) and the World Health Organization (WHO) revised glossary on ART terminology. *Human Reproduction*, 24(11), 2683–2687.

PART 3

Risk and regulation

CAM products, practitioners and the state

9

MAKING CAM AUDITABLE

Technologies of assurance in CAM practice today

Ayo Wahlberg

I Introduction

The principal purpose of regulation of any healthcare profession is to protect the public from unqualified or inadequately trained practitioners. The effective regulation of a therapy thus allows the public to understand where to look in order to get safe treatment from well-trained practitioners in an environment where their rights are protected. It also underpins the healthcare professions' confidence in a therapy's practitioners and is therefore fundamental in the development of all healthcare professions … High quality, accredited training of practitioners in the principal CAM disciplines is vital in ensuring that the public are protected from incompetent and dangerous practitioners.

(House of Lords 2000: 5.1, 6.1)

Whether CAM is dangerous or not has been and remains a contentious matter among CAM practitioners, medical doctors, regulators and patients alike. For some, all CAM (however defined) is dangerous, 'like bringing back bleeding with leeches … developed before we understood the causes of disease, before germ theory' (Dawkins cited in Clements 2007). For others, it is those CAMs that 'lack any credible evidence base' (House of Lords 2000: 2.1), located at the bottom of safety–efficacy hierarchies that are dangerous (if only because their use can delay credible treatment). And still others see CAM as exactly an antidote to the dangers of modern medicine, 'a kinder alternative to mainstream medicine [providing] a safe, gentle and effective approach to health care' (NIMH 2004).

In this chapter, rather than approaching the regulation of CAM as an arena of competing interests, boundary building and gate-keeping (cf. Saks 1995, 2003; Cant and Sharma 1996; Welsh *et al.* 2004; Cohen 1998), I will approach CAM as a problematic of government, which is to say as an assemblage of 'assorted attempts at the calculated administration of diverse aspects of conduct through countless, often competing, local tactics of education, persuasion, inducement, management, incitement, motivation and encouragement' (Rose and Miller 1992: 175). My analysis will focus on regulatory developments surrounding CAM in the United Kingdom over the last three decades or so as various CAM therapies have debated, adopted, rejected or been denied statutory regulation, with many opting for voluntary self-regulation.

Debates around the regulation of CAM practitioners, both generally and within different CAM therapies, have been polemic to say the least: 'allowing this bizarre pseudo-regulation to continue risks legitimising a whole range of bogus medical practices' (Robbins 2010); 'State regulation does not ensure the public's safety ... and results in considerable amounts of time and tax payer's money being wasted' (Save Our Herbs 2012); 'The state is attempting to impose Statutory Regulation on herbalists under the pretext of "protecting the public" without providing a scrap of evidence that we have ever posed a risk' (Herbarium 2009); 'regulation is the best way to safeguard the public' (ATCM 2010). Whatever positions there may be, it is clear that CAM in the UK is in a regulatory moment as an on-going process involving ministries, government agencies, CAM organisations, practitioners and others unfolds.[1] Indeed the task of this chapter is not to determine what form of regulation is most appropriate or suitable for CAM, or indeed whether it is appropriate to regulate CAM, rather it is to examine the conditions of possibility of CAM's regulatory moment – how is it that CAM practice today is something that must be regulated rather than actively marginalised or prohibited as a matter of public protection?

There are three key arguments I will be making to shed light on this regulatory moment. First, I will argue that once CAM in the UK was, in a sense, welcomed 'into the fold' somewhere around the early 1990s (however contentiously), it became amenable to the kind of 'audit society' or 'audit culture' whose origins Michael Power (1999), Marilyn Strathern (2000), Cris Shore and Susan Wright (1999) have traced to exactly the same period. Moreover, calls to regulate CAM have also come at a time when the biomedical profession itself has been under increasing pressure to improve the auditing of its members in the wake of a series of high-profile scandals. Medical practice, whether orthodox or unorthodox, must be accountable. Second, I will argue that, since the early 1990s, 'the Council' has emerged as a central *dispositif* or grid for CAM through which the 'competent and responsible practitioner' comes to be made up and managed as a counterpoint to the 'incompetent and dangerous practitioner' identified by regulatory authorities as a hazard to the public's health. The task of councils is to oversee, certify, sanction and discipline in a way that is visible to members of the public. Finally, I will argue that the council as *dispositif* operates through what might be termed *technologies of assurance* – understood as an assemblage of strategies, techniques, institutions and problematisations through which certain activities and/or actions come to be vouched for over others. In this particular case, it is the ethical and professional competence of certain individuals that is to be vouched for over others as practitioner associations are called upon to police their own members through the formulation of codes of ethics and practice, the accreditation of CAM teaching courses, the definition of dishonourable conduct and professional and ethical misconduct, the establishing of ethics committees, as well as through the implementation of disciplinary and complaints procedures as a way to 'censure, suspend or expel' members if deemed necessary.

To make these arguments, I will trace CAM regulation as it has unfolded in and between five particular arenas. First, the House of Lords has been particularly instrumental in debating and making recommendations about the regulation of CAM, especially after it organised a series of debates on natural medicine in the 1980s and culminating in the publication of a Select Committee report on complementary and alternative medicine in 2000. Tracing CAM debates in the House of Lords can give us a sense of how a regulatory imperative has emerged around CAM. Second, the British Medical Association (BMA) as a representative of the UK's biomedical profession has often been a vocal critic of CAM practice, while at the same time serving as a model for other CAM associations. As we will see, the BMA has changed its tactics towards CAM considerably over the last decades. Third, since the 1990s, a series of associations and regulatory working groups have been formed around various forms of CAM with a remit to propose an appropriate form of regulation for their profession. Such working groups often consist of representatives from different and sometimes competing CAM groupings. The formation and activities of working groups have been particularly divisive as different views on the most appropriate form of regulation for a therapy circulate. Fourth, as the responsible agency for implementing and overseeing regulation of medical professions in the United Kingdom, the Department of Health has stepped up efforts to regulate CAM, especially in the aftermath of the House of Lords Select Committee report which recommended regulation of some forms of CAM. Finally, a number of non-governmental organisations and individuals have contributed to regulatory discussions by publishing reports, by establishing websites or through the media. It is the assorted attempts at the calculated administration of CAM conduct currently playing out within these arenas that I will analyse in the following.

II 'They must put their own house in order' – confusion in the CAM marketplace

Ever since the 'Act to regulate the qualifications of practitioners in medicine and surgery' came into force in 1858, one of the central objectives of UK statutory medical regulation has been to enable 'Persons requiring Medical Aid ... to distinguish qualified from unqualified Practitioners' (Great Britain Parliament 1858). Although a number of CAM therapies have a long history of organisation and self-regulation in the United Kingdom, it was not until 1986 that a series of state-supported efforts aimed at helping the public to know where to look for safe and competent CAM treatment would be set in motion (Wahlberg 2007) (see Box 9.1). It was in this year that the Board of Science of the British Medical Association published its report on *Alternative Therapy* (BMA 1986). The report had been commissioned by the Prince of Wales, an advocate of CAM, while he was President of the BMA in the early 1980s. Yet when published, the report was read by many as an attack on CAM.[2] Reacting to the report, Harold Wicks of the Research Council for Complementary Medicine suggested that 'by being negative and dismissive the report will separate the orthodox from the complementary practitioner. That is not in the public interest' (cited in Veitch 1986). Nonetheless, chairman of the Board of Science of the BMA Professor James Paine did hint that regulation might be the way forward for some therapies: 'The ordinary citizen is in no position to decide whether an acupuncturist has been trained or whether he has been off on a weekend course and come back with an armful of needles' (ibid.).

Box 9.1 Regulating CAM practice in the UK – some milestones

September 1982 – the Institute for Complementary Medicine is formed 'to provide the public with information on all aspects of the safe and best practice of complementary medicine through its practitioners, courses and research'.

February 1985 – the Council for Complementary and Alternative Medicine is launched by former Prime Minister Lord Home as 'the first national association of professional bodies of complementary and alternative medicine that have substantial training and comprehensive codes of ethics and practice'.

May 1986 – the Board of Science Working Party on Alternative Therapy of the British Medical Association (BMA) publishes its report *Alternative Therapy*, suggesting that 'growing interest in complementary medicine' is a 'passing fashion', citing their duty to warn patients 'that consultation with practitioners of some alternative therapies may be attended by the risk of great harm' (BMA 1986: 1, 73–74).

June 1992 – the British Complementary Medicine Association formed 'to help protect the public by maintaining a register of suitably qualified practitioners of complementary medicine'.

July 1993 – the Osteopaths Act is passed, leading to the formation of the General Osteopathic Council with a remit 'to protect the public and maintain the reputation of the profession'.

July 1993 – the BMA changes tactics, calling for 'good practice' in the CAM field in their report *Complementary Medicine: New Approaches to Good Practice*, arguing that 'doctors have a duty to… safeguard the public health and, to this end, it is important that patients are protected against unskilled or unscrupulous practitioners of health care' (BMA 1993: 2).

July 1994 – the Chiropractors Act is passed, leading to the formation of the General Chiropractic Council with a remit 'to protect the public by establishing and operating a scheme of statutory regulation for chiropractors, similar to the arrangements that cover other health professionals'.

April 1996 – Department of Health-commissioned report *The Regulation of Health Professions: A Review of the Professions Supplementary to Medicine Act (1960)* suggests that 'Statutory regulation is the route through which the "newly emerging" professions or alternative/complementary medical professions are seeking regulation'.

January 1997 – Department of Health publishes commissioned report *Professional Organisation of Complementary and Alternative Medicine in the United Kingdom* 'to throw light on approaches towards coordinating activity and encouraging responsible practice'.

November 2000 – the House of Lords Select Committee on Science and Technology publishes landmark report *Complementary and Alternative Medicine*, arguing that 'the use of complementary and alternative medicine (CAM) is widespread and increasing across the developed world… rais[ing] significant issues of public health policy such as whether good structures of regulation to protect the public are in place'. Acupuncture and herbal medicine are singled out as 'two therapies which are at a stage where it would be of benefit to them and their patients if the practitioners strive for statutory regulation'.

March 2001 – Department of Health publishes the Government's response to the House of Lords report, concurring that 'it would be desirable to bring both acupuncture and herbal medicine within a statutory framework as soon as practicable'. They also suggest that 'the Government is prepared to consider the possibility of extending statutory regulation for other therapies if there is a case for it' and 'there is a unified professional body which has the support of most members of its profession for pursuing that option'. As a minimum, 'the Government … strongly encourages the regulating bodies within each therapy to unite to form a single body to regulate each profession'.

January 2002 – Herbal Medicine Regulatory Working Group formed to 'support and promote moves towards unification within a federal structure of the herbal practitioner profession'.

September 2002 – Acupuncture Regulatory Working Group (ARWG) formed.

2005 – the Department of Health pledges £900,000 to the Prince of Wales Foundation of Integrated Health to advance work on the regulation of CAM practitioners.

September 2005 – publication of the Stone report, which makes proposals for a federal voluntary regulatory structure for complementary healthcare professions. The report was commissioned by the Prince of Wales's Foundation for Integrated Health. The Foundation also publishes *Complementary Healthcare: A Guide for Patients* 'to give you enough information to help you choose a complementary therapy that is right for you and find a properly trained and qualified practitioner of that therapy'.

2007 – Professor Dame Joan Higgins chairs the Federal Working Group (FWG) to follow up on the Stone report proposals, eventually leading to the launching of the Complementary and Natural Healthcare Council (CNHC).

October 2007 – the General Regulatory Council for Complementary Therapists (GRCCT) is launched.

April 2008 – the Complementary and Natural Healthcare Council (CNHC) is set up.

It was exactly this problem of knowing where to look that was again highlighted by the chair of the British Complementary Medicine Association (BCMA) at its launch a few years later in June 1992: 'The position of the consumer is one of confusion and vulnerability at present; where else can you be a consultant overnight except in alternative therapy?' (cited in Westcott 1992: 19). Eight years later, the House of Lords Select Committee's report on CAM concurred, arguing that lack of regulation 'inevitably, gave rise to considerable public confusion amongst members of the public' and consequently that 'the effective regulation of a [CAM] therapy … allows the public to understand where to look in order to get safe treatment from well-trained practitioners' (House of Lords 2000: 5.12, 5.1). And more recently, the Affiliation of Crystal Healing Organisations has referred to 'national concerns … mainly centred around the safety of the public and how they can distinguish between a well-trained practitioner and people who have only taken a short course' (ACHO 2012).

And so we can see how the lack of a regulated CAM field came to be framed as a political problem of public protection. So, how is it that the mid-1980s marked a tactical turning point when it came to protecting the public? Part of the answer is undoubtedly to be found in the question put by Lord Prys-Davies to his peers during a House of Lords debate on Natural Medicine on 27 February 1985: 'why has a trickle of interest in alternative medicine become, in recent years, a flood?' (House of Lords 1985: 985) Like in many other countries, policymakers in the UK were coming to terms with what the BMA called a 'growing interest' in CAM during the 1980s. If there indeed was a flood of patients consulting CAM practitioners, just what kind of a marketplace was it they were entering? Lord Winstanley gave his frank assessment in the same House of Lords debate:

> Here in Britain nearly all these professions (if that is the right word) of alternative medicine are at present in an uncontrolled state, similar to the uncontrolled state of the estate agents. For years and years, in your Lordships' House and in another place, Members have been talking about the need for some kind of regulation of the estate agents. It cannot be done until they put their own house in order. The same applies to some of the practitioners who have real skills and real ability. But they, too, collectively, must put their own house in order. Until their ranks are organised and their people are trained and registered, they cannot really be let in, if I may use that phrase, if the public are to be protected against fraud, exploitation and incompetence.
>
> *(House of Lords 1985: 975)*

The decades that have followed might well be described as a more or less concerted effort to put the 'CAM house in order'. The first challenge facing CAM practitioners has been what the House of Lords Select Committee described as 'considerable fragmentation, sometimes resulting in several bodies, each with different training and educational requirements, codes of practice and complaints procedures, representing therapists in the same field' (House of Lords 2000: 5.11). In its response to the House of Lords report, the Department of Health decried such a state of affairs: 'stakeholders clearly deserve better than the current fragmented regulation of certain CAM therapies. The Government therefore strongly encourages the regulating bodies within each therapy to unite to form a single body to regulate each profession' (Department of Health 2001: 7).

Looking at the last twenty years, regulatory authorities have begun ranking different forms of CAM according to their regulatory maturity. In such accounts, a regulatory continuum is invoked beginning with the formation of affiliations and associations of CAM practitioners, such as the Affiliation of Crystal Healing Organisations, the British Complementary Medicine

Association or the Aromatherapy Council. The next stage is when CAM practitioners bring fragmented organisations together to form regulatory working groups, such as the Herbal Medicine Regulatory Working Group, the Acupuncture Regulatory Working Group, the Reiki Regulatory Working Group or the Working Group for Hypnotherapy Regulation. The task facing such working groups is to decide upon a regulatory model suitable for their therapy, a task that has proven divisive. CAM therapies can choose between maintaining status quo, pursuing a path of statutory regulation or opting for voluntary self-regulation. Chiropractors and osteopaths were the first to pursue and achieve statutory regulation in 1993 and 1994, respectively, leading to the formation of the General Chiropractic Council and the General Osteopathic Council. Next in line, not least after they were singled out in the Select Committee report on CAM as the 'two therapies which are at a stage where it would be of benefit to them and their patients if the practitioners strive for statutory regulation' (House of Lords 2000: 5.53), are herbal medicine and acupuncture (together with traditional Chinese medicine [TCM] since TCM practitioners use both forms of CAM), although it is unclear yet whether they will fall under the remit of the Health Professions Council (HPC) or some other form of council. The HPC is an umbrella council which regulates seventeen different health and care professions. Most recently, the General Regulatory Council for Complementary Therapies (in 2007) and the Complementary and Natural Healthcare Council (in 2008) have been formed to regulate therapies like Alexander technique, aromatherapy, Bowen therapy, craniosacral therapy, reflexology and healing.

The process remains on-going and both the Department of Health and the Prince of Wales Foundation for Integrated Health (PWFIH) have suggested we can speak of 'the stage various therapies have reached in their professional organisation' (Department of Health 2001: 4) or the 'different stages of developing voluntary systems of regulation' (PWFIH 2005: 13). But the process has, as noted earlier, also been divisive for many practitioners of CAM, leading some to resign from their practitioner associations in protest while others passionately advocate specific forms of regulation. Within herbal medicine, for example, a drive towards statutory regulation by some herbal practitioners has been disparaged by others (see Griggs 1997; Save Our Herbs 2012).

Each council, affiliation or working group has had a particular history involving forms of negotiation, bureaucratic hurdles, factions, lobbying, etc. not least *vis-à-vis* regulatory agencies like the Department of Health, National Institute for Health and Clinical Excellence, Medicines and Healthcare Products Regulatory Agency and the National Health Service. Particularities notwithstanding, we can nonetheless point to a common point of departure for each of these diverse groupings, namely an impetus (whether imposed or generated from within) to overcome fragmentation and confusion; to help the public know where to look.

And so the drive to regulate CAM, which began in the late 1980s, marks a significant shift in government-led efforts to protect the public. As put by Health Minister John Hutton in 2004, 'It is no longer appropriate for statutory regulation to be restricted to orthodox healthcare professionals such as doctors, nurses and physiotherapists' (Department of Health 2004: 3). Regulating CAM as a matter of protecting the public is premised on the possibility of determining what a competent, skilled and responsible CAM practitioner is. And it is this acceptance that has been attacked by a vocal group of critics who argue that regulating CAM is akin to legitimising superstition: 'you cannot start to think about a sensible form of regulation unless you first decide whether or not the thing you are trying to regulate is nonsense' (Colquhoun 2009); 'How does a regulator decide what is good practice and what is charlatanry when none of it has peer-reviewed, scientific evidence that it works?' (Toynbee 2008). But for now, their protests have not seemed to dent the regulatory momentum around CAM accounted for above. One key reason for this is to be found in the resulting novel regulatory separation of ethical and professional practice from the highly contentious question of efficacy. In a recent reply to a letter from one of the vocal critics of CAM regulation, a Department of Health representative suggested that:

> Professional regulation, whether statutory or in this case, voluntary, is about protecting the public, not about the efficacy of the therapies involved. Registration will mean that a practitioner has met certain entry standards (for instance, has an accredited qualification) and subscribes to a set of professional standards. In this way, the public will have the reassurance that any registered practitioner they choose meets these criteria and that practitioners would be subject to fitness to practise procedures should they behave inappropriately.
>
> *(cited in* Thinking is Dangerous *2009)*

Official recognition of such a thing as a 'qualified CAM practitioner' has been central to the CAM regulatory moment. For, once invited to reassure members of the public through a system of qualification, CAM therapies are in effect a part of accepted health care provision. And as we will see in the following, once accepted, CAM practitioners are expected to take active measures to assure people that they are fit to practice.

III 'Anyone could set themselves up tomorrow as a practitioner' – separating the wheat from the chaff

Now if CAM practitioners are in fact currently in the process of being 'let in', then we must account not only for this novel rationality of public protection – i.e. to regulate rather than actively marginalise or prohibit CAM – that has made space for the figure of the 'ethically responsible and competent CAM practitioner' but also for the particular configuration this political rationality has taken. The council, I argue, has emerged not so much as a model, but rather as a central *dispositif* in the regulation of CAM; a grid through which ethically responsible and competent CAM practitioners are made up and managed. It was Foucault who proposed that a *dispositif* can be thought of as 'a thoroughly heterogeneous ensemble consisting of discourses, institutions, architectural forms, regulatory decisions, laws, administrative measures, scientific statements, philosophical, moral and philanthropic propositions.... The apparatus itself is the system of relations that can be established between these elements' (Foucault 1980: 194). The Council, as we will see, is the apparatus that has emerged through three decades of parliamentary debates, regulatory decisions, administrative measures, institutions, etc. surrounding CAM

When we look at the series of state-sanctioned regulatory initiatives around CAM in the UK, we should not be surprised to learn that they have been cotemporaneous with what Michael Power has called an 'audit explosion':

> During the late 1980s and early 1990s, the word 'audit' began to be used in Britain with growing frequency in a wide variety of contexts. In addition to the regulation of private company accounting by financial audit, practices of environmental audit, value for money audit, management audit, forensic audit, data audit, intellectual property audit, medical audit, teaching audit, and technology audit emerged and, to varying degrees, acquired a degree of institutional stability and acceptance.
>
> *(Power 1999: 3)*

We can surely add CAM audit to this list. Indeed, referring to the work initiated by the Council for Complementary and Alternative Medicine already in 1985, Lord Kindersley argued in a House of Lords debate on complementary medicine held on 11 November 1987 that:

> different groups within complementary medicine have recently taken it upon themselves to establish an independent audit of their existing colleges and training centres with the aim of raising all to an acceptable level. As each group achieves this target within their own register, I hope that Parliament will give statutory recognition to the standards achieved. In this process it will be vitally important that those skilled practitioners of many years' experience do not find themselves left out in the cold.
>
> *(House of Lords 1987: 1382)*

If an initial strategy for helping the public to know where to look has been to overcome the confusion of fragmentation by encouraging unification of CAM therapies into single institutions, then an equally important task has been that of helping the public on an individual basis to distinguish the competent and responsible from the incompetent and unscrupulous ones. The task is twofold: on the one hand, one needs to ensure that practitioners are qualified (i.e. professionally competent) and on the other that they are responsible (i.e. ethically competent). In the UK, common law allows anyone to practice CAM as long as they do not falsely claim a statutorily protected title (e.g. osteopath and chiropractor are protected by law), dispense prescription medications or carry out certain invasive procedures that are limited by law to particular professions. Since the practice of most CAM therapies does not involve transgressing any of these statutory restrictions, it is not immediately clear how a member of the public would be able to distinguish between a qualified and an unqualified CAM practitioner (except in osteopathy and chiropractic), a situation that a number of CAM practitioners and others have been unsatisfied with:

> It's absurd – and dangerous too – that [anyone] could set themselves up tomorrow as a practitioner of herbal medicine. They could gain access to powerful herbs such as belladonna and ephedra, and give those to patients without any training or quality control at all. That has to stop.
>
> *(Michael Dixon, cited in Adams 2009)*

This, then, is where the council as *dispositif* comes in as an apparatus of assurance. In July 2006, the Chief Medical Officer (CMO) of the UK proposed

> to strengthen the system to assure and improve the performance of doctors and to protect the safety of patients [so that] patients, the public, the medical profession, employers and other contracting organisations become able to trust that every doctor will deliver good clinical care throughout their careers.
>
> *(Department of Health 2006: vi)*

While the CMO's report was directed at the biomedical profession following a series of high-profile scandals involving doctors who were deemed unfit to practice, the proposed emphasis on assurance and trust is just as relevant, if not more so bearing in mind on-going controversy, in the field of CAM regulation.

As argued by the Reflexology Forum, one of the main organisations representing reflexologists in the UK, 'Whenever you see a Reflexologist you need to feel confident that the person treating you meets professional standards. You also need to know that someone will take action if things go wrong. That is where regulation is important' (Reflexology Forum 2012). Similarly, one of the acupuncturists responding to the government's consultation on statutory regulation for herbal medicine and acupuncture suggested that once statutorily regulated through a council 'the public can be assured that any acupuncturist that they choose to visit fulfils the minimum criteria of competence required by the regulatory body' (Department of Health 2011: 12). The UK-based International Federation of Reflexologists agrees, suggesting that assurance and accountability are at the heart of what the General Regulatory Council for Complementary Therapies (GRCCT) stands for: 'If a patient/client or a member of the medical profession calls a GRCCT registered therapist they can be reasonably assured that he/she is properly trained, insured and accountable for their actions' (IFR 2012).

It is in this sense that CAM regulation has come to take the form of the audit. Bearing in mind the complexities of modern 'audit societies', individuals have, in a sense, outsourced verification to other agencies. Michael Power and Marilyn Strathern both note, by recourse to Mary Douglas, how 'people are constantly checking up on each other, constantly monitoring the ongoing stream of communicative exchanges and accounts that make up daily life' (Power 1999: 1) as 'accountability is part of the general fabric of human interchange' (Strathern 2000: 4). Yet in the bustle of complex urban life where individuals rarely have personal relations with the people providing them with goods and services (including medical services), the quality marks, kite marks, certifications and labels that audit processes can culminate in have become proxies or vouchers for that which is good, proper, correct and therefore trustworthy. This is exactly what is currently happening within the CAM field. The public, it is argued, are to feel confident that when they choose a certified CAM practitioner, she or he is both 'fit to practice' and 'ethically responsible'. Thus, it is not up to the individual to laboriously separate the wheat from the chaff each time he or she would like to consult a CAM practitioner, instead rituals of verification are being put into place on their behalf.

As we will see in the following section, the council has become the locus of such rituals of verification. The council oversees, certifies, adjudicates, sanctions and disciplines as a matter of assurance and through a series of procedures and practices. If not anyone should be allowed to set themselves as a CAM practitioner, then criteria as well as procedures for checking these are needed to decide who it is that should be allowed to do so.

IV 'It is the incompetent and the irresponsible we need to stop' – certification and sanctioning of CAM practice

In this final section of this chapter, I will turn my attention to just how various CAM therapies have internalised the very dividing practices that at one time kept them from playing an active part in the delivery of health care in the UK (see Saks 1995; Brown 1982, 1985; Wallis and Morley 1976; Wahlberg 2007). To be sure, a number of CAM therapies in the UK have very long histories of self-organisation, which has involved the development of education programmes as well as policing of members' practice (see Wahlberg 2007). However, as we have seen, it was not until the 1980s that such activities would gain any kind of official sanctioning from the state. What is more, as we will see, it is safe to say that there has been a significant intensification of efforts to ensure that CAM practitioners are competent and responsible in the past decade or so.

How then can one ensure that CAM practitioners are competent and responsible? In an 'audit society' like the UK's, this task has revolved around making CAM practice auditable, which is to say making CAM practice amenable to measurement, verification and validation. As

Michael Power notes, 'a new market for assurance services has emerged which demands a tight coupling between quality performance, however that is to be defined, and processes to ensure that this performance is visible to a wider audience' (Power 1999: 60). It is within this market for assurance services that the General Osteopathic Council, the General Chiropractic Council, the Health Professions Council, the General Regulatory Council for Complementary Therapies and the Complementary and Natural Healthcare Council have emerged as they work to make CAM practice auditable. About such processes, Strathern argues:

> Where audit is applied to public institutions – medical, legal, educational – the state's overt concern may be less to impose day-to-day direction than to ensure that internal controls, in the form of monitoring techniques, are in place. That may require the setting up of mechanisms where none existed before, but the accompanying rhetoric is likely to be that of helping (monitoring) people help (monitor) themselves, including helping people get used to this new 'culture'.
>
> *(Strathern 2000: 3–4)*

Let us take a closer look at how the various CAM councils are currently setting up monitoring mechanisms. The first point to be made about councils and the technologies of assurance that they are built up around is that they make no guarantees. Indeed this is one of the arguments made by opponents of statutory regulation:

> The UK government is of the opinion that statutory regulation of Herbalists will protect the public from serious harm. However, has statutory regulation of the NHS, Banking and Pension industries protected the public? No, it most certainly has not! Even now, after so called 'improved' guidelines resulting from the behaviour of Harold Shipman, abuse and cruelty on the part of medical staff is still being reported.
>
> *(Save Our Herbs 2012)*

What the setting up of a council does instead is provide assurance by *vouching* for the professional and ethical competence of registered members as a matter of public protection. As the reflexologists quoted earlier put it, choosing a certified practitioner means that you 'can be reasonably assured [that your practitioner] is properly trained, insured and accountable for their actions'. What this means is that there are *systems* in place to check that a practitioner is qualified as well as to respond when something goes wrong. While each therapy is currently in the process of developing and refining its regulatory procedures, we can point to a range of common features of the systems that are currently being set up which relate to certification (i.e. recognised entry into a particular CAM therapy) on the one hand, and punishing (i.e. suspension or expulsion from that therapy) on the other.

1 Accreditation and registration

One of the foremost tasks of a council is to establish and maintain a register of competent practitioners. It is this act of gatekeeping that is aimed at providing the public with confidence in a specific therapy, as it is only qualified practitioners who will be allowed to register and conversely anyone deemed not qualified will be excluded. To operate a register, two important kinds of audits are required. First, an audit of the schools or colleges that provide a CAM degree, and second an audit of the person who applies for membership in a council's register. Accreditation is the form of the audit of CAM degrees. The General Chiropractic Council, for example, has developed a set of 'Degree Recognition Criteria', the Herbal Medicine Regulatory Working Group has proposed an 'Accreditation Handbook' and the Aromatherapy Council has developed a 'Core Curriculum'. Each specifies the criteria required to become an accredited provider of a degree which is then recognised by the respective council. In recent years, a number of universities in the United Kingdom have begun offering degrees in, for example, acupuncture, aromatherapy, homeopathy, Ayurvedic medicine and Chinese herbal medicine. And not without controversy:

> What would you think if your child went off to university to be taught that amethyst crystals 'emit high yin energy'? … For more than a decade, 'facts' such as these have been peddled by more than a dozen fully accredited, state-funded British universities. … Indeed, since the mid-1990s, such ideas have been presented and taught as if they were real medicine. … It may seem harmless and even a welcome alternative to traditional perspectives. But teaching people that homoeopathy is evidence-based when it isn't, and encouraging students to distrust the scientific method, not only runs counter to reason, but can be dangerous.
>
> *(Colquhoun 2012)*

Those critics who have dismissed regulation of CAM as nonsense have also argued that accreditation is dangerous. Yet this is exactly what all forms of CAM therapy are being encouraged to do, to accredit their courses as a way to assure members of the public that practitioners have trained properly. Yet, as pointed out by the General Chiropractic Council, 'successfully completing a recognised degree programme does not guarantee that someone will become registered as a chiropractor. It shows us that the applicant has met the degree programme outcomes and so is eligible to apply for registration' (GCC 2012).

Eligibility is the first step as individuals with recognised degrees must then apply to be included on a council's register, as the council not only wants assurance of professional competence (which a degree stands for) but also of an individual's ethical standing, as an applicant must also submit a character reference, 'give information about any allegations of professional negligence considered by a civil court' and declare any criminal convictions. In this way, application forms, accreditation reports, recognition visits, interviews and documentation requirements are the micro-components of the technologies of assurance which vouch for certain degree courses or individuals as they generate audit trails which can be checked and verified. Papers must be in order. Yet, the auditing of competence does not always end with registration. As statutorily regulated professionals, osteopaths and chiropractors are required to engage in continual professional development (CPD) and

> by 30 November each year registrants must send [the council] a completed CPD summary sheet, listing learning activities completed, if they wish to remain on the Register for the following year. … Registrants must complete 30 hours of CPD each CPD year – 15 hours of this must include learning with others.
>
> *(GCC 2012; see also Clarke et al. 2004)*

A council will usually have an Education Committee responsible for accrediting recognised degrees as well as overseeing continued professional development of members. Such committees assure that both the programmes which lead to qualified practitioner status and the individuals who apply for membership of a register are fit for purpose/practice (see Figure 9.1).

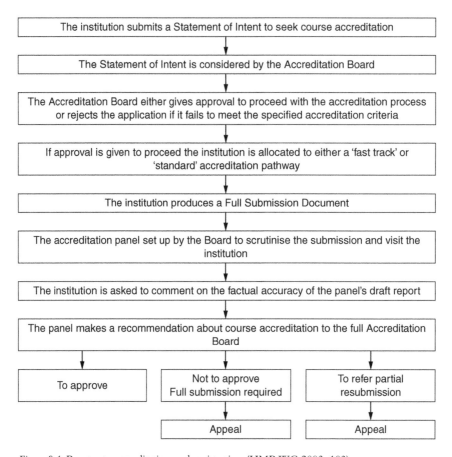

The institution submits a Statement of Intent to seek course accreditation

The Statement of Intent is considered by the Accreditation Board

The Accreditation Board either gives approval to proceed with the accreditation process or rejects the application if it fails to meet the specified accreditation criteria

If approval is given to proceed the institution is allocated to either a 'fast track' or 'standard' accreditation pathway

The institution produces a Full Submission Document

The accreditation panel set up by the Board to scrutinise the submission and visit the institution

The institution is asked to comment on the factual accuracy of the panel's draft report

The panel makes a recommendation about course accreditation to the full Accreditation Board

To approve

Not to approve
Full submission required

To refer partial
resubmission

Appeal

Appeal

Figure 9.1 Routes to accreditation and registration (HMRWG 2003: 103).

2 Auditing conduct

Once certified, members can practice as qualified practitioners of a given CAM therapy. Yet, as discussed earlier, since audited assurance practices are not guarantees, malpractice, misconduct or inappropriate behaviour on the part of a registered practitioner can happen. And as noted in the Chief Medical Officer's report on 'Trust, Assurance and Safety' from 2006, it is in these situations that a council must act robustly if the confidence of the public is to be maintained. Councils will therefore often include an Investigating Committee, a Professional Conduct and Competence Committee and/or an Ethics Committee. If a complaint is made, the Investigating Committee will make an initial assessment and decide whether the case should be referred to the Professional Conduct and Competence Committee, who have the power to admonish, impose conditions of practice, suspend or strike off a practitioner. Further to the efforts which aim to define the specific competences/qualifications which give an individual access to a particular title discussed above, technologies of assurance also operate through the development and installing of 'procedures to protect patients and the public from individuals it deems unfit to practise' (HMRWG 2003: 19). In the words of Professor George Lewith, a long-time advocate of CAM in the UK: 'It is the incompetent and the irresponsible we need to stop. Not the well-trained, dedicated herbalists who put their patients first' (cited in BBC 2009).

These then, are the ways in which the council as *dispositif* work. Rather than through Draconian measures, paths of accreditation and registration work by educating, persuading, inducing and motivating to shape the conduct of CAM practitioners. Making CAM auditable does not in any way guarantee competent and ethical practice; what it does is makes visible the ways in which competences of practitioners are vouched for through an assemblage of technologies of assurance – accreditation, registration and disciplining.

V Conclusions

The regulation of CAM, it appears, is here to stay. What I have shown in this chapter is how it has become possible to regulate a range of CAM therapies which not too many years ago remained ostracised from any state-sanctioned forms of recognition. This has certainly changed in the last thirty years or so. What I have suggested is that the following conditions can help us account for this change. First, a shift in public protection rationalities in the medical regulation sphere has allowed CAM regulation to replace CAM marginalisation or prohibition as the preferred centralised approach in the UK. This shift, in turn, has been made possible through a tactical separation of practitioner competency from the very contentious question of efficacy. Notwithstanding unsettled debates about the efficacy of CAM therapies, the figure of the 'qualified and ethically responsible' CAM practitioner is now feasible. And since we can now speak of a qualified and responsible CAM practitioner, the CAM field has become amenable, indeed answerable, to the requirements of audit – accountability, transparency, verifiability, etc. In this sense, CAM is no different than the biomedical or banking professions.

Some have suggested that CAM councils have been modelled on the General Medical Council. While this may be the case, I have argued that we gain more analytical traction from conceptualising the council as a *dispositif*, an apparatus of assurance which operates through technologies of assurance which vouch for certain activities and/or actions over others. Having been 'let in', lawmakers have called on CAM practitioners to 'put their house in order' and this is exactly what has characterised the last two decades or so. Vocal critics of CAM regulation remain, and the process has been both polemic and divisive among CAM practitioners. But this has not changed the fact that in an audit society, patients, regulators and health care personnel alike demand assurance that those providing medical care are competent and responsible.

Notes

1 In this chapter, I will be focusing on the regulation of CAM practice and will not be discussing the regulation of CAM products, which is an equally important aspect of CAM regulation.
2 On 13 May 1986, *The Guardian* ran the story 'BMA's wounding verdict on rival healers/Alternative medicine dismissed as ineffective' (Veitch 1986), while *The Times* ran with 'Doctors warn patients of risk from some alternative medicines' (Timmins 1986).

References

ACHO (2012) 'Voluntary self regulation – VSR', Affiliation of Crystal Healing Organisations, www.crystal-healing.org/documents-and-forms, accessed on 30 December 2014.
Adams, Michael (2009) '"Nonsense" alternative medicines should not be regulated', *The Daily Telegraph*, 17 December 2009.
ATCM (2010) 'Statutory regulation is the best way to safeguard the public', The Association of Traditional Chinese Medicine's Response to Department of Health Press Release – Next Steps for Complementary Therapy, 1 April 2010, available at www.atcm.co.uk/.

BBC (2009) 'Prince's herbal medicine appeal', *BBC News*, http://news.bbc.co.uk/go/pr/fr/-/2/hi/health/8388985.stm, accessed on 29 March 2011.

BMA (1986) *Alternative therapy*, London: British Medical Association.

BMA (1993) *Complementary medicine: new approaches to good practice*, Oxford: Oxford University Press.

Brown, P. S. (1982) 'Herbalists and medical botanists in mid-nineteenth-century Britain with special reference to Bristol', *Medical History*, 26(4), 405–420.

Brown, P. S. (1985) 'The vicissitudes of herbalism in late nineteenth- and early twentieth-century Britain', *Medical History*, 29(1), 71–92.

Cant, S. and Sharma, U. (1996) 'Professionalization of complementary medicine in the United Kingdom', *Complementary Therapies in Medicine*, 4, 157–162.

Clarke, D. B., Doel, M. A. and Segrott, J. (2004) 'No alternative? The regulation and professionalization of complementary and alternative medicine in the United Kingdom', *Health & Place*, 10(4), 329–338.

Clements, A. (Producer) (2007) *Slaves to superstition. Enemies of reason*, 20 August, London: Channel 4.

Cohen, M. H. (1998) *Complementary and alternative medicine: legal boundaries and regulatory perspectives*, Baltimore; London: Johns Hopkins University Press.

Colquhoun, D. (2009) 'Editorial: secret remedies: 100 years on', *British Medical Journal*, 339, b5432.

Colquhoun, D. (2012) 'Complementary medicine courses in universities: how I beat the varsity quacks', *Telegraph*, 31 January 2012, www.telegraph.co.uk/science/science-news/9051103/Complementary-medicine-courses-in-universities-how-I-beat-the-varsity-quacks.html, accessed on 10 October 2012.

Department of Health (2001) 'Government response to the House of Lords Select Committee on Science and Technology's report on complementary and alternative medicine', presented to Parliament by the Secretary of State for Health by command of Her Majesty, March 2001.

Department of Health (2004) *Regulation of herbal medicine and acupuncture. Proposals for statutory regulation.* Consultation 34352. March 2004. Leeds: Department of Health.

Department of Health (2006) *Good doctors, safer patients. Proposals to strengthen the system to assure and improve the performance of doctors and to protect the safety of patients – a report by the Chief Medical Officer*, London: COI.

Department of Health (2011) 'Statutory regulation of practitioners of acupuncture, herbal medicine, traditional Chinese medicine and other traditional medicine systems practised in the UK', analysis report on the 2009 consultation.

GCC (2012) 'Education', www.gcc-uk.org/page.cfm?page_id=25, accessed on 9 January 2013.

Great Britain Parliament (1858) 'An act to regulate the qualifications of practitioners in medicine and surgery', CAP. XC, 2 August.

Griggs, B. (1997) *New green pharmacy: the story of Western herbal medicine*, London: Vermilion.

Herbarium (2009) Blog, http://theherbarium.wordpress.com/2009/02/01/network-of-transition-herbalists/, accessed on 4 January 2012.

HMRWG (2003) 'Recommendations on the regulation of herbal practitioners in the UK: a report from the Herbal Medicine Regulatory Working Group', London: Department of Health, European Herbal Practitioners Association & Prince of Wales's Foundation for Integrated Health.

House of Lords (1985) 'Debate on natural medicine', 27 February 1985, vol. 460 cc970–992.

House of Lords (1987) 'Debate on complementary medicine', 11 November 1987, vol. 489, cc1379–1416.

House of Lords (2000) 'Complementary and alternative medicine', London: Science and Technology Committee.

IFR (2012) 'Regulation – what is it?', available at www.intfedreflexologists.org/pdf/regulation.pdf, accessed on 12 January 2013.

NIMH (2004) 'What is herbal medicine?', www.nimh.org.uk/features.html, accessed on 6 December 2004.

Power, Michael (1999) *The audit society: rituals of verification*, Oxford: Oxford University Press.

PWFIH (2005) *Complementary healthcare: a guide for patients*, London: Prince of Wales's Foundation for Integrated Health.

Reflexology Forum (2012) 'Voluntary regulation of reflexologists', available at www.reflexologyforum.org.uk, accessed on 22 December 2014.

Robbins, Martin (2010) 'Quacks fly in all directions as alternative medicine regulation fails', Lay Scientist blog, *Guardian*, www.guardian.co.uk/science/2010/apr/16/quacks-alternative-medicine-regulation, accessed on 30 March 2011.

Rose, N. and Miller, P. (1992) 'Political power beyond the state: problematics of government', *British Journal of Sociology*, 43(2), 172–205.

Saks, M. P. (1995) *Professions and the public interest: medical power, altruism and alternative medicine*, London; New York: Routledge.

Saks, M. P. (2003) *Orthodox and alternative medicine*, London: Sage.

Save Our Herbs (2012) 'Myths', www.saveourherbs.org.uk/Myths.html, accessed on 10 January 2012.

Shore, C. and Wright, S. (1999) 'Audit culture and anthropology: neo-liberalism in British higher education', *Journal of the Royal Anthropological Institute*, 5(4), 557–575.

Strathern, M. (ed.) (2000) *Audit cultures: anthropological studies in accountability, ethics and the academy*, London: Routledge.

Thinking is Dangerous (2009) 'Department of Health response to CNHC letter', posted on Thinking is Dangerous blog, 12 March, http://thinking-is-dangerous.blogspot.dk/2009/03/department-of-health-response-to-cnhc.html, accessed on 5 December 2012.

Timmins, N. (1986) 'Doctors warn patients of risk from some alternative medicines', *The Times*, 13 May.

Toynbee, P. (2008) 'Quackery and superstition – available soon on the NHS', *Guardian*, 8 January.

Veitch, A. (1986) 'BMA's wounding verdict on rival healers/Alternative medicine dismissed as ineffective', *Guardian*, 13 May.

Wahlberg, A. (2007) 'A quackery with a difference – new medical pluralism and the problem of "dangerous practitioners" in the United Kingdom', *Social Science & Medicine*, 65(11), 2307–2316.

Wallis, R. and Morley, P. (1976) *Marginal medicine*, London: Owen.

Welsh, S., Kelner, M., Wellman, B. and Boon, H. (2004) 'Moving forward? Complementary and alternative practitioners seeking self regulation', *Sociology of Health and Illness*, 26, 216–241.

Westcott, P. (1992) 'New code of conduct for safe alternatives', *Daily Mail*, 16 June.

10

THE HARM PRINCIPLE AND LIABILITY FOR CAM PRACTICE

A comparative analysis of Canadian and United States health freedom laws

Irehobhude O. Iyioha

I Introduction

Healthcare pluralism in Canada, as well as the United States, is on a continuous rise. Data from the United States show that in 2007 almost four in ten Americans used complementary and alternative healthcare.[1] Expenditure on Complementary and Alternative Medicine (CAM) in the US amounted to about $34 billion in out-of-pocket spending in 2007, with $11.9 billion spent on visits to practitioners.[2] The US data also indicate that, while about 27.4 percent of the adult population used CAM for health promotion, 17.4 percent used CAM for treating disease or illness.[3]

A study by the Fraser Institute in Canada shows that 74 percent of Canadians use complementary and alternative health services, while 71 percent have used natural health products to combat chronic and debilitating medical conditions.[4] The study reports that other patrons have used natural health products simply for preventive healthcare purposes.[5] According to a different study by Health Canada, 81 percent of Canadians are convinced that there will be an increase in the use of natural health products over the next ten years.[6] In spite of the rising profile of medical pluralism in Canada, restrictive federal and provincial laws and policies place complementary and alternative health services and products out of the reach of many Canadians and impede the practice of complementary and alternative medicine by many Canadian health practitioners.

The traditional definition of medical negligence or medical malpractice, which renders a physician's practice of CAM a standard case of deviation from acceptable practice standards, further inhibits the professional autonomy of physicians interested in practicing CAM or integrated medicine. However, recent legislative changes, such as amendments to the Medical Acts or health professions legislation of some Canadian provinces, attempt to ease the contentious relationship between the biomedical institution and CAM practice by recognizing – without actually espousing – the practice of CAM through the circuitous approach of modifying the grounds on which biomedical healthcare professionals may become liable for medical malpractice.

For example, amendments to Medical Acts in Alberta, Ontario, British Columbia and Manitoba provide that physicians will not be liable for unprofessional conduct solely on the basis of departing from the prevailing medical practice or practicing non-traditional therapies. These provisions in Canadian law are modeled after similar provisions in Acts regulating medical practice in several states in the United States (US), including Oklahoma, Texas, Washington, Oregon, New York, North Carolina, Massachusetts, Georgia, Colorado and Alaska. Today, while a good number of laws and legislative amendments, which are denoted as health freedom laws, in the US as well as Canada provide that physicians will not be liable for unprofessional conduct for practicing a non-traditional therapy except *where the chosen therapy poses a greater risk to the patient than the conventional therapy*, Alaska's health freedom provision (and before the recent amendment following a key legal decision, North Carolina's) has a different proviso which makes physicians automatically liable for use of a non-conventional therapy *where the patient is harmed*. Washington's health freedom law incorporates both types of provisos, attaching liability to a physician's use of a non-traditional therapy only where it results in harm or creates unreasonable risk.

Denoting these provisos as the "harm principle", this chapter explores the critical implications of the principle alongside the disparities between the two variants of the provisos and their impact on the practice of CAM and integrated medicine. The chapter contends that, in deviating from the traditional standards for a finding of liability for medical negligence or malpractice, the provisos draw a subtle hierarchy between CAM and biomedicine and further impede the practice of CAM. While outlining the impact of the provisos on the integration of CAM and biomedicine, the chapter outlines how the health freedom provisos reinforce the co-option model of CAM integration – a model involving the practice of validated CAM therapies by biomedical practitioners, and fundamentally excludes non-biomedically trained CAM practitioners from hospital-centered CAM practice.

It is noteworthy that there seems to be a gradual trend in legislation towards the more nuanced provision that emphasizes the degree of risk of a CAM therapy comparative to standard or recognized treatment as the fulcrum in the determination of professional liability – a trend that appears to have been spurred, at least in the case of North Carolina, by adverse judicial opinion. However, it remains important to deconstruct the inherent problems and limitations of the harm provisos in order to serve as a decision-making guide for future US and Canadian state and provincial legislatures that are yet to adopt a health freedom law.

The analysis and perspectives enunciated in this chapter draw from law and ethics – from the analytical tools provided in the law of professional negligence and the ethical principles of non-maleficence and, inferentially, autonomy. These disciplines collectively illuminate the approach adopted and thesis herein espoused. Given the nature of the subject of complementary and alternative medicine – a subject imbued with the complexities that trail health policy and health law studies – and its dependency on law for legitimacy, the analysis of the harm principle through legal and ethical lenses is fundamental to achieving the ultimate goal of validation and legitimization of CAM.

The discussion is set out in three sections. The following section defines and examines health freedom laws in Canada and the United States. Next, in the context of a general overview of malpractice in CAM practice, the "harm principle" is analyzed with some focus on the similarities and differences between the two versions of the harm principle adopted by US states and Canadian provinces. The section also examines the implications of the provisos within medical negligence law. Following the discussion of the harm principle, the section highlights the slippery-slope effect of the amendments towards the co-option model of medical integration, and evaluates the impact of the amendments on the growth and development of the field of CAM. The concluding section discusses possible legislative and interpretive reform of the harm principle with primary focus on the importance of minimum standards of acceptable medical practice as part of the evaluation of a healthcare professional's liability for the practice of CAM.

II Health freedom laws in Canada and the United States

Medical malpractice or medical negligence more generally occurs when a healthcare practitioner provides a treatment that deviates from acceptable standards of medical practice and the treatment causes harm to the patient. This universal definition under the law of torts of which negligence is one of several subjects implies that physicians practicing CAM – a constellation of practices which, in many respects, do not conform to the theories of biomedicine – deviate from the standards of biomedical practice, *stricto sensu*.[7] Health freedom laws in the context of physicians' liability for the practice of CAM are legislative attempts to extend the boundaries of physicians' scope of practice to accommodate (the increasing occurrence of) CAM practice by physicians without the automatic liability that traditionally attaches to such practice.

Generally, health freedom laws (or medical freedom laws as they are also called) are laws or legislative amendments that protect the freedom of patients to make decisions about the type of healthcare or health services they should receive and the autonomy of health professionals to provide those services. This omnibus definition recognizes the variation in the laws that have been labeled "health freedom laws". Hence, it places within the taxonomy of "health freedom laws" or "medical freedom laws" legislative provisions and statutes that are passed with the objective of broadening patients' access to complementary and alternative therapies – amendments that are directed at alleviating the risk of professional liability for physicians who practice CAM.

Laws crafted to overturn the specter of prosecution under which unlicensed CAM providers practice their profession are another example of health freedom laws. Thus, some health freedom laws, such as Minnesota's *Complementary and Alternative Health Care Freedom of Access Law* (CAHFAL), signed into law by Governor Jesse Ventura in 2000, also aim to allow unlicensed CAM practitioners to practice as long as they do not carry out certain restricted procedures such as surgeries and x-rays or prescribe certain drugs, while guaranteeing reimbursement through third-party insurers to licensed providers. Such laws, as in the case of Minnesota's CAHFAL, often have built-in protective mechanisms for the public, including provisions for full disclosure of practitioners' practice and training as well as enforcement mechanisms to prevent fraud and harm.

Interestingly, also labeled as "health freedom laws" are state statutes in the US that focus on undermining, through counter-legislative provisions, the validity of the United States' *Patient Protection and Affordable Care Act* (PPACA). The PPACA, which was signed into law by President Obama on March 23, 2010, was heralded by controversies, legal and otherwise, led by both political figures and the laity and in its wake by legal and constitutional challenges regarding the individual health insurance mandate provided by the law. Also the subject of challenge were the scope of congressional powers and the right of states over healthcare, amongst other issues. Besides several court challenges instituted by some states, there have also been new state laws promulgated to negate several key provisions of the Act, such as its mandatory healthcare insurance provision. This latter group of statutes, with the underlying objective of challenging the alleged restriction of rights under the PPACA, is beyond the focus of this chapter.[8]

The underlying objective of health freedom laws coming within the first two categories outlined above is to provide broader freedom for health professionals and patients interested in non-mainstream therapies. Central to the discussion in this chapter are amendments specifically designed, at least apparently, to limit the risk of professional liability for physicians practicing

CAM or other experimental therapies. A number of states in the US, including New York, North Carolina, Oklahoma, Texas, Washington, Oregon, Massachusetts, Georgia, Colorado and Alaska, have passed health freedom laws that redefine the threshold of liability for physicians interested in practicing CAM, though with different wordings, and therefore, as argued below, different legal effects. In some cases, as in the case of Minnesota's CAHFAL, a health freedom statute or proviso is the result of collective efforts through mobilizations by concerned practitioners or patron groups to challenge the status quo following high-profile litigations against CAM practitioners.[9] It could arise from the sometimes-incessant disagreements between boards of medical examiners and associations or professional bodies representing alternative healthcare practitioners.[10]

Health freedom laws provide that physicians will not face disciplinary action or be held liable for malpractice for merely using an unconventional or a non-traditional therapy. The caveat, as outlined in Alaska's health freedom law, is that the practitioner will be guilty of misconduct where the treatment administered results in harm. This is one of two dominant versions of the harm principle. The classification of the principles into two groups is primarily for convenience. In actuality, the "harm" and "risk" provisos come in a spectrum of types. Some other statutes have a more nuanced, and perhaps tolerant, version of the proviso. For example, the harm principle under Colorado's *Medical Practice Act*, which of course comes under the section on what constitutes "unprofessional conduct", is stipulated as follows:

> "Unprofessional conduct" as used in this article means:...
>
> (3)(a) For purposes of this section, "alternative medicine" means those health care methods of diagnosis, treatment, or healing that are not generally used but that provide a reasonable potential for therapeutic gain in a patient's medical condition that is not outweighed by the risk of such methods. A licensee who practices alternative medicine shall inform each patient in writing, during the initial patient contact, of such licensee's education, experience, and credentials related to the alternative medicine practiced by such licensee. The board shall not take disciplinary action against a licensee solely on the grounds that such licensee practices alternative medicine.[11]

While Colorado's law does not expressly adopt either of the provisos verbatim, it does implicitly impose disciplinary actions by the board where a licensee practices an alternative therapy that is outweighed by the risks associated with the therapy.

Another interesting formulation of the proviso is to be found in Washington's health freedom provision. The Washington provision combines both forms of the principle into a rule that *simpliciter* attaches liability to either the occurrence of harm or to the use of a therapy that creates an unreasonable risk. According to the law, the administration of a "non-traditional treatment" is not by itself proof of malpractice, provided the treatment *does not result in harm* or *create unreasonable risk* to a patient.[12] Thus, a physician would be liable for malpractice if an applied alternative therapy causes harm *simpliciter*.

Some other laws provide, equally tolerantly, that physicians will be liable for professional misconduct only where the non-traditional treatment *poses a greater risk to the patient than the traditional or conventional treatment*. The *Medicine and Allied Occupations Act* of North Carolina now has a health freedom amendment of the tolerant category. Section 90–14 of the law, which outlines the disciplinary powers of the North Carolina Medical Board, provides as follows:

> The Board shall not revoke the license of or deny a license to a person, or discipline a licensee in any manner, solely because of that person's practice of a therapy that is

experimental, nontraditional, or that departs from acceptable and prevailing medical practices unless, by competent evidence, the Board can establish that the treatment has a safety risk greater than the prevailing treatment or that the treatment is generally not effective.[13]

Prior to the amendment that gave rise to the above new provision – a move inspired by a judicial decision,[14] a physician was guilty of professional misconduct based on "departure from, or failure to conform to, the standards of acceptable and prevailing medical practice ... irrespective of whether or not a patient" was injured by the therapy.[15] As evident in the case of *Re Guess*, the old rule could have a deleterious effect on practitioners, as well as their patients, whose conducts did not otherwise constitute a breach of clinical standards.

Employing legislative language similar to that used in the "tolerant" version of the harm principle in the US, the relevant Acts regulating physician practice of the Canadian provinces of Ontario, British Columbia, Alberta and Manitoba stipulate that non-conventional practice by provincial physicians will not result in liability except to the extent that the therapy constitutes a higher risk alternative compared to the conventional treatment. According to section 5.1 of Ontario's *Medicine Act*:[16]

> A member shall not be found guilty of professional misconduct or of incompetence under section 51 or 52 of the Health Professions Procedural Code solely on the basis that the member practices *a therapy that is non-traditional or that departs from the prevailing medical practice unless there is evidence that proves that the therapy poses a greater risk to a patient's health than the traditional or prevailing practice.*[17]

In Alberta, section 5 of Schedule 21 of Alberta's *Health Professions Act*[18] provides:

> Despite anything in this Act, a regulated member is not guilty of unprofessional conduct or of a lack of competence solely because the regulated member employs a therapy that is non-traditional or departs from the prevailing practices of physicians, surgeons or osteopaths unless it can be demonstrated that the therapy has a safety risk for that patient that is unreasonably greater than that of the traditional or prevailing practices.[19]

Section 25.4 of British Columbia's *Health Professions Act, 1996* stipulates:

> The college must not act against a registrant or an applicant for registration solely on the basis that the person practises a therapy that departs from prevailing medical practice unless it can be demonstrated that the therapy poses a greater risk to patient health or safety than does prevailing medical practice.[20]

A similarly worded provision is contained in section 185 of Manitoba's proposed *Regulated Health Professions Act*.[21] These provisions convey the same rule. Except to the extent that it is unclear whether the law conceives the traditional or prevailing therapy as biomedical, this version of the harm principle apparently aims to ensure that patients receive treatment that poses the least risk to the patient's health and safety. With the lack of clarity on whether the legislative intent is to allow "prevailing" or "traditional treatment" to be defined as either biomedical or CAM, it is debatable whether the phrases should be construed as such.

A more progressive interpretation is the non-discriminatory reading, that is "traditional" or "prevailing" treatment should be taken to mean treatment that is either biomedical or CAM.

This construction of the phrases accommodates a future in which the biomedical community would accept specific validated CAM therapies as the standard therapies for particular conditions. In fact, there are early judicial and legislative signs indicating the likelihood of such a future when both law and medical norms would evolve to hold physicians to a higher standard of care requiring full disclosure of procedures or treatments which are currently described as non-conventional or fringe and hold physicians liable for failure to do so. The US case of *Gemme v Goldberg*[22] illustrates this point. In that case, a physician who did not inform his patient that surgery was elective and that the patient could opt for an alternative treatment was held to have breached the informed consent rule. According to the court, the jury could have decided that the physician had breached the informed consent obligation by neglecting "to disclose a viable alternative that might have produced a less perfect result but may have represented a safer or less invasive procedure".[23]

An important legislative pointer to the broader meaning of "prevailing" or "traditional" medical practice may be found in British Columbia's *Health Professions Act, 1996*.[24] As already observed, section 25.4 of the Act provides that the "College" will not indict registrants or applicants "solely" on the ground that the registrant practices a therapy that "departs from prevailing medical practice unless it can be demonstrated that the therapy poses a greater risk to patient health or safety than does prevailing medical practice".[25] The Act includes in its definition of "college" the British Columbia College of Chiropractors, the College of Dental Surgeons of British Columbia, the College of Surgeons and Physicians of British Columbia, the College of Pharmacists of British Columbia, and any other college "continued under" section 15(1) of the Act.[26] The inclusion of the College of Chiropractors in the definition may be taken to suggest that "prevailing medical practice" could refer to either CAM or biomedicine. Yet, it remains unclear whether statutorily unregulated CAM practices in British Columbia would be classified as "prevailing medical practice". Canadian health freedom provisions would stand in contrast to some in the US if "prevailing medical practice" does not include unregulated CAM practices, considering that statutes denoted as health freedom laws in the US also include statutes or provisions authorizing unregulated CAM providers to practice within defined scopes and guidelines.

Although the harm principle may serve as a welcome legislative attenuation of the hitherto "strict liability"[27] imposed on physicians who practiced outside their professional boundaries, the law insists on a number of safeguards for patients. Generally, physicians practicing within the area of CAM or integrated medicine must comply with the informed consent principle, providing patients complete information on the benefits and risks of the proposed treatment. Physicians are also required to conduct appropriate examination and testing, provide follow-up patient monitoring and keep medical records.[28] In fact, the health freedom laws of some states, such as Texas and Louisiana, require physicians interested in administering a CAM therapy to conduct comprehensive examination, offer an appropriate diagnosis and treatment program, and carry out patient reviews, as well as comprehensive and accurate record keeping.[29]

Therefore, although physicians have some more latitude to practice CAM either as an individual therapy or as part of a broader biomedical regimen, they are required to continue to follow traditional clinical, ethical and legal guidelines. This point was made clear in *Ravikovich v College of Physicians and Surgeons of Ontario*,[30] a case involving a physician who was indicted for violating professional standards of practice. The physician was alleged to have used methods of diagnosis and treatment with no scientific validity. Although the disciplinary committee of the College found him guilty of professional misconduct, the committee stipulated, while acknowledging the harm principle, that the use of an unconventional therapy is not of itself evidence of professional incompetence.[31]

III The harm principle

The provisions discussed above identify the occurrence of harm or presence of risk of harm greater than that associated with the prevailing regimen as the legal threshold for a finding of liability. This strict requirement of injury or of a greater risk of harm for a finding of liability for CAM practice is, as evident in the foregoing discussion, herein described as the "harm principle". The legislative focus on the occurrence of harm is hardly surprising. As Beauchamp and Childress have noted, the doctrine of non-maleficence, which prohibits us from harming others, is in the realm of medical ethics a principle that "has been treated as effectively identical to the celebrated maxim *Primum non nocere:* Above all [or first] do no harm".[32] The Hippocratic Oath itself includes the principle of non-maleficence as well as the doctrine of beneficence: "I will use treatment to help the sick according to my ability and judgment, but I will never use it to injure or wrong them."[33] The ethical principle of non-maleficence binds physicians to a duty of assessing the likely risks of a therapy or medical procedure before using the therapy or carrying out the procedure. The obligations imposed by the principle include both the duty to avoid inflicting harm on others and the duty to avoid imposing risks of harm.[34] Thus, the two primary versions of health freedom laws – the first basing liability strictly on the occurrence of harm and the second requiring that the alternative therapy does not pose a greater risk than the prevailing therapy – are subsumed under the doctrine of non-maleficence.

As is further elucidated below, both provisos are problematic, the former more so than the latter. However, considering the role of medical professional monitoring boards in professional output regulation, it can be contended that the goal of patient safety is central to health freedom provisos, especially those legislative amendments that focus on the occurrence of harm *simpliciter* for a finding of professional misconduct. The version of the harm principle that advises against the use of a therapy that poses a higher or greater risk of injury to a patient than the conventional treatment is arguably a reasonable standard expected of physicians, especially considering the ethical guidelines within which physicians must operate. However, both forms of the principle are contentious, with the "greater risk" proviso debatably raising some challenging questions with no straightforward answers.

The primary problem that the provisos raise is the absolutism in the treatment of the occurrence of medical harm. Underlying the first proviso – that is, the construction that invokes legal liability on the mere occurrence of harm – is the assumption that all medical harms are culpable. The factual and legal foundations of this version of the principle are flawed because the proviso, *prima facie*, ignores the justificatory and excusatory conditions in the occurrence of medical harm. Under the tort of negligence, a medical practitioner is guilty of professional negligence only after an assessment of a number of factors:[35]

1   The existence of a duty of care as between the health provider and the patient;
2   Breach of the duty of care;
3   The occurrence of injury or harm;
4   The existence of a nexus between the breach and the injury.

These four factors simply require a health provider to have a duty of care to the patient, a requirement satisfied by the provider–patient relationship that exists between the parties; that the provider breach that duty of care through negligent or fault-based action; that the patient suffer harm or injury; and that the harm or injury be the result of the breach of duty. Hence, critical to this process of assessment is the existence of "fault" in the conduct of the professional – that is, the existence of a connection between the violation of a medical standard and the occurrence of harm. The "fault" requirement distinguishes harm that is the result of a breach of the minimum standards of care required by the medical professional body from injury that is within the foreseeable outcomes or side-effects of a therapy administered or procedure conducted non-negligently. Thus, a successful cause of action in negligence would require proof that a given healthcare professional failed to meet the expectations of his or her professional peers in the treatment of the patient. This traditional understanding of liability rules therefore calls into question the utility – and perhaps, objective – of the impugned form of the harm principle under health freedom laws.

As Beauchamp and Childress have noted:

> A harm is a thwarting, defeating, or setting back of some party's interests, but a harmful action is not always a wrong or unjustified. Harmful actions that involve justifiable setbacks to another's interests are not wrong – for example ... justified punishment of physicians for incompetence or negligence.... Nevertheless, the principle of nonmaleficence is a prima facie principle that requires the justification of harmful actions.[36]

Thus, whether the "agent of harm" is legally responsible for the harm[37] depends on the result of a legal equation animated by the standard of due care and defined in the four elements for proof of liability outlined above. Indeed, the spheres of law and morality both identify "a standard of due care that determines whether the agent who is causally responsible for the risk is legally or morally responsible as well".[38] According to Beauchamp and Childress, "this standard is a specification of the principle of nonmaleficence".[39] The standard of due care requires a health provider to practice with proper care within established professional guidelines to avoid causing harm to a patient.

Another component of the standard of due care, which arguably problematizes the second version of the harm principle, is that health providers must ensure the goals of treatment "justify the risks" imposed to attain the goals.[40] A serious or grave risk must, therefore, be proportionate to the goals sought to be achieved, and be undertaken with due care, if the agent is to avoid violating moral and legal rules.[41] In the present context, whether or not the choice of an alternative therapy with higher safety risks than the prevailing treatment would meet this proportionality test would depend on the given circumstance. A few questions help place the challenges with this proviso in some perspective: If the alternative therapy would serve a "commensurately momentous"[42] goal desired by the given patient in spite of its higher safety risks, does the proportionality test thereby displace the requirements of the health freedom law? If the goal of the alternative therapy is commensurate with the greater risks imposed by the treatment – and therefore meets the proportionality test, is the health freedom proviso thereby displaced? Or, perhaps, the more fundamental question is whether there is ever to be a (CAM treatment) goal that is so momentous that the CAM therapy is acceptable, in spite of possessing a higher risk than the conventional treatment, as a preferred alternative to the prevailing option.

Overall, the rules regarding harm, risks of harm and liability can be stated simply: even if the therapeutic encounter or relationship between a health provider and the patient "proves harmful or unhelpful, malpractice occurs *if and only if* physicians do not meet professional standards of care".[43] The question that arises, therefore, is: should a provider who administers a CAM therapy with the appropriate care, complying with appropriate standards, and avoiding the imposition of an unreasonable risk on the patient comparative to the goals sought to be achieved be held liable in negligence (or for malpractice) based on the mere occurrence of an adverse consequence? A "yes" answer – which is the response provided by the impugned health freedom laws in their current construction – flagrantly disregards the four factors identified above.

As Sharpe and Faden have noted, the first of two principal justifications for "harm-causing actions and the imposition of risk" is valid consent by a competent patient or consent by a surrogate.[44] The assumption of risk principle further explicates this first justification. The principle, which is an absolute defense to malpractice,[45] allows patients to voluntarily consent to the risks that may arise from a medical procedure. The consent is, however, conditional on the physician's full disclosure of all likely or foreseeable risks associated with the given procedure. The second justification is that the expected harm is central to achieving patient health benefit and "is proportionately less harmful than the condition for which the patient sought care".[46] Elsewhere, I have discussed informed consent and patients' interest in self-determination, which come within the first of the justifications for medical injury indicated above;[47] however, the central theme of the present discourse is more closely linked to excusatory grounds.

Excusatory conditions for liability recognize the agency of intervening factors in the occurrence of harm. These factors are usually beyond the direct or immediate control of the medical actor. Legally accepted excusatory grounds, which often include systemic failures or unforeseeable medical outcomes, do not represent a denunciation of the ethics of non-maleficence or beneficence.[48] The physician retains understanding – expectedly at least – of the "priority"[49] of these ethical principles, but appeals for an appreciation of the exigencies of the circumstances under which the harm occurred. The impugned version of the harm principle discounts important excusatory conditions for harm, such as unfortunate shortcomings in the best available medical information, fiscal problems and managerial or systemic difficulties beyond the control of medical personnel, inadequate public resources and "good-faith error", amongst others.[50] By creating a rule that disregards these possibilities and imposes a strict liability standard on practitioners on the mere occurrence of harm, the law rules out the possibility of an unforeseen adverse outcome from CAM practice that is not based on fault, which can happen in normal, everyday CAM practice, and which is in fact traditional in biomedical practice. By implication, therefore, the proviso creates a higher standard of liability for CAM practice than the traditional standard under negligence or malpractice law.

IV The harm principle: impact on integrated medical practice

While the underlying objective of the harm principle may be patient safety, its effect on integrated medical practice can hardly be overlooked. The problematic requirement that unprofessionalism will be determined in the context of CAM or integrated medical practice by the sole occurrence of injury creates a legal problem and burden that interested or would-be practitioners of CAM may not be ready to bear. Besides creating a hierarchy between the two systems of medical practice, the requirement reifies the uncomplimentary characterization of CAM as practice " 'deviating' from or operating 'below' the standard of biomedicine" – deviation that is tolerated except where harm occurs.[51] This characterization hardly enhances the development of CAM or integrated medicine as legitimate fields of medical practice. It is noteworthy, however, that at least one CAM and integrated medicine scholar espouses the harm principle. Michael Cohen suggests that medical negligence law should be reconceptualized to incorporate the type of amendments in health freedom laws; that is, the standard for a finding of negligence should be amended to de-emphasize the aspect of the rule that requires "deviation from minimum standards of acceptable practice" while accentuating the resultant injury.[52] By implication, this would lead to a reconstruction of the age-old standard of negligence in which case liability attaches to the conduct of an agent on the mere occurrence of harm, rather than on deviation from the standards acceptable in the given profession of the agent in order to accommodate the emerging set of health freedom provisos.

This recommendation, itself reflective of the harm principle, may be interpreted – at one level – as a legitimate cautionary proviso which, through its stipulation of a different standard of liability for CAM practice, fulfills the objective of patient safety to the extent that it dissuades potentially interested physicians from CAM practice except after a thorough consideration of the utility, safety and effectiveness of the chosen therapy. At another level, however, it achieves the result of impeding CAM practice and integrated medicine. Fear of automatic liability that attaches to the occurrence of harm, no matter how minor, can stifle medical practice.[53] While a similar assertion may be made within the arena of biomedical practice, the difference is simply that the law of medical negligence or malpractice provides a different, more nuanced, better considered criteria for professional medical liability. Thus, while the evolving nature of many CAM therapies might influence a reading of Cohen's suggestion and the identical statutory requirement as a reasonable compromise in a world where regulatory authorities are constantly combating the upshots of an asymmetrical healthcare market, it is hardly an over-amplification of the deleterious impact of biomedical laws on the development of CAM to argue for a reasonable reformulation of the harm principle. Such reformulation, it is hoped, would serve the goals of both patient safety and the growth of the field of CAM.

Finally, the acknowledgement of the practice of CAM by biomedical practitioners – and, specifically, the ostensive authorization of the practice by and within the traditional medical establishment – through the instrumentation of health freedom laws is analogous to the "co-option"[54] of CAM into biomedicine. As I have observed elsewhere, the state policy "to support through legislative provisos the delivery" of CAM by physicians "is hardly different from the state's predilection towards the model of co-option in which biomedical professionals exclusively provide alternative medical services".[55] Health freedom laws by design "accommodate" the delivery of CAM by biomedical professionals who have acquired the skill to do so.[56] While the delivery of CAM by biomedically trained health professionals has its rewards in terms of safety and quality assurances that may be non-existent with some unlicensed CAM practitioners, the moral problem lies with the "concomitant denial of legitimacy"[57] to CAM practitioners, the systemic and regulatory hiatuses in the field of CAM, and the consequent diminished status of the CAM paradigm.

V Reforming the harm principle

Any recalibration of the harm principle to ensure that health freedom laws serve the objectives of protecting freedoms and ensuring access must be founded on an "egalitarian framework"[58] that recognizes that the institutional changes in healthcare delivery are the corollary of patients' aspirations and choices. The increasing physician and provider interest in CAM and other alternative therapies and the associated emerging evolution in the delivery of care involving a transition to more integrated forms of healthcare and greater attention to patients' needs are influenced by the patient-led interest in the personalized care embodied in CAM. As patients continue to opt for alternative medical options or seek these options when all else has failed, it is necessary to have laws that facilitate these needs while addressing the thorny and inescapable issue of provider liability. It is equally important, however, that due consideration is given to the law's interest in patient safety. Unfortunately, the difficulty of balancing patient safety and patient choices is evident in the longstanding conflict between the ethical principles of beneficence and autonomy.[59] Nevertheless, considering the evolving and unproven nature of many CAM therapies, it is important that the conflict is resolved with a primary focus on protecting patients' safety and wellbeing, without necessarily sacrificing the autonomy of patrons and practitioners. A reasonable compromise may be reached by prioritizing well-founded medical and legal rules for healthcare delivery.

The proposition, therefore, is that the harm principle may reasonably be reformulated around breach of the standard of care. Adjudication and possible legislative amendment of the principle should be based on the failure of a physician to meet minimum acceptable medical standards. This ground of assessment of a physician's liability reflects the central role of "fault" or "blameworthiness" in imputing liability on an otherwise cautious and principled practitioner. On the basis of this assessment, the medical disciplinary tribunals or courts would have to consider whether the physician has complied with relevant professional guidelines for the administration of a particular treatment. For example, has the physician ascertained the safety of the CAM therapy? Is the physician properly informed about and trained in the administration of the therapy? Did the physician record the clinical state of the patient and changes in the state? Did the physician refer the patient to another physician or specialist when the clinical indications necessitated such referral? Some of these guidelines were laid down for physicians practicing non-traditionally in the Ontario case of *Ravikovich*. According to the disciplinary committee of the college:

> The drug must be proven safe. The physician must record in considerable detail the clinical state of the patient and the changes in this state, both good and bad, that are produced by the medication. The physician should be aware of all of the pertinent publications that bear on the clinical problem as well as on the proposed treatment.[60]

Furthermore, in consonance with the substance of the less contentious version of the harm principle, judges may assess whether the CAM therapy chosen by the physician was indeed the ideal choice, considering safety, benefits, possibility of harm and treatment goal, among several of the prevailing options – options that include CAM or biomedicine. In line with this arm of the harm principle, Cohen has suggested three factors to be evaluated by the courts determining malpractice liability in the alternative medical context:

> (1) the risk of danger or injury created by the specific therapy, (2) the extent to which the patient's condition was likely to result in death or disability irrespective of complementary or alternative care, and (3) the extent to which the complementary and alternative therapy displaced conventional care and the extent to which the neglect of conventional care was the actual and proximate cause of the injury.[61]

Underlying the first factor and central to the suggestions outlined above, is that the CAM therapy administered by a physician should be backed by evidence of safety and effectiveness and the associated risks should be commensurate with the treatment goal. It should also pose less risk of harm than other "traditional" options, and going further than the first factor and the provisos, these options should include both CAM and biomedical options.

Therefore, unlike Cohen's third proposition, which arguably[62] suggests biomedicine as the standard to which physicians must have first recourse, adjudicators should determine whether the therapy employed by the physician displaced a more effective or less risky therapy – *whether biomedicine or CAM*.[63] This suggestion counters the hierarchical subtext of the harm principle.[64] Thus, central to one of my suggestions above – specifically assessment of whether the CAM therapy administered by the physician is the safest and most effective choice among different options – is the legal requirement that the physician must not be negligent in choosing a therapy or course of treatment.[65]

The ideal of protecting patients' wellbeing and ensuring safety must be pivotal to the practice of CAM, especially as patient advocacy groups and practitioners continue to advocate for legitimacy for CAM and integrated medicine. While the harm principle ostensibly recognizes the importance of patient safety and wellbeing to medical practice, the goal will be better served by legislative and judicial focus, not mechanically on the occurrence of adverse results, but on the underlying causes of those outcomes and the extent to which practitioners' non-adherence to the medico-legal and ethical standards that govern medical practice or specific procedures created the result. Such an interpretive approach serves the interests of both patients and practitioners interested in CAM, and better fosters the growth of the field.

Notes

1 P. M. Barnes, B. Bloom and R. Nahin, "Complementary and Alternative Medicine Use Among Adults and Children: United States, 2007" (2008) *CDC National Health Statistics Report* #12.

2 R. Nahin, P. M. Barnes, B. J. Stussman and B. Bloom, "Costs of Complementary and Alternative Medicine (CAM) and Frequency of Visits to CAM Practitioners: United States, 2007" *National Health Statistics Report* #18.

3 M. A. Davis, A. N. West, W. B. Weeks and B. E. Sirovich, "Health Behaviors and Utilization among Users of Complementary and Alternative: Medicine for Treatment versus Health Promotion" (2011) 46(5) *Health Services Research* 1402–1416.

4 Esmail Nadeem, "Complementary and Alternative Medicine in Canada: Trends in Use and Public Attitudes: 1997–2006" (2007) 87 *Public Policy Sources* 1–53.

5 Ibid.

6 Health Canada Baseline Natural Health Products Survey Among Consumers: *Final Report, 2005*, online: Health Canada, www.hc-sc.gc.ca/dhp-mps/alt_formats/hpfb-dgpsa/pdf/pubs/eng_cons_survey-eng.pdf ["Health Canada Report"].

7 See M. H. Cohen, *Beyond Complementary Medicine: Legal and Ethical Perspectives on Health Care and Human Evolution* (Ann Arbor: The University of Michigan Press, 2003) ["Cohen, *Beyond Complementary Medicine*"]; see also Irehobhude O. Iyioha, *Health Governance, Medical Pluralism and the Politics of Integration: A Legal Theory for Increasing Access to Healthcare* (UBC Libraries: PhD Dissertation, 2010) ["Iyioha, *Health Governance*"].

8 If the legal challenges against the PPACA (most of which revolve around the individual mandate) are resolved in favor of the Act – just as Congress' power to enact the individual mandate has been upheld – then these newly styled "health freedom laws" promulgated to negate provisions of the PPACA will be rendered ineffective based on the Supremacy Clause of the United States Constitution, under which federal laws are the Supreme Law of the Land: US Const. Art. VI, cl. 2: See H. Chaikand, C. W. Copeland, C. S. Redhead and J. Staiman, "PPACA: A Brief Overview of the Law, Implementations, and Legal Challenges" (CRS Report for Congress, 2011), online, http://nationalaglawcenter.org/wp-content/uploads/assets/crs/R41664.pdf (last accessed May 20, 2014).

9 See *Health Freedom States*, online, www.cancure.org/legislation_already_passed.htm (last accessed May 20, 2014).

10 Ibid.

11 Col. Rev. Stats., Title 12, Art. 36., §12-36-117.

12 Wash. Rev. Code Ann. S. 18.130.180(4). Emphasis supplied.

13 N.C. Gen. Stat. 90-14(a)(6).

14 *Re Guess*, 393 S.E.2d. In *Re Guess*, a physician who administered homeopathy to his patients after they failed to respond to biomedical treatment was indicted for unprofessional conduct. The North Carolina Board of Medical Examiners indicted the physician for departing from "standards of acceptable and prevailing medical practice in North Carolina". In refuting the charge that homeopathy was not an "acceptable and prevailing" therapy in North Carolina, Guess provided evidence that homeopathy is recognized in three US states and several foreign countries. Guess' patients testified to the benefits they had derived from Guess' treatment and that they had not been harmed by it. In spite of these testimonies, the board revoked his license. On appeal, the court citing the harm exception observed that the board "neither charged nor found that Dr. Guess's departure from approved and prevailing medical practice either endangered or harmed his patients or the public". Reversing the board's decision, the court held that the physician's license would be appropriately revoked if his practice causes harm to the public. According to the court, "conduct that is merely different from that of other practitioners" is not a sufficient ground for revoking a physician's license. On further appeal, the North Carolina Supreme

Court decided that the law did not require proof of harm to support a finding that a physician was liable for misconduct in the circumstances outlined in the relevant legislation.

15 See N.C. Gen. Stat. 90-14(a)(6).
16 S.O. 1991, c. 30.
17 Ibid., s. 5.1.
18 *Health Professions Act*, RSA 2000, c H-7.
19 RSA 2000 c. H-7 Sched. 21 s. 5; 2008 c 34 s. 30. Bill 209, which contained this amendment, was passed by the Alberta legislature in April 1996.
20 S. 25.4, RSBC 1996, c. 183.
21 S.M. 2009, c. 15, Bill 18, 3rd Session, 39th Legislature. Assented to June 11, 2009.
22 *Gemme v Goldberg*, 626 A.2d 318 (Conn. App. Ct. 1993) ["*Gemme v Goldberg*"].
23 *Gemme v Goldberg* at 326.
24 S. 25.4, RSBC, 1996.
25 Ibid.
26 S. 15.1, ibid.
27 "Strict liability", which is liability without fault under Canadian tort law, is used here to capture the nature of the general rule that health professionals cannot practice outside their professional scopes of practice without incurring malpractice liability. Fault-based liability, of course, involves negligent actions or the intention to harm. As already discussed above, physicians were *stricto sensu* liable for malpractice for practicing CAM whether or not they conducted the CAM practice negligently. The mere act of deviation from what is considered "standard or prevailing practice" was sufficient to incur liability.
28 Joseph A. Barrette, "Complementary and Alternative Medicine" in S. S. Sanbar, *Legal Medicine* (Philadelphia: Mosby/Elsevier, 2007) at 69 ["Sanbar, *Legal Medicine*"]; *Gonzalez v New York Department of Health*, 232 A.D. 2D 886 (3d Dept. 1996).
29 La Reg. tit. 46, §7103–7107 (2001) (Professional and Occupational Standards); Sanbar, *Legal Medicine*, ibid. at 69.
30 *Ravikovich v College of Physicians and Surgeons of Ontario*, [1997] OJ No 1625 (CA) (QL) ["*Ravikovich*"].
31 This principle is recognized under Ontario Law: O. Reg 52/95, made under the *Medicine Act*, 1991.
32 Tom L. Beauchamp and James F. Childress, *Principles of Biomedical Ethics*, 7th edn (Oxford: Oxford University Press, 2013) at 150 ["Beauchamp and Childress, *Principles of Biomedical Ethics*"].
33 Ibid.
34 Ibid. at 154.
35 I. O. Iyioha, "Medical Negligence" in I. O. Iyioha and R. N. Nwabueze, eds., *Comparative Health Law and Policy: Critical Perspectives on Nigerian and Global Health Law* (Farnham: Ashgate, 2015) ["Iyioha and Nwabueze, *Comparative Health Law and Policy*"].
36 Beauchamp and Childress at 153.
37 Ibid. at 154.
38 Ibid.
39 Ibid.
40 Ibid. at 154–155.
41 Ibid. at 155.
42 Ibid. at 155.
43 Ibid. Emphasis added.
44 V. A. Sharpe and A. I. Faden, *Medical Harm: Historical, Conceptual, and Ethical Dimensions of Iatrogenic Illness* (Cambridge: Cambridge University Press, 1998) at 124 ["Sharpe and Faden, *Medical Harm*"].
45 *Schneider v Revici*, 817 F.2d 987(2nd Cir 1987). See also Iyioha, *Health Governance*, supra; I. O. Iyioha, "Medical Integration: Law and Policy on Alternative and Integrative Medical Practice" in Iyioha and Nwabueze, *Comparative Health Law and Policy*.
46 Ibid.
47 Iyioha, *Health Governance*, ibid.; Irehobhude O. Iyioha, "Informed Choice in Alternative Medicine: Expanding the Doctrine Beyond Conventional Alternative Therapies" (2007) 5:2 *ICFAI Journal of Health Care Law* 8 (Reprinted in S. Sudarshan, ed., *Consent in Law: Problems and Perspectives*, Hyderabad: ICFAI University Press, 2008).
48 Sharpe and Faden, *Medical Harm* at 132.
49 Ibid.
50 Ibid.

51 Iyioha, *Health Governance* at 368, 370.
52 Cohen, *Beyond Complementary Medicine* at 23–34; Iyioha, *Health Governance* at 367.
53 For more on this issue, see Iyioha, *Health Governance, supra.*
54 For a discussion of the co-option model of integration, see D. J. Tataryn and M. J. Verhoef, "Combining Conventional, Complementary and Alternative Health Care: A Vision of Integration" in *Perspectives on Alternative and Complementary Health Care: A Collection of Papers Prepared for Health Canada* (Ottawa: Health Canada, 2001); see also Iyioha, *Health Governance*, chapter 5.
55 See ibid., Iyioha, *Health Governance.*
56 Iyioha, *Health Governance* at 369.
57 Ibid.
58 Iyioha, *Health Governance* at 371.
59 A discussion of this ethical conflict is beyond the scope of this paper. For a comprehensive discussion of this and medical ethics generally, see Beauchamp and Childress, *The Principles of Biomedical Ethics, supra.*
60 College of Physicians and Surgeons of Ontario, Discipline Committee Decisions: Dr. Felix Ravikovich (undated) (www.cpso.on.ca) Reported in: CPSO, Member's Dialogue, January 1996: Case no. 4.
61 Cohen, *Beyond Complementary Medicine* at 34.
62 Cohen's meaning is disputable depending on whether the author employs "conventional care" to simply mean "biomedicine" or whether the term is to be read as an omnibus expression for both biomedicine and CAM.
63 Iyioha, *Health Governance* at 373.
64 Ibid.
65 Ibid.

References

Barrette, Joseph A. "Complementary and Alternative Medicine" in S. S. Sanbar, *Legal Medicine* (Philadelphia: Mosby/Elsevier, 2007).

Beauchamp, T. L. and Childress, J. F. *The Principles of Biomedical Ethics*, 7th edn (New York: Oxford, 2013).

Chaikand, H., Copeland, C. W., Redhead, C. S. and Staiman, J. "PPACA: A Brief Overview of the Law, Implementations, and Legal Challenges" (CRS Report for Congress, 2011), online, www.nationalaglawcenter.org/assets/crs/R41664.pdf.

Cohen, M. H. *Beyond Complementary Medicine: Legal and Ethical Perspectives on Health Care and Human Evolution* (Ann Arbor: The University of Michigan Press, 2003).

College of Physicians and Surgeons of Ontario, Discipline Committee Decisions: Dr. Felix Ravikovich (undated) (www.cpso.on.ca) Reported in: CPSO, Member's Dialogue, January 1996: Case no. 4.

Gemme v Goldberg, 626 A.2d 318 (Conn. App. Ct. 1993).

Gonzalez v New York Department of Health, 232 A.D. 2D 886 (3d Dept. 1996).

Health Canada Baseline Natural Health Products Survey Among Consumers: *Final Report, 2005*, online: Health Canada, www.hc-sc.gc.ca/dhp-mps/alt_formats/hpfb-dgpsa/pdf/pubs/eng_cons_survey-eng.pdf.

Health Professions Act, RSBC 1996, c. 183.

Health Professions Act, RSA 2000, c. H-7.

Health Professions Act, RSA 2000 c. H-7 Sched. 21 s. 5; 2008 c. 34 s. 30.

Iyioha, Irehobhude O. "Medical Negligence" in Iyioha, I. O. and Nwabueze, R. N. (eds) *Comparative Health Law and Policy: Critical Perspectives on Nigerian and Global Health Law* (Farnham: Asgate, 2015).

Iyioha, Irehobhude O. *Health Governance, Medical Pluralism and the Politics of Integration: A Legal Theory for Increasing Access to Healthcare* (UBC Libraries: PhD Dissertation, 2010).

La Reg. tit. 46, §7103-7107 (2001) (Professional and Occupational Standards).

Medicine Act, S.O. 1991, c. 30.

Nadeem, Esmail "Complementary and Alternative Medicine in Canada: Trends in Use and Public Attitudes: 1997–2006" (2007) 87 *Public Policy Sources* 1–53.

N.C. Gen. Stat. 90-14(a)(6).

Ontario Law: O. Reg 52/95, made under the *Medicine Act*, 1991.

Patient Protection and Affordable Care Act (PPACA).

Ravikovich v College of Physicians and Surgeons of Ontario, [1997] OJ No 1625 (CA) (QL).

Re Guess, 393 S.E.2d.

Sharpe, V. A. and Faden, A. I. *Medical Harm: Historical, Conceptual, and Ethical Dimensions of Iatrogenic Illness* (Cambridge: Cambridge University Press, 1998).

Tataryn, D. J. and Verhoef, M. J. "Combining Conventional, Complementary and Alternative Health Care: A Vision of Integration" in *Perspectives on Alternative and Complementary Health Care: A Collection of Papers Prepared for Health Canada* (Ottawa: Health Canada, 2001).

Wash. Rev. Code Ann. S. 18.130.180(4).

11

RISK AND REGULATION

CAM products, practitioners and the state – perspectives on 'risk' and 'protection of the public' in the Australian media

Monique Lewis

I Introduction

This chapter has arisen from my research into mainstream newspaper reports on herbal medicine in Australia. The objectives were to determine the dominant topics and frames that occurred in media reports about herbal medicine over a five-year period, and to measure the prevalence of risk references in newspaper reports during this timeframe. Sociological investigations into media representations of herbal medicine (and CAM, more broadly) are not common. My research attempts to address a gap in the research, using an interdisciplinary approach that draws from sociological theories of health, medicine and CAM, as well as media and risk. The research systematically measures the frequency of various themes and framings, using content analysis.

Consistent and vigilant attention to and commentary about CAM news frames can contribute to supporting a critical literacy of health issues as well as what the media tells us about them. Media framing analysis highlights the importance of understanding news culture and news-making in a broader sociopolitical and cultural context that considers the news institutions and journalists themselves (subject to timing and opportunity), as well as those news sources or 'claims-makers' who communicate their messages to media and compete to have their 'reality' dominate the news frame (Johnson-Cartee, 2005).

As a marginalised form of medicine, exploration of these representations reveals the tenuous position of herbal medicine in the context of mainstream Australian healthcare. My findings demonstrate the extent to which the stigmas of benignity and the placebo effect have subsided (although certainly not disappeared), making way for an increasing recognition of plants as substances that are pharmacologically active and potent. These representations occur in both scientific and lay discourses (Lewis, 2011a), although this chapter focuses on the lay discourses found in mainstream news reports. Through the analysis of media representations, it becomes apparent that risk discourses have ultimately helped rather than hindered this more recent positioning of herbal medicine in the Australian healthcare landscape. At the same time, herbal medicines remain peripheral to mainstream Australian healthcare. The omission of any herbal medicine products from the Australian Pharmaceutical Benefits Scheme (PBS),[1] and the fact that herbal medicine practitioners and naturopaths are unregulated and excluded from the government's Medicare scheme, draws a picture of herbal medicine's marginalised position in the healthcare context.

The media representations of herbal medicine under analysis here do demonstrate sociopolitical responses from a range of stakeholders in the face of a 'CAM uprising' which poses a substantial challenge to biomedical dominance in Australian society and culture.

This chapter first addresses the relevance of understanding media literacy and the news construction process in a world of ever-flowing news stories, which is a driving force of my research. I contextualise the modernisation of herbal medicine in Australia, offering insight into the consequences of its scientisation, pharmaceuticalisation and commercialisation. I also highlight the subsequent tensions that have arisen between evidence-based medicine (EBM) and traditional herbal medicine researchers and practitioners. The issues surrounding the culture and politics of risk are presented, drawing from risk society and complexity theories. These are particularly useful in understanding the challenges posed by herbal medicine to biomedical hegemony, and the rhetorical tactics that arise in response to these challenges. An overview of other CAM media research is provided, presenting the range of findings of other relevant media research to date, some of which are contradicted by my findings. The method of content analysis that considered both manifest and latent codes is then described, followed by the research findings.

II Background

Despite the increasing proliferation of peer-review articles and scholarly books about CAM therapies, practice and usage, the sociology of CAM is still a very young sub-discipline. Given the well-documented burgeoning application of CAM therapies worldwide, whether practitioner-based or self-prescribed, the particular phenomenon of CAM in the media remains relatively unexplored, with barely a 12-year history in the Western scholarly literature (Lewis, 2011a; Weeks & Strudsholm, 2008). Sociological explorations of CAM and media are relevant for a range of reasons that encompass issues of health and media literacy, influences on health choices and behaviours, policy-making, the politics of representation and expert versus lay knowledges.

Sociological analyses of risk discourse and CAM are also limited, with the exception of Broom and Adams (2009), Broom and Doron (2013), Lewis (2011a, 2011b) and O'Neill (1994) and, to an extent, Connor (2012). Although often essential in maintaining the safety of a society's citizens, risk discussions are not always directed towards enhancing our understanding of what is safe and what is dangerous, or potentially so. In these conversations, we need to pose questions that identify which risks are under the microscope, who is identifying and discussing them, and how the debates or issues about risk are being represented or constructed (Kitzinger, 1999a). Such an approach reveals much about the complexities of risk discourses, taking into account the dynamics of government regulation, professional tensions, professional boundary-making and moral governance.

In this chapter, I apply a social constructionist perspective to understanding CAM media representations. Social constructionism in media analysis regards media texts as part of a construction process influenced by news-makers and news institutions, sources and 'claims-makers'. However, I am cognisant of the varying extremes this constructionist stance can take, wary of surrendering to the postmodern realms of relativism and the view that *all* realities are purely constructs, based on individual subjective experiences.[2] The relativist assumption, as Philo and Miller (2001) point out, can potentially lead to a dead end, theoretically speaking, in which social action becomes discouraged as the focus is taken off the role of power relations. I tend to agree with Philo and Miller, and believe a more helpful and useful schema is one that approaches media as a powerful sociocultural, political and economic phenomenon, where society's groups or individuals often battle to have their own truth emerge most prominently.

This approach highlights the subjectivities inherent in any knowledge-forms, including scientific knowledge, which cannot be assumed to operate in a vacuum, untainted by social, cultural, economic or political influences. Notably, in a world of competition for funding and professional and academic territoriality and positioning, efforts surrounding the development, enhancement and promotion of scientific knowledge must be recognised as highly subjective.

III The power of media representations

In an information-driven society with the 'need to know' as an integral part of our social development (Hudson, 2006), media literacy is essential. Numerous scholarly writings on health media reporting tend to carry consensus on a key point: the lack of 'accuracy' (Bubela, Caulfield & Boon, 2006b; Gerbner, Gross, Morgan & Signoriellei, 1981; Karpf, 1988; MacDonald & Hoffman-Goetz, 2002; Moynihan, Bero, Ross-Degman & Henry, 2000; Oxman *et al.*, 1993; Schudson, 2002; Schwartz & Woloshin, 2004; Signoriellei, 1993; Stryker, 2002; Voss, 2002; Wilson, Bonevski, Jones & Henry, 2009; Woloshin & Schwartz, 2006). Given the pervasive presence of new and various media forms in our daily lives, and the subsequent and constant flow of new information that is incessantly and so readily available to us, we may accept that inaccuracies in reports about health issues are 'almost inevitable', as Seale (2010) suggests. Media sociologist Jenny Kitzinger has pointed out the limitations of focusing solely on the matter of 'accuracy' in media reporting and reflects on the value of accepting media as a 'legitimate alternative space for debate' rather than 'an inadequate transmitter of information' (Kitzinger, 1999b). Whilst this pragmatic, sceptical approach may save us all a lot of grief in our reading of media messages, it is not necessarily effective in practice, as audience reception research of health messages indicates (Clarke, Arnold, Everest & Whitfield, 2007; Davin, 2005; DeSilva, Muskavitch & Roche, 2004). In fact, our scepticism and critical appraisal of the media messages we receive with such frequency are not what one might assume, considering the prominent role media plays in many of our lives. A recent survey of 25 countries by public relations firm Edelman, which measured people's levels of 'trust' towards different institutions, pointed towards an actual *rise* in people's levels of trust towards the media (and a decline in trust of other institutions, notably government), especially towards social media and, perhaps surprisingly, more traditional forms of television, radio and newspaper reporting (Edelman, 2012).

Whilst accuracy and quality of reporting about health issues draws necessary attention in academic literature, there is substantially more to consider. News reporting is not simply a matter of journalists assembling a series of narrativised 'facts' for audiences, as we well know. Also to consider is the interweaving and embedding of perspectives, discourses, systems of knowledge, rhetorics and even ideologies that are typically being reproduced and reinforced, and which contribute to the construction of certain realities or 'truths' (Lewis, 2011a; Seale, 2003). Other discourses or perspectives may be incorporated into the media story; however, it is understanding the dominant 'frame' – those selected aspects of a perceived reality which are most prominent – that offers a richer, more comprehensive level of insight into media representations (Entman, 2007).

Although the extent to which news sways audiences is a contentious topic, there has been a substantial amount of research to demonstrate just how much media messages can and do influence people (Clarke *et al.*, 2007; Iyengar, 1994; Kitzinger, 1999b; Philo, 1993) as well as institutions and organisations (Gans, 2003). News is a genre that we are more likely to take seriously than other genres, and we tend to have faith in it as an objective representation of facts (Philo & Miller, 2001; Schudson, 2003). News journalists may also be less aware of their engagement in the framing process than if they were writing an opinion piece, a blog or a piece of political satire, for example (Entman, Matthes & Pellicano, 2009). Mainstream news has been shown to set the agenda for how other forms of media, such as blogs, may cover an issue (Lee, 1996; Lee, 2007).

In 2003, Australia experienced an unprecedented recall of over 1600 therapeutic products, most of which were herbal medicines (HM) and nutritional supplements manufactured by a company called Pan Pharmaceuticals. The recall incident received saturation media coverage and brought about policy changes in relation to the way in which HM and CAM are regulated in Australia. Although the event was based on a risk episode relating to Pan's poor manufacturing practices and falsification of product testing results, the effect was the adoption of broader issues about HM and CAM in Australia by the media. Dramatically, the recall, with an initial magnitude of 219 products, occurred in conjunction with the suspension of the manufacturing licence of Pan Pharmaceuticals after it was determined by the Therapeutic Goods Administration (TGA) and an independent expert advisory committee that the products, manufactured by Pan Pharmaceuticals, posed a risk to consumers, given the 'serious safety and quality breaches' by Pan (TGA, 28 April 2003). The initial recall figure of 219 products multiplied over the following weeks as further products manufactured by Pan were identified. The Pan incident has been noted as the largest medicines recall of its kind in Australasian history (Croucher, 2009; Eagle, Hawkins, Rose & Kitchen, 2004).

As a direct consequence of the Pan event, the Australian government made amendments to the Therapeutic Goods Act 1989, which increased penalties for offences by manufacturers under the Act and added offences to the Act regarding falsification of documents. Further amendments gave the TGA greater enforcement powers to ensure compliance with the Act, including the ability to administer on-the-spot fines to non-compliant companies (2006). To the benefit of industry and universities, research funding arose in the wake of Pan, following the recommendations by an Expert Committee on Complementary Medicines. In November 2006, the Federal government committed $5 million for National Health and Medical Research Council (NHMRC) grants for CAM research and the establishment of the National Institute of Complementary Medicines (NICM) in 2007, which received $4.6 million from federal and state governments.

The role played by the media in the Pan event – which was indeed also a media event – is suggestive of the potential influence of news reports on public policy. As Gans (2003: 98) has pointed out, although news media cannot control their audiences and may not even be able to attract their attention to political news, public officials still need to act 'as if an audience is paying attention'.

IV Scientisation and pharmaceuticalisation

Herbal medicine is evolving as one of the more broadly 'acknowledged' CAM therapies by governments and even some of the more historically reluctant biomedically based institutions. Studies have suggested that between 16 and 23 per cent of Australians use Western herbal medicine products (MacLennan, Myers & Taylor, 2006; Xue, Zhang, Lin, Da Costa & Story, 2007; Zhang, Story, Lin, Vitetta & Xue, 2008), with a cross-sectional population survey of 2526 people in the state of Victoria indicating the highest users were women, adults aged between 35 and 54 years of age and people with a higher education qualification (Zhang *et al.*, 2008). Over 90 per cent of the users reported to have found the herbs beneficial, the most common of which were aloe vera, garlic, green tea, chamomile, Echinacea and ginger (Zhang *et al.*, 2008: 1008).

Zhang and colleagues (2008) note even higher rates for garlic and Echinacea use in an earlier survey of a rural community in New South Wales (Wilkinson & Simpson, 2001). Half of the people in the Zhang study self-prescribed their herbal medicine products (Zhang *et al.*, 2008: 1008).

As acknowledged pharmacologically active substances, plants are gaining more acceptance in the context of pharmacy and phytochemistry and, gradually, gaining credibility within the bio-medical paradigm (Lewis, 2011a: 4). For example, in the laboratory, plant medicines can be 'reduced' to their active constituents, via the scientific technologies of high performance liquid chromatography and nuclear magnetic resonance, thus providing the logic and rationale for the effectiveness of the herb in relation to specific conditions or symptoms. Researchers can system-atically measure the effectiveness of botanical medicines through randomised, controlled, double-blind clinical trials. Based on this systematic approach as a gold standard, the US Federal Drug Administration (FDA) has recently approved America's first oral herbal medicine, Cro-felemer (also known as Fulzaq), derived from an Amazon tree, for the relief of diarrhoea in HIV patients. Whilst there are no prescription-only botanical products in Australia, Omacor, a fish oil-derived medicine, was approved by the TGA as a prescription medicine in 2011.

The research activities associated with herbal medicines demonstrate what has been referred to as 'pharmaceuticalisation', the process of investigating herbal medicines using the tools of modern pharmacological research and medical clinical trials as a basis for acceptance (Lewis, 2011a: 4). The evidence-based approach to understanding herbal medicine's effectiveness has received criticism from herbalists and CAM sociologists, largely based on the contended incom-mensurability between the principles of evidence-based medicine and those of vitalism (Evans, 2008a, 2008b; Kim, 2007; Jagtenberg *et al.*, 2006; Coulter & Willis, 2004; Jagtenberg & Evans, 2003; Van Marie, 2002). Evidence-based medicine is guided by the results of systematic meas-urement in the biomedical frameworks of randomised controlled trials that are double-blinded and preferably subjected to meta-analyses. Vitalism in herbal practice, in contrast, is guided by the focus to strengthen the body's own innate natural healing capacities using traditional know-ledge of plant medicines as well as clinical experience.[3]

Kim (2007) argues that, problematically, the laboratory becomes something of an assembly line, a 'political machine' dedicated to proving that the medicines work – resulting in an 'iden-tity crisis' for Korean medicine that involves the decoupling of herbal theory and herbal mater-ials as the research agenda is purely based on the 'chemical activities' of the herbs alone, rendering obsolete any questions of the 'qi', flavour, ascension and descension, and tract affinity that is present in the philosophy of Chinese and Korean medicine (2007: 863–864). While traditional-ists of herbal medicine practice and philosophies may lament such reductionism, an evidence-based approach offers a basis for acceptance that becomes impossible to refute within the scientific and biomedical community and gatekeepers. The problem of 'incommensurability', at least from the biomedical perspective, becomes irrelevant (Willis & White, 2004). Therefore, while herbal therapies may be accepted into the mainstream using an EBM approach, the philo-sophies underlying their usage may not be considered at all. This is demonstrative of herbal medicine gaining acceptance, but only on the terms dictated by biomedicine.

The definition of pharmaceuticalisation is not restricted to the incorporation of scientific methods alone. It also takes into account the commercialisation of herbal medicine and the sub-sequent marketing tactics, which employ trademark pharmaceutical-style branding of products, using product names that resemble pharmaceutical medications, thus appealing to the con-temporary 'pharma brandscape' (Robins, 2006) and drawing from a range of symbols in lan-guage and imagery to create an authentic 'aura' of science. For example, a contemporary print advertisement for a herbal medicine or nutraceutical product often features symbols that align it with a peer-reviewed journal article, such as numbered citations within the promotional text accompanied by a reference list at the end.

Pharma-branding and pharmaceuticalisation are important elements to consider in understanding the evolution of botanical medicine's commercial and academic success in industrial modernity. It is also a reason for much criticism levelled at the industry in Australia, as having 'Listed' (labelled as AUST L) medicine status on the Australian Register of Therapeutic Goods (ARTG) has been criticised as an illegitimate and unethical 'free ticket', an unacceptable appropriation of pharmaceutical tactics, without the strict testing requirements that gain a pharmaceutical product entry into the market (see Harvey, Korczak, Marron & Newgreen, 2007). Listed complementary medicine products are not individually evaluated for efficacy by the TGA, and Harvey *et al.* (2008) argue that, contrary to the claims of the TGA, they are not appropriately evaluated for quality and safety. The TGA relies on sponsors holding information to substantiate any claims that are made and does not have the capacity to individually assess such a vast range of AUST L products. In contrast, registered products ('AUST R'), of which there are currently 30 in Australia, do receive individual government evaluation for the marketplace, based on the ingredients or indications that are considered by the TGA to hold a higher level of risk.[4]

The next section provides a historical and sociological context for understanding risk in contemporary society, and the limitations of understanding risk through scientific reductionism alone.

V The culture and politics of risk

The twentieth century, a 'golden age' of science, medicine, technology and industrialisation, was also a period that became increasingly characterised by mistrust of the expert knowledge that had been assuring us of the safety of thalidomide, tobacco, nuclear power and reprocessing plants, the insecticide dichlorodiphenyltrichloroethane (DDT) and, more recently, the ideology of a free-market economy (Lewis, 2011a: 67). Risks and side-effects, at the regulatory level at least, were deemed part and parcel of having access to new technologies and potent medicines. However, with increasing public awareness of the impact of these biological and environmental risks, frequently perceived as being tainted by commercial interests, a risk society emerged, strongly characterised by an increasing mistrust towards expert scientific knowledge and advice (Giddens, 1990; Beck, 1992, 1999; Wynne, 1996).

In Western industrialised societies, 'risk assessment' demonstrates the endeavour to quantify 'probabilities and consequences' from the processes we undertake in our daily lives (Wynne, 1987: 2). However, scientific reductionism provides a limited way of understanding risk and 'failure' in risk management, as illustrated by complexity theory. The complexity systems approach, extensively theorised by Dekker, demands sociocultural, political, environmental and economic scrutiny of the entire complex system involved (such as medicine or aviation, for example) rather than the individual components of the system (like an individual nurse or a pilot) that may have resulted in a risk event, or the 'drift into failure' (Dekker, 2011). Dekker's work explores the consequences of how an organisation like a hospital can engage in activities reminiscent of sixteenth-century 'witch hunts' when, for example, a nurse fatally administers the wrong medicine to a patient:

> Inventing and accentuating deviance by identifying witches (or, in late modernity, criminally deviant nurses) served functions of setting moral boundaries, which augmented cohesion among the 'non-deviant' and reinstated a chimera of control over destiny in an otherwise complex and confusing world.
>
> *(Dekker, 2007: 469)*

Dekker's observations on risk and human error highlight the limitations of relying on science to understand risk, as well as the boundary work that goes on, in which risk rhetorics become employed to unite the 'non-deviant' in a moral struggle, and sift out the 'deviant' from the ranks. Risk rhetorics are used in the 'manufacturing of believable deviance' – and are a tactic to regain control in the face of the 'erosion or absence of moral norms governing social interaction and accountability' (Dekker, 2007: 469).

An analogy can be made here with CAM. In the face of a 'CAM uprising', which challenges biomedical practice and knowledge systems, the moral order is clearly disrupted, and rhetorical tactics are employed to reassert control in influencing our therapeutic choices. In the field of oncology in Australia, risk is used as a rhetorical device to divert patients away from using CAM, despite the lack of knowledge or evidence for doing this (Broom & Adams, 2009). This has been seen in India as well, where oncologists were found to refer to 'pollution' and 'toxicity' as the main dangers of the CAM therapies that their patients were using (Broom & Doron, 2013).

VI An overview of CAM media research

My own primary research focuses on news stories about herbal medicine in mainstream Australian newspapers. Mainstream newspapers (both online and print) play an important role in setting the news agenda and have a substantial influence on politicians and opinion-leaders (ABA, 2000; Nichols, 2007; Pearson & Brand, 2001: 9). In print journalism, there are also fewer available resources for embellishments to the story, as with television news and current affairs reporting in particular. Research of health reporting in Australia has indicated that newspapers provide a higher 'quality' of news presentation (Bonevski, Wilson & Henry, 2008: 6; Wilson *et al.*, 2009: 4), which also applies to articles about CAM (Bonevski *et al.*, 2008).

A number of studies have indicated trends in media reports on CAM, finding that articles were largely positive and uncritical about CAM, with under-representation of negative reports (Weeks & Strudsholm, 2008; Ernst, 2004; Kava, Meister, Whelan, Lukachko & Mirabile, 2002; Milazzo & Ernst, 2006; Shaw, Zhang & Metallinos-Katsaras, 2009). Content analyses looking at representations of dietary supplements (Kava *et al.*, 2002; Shaw *et al.*, 2009) and antioxidants (Lewis, Orrock & Myers, 2010; Uusitalo, Ovaskainen & Prattala, 2000) have referred to other problems with media reports in terms of accuracy and product claims (Shaw *et al.*, 2009), omission of information about safety (Kava *et al.*, 2002; Shaw *et al.*, 2009) and confusing and conflicting information from expert claims-makers (Uusitalo *et al.*, 2000).

In Canada, researchers have investigated herbal medicine reports specifically (Bubela, Boon & Caulfield, 2008; Bubela, Caulfield & Boon, 2006a, 2006b; Bubela, Koper, Boon & Caulfield, 2007), framing their research around errors of omission and under-reporting of risk, as well as the lack of disclosure of clinical trial funding and potential conflicts of interest discovered in the articles. In contrast to the findings of the content analyses cited above, these Canadian researchers revealed that newspaper coverage of herbal remedy clinical trials was more negative, particularly in comparison to pharmaceutical trials.

Two separate studies took into account reports on risk as well as benefits, which were based on articles referring to CAM usage and cancer (Weeks, Verhoef & Scott, 2007; Mercurio & Eliott, 2009). Both studies found that reports about risk in relation to CAM usage were outweighed by stories about benefits, as well as a predominance of personal anecdotes and biomedical practitioners as sources.

A study by this author that specifically investigated the biomedical media genre yielded quite different findings (Lewis, 2011a). This longitudinal content analysis of Australia's primary peer-reviewed medical publication, the *Medical Journal of Australia*, found that risk was the dominant issue in articles about CAM or herbal medicine over a 42-year period (Lewis, 2011a). This study was a precursor to the newspaper content analysis discussed in the following section.

My study is distinct for its specific investigation of the mainstream news genre in an Australian context, and its breadth of coding categories that covered issues of risk, efficacy, research, regulation, industry and ethics. Additionally, this study also took into account the key sources used in each article and sought to determine which themes and framings occurred most frequently amongst source categories, also considering positive and negative intonation of both articles and headlines.

Additionally, I was particularly interested in how mainstream news stories about risk were framed, and whether these risk-based articles were prevalent in comparison to other themes. This research has been the first of its kind to consider risk in relation to herbal medicine discourse in Australian mainstream news and offers insight into how and why such representations contribute to the construction of herbal medicine risk. Risk representations may influence people's usage of herbal medicine, its acceptance by the mainstream health professions, its place in the Australian healthcare system and the formulation of public policy.

VII Method: content analysis of mainstream Australian newspapers

The study was a content analysis of news reports in 18 mainstream national and metropolitan Australian newspapers about herbal medicine, from January 2005 to May 2010. Content analysis is useful as a method for mapping the frequency of ideas, opinions and political leanings in texts (Krippendorff, 2004: xiii–xiv). It is also a powerful method for making explicit facts about content, which may not be immediately obvious (Stokes, 2003: 66). This was a mixed methods approach, using both manifest and latent content analysis. Manifest analysis involves systematically counting the literal or denotative meanings that are explicit with the text, whereas latent analysis explores the less obvious connotative meanings behind the words, or the way in which the story is framed.

For the manifest analysis, 45 coding categories were devised in order to measure their frequency of reference during the period of analysis. The codes covered issues of herbal medicine risk, benefit, quality, regulation and research, as well as items that were sociocultural and political in nature. For the latent analysis, 55 codes were devised to measure the frequency of particular themes, how the stories were framed, positive and negative intonation, as well as the main sources of information used by the journalist.

Australian daily metropolitan and national newspapers were selected for the study, excluding *The Australian Financial Review*, which is more oriented towards business and finance than general news stories. Factiva, Newsbank and Fairfax newspaper databases were searched from the period 1 January 2005 until 30 April 2010.[5] From the searches of these databases, 401 articles were sourced, which after applying the inclusion and exclusion criteria, were reduced to a total of 139 articles.

The data for both manifest and latent analyses was interpreted using a univariate technique (for example, the occurrence of the news frame: 'HM is effective') as well as a multivariate approach, which examined the news frame, as well as whether the story was positive or negative, and the main sources used in the news story. Two coders were used to establish intercoder reliability. Coding was undertaken independently with 14 per cent overlap for the reliability test. The reliability study showed a substantial level of intercoder agreement (0.68 for manifest codes and 0.72 for latent). The finalised manifest and latent codings were entered into an SPSS database for descriptive data analysis.

VIII Findings

In this section, I will present the results from the content analysis and discuss the findings. Given that risk was a prominent feature of the findings, the discussion will focus on the different types of risk representations that occurred. The level of references to efficacy are also significant, particularly given the high rate of risk framings, and will be presented in this section.

Figure 11.1 indicates that the year 2005 saw the greatest proportion of articles about herbal medicine (35/139) followed by 2006 (28/139 articles). In both 2007 and 2008, there were 25 articles, with the lowest proportion of articles in the study occurring in 2009 (17/139). It is important to note that the 2010 period measured only extends to the end of April, which was the cut-off point for the data collation.

There was a high rate of negativity in headlines (63.3 per cent) and article tone (53.2 per cent) overall. Little distinction was found between how tabloid and broadsheets reported on herbal medicine. Negativity, conflict and drama are important values in the news-making culture (Johnson-Cartee, 2005). News reports about herbal medicine also satisfy the values of relevance and social impact, given its increasing popularity. However, this explanation offers only a partial insight into the nature of the reports, as a risk report does not necessarily come with an overall negative message or intonation. For example, a 2008 study by Bubela, Boon and Caulfield that compared newspaper reports between pharmaceutical and herbal medicine clinical trials demonstrated that the pharmaceutical reports were more likely to be positive and at the same time they were also more likely to refer to risks than the herbal medicine reports. Reference to risk does not necessarily mean that a negative tone prevails, or that risk is the main message. This point offers insight into the complexities of both the research and interpretation process, and highlights why it is so important to take into consideration the prevalent framings.

The negative intonation found in the majority of news reports was also accompanied by a high level of risk items and framings. Table 11.1 shows the results from the manifest analysis based on the five most mentioned items during the period of analysis.

In the manifest analysis (Table 11.1), the most frequent items were the general risk of a herbal medicine product or practitioner (41 per cent), followed by adverse events (33.1 per cent), acknowledgement of efficacy (28.1 per cent), reference to research results (23 per cent) and the need for regulation (22.3 per cent). When manifest codes about risk were clustered, there was a

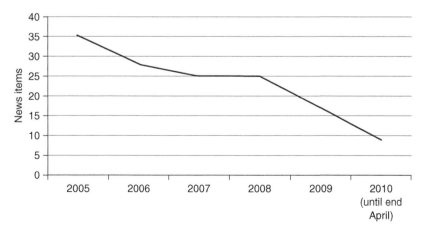

Figure 11.1 Longitudinal frequency of news articles about herbal medicine from January 2005 to end of April 2010.

Table 11.1 Individual items most frequently mentioned in news articles, 2005–2010 (manifest analysis)

Issue coded	Frequency of reference
Risk HM (general risk of HM or general/specific risk of HM practitioner)	41% (57/139)
Adverse events	33.1% (46/139)
Effective	28.1% (39/139)
Research results	23% (32/139)
Regulation needed	22.3% (31/139)
Popularity of HM	18.7% (26/139)
Unscrupulous marketing	18.7% (26/139)
Vulnerable consumers	15.1% (21/139)
Costs/expenditure	13.8% (19/139)
Drug interactions	10.8% (15/139)

frequency of 67.5 per cent, more than double that of clustered 'benefit' codes (see Table 11.2).[6] However, 22.3 per cent of these were stories about the manslaughter and sexual assault trials for two practitioners.

Table 11.2 shows the results for the news frames. The framing of herbal medicine as a product or therapy that is associated with risk was the most pervasive frame in the news reports in mainstream national and metropolitan Australian newspapers over the past five years. Corruption, consumer vulnerability and negligent practitioners were the other main frames used in news discourse about herbal medicine, frames which are related to risk. If the articles based on two prominent court cases during the period of analysis are excluded from the manifest codings, the most commonly mentioned risk is adverse events (33.1 per cent), rather than practitioner

Table 11.2 Frequency of news frames

Frame	Frequency
Risk	38.8% (54/139)
Corruption	25.9% (36/139)
Vulnerable consumer	25.2% (35/139)
HM is effective	20.9% (29/139)
Negligent practitioner	15.1% (21/139)
Regulation necessary for public safety	14.4% (20/139)
Popular HM	12.2% (17/139)
Critique of funding/regulation	10.8% (15/139)
Positive scientific research	8.6% (12/139)
Negative scientific research	7.9% (11/139)
Hope of new research	6.5% (9/139)
HM not effective	5% (7/139)
HM becoming mainstream	3.6% (5/139)
HM more effective/safer than biomedicine/pharmaceuticals	3.6% (5/139)
Business disadvantaged by regulation	3.6% (5/139)
Lucrative industry	2.9% (4/139)
Collaboration	2.9% (4/139)
Beneficial new product	0.7%(1/139)
Research funds needed	0%

risk (41 per cent). While adverse events were mentioned far more often than other risk items, the actual reasons for the adverse events (for example, allergic reactions or toxicity of the plant) were less likely to be mentioned.

Such frequent attention to the 'dodgy practitioner', who has questionable ethics or is being taken to court, has contributed to the risk construction process in Australian news reports in recent years. The 'dodgy practitioner' theme is also popular in news reports about biomedical practitioners, as media representation research has shown (Entwistle & Sheldon, 1999; Lupton & McLean, 1998); however, it is important to note that these frames do not dominate other news about doctors or biomedicine (Lupton & McLean, 1998). Stories about deviant practitioners essentially hold a 'watchdog' function, in which the journalist highlights immorality and reinforces the preservation of moral norms and standards (Gans, 2003, Lewis, 2011a). The complexities of understanding these risk representations are further highlighted by the fact that, despite the proliferation of the 'quack' frame in this particular study, herbal medicine practitioners are also the most highly cited practitioner group in the whole analysis.

In the newspaper findings, we can observe how Australian herbal medicine practitioners may in fact harness the risk agenda in order to legitimise their professional activities, thus contributing to the construction of a risk discourse that is beneficial to them. The Australian Register of Naturopaths and Herbalists (ARONAH), a group advocating registration for these practitioners, appropriated the 'dodgy practitioner' theme to highlight the need for regulating the profession via registration, to ensure the public would not be vulnerable to the unqualified and unethical:

> 'Currently, anyone can hang out their shingle as a herbalist or naturopath and practice without any training whatsoever, and with little accountability. The public is increasingly turning to herbalists and naturopaths so continuing along those lines is clearly untenable', Ms Doolan said.
>
> *(ARONAH media release, 2009)*

The framing of the articles resulting from the ARONAH media release were more oriented towards 'regulation is necessary for public safety' and 'herbal medicine is effective' framings, rather than a broader risk frame; however risk was woven into the articles through the symbol of the 'quack'. Wahlberg (2007: 2315) has noted that the definition of today's dangerous practitioner is now far broader, encompassing both biomedical and CAM practitioners. Instead of the CAM quack, the focus is on whether the practitioner is irresponsible, incompetent or unscrupulous.

Despite the frequency of news stories mentioning adverse events, the actual reason for a herbal medicine product to cause an adverse event was less likely to be mentioned. This satisfies news values of simplicity and journalists' preference for monocausal explanations in news reporting (Stallings, 1990). At the same time, it may suit the needs of claims-makers who may work with the news-makers (for example, via media release or interview) to ensure a risk message dominates the report. Clearly, there is a pattern of news discourse mentioning the dangers of herbal medicine (as a 'sweeping risk' narrative) or practitioners more often than those narratives that consider 'specific risk' attributes of herbal medicine products.

The most frequently specified adverse events were herb–drug interactions (10.8 per cent), toxicity (7.9 per cent) and contamination (7.9 per cent). In a separate study of the *Medical Journal of Australia* by Lewis (2011a), adverse events were the most frequently mentioned item across all articles. This is unsurprising, given that ensuring safety (as well as quality and efficacy) in medicines is a priority defined in the National Medicines Policy[7] and regarded as a government responsibility. At the same time, it must be acknowledged that the high rate of reference to adverse events reflected in both studies is disproportionate to the actual occurrence of adverse events caused by herbal medicines in Australia, particularly in light of the very high rate of iatrogenic injury caused by pharmaceutical products (Roughhead & Semple, 2002: 17). This point about comparative risk or risk ratios was not commonly mentioned in news stories (Lewis, 2011a: 238).

To further explore how herbal medicine risk is talked about, the risk-based stories in this study can be distinguished between 'sweeping risk' stories, which are characterised by the generalisations made about the danger of herbal medicine or CAM products, and 'specific risk' stories, which identified the particular herbal medicine products attributed to the adverse reaction/s. For example, the 'sweeping risk' frame is exemplified in the following article excerpts:

> Some popular herbal remedies can be dangerous, even lethal, contrary to the perception that they are a safer alternative to conventional medicine, a University of Adelaide researcher has warned.
>
> *(Miller, 2010b: 3)*

> The Victorian Cancer Council has declared war on 'cancer quacks' by urging patients to rigorously question 'miracle cures' such as macrobiotic diets and herbal remedies, and to talk to their doctors about them.
>
> *(Medew, 2009: 3)*

> The National Prescribing Service research found complementary medicine was taken by 67 per cent of Australians – a 2004 survey found that half the population did. But many were unaware of risks such as side effects, toxicity and allergies.
>
> *(Miller, 2008: 3)*

> The move [to regulate CAM] comes as many alternative therapies are being revealed as, at best, useless and in some cases dangerous.... Laboratory tests commissioned by the Sunday Herald Sun this week found Chinese herbs bought from two Melbourne outlets contained rat faeces and potentially harmful bacteria.
>
> *(Hinde, 2006: 11)*

This 'sweeping risk' approach is useful for news makers, precisely because it carries ambiguity by not specifying *which* complementary medicines or *which* herbs are under scrutiny. This ambiguity means the story will hold appeal for a broader range of audiences (Johnson-Cartee, 2005: 65). Common treatment recommendations or suggested ways of dealing with the problem being reported (in this case, the risk of using herbal medicine) is for more stringent regulatory controls of herbal medicine or CAM products, or for readers to simply beware, probably not take them and be certain to 'talk to their doctors'. This coheres with reinforcing the hierarchical importance of the doctor in healthcare, typically expressed by a biomedical source from a hospital or university. When sweeping risk stories occur, the source is usually a biomedical researcher or practitioner from a university, a hospital or a medical journal. The model of reporting used in these sweeping risk stories tends to be based on an authoritative style of communication, which Briggs and Hallin (2007) refer to as something of a more outdated 'biomedical-authoritative' model. While we also hear plenty of stories about dangers associated with specified pharmaceutical products, these articles are unlikely to generalise about the dangers of 'pharmaceuticals' per se. This would very quickly be exposed as irresponsible journalism.

In contrast to the sweeping risk frames, 'specific risk' frames were also frequent in risk stories, typically reporting on toxicity, adulteration and unsafe dosages:

> Common over-the-counter herbal remedies [black cohosh products] used by hundreds of women to relieve symptoms of menopause have been linked to at least four cases of liver failure requiring transplants.
>
> *(Crouch, 2007: 12)*

> The nation's drug watchdog is being asked to ban the sale of a herbal weight-loss product on the grounds that it could harm or even kill people, amid claims an active ingredient has been linked to cases of heart complaints overseas.
>
> *(Cresswell, 2009: 3)*

> Malaysia has banned a local herbal medicine after it was found to contain chemicals used in the anti-impotency drug Viagra … the purported herbal medicine, whose manufacturers claimed it promoted general health, was found to be mixed with tadalafil and sildenafil – chemicals that went into making Viagra.
>
> *(Unattributed, 2006: 34)*

> They are called 'Giggle' – but these pills are anything but a laughing matter with a man hospitalised after taking just one of the latest over-the-counter highs that packs the punch of 20 coffees.
>
> *(Jones & Miles, 2009: 2)*

Specific risk stories typically address an audience that is 'actively responsible, information-seeking and self-regulating', rather than 'passive' recipients of health information from an authoritative biomedical source. Unlike the sweeping risk stories, the specific risk stories are more likely to offer alternative viewpoints from the risk frame and are less likely to convey consumers as vulnerable or ignorant. These stories also function to filter warning messages from the TGA about adverse events or recalled herbal medicine products.

This contrast between specific and sweeping risk stories highlights the complexities in understanding how herbal medicine is portrayed in the media and the diverse ways in which risk can be constructed. The articles also demonstrate different approaches to herbal medicine users – who are constructed in the news stories as either passive patients, ignorant of the potential dangers presented by herbal medicine, or as neoliberal subjects, requiring advice in the quest for being active, responsible and self-governing citizens.

IX Sources in risk reports

The sources journalists use in their stories are of course an integral part of the news production process. Taking into account how often different sources and claims-makers are heard, and in what types of stories about herbal medicine, provides valuable insight into the role these sources play in the news articles. The most prominent voices across all article frames were the police and courts (29.5 per cent), universities (25.9 per cent), government (20.9 per cent) and herbal medicine/CAM practitioners (Figure 11.2). Stories with the efficacy frame typically cited or quoted university-based CAM researchers and herbal medicine practitioners. Herbal medicine/CAM practitioners were the most cited practitioner voice across all articles, more than double the frequency of biomedical practitioners. Contrary to other research findings based on CAM media

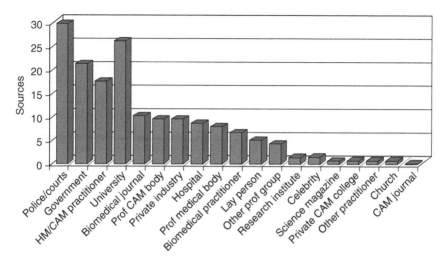

Figure 11.2 Frequency of main source for all news articles (latent analysis).

investigations in Canada and Australia (Mercurio & Eliott, 2009; Weeks & Strudsholm, 2008), lay people and celebrities rarely appeared. CAM journals were not cited as a source in any of the news stories (Figure 11.2).

1 Risk sources

When risk stories were isolated, the main sources and spokespeople referred to were government, universities (mostly from biomedical research) and hospitals (see Table 11.3). Although less frequent as a source overall, hospital sources (only 8.6 per cent) had the most risk frames, which is hardly surprising, given their role at the frontline for serious adverse events. Reports included specific warnings from senior hospital officials after one man's adverse event from taking a recreational guarana-based herbal 'giggle' pill (Jones & Miles, 2009; Miles & Elsworth, 2009) and a broad warning from a senior immunologist about the 'Russian-roulette' risk of taking 'alternative' therapies like Echinacea if you suffer from hay fever (Unattributed, 2005: 19). Articles using hospital sources also included the black cohosh stories, which despite carrying a risk frame did not challenge the validity of women taking black cohosh for menopausal symptoms, acknowledging its 'traditional

Table 11.3 Sources with highest proportion of risk frames

Source	No. articles	Percentage
Hospitals	10/12	83.3
Professional CAM bodies	7/13	53.9
Government	14/29	48.3
Professional medical bodies	5/11	45.5
Biomendical practioners	4/9	44.4
Biomedical journals	6/14	42.9
Universities	14/36	38.9
HM practioner	6/24	25

use by indigenous North Americans' (AAP, 2008: 5). The black cohosh articles characterise a significant attitudinal shift towards herbal medicine reflected by the voice of the hospital physician, through which a product like black cohosh becomes a valid medicine, despite its potential toxicity. The acknowledged potency of the plant imbues it with medical meaning (Lewis, 2011a).

Government sources in articles were typically from the TGA and health government ministers or officials. The high frequencies of government sources in risk stories reflect the importance journalists attribute to government regulators and policy-makers as a source. Government regulatory activities, their media releases about health warnings or published reports and speeches by health ministers each become part of the dynamic process of risk construction. Commonly in health reporting, the government role represented is that of a 'watchdog', reinforcing the message that the government's job is to ensure the quality, safety, efficacy and availability of therapeutic goods in Australia (TGA, 2004: 4). The typical government story functions as a 'top-down' consumer health warning of possible adverse effects. It should be noted that this type of watchdog story is not specific to herbal medicine stories and may also be associated with *any* medicines or medical products.

University status is a powerful asset for claims-makers about herbal medicine in general, including those defining risk. Stories citing university sources featured sweeping risk and practitioner risk items, as well as risks caused by adverse events, drug interactions, contamination and toxicity. The risk frame was used in 14/36 (38.8 per cent) articles citing universities. A series of articles based on the publication of a peer-reviewed article by a professor from the University of Adelaide resulted in the most intensive period of risk coverage citing a university source, with five mainstream newspapers taking up the story as well as radio and television current affairs programmes. Sweeping risk headlines ensued: 'Herbal medicines can kill: researcher' (Miller, 2010a: 2); '"Natural" remedies can prove lethal: research' (Miller, 2010b: 3); 'Deadly remedies' (Unattributed, 2010a: 9); 'Herbal mix can be lethal' (Watson, 2010: 5); 'Herbal cures "a toxic mix"' (Cresswell, 2010: 7); and 'Herbs lethal if misused' (Unattributed, 2010b: 18). Professor Byard's research gave a novel edge to the herb-risk frame, with a lead-in reference to the difficulties facing forensic pathologists testing for toxicity caused by herbal medicines in autopsies. It also satisfied numerous news values, including risk, negativity, human interest, victims and the conflict with 'popular' belief about the safety of herbal medicines. The authoritative and legitimising voice of scientific expertise and peer review is added to the mix. The Byard stories also created space for counter-claims to be heard, which provided a conflicting opinion, albeit one that was subordinate to the main sweeping risk frame. These counter-claims came from a university-based professor of complementary medicine, the president of the National Herbalists' Association of Australia (NHAA) and the former Dean of a private CAM college.

The distinction in tone and framing between articles citing biomedical researchers or CAM researchers in universities is worthy of attention. News stories quoting or citing biomedical researchers were more likely to carry a negative tone and a risk frame, and tended to report more negative findings from scientific research. In contrast, articles citing CAM researchers were substantially more positive, and more likely to refer to efficacy. Either way, the university voice is a privileged one that carries the power to influence news framing. The difference that is highlighted between the two research cultures is an interesting one and warrants further investigation, although it is not within the scope of this research.

Amidst these discrepancies between university sources, there is not yet the data to adequately determine why negative tone and risk reportings are far more aligned with biomedical sources, or why positive articles and efficacy stories are associated more strongly with CAM research sources. Some scholars point towards the bias of biomedical journals (Bubela *et al.*, 2006a, 2006b; Caulfield & DeBow, 2005; Eskinazi & Muehsam, 1999; Polich, Dole & Kaptchuk,

2010; Resch, Ernst & Garrow, 1997) which influence news reports, although in my study only 10 per cent of articles cited research from biomedical journals as a major source. Other studies have suggested that CAM journals, an important site for CAM researchers to publish their research, are more biased towards positive findings (Coelho, Pittler & Ernst, 2007). What my findings may suggest is that news-makers may carry assumptions about the links between bio-medical researchers and negativity, and CAM researchers and positivity, and reproduce these assumptions in the news construction process. Either way, the voice of the university researcher is privileged in health reporting (See Lewis (2011a) for elaboration on source categories from this content analysis).

2 *Efficacy*

From the results, risk-oriented news frames do not tell the whole story. Importantly, efficacy emerged as a frequent item in both latent and manifest analyses, favouring university-based CAM researchers or herbal medicine practitioners as sources. As Tables 11.1 and 11.2 show, stories with framings supporting the effectiveness of herbal medicine appeared 20.9 per cent (29/139 articles) of the time and stories acknowledged efficacy or potential efficacy in 28.1 per cent (39/139) of all articles. Clearly, the idea that herbal medicines work is abundant in Austral-ian mainstream news discourse. I would suggest that the increasing adaptation of efficacy fram-ings is a result of the risk discourse.

Efficacy stories tended to quote university researchers, particularly those from CAM research centres or departments, and herbal medicine practitioners. Most of the articles featuring quotes from ordinary people had efficacy framings. Contradicting other Australian and UK-based research into CAM media reporting, the voices of ordinary people as 'lay heroes' were not common. This could be a consequence of distinguishing 'herbal medicine' from stories that are more broadly about CAM, as well as restricting the investigation to the news genre, specifically.

The growing acceptance that herbs as pharmacologically active substances carry potency that can injure or even kill someone is also accompanied by the notion that they are meaningful medical substances with clout. As the acceptance of their potency increases, so too do the per-ceived proportions of efficacy and risk; this is the risk–efficacy interface. If we look at the research findings of Braun (2006) and Lin *et al.* (2005), we can see evidence of this risk–efficacy correlation being made by hospital physicians and pharmacists as well as general practitioners who were surveyed or interviewed about their perceptions of different complementary thera-pies. Arguably, an association of risk about botanicals has served to convince medical practition-ers of their potential usefulness.

X Conclusion

Medicinal plants have emerged in the twenty-first century as recognised pharmacologically active and potent substances, gradually shedding the stigma of benignity and the placebo effect. The risk discourse that abounds in media discussions about plant medicines does not necessarily negate their use, nor has it appeared to have impacted on the frequency with which people take them. Even during the Pan Pharmaceuticals product recall, in 2003, people continued to take their vitamins and herb products, even though they were aware they had been recalled (Eagle *et al.*, 2004; Needham, 2003) Plants have re-emerged from their twentieth-century 'eclipse', with a new-found medical meaningfulness, but as I have referred to elsewhere, they have become 'tenuous, confusing and ambiguous substances for the modern pharmaceutically-driven phar-macopoeia' (Lewis 2011a).

In Australia, herbal medicine is accepted as a therapeutic substance at the level of government (reflected by the Therapeutic Goods Act), and at the level of postgraduate education and research, as reflected by programmes like the Master of Herbal Medicine at the University of Sydney and the Master of Health Sciences at the University of New England. Medicinal plant products are also heavily commercialised and increasingly commoditised products in the Australian marketplace.

In Australian news reports, risk constructions occur in a range of ways and with different claims-makers, with different agendas. Scientific knowledge plays a pivotal role in risk constructions and is harnessed by these different stakeholder groups, who employ a range of rhetorical tactics to firstly grab media attention and then to have their way of seeing things – their 'truth' – dominate the framing of the article. Importantly, it is most often the privileged and elite voices that are heard in risk reports – typically arising from hospitals, government and universities. Audiences have to struggle to negotiate their way through these multiple risk representations, as well as the other topics and frames that they encounter, as they formulate their opinions and decide whether or not to use herbal medicines.

The construction of risk about herbal medicines is integral to its move towards mainstreaming. Certain groups – researchers and practitioners in particular – have learned how to effectively appropriate risk discourse as a strategy to highlight the benefits of herbal medicine products and practice, and the important role it may play in the modern Australian healthcare system. Ultimately, it is likely that this process of embracing or appropriating risk discourse will continue to contribute to the mainstreaming and acceptance of herbal medicines into the modern, medicalised, healthcare system of Australia.

Acknowledgement

I would like to thank Amanda Wilson from the University of Newcastle for generously offering her wisdom and collaboration in the pilot and intercoder reliability studies for the newspaper content analysis. It was an honour to collaborate with her.

Notes

1 The Pharmaceutical Benefits Scheme (PBS) is a government-funded programme that subsidises the costs of listed pharmaceutical medicines.
2 For elaboration on distinctive levels of constructionism, see Lupton (1999).
3 For a more in-depth discussion of vitalism in relation to herbal practice, see Evans (2008b).
4 www.tga.gov.au/industry/cm-basics-registered.htm#.UsD3KWQW3q8.
5 For the complete list of search terms, see Lewis (2011a, Section 4.8.4, page 137).
6 For a comprehensive account of the results for all 45 codes, see Lewis (2011a: 210–211).
7 www.health.gov.au/internet/main/publishing.nsf/Content/National+Medicines+Policy-2.

References

AAP. (2008, 7 April 2008). Alert on herbal remedy, News. *The Australian*, p. 5.
ABA. (2000). *Revised Project Brief*. Sydney: Australian Broadcasting Authority.
Beck, U. (1992). *Risk Society: Towards a New Modernity*. London: Sage Publications.
Beck, U. (1999). *World Risk Society*. Cambridge: Polity.
Bonevski, B., Wilson, A. & Henry, D. A. (2008). An analysis of news media coverage of complementary and alternative medicine. *PLoS ONE, 3*(6), e2406 (2401–2407).
Braun, L. (2006). *Complementary Medicines in Hospitals: a Focus on Surgical Patients and Safety*. PhD, RMIT University, Melbourne.

Briggs, C. L., & Hallin, D. C. (2007). Biocommunicability: The neoliberal subject and its contradictions in news coverage of health issues. *Social Text, 25*(4), 43–66.

Broom, A., & Adams, J. (2009). Oncology clinicians' accounts of discussing complementary and alternative medicine with their patients. *Health, 13*(3), 317–336.

Broom, A., & Doron, A. (2013). Traditional medicines, collective negotiation, and representations of risk in Indian cancer care. *Qualitative Health Research, 23*(1), 54–65.

Bubela, T., Boon, H. & Caulfield, T. (2008). Herbal remedy clinical trials in the media: A comparison with the coverage of conventional pharmaceuticals. *BMC Medicine, 6*(35).

Bubela, T., Caulfield, T. & Boon, H. (2006a). Media portrayal of conflicts of interest in herbal remedy clinical trials. *Health Law Review, 15*(1), 9–11.

Bubela, T., Caulfield, T. & Boon, H. (2006b). Trends in evidence based medicine for herbal remedies and media coverage. *Health Law Review, 15*(1), 3–6.

Bubela, T., Koper, M., Boon, H. & Caulfield, T. (2007). Media portrayal of herbal remedy versus pharmaceutical clinical trials: Impacts of decision-makers. *Medicine and Law, 26*(2), 363–373.

Caulfield, T., & DeBow, S. (2005). A systematic review of how homeopathy is represented in conventional and CAM peer reviewed journals. *BMC Complementary and Alternative Medicine, 12*.

Clarke, J. N., Arnold, S., Everest, M. & Whitfield, K. (2007). The paradoxical reliance on allopathic medicine and positivist science among skeptical audiences. *Social Science & Medicine, 64*, 164–173.

Coelho, H., Pittler, M. & Ernst, E. (2007). An investigation of the contents of complementary and alternative medicine journals. *Alternative Therapies in Health and Medicine, 13*(4), 40–44.

Connor, L. (2012). Relief, risk and renewal: Mixed therapy regimens in an Australian suburb. In J. Adams, G. J. Andrews, J. Barnes, A. Broom & P. Magin (Eds), *Traditional, Complementary and Integrative Medicine*. Hampshire, UK: Palgrave Macmillan.

Coulter, I., & Willis, E. (2004). The rise and rise of complementary and alternative medicine: A sociological perspective. *Medical Journal of Australia, 180*(11), 587–589.

Cresswell, A. (2009, 8 April 2009). Ban urged on weight-loss medicine, News. *The Australian*, p. 3.

Cresswell, A. (2010, 9 February 2010). Herbal cures 'a toxic mix', News. *The Australian*, p. 7.

Crouch, B. (2007, 24 June 2007). Herb warning: Liver failure link to natural remedy, June. *Sunday Mail*, p. 12.

Croucher, G. (2009). *A Challenging Communications Environment: Public Information and Pan Pharmaceuticals*. Paper presented at the Australian Political Studies Association Conference 2009, Macquarie University, Australia.

Davin, S. (2005). Public medicine: The reception of a medical drama. In M. King & K. Watson (Eds), *Representing Health: Discourses of Health and Illness in the Media*. Palgrave: Macmillan.

Dekker, S. (2007). Discontinuity and disaster: Gaps and the negotiation of culpability in medication delivery. *Journal of Law, Medicine & Ethics, 35*(3), 463–470.

Dekker, S. W. A. (2011). *Drift into Failure: From Hunting Broken Components to Understanding Complex Systems*. Farnham, UK: Ashgate Publishing Co.

DeSilva, M., Muskavitch, M. A. & Roche, J. P. (2004). Print media covergae of antibiotic resistance. *Science Communication, 26*(1), 31–43.

Eagle, L., Hawkins, J., Rose, L. C. & Kitchen, P. J. (2004). *Product Withdrawal Pandemonium: Marketing Communication Implications from the Pan Pharmaceuticals Product Withdrawals*. Manawatu: Massey University.

Edelman. (2012). *Executive Summary, Edelman Trust Barometer: 2012 Annual Global Study*. Edelman.

Entman, R. M. (2007). Framing bias: media in the distribution of power. *Journal of Communication, 57*, 163–173.

Entman, R. M., Matthes, J. & Pellicano, L. (2009). Nature, sources and effects of news framing. In K. Wahl-Jorgensen & T. Hanitzsch (Eds), *The Handbook of Journalism Studies*. New York: Routledge.

Entwistle, V., & Sheldon, T. (1999). The picture of health? Media coverage of the health service. In B. Franklin (Ed.), *Social Policy, Media and Misrepresentation*. Florence, USA: Routledge.

Ernst, E. (2004). The British press and CAM. *Focus on Alternative and Complementary Therapies, 9*(4), 259–260.

Eskinazi, D., & Muehsam, D. (1999). Is the scientific publishing of complementary and alternative medicine objective? *Journal of Alternative & Complementary Medicine, 5*(6), 587–594.

Evans, S. (2008a). *Challenge, Tension and Possibility: An Exploration into Contemporary Western Herbal Medicine in Australia*. PhD thesis, Southern Cross University, Lismore.

Evans, S. (2008b). Changing the knowledge base in Western herbal medicine. *Social Science & Medicine, 67*(12), 2098–2106.

Gans, H. J. (2003). *Democracy and the News*. Cary, NC, USA: Oxford University Press.

Gerbner, G., Gross, L., Morgan, M. & Signoriellei, N. (1981). Health and medicine on television. *New England Journal of Medicine, 305*(15), 901–904.

Giddens, A. (1990). *The Consequences of Modernity*. Cambridge: Polity Press.

Harvey, K., Korczak, V., Marron, L. & Newgreen, D. (2007). Commercialism, choice and consumer protection: regulation of complementary medicines in Australia. *Medical Journal of Australia, 188*(1), 21–25.

Hinde, S. (2006, 13 August 2006). Herbal potions to be regulated, News. *The Sunday Herald Sun*, p. 11.

Hudson, H. (2006). Universal access to the new information infrastructure. In L. Lievrouw & S. Livingstone (Eds), *The Handbook of New Media: Updated Student Edition*. Thousand Oaks, CA: Sage.

Iyengar, S. (1994). *Is Anyone Responsible? How Television Frames Political Issues*. Chicago and London: University of Chicago Press.

Jagtenberg, T., & Evans, S. (2003). Global herbal medicine: A critique. *The Journal of Alternative and Complementary Medicine, 9*(2), 321–329.

Jagtenberg, T., Evans, S., Grant, A., Howden, I., Lewis, M. & Singer, J. (2006). Evidence-based medicine and naturopathy. *Journal of Alternative & Complementary Medicine, 12*(3), 323–328.

Johnson-Cartee, K. S. (2005). *News Narratives and News Framing*. Lanham, US: Rowman & Littlefield Publishers.

Jones, G., & Miles, J. (2009, 29 September 2009). Health risk in a Giggle pill that can kill, News. *The Daily Telegraph*, p. 2.

Karpf, A. (1988). *Doctoring the Media: The Reporting of Health and Medicine*. London: Routledge.

Kava, R., Meister, K. A., Whelan, E. M., Lukachko, A. M. & Mirabile, C. (2002). Dietary supplement safety information in magazines popular among older readers. *Journal of Health Communication, 7*, 13–23.

Kim, J. (2007). Alternative medicine's encounter with laboratory science: The scientific construction of Korean medicine in a global age. *Social Studies of Science, 37*, 855–880.

Kitzinger, J. (1999a). Researching risk and the media. *Health, Risk & Society, 1*(1), 55–69.

Kitzinger, J. (1999b). A sociology of media power: Key issues in audience reception research. In G. Philo (Ed.), *Message Received: Glasgow Media Group Research 1993–1998*. Harlow: Longman.

Krippendorff, K. (2004). *Content Analysis: an Introduction to its Methodology* (2nd edn). Beverley Hills: Sage.

Lee, C. (1996). Choose your potions: In South Korea, a turf war pits old medicine against new. *Far Eastern Economic Review, 159*(Sep 19), 50–51.

Lee, J. K. (2007). The effect of the internet on homogeneity of the media agenda: A test of the fragmentation thesis. *Journalism and Mass Communication Quarterly, 84*(4), 745–760.

Lewis, M., Orrock, P. & Myers, S. P. (2010). Uncritical reverence in CM reporting: Assessing the scientific quality of Australian news media reports. *Health Sociology Review, 19*(1), 57–73.

Lewis, M. (2011a). *Herbal Medicine and Risk Constructions: Representations in Australian Print Media*. PhD thesis, Southern Cross University, Lismore, Australia. Retrieved from http://epubs.scu.edu.au/theses/247/.

Lewis, M. (2011b). Risk and efficacy in biomedical media representations of herbal medicine and complementary and alternative medicine (CAM). *Journal of Evidence-Based Complementary & Alternative Medicine, 16*(3), 210–217.

Lin, V., Bensoussan, A., Myers, S. P., McCabe, P., Cohen, M., Hill, S. & Howse, G. (2005). *The Practice and Regulatory Requirements of Naturopathy and Western Herbal Medicine*. Melbourne: La Trobe University.

Lupton, D. (1999). *Risk*. Florence, US: Routledge.

Lupton, D., & McLean, J. (1998). Representing doctors: Discourses and images in the Australian press. *Social Science & Medicine, 46*(8), 947–958.

MacDonald, M. M., & Hoffman-Goetz, L. (2002). A retrospective study of cancer information in Ontario daily newspapers. *Canadian Journal of Public Health, 93*(2), 12.

MacLennan, A. H., Myers, S. P. & Taylor, A. W. (2006). The continuing use of complementary and alternative medicine in South Australia: Costs and beliefs in 2004. *Medical Journal of Australia, 184*(1), 27–31.

Medew, J. (2009, 24 April 2009). Warning on 'quack' remedies for cancer, News. *The Age*, p. 3.

Mercurio, R., & Eliott, J. A. (2009). Trick or treat? Australian newspaper portrayal of complementary and alternative medicine for the treatment of cancer. *Supportive Care in Cancer*, 27 November 2009, 1–14.

Milazzo, S., & Ernst, E. (2006). Newspaper coverage of complementary and alternative therapies for cancer – UK 2002–2004. *Supportive Care in Cancer, 14*, 885–889.

Miles, J., & Elsworth, S. (2009, 29 September 2009). Giggle pills no joy for heart, News. *Hobart Mercury*, p. 7.

Miller, N. (2008, 21 November 2008). Caution prescribed for herbal medicine users, News. *The Age*, p. 3.

Miller, N. (2010a, 9 February 2010). Herbal medicines can kill: researcher, News. *The Sydney Morning Herald*, p. 2.

Miller, N. (2010b, 9 February 2010). 'Natural' remedies can prove lethal: research, News report. *The Age*, p. 3.

Moynihan, R., Bero, L., Ross-Degman, D. & Henry, D. (2000). Coverage by the news media of the benefits and risks of medications. *The New England Journal of Medicine, 342*(22), 1645–1650.

Needham, K. (2003, 7 May 2003). Consumers keep taking the tablets, despite recall, News. *The Sydney Morning Herald*. Retrieved from www.smh.com.au/articles/2003/05/06/1051987703188.html.

Nichols, J. (2007). Newspapers ... And After? *The Nation*. http://www.thenation.com/article/newspapersand-after.

O'Neill, A. (1994). Danger and safety in medicines. *Social Science & Medicine, 38*(4), 497–507.

Oxman, A. D., Guyatt, G. H., Cook, D. J., Jaeschke, R., Heddle, N. & Keller, J. (1993). An index of scientific quality for health reports in the lay press. *Journal of Clinical Epidemiology, 46*(9), 987–1001.

Pearson, M., & Brand, J. (2001). *Sources of News and Current Affairs*. Sydney: Bond University, Centre for New Media Research and Education.

Philo, G. (1993). Getting the message: Audience research in the Glasgow University Media Group. In J. Eldridge (Ed.), *Getting the Message: News, Truth and Power*. New York: Routledge.

Philo, G., & Miller, D. (2001). *Market Killing: What the Free Market Does and What Social Scientists Can Do About It*. Essex: Longman.

Polich, G., Dole, C. & Kaptchuk, T. (2010). The need to act a little more 'scientific': Biomedical researchers investigating complementary and alternative medicine. *Sociology of Health & Illness, 32*(1), 106–122.

Resch, K., Ernst, E. & Garrow, J. (1997, 20 September 1997). *Does Peer Review Favour the Conceptual Framework of Orthodox Medicine? A Randomised Controlled Study*. Paper presented at the The International Congress on Biomedical Peer Review and Global Communications, Prague, Czech Republic.

Robins, R. (2006). Brand matters: The lingua franca of pharmaceutical brand names. *Brand Channel*. Retrieved from www.brandchannel.com/papers_review.asp?sp_id=1233.

Roughead, L., & Semple, S. (2002). *Second National Report on Patient Safety: Improving Medication Safety*. Canberra: Australian Council for Safety and Quality in Healthcare.

Schudson, M. (2002). The news media as political institutions. *Annual Review of Political Science*(5), 249–269.

Schudson, M. (2003). *The Sociology of News*. New York: W. W. Norton & Co Inc.

Schwartz, L. M., & Woloshin, S. (2004). The media matter: A call for straightforward medical reporting. *Annals of Internal Medicine, 140*(3), 226.

Seale, C. (2003). Health and media: An overview. *Sociology of Health & Illness, 25*(6), 513–531.

Seale, C. (2010). How the mass media report social statistics: A case study concerning research on end-of-life decisions. *Social Science & Medicine, 71*(5), 861–868.

Shaw, P., Zhang, V. & Metallinos-Katsaras, E. (2009). A content analysis of the quantity and accuracy of dietary supplement information found in magazines with high adolescent readership. *Journal of Alternative & Complementary Medicine, 15*(2), 159–164.

Signoriellei, N. (1993). *Mass Media Images and Impact on Health*. Westport Connecticut: Greenwood Press.

Stallings, R. A. (1990). Media discourse and the social construction of risk. *Social Problems, 37*(1), 80–95.

Stokes, J. (2003). *How to Do Media and Cultural Studies*. London: Sage Publications.

Stryker, J. E. (2002). Reporting medical information: Effects of press releases and newsworthiness on medical journal articles' visibility in the news media. *Preventive Medicine, 35*, 519–530.

TGA. (28 April 2003). *National Medicines Regulator Suspends Drug Company's Manufacturing Licence*. Canberra: Therapeutic Goods Administration (TGA).

TGA. (2004). *The Therapeutic Goods Administration's risk management approach to the regulation of therapeutic goods*. Canberra: Department of Health and Ageing.

Unattributed. (2005, 9 July 2005). Echinacea can be life-threatening, News. *The Daily Telegraph*, p. 19.

Unattributed. (2006, 12 January 2006). Asia-Pacific 'stiff' tonic not what it seemed, News. *The Advertiser*, p. 34.

Unattributed. (2010a, 9 February 2010). Deadly remedies, News. *The Daily Telegraph*, p. 9.

Unattributed. (2010b, 2 February 2010). Herbs lethal if misused, News. *Herald-Sun*, p. 18.

Uusitalo, L., Ovaskainen, M.-L. & Prattala, R. (2000). Antioxidants in the Finnish press: A battlefield of alternative and conventional medicine. *Health Promotion International, 15*(1), 71–78.

Van Marie, E. (2002). *Re-presenting Herbal Medicine as Phytotherapy: A Strategy of Professionalisation Through the Formation of 'Scientific' Medicine*. PhD thesis, University of Leeds, Leeds.

Voss, M. (2002). Checking the pulse: Midwestern reporters' opinions on their ability to report health care news. *Research and Practice, 92*(7), 1158–1160.

Wahlberg, A. (2007). A quackery with a difference: New medical pluralism and the problem of 'dangerous practitioners' in the United Kingdom. *Social Science & Medicine, 65,* 2307–2316.

Watson, C. (2010, 2 February 2010). Herbal mix can be lethal, News. *The Advertiser,* p. 5.

Weeks, L. C., & Strudsholm, T. (2008). A scoping review of research on complementary and alternative medicine (CAM) and the mass media: Looking back, moving forward. *BMC Complementary and Alternative Medicine, 8*(43).

Weeks, L. C., Verhoef, M. & Scott, C. (2007). Presenting the alternative: Cancer and complementary and alternative medicine in the Canadian print media. *Supportive Care in Cancer, 15,* 931–938.

Willis, E., & White, K. (2004). Evidence-based medicine and CAM. In P. Tovey, G. Easthope & J. Adams (Eds), *The Mainstreaming of Complementary and Alternative Medicine: Studies in Social Context.* London: Routledge.

Wilkinson, J., & Simpson, M. (2001). High use of complementary therapies in a New South Wales rural community. *Australian Journal of Rural Health, 9*(4), 166–171.

Wilson, A., Bonevski, B., Jones, A. & Henry, D. (2009). Media reporting of health interventions: Signs of improvement, but major problems persist. *PLoS ONE, 4*(3), 1–5.

Woloshin, S., & Schwartz, L. M. (2006). Media reporting on research presented at scientific meetings: More caution needed. *Medical Journal of Australia, 184*(11), 576–580.

Wynne, B. (1987). *Risk Management and Hazardous Waste: Implementation and the Dialectics of Credibility.* London: Springer-Verlag.

Wynne, B. (1996). May the sheep safely graze? A reflexive view of the expert-lay knowledge divide. In S. Lash, B. Szerszynski & B. Wynne (Eds), *Risk, Environment and Modernity: Towards a New Ecology.* London: Sage Publications.

Xue, C. C., Zhang, A. L., Lin, V., Da Costa, C. & Story, D. F. (2007). Complementary and alternative medicine use in Australia: A national population-based survey. *The Journal of Alternative and Complementary Medicine, 13*(6), 643–650.

Zhang, A. L., Story, D. F., Lin, V., Vitetta, L. & Xue, C. C. (2008). A population survey on the use of 24 common medicinal herbs in Australia. *Pharmacoepidemiology and Drug Safety, 17,* 1006–1013.

12

TRADITIONAL MEDICINE AND THE LAW IN KENYA

John Harrington[1]

I Introduction

After decades of repression, neglect and occasional verbal support, the Kenyan authorities are now actively seeking to modernize and reconstruct both traditional medical practice and the manner in which traditional medical knowledge is utilized and transmitted. This chapter examines the most important of these initiatives, setting them in the context of broader legal developments at national level and relating them to changes in global governance and in international political economy more broadly. The chapter is structured as follows. Section II reflects on the definition of traditional medicine, highlighting its conceptually residual nature as the subordinated other of Western biomedicine. Section III examines the history of official attitudes to traditional medicine from the early colonial period at the end of the nineteenth century to the early decades of independence since 1964. Surprisingly, perhaps, it will be seen that there was a significant degree of continuity between the colonial association of traditional medicine with witchcraft and the post-colonial desire to modernize health care by eliminating indigenous practices. Section IV provides an overview of the nature and extent of traditional medical practice in contemporary Kenya. Though a vital source of health care for a majority of the population, particularly the poor and those living in remote areas, practice is increasingly stratified. Urban clinics present a commercial face to patients quite at odds with the popular image of the individual healer embedded in a rural community. The rest of the chapter considers three significant aspects of the legal engagement with traditional medicine. Section V reviews the current, weak system for licensing practitioners, as well as recent policy and legislative initiatives to discipline traditional practice by integrating it into the national health system. These plans lay at least as much emphasis on the materials used in treatment as on the work of healers themselves. This theme is elaborated in Section VI, which considers the pressure placed on wild plant resources by the growing commercialization of traditional healing. Section VII examines a further resource-related problem, namely the threat that traditional knowledge and genetic resources will be appropriated by foreign researchers or companies without due consent being obtained or compensation being rendered. International agreements have significantly influenced Kenyan law on this area, though considerable problems of implementation remain and there have been a number of documented cases of unauthorized appropriation. Intellectual property (IP) reforms, proposed in response to this problem, are also considered, along with recent projects to develop a herbal products industry on the basis of extant traditional medical knowledge. Section VIII reflects on the broad trend of regulation in the sector with reference to the model of bio-political governance developed by Rose and Miller. Considered thus, diverse initiatives can be said to problematize different aspects of traditional medicine and to propose a rationalization of practice or medical products in response. I argue that the law plays a two-fold role in these problematizations, functioning as a technical means of reform, but also as a normative source of the goals to which reform programmes are oriented.

This research is based on an extensive review of published literature concerning the regulation of traditional medicine in Kenya. It draws on academic studies of modern Kenyan history and politics, as well as more specific work on the health care system since the beginning of the colonial period in the late 1800s. Existing law and current developments were tracked through a review of official legal materials and the grey literature, i.e. policy documents produced by Kenyan ministries and parastatal bodies, as well as by international and regional organizations. Given the diverse issues raised by traditional medicine – from the regulation of practice, to the control of access to resources, to intellectual property rights – a wide range of such sources was consulted. However, official documents are not always readily available. Consequently, this survey was complemented by a series of interviews conducted with public servants, prominent healers and lawyers working in the public sector or in private practice. As well as providing useful insights and background on legislative and policy developments, interviewees were also able to help locate otherwise unavailable material.

II Defining 'traditional medicine': subordinate and supplementary

The World Health Organization has stated that traditional medicine is difficult to define positively with any precision including as it does 'a diversity of health practices, approaches, knowledge, and beliefs incorporating plant, animal, and/or mineral-based medicines; spiritual therapies; manual techniques; and exercises' (WHO 2001: 1–2). As Stacey Langwick has noted, the terms used in Kiswahili for traditional medicine – *dawa za asili*, *dawa za jadi* and *dawa za kienyeji*[2] – all come with connotations of inheritance. As such, they can be contrasted with the term for biomedicine – *dawa za kisasa*, literally 'medicine of the present' (Langwick 2008: 437). It is important to note that traditional medical practices are not fixed, but are rather subject to continuous improvement by practitioners in each generation. 'Traditional' can be taken then to refer not to the antiquity of the knowledge but to the manner in which it is transmitted (Correa 2002: 18).

An understanding of traditional medicine cannot simply proceed from a stipulation or simple translation, however. Rather, account has to be taken of the specific colonial and post-colonial history of power and domination which shapes the therapeutic field in Kenya as elsewhere. Thus, where 'Western medicine' is taken to be a unified system based on a universally valid scientific knowledge and method of inquiry, 'African medicine' has been represented as a heterogeneous set of healing practices each proper to a specific ethnic group, rooted in local cultures and religious beliefs, transmitted ineffably by way of 'collective memory' rather than by formal training and instruction (see Sujatha 2011: 195; Arihan and Gençler Özkan 2007: 136).

Since the inception of colonialism, biomedicine has promised a great deal to Africans (Vaughan 1991). Though it has certainly delivered on much of this promise, its shortcomings have also been painfully apparent. The latter have been a consequence of political and economic circumstances (e.g. the withdrawal of already meagre state health provision under structural adjustment programmes) or of the insufficient reach of scientific medicine (e.g. the stalled development of drugs aimed at tropical illnesses) (Anangwe 2008). As will be seen later, traditional medicine has been conceived of in this context as a subordinate, but still helpful supplement, making good the practical and scientific deficiencies of orthodox medicine (Langwick 2008: 428). On this view, it should function as a guide to the discovery of new drugs or as a source of cheap and widely accessible health care which is culturally acceptable to most ordinary people functioning in an ancillary role to biomedicine or (Hoff 1993).

III Historical background: 'tribalism', 'witchcraft' and modernization

The British colonial authorities expressed their understanding of traditional medicine in the Kenyan *Medical Practitioners and Dentists Ordinance* of 1910, which permitted

> the practice of systems of therapeutics according to Native … methods by persons recognised by the community to which they belong to be duly trained in such practice; provided that nothing in this section shall be construed to authorise any person to practice native … systems of therapeutics except amongst the community to which he belongs…[3]

This provision effectively meant that local healers would not be allowed to integrate Western techniques, instruments or medicines into their practice. As well as bolstering the prestige of the new biomedicine, it thus also secured the monopoly position of registered doctors. By confining healers to their ethnic groups, the Ordinance contributed to the creation and reification of 'tribal' identities which were central to British strategies of 'indirect rule' across Africa (see Mamdani 1996). However, this essentializing move did not accord with the reality of traditional medical practice then or in the present day. Historically, many healers have travelled from their home area to learn their craft from more experienced practitioners belonging to another ethnic group (see Rekdal 1999). Equally, healers from beyond the locality, often far beyond, were and still are seen as being especially effective. For example, Tanzanian healers or those from, say, the coastal region of Kenya working in Nairobi advertise their specific origins prominently. More-over, in the multi-ethnic slums of Kenya's growing cities, healers seek to build their reputations among people of all backgrounds (Iliffe 1998: 191). Patients themselves are commonly uncon-strained by 'tribal' categories or by the barrier between 'Western' and 'African' medicine in their pluralistic selection and combination of therapies (Burris interview, 30 January 2013).

The terms of the *Medical Practitioners and Dentists Ordinance* indicate that at least formally the colonial administration was willing to tolerate traditional medicine within significant limits. By contrast, missionaries, who delivered the bulk of biomedical care before independence, were much more forceful opponents (see Iliffe 1998: 19; Kimani interview, 26 March 2012). Local converts, including those recruited to work in missionary medical facilities, were particularly vociferous (Vaughan 1991: 55). This tension is still evident in contemporary Kenya, with the evangelical churches popular in urban slums condemning traditional medicine as ungodly (Burris interview, 30 January 2013). In response, it has been emphasized that both the Bible and the Koran refer to the use of herbal medicines.[4] While the above cited provision of the *Medical Practitioners and Dentists Ordinance* is no longer part of Kenyan law, its underlying association of traditional medicine with local cultures, as opposed to science, continues to shape official insti-tutional arrangements. Most obviously, the system for licensing traditional practitioners is the responsibility of the Ministry of Culture, not the Ministry of Health or one of the state medical boards. As will be seen, recent reform initiatives are seeking to change this.

Of still greater practical and ideological salience has been the *Witchcraft Ordinance* (now *Act*), passed in 1925 and still in force. In principle, this is aimed not at stopping healing work (*uganga*), but at suppressing sorcery, accusations of witchcraft (*uchawi*) and the use of witchcraft to discover crimes.[5] The latter have often led to the murder of the people so accused.[6] In addition to the everyday maintenance of order, the Ordinance was also motivated by a fear that diviners would mobilize resistance to colonial rule, as had happened during the Maji Maji rebellion in early twentieth-century Tanganyika (Langwick 2011a: 42). According to prominent contemporary healers, one effect of the legislation has been to confuse *uchawi* and *uganga* and to extend the stigma of sorcery and criminality to wholly benevolent traditional healing (Mwangi interview, 10 April 2012; Maina Mwea interview, 29 January 2013). Inaccurate and pejorative references to healers as 'witchdoctors' are common, not only among foreigners, but also on the part of educated Kenyans.[7] There is particular resentment at healers' use of the title 'Doctor', even though this is prohibited for anyone except a registered medical practitioner (Taracha interview, 25 July 2013).[8]

In addition to colonial and missionary influences, much hostility to traditional medicine has come from the distinctive modernizing vision of many leading medical professionals and of the Kenyan elite more generally. That vision was shaped in turn by Kenya's distinctive path to independence. During the 1950s, Mau Mau insurgents, confined to the mountains and forests, had of necessity to treat themselves with herbal remedies (Jackson 2003; Butungi 2010). In government-controlled areas, by contrast, state and missionary clinics were only open to civilians willing to pledge their loyalty to the Crown (Kimani interview, 26 March 2012). The widespread characterization of Mau Mau, by Kenyan loyalists and the British administration, as a regression to the 'primitive and barbaric' contributed to the stigmatization of the traditional beliefs and practices, including healing practices, with which the movement was associated (Githae interview, 22 April 2013; Lonsdale 1990). The defeat of the guerrillas paved the way for a transfer of power to conservative nationalists in 1963, including first President Jomo Kenyatta, who denounced Mau Mau as a 'disease' and urged Kenyans instead to work hard to build the new nation (Clough 2003: 256). Kenyatta himself drew on this idiom to condemn 'medicine men' in 1969 as 'lazy cheats who want to live on the sweat of others' (Iliffe 1998: 191). Kenyatta's views were shared by those doctors and functionaries who took administrative control of the health system at independence. A senior official in 1970 was typical in stating that the policy of the Health Ministry was 'to discourage the use of native medicines as far as possible' (Iliffe 1998: 191). As Ombongi has noted, 'the independent state inherited [and extended] the modernizing mentality of the late colonial period' (2011: 362). By contrast with more radical regimes, such as that of Kwame Nkrumah in Ghana and Julius Nyerere in Tanzania, its African nationalism was asserted by removing racial barriers to practising and accessing biomedicine rather than through the promotion of indigenous healing practices (Owoahene-Acheampong and Vasconi 2010; Langwick 2010).

The attitude of the state to traditional medicine began to change somewhat in the late 1970s under the influence of the Alma Ata Declaration of the World Health Organization on the policies and strategies needed to realize 'an acceptable level of health for all the people of the world' by the year 2000 (Ng'etich 2008: 25). The Declaration expressly identified a role for 'traditional practitioners' in delivering primary care, albeit they would be involved only 'as needed' and subject to suitable training and the technical direction of public health specialists and medics.[9] Kenya's response to the Declaration was particularly focused on the area of immunization (Ndege 2001: 139). But in its National Development Plan for 1979–1983, the government also gave unprecedented acknowledgment to the major contribution made by traditional medicine to primary health care. The Plan called for research to 'evaluate [its] role and functions and to determine [its] usefulness' (quoted in NCAPD 2005: 1). Some studies were carried out, localized efforts were made to coordinate the work of healers and doctors and a curriculum established for training traditional birth attendants (Kimani 1981: 421). A Traditional Medicines and Drugs Research Centre was established as part of the Kenya Medical Research Institute (KEMRI) in 1984 (Ombongi 2011: 364).[10] Beyond these piecemeal initiatives, however, the state's commitment was largely verbal. A task force established to build cooperation between healers and doctors in 1989 was also fruitless (Ng'etich 2008: 26). Other African jurisdictions such as Zimbabwe (in 1981), Ghana (in 2000), Tanzania (in 2002) and South Africa (in 2004) have pushed ahead of Kenya in enacting comprehensive legislation on the sector and (with varying degrees of success) in including it within the official health care system (Chavunduka 1986; Owoahene-Acheampong and Vasconi 2010).

Since the 1980s, official attitudes in Kenya have been ambivalent. On the one hand, for example, it is claimed that healers may be able to contribute to treating non-communicable diseases (Kimani interview, 26 March 2012). In particular, with the spread of HIV infection in the 1980s, herbal remedies have been seen as a means of boosting the immunity of people living with the virus and the holistic approach of healers has been recommended as a means of delivering client-centred care (Burris interview, 30 January 2013; UNAIDS 2000). On the other hand, unfounded claims that healers could effect a complete cure for AIDS, as well as their association with harmful practices such as female genital mutilation, led to renewed calls for traditional medicine to be banned (Kareithi 2009; Kimani interview, 26 March 2012). The last decade has seen a more positive approach to traditional medicine on the part of state bodies and political leaders. This has facilitated several important reform initiatives, including detailed policy papers on traditional medical knowledge and a number of bills for the regulation of practice. These will be discussed later. It should, however, be noted that state commitment has been neither sufficiently consistent nor sufficiently widespread across different institutions to enable any of these initiatives to succeed thus far.

IV Traditional medicine in Kenya today: practitioners and patients

It is estimated that there are currently around 40,000 traditional practitioners working in Kenya (Lambert and Leonard 2011: 4).[11] Their work is marked by considerable diversity. Of a nationwide sample, 64 per cent had more than one specialization. They included herbalists (98 per cent), traditional birth attendants (26 per cent), bone setters (38 per cent) and spiritualists or faith healers (22 per cent) (Lambert and Leonard 2011: 20).[12] There are also important differences in the degree of commercialization of healers' work. In rural areas, most practise in their villages and are known by reputation. They collect raw materials from local forests and process them themselves, grinding powders and bottling decoctions (Prince and Geissler 2001). Payment is often in kind (a goat or a chicken, for example) and normally made when there is a successful outcome, rather than in advance or on the administration of therapy, as is the case with biomedical practitioners (Leonard 2003). Many individual healers also practice in this way in towns and cities (TICAH 2010: 7). Their reputation is spread by word of mouth, though many also advertise by way of painted signs nailed to trees and telegraph poles (Gudacha interview, 21 February 2013).

Medicinal liquids and powders are sold at herbal clinics which offer individual patient consultation or direct to the consumer in local open markets (Majtenyi 2012). A few larger scale enterprises have invested in the production, packaging and marketing of pills, lotions and creams with standard dosages and greater stability (Muriuki, Franzel, Mowo, Kariuki and Jamnadass 2012: 118).[13] These firms advertise through websites, social media and the national newspapers.[14] Notwithstanding the varying degrees of commercialization, healers of all types affirm that therapeutic beneficence, rather than financial gain, is their primary motive (Githae interview, 22 April 2013; Gudacha interview, 21 February 2013).

Becoming a healer in the rural areas often involves carrying on a family tradition. Normally this is not a matter of simple choice, but of being called in a dream or when an individual is picked out by an established practitioner as being particularly adept and of good character. Initiation follows an apprenticeship model.[15] For example, where a child is especially close to his grandmother, herself a healer, he may accompany her to the forest to collect plants and help in the preparation of remedies from an early age (Prince and Geissler 2001: 53). Formal training in traditional medicine is not available in Kenya (TICAH 2010: 5). Indeed apart from courses on pharmacognosy and community medicine, traditional healing is also absent from the curriculum of the country's medical schools.[16]

Healers themselves are widely perceived to be uneducated. Lambert and Leonard's survey found that 66 per cent had received no more than primary schooling (2011: 19). By contrast a number of the larger scale practitioners previously mentioned have university-level qualifications in pharmacy or the natural sciences. These qualifications are displayed in their promotional material (e.g. Maina Mwea interview, 29 January 2013; Githae interview, 22 April 2013). However, they too reported having been called in some way to the vocation of healing. Thus, one, a qualified pharmacist, found that standard medicines had failed to relieve his wife's migraines. On the advice of an aunt, he consulted a 'medicine man', who successfully treated his wife. After this revelation, he decided that he would no longer work in conventional medicine. He spent three years as an apprentice to a healer in a rural area, returning to Nairobi to build a successful herbal medicine practice (Maina Mwea interview, 29 January 2013).

It is estimated that over 70 per cent of the Kenyan population relies on traditional medicine as its primary source of health care, while more than 90 per cent use medicinal plants at one time or another (IEA 2011b: 11). Although the great bulk of state health care resources are allocated to the delivery of biomedical care, traditional healers are considerably more accessible to ordinary Kenyans, particularly in remote, rural areas. While the doctor–patient ratio is approximately 1:33,000, that for traditional healers is 1:950.[17] Moreover, healers report that their patients tend to have lower incomes and be less educated than the average Kenyan (Lambert and Leonard 2011: 19). They are consulted, for example, where the supply of biomedicines in public hospitals is exhausted – so-called 'stock-outs' (Khayeka interview, 31 June 2013). Nonetheless, the fact that most charge a fee means that they are not always more affordable than licensed doctors, who may be subsidized or working on a voluntary basis. Furthermore, traditional medical care is not covered by private or public health insurance in Kenya (Ng'etich 2008: 31). This commercial dimension is particularly notable in towns and cities where healers are also consulted by middle class and wealthy Kenyans, including, it is alleged, senior politicians (Ng'etich 2008: 28; Maina Mwea interview, 29 January 2013). Thus, contrary to the idealization of traditional medicine as a holistic, non-market alternative to commodified biomedicine, it is clear that there is a stratified market for both forms of care in Kenya (TICAH 2010: 5). As one expert put it, in 'the urban areas healers compete with medical doctors' as well as unlicensed for-profit clinics; 'in the rural areas they compete with poverty' (Senior Kenyan Research Scientist interview, 26 February 2013).

Healers themselves report that malaria is by some margin the condition which they treat most often, but patients also commonly present with typhoid, worms, gynaecological problems and colds (Kareru, Kenji, Gachanja, Keriko and Mungai 2007: 86).[18] Twenty-eight per cent of births are assisted by traditional birth attendants, though this figure is above 40 per cent for women with no formal education and those in the lowest wealth quintile (KNBS 2009: 122). While healers are also consulted for more serious infectious conditions like tuberculosis, it appears that patients are rather more likely to attend biomedical medical facilities in such cases (Lambert and Leonard 2011: 29). It should be added that much use of traditional medicines is in the form of self-care and, thus, genuinely beyond the market (TICAH 2010: 5). While healers are often possessed of their own esoteric knowledge, many herbs are known to all the local community for their healing properties (Correa 2001: 4; Prince and Geissler 2001: 448). Clearly self-treatment of this sort is much more difficult in urban than in rural areas where medicinal plants grow wild (TICAH 2010: 7).

V Licensing, regulation and legislative reform

According to the tripartite categorization developed by the World Health Organization, Kenya can be said to operate a 'tolerant' regime for the regulation of traditional medicine (WHO 2002: 8–9). Though practice is not proscribed by law, neither is it officially included, much less fully incorporated into the health care system, as is the case in China, Korea or Vietnam. There is no formal, comprehensive system for licensing and disciplining practitioners. Rather they are subject to a relatively 'light-touch' system of registration by the Ministry of Culture. Before issuing a certificate of registration, the Ministry requires testimony of good character from the local Chief (the lowest administrative level in the Kenyan state), as well as a letter stating that the healer's plants have been analysed at a recognized centre (Mwangi 2012: 22). The latter include the Centre for Traditional Medicine and Drug Research at KEMRI and departments of botany at a number of universities (Gemson 2013). Though staff at these centres aspire to test plants for toxicity, efficacy, dosage and stability, they are currently prevented from doing so by a lack of resources. Instead they draw on their own experience and on the body of tests carried out under previous drug development initiatives (Matu interview, 21 May 2013). This information is used to question the healer regarding the origin, identity and uses of the plant. Where the latter is known to be toxic or inefficacious against the conditions mentioned, the healer will be informed that any letter issued will not be supportive of their application to the Ministry of Culture (Matu interview, 21 May 2013). The lack of an effective system of enforcement means, however, that they are unlikely to be impeded from practising (Gemson 2013). Instead, registration is useful to healers in so far as local councils make it a precondition of issuing them with a licence to trade. It can also provide a means of deflecting corrupt officials seeking bribes. In practice, certificates are more likely to be acquired by urban practitioners than their rural counterparts, often being prominently displayed in herbal clinics to bolster the healer's credibility (Maina Mwea interview, 29 January 2013).

As well as attesting to the status of the applicant themselves, the process of certification is also seen as an admittedly weak means of screening out fake healers and those who simply deal in traditional remedies as commodities (see Anon 2012). Administrators, scientists and healers' leaders explain the proliferation of fake healers as resulting from processes of urbanization and commercialization, which have undermined the legitimacy of practitioners and the authenticity of their remedies (Matu interview, 21 May 2013; Matoke interview, 31 January 2013). The official response to these processes has not been to attempt to refurbish traditional practice and medical knowledge. Instead reformers within the state and their interlocutors in civil society, with guidance from the WHO Regional Office for Africa and support from the World Bank, have promoted the rationalization of traditional medicine (see WHO-AFRO 2010; KWG-MAPS 2011). This is manifested in a drive to discipline healers through diverse local and nationwide schemes to train them in hygiene and record keeping and in a broader aspiration to raise the average level of their general education.[19] It is also evident in official policies to standardize the production, labelling and marketing of herbal medicines through the implementation of good manufacturing practice (see NCAPD 2005: 21). Research and development carried out in Kenyan laboratories will, it is hoped, be the cornerstone of traditional medicine in the future, proving that it isn't mere 'hocus pocus' (Mwangi 2012: 15–16). Ministers and interested parliamentarians agree that it is only thus that quacks can be suppressed and dangerous procedures eliminated allowing healers to make their contribution to the health of the nation (Mwangi 2012: 25).[20] In effect, a new social and semantic context is to be created for traditional medicine. Inherited forms of authority will be replaced with legally based requirements that would allow patients to 'read off' the credibility of practitioners and products from certificates and labels themselves underwritten by state-backed science (Ng'etich 2005: 10).[21]

In pursuing this project, Kenyan reformers have drawn inspiration from the modernization of traditional Chinese medicine (TCM) after the communist revolution of 1949.[22] They observe how TCM has been subjected to a dense regime of regulations backed by criminal and civil sanctions, allowing it to be integrated into the national health system and forming the basis for a profitable export industry in herbal remedies.[23] As in other areas of political and economic development, China is taken to exemplify how the dependency and inequality which have marked Kenya's relationship with the West since the colonial period may be overcome.[24] Interest in TCM has been fostered by the Chinese embassy, which funds Kenyan government officials, scientists and healers to undertake study trips, visiting the national Institute of Traditional Medicine and dedicated hospitals, as well as cultivation and production facilities.[25] Many are impressed with the equality of status which traditional Chinese medicine has achieved with biomedicine. They note with approval that both are governed from the health ministry in Beijing, rather than the culture ministry as in Nairobi, the colonial association of traditional medicine with a pre-scientific culture having been rejected.[26]

The last fifteen years have seen a number of policy and legislative initiatives in relation to the regulation of traditional medical practice in Kenya. That none has so far been realized is significantly due to a fragmentation of responsibility within the state. Different ministries and agencies have commissioned detailed policies and draft bills, each informed by the distinctive expertise of international bodies, such as the World Health Organization and the World Intellectual Property Organization. This diversity of perspective is reinforced by the conflicting interests of the professional and commercial groups most closely engaged with those particular state bodies. To take the most important example, the Ministry of Health enjoys close relations with the established medical professions, which are, as has been noted above, generally antipathetic to traditional medicine. Unsurprisingly, a draft bill of 2002 originating in the Ministry took a harshly punitive approach to regulation in line with the express wishes of the Kenya Medical Association, leading in turn to its rejection by healers (Chege 2002; Mwangi interview, 10 April 2012). Equally, legislation based on the National Policy on Traditional Medicine and Medicinal Plants,[27] sponsored by the Ministry of Planning, was shelved in 2009 for lack of support from the Ministry of Health (Otswong'o interview, 11 July 2013).

The failure of a unified and representative national healers' association to emerge in Kenya has also been a significant obstacle to reform (Ominde-Ogaja interview, 19 February 2013). Numerous rival bodies have contended for official attention, often mutually suspicious of each other and sometimes divided on ethnic lines (Burris interview, 30 January 2013; NCAPD 2005: 22). In 2010, for example, the failure of the leadership of the National Traditional Health Practitioners' Association (NATHEPA) to bring its mid-ranking members with it blocked the progress of a draft bill based on the National Policy on Traditional Knowledge, Genetic Resources and Traditional Cultural Expressions (Otswong'o interview, 11 July 2013).[28] NATHEPA has since been reformed as the Herbalists Society of Kenya, an umbrella organization for diverse local groups.[29] This lack of unity is exacerbated by the tendency of ministries and other state agencies to call forth new associations as their preferred interlocutors in relation to specific reform initiatives (Matoke interview, 31 January 2013). Unsurprisingly, perhaps, rural healers, who make up the majority of practitioners, are likely to view such groups as largely Nairobi-based phenomena, when they know about them at all (Ng'etich 2005: 28; Khayeka interview, 31 June 2013).

Impetus for the reform initiative currently in progress has been provided by Kenya's Constitution of 2010. While this devolves responsibility for almost all health care delivery to forty-seven newly created counties, it reserves the setting of policy, including professional regulation, for the national authorities.[30] A draft Health Bill aimed at implementing this devolved regime imposes an obligation on the government to create a traditional healers' council tasked with maintaining a register, licensing practitioners and securing quality control over practitioners.[31] The details of these standards, as well as guidelines requiring healers to refer their patients to 'conventional' health care facilities, are to be developed by the Ministry of Health in consultation with stakeholders (see Tolo 2014: 4–5). As discussed above, healers have welcomed this planned shift in responsibility from the Ministry of Culture and to the Ministry of Health (see Abuje 2012). The input of a representative association will again be required as the committees of the traditional healers' council are constituted and a code of ethics developed (Ruchira interview, 12 February 2013; Ominde-Ogaja interview, 19 February 2013). In order to achieve a rationalization of herbal products in tandem with the planned regulation of practitioners, the Ministry has also established a dedicated Technical Working Group drawn from state agencies and universities. The Group has already produced draft guidelines for the registration, licensing and testing of such products (see Tolo 2014: 5).

VI Access to medical materials and conservation

Kiswahili speakers often say '*miti ni dawa*', trees are medicine. Among the most popular sources of traditional remedies in Kenya is the East African greenheart or muthiga tree (*Warburgia ugandensis*), which has been found to contain anti-microbials (McMullin *et al.* 2012: 196). Its bark is used in powdered form to treat colds and sinus infections and as a decoction against malaria. For chest complaints, it is either chewed or burnt and the smoke inhaled. Twigs used as toothbrushes appear to prevent periodontal diseases.[32] Other well-known sources include the neem tree (*Azadirachtica indica*), known in Kiswahili as *mwarubaini* since it is said to cure forty different complaints, and red stinkwood (*Prunus africanus*) taken as an infusion against stomach-ache, an appetite stimulant and a treatment for benign enlargement of the prostate.[33]

In most cases, these materials are collected by healers themselves or by traders who make a living out of selling them on (McMullin *et al.* 2012: 189). However, supply has become increasingly limited due to unsustainable harvesting practices. Bark and roots are preferred by Kenyan healers, though removing leaves, flowers or seeds would cause considerably less damage to plants. A great deal of the harvested material is wasted in any event (Muriuki *et al.* 2012: 122). Specific practices of ring-barking (removing all the way around the trunk) and repeated bark-stripping often lead to the death of the tree due to loss of moisture and the incursion of bacteria (McMullin *et al.* 2012: 204; Chege interview, 22 November 2013). Since trees often take years to mature, natural replacement is insufficient to compensate for this depletion. Coupled with the cost of inputs, this means that there is little profit in sustainable cultivation, which has been slow to develop in Kenya. Moreover, many healers favour plants harvested in the wild assuming that these are purer and more potent (Muriuki *et al.* 2012: 124). As a result, a vicious circle is observed whereby overharvesting in the wild leads to scarcity, which drives up prices, creating a further incentive to overharvest (Cunningham 1998: 123, 124). Growing demand in cities and towns has the unfortunate effect of depleting the resources available to rural healers, diminishing their ability to meet the primary health needs of local populations who are already under-served by the official health care system (Cunningham 1998: 125). In response to these threats, the National Policy on Traditional Medicine and Medicinal Plants recommended programmes to document current availability of plants, to develop an 'agro-industrial system' of cultivation and to promote nurseries and home herb gardens (NCAPD 2005: 10, 13, 15).

Access to medical materials is also dramatically constrained by the loss of formerly common lands, including forests. Currently only 1.7 per cent of Kenya's landmass is forested, with 5,000 hectares disappearing each year (NEMA 2011: 86, 101). Article 69(1)(b) of the Constitution commits the state to raise this to 10 per cent, but that will be difficult to achieve even in the medium term (KFS n.d.). As well as agriculture and logging, much has been lost to landgrabbing, the besetting vice of Kenya's political and business elite in the decades since independence (see Harrington and Manji 2013). Even when forests have been secured for more benign purposes, the same effect is observable. Thus, both British and independent administrations, acting in the name of wildlife conservation, excluded local communities from forests (Lumumba interview, 29 August 2013). The enduring colonial doctrine that ultimate title rests with the state has allowed customary rights to gather medical and other materials to be set aside in these cases.[34] The *Forests Act 2005* sought to mitigate this by allowing the establishment of Community Forest Associations (CFA), which could take over authority to manage local forests, including the determination of user rights such as the 'collection of medicinal herbs'.[35] In some districts, such as Kakamega and Malindi, effective local groups have taken on this role, paying specific attention to the needs of healers and patients (IEA 2011b: 64–66). Elsewhere, the consequences have been ambivalent to say the least. For example, Karura forest in Nairobi was saved from landgrabbing by civil society activists. Now managed by a CFA, it has been fenced off so as to exclude violent criminals and illegal loggers (KFS 2010: 17, 41). While the Association's management plan commits it to the 'protection of traditional interests', in practice the effect of the fence has been to privilege the recreational needs of middle class and expatriate Nairobians (KFS 2010: 61, 41). Unable to afford the entrance fee, local healers, who had long gathered material from the *muthiga* and other trees in the forest, are wholly excluded (Chege interview, 22 November 2013).

VII Biopiracy, intellectual property and commercialization

Kenya's natural resources have also been targeted by international companies seeking the impetus for new drug development and other commercial products. In 1995, the German company Bayer filed a patent on a process for the biosynthesis of acarbose, a drug which regulates the entry of glucose into the blood system and is prescribed for type II diabetics. It was later confirmed that the process utilized a type of bacteria (*Actinoplanes sp.*) originally taken from Lake Ruiru in Kenya. Though sales of acarbose were worth US$379 million in 2004, none of these benefits were shared with the local community (McGown 2006: 11). In a second case, the US biotech company Genencor informed its shareholders that it had licensed enzymes capable of fading denim jeans to Proctor and Gamble for use in their detergent powder 'Tide'. The enzymes had been discovered in a microbe, removed without authorization, from Lake Bogoria in the Rift Valley (IEA 2011b: 6–7). Though the genetic resources acquired in these cases had not previously been used by local healers, the ease with which they were extracted is a matter of concern to Kenyan officials concerned with traditional medicine and to healers themselves (Ominde-Ogaja interview, 19 February 2013; Githae interview, 22 April 2013). Elsewhere in Africa ethno-botanists have enrolled local healers as sometimes unwitting guides to bioprospecting on behalf of foreign companies. This is how the rosy periwinkle (*Vinca sp.*) was identified in Madagascar as a source of vinblastine and vincristine. Used to treat childhood leukaemia and Hodgkin's disease, respectively, these earned the Eli Lilly corporation around $100 million per year in 2004. No compensation has been paid to the healers or their community (McClelland

2004). Since then some bioprospecting companies have developed voluntary remuneration schemes, though these have been criticized on both ethical and business grounds (Peterson 2001; Clapp and Crook 2002).

Such unlicensed and unremunerated extraction has been condemned as a new form of 'colonial pillaging' (IEA 2009: 3; Government of Kenya 2009: 6).[36] The Convention on Biodiversity (CBD) 1992, ratified by Kenya in 1994, addresses this problem by rejecting the notion that biodiversity is part of the common heritage of mankind, available for exploitation by those best equipped to do so (see Timmermans 2003: 747). Instead it recognizes the sovereign right of states to exploit their own resources (Article 3). This privileging of the nation state is supplemented by the imposition of an obligation on parties

> to respect, preserve and maintain knowledge, innovations and practices of indigenous and local communities embodying traditional lifestyles relevant for the conservation and sustainable use of biological diversity [and] to promote their wider application with the approval and involvement of the holders of such knowledge.
>
> *(Article 8j)*

Specific measures are mandated to provide for: 1) prior informed consent to the extraction and use of genetic resources; and 2) the fair and equitable sharing of the benefits from the use of genetic resources (Article 15). Kenya has recognized these principles in its Constitution[37] and in dedicated regulations.[38] Permission to access genetic resources will only be issued by the National Environment Management Agency (NEMA) where it is shown that consent has been obtained and that monetary (e.g. up-front and milestone payments, as well as royalties) and non-monetary (e.g. academic collaboration and technology transfer) compensation will be facilitated. However, the Regulations do not clarify precisely who should give consent or with whom benefits should be shared (IEA 2009: 10). Moreover, a continuing jurisdictional overlap between NEMA and other state agencies has allowed researchers to circumvent the Regulations (IEA 2009: 9; Munyi interview, 1 October 2013). As a result, experts have argued that few real benefits have accrued to ordinary Kenyans since the ratification and implementation of the CBD (Mutta and Munyi 2010: 8).

Strategies focused on patent law have been considered as a necessary complement to the CBD regime in empowering local communities (see IEA 2011a). Prior publication in a database, for example, would destroy the element of novelty required for the grant of a patent, removing the incentive for outsiders to misappropriate traditional knowledge (Timmermans 2003: 752).[39] Publication would also have the salutary effect of widening access to traditional remedies, though there would be little financial return on this to the community or its healers. Alternatively, patent applicants could be required to disclose the origin of materials or traditional knowledge used in making an invention, as well as evidence of prior informed consent (IEA 2009: 6) However, the changes to Article 27 of the WTO's Trade Related Intellectual Property Agreement (TRIPs), which would permit such a requirement, have been resisted by the United States and other developed countries (Correa 2001: 7). Allowing healers themselves to claim IP rights might incentivize the development of traditional medical knowledge and encourage younger members of the community to acquire it (Correa 2002: 10). But most traditional knowledge is socially produced and, therefore, not readily compatible with the individualized view of innovation on which the patent system rests (Timmermans 2003: 748; Government of Kenya 2009: 16).[40]

In response to the shortcomings of the orthodox IP regime, countries such as Costa Rica, the Philippines and Thailand have moved to establish so-called *sui generis* rights (see Correa 2001:

12–15).[41] Such a system has also been proposed by the Kenya Copyright Board in a recent draft bill based on the National Policy on Traditional Knowledge, Genetic Resources and Folklore (Government of Kenya 2009).[42] This would vest control over the use of traditional knowledge in 'local and traditional communities', who may exploit it themselves or license commercial firms to do so. A National Competent Authority would be charged with ensuring that the prior informed consent of the community had been obtained and that arrangements for the equitable sharing of benefits are in place. The draft is marked by a number of definitional problems, however. Most seriously, identification of the 'community' which owns the knowledge is left to customary law, even though the latter is often uncertain and unlikely to deal with the con-stitutional question of group definition in any case (Jones 1996: 132; IEA 2011a: 6). In any case, effective ownership presumes clear structures of representation and a leadership capable of enforcing property and contractual rights, though these are generally lacking even among Kenya's more tightly knit communities (Ng'etich 2005: 9; IEA 2011a: 7). There are also likely to be numerous claims to ownership of the same knowledge, since, as was noted above, members of different ethnic groups live alongside each other in many parts of the country (IEA 2011a: 6).[43] Whenever these problems mean that 'traditional owners' cannot be identified, the Author-ity is to hold and, presumably, exploit the knowledge 'on behalf of the people of Kenya'. Com-pulsory licences for processing may also be issued where the knowledge is 'not being sufficiently exploited' by the community.[44]

In many cases, then, traditional medical knowledge ends up being directly subject to the dominion of the state (see Mills 1996: 71). This is consistent with official policies over the last ten years which have envisioned it as providing the foundation for an export-focused herbal products industry, with the potential to contribute to 'accelerated socio-economic develop-ment' in Kenya (NCAPD 2005: vii; Government of Kenya 2009: 12, 3; Ministry of State for National Heritage and Culture 2012: 8).[45] Central to these proposals is the standardization of cultivation, production, packaging and marketing, increasingly demanded for entry into developed country markets (NCAPD 2005: 20; Ministry of State for National Heritage and Culture 2012: 13–14; Hughes 2011). As with patient safety, the ideal product is foregrounded, obscuring the healer on whose knowledge and experience it is based (Burris interview, 30 January 2013). Indeed, 'the secretiveness of practitioners' itself is seen as a significant obstacle to commercialization (NCAPD 2005: 6; Ministry of State for National Heritage and Culture 2012: 7). An extension of IP rights would, it is claimed, give them a sufficient sense of security to share their knowledge for the greater good as envisaged by Article 11(2)(c) of the Constitution and the government's medium-term economic plan *Vision 2030* (Mwangi 2012: 34; Government of Kenya 2012: 22). Traditional medicine is, thus, to be moved 'out of the informal economy' and reconstructed as 'legally regulated, scientifically driven and commercially informed' (Taracha interview, 25 July 2013; Government of Kenya 2009: 12; IEA 2011b: 12). Communities and traditional practitioners have been offered little scope to refuse this drive for commodification, though the latter may be inconsistent with the altruistic relations in which healing is often embedded, at least in rural areas (Correa 2002: 46; Ng'etich 2005: 10).

VIII Discussion: problematizing traditional medicine

Few of the initiatives to reform traditional medicine discussed above have as yet come to fru-ition. Nonetheless it is clear that, after decades of hostility or at best superficial support, the sector is now the object of a consistent 'quest for governance' on the part of the Kenyan state (Ng'etich 2008: 26). The nature of this quest and the role of law within it can be usefully elabor-ated in terms of the theory of biopolitical government developed by Rose and Milller (1992).[46]

On that account, governmental strategies are realized across two dimensions: (1) a normative focus on the principles and goals guiding human behaviour; and (2) an epistemological concern with strategies of rule and the objects at which they are directed. These dimensions are combined in 'problematizations' identifying the failures of organization, behaviour and regulation which lead specific activities to fall short of greater biopolitical goals (Bacchi 2012). Expert knowledges are central to the construction of such problem-fields (see further Henderson, Coveney, Ward and Taylor 2009).

The state's new posture towards traditional medicine has been supported in part by regional, continent wide and international initiatives – for example, the creation of an East African Network on Traditional Plants and Traditional Medicine in 2003, the African Union's declaration of 2001–2010 as the Decade of African Traditional Medicine and the Beijing Declaration adopted by the WHO Congress on Traditional Medicine in 2008 (see Langwick 2011b: 265). Each provides a set of non-legal or soft-law goals for the development of policy in this area. A further impetus has been provided by the coming into force of a new Kenyan constitution in 2010. The constitution is widely seen as re-founding the Kenyan republic after decades of authoritarianism and social injustice (see Harrington 2014: 116). Its passage is specifically interpreted by many healers as effecting a clear break with the hostility of colonial and post-colonial regimes to the practice of traditional medicine (Githae interview, 22 April 2013; Matoke interview, 31 January 2013). They note in particular Article 11, which positively affirms culture as 'the foundation of the nation' and recognizes the contribution of 'indigenous technologies' to national development.[47]

Of more concrete significance perhaps is the Bill of Rights, which guarantees citizens the right to the highest attainable standard of heath (Article 43(1)(a)) and obliges the state to protect the health and safety of consumers and their right to goods and services of reasonable quality (Article 46(1)).[48] These provisions do not function simply to ratify traditional medicine as currently practised. Rather, they provide normative force for its problematization as a potential threat to patient welfare and its reconstruction as a reliable element of the health care system according to senior administrators (Ominde-Ogaja interview, 19 February 2013). This view is shared by civil society groups, who have contemplated litigation to compel the government to legislate on the basis that healers, fake or genuine, are endangering the right to health of people living with HIV/AIDS by persuading them to abandon orthodox anti-retroviral therapies in favour of unproven 'miracle' cures (Ogendi interview, 25 February 2013; Kenya AIDS Law Project 2013).

The 'public health' problematization has been manifest in the range of initiatives addressing the 'safety, competency and quality' of traditional practitioners and the medicines they use (Wahlberg 2006: 137). Consistent with what Rose and Miller term 'neo-liberal' modes of government, these strategies commonly aim to mobilize the self-regulating capacities of non-state social groups and to remould the subjectivities of individual actors (Rose and Miller 1992: 179). Training in record keeping, hygiene and sustainable harvesting clearly aims at producing healers who discipline themselves in these aspects of their work. Moreover, as was seen above, governmental officials seek a united healers association, not only as an interlocutor in the reform process, but also as a source of authentic ethical guidance and discipline for practitioners. The prominence of self-regulation in these strategies should not obscure the importance of formal law. Indeed, a lack of legislation is itself identified as contributing to the health problem posed by traditional medicine and to Kenya's failure to profit from its indigenous knowledge (Matoke interview, 31 January 2013). Consequently, statute-based regulation, giving coercive force to professional standards, is a central objective of both healers and concerned officials.

Traditional medicine in Kenya is the site of other problematizations, oriented to a range of goals beyond public health.[49] Thus, a lack of product standardization and clearly defined intellectual property rights are seen to hinder commercialization; the unsustainable harvesting practices of healers engage the value of environmental protection; and the threat of 'biopiracy' is framed in terms of sovereignty over resources (NCAPD 2005: 2; Mwangi 2012). All of these concerns are further inscribed within the 'master frame' of national economic development which has been the raison d'être of Kenya, like most other post-colonial states, since independence (Branch and Cheeseman 2010; Harrington and O'Hare 2014). As with health, normative underpinnings for these goals are provided by international agreements (e.g. the Convention on Biological Diversity and the TRIPs Agreement) and by the Kenyan constitution itself. The latter expressly obliges the state to 'protect the intellectual property rights of the people of Kenya' and to ensure 'sustainable exploitation' of natural resources and 'the equitable sharing of the accruing benefits'. Indeed, its first article is a general declaration of popular sovereignty.[50]

These problematizations of traditional medicine derive much of their rhetorical force from the sense of impending loss communicated by commentators and policy makers. Thus, indigenous knowledge is represented as 'an invaluable heritage … gained over thousands of years', but threatened with loss through a failure to ensure its transmission to the next generation of practitioners (Mwangi 2012: 9, 34). Kenyan resources and the income which can be derived from them may be unwittingly surrendered to foreign biopirates (see NCAPD 2005: 4; Government of Kenya 2009: 8). Customary law prohibitions which protect biodiversity and access to medical materials have fallen into disuse and are ignored (Mutta and Munyi 2010: 5). The integrated, holistic and stable context for the practice of traditional medicine, which protected patients against harm and exploitation, is alleged to be dissolving under pressure of urbanization and commercialization (see supra section V). Such concerns have led one eminent scholar and practitioner of traditional medicine to argue that his contemporaries are under an 'academic, moral and practical obligation to salvage' this aspect of the national heritage (Mwangi 2012: 11). Kenya's commercial healers draw on this sense of traditional medicine as distinctively African and ancient, using maps of the continent and images of village life, as well as slogans such as 'Back to the Roots', in marketing their clinics.[51] At the same time, however, they are increasingly investing in mechanized production and the delivery of standardized products. Thus, together with their partners in various state bodies, they aim not so much at 'salvaging' as 'reconstructing' traditional medicine by making it fit for 'modern' conditions, thereby intensifying the process of change. The necessity of standardizing inherited practices in order to save them and make them 'exploitable' has also been expressed by MPs debating the regulation of traditional medicine.[52]

Problematizations of traditional medicine, as regards patient safety, conservation, biopiracy or commercialization, are also articulated generically in terms of the opacity of practitioners and their therapies to state agencies. It has been noted that the ingredients of herbal products are a matter of guesswork since there are no machines to test them; healers' knowledge is unwritten, passed on by elderly relatives and kept secret for fear of intellectual property theft (Anon 2010b). Reform proposals can thus be seen as strategies for making traditional medicine 'readable' by the state and the market. This 'project of legibility', to use Scott's term, is to be realized through the creation of new legal forms or the imposition of penal sanctions (see Scott 1998: 80, 82). Thus, the obscurity of the healer–patient relationship is to be removed through an obligation to keep records of consultations; the plants used by healers are being catalogued by Kenyan scientists and international agencies (see Ongugo, Mutta, Pakia and Munyi 2012: 9); intellectual property reforms, whether the extension of existing forms or the creation of *sui generis* rights, are proposed in order to clarify ownership and thus allow markets in herbal products to develop (NCAPD 2005: 41); and the dosage and contents of traditional medicines are to be made visible to consumers through standardized production and packaging (NCAPD 2005: 34; Anon 2010b).

Scott notes that such legibility can only be achieved through eliminating local particularities and individual idiosyncrasies (1998: 81). The embodied (and therefore obscure), 'practical' knowledge of healers is to be supplanted by the codified (and therefore legible) 'technical' knowledge of state and private sector experts (see Oakeshott 1962).

This trend has two important implications. First, as already noted, it enables state agencies to focus increasingly on the products associated with traditional medicine, rather than on its practitioners. Various strategies of documentation and standardization will allow potentially valuable knowledge to be prised away from 'secretive' healers seen as hoarding resources on which the nation as a whole has a claim (NCAPD 2005: 5; Langwick 2011b: 277). Second, in response to this tendency, prominent healers have repositioned their practice by identifying exclusively with those forms of practice most legible to the state. They distinguish themselves not only from quacks, but also from spiritualists and faith healers whose therapeutics cannot be immediately re-read in terms of scientific biomedicine (see Adams 2002: 667). This is reflected in the pervasive use of the term 'herbalist' to describe healers, their clinics and professional associations.

The foregoing review indicates that the problematization of traditional medicine in Kenya has widened and deepened considerably over the last fifteen years. The hostility of the authorities in the colonial and early post-colonial periods was based upon a fairly simplistic representation of traditional medicine as evil, subversive or, at best, a 'tribal' residue. Legal and societal responses to it were correspondingly undifferentiated: criminal repression, religious denunciation or limited tolerance. More recent policy proposals are considerably more detailed. They are informed by quite distinct disciplines (e.g. botany, public health, marketing), promoted by diverse state institutions (e.g. ministries of health, trade, agriculture and forestry) and oriented by a range of normative goals and principles. Where traditional medicine was previously only visible to the state in outline, it has emerged as the object of an increasingly discriminating regime of visibility (Scott 1998: 51–52). Legal norms and legal technologies play a significant role in this regime.

IX Conclusion

This chapter has examined developments in the legal regulation of traditional medicine in Kenya. Three main modes of state engagement were observed. Repression and exclusion in the colonial period was followed by official indifference in the early decades of independence. Current initiatives signal a more intensive and wide-ranging engagement. As Vincanne Adams (2002) has argued, policing the line between reason and magic, between the scientific and the traditional has long been a central task of the state. This task has specific salience in African nations. Like the late colonial regimes to which they succeeded, the independent states created in the 1950s and 1960s saw themselves as agents of modernization and development (Vaughan 1991). Biomedicine was central to these strategies. States committed themselves to make adequate biomedical care available to all citizens as a 'fruit' of independence (Ndege 2001). More broadly, acceptance of the scientific worldview purveyed by biomedicine was taken to be a key marker of the modernity of a given individual and of the nation as a whole (Geissler 2011). The state's role as the central agent of development and modernization was undermined in the 1980s as much of Africa was beset by economic and political crisis (Ferguson 2006). Ensuing programmes of structural adjustment, democratization and governance reform shrank the capacity of the public sector, privileging corporate actors and civil society organizations instead (see Harrington 2004). However, as has been seen, the role of the state has not so much been abolished as reconfigured. It is now focused on creating, enabling and regulating markets in services, such as health, which it previously supplied directly to citizens. Thus, the problematizations of traditional medicine considered in this chapter involve drawing the line between what may be safely and securely traded and what may not. The distinction between the rational and the irrational, the salutary and the dangerous remains central to the state's historic tasks of modernization and development. But under neo-liberal circumstances, these tasks can only be realized through the orderly functioning of the market.

Notes

1 This chapter could not have been written without the invaluable research assistance of Elizabeth Storer, Graduate Attachée at the British Institute in Eastern Africa, Nairobi (2013). Thanks to Ambreena Manji and Maria Stuttaford for their comments on earlier drafts. The usual disclaimer applies. This research was carried out under Research Authorization NACOSTI/P/14/0818/628 issued by the Kenyan National Council for Science, Technology and Innovation.

2 These mean 'original', 'customary' and 'local medicine', respectively (Langwick 2008: 437).

3 See further Iliffe (1998: 28–29).

4 See, for example, *Kenya National Assembly Debates*, 25 November 2009, 4049 (Nicholas Gumbo MP, referring to Exodus 15:25, Kings II 20:7, Revelation 22:2 and Isaiah 38:1–2). For sources in the Koran and Islamic tradition (Hadith), see Marwat, Khan and Rehman (2008).

5 See, respectively, ss. 2, 7, 6 *Witchcraft Act* Cap 67. Langwick argues that the concept of 'witchcraft' is distinctively European origin, mapping only loosely on to prior African belief systems (2011a: 46).

6 For example, *Chivatsi v Republic*, Court of Appeal at Mombasa Criminal Appeal No. 77 of 1989 [1990] KLR 529.

7 See, for example, Makori (2013), Anon (2010a).

8 See s. 22(2) *Medical Practitioners and Dentists Act* Cap 253. Of equal import are s. 19(1) and s. 35(a) *Pharmacy and Poisons Act* Cap 244, which limit the conduct of business as a pharmacist and the manufacturing of medicinal substances, respectively, to those registered under the Act. Healers certainly engage in all such activities. The extent to which the law is enforced against them is unclear.

9 Declaration of Alma-Ata, International Conference on Primary Health Care, Alma-Ata, USSR, 6–12 September 1978.

10 KEMRI's founder, Professor Kihumbu Thairu, had written in 1975: 'We should be proud of our medicine men. It is they who bore the torch of medical knowledge in the pre-microscope days in our society' (quoted in Ombongi 2011: 364).

11 In the absence of a formal system of registration, this estimate is necessarily a very rough one.

12 $n = 254$.

13 The Commonwealth Secretariat has provided some support for the installation of mechanized processing facilities: see 'Dr Jack Githae – SAMTECH', 17 December 2012: available at www.youtube.com/watch?v=71qFALMAd5I (last accessed 16 April 2014).

14 See, for example, the Kenya Alternative Medicine Initiative website: www.secretcures.co.ke (last accessed 16 April 2014).

15 Seventy-four per cent of the traditional practitioners surveyed by Lambert and Leonard were training between one and three apprentices (2011: 4).

16 This reflects the pattern of subordination mentioned above. Community medicine casts traditional healers as supporting orthodox health care workers, while pharmacognosy is concerned with the identification of new therapies in natural substances.

17 Africa Health Workforce Observatory – Human Resources for Health Country Profile: Kenya – March 2009, quoted in Lambert and Leonard (2011: 29).

18 It should be noted that popular understandings of 'malaria' in East Africa are broad and fluid; see Muela, Ribera, Mushi and Tanner (2002).

19 Such workshops have been organized by the Jomo Kenyatta University of Agriculture and Technology in Nairobi and by Kenya Working Group on Medicinal and Aromatic Plants across the country (Gemson 2013; KWG-MAPS: 2011).

20 See *Kenya National Assembly Official Report*, 13 August 2008, 2593 (Minister for Medical Services Anyang Nyong'o); 25 November 2009, 4049 (Mr Gumbo MP).

21 See more generally Henkel (2013).Note also that healers, fake or not, sometimes combine 'Western' pharmaceuticals with more traditional herbal remedies. This is seen as a particular source of risk to patients; see, for example, Anon (2010b).

22 The views on TCM reported in this paragraph are drawn from: Matoke interview, 31 January 2013; Matu interview, 21 May 2013; Mwangi interview, 10 April 2012; Ominde-Ogaja interview, 19 February 2013; Taracha interview, 25 July 2013.

23 See further Schroeder (2002).

24 An orientation to China and a corresponding distrust of the West have been prominent in parliamentary debates on traditional medicine; see *Kenya National Assembly Debates*, 25 November 2009, 4440, 4449 (Mr Mwira MP, Mr Shakeel MP).

25 Kenyan students have also been supported by doctoral scholarships to study traditional medicine in China (Kimani interview, 26 March 2012).

26 It should be noted, on the other hand, that healers also see TCM as a source of competition in East Africa itself (Jamah 2012; Hsu 2002) and that allegations of fakery have been raised against local TCM firms (Wan 2014).

27 See NCAPD (2005).

28 This policy was developed under the auspices of the Attorney General's office; see Government of Kenya (2009).

29 The Kenya Working Group on Medicinal and Aromatic Plants mentioned above relied on NATHEPA to select healers for funded training in plant conservation and record keeping. However, trainers noted a 'lack of organizational cohesiveness and a tendency to dispute which threatened the running of some workshops'; see KWG-MAPS (2011: 5, 13).

30 Article 186(1) and Schedule 4, Parts I.28 and II.2.

31 The discussion in this paragraph refers to the version of the draft dated 29 July 2013. A copy is on file with the author.

32 World Agroforestry Centre, *Agro-Forestry Tree Database: Warburgia ugandensis* (Nairobi n.d.): www.worldagroforestry.org/treedb/AFTPDFS/Warburgia_ugandensis.pdf (last accessed 16 April 2014).

33 World Agroforestry Centre, *Agro-Forestry Tree Database: Azadirachta indica* (Nairobi n.d.): www.world-agroforestry.org/treedb/AFTPDFS/Azadirachta_indica.pdf (last accessed 16 April 2014). World Agroforestry Centre, *Agro-Forestry Tree Database: Prunus africana* (Nairobi n.d.): www.worldagroforestry.org/treedb/AFTPDFS/Prunus_africana.pdf (last accessed 16 April 2014).

34 This doctrine remains part of Kenyan law: s. 20 *Forests Act 2005*. On customary rights in this context, see Mutta and Munyi (2010: 15). Management of Kenya's forests is hindered by the overlapping jurisdiction of several state agencies in this area (NEMA 2011: 106).

35 Ss. 45, 46(2)(a) *Forests Act 2005*. See further, Kenya Land Alliance (2006).

36 See also *Kenya National Assembly Debates*, 9 December 2009, 4449, 4452 (Mr Shakeel MP, Mr Maina MP).

37 Articles 11(3)(a), (b) and 69(1)(a).

38 Regs 9, 20 *Environmental Management and Co-ordination (Conservation of Biological Diversity and Resources, Access to Genetic Resources and Benefit Sharing) Regulations 2006*.

39 The requirements for the issuing of a patent in Kenya are laid down in s. 23 *Industrial Property Act* Cap 509.

40 Although no patents have been filed in Kenya by healers to date, a few utility models (or 'petty patents') have been recognized (Otswong'o interview, 11 July 2013). These are cheaper and easier to obtain than patents, though they offer only ten instead of twenty years' protection; s. 82(1), (2) *Industrial Property Act* Cap 509.

41 Such rights are also included in the Organization of African Unity (now the African Union) *Model Law for Protection of the Rights of Local Communities, Farmers and Breeders, and for the Regulation of Access to Biological Resources* (2000); see further Wekesa (2009: 290).

42 A copy of the draft bill from May 2013 is on file with the author.

43 The potential for an entrepreneurial creation of ethnic identities to profit from such rights and the ensuing risk of political conflict has been noted by Lynch (2011).

44 For equivalent provisions in Thailand, see Kuanpoth (2008: 80).

45 There are already small programmes for the development of herbal products at KEMRI and a number of Kenyan universities; see Anon (2013).

46 For a useful application of this approach to the regulation of traditional medicine in Vietnam, see Wahlberg (2006).

47 See Articles 11(1) and 11(2)(b), respectively.

48 For a review of the relevance of the right to health for access to and practice of traditional medicine, see Harrington *et al.* (2014).

49 On the relationship between multiple problematizations of a single issue, see Dent (2009).
50 See Articles 40(5), 69(1)(a) and 1(1), respectively.
51 Advertising flyer for Dr Maina's Herbals (copy on file with author). Parliamentarians also emphasize their pride in 'African' or 'our' medicine, often referencing the medical practices of their own ethnic groups and mentioning childhood encounters with local healers; see, for example, *Kenya National Assembly Debates*, 9 December 2009, 4442, 4446, 4448 (Mr Khalwale MP, Mr Baya MP, Mr Bifwoli MP).
52 See *Kenya National Assembly Debates*, 9 December 2009, 4438 (Mr Mwiria MP).

Bibliography

Abuje, J. (2012) 'Traditional Medicine Practitioners Upbeat Over New Health Bill', *Africa Science News*, 16 October: www.africasciencenews.org/en/index.php?option=com_content&view=article&id=650:traditional-medicine-practitioners-upbeat-over-new-health-bill&catid=63:health&Itemid=114 (last accessed 16 April 2014).

Adams, V. (2002) 'Randomized Controlled Crime: Postcolonial Sciences in Alternative Medicine Research', 32 *Social Studies of Science* 659–690.

Anangwe, A. (2008) 'Health Sector Reforms in Kenya: User Fees', in M. Sama and V. K. Nguyen (eds), *Governing Health Systems in Africa* (Dakar: Codesria), 44–59.

Anon (2010a) '"Witch Doctors" Out to Defraud Public Seized', *Daily Nation*, 24 January.

Anon (2010b) 'Herbal Medicine Set for Regulation', *Business Daily*, 27 October.

Anon (2012) 'Africa: Snake Oil Salesmen and Dodgy HIV "Cures"', IRIN, 19 January: www.irinnews.org/report/94679/africa-snake-oil-salesmen-and-dodgy-hiv-quot-cures-quot (last accessed 16 April 2014).

Anon (2013) 'The TMDDP Exhibits at the Nairobi Trade Fair', 1(1) *Traditional Medicine and Drug Development Programme Newsletter* 6: www.kemri.org/dmdocuments/TMDDP%201st%20Newsletter%202013.pdf (last accessed 16 April 2014).

Arihan, O. and A. Gençler Özkan (2007) 'Traditional Medicine and Intellectual Property Rights', 36 *Journal of Faculty of Pharmacy of Ankara University* 135–151.

Bacchi, C. (2012) 'Why Study Problematizations? Making Politics Visible', 2 *Open Journal of Political Science* 1–8: http://dx.doi.org/10.4236/ojps.2012.21001 (last accessed 20 June 2014).

Barnett, A. (2004) 'Multi-Million Bio-Piracy Lawsuit Over Faded Jeans and African Lakes', *The Observer*, 5 September.

Branch, D. and N. Cheeseman (2010), 'Introduction: Our Turn to Eat', in D. Branch, N. Cheeseman and L. Gardner (eds), *Our Turn to Eat: Politics in Kenya Since 1950* (Berlin: Lit Verlag 2010), 1–10.

Butungi, C. (2010) 'Greenheart the Wonder Tree, Can Sprout Money if Spared the Axe', *East African*, 30 August.

Chavunduka, G. (1986) 'Zinatha: The Organisation of Traditional Medicine in Zimbabwe', in M. Last and G. L. Chavunduka (eds), *The Professionalisation of African Medicine* (Cambridge: Cambridge University Press), 29–51.

Chege, K. (2003) 'Kenyan Parliament to Debate Traditional Medicine', *SciDevNet*, 24 December: www.scidev.net/en/news/kenyan-parliament-to-debate-traditional-medicine.html (last accessed 16 April 2014).

Cho, H.-J. (2000) 'Traditional Medicine, Professional Monopoly and Structural Interests: A Korean Case', 50 *Social Science and Medicine* 123–135.

Clapp, R. A. and C. Crook (2002) 'Drowning in the Magic Well: Shaman Pharmaceuticals and the Elusive Value of Traditional Knowledge', 11 *Journal of Environment Development* 79–102.

Clough, M. S. (2003) 'Mau Mau and the Contest for Memory', in E. S. Atieno Odhiambo and J. Lonsdale (eds), *Mau Mau and Nationhood. Arms, Authority and Narration* (Oxford: James Currey), 251–267.

Correa, C. M. (2001) *Traditional Knowledge and Intellectual Property. Issues and Options Surrounding the Protection of Traditional Knowledge. A Discussion Paper* (Geneva: Quaker United Nations Office).

Correa, C. M. (2002) *Protection and Promotion of Traditional Medicine – Implications for Public Health in Developing Countries* (Geneva: South Centre).

Coveney, J. (2008) 'The Government of Girth', 17 *Health Sociology Review* 199–213.

Cunningham, A. (1998) 'An Africa-Wide Overview of Medicinal Plant Harvesting, Conservation and Healthcare', in FAO, *Medicinal Plants for Forest Conservation and Healthcare* (Rome: Food and Agricultural Organization), 116–129.

Dent, C. (2009) 'Copyright, Governmentality and Problematisation: An Exploration', 18 *Griffith Law Review* 129–150.

Ferguson, J. (2006) *Global Shadows. Africa in the Neo-Liberal World Order* (Durham, NC: Duke University Press).

Fortunate, E. (2012) 'Health Clinics Run by Quacks in Many City Slums', *Daily Nation*, 28 February.

Geissler, P. W. (2011) 'Parasite Lost: Remembering Modern Times with Kenyan Government Medical Scientists', in P. W. Geissler and C. Molyneux (eds), *Evidence, Ethos and Experiment. The Anthropology and History of Medical Research in Africa* (New York: Berghahn), 297–332.

Gemson, S. C. (2013) 'Herbal Medicine Industry in Dire Need of Regulation', *Daily Nation*, 19 February.

Government of Kenya (2009) *National Policy on Traditional Knowledge, Genetic Resources and Traditional Cultural Expressions*, submitted to the Intergovernmental Committee on Intellectual Property and Genetic Resources, Traditional Knowledge and Folklore, World Intellectual Property Organization, 16th Session, Geneva, 3–7 May 2010, WIPO/GRTKF/IC/16/INF/25.

Government of Kenya (2012) *Sessional Paper No. 10 of 2012 on Kenya Vision 2030* (Nairobi).

Harrington, J. (2004) 'Medical Law and Health Care Reform in Tanzania', 7 *Medical Law International* 207–230.

Harrington, J. (2014) 'Access to Essential Medicines in Kenya: Intellectual Property, Anti-Counterfeiting and the Right to Health', in M. Freeman, B. Bennett and S. Hawkes (eds), *Law and Global Health. Current Legal Issues, vol. 16* (Oxford: Oxford University Press), 94–118.

Harrington, J. and A. Manji (2013) 'Satire and the Politics of Corruption in Kenya', 22 *Social and Legal Studies* 3–23.

Harrington J. and A. O'Hare (2014) 'Framing the National Interest. Debating Intellectual Property and Access to Medicines in Kenya', 17 *Journal of World Intellectual Property* 16–31.

Harrington, J., M. Stuttaford, S. Al Makhamreh, F. Coomans, C. Himonga and G. Lewando Hundt (2014) 'The Right to Traditional, Complementary, and Alternative Health Care', 7 *Global Health Action*: 24121: http://dx.doi.org/10.3402/gha.v7.24121.

Henderson, J., J. Coveney, P. Ward and A. Taylor (2009) 'Governing Childhood Obesity: Framing Regulation of Fast Food Advertising in the Australian Print Media', 69 *Social Science and Medicine* 1402–1408.

Henkel, A. (2013) 'Geneaology of the Pharmacon: New Conditions for the Social Management of the Extraordinary', 8 *Management and Organizational History* 262–276.

Hoff, W. (1993) 'Traditional Healers and Community Health', 13 *World Health Forum* 182–187.

Hsu, E. (2002) '"The Medicine from China has Rapid Effects": Chinese Medicine Patients in Tanzania', 9 *Anthropology and Medicine* 291–313.

Hughes, D. (2011) 'New EU Regulations on Herbal Medicines Come into Force', *BBC News*, 30 April: www.bbc.co.uk/news/health-13215010 (last accessed 15 May 2014).

IEA (2009) 'Biodiversity Related International Initiatives and National Policy Coherence for Development and Poverty Reduction in Kenya', *Trade Notes, No. 23* (Nairobi: Institute of Economic Affairs).

IEA (2011a) 'Protecting Traditional Knowledge and Associated Genetic Resources in Kenya: What a Community Needs to Know', *Trade Notes, No. 31* (Nairobi: Institute of Economic Affairs).

IEA (2011b) *Biodiversity, Traditional Knowledge and Intellectual Property in Kenya: The Legal and Institutional Framework for Sustainable Economic Development* (Nairobi: Institute of Economic Affairs).

Iliffe, J. (1998) *East African Doctors: a History of the Modern Profession* (Cambridge: Cambridge University Press).

Jackson, K. (2003) '"Impossible to Ignore their Greatness"; Survival Craft in the Mau Mau Forst Movement', in E. S. Atieno Odhiambo and J. Lonsdale (eds), *Mau Mau and Nationhood. Arms, Authority and Narration* (Oxford: James Currey), 176–190.

Jamah, A. (2012) 'Herbal HIV Drugs from China for Kenyan Market', *The Standard*, 3 April 2012.

Jones, P. W. (1996) 'Indigenous Peoples and Intellectual Property Rights', 4 *Waikato Law Review* 117–140.

Kareithi, A. (2009) 'How Herbalists Con Kenyans', *The Standard*, 11 February.

Kareru, P. G., G. M. Kenji, A. N. Gachanja, J. M. Keriko and G. Mungai (2007) 'Traditional Medicines among the Embu and Mbeere Peoples of Kenya', 4 *African Journal of Traditional Complementary and Alternative Medicine* 75–86.

Kenya AIDS Law Project (2013) *Access to Medicine Program – Adherence Campaign Report*, 10 April (Nairobi) [copy on file with author].

Kenya Land Alliance (2006) *Challenges Facing the Implementation of the Forest Act* 2005 (Nairobi): www.mokoro.co.uk/files/13/file/lria/kla_land_update5.2forest.pdf (last accessed 16 April 2014).

KFS (2010) *Karura Forest Strategic Management Plan 2010–2014* (Nairobi: Kenya Forest Service) [copy on file with author].

KFS (n.d.) 'Kenya Needs Ksh 7.6 Billion to Reach 10% Forest Cover by the Year 2030' (Nairobi: Kenya Forest Service): www.kenyaforestservice.org/index.php?option=com_content&view=article&id=254:kenya-needs-ksh-76-billion-to-reach-10-forest-cover-by-the-year-2030&catid=223:hict&Itemid=98 (last accessed 16 April 2014).

Kimani, V. (1981) 'Attempts to Co-ordinate the Work of Traditional and Modern Doctors in Nairobi in 1980', 15B *Social Science and Medicine* 421–422.

KNBS (2009) *Kenya Demographic and Health Survey 2008–9* (Nairobi: Kenya National Bureau of Statistics).

Kuanpoth, J. (2008) 'Intellectual Property Protection after TRIPS: An Asian Experience', in J. Malbon and C. Lawson (eds), *Interpreting and Implementing the TRIPS Agreement* (Cheltenham: Edward Elgar), 71–96.

KWG-MAPS (2011) *Kenya Working Group on Medicinal and Aromatic Plants: Training Report, Components A and B* (Nairobi: World Bank and Japanese Social Development Fund) [copy on file with author].

Lambert, J. and K. Leonard (2011) *The Contribution of Traditional Herbal Medicine Practitioners to Kenyan Health Care Delivery: Results from Community Health-Seeking Behaviour Vignettes and a Traditional Herbal Medicine Practitioner Survey* (Washington DC: World Bank).

Langwick, S. A. (2008) 'Articulate(d) Bodies: Traditional Medicine in a Tanzanian Hospital', 35 *American Ethnologist* 428–439.

Langwick, S. A. (2010) 'From Non-Aligned Medicines to Market-Based Herbals: China's Relationship to the Shifting Politics of Traditional Medicine in Tanzania', 29 *Medical Anthropology: Cross Cultural Studies in Health and Illness* 15–43.

Langwick, S. A. (2011a) *Bodies, Politics and African Healing: The Matter of Maladies in Tanzania* (Bloomington, Ind.: Indiana University Press).

Langwick, S. A. (2011b) 'Healers and Scientists: The Epistemological Politics of Research about Medicinal Plants in Tanzania or Moving Away from Traditional Medicine', in P. W. Geissler and C. Molyneux (eds), *Evidence, Ethos and Experiment. The Anthropology and History of Medical Research in Africa* (New York: Berghahn), 263–296.

Leonard, K. (2003) 'African Traditional Healers and Outcome-Contingent Contracts in Health Care', 71 *Journal of Development Economics* 1–22.

Lonsdale, J. (1990) 'Mau Maus of the Mind: Making Mau Mau and Remaking Kenya', 31 *Journal of African History* 393–421.

Lynch, G. (2011) 'Kenya's New Indigenes: Negotiating Local Identities in a Global Context', 17 *Nations and Nationalism* 148–167.

Majtenyi, C. (2012) 'Kenya Considers Policy to Regulate Traditional Medicines', *Voice of America News*, 29 May: www.voanews.com/content/kenya-considers-policy-to-regulate-traditional-medicines/1120662.html (last accessed 16 April 2014).

Makori, N. (2013) 'Herbalist's Concoction Kills Five Family Members', *The Standard*, 15 January.

Mamdani, M. (1996) *Citizen and Subject. Contemporary Africa and the Legacy of Late Colonialism* (Oxford: James Currey).

Marwat, S. K., M. A. Khan and F. Rehman (2008) 'Ethnomedicinal Study of Vegetables Mentioned in the Holy Qura'n and Ahadith', 12 *Ethnobotanical Leaflets* 1254–1269: www.ethnoleaflets.com/leaflets/marwat.htm (last accessed 16 June 2014).

McClelland, L. (2004) 'Bioprospecting: Market-Based Solutions to Biopiracy', 8 *UCLA Journal of Law and Technology*: www.lawtechjournal.com/notes/2004/08_040809_mcclelland.php (last accessed 16 April 2014).

McGown, J. (2006) *Out of Africa: Mysteries of Access and Benefit Sharing* (Washington DC: Edmonds Institute).

McMullin, S., J. Phelan, R. Jamnadass, M. Iiyama, S. Franzel and M. Nieuwenhuis (2012) 'Trade in Medicinal Tree and Shrub Products in Three Urban Centres in Kenya', 21 *Forests, Trees and Livelihoods* 188–206.

Mills, S. (1996) 'Indigenous Music and the Law: An Analysis of National and International Legislation', 28 *Yearbook for Traditional Music* 57–86.

Ministry of State for National Heritage and Culture (2012) *The Natural Products Industry Policy* (Nairobi).

Muela, S. H., J. M. Ribera, A. K. Mushi and M. Tanner (2002) 'Medical Syncretism with Reference to Malaria in a Tanzanian Community, 55 *Social Science and Medicine* 403–413.

Muriuki, J., S. Franzel, J. Mowo, P. Kariuki and R. Jamnadass (2012) 'Formalisation of Local Herbal Product Markets Has Potential to Stimulate Cultivation of Medicinal Plants by Smallholder Farmers in Kenya', 21 *Forests, Trees and Livelihoods* 114–127.

Mutta, D. and P. Munyi (2010) 'Protecting Maasai and Mijikenda Healers' Rights', in International Institute for Environment and Development (ed.), *Protecting Community Right over Traditional Knowledge Implications of Customary Laws and Practices* (London: IIED), 15–16.

Mwangi, J. (2012) 'Herbal Medicines: Do They Really Work?' *Inaugural Lecture, University of Nairobi*, 14 March [copy on file with author].

NCAPD (2005) *National Policy on Traditional Medicine and Medicinal Plants* (Nairobi: National Coordinating Agency for Population and Development) [copy on file with author].

NCAPD (2008) *Seeking Solutions for Traditional Herbal Medicine: Kenya Develops a National Policy. Policy Brief No. 1* (Nairobi: National Coordinating Agency for Population and Development).

Ndege, G. O. (2001) *Health, State and Society in Kenya* (Rochester, NY: University of Rochester Press).

NEMA (2011) *Kenya – State of the Environment and Outlook 2010: Supporting the Delivery of Vision 2030* (Nairobi: National Environmental Management Agency).

Ng'etich, K. (2005) *Indigenous Knowledge, Alternative Medicine and Intellectual Property Rights: Concerns in Kenya*, paper presented to 11th CODESRIA General Assembly, Maputo, Mozambique, 6–10 December [copy on file with author].

Ng'etich, K. (2008) 'Governing the Traditional Health Care Sector in Kenya: Strategies and Setbacks', in M. Sama and V. K. Nguyen (eds), *Governing Health Systems in Africa* (Dakar: CODESRIA), 25–33.

Oakeshott, M. (1962) *Rationalism in Politics and Other Essays* (London: Methuen).

Ombongi, K. S. (2011) 'The Historical Interface Between the State and Medical Science in Africa: Kenya's Case', in P. W. Geissler and C. Molyneux (eds), *Evidence, Ethos and Experiment. The Anthropology and History of Medical Research in Africa* (New York, Oxford: Berghahn), 353–372.

Ongugo, P., D. Mutta, M. Pakia and P. Munyi (2012) *Protecting Traditional Health Knowledge in Kenya. The Role of Customary Laws and Practices* (London: IIED).

Owoahene-Acheampong, S. and E. Vasconi (2010) 'Recognition and Integration of Traditional Medicine in Ghana: A Perspective', *26 Research Review* 1–17.

Peterson, K. (2001) 'Benefit Sharing for All? Bioprospecting NGOs, Intellectual Property Rights, New Governmentalities', 24 *PoLAR: Political and Legal Anthropology Review* 78–91.

Prince, R. and P. W. Geissler (2001) 'Becoming "One Who Treats": A Case Study of a Luo Healer and Her Grandson in Western Kenya', 32 *Anthropology and Education Quarterly* 447–471.

Rekdal, O. B. (1999) 'Cross-Cultural Healing in East African Ethnography', 13 *Medical Anthropology Quarterly* 458–482.

Rose, N. and P. Miller (1992) 'Political Power Beyond the State: Problematics of Government', 43 *British Journal of Sociology* 173–205.

Schroeder, T. (2002) 'Chinese Regulation of Traditional Chinese Medicine in the Modern World: Can the Chinese Effectively Profit from One of Their Most Valuable Cultural Resources?' 11 *Pacific Rim Law and Policy Journal* 687–716.

Scott, J. C. (1998) *Seeing Like a State. How Certain Schemes to Improve the Human Condition Have Failed* (New Haven, Conn.: Yale University Press).

Sujatha, V. (2011) 'Innovation Within and Between Traditions: Dilemma of Traditional Medicine in Contemporary India', 16 *Science, Technology and Society* 191–213.

TICAH (2010) *Trust for Indigenous Culture and Health Final (Year 2) Report to the Rockefeller Foundation – Valuing Traditional Medicine* (Nairobi: Trust for Indigenous Culture and Health) [copy on file with author].

Timmermans, K. (2003) 'Intellectual Property Rights and Traditional Medicine: Policy Dilemmas at the Interface', 57 *Social Science and Medicine* 745–756.

Tolo, F. M. (2014) 'The Kenya Health Bill 2012 on Traditional Medicine', 2(1) *KEMRI Natural Products Newsletter* 4–5: www.kemri.org/dmdocuments/TMDDP%202nd%20Newsletter%202014.pdf (last accessed 16 April 2014).

UNAIDS (2000) *Collaboration with Traditional Healers in HIV/AIDS Prevention and Care in Sub-Saharan Africa. A Literature Review* (Geneva: United Nations AIDS Programme).

Vaughan, M. (1991) *Curing their Ills. Colonial Power and African Illness* (Cambridge: Polity).

Wahlberg, A. (2006) 'Bio-politics and the Promotion of Traditional Herbal Medicine in Vietnam', 10 *Health* 123–147.

Wan, J. (2014) 'Get Rich or Die Trying: The Chinese Herbal Medicine "Death Sentence" in Uganda', *Think Africa Press*, 3 June: http://thinkafricapress.com/uganda/get-rich-or-die-trying-chinese-herbal-medicine-death-sentence-uganda (last accessed 20 June 2014).

Wekesa, M. (2009) 'Traditional Knowledge – the Need for a Sui Generis System of IPR Protection', in M. Wekesa and B. Sihanya (eds), *Intellectual Property Rights in Kenya* (Nairobi: Konrad Adenauer Stiftung), 267–298.

WHO (2001) *Legal Status of Traditional Medicine and Complementary/Alternative Medicine: A Worldwide Review* (Geneva: World Health Organization).

WHO (2002) *Traditional Medicine Strategy 2002–2005* (Geneva: World Health Organization).

WHO-AFRO (2010) 'Special Issue: Regulation of Traditional Medicine in the WHO African Region', 13 *The African Health Monitor*. www.aho.afro.who.int/en/ahm/issue/13 (last accessed 16 April 2014).

Interviews

(affiliations as at date of interview)

Dr Mary Ann Burris, Director of the Trust for Indigenous Culture and Health (TICAH), Kenya – 30 January 2013.

John Chege, Chief Scout, Karura Forest, Nairobi – 22 November 2013.

Dr Jack Githae, Traditional Healer and Director of the School of Alternative Medicine and Technology (SAMTECH), Nyeri – 22 April 2013.

Alhonse Gudacha, Traditional Healer in Muthaiga District, Nairobi – 21 February 2013.

David Khayeka, Traditional Healer, Magagori District, Kakamega County – 31 June 2013.

Dr Violet Kimani, Senior Lecturer, School of Public Health, University of Nairobi – 26 March 2012.

Odenda Lumumba, Chairman, Kenya Land Alliance – 29 August 2013.

Maina Mwea, Traditional Healer and Proprietor of *Dr Maina Herbals*, Nairobi – 29 January 2013.

Lydia Matoke, Traditional Healer and Chairperson, Herbalists Society of Kenya – 31 January 2013.

Dr Esther Matu, Senior Research Officer at Centre for Traditional Medicine and Drug Research, Kenya Medical Research Institute (KEMRI) – 21 May 2013.

Peter Munyi, Partner, Sisule, Munyi, Kilonzo Advocates, Nairobi, former legal consultant to International Centre for Insect Physiology and Ecology (ICIPE) – 1 October 2013.

Professor Julius Mwangi, Professor of Pharmacognosy, University of Nairobi – 10 April 2012.

Paul Ogendi, Programmes Officer, Kenya AIDS Law Project – 25 February 2013.

Dr Elizabeth Ominde-Ogaja, Deputy Chief Pharmacist, Ministry of Medical Services, Nairobi – 19 February 2013.

Frederick Otswong'o, Partner Random Forks Law Firm, former Patent Inspector, Traditional Knowledge and Genetic Resources Unit, Kenya Industrial Property Institute (KIPI) – 11 July 2013.

Didi Ruchira, Homeopathist and Founder of Abhalight Foundation – 12 February 2013.

Senior Kenyan Research Scientist, working nationally and internationally in the field of traditional medicine – 26 February 2013 [this interview was granted on condition of anonymity].

Dr Evans Taracha, Chief Researcher, Institute of Primate Research, National Museums of Kenya – 25 July 2013.

13

REGULATION OF COMPLEMENTARY MEDICINES IN AUSTRALIA

Influences and policy drivers

Michael Dodson

I Introduction

The regulatory landscape for complementary medicines in Australia has been influenced by a variety of key stakeholders within the context of a constantly evolving political backdrop. This chapter aims to provide the reader with an understanding of the way complementary medicines are regulated in Australia, and the factors that have helped shape this process. Section II aims to provide the reader with an outline of the current regulatory framework for therapeutic goods in Australia and how complementary medicines are regulated within this framework. Section III outlines the key stakeholder groups and political factors that have been influential in determining the nature of the system, degree of regulatory oversight and process involved in the regulation of complementary medicines. As these forces are inextricably linked, the subsequent sections consider policy and policy drivers, within their relative historical context (Section IV), and potential future developments in regulatory policy based on current political and social trends (Section V).

II The Australian regulatory framework

1 The regulation of medicines in Australia

The Therapeutic Goods Administration (TGA) is responsible for the regulation of therapeutic goods in Australia. This is achieved through administration of the *Therapeutic Goods Act 1989* (the Act) and the *Therapeutic Goods Regulations 1990* (the Regulations). Under the Act, the TGA is responsible for ensuring that therapeutic goods available for supply in Australia are safe and fit for their intended purpose (1). The definition of therapeutic good under the Act includes goods that are represented to be, or likely to be taken to be, for therapeutic use (unless specifically excluded), where therapeutic use refers to use in or connection with:

- preventing, diagnosing, curing or alleviating a disease, ailment, defect or injury in persons or animals; or

- influencing, inhibiting or modifying a physiological process in persons or animals; or
- testing the susceptibility of persons or animals to a disease or ailment; or
- influencing, controlling or preventing conception in persons; or
- testing for pregnancy in persons; or
- the replacement or modification of parts of the anatomy in persons or animals.

This definition is therefore broad and includes goods that may be involved in sustaining health as well as treating and/or preventing illness. This includes products containing nutrients that are presented or likely to be taken for use in achieving health benefits unless excluded by means of inclusion in the Australia New Zealand Food Standards Code as defined in subsection 3(1) of the Australia New Zealand Food Authority Act 1991.

The Therapeutic Goods Act 1989 requires that therapeutic goods that are imported or manufactured for supply in Australia be included in the Australian Register of Therapeutic Goods (ARTG),[1] unless they are specifically exempted from this requirement by Schedule 5 of the Therapeutic Goods Regulations 1990.

The TGA adopts a risk-based approach to the regulation of therapeutic goods that is applied to products prior to marketing (pre-market) and once they are on the market (post-market). Risk stratification takes into account a number of factors associated with the potential for adverse outcomes associated with use of a product, such as the toxicity of the ingredients, potential for interactions with other foods or therapeutic products, dosage form, approved use of the product and potential for non-compliance or off-label use.

Low-risk medicines receive a lesser degree of pre-market scrutiny than high-risk products, and may be listed (Aust L) on the ARTG following an automated process that relies largely upon self-certification that the product meets the certain requirements specified in the Act. During this process, sponsors are required to certify that the product contains only ingredients approved for use in listed medicines, that products have been manufactured according to Good Manufacturing Process (GMP) and that they hold evidence to support any claims being made. Indications for listed medicines may not refer to disorders that require health practitioner involvement ('serious disorders') (2). During the listing process, sponsors may enter indications by choosing from a list of prescribed 'standard'' indications, or entering their own unique indications in a free text field. Products carrying a higher risk are comprehensively assessed by the TGA with respect to safety, quality and efficacy prior to their inclusion on the ARTG. If found to comply, they are registered (Aust R) on the ARTG.

Post-market activities relate to the monitoring of the continuing safety, quality and efficacy of listed and registered therapeutic goods once they are on the market (3). In order to ensure compliance with requirements, the TGA performs audits of GMP and carries out targeted and random assessments of products in the marketplace. These assessments may involve assessment of labels, promotional material[2] and/or laboratory testing. In addition, listed medicines are subject to targeted and random desk-based audits that assess the accuracy of certification by sponsors at the time of listing. These controls are supplemented by a pharmacovigilance programme that considers adverse events reported to the TGA by consumers, health professionals, the pharmaceutical industry, international medicines regulators or medical and scientific experts on TGA advisory committees. An effective, responsive and timely recall process is in place that facilitates rapid removal of unsafe products from the marketplace.

2 *The regulation of complementary medicines*

The Regulations consider a complementary medicine to be 'a therapeutic good consisting wholly or principally of 1 or more designated active ingredients, each of which has a clearly established identity and a traditional use' (4). Most complementary medicines are listed medicines and most listed medicines are complementary medicines. Schedule 4 of the Regulations specifies that listed medicines are preparations containing as their therapeutically active ingredients only vitamins, minerals and certain herbal substances, but it also includes certain other groups of therapeutically active products, such as sunscreens.

Responsibility for regulation of complementary medicines is centred within the Office of Complementary medicines. Part 2 of Schedule 10 of the Regulations provides for the Office of Complementary Medicines to evaluate complementary medicines, excipients in complementary medicines and therapeutic goods referred for evaluation to the Office of Complementary Medicines by other offices within the Therapeutic Goods Administration. The Advisory Committee for Complementary Medicines (ACCM) provides expert advice to the Office on matters relating to complementary medicines.

III Influences and policy drivers for change and innovation in the regulation of complementary medicines in Australia

Drivers for change in complementary medicines regulation in Australia are conveniently considered in terms of the influences of stakeholder groups that provide input into government policy, and the broad social and political backdrop that provides the impetus for change and engagement with those stakeholder groups. Section 1 outlines the key stakeholder groups that have engaged, and continue to engage, with government on matters related to complementary medicines regulation. Section 2 then provides the reader with an insight into the broader political trends and major policy initiatives that have impacted upon the way complementary medicines are regulated.

1 Key stakeholders

1.1 Government

The Therapeutic Goods Administration is broadly divided into pre-market and post-market divisions that report to an executive comprising the National Manager, Principal Medical Adviser, Principal Legal Adviser, Chief Regulatory Officer and Chief Operating Officer. The pre- and post-market divisions are responsible respectively for the evaluation of therapeutics prior to marketing and the oversight of marketed products. Different offices within the pre-market division bear responsibility for different types of therapeutic goods, such as prescription medicines, complementary medicines and medical devices. The regulatory functions of the pre- and post-market divisions are supported by legal, financial, information technology, communication and administrative resources. A number of internal committees with representation from all offices within the TGA exist in order to ensure that regulatory practices within the TGA remain consistent.

The TGA is a division of the Department of Health and Ageing and interacts with other divisions of the department, such as the Regulatory Policy Governance Division (RPGD) for policy matters relating to the development of regulatory best practice across the health portfolio. The TGA also interacts with statutory authorities and other government departments. Key here are interactions between the TGA and Food Standards Australia and New Zealand (FSANZ) in relation to the food–medicine interface, and interactions between the TGA and the National Health and Medicine Research Council (NHMRC) regarding the establishment of standards of evidence assessment. The TGA is also integral to the ongoing refinement of the

National Medicines Policy (NMP) that strives to ensure access and quality use of medicines by Australians. The NMP includes complementary medicines and provides an important mechanism by which the access and information needs of consumers and health professionals can be recognised and addressed.

The TGA engages with a number of external committees that provide advice and recommendations relating to regulatory matters. These 'expert committees' are established under legislation. Their membership (also specified in legislation) includes experts in various aspects of therapeutic goods regulations that are of relevance to each committee's terms of reference, as well as nominees of organisations that represent the therapeutic goods industry, and consumers of health services. Committees that are of particular relevance to complementary medicines include the Advisory Committee on Complementary Medicines (ACCM), the Therapeutic Goods Committee (TGC), the Therapeutic Goods Advertising Code Council (TGACC) and the Complaints Resolution Panel (CRP).

The ACCM was established to advise and provide recommendations to the Minister for Health and Ageing on matters related to complementary medicines regulation (5). Members of the committee have expertise in complementary medical practice, manufacture of medicines, consumer issues, general medical practice in Australia, herbal medicine, naturopathy, nutrition and nutritional medicine, pharmacology, pharmacognosy, toxicology and/or epidemiology (6). The TGC advises and provides recommendations to the Minister for Health and Ageing on the adoption of standards and requirements for therapeutic goods relating to labelling, packaging and manufacture (7). The committee's expertise spans manufacturing, microbiology and virology, biomedical engineering, biological safety of biomaterials, biotechnology, pharmaceutical science and/or community or hospital pharmacy practice (8).

The TGACC is responsible for ensuring that the Therapeutic Goods Advertising Code is current and relevant, and reflects community values. It provides recommendations to the Minister of Health and Ageing about the advertising of therapeutic products to consumers and consists of twelve members representing the manufacturing and supplier sector, the advertising industry, consumers, healthcare professionals and government (9). The CRP comprises representatives from industry, consumers, advertising agencies, healthcare professionals and government and is chaired by a person elected by the TGACC. The Panel considers complaints made in relation to advertisements for therapeutic goods and refers its decisions to the TGA for action (10).

The TGA also has regular bilateral interactions with its international counterparts and the complementary medicines industry.

1.2 Consumers

The Consumers Health Forum of Australia (CHF) is the national peak body representing the interests of Australian healthcare consumers (11). The CHF was established in 1987 to ensure consumer representation in health matters, the CHF aims to achieve safe, quality, timely healthcare for all Australians, which is supported by accessible health information and systems. The CHF has been actively involved in the development of the NMP, and in developing TGA policy through submissions to public consultations and in nominating consumer representatives for TGA external committees, including the ACCM.

Formerly known as the Australian Consumers Association, CHOICE was founded in 1960 and is now the largest consumer organisation in Australia (12). CHOICE empowers consumers to get the most out of all their purchasing decisions by providing advocacy, information and advice (13). Like the CHF, CHOICE participates actively in matters related to therapeutic goods regulation through nominating membership for TGA committees and the preparation of submissions for public consultations. In recent years, the Australian Skeptics have shown an increasing interest in complementary medicines and have provided input into public consultations relating to complementary medicines reform. Consumers can also provide individual input through application for membership to committees as consumer reps and through submissions to public consultations.

1.3 Industry

Four key industry bodies represent the sponsors of therapeutic goods regulated by the Therapeutic Goods Administration: the Australian Self-Medication Industry (ASMI), the Complementary Healthcare Council (CHC), Medicines Australia and the Medical Technology Association of Australia (14). Two of these peak bodies, ASMI and CHC, have been particularly influential in the evolution of complementary medicines regulation in Australia. ASMI and its predecessor, Proprietary Medicines Association of Australia (PMAA) have broadly represented the makers of non-prescription medicines in Australia, and the Complementary Healthcare Council and its predecessor, Nutritional Foods Association of Australia, have represented, more specifically, the makers of complementary medicines. Both interact regularly with the TGA in a number of fora including:

- regular government-industry meetings
- representation on expert committees and working groups
- attendance at conferences/training days
- private audience
- submissions to industry and public consultations.

As a result of the intimacy of relationships, ASMI and CHC have been well placed to influence TGA policy relating to complementary medicines and both have been important players in the unfolding of the Australian approach to complementary medicines regulation. The complementary medicines industry in Australia includes a diversity of large, medium-sized and small businesses. Although any of these can provide input into TGA policy through submissions to public consultations of direct contact with the TGA, the larger companies tend to be better resourced to provide strategic input directly and through their relationships with ASMI and CHC.

1.4 Health professionals

Health practitioner groups enjoy wide representation on TGA expert committees. For example, ACCM includes representation from the medical profession, herbal medicine, naturopathy, nutrition and nutritional medicine. Health professionals and their representative bodies are also able to provide input into TGA policy via submissions to public consultations. Certain health practitioners and academics have also been advocates in their own right for change in complementary medicines regulation in Australia. One such advocate has published widely on the limitations of the current regulatory framework for complementary medicines regulation in Australia (15).

2 The political context

2.1 Broad political trends

The underlying political climate necessarily plays an important role in the evolution of regulatory policy. Prompted by a pervasive sense of national stagnation that accompanied poor GDP growth and high unemployment in the early 1980s, support grew for freer trade and a more market-oriented economy (16). The middle and late 1980s were characterised by liberal economic reforms by the newly elected labour government that failed and were replaced with more moderate economic reforms characterised by low inflation and high productivity coupled with market deregulation, which proved more effective in shoring up the national economy under increasing pressures of globalisation (16).

These reforms generated significant growth in economic activity, employment and household disposable income that was maintained and administered during the late 1990s and early 2000s by a liberal government that was elected to power in 1996. The nation's strong economic position led to a reduction in political and business incentive to engage in new productivity-enhancing reforms and prompted the government to embark upon tax reform that culminated in the introduction of a goods and services tax in 2000. International relationships received increasing attention and brought with them increased participation in global affairs, including involvement in wars in Iraq and Afghanistan.

In 2007, the Australian Labour Party was returned to power and initiated a series of reviews that targeted the health and education sectors. Health system reform followed, with the development of a blueprint for hospital funding reform, the formation of interdisciplinary local health networks and the formulation of a preventative health strategy. Another important focus of the current government has been on transparency of process and ensuring that the voices of consumers are heard.

2.2 Policy initiatives impacting upon complementary medicines regulation

In Australia, complementary medicines are regulated as therapeutic goods. As such, their regulation is influenced by broad regulatory policy initiatives that apply to therapeutic goods, such as the decision to work towards a joint regulator for therapeutic goods across both Australia and New Zealand (2.2.1) and the development of a National Medicines Policy (2.2.2). In addition, as many ingredients used in complementary medicines may be derived from natural sources and/or included in foods, complementary medicines regulation in Australia is also influenced by policy addressing the regulation of foods (2.2.3).

2.2.1 Joint regulator for therapeutic goods in Australia and New Zealand (ANZTPA)

In 1991, the health ministers of Australia and New Zealand agreed to consider options that would enable the harmonisation of therapeutic products regulation (17). This would provide therapeutic goods that were evaluated and licensed in Australia or New Zealand with access to both markets, in effect creating a single marketplace for therapeutic goods and bringing them in line with other goods under the proposed Trans-Tasman Mutual Recognition Arrangement (TTMRA). The Trans-Tasman Mutual Recognition scheme came into effect on 1 May 1998, following the gazettal of the *Trans-Tasman Mutual Recognition Act 1997* (the TTMR Act). The TTMRA was to give effect to two mutual recognition principles relating to the sale of goods and the registration of occupations such that most goods that could legally be sold in Australia could also be sold in New Zealand, and vice versa. Therapeutic products were exempted from the TTMRA because of significant differences in regulation between the two countries (18).

Baume encouraged the TGA to continue to consider the proposal and work commenced to explore the feasibility of a joint regulatory agency for therapeutic goods (19). In late 2003, both countries signed a treaty providing for the creation of a joint agency, which would essentially replace the existing TGA and its New Zealand equivalent (Medsafe) (20, 21). The joint agency would include all classes of therapeutic goods, including complementary medicines, and would align pre-market evaluation, post-market monitoring and enforcement, heralding an unparalleled degree of regulatory integration between any two countries in the world (22, 23). The ANZTPA was to be established by Australia as a body corporate under Australian legislation to administer the joint scheme in both countries (20). The ongoing cost of regulation was to be recovered from industry (24).

Extensive consultation with industry for the new regulatory scheme occurred in 2005 and early 2006 (25, 26) and, in 2006, steps were taken to introduce implementation legislation in New Zealand and draft legislation was released in Australia (27, 28). However, the joint initiative was suddenly put on hold when the New Zealand government announced on 16 July 2007 that it was not able to secure passage of the legislation through parliament due to opposition from minor party members of parliament, including the Greens, the National Party and ACT New Zealand (17, 29). This dissent was rooted in concerns surrounding the way complementary medicines would be regulated under the joint scheme (30).

The approach to regulation of complementary medicines was one of the most controversial aspects of the joint regulatory scheme in New Zealand (31). Unlike Australia, New Zealand had not required pre-market approval for certain complementary medicines (dietary supplements) which were regulated under food legislation. Under the joint regulatory scheme, however, these products were to be regulated as therapeutic goods by the ANZTPA (31). Despite suspension of the joint initiative, the underlying Treaty between Australia and New Zealand remained in place, allowing both countries to resume negotiations at any time (30).

Following the withdrawal of NZ support for the joint agency, the Australian Productivity Commission considered various options of approaching the regulation of therapeutic goods within the context of Australia–New Zealand trade. The report supported the progression of unilateral reform within Australia and New Zealand during suspension of the joint effort and advocated for resumption of negotiations between the Australian and New Zealand governments to establish a joint regulatory scheme for therapeutic products, and a joint agency to oversee the scheme, as soon as feasible after the 2008 New Zealand national election (32). In Australia, industry remained supportive of the ANZTPA idea despite ongoing concerns regarding the way complementary medicines would be regulated (32, 33: pp. 141–2). The complementary medicines industry also highlighted the uncertainty created by the suspension of activities and urged the governments of Australia and New Zealand to resume negotiations as a matter of urgency or to abandon the project (32: p. 143).

However, it was not until 2011 that the Australian and New Zealand governments agreed to revive the initiative to form a joint regulatory agency and to proceed with a joint scheme for regulation of therapeutic goods that would be implemented in a three-stage approach over a period of up to five years. The process was to begin with increased work-sharing and joint operations, the establishment of a single entry point for industry and the development of a common trans-Tasman regulatory framework. Once established, the integration of business processes would culminate in the establishment of a single regulator that would 'provide health benefits for consumers, reduce regulatory costs for industry and greater efficiency for governments' (30).

Despite the ultimate goal of a single regulator for all classes of therapeutic goods, complementary medicines have been left out of the first stages of the joint scheme whilst both countries progress their own reforms relating to the regulation of complementary medicines. In New Zealand, this has involved the development of a stand-alone framework for domestic regulation of low-risk complementary medicines that was to be reviewed in five years, at which time a decision would be made to incorporate complementary medicines regulation into the joint agency or maintain a separate scheme for certain natural health products in New Zealand (30).

2.2.2 National Medicines Policy and Quality Use of Medicines

The National Medicines Policy (NMP) is a framework based on partnerships between the Australian federal government, state and territory governments, the medicines industry, health educators, healthcare providers, suppliers, consumers and the media which aims to improve positive health outcomes for all Australians through ensuring access to, and appropriate use of, medicines (24). The NMP has four central objectives:

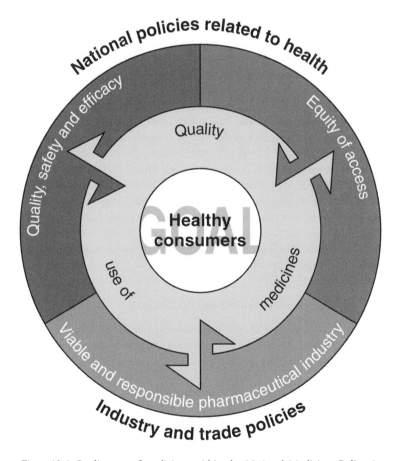

Figure 13.1 Quality use of medicines within the National Medicines Policy (*source: Commonwealth Department of Health and Ageing 2002, The National Strategy for Quality Use of Medicines, Canberra. Copyright, Commonwealth of Australia*).

- timely access to the medicines that Australians need, at a cost individuals and the community can afford
- medicines meeting appropriate standards of quality, safety and efficacy
- quality use of medicines
- maintaining a responsible and viable medicines industry (34).

The development of an Australian National Policy on Medicines followed Australia's participation in the 39th World Health Assembly, held in 1986, which called on governments to implement a National Medicinal Drug Policy (35). Within two years, the Australian government had voiced its support for such a policy and, by 1991, the Australian Pharmaceutical Advisory Council (APAC) had been formed in an effort to garner stakeholder input into the development of the policy (35). APAC brought together key stakeholders from the medical, nursing and pharmacy professions, as well as industry, consumers and government (36, 37).

The Commonwealth government established an additional advisory group, the Pharmaceutical Health and Rational Use of Medicines (PHARM) Committee, which was tasked to improve pharmaceutical education. PHARM went on to formulate a policy on the Quality Use of Medicines (QUM) that was endorsed by federal government in 1992, giving rise to the *National Strategy for Quality Use of Medicines* (36, 38). In this strategy, the term 'medicine' included prescription, non-prescription and complementary medicines (24: p. 41). The strategy provided a framework to improve the use of medicines in Australia and, in concert with other policies and government initiatives, contributed to the formulation of the Australian National Medicines Policy in 1999 (35, 39). The complete and revised NMP was formally launched on 10 December 1999 (34).

The structures that support the NMP were revised in 2009 and efforts were made to enhance partnerships with key stakeholders and facilitate stakeholder input into the principles, policy and practice of the NMP. Key to this approach was the inception of annual NMP Partnerships Fora that would bring together members of federal and state/territory governments with consumer, clinical practice and medicines-industry stakeholders. The first annual NMP Partnerships Forum was hosted by the NMP Executive and Committee on 29 June 2009 in Canberra and identified a number of key priority areas, which included the integration of medicines policy into the government's health reform (40). The 2010 Forum brought with it an increasing focus on communication between health professionals and consumers, and improving consumer health literacy, whilst the 2011 Forum provided stakeholders with the opportunity to discuss methods for assessing the safety and effectiveness of medicines in practice (41, 42).

2.2.3 Food regulation and health claims

Food Standards Australia New Zealand (FSANZ) was established in 2002 following a concerted effort to harmonise food standards, reduce compliance costs and remove regulatory barriers to trade in food between Australia and New Zealand (43). This was made possible by the signing of an *Agreement between Australia and New Zealand establishing a System for the Development of Joint Food Standards* (the Treaty) on 5 December 1995 to establish a joint Australian New Zealand Food Standards Code and the formation of the first bi-national government agency between Australia and New Zealand. The joint *Australia New Zealand Food Standards Code* was introduced on 24 November 2000 and two years later FSANZ was established as the bi-national food regulator (43).

Vitamins, minerals and certain plant-derived substances represented to be, or likely to be taken to be, for therapeutic use are regulated as complementary medicines. However, these substances may also be present in foods, where they fall under the jurisdiction of FSANZ. This creates a regulatory watershed zone where the critical step is determining whether a marketed product should be regulated as a food or a medicine. Key factors in determining the regulatory jurisdiction of a marketed product are:

- route of administration: if administered by a non-oral route, the good is unlikely to be a food
- whether the good is captured by a Section 7 declaration: under a Section 7 declaration, certain ingredients may be explicitly determined not to be therapeutic goods
- whether the good is captured by a food standard: if captured by a food standard, the good is likely to be a food
- whether there is a tradition of use as a food or a medicine: a traditional of use as a medicine or food supports a contemporary use as a medicine or food
- whether the presentation of the good makes it likely to be taken for therapeutic use (for example, therapeutic claims, product name, dosage form and dosage instructions, label and container, and any advertising and promotional material).

Because of the complexity and subjectivity of the food–medicine interface, policy change by either the TGA or FSANZ that impacts upon the interface has the potential to displace from one jurisdiction to the other. Such policy change may include Section 7 declarations by the TGA or changes in the food standard and the approach to health claims by FSANZ. Whether a product is a food or medicine has important implications as the regulatory requirements may be significantly different. For example, medicines, but not foods, are required to be manufactured according to principles of Good Manufacturing Practice.

The approach taken by FSANZ with respect to food health claims also impacts upon complementary medicines regulation. This is important as the opportunity for foods to make health claims makes it more attractive for industry sponsors to market health products as health foods rather than complementary medicines because of differences in regulatory requirements. In 2003, the Australia and New Zealand Food Regulation Ministerial Council (ANZFRMC) issued a nutrition, health and related claims policy guideline. The policy aimed to ensure that claims made on foods or in advertising are true, scientifically substantiated and not misleading. After a series of public consultations, FSANZ released a draft standard and guideline(s) for nutrition, health and related claims that resembled the TGA approach to complementary medicines regulation in that it permitted industry self-substantiation for low-level health claims but required pre-market assessment and approval by FSANZ of high-level health claims (44).

Following further consultation and critique by the ANZFRMC, FSANZ began revising the text and structure of the draft standard for the purpose of improving clarity and ensuring its enforceability. This required a revision of the approach for regulating health claims that would require all food–health relationships underpinning health claims to be pre-approved. The revised draft standard proposed 115 pre-approved food–health relationships that could be used by industry without further assessment. Industry would also be able to submit confidential applications for new food–health relationships through a 'high level health claim variation' process (44).

IV The evolution of complementary medicines regulation in Australia

1 The establishment of a national framework for the regulation of complementary medicines

The push for a regulatory framework that recognised complementary medicines began in the mid-1980s. At that time, the regulation of therapeutic goods was achieved through a complex arrangement between states, territories and the Commonwealth that was underpinned by the *Therapeutic Goods Act 1966* and additional state-based legislation. The *Therapeutic Goods Act 1966* set out standards relating to the composition, strength, potency, stability, sterility, quantity, quality, method of preparation and labelling and packaging of therapeutic goods that were imported, subject to interstate trade, included in the Pharmaceutical Benefits Scheme or supplied to Commonwealth agencies, and required such therapeutic goods to be included on the National Register of Therapeutic Goods (45). The involvement of states and territories in the regulation of therapeutic goods that fell outside this jurisdiction resulted in a situation where gaps, overlaps and inconsistencies in regulatory oversight developed (46). Complementary medicines represented one sector that had flourished in the absence of regulatory oversight. However, as claims associated with complementary medicine products become more extravagant, concerns grew regarding their effectiveness, safety and quality (46).

Increasing discontent led to the initiation of a series of reviews of the regulation of therapeutic goods, including *The Public Service Board Review of Drug Evaluation Procedures* (1987) and *Therapeutic Goods – A Review of the Therapeutic Goods Evaluation and Testing Program* (1988). The latter called for a Bill to be introduced to provide uniform national legislation for the evaluation and registration of therapeutic goods, the application of standards and testing procedures, the licensing and inspection of manufacturers and wholesalers, and the monitoring of advertisements for compliance with national guidelines. The report also recommended that a system of fees be introduced for the licensing of manufacturers, evaluation of therapeutic goods and the entry of therapeutic goods onto the National Register of Therapeutic Goods (45).

In response to these reports, the Therapeutic Goods Administration was established from the Therapeutics Division of the Department of Community Services and Health in August 1989 and the Therapeutic Goods Bill 1989 was introduced into the House of Representatives in October 1989. The passing of the Bill resulted in the Therapeutic Goods Act 1989 (The Act) and the Therapeutic Goods Regulations (1990), which came into effect, following a series of amendments, on 15 February 1991.

The Act provided a broad definition of therapeutic goods and gave the Commonwealth coverage of all therapeutic goods, including complementary medicines. It introduced a risk-based approach to the regulation of therapeutic goods, where products representing a lower level of risk to the public were subject to a lower level of regulation. All therapeutic goods, unless exempted, were to be entered on the Australian Register of Therapeutic Goods (ARTG) prior to their supply into the Australian market, and a new level of entry into the ARTG was created where certain low-risk medicines could be 'listed' through largely a self-assessment process. The need to cater for the particular requirements of complementary medicines was increasingly recognised and a series of amendments to the Act and its Regulations during 1990 included the establishment of the Traditional Medicines Evaluation Committee (TMEC) to evaluate traditional medicines for registration and would include representatives of the manufacturers and practitioners (46). TMEC met for the first time on 22 February 1991, just one week after the Act had come into effect (46).

The Act also made reference to parts of the Therapeutic Goods Advertising Code (the Code), bestowing upon it a degree of legal underpinning. The Code had existed as a guidance document since its development and inception in the 1970s by the first Therapeutic Goods Advertising Code Council (TGACC) (47).

In 1991, Professor Baume was commissioned to perform a review of the Therapeutic Goods Administration and its processes (19). The review critically assessed TGA processes and provided recommendations for improvement that focused largely on the evaluation of prescription medicines and provided little advice regarding the evaluation or post-market monitoring of complementary medicines.

Although largely silent with respect to complementary medicines regulation, the Baume review foreshadowed major reform of the TGA that was geared towards improving access of the Australian population to new drugs of proven quality, safety and efficacy. Reforms initiated by the TGA included the introduction of an Electronic Lodgement Facility (ELF) in 1996 to streamline the submission process for listed medicines and a series of changes to the arrangements for dealing with issues related to the advertising of therapeutic goods. This became necessary when the organisation hitherto responsible for advertising-related matters, the Media Council of Australia (MCA), ceased operations at the end of 1996. Arrangements were made for administration of the code by the TGA in conjunction with an industry collegiate formed by the Proprietary Medicines Association of Australia (now the Australian Self-Medication Industry) and the Nutritional Foods Association of Australia (now the Complementary Healthcare Council). This was achieved through a series of changes to the Therapeutic Goods Act and Regulations in December 1997 (Amendment 400). Amendment 400 formalised the TGACC and its responsibilities to ensure that the Code remained current and relevant, and reflected community values and standards, to ensure a level playing field for all advertisers and to provide advice to the Minister about advertising matters (48). It also gave rise to the Complaints Resolution Panel (CRP) with responsibility for assessing advertising-related complaints and provided for the formal approval of mainstream print advertisements for therapeutic goods by the industry collegiate (48).

However, it was not until a subsequent review, conducted by KPMG in 1997, that attention within the TGA turned towards reform in the regulation of complementary medicines (49). This occurred within the context of increasing interest in complementary medicines, which included a show of interest from the Australian government in the form of an *Alternative Medicines Summit*, aimed at improving access to alternative medicines (50). The KPMG report included a number of recommendations that impacted directly upon the regulation of complementary medicines, and included the following:

- review of the claims allowed for listed medicines, and the development of a system for claims for listed products that allows for an acceptable degree of flexibility
- the adoption of a hierarchy of evidence to support therapeutic claims, such that a lower level of evidence be tolerated in support of low-risk medicines purporting to treat non-serious conditions
- review and amendment of the ELF for listing of medicines on the ARTG
- development of a revised definition for herbal products and the consideration of issues relating to the safety and quality of herbal substances
- disbandment of TMEC and the establishment of a new committee, the Complementary Medicines Evaluation Committee (CMEC), to advise on issues relating to complementary medicines
- consideration of strategies for working with international regulators, and the development of additional consultation mechanisms between TGA and the complementary medicines industry

- improvement of the controls on advertising therapeutic goods to consumers
- provision of information in relation to decisions about products at the food/medicine interface.

Over the next five years, a series of reforms were initiated to address the recommendations of the KPMG report. Central to the reform process was the formation of 'The Parliamentary Secretary's Working Party on Complementary Medicines'. The working party included representatives from the TGA, major complementary medicines companies (Blackmores, Hilton Lifestream and Smithkline-Beecham), industry peak bodies (Nutritional Foods Association of Australia, Proprietary Medicines Association of Australia) and consumer representative bodies (Consumer Health Forum). The working party met for the first time on 16 December 1998 to provide a strategy that would shape the approach towards reform. This strategy included as its centrepiece a shift in emphasis from pre-market evaluation to post-market monitoring for low-risk products, a cooperative approach with industry and recognition of the need for government and industry to uphold consumer confidence through appropriate evaluation of therapeutic goods, ensuring standards of manufacturing quality were met, and the substantiation of therapeutic claims made in the marketplace.

The CMEC soon replaced the TMEC and a complementary medicines section was established within the TGA to deal specifically with issues relating to the regulation of complementary medicines and to provide technical and secretariat support for the CMEC (46). The required membership of the committee was formalised and expanded to include representation from individuals with qualifications and expertise in toxicology, pharmacology, pharmacognisance and a variety of complementary medicine paradigms, such as traditional Chinese medicine, Western herbal medicine, naturopathy, homoeopathy and nutritional medicine. The functions of CMEC were also expanded, such that the committee could now provide scientific and policy advice regarding product claims, in addition to advice relating to the safety, quality and efficacy aspects, of complementary medicines. The CMEC subsequently became recognised as a statutory expert committee, which brought it the same level of recognition as the Health Minister's other therapeutic expert advisory committees.

Under the direction of the working party, the complementary medicines section was expanded and given increasing autonomy within the TGA. From it, the Office of Complementary Medicines was established in 1999. A requirement for listed medicines to be supported by appropriate evidence or information was incorporated into the Act in April 1999, and a guideline was developed that incorporated a hierarchical model for evidence required to support indications and claims made by listed complementary medicines. A post-market review section was created and charged with the responsibility of performing random and targeted audits of products listed on the ARTG. A major overhaul of the ELF was also undertaken in an effort to streamline the listing process. This included the development of a list of standard Indication Codes to be included in the ELF.

The KPMG review had also stressed the need for increasing cooperation and consultation with key stakeholders, clarification of the food medicine interface and increased scrutiny of advertising of claims. A formal TGA-industry consultative group, the Complementary Healthcare Consultative Forum (CHCF), was established and met for the first time on 1 July 1999 (51). The CHCF included representation from government (TGA, FSANZ, DISR, states and territories), healthcare practitioners, consumers, academia and industry peak bodies (CHC and ASMI), and was intended to facilitate consultation and promote constructive relations between government and the complementary healthcare sector on broad policy, regulatory performance and other related issues (52). In collaboration with FSANZ and ACCC, respectively, attempts were made to clarify the food–medicine interface and to develop more robust mechanisms for dealing with issues related to the advertising of therapeutic goods. The latter precipitated a major review of all advertising arrangements by the TGACC during 1999. This resulted in the replacement of the existing prescriptive advertising code with a principles-based code and the expansion of the approval and complaints processes to include other forms of therapeutic goods advertising (53).

By the end of 2003, the Office of Complementary Medicines was accountable for a regulatory framework for complementary medicines that was broadly consistent with the current system, being characterised by a co-regulatory approach between government and industry, a hierarchy of evidence for claims that was related to risk, rapid market entry through a self-certification listing process and enhanced post-market surveillance for low-risk complementary medicines, and a statutory expert committee with sufficient expertise to provide guidance to the Office with respect to a diversity of technical matters that may arise during administration of the Act.

2 Shaping the landscape: review, reform and the regulation of complementary medicines

In April 2003, the failure of a medicine manufacturer to maintain appropriate manufacturing and quality control standards prompted the TGA to initiate the recall of more than 1600 complementary medicines from the Australian marketplace (54). This represented the largest recall of medicines ever in Australia, and it led consumer groups, health professionals, researchers and practitioners to voice concerns regarding the level of trust that can be placed in complementary medicines (55).

In an effort to restore consumer and healthcare practitioner confidence in the safety and quality of complementary medicines, the Australian government established the Expert Committee on Complementary Medicines in the Health System (ECCMHS) (55). Comprising members from industry, academic and clinical environments with expertise in the manufacture, pharmacology, toxicology, clinical evaluation and quality use of complementary medicines, the ECCMHS was asked to review the regulatory system for complementary medicines in order to ensure that the central objectives of the National Medicines Policy would be met in relation to complementary medicines (24: p. 7). These objectives would only be met if a coordinated national approach was taken to ensure that regulatory controls were in place to guarantee that safe, efficacious and high-quality complementary medicines were provided to consumers in a timely manner and in an environment that facilitated access and informed self-choice.

The ECCMHS met for the first time in June 2003 and released its review three months later. It found that a single regulatory framework for medicines was appropriate for the regulation of complementary medicines in Australia and advocated that the current two-tiered, risk-based regulatory system for complementary medicines should be maintained, but with some enhancements, which included increased auditing of sponsors of listed complementary medicines to ensure that evidence of efficacy was held. The committee made a total of forty-nine recommendations relating to national regulatory controls for complementary medicines, adverse reactions, information and advertising, healthcare practitioners, industry, and administrative and advisory mechanisms.

Key recommendations included:

- the introduction of legally enforceable quality standards for ingredients in complementary medicines to ensure appropriate safety and quality

- legislative underpinning for the TGA's *Guidelines for Levels and Kinds of Evidence to Support Indications and Claims* and a requirement for sponsors to submit to the TGA a summary of the evidence held in support of the efficacy of complementary products included on the ARTG without formal assessment
- an increase in random and targeted assessments of the evidence to support the indications and claims held by sponsors for listed medicines
- regulation of homoeopathic medicines and related remedies making therapeutic claims to ensure they meet appropriate standards of safety, quality and efficacy
- an increase in penalties if a sponsor refuses to provide requested information that supports claims made by the sponsor
- review of the registration process for complementary medicines
- the development of a strategy to improve the quality and proportion of complementary medicine adverse reaction reports by health professionals and consumers to the TGA
- improved handling of adverse reactions associated with complementary medicines and inclusion of complementary medicines in the national pharmacovigilance guideline
- appropriate regulatory activity to prevent the sale of illegal complementary medicines
- the adoption of nationally consistent therapeutic goods legislation by all states and territories in order to ensure consistent standards of quality, safety and efficacy and a fair and competitive environment for the supply of medicines in Australia
- identification of incentives to encourage innovation and research in complementary medicines, including data protection and market exclusivity
- inclusion of members with expertise in complementary medicines on all bodies that advise on the research and use of medicines (including APAC and the PHARM Committee)
- the introduction of standardised training, certification and regulation of complementary healthcare practitioners that includes requirements for ongoing education and compliance with a code of ethics
- commitment to complementary medicines research with dedicated funding to create a database of researchers and centres of excellence and formal links with appropriate international centres involved in complementary medicine research
- the explicit incorporation of complementary medicines into the NMP and *The National Strategy for Quality Use of Medicines* (QUM), and the devotion of specific resources to projects that would determine the complementary medicines information and skill needs of healthcare professionals and consumers, and the research needs of the complementary medicines industry.

The TGA was charged with responsibility for coordinating the implementation of its response and appointed the Complementary Medicines Implementation Reference Group (CMIRG) in July 2005 to help advise and oversee this work. Further input came from APAC, which set up a working party to contribute to the implementation of the government response (56).

Following stakeholder consultation in Australia and New Zealand to help inform its response to the recommendations of the ECCMHS, the Australian government released a progress report in 2006 in which it accepted thirty-five of the forty-nine ECCMHS recommendations, and accepted one additional recommendation in principle. One recommendation relating to complementary medicine research funding was not accepted and the remaining twelve recommendations (largely relating to the regulation of complementary medicine health practitioners) were considered to be outside the direct responsibility of the Australian government (56).

By February 2006, implementation of nineteen of the recommendations was underway, two regarding improved reporting of adverse events related to complementary medicines had been completed, and specific plans and timelines were in place for all remaining recommendations to be addressed by the Australian government (56). It was recognised, however, that the implementation of the proposed joint Australia–New Zealand regulatory scheme for therapeutic products was likely to impact upon the completion date for many of the recommendations.

The response to the report from stakeholders was mixed and likely to have been influenced by ambivalence and uncertainty surrounding the impending joint regulatory scheme. There were concerns that the regulatory framework for mainstream medicines may not provide sufficient flexibility to cater for the unique properties of complementary medicines. Support for a new regulatory agency that was dedicated to complementary medicines grew within the industry sector and was championed by the CHC (57). Supporters drew upon the recognition of 'natural health products' by the Canadian government and the establishment of a new regulatory authority called the Directorate of Natural Health Products within Health Canada as a precedent to the initiative (57). The Australian government, however, expressed concerns about the industry proposal and, upon consideration of advice from APAC, made it clear that a separate regulatory system for complementary medicines would not be created. It was felt that public confidence in complementary medicines was best achieved under a single national medicines policy by a single national regulator, the TGA (58).

Following the suspension of the ANTZPA process, Senator McLucas, the then Parliamentary Secretary for Health and Ageing, took the opportunity to progress a number of deregulatory reforms that did not depend upon the establishment of a joint agency. These included changes to legislation and policy to allow new default standards for therapeutic goods and to increase transparency by enabling the TGA to publish more information about its processes and decisions (14).

Another focus activity was the list of standard indications included in ELF. In conjunction with industry, the TGA began the process of reviewing the current list of standard indications with a view to rationalising the list and expanding it. This would ideally result in a system with a comprehensive list of standard indications such that sponsors would not need to use the free text field to enter novel indications. The free text field had become problematic as it provided little protection against the entry of indications that referred to serious disorders (and were therefore not appropriate for low-risk listed medicines) or additional information that was used for marketing purposes but did not describe a therapeutic use.

However, despite these changes, a number of recommendations from the ECCMHS review remained outstanding. A member of CMIRG expressed her concerns regarding the lack of government feedback to CMIRG members since the final CMIRG meeting and failure to progress the implementation of seventeen outstanding ECCMHS recommendations (59). Amongst these outstanding recommendations was the government's undertaking to implement a process requiring sponsors to submit to the TGA a summary of the evidence held by the sponsor in support of the efficacy of complementary medicines included on the ARTG, and its commitment to prescribe the 'Levels and kinds of evidence' document in the Therapeutic Goods Regulations. It is, however, of note that these recommendations were to be implemented under arrangements for the stalled trans-Tasman therapeutic products regulatory agency (56).

Concern grew regarding the validity of the claims made by listed complementary medicines. Complementary medicines claiming to produce or assist with weight loss posed a particular problem (15). The TGA responded by drafting and consulting publicly on a specific document that provided guidance for sponsors in relation to the evidence needed to substantiate listed weight loss products. The responses to the document from industry and public health advocates were polarised. Industry saw the document as overly prescriptive and rigorous, whilst others remained concerned about limitations of the document, including the lack of an implementation plan, and complained about the lack of transparency in the consultation process (15).

A major internal restructuring of the TGA in 2010 resulted in a separation of pre- and post-marketing decision-making within the TGA. As part of this process, the responsibility for decisions on safety issues related to marketed complementary medicines was transferred from the Office of Complementary Medicines to the new Office of Product Review. However, validation of sponsor self-certification during the listing process remained the responsibility of the Office of Complementary Medicines.

The regulation of complementary medicines came to public attention in Australia when the Department of Health and Ageing reported in late 2010 that as many as 90 per cent of products reviewed over the past twelve months were found to be non-compliant with regulatory requirements, despite self-certification during the listing process (50). Of products selected randomly for review, approximately a third were found to be non-compliant with respect to manufacturing or quality standards, a third were non-compliant with labelling requirements and almost half were making claims that were not backed by sufficient evidence (50). These concerns triggered a review of the regulatory framework for complementary medicines by the Auditor-General (50). The review identified a number of weaknesses in the current regulatory framework for listed complementary medicines and made five recommendations aimed at strengthening the integrity and transparency of the framework by building upon the existing systems and processes and developing more efficient work practices:

- to achieve timely completion of key guidance material for complementary medicines
- to improve the integrity of the self-assessment process for listing complementary medicines on the ARTG; this was to be achieved by progressing the standard indications project, thereby creating a comprehensive list of standardised indications for sponsors to select from when listing a product on the ARTG
- to provide information to the Australian public about post-market reviews on listed medicines
- to develop risk profiles of sponsors and the most significant characteristics of medicines in order to inform post-market reviews and improve compliance of sponsors with the regulatory framework
- to adopt a standard operating procedure for completing investigations of advertising breaches that would provide timelines for completing investigations and enable the identification of investigations and trends in non-compliance.

The Auditor-General also noted the failure of the TGA to account for the previous ECCMHS recommendation for sponsors to submit summaries of evidence to the TGA at the time of listing complementary medicines on the Australian Register of Therapeutic Goods (ARTG) and advocated for such a process to be implemented so that this information would be available to consumers.

The Australian government agreed to all five recommendations of the Auditor-General's report but remained silent on the issue of evidence summaries. An expert committee, the Informal Working Group on Complementary Medicines, was established to provide additional information into mechanisms by which the Auditor-General's recommendations could be achieved. Including representation from consumers, healthcare professionals and the complementary medicines industry, the Informal Working Group recommended that the TGA:

- provide increased information on labels and the TGA website
- modify the ELF to include restriction or elimination of access by sponsors to 'free text' and provide guidance and cautionary notes for sponsors

- update 'Guidelines for levels and kinds of evidence' and include 'Guidelines for levels and kinds of evidence' in regulation
- review the standard indications project based on the document 'Guidelines for levels and kinds of evidence'
- apply, enforce and publicise sanctions and penalties for products that are removed from the ARTG as a result of regulatory action
- enhance sanctions and penalties for repeated breaches of compliance (as well as strengthening sanctions and penalties for advertising) (60).

The Auditor-General's audit of complementary medicines regulation and the deliberations of the Informal Working Group occurred within the context of a series of reviews of TGA processes and decision-making during 2010 and 2011. Other reviews that impacted significantly on the regulation of complementary medicines focused upon the transparency of the Therapeutic Goods Administration, the promotion of therapeutic products and the regulatory framework for advertising therapeutic goods. The outcomes and recommendations of these reviews were bundled together and addressed in a major document titled 'TGA reforms: A blueprint for TGA's future', which would potentially reshape the way the TGA regulated therapeutic goods (60). Meanwhile, the announcement of the recommencement of the ANZTPA process indicated that these reforms would need to be broadly consistent with the approach of the pending joint agency for all types of therapeutic goods except complementary medicines.

V Complementary medicines regulation of tomorrow: a harmonised approach?

The TGA's response to the Auditor-General's report was swift. A dedicated team was assembled and a strategy developed that would address each recommendation. By April 2012, a draft of a revised evidence document was available for public comment on the TGA website and work had begun on expanding the list of available standard indications and enhancing the ELF. The intensity of work continued during the second half of 2012, bringing with it further rounds of public consultation on revised guidance material, the reform of post-market review processes and the publication of increasing amounts of information relating to the work processes and decisions of the Office of Complementary Medicines.

The approach to substantiation of claims has been to maintain the reliance upon sponsor self-certification, but to revise the degree of rigour involved in the assessment of evidence and to embed the document within legislation so as to enhance the ability of the TGA to act in cases when claims are unsubstantiated. The first revision of the evidence document required sponsors to complete a full systematic review before determining whether an indication or claim was supported by evidence (61). A subsequent revision of the document incorporated an approach whereby certain 'Sources of Established Evidence' (SEE), such as authoritative reviews and traditional pharmacopoeia, were considered acceptable by the TGA as evidence in their own right. Claims or indications that were included in a SEE would therefore be considered to be substantiated without the need for additional review by sponsors (62).

The approach to standard indications and the ELF has been to embark upon a suite of changes that would result in a system with enhanced usability and functionality that provides sponsors with a comprehensive list of standard indications at the expense of the free text field. A mechanism will exist that enables sponsors to apply for additional indications to be added to the list following TGA scrutiny. Such a system is only likely to be considered acceptable by industry if an efficient mechanism is in place for assessing applications for new listable indications and some flexibility between indications listed on the ARTG and claims included on product labels is permitted. Failure to incorporate these concepts into the ELF and regulatory framework may result in a system that stifles innovation and is cumbersome and overly restrictive. Consultation on the list of standard indications is scheduled for the second half of 2012, with a view to effecting the outcome within an appropriate legislative framework by mid-2013.

With increasing pressure to improve compliance of listed medicines and to provide consumers with increasing amounts of useful information, the TGA post-market review processes have been reviewed and published on the TGA website (63). The required business process reforms and IT changes are currently being put in place to enable the TGA to publish the results of compliance reviews in a timely manner and to use the results of reviews to gather risk-profiling information that will help inform future reviews.

Just how successful the current suite of reforms will be in terms of improving the effectiveness, efficiency and transparency of the regulation of complementary medicines in Australia remains to be seen. For current reforms to take root, further consultation is required, as are a number of mandatory processes, such as formal assessment of the likely effects of change on industry viability. Once these are negotiated, legislative changes will be required to embed reform within the legislation for therapeutics goods regulation.

The standard indications project and the incorporation of SEE within the evidence requirements for listed complementary medicines represent two key approaches that could potentially facilitate listings for medicines that are claiming well-established, listable therapeutic benefits. The suite of reforms provides an ideal opportunity for the TGA to bring together these concepts and instil within the ELF a set of standard indications derived from SEE that were only accessible to sponsors when the product being listed met the criteria outlined in the SEE (such as ingredient, preparation, dose and dosing regime). This could potentially save TGA the resources currently required to assess evidence during post-market reviews, and also save industry the resources required to source indications from SEE. Such an approach would also be advantageous in facilitating international harmonisation if a set of established claims and sources of acceptable evidence can be agreed upon by nations around the world. Indeed, a cooperative of international regulators is currently engaged in a project that aims to identify commonly agreed up sources of 'pre-cleared' information or evidence.

As current reforms surrounding health claims made by foods in Australia and New Zealand, as well as in other jurisdictions such as Europe, are moving towards systems that incorporate accepted claims for certain ingredients, a similar approach in Australia would seem fitting. It would also facilitate harmonisation across the food–medicine boundary. For example, the TGA could import food claims evaluated by FSANZ into ELF, and include FSANZ reviews as SEE, in order to create a consistent approach to evidence requirements surrounding health claims. This could also occur for international regulators such as the European Food Safety Authority, where much work has recently occurred in establishing prescribed lists of ingredient-linked claims.

It also remains to be seen just how complementary medicines regulation will be placed within a joint Australia and New Zealand regulator. Complementary medicines reform is currently occurring separately in Australia and New Zealand, in isolation from the joint agency venture. However, what eventuates following the New Zealand review of its regulatory framework for complementary medicines in five years' time cannot be foreshadowed. It is possible that separate schemes for complementary medicines regulation may persist alongside joint regulatory schemes for mainstream therapeutics and foods. Such an arrangement would not be entirely without precedent. For example, the regulation of foods by FSANZ provides for a number of controls that are shared between Australia and New Zealand, such as controls on the use of ingredients, the composition of certain foods and labelling for both packaged and unpackaged food, but performs additional functions in Australia, such as the preparation of standards across the food supply chain (production, processing and food hygiene) and the setting of residue limits for agricultural and veterinary products. In New Zealand, these activities are undertaken by the New Zealand Ministry for Primary Industries (64). However, it is also possible that greater efficiencies and improved regulation may be found by integrating complementary medicines regulation into the joint regulatory framework for therapeutics, or conversely aligning the regulation of complementary medicines more closely with that of health foods.

VI Conclusion

This chapter has provided insight into the complex interplay between government, industry and community in shaping regulatory policy. Over the past thirty years, complementary medicines regulation has evolved through processes of national systematisation, deregulation, incremental improvements in efficiency and, most recently, increasing transparency. These phases have been consistent with broad underlying political trends, fuelled by public expectations that have led to formal reviews, and translated into policy with input from key stakeholders. The implications of this are significant, particularly in the context of potential future developments in the regulation of medicines in Australia. The fate of complementary medicines within the envisaged joint Australia and New Zealand therapeutic goods regulator is uncertain. Separation of complementary medicines regulation would mean that the key influences on evolving policy would remain largely unchanged; however, inclusion of complementary medicines within the joint agency would introduce new influences from New Zealand.

Notes

1 The TGA maintains the Australian Register of Therapeutic Goods (ARTG), a database that includes details of all therapeutic goods that are imported into, supplied in or exported from Australia. It is a legal requirement that, unless specifically exempt or excluded, all therapeutic goods are included on the ARTG prior to their supply.
2 Controls for the advertising of therapeutic goods are also in place. In Australia, all advertisements for therapeutic goods that are directed to the public must comply with provisions of the Act, the Regulations and the Therapeutic Goods Advertising Code (TGAC).

References

1 Therapeutic Goods Administration. Industry: Regulation Basics. Department of Health and Ageing, Australian Government; 2012 [cited 2012 4 September]. Available from: www.tga.gov.au/industry/basics.htm.
2 Therapeutic Goods Regulations. Schedule 4. Part 1. Listable substances (1990).
3 Therapeutic Goods Regulations. Schedule 4. Therapeutic goods required to be included in the part of the Register for listed goods (1990).
4 Therapeutic Goods Regulations. Part 1 Preliminary. 2 Interpretation (1990).
5 Therapeutic Goods Regulations. Regulation 39A (1990).
6 Therapeutic Goods Regulations. Regulation 39B (1990).
7 Therapeutic Goods Administration. Therapeutic Goods Committee; 2011 [cited 2012 4 September]. Available from: www.tga.gov.au/about/committees-tgc.htm.
8 Therapeutic Goods Regulations. Regulation 34B, (1990).
9 Therapeutic Goods Advertising Code Council. TGACC Members; 2012 [cited 2012 8 September]. Available from: www.tgacc.com.au/members.cfm.
10 Complaints Resolution Panel. About CRP; 2012 [cited 2012 8 September]. Available from: www.tgacrp.com.au/index.cfm?pageID=2.

11 Consumer Health Forum. What We Do; 2012 [cited 2012 8 September]. Available from: www.chf. org.au/who-we-are.php.

12 Australian Competition and Consumer Commission. Product Safety Australia. CHOICE, Australian Consumers Association; 2012 [cited 2014 6 December]. Available from: www.productsafety.gov.au/content/index.phtml/itemId/980134.

13 CHOICE. CHOICE; The People's Watchdog. About Us; 2012 [cited 2012 10 September]. Available from: www.choice.com.au/about-us.aspx.

14 McLucas J. Future Directions in Therapeutic Regulation: Keynote address to the Australian Self-Medication Conference. Australian Self-Medication Conference; Australian Technology Park Conference Centre; 2008.

15 Harvey K, Korczak V, Marron L, Newgreen D. Commercialism, choice and consumer protection: regulation of complementary medicines in Australia. Medical Journal of Australia. 2008; 188:21–5.

16 Kelly, P. The politics of economic change in Australia in the 1980s and 1990s. In: Gruen, D. and Shrestha, S., eds. The Australian Economy in the 1990s. Sydney: Reserve Bank of Australia; 2000.

17 von Tigerstrom B. Globalisation, harmonisation and the regulation of therapeutic products: the Australia and New Zealand Therapeutic Products Authority project in global context. Canterbury Law Review. 2007; 13:287–314.

18 Trans-Tasman Mutual Recognition Act, Part IX Schedule 3, Annex 1 (1997).

19 Baume P. A Question of Balance: Report on the Future of Drug Evaluation in Australia. Canberra: Australian Government Publishing Service; 1991.

20 Australian and New Zealand Governments. Agreement between the Government of Australia and the Government of New Zealand for the Establishment of a Joint Scheme for the Regulation of Therapeutic Products; 2003.

21 King A, Worth T. Australia and New Zealand Sign Treaty to Regulate Medicines and Therapeutic Products (media release). Wellington and Canberra; 2003.

22 King A, Worth T. Health Committee, Forty-seventh Parliament, Inquiry into the Proposal to Establish a Trans-Tasman Agency to Regulate Therapeutic Products. Wellington and Canberra; 2003.

23 World Health Organization. Medicines Strategy 2004–2007 – Countries at the Core. Geneva: WHO; 2004.

24 Expert Committee on Complementary Medicines in the Health System. Complementary Medicines in the Australian Health System. Canberra: ECCMHS; 2003.

25 Australia New Zealand Therapeutic Products Agency. Consultation Begins on Proposed Australia New Zealand Therapeutic Products Regulatory Scheme. Canberra and Wellington: Australian and New Zealand Governments; 2006 [cited 2014 6 December]. Available from: http://anztpa.gov.au/archive/anztpa-121127/media/060523cons.htm.

26 Department of Health and Ageing. Annual Report 2005–06: Outcome 01 Population Health. Canberra: Australian Government; 2009.

27 King A. Therapeutics Products and Medicines Bill (media release). Wellington; 2006.

28 Mason B. New Therapeutic Products Exposure Bill (media release). Canberra; 2007.

29 Health Freedom New Zealand. Anti-Vitamin bill; 2009 [cited 2014 6 December]. Available from: www.healthfreedom.co.nz/anti-vitamin-bill.html.

30 Therapeutic Goods Administration. Australia New Zealand Therapeutic Products Agency (ANZTPA) Factsheet. Canberra; 2011 [cited 2014 6 December]. Available from: www.health.gov.au/internet/main/publishing.nsf/Content/407F341155162622CA257BF0001C965B/$File/ANZTPA%20Factsheet.pdf.

31 Faunce T, Johnston K, Bambrick H. The Trans-Tasman Therapeutic Products Authority: potential AUSFTA impacts on safety and cost-effectiveness regulation for medicines and medical devices in New Zealand. Victoria University Wellington Law Review. 2006; 37:365.

32 Productivity Commission. Review of Mutual Recognition Schemes; Research Report. Canberra; 2009.

33 Australian Self Medication Industry. Response to Productivity Commission's Draft Report on Mutual Recognition; 2008 [cited 2012 9 October]. Available from: www.pc.gov.au/__data/assets/pdf_file/0011/84728/subdr60.pdf.

34 Department of Health and Ageing. National Medicines Policy document. Canberra: Australian Government; 1999 [cited 2014 6 December]. Available from: www.health.gov.au/internet/main/publishing.nsf/Content/national-medicines-policy.

35 Department of Health and Ageing. National Medicines Policy Overview Canberra: Australian Government; 2011 [cited 2012 9 October]. Available from: www.health.gov.au/internet/main/publishing.nsf/content/National+Medicines+Policy-2.

36 Mant A. Quality use of medicines: ten years down the track. Australian Prescriber. 2001; 24:106–7.

37 Department of Health and Ageing. Guiding Principles for Medication Management in the Community. Canberra: Australian Government; 2006 [cited 2014 6 December]. Available from: www.health.gov.au/internet/main/publishing.nsf/Content/apac-publications-guiding.

38 Quality Use of Medicines and Pharmacy Research Centre. Measurement of the Quality Use of Medicines Component of Australia's National Medicines Policy. Second Report of the National Indicators. University of South Australia; 2003.

39 Medicines Australia. Quality Use of Medicines and the Medicines Industry; 2005 [cited 2012 6 October]. Available from: http://medicinesaustralia.com.au/files/2012/05/MA_QUM_External_Reduced.pdf.

40 Australian Government. Outcome Statement. National Medicines Policy Partnerships Forum, 29 June 2009; Old Parliament House, Canberra; 2009.

41 Australian Government. Outcome Statement. National Medicines Policy Partnerships Forum, 30 June 2010; Citigate Central, Sydney; 2010.

42 Australian Government. Outcome Statement. National Medicines Policy Partnerships Forum, 29 July 2011; Old Parliament House, Canberra; 2011.

43 Food Standards Australia and New Zealand. History of FSANZ. Canberra; 2012 [cited 2012 20 October]. Available from: www.foodstandards.gov.au/scienceandeducation/aboutfsanz/background/historyoffsanz.cfm.

44 Food Standards Australia and New Zealand. Historical Development of Draft Standard 1.2.7 – Nutrition, Health and Related Claims. Canberra; 2012 [cited 2012 20 October]. Available from: www.foodstandards.gov.au/consumerinformation/nutritionhealthandrelatedclaims/healthclaimsstandard5081.cfm.

45 Therapeutic Goods Bill 1989 (1989).

46 McEwen J. A History of Therapeutic Goods Regulation in Australia. Canberra: Commonwealth of Australia; 2007.

47 Therapeutic Goods Advertising Code Council. A Brief History of the TGACC; 2012 [cited 2012 20 October]. Available from: http://tgacc.com.au/history.cfm.

48 Therapeutic Goods Regulations (Amendment) No 400 (1997).

49 KPMG. Review of Therapeutic Goods Administration/KPMG [Management Consulting] on behalf of the Department of Health and Family Services. Sydney; 1997.

50 Australian National Audit Office. The Auditor-General Audit Report No. 3 2011–12 Performance Audit. Therapeutic Goods Regulation: Complementary Medicines. Canberra; 2011.

51 Tambling G. Opening Address. Complementary Healthcare Consultative Forum. Canberra: Commonwealth of Australia; 1999.

52 Parliament of Australia. Questions on Notice Health: Complementary Healthcare Consultative Forum. Question No. 2387. Canberra; 2004.

53 Therapeutic Goods Advertising Code Council. A Brief History of the TGACC; 2012 [cited 2012 28 October]. Available from: http://tgacc.com.au/history.cfm.

54 Therapeutic Goods Administration. Pan Pharmaceuticals Limited: Regulatory Action and Product Recall Information; 2003 [cited 2012 27 October]. Available from: www.tga.gov.au/safety/recalls-medicine-pan-030428.htm.

55 Therapeutic Goods Administration. Expert Committee on Complementary Medicines in the Health System; 2011 [cited 2012 29 October]. Available from: www.tga.gov.au/archive/committees-eccmhs.htm.

56 Department of Health and Ageing. Implementation of the Government Response to the Recommendations of the Expert Committee on Complementary Medicines in the Health System. Progress Report. Canberra: Commonwealth of Australia; 2006.

57 Blackmore M. Government Health Policy and Complementary Medicines. Desana WholeHealth Life Regeneration; 2003 [cited 2012 29 October]. Available from: http://desana.com.au/features/pandemonium.

58 Worth T. Media Release: Government Supports TGA Oversight of Complementary Medicines. Canberra: Australian Government; 2003 [cited 2012 3 July]. Available from: www.health.gov.au/internet/main/publishing.nsf/Content/health-mediarel-yr2003-tw-tw03028.htm.

59 Robertson G. Submission: Transparency Review of the Therapeutic Goods Administration; 2011 [cited 2014 6 December]. Available from: http://tga.gov.au/sites/default/files/review-tga-transparency-1101-submission-geraldine-robertson.pdf.

60 Australian Government. TGA Reforms: A Blueprint for TGA's Future. Canberra: Commonwealth of Australia; 2011.

61 Therapeutic Goods Administration. Evidence Required to Support Indications for Listed Medicines (Excluding Sunscreens and Disinfectants) – Draft. In: Department of Health and Ageing, editor. Canberra: Commonwealth of Australia; 2012.

62 Therapeutic Goods Administration. Consultation: Evidence Required to Support Indications for Listed Medicines (Excluding Sunscreens and Disinfectants); 2012 [cited 2012 16 September]. Available from: www.tga.gov.au/newsroom/consult-cm-evidence-listed-medicines-120827.htm.

63 Therapeutic Goods Administration. Listed Complementary Medicine Compliance Reviews; 2012 [cited 2012 18 September]. Available from: www.tga.gov.au/industry/cm-basics-regulation-compliance-reviews.htm.

64 Food Standards Australia and New Zealand. Food Standards Australia and New Zealand: What We Do. FSANZ website: FSANZ; 2012 [cited 2013 18 February]. Available from: www.foodstandards.gov.au/scienceandeducation/aboutfsanz/whatwedoanddontdo.cfm.

14

INTUITIVE SPIRITUAL MEDICINE

Negotiating incommensurability

Ruth Barcan

I Introduction

This chapter draws on qualitative interviews with a small number of Australian spiritual healers and medical clairvoyants in order to reflect on the particular conundrums posed by forms of healing that are marginal to mainstream biomedicine and paradigmatically starkly different from it, and yet which co-exist with it in subterranean form in many modern Western societies. It focuses on practices in which healers claim to offer insights, interpretation and guidance, be that diagnostic information, treatment suggestions or metaphysical interpretations of illness, and asks: is it desirable, and indeed even *possible*, that such practices be formally regulated?

Asking this involves confronting a situation where positions can be entrenched, opinions strong and public debate occasionally venomous. In such a climate, it is difficult to cut through the strong emotions evidently aroused by the various forms of what we might for the moment call 'spiritual medicine', but the task is important, both to ensure patient safety and to rise to the intellectual challenge of understanding these practices in all their complexity. For, although public debate all too often construes the medical dimensions of the so-called 'spiritual revolution' (Heelas *et al.* 2005) as a contest between rationality and its others (superstition, nonsense, religion or emotion), the *social* truth of spiritual medicine as a lived practice is far more complex.

The perspectives and methods afforded by Gender and Cultural Studies provide one way of opening out this complexity. They are particularly suited to practices with a degree of secrecy, perhaps even shame, surrounding them, for Gender and Cultural Studies is committed to taking seriously the seemingly 'quaint', 'naive', 'outrageous' or 'unthinkable' (Hodge 1995: 37), mining them both for their intrinsic value and for what they might reveal about a putative mainstream. Gender and Cultural Studies also insists on the importance of understanding the intricate processes by which social actors forge meaning out of practice. Yet despite what might therefore be imagined to be a disciplinary predisposition to view the practices of spiritual medicine with potential sympathy, Cultural Studies has had its own ambivalence, to say the least, about taking spiritual practices seriously (Frow 1998; Barcan 2011; Barcan and Johnston 2011). A more specifically feminist ethnographic commitment to valuing stigmatized, feminized practices is needed to remedy this rather programmatic squeamishness.

Through a focused study of practices in which people understand healing to involve the passing on of non- or supra-rational guidance (practices I will call, rather loosely, 'intuitive spiritual medicine'), this chapter aims to shed light on how a small group of Australian practitioners understand the epistemology and the ethics of their practice and, through this, to tease out some of the reasons that formal regulation of these practices is difficult. A qualitative study of somewhat 'peripheral' forms of spiritual-medical practice pushes to the forefront the complexity of medical pluralism as an everyday lived reality, forcing us to engage less with big discourses about superstition or reason than with the intricacy of people's engagement with multiple health-care practices, multiple authorities and indeed multiple rationalities, logics and epistemologies.

Qualitative data is drawn from a series of practitioner interviews carried out intermittently between 2004 and 2010, as part of a 'Bodies of Knowledge' research project conducted at the University of Sydney, which studied CAM therapies as embodied experiences that open out different forms of knowledge of the body and the world.[1] The interviewees were clairvoyants and healers who self-identify as part of the New Age/alternative health movement; the project did not address other contexts in which interpretive healing practices occur, such as within specific organizations like the Spiritualist Church, or within ongoing lineages of practice in migrant communities. Since the interviews were a subset of a larger project on the embodied experiences offered by CAM therapies, sample size is small: six interviews of up to two hours each, plus participant observation in healing sessions. This, along with the Australian location, means that the conclusions cannot be considered generalizable, but the interviews are nonetheless very illuminating, offering some close-up insights into the daily workings of practices that normally remain quite hidden from mainstream view.

In this chapter, I claim that practices like medical clairvoyance and spiritual healing are important not despite, but in fact *because* of, their relatively peripheral social status. They are a particularly vexing, and particularly interesting, case for those concerned with the politics of integrative medicine, raising ethical and regulatory questions that can be only uneasily resolved, given the fundamental conflict between a medicine that is secular and one that is spiritually based. Despite my emphasis on incommensurability, it is important to recall the points of homology and convergence between these seemingly divergent medical approaches. The New Age, after all, has reshaped elements of traditional spiritual practice through contemporary cultural filters like individualism, neoliberalism, psychoanalysis and consumerism, and so it is unsurprising that some of its core precents should tally with dominant cultural logics. Understanding these practices thus involves keeping two somewhat opposing perspectives in tension: the stark paradigmatic differences between spiritual medicine and biomedicine but also their occasional points of congruence or overlap.

The first half of the chapter considers why formal regulation of intuitive spiritual medicine is difficult. It canvasses some differences between the assumptions, values and even goals of intuitive medicine and biomedicine that are so fundamental as to call into question the amenability of these healing practices to regulation within the rationalist and individualist frames of conventional biomedical ethics and legal protections. The second half draws on the thoughts and practices of the interviewees to delineate several possible avenues for enhancing intuitive healing practice, arguing that there is likely to be a larger role for professionalization strategies than for restrictive forms of regulation. The chapter concludes with the suggestion that the best strategies to ensure patient safety and professional ethics, along with the best hopes for an enriched medicine, are likely to be ones that involve cooperative practice rather than the maintenance of separate non-communicating spheres of practice. These, however, are fraught with difficulty, and it is indubitable that intuitive medicine and spiritual healing will also continue to be practised in private, even subterranean, ways.

II Background

There are many types of sacred medicine practised in contemporary Western societies. This chapter focuses on practices involving the passing on of information that is believed to be obtained through supra-rational or other-than-human (Hume 2007: 78) ways, since they pose quite particular problems for a health-care system in which medical authority is officially understood to be based on the certified acquisition of a body of rational knowledge.[2] I am broadly grouping together spiritual-therapeutic encounters in which the practitioner passes on 'guidance' believed to have emanated either from the client's unconscious and/or from some form of external spiritual force. This guidance takes a variety of forms and may include material that is diagnostic in nature, or that contains advice about treatment. It may or may not be predictive in nature, and it may sometimes be accompanied by a healing procedure or ritual.

Two contemporary labels under which such guidance occurs in a healing context are medical clairvoyance and spiritual healing. Medical clairvoyance, also known as medical intuition, is a specialized use of clairvoyance for medical or health purposes. It may take place as part of a broader clairvoyant reading, but there are also some clairvoyants who specialize in medical or health matters, some of whom label themselves 'medical intuitives'. Spiritual healing is a form of bodily treatment involving the channelling or direction of 'external' energies for the purposes of healing. Although the passing on of supra-rational guidance is not always part of spiritual healing, it is a reasonably common component of practices that go by this name. This definitional blurriness points to the fact that healing practices go by a variety of names and are often customized by the practitioners, a fact that is of relevance when considering professional regulation. For the purposes of this chapter, we might consider the types of practices I am describing as forms of 'intuitive spiritual medicine', since, whatever their differences, they all rely on the centrality of intuition as a sacred perceptual capacity. My use of the term 'medicine' is not intended to imply endorsement. Rather, I use it symptomatically, the intention of the chapter being, in fact, to point to the difficulties and predicaments that arise when spiritual techniques begin to blur into or overlap with mainstream medical ones.

Interpretive intuitive healing practices, despite their socially peripheral status, have some links to the medical mainstream. First, most clients of intuitive spiritual medicine also make use of biomedicine. Many would seem to have substantial personal investments in rationalism, insofar as there is, according to my interviewees, no shortage of clients coming from the supposedly ultra-rational professions like law and indeed medicine itself. (Most interviewees reported doctors and medical specialists among their clientele, as part of a seemingly broad demographic mix including politicians, teachers, nurses, sex workers and media personalities.) But the links with biomedicine go further than that, in that there exist formal and informal collaborations between healers or medical intuitives and physicians. In Australia at least, such collaborations tend to be invisible, even clandestine; they are not of the spectacular variety peppered across US popular culture, where one or two 'celebrity' medical intuitives work openly alongside medical doctors. Australian doctors are, according to one interviewee, inquisitive but wary. But semi-regular forms of collaboration nonetheless exist, usually behind the scenes, through personal relationships between clairvoyants/healers and doctors.

The co-existence and subtle communication between two radically different medical cosmologies in a modern Western nation like Australia – one systematized, legitimated and state-sanctioned, the other operating predominantly in the sphere of private belief and practice – is not, of course, the only way in which radically different medical practices may co-exist within a society. Medical pluralism works differently depending on the histories of colonization, dispossession, migration and globalization of any society. Many societies outside the West have had medical pluralism forced on them as a historical inevitability through the operations of colonialism and/or globalization, though the extent to which biomedicine displaces existing medicine varies according to context.

In modern Western societies, clairvoyant practices, as descendants of traditional, sacred or occult medicines, have persisted alongside (or underneath) the rise to dominance of rational knowledge and scientific medicine. Indeed, the shape they take in modern societies has really been brought into being *by* this dominance, insofar as the rise of science relegated non-scientific thinking to a separate sphere and created a newly demarcated realm of occult, mystical or faith-based practice. But technological advances did not simply dispel magical thinking; nineteenth-century visual technologies like the X-ray, for example, could, for those so inclined, foster a sense of a mysterious unseen world invisible to the human eye (Keller 2008: 19). Still and all, the rise to dominance of secular rationalism and its medicine meant that a hard science coded as masculine became delineated from a feminized supernatural, leaving clairvoyant practices to function as enticing yet stigmatized and sometimes clandestine healing practices. For that reason, today, although they enjoy a degree of public visibility in the form of advertisements or low-brow television programmes, as seriously performed healing practices they tend to take place either in non-public locations or in contexts that grant them legitimacy through community. Common contexts are: private homes, where single operators, usually women, offer clairvoyant/spiritual services in unmarked premises; New Age or alternative fairs or expos (e.g. Mind-Body-Spirit festivals or psychic fairs); formal settings (e.g. the Spiritualist church); and particular, countercultural, towns, regions or suburbs.

Today, the contemporary tussle between the masculine world of scientific rationality and its feminized foil has become more strident. The turn of the twenty-first century saw the emergence of public concern about the perils of the rise of unreason and the need to reclaim scientific rationality from the seductions of emotionality, superstition or religious belief (see, for example, Scruton 1999; Wheen 2004; Dawkins 2006; Hitchens 2007; for an analysis of this discourse, see Barcan 2009a). In such a climate, where the defence of reason is presented as an urgent necessity, it is important to be open about one's investments. In any case, recognizing and communicating one's speaking position is a taken for granted part of Gender and Cultural Studies work. In that spirit, then, it should be noted that this chapter does not set out to debunk or ridicule sacred medicine as practised in modern societies. Rather, it aims to reflect on some of the problems posed by the incommensurability of medical cosmologies. The rise of a significant demographic who move across multiple health practices and systems of care in largely invisible and unmonitored ways is sufficient to warrant consideration from social scientists and cultural analysts. This interest is even greater if one is prepared to grant even a measure of epistemological legitimacy to these practices, in which case the issue is not just a sociological interest in the limits of medical pluralism and the governance strategies of state-sponsored health-care systems, nor a purely regulatory agenda (how to manage, if not stamp out, practices that would seem to a biomedical hard line to be self-evidently delusional or damaging). Rather, if one remains at least agnostic about the potential benefits of such practices then the questions become more complex: how, given the incommensurability of the logics that underpin them, might one manage – indeed, facilitate – such transactions across epistemologies? How might one enrich their ethical base and professionalize them without losing exactly that which is most distinctive about them? For those prepared to countenance their potential use and efficacy (among whom I number myself), there is a medical issue at stake beyond that of safety: how one might facilitate an enriching cross-fertilization across a seeming gulf.

III Regulation: why it is difficult

This section describes some of the reasons that regulation of intuitive spiritual medicine is difficult: its different epistemological base from biomedicine (different assumptions, values and goals); its different idea of competency (which is understood as a gift rather than the acquisition of technical knowledge or skills); and the private, individualized contexts of much healing practice (i.e. its marginal social status).

1 Different epistemological bases

Traditional medicines, says Eric de Rosny, have three main things in common: they are 'essentially *sacred* medical practices; all of them have a *social* dimension; and they are based on the *power* of the person giving the treatment' (1998: 9, original italics). These three qualities point to an incompatibility between the epistemological base of biomedicine and that of intuitive spiritual medicine. They are fundamentally different spheres of discourse and practice, animated by different logics. As the clairvoyant Mary put it:

> I think that people who come know that I'm not a medically qualified practitioner and that the advice is from a different sort of realm altogether. It's like a spiritual realm. So hopefully they will understand that it's not something which is scientific.

The sacred base of intuitive medicine is starkly at odds with the avowed secularism of biomedicine, which hasn't expunged spiritual or religious belief so much as sidelined it, relegating it to a minor, feminized, adjunctive or palliative role.[3] By contrast, intuitive spiritual medicine centralizes the sacred as both the ultimate *source* of knowledge and a means of its transmission, and it relies on the cultivation of the practitioner's own spiritual sensibilities and capacities. This blurring between spiritual and healing practices makes intuitive spiritual medicine ill-suited to a medico-legal system predicated on the essentially *private* nature of religious belief (Carrette and King 2005) and on the biomedical model of illness, in which the multifaceted nature of dysfunction that characterizes holistic views of illness is typically greatly reduced.

This second, social, aspect of traditional medicine – its embrace of much wider definitions of both health and disease than biomedicine (Chauvet and Miklós 1998: vii) – has been taken up in the syncretic holism of the New Age, in which disease is a sign of dis-ease (Hay 1987), and is understood as something more than a purely organic, mechanical dysfunction. In keeping with the pre-modern conception of illness as essentially social (de Rosny 1998: 9), the New Age sees illness as enmeshed in other dimensions of social life, like relationship problems, job worries, family dynamics or financial worries. In much New Age thought, *all* illness has a metaphysical cause (Hay 1987). Within this holistic paradigm, the remit of the healer extends well beyond the physical, and the goal of a consultation may be similarly expanded, since within a spiritual logic, healing is not the same as physical cure (Barcan and Johnston 2011). Healing essentially means reconciliation, which may occur on a physical, mental, emotional, social or spiritual plane, and may not always involve the eradication of disease. Indeed, in some cases even death itself – a peaceful, reconciled death – may be understood as a form of healing, in stark contrast to the triumphalist aspirations typifying the biomedical paradigm. Thus, the very *goals* of biomedicine and sacred medicine are not always aligned (Brown 2000: 171).

This social character of both health and illness does not necessarily present a regulatory problem per se for biomedicine, since many practices accepted as adjuncts by state health-care systems (e.g. psychology, counselling or massage) may take amelioration or improvement in

'subjective wellbeing' as their aim. The difficulty arises when naïve or dogmatic spiritual practitioners may insist that *only* a metaphysical explanation will do, and may either explicitly or
tacitly countermand other forms of explanation and treatment. To my mind, this difficulty, with
its potential for medical harm, points to the value of strategies involving close cooperation
between spiritual medicine and biomedicine rather than their relegation to separate spheres.

2 Different ideas of competency

The third element of de Rosny's characterization of traditional medicine – that it is 'based on the
power of the person giving the treatment' (1998: 4) – is, perhaps, at the core of the regulatory conundrums raised by the difference between intuitive medicine and biomedicine. Spiritual/clairvoyant
therapies are organized around a perceptual capacity – intuition – rather than around training in a
specific knowledge base or in practical techniques, though these are of course developed through
practice. Their sacred character means that their relations to knowledge and authority differ from
those in biomedicine in two ways: the *source* of medical knowledge and the means of *accessing* that
knowledge. In spiritual medicine, knowledge is not rationally produced but spiritually derived:

> Everything that I know about the psychic realm or the spiritual realm or healing or health
> or whatever you call it, probably 99 per cent of what I actually know – logically know
> – is given psychically. Often I have to unlearn what I think I knew from other means.
> I've learnt so much about who we are physically and mentally and emotionally and the
> intricate workings of how we're put together which no textbook could ever teach.
>
> *(Mary)*

Most New Age-inspired alternative therapies view rational knowledge as limited and/or
counter-productive because reasoning works with chains of cause and effect that are patterned
and familiar. In such a context, medical knowledge can actually be a *hindrance*, since it may discourage receptivity to the unknown:

> The[re is] one thing I've very consciously avoided doing. When I got more involved
> with the medical side, I was very tempted to go and do anatomy and physiology. What
> happens then is that your own logical brain gets in the way of what you are seeing. So
> you might see somebody who has a problem, and your logic says, 'If there's a problem
> in that area, it has to be this'.... So by not doing medicine and very definitely refusing
> to do anatomy and physiology and all the rest of it, what I see is what is actually *there*,
> rather than what I expect to be there.
>
> *(Glen Margaret)*

Spiritual practitioners believe they are accessing a universal consciousness that transcends linear
time and geographical space. They may also claim to be receiving information from specific
spiritual entities – deceased relatives, spirit guides, angels and so on. Access to this supra-rational
knowledge is less a matter of training than of receptivity. It is a sensitivity that is *given* rather than
acquired:

> RUTH: Do you see your ability as a gift?
> MARY: Oh yeah, it's a gift, it's a definite gift. It was just given to me. Even *that*
> was given to me – the fact that I was going to receive this gift. I was told I was
> going to.

My interviewees all saw some role for training and experience in the development and refinement of this gift. Some saw their clairvoyant intuition as completely discrete from everyday empathy and intuition; others considered that they blurred into each other somewhat. Despite these differences, which I have elaborated in detail elsewhere (Barcan 2009b), all of them saw intuition as a quite separate capacity from rational knowledge and as something that could not be equally, predictably and rationally acquired.

The idea of an unteachable,[4] unquantifiable gift is fundamentally incompatible with the skills-based approach that dominates contemporary professional life and managerial discourse, where expertise is configured as a set of core competencies that can be measured against key performance indicators. Its very existence is highly contested. Even for those who believe in it, intuition, as a sacred, holistic, embodied, intersubjective and context-dependent faculty, is fundamentally unamenable to the specifying, systematizing and monitoring procedures that are the basis of conventional medical regulation.

From this fundamental epistemological incompatibility – in which knowledge is understood to derive from different sources and processes (peer review, reasoned debate, the systematic accumulation of evidence on the one hand, versus spiritual authority on the other) – spring both medical and ethical difficulties. The most significant medical question is that of the truth or otherwise of the information passed on by the practitioner. From the client's point of view, making judgments about the accuracy of information provided is one of the pleasures, burdens and obligations of the process. Practitioners themselves are not immune from self-questioning about their own fallibility.[5] But how would accuracy be able to be rendered in a manner amenable to biomedical criteria? Whereas biomedical competence is seemingly assessable by a body of peers in relation to determinable criteria of knowledge and practice, no such criteria and no such jury of peers exist in any formal sense in spiritual practice.

In any case, clairvoyant practice is underpinned by a logic in which the very idea of 'accuracy' is rendered difficult. While a medical diagnosis is often able to be verifiably true or false, the holistic logic in which clairvoyants work, according to which illness might be bound up in a host of psychological, familial, financial or work issues, means that truth is neither singular, nor static (the very act of speaking it may alter it), nor even the *sine qua non* of healing. There is, therefore, a certain structural irrefutability to the narrative and interpretive processes of intuitive medicine, in that particular propositions may not always in any simple way be falsifiable and, even if they are, the client may still interpret the process as a 'healing' one. The very process of receiving information may be therapeutic regardless of the accuracy of the information, given the rich affective and bodily experience of the 'transmission' process, where the client may well feel nurtured and supported by the very process of prolonged, caring attention and the transformative experience of entering the 'heterotopic' space (Foucault 1986)[6] of the healing room – a space outside the habits, constraints, limits and rules of everyday rationality.

Having said that, it is also the case that both practitioners and clients are bound together in a search for revealed truth, and are of course reassured and pleased by revelations that turn out to be empirically verified (either by subsequent biomedical diagnosis or by evident cure). The revelation of truths is a source of potential delights, and helps feed the word-of-mouth processes by which clients discriminate 'good' healers from 'bad'.

Another regulatory conundrum derives from the fact that the clairvoyant is not, in a sense, the originator of the knowledge. She[7] conceives of herself as a channel or conduit for information coming from 'elsewhere'. This model of the self as a channel is quite different from the agentic neo-liberal self on which legal liability and conventional professional ethics repose:

RUTH: You also give guidance on health issues. I wonder, what would the medical fraternity think about your advice? Are there lines you need to steer away from to protect yourself legally? Do you feel protected in that regard or what do you think the ethics of that are?

MARY: I think that's a good question. Well, first of all, it's not me. I, Mary, don't give this advice. It comes *through* me. But that would be very hard to argue in law, of course it would. That's my understanding of it – it's not me. So if I'm delivering, I'm the messenger. If I'm delivering information I am certain that it's come from the right source and [I also get that confirmation] through feedback [from clients].

So, interpretive spiritual practices are underpinned by an ambiguous relation to the question of responsibility and of medical accuracy. On the one hand, the search for truth structures the process; on the other, the process of *healing* may not be contingent on truth. For, even though some practitioners, like Mary, see their process as one of 'delivery', the content of the information and the process of passing it on are not one and the same thing. The communication process is not a neutral delivery of information, but rather an intersubjective exchange that may itself be transformative. Viewed this way,[8] a clairvoyant reading emerges as a complex mixture: allegedly supra-rational knowledge authoritatively delivered in a richly intersubjective context by a practitioner whose role is central, but who nonetheless conceives of it as catalytic rather than directly curative, and who does not see herself as ultimately responsible for the information provided or for its impacts: '[As a client], you've got to be very careful who you go to and you have to take responsibility ultimately for any information that you've been given. You decide' (Mary). This particular spiritual logic happens to sit well with the consumerist and neo-liberal principles of caveat emptor, but less easily with a medico-legal prohibition on diagnosis by CAM practitioners.

In the New Age context, then, there is some congruence between the logic of medical pluralism and that of consumerism, where 'health consumers' have the freedom to select and combine different health-care options, even across paradigmatic gulfs. The development of savvy consumers is part of the everyday processes by which people actively negotiate choices in a medical pluralist society. As Mary put it: 'I think the best way to select a psychic is by word of mouth. [Recommendations] have to come from somebody who has had a really helpful, positive experience. I think that [otherwise] we take a risk.' Such strategies work best, of course, for those who have strong social networks, rather than for the isolated, the alienated or the socially disenfranchised and they are, in any case, no basis for the regulation of a state-sanctioned health-care system. A further paradox interior to the spiritual logic is that one of the ways one might make good choices about intuitive medicine is by having good intuition oneself. Mary described to me an occasion when she herself visited a clairvoyant she didn't know: 'I went on spec. I thought, "Wow, she's going to be really good, I'm going to go there", so I did. And you know, my own psychic guidance was right, because she *was* fabulous; she was amazing.' The difficulty is that both of these ways of negotiating choice across different paradigms – robust social networks and having a good inner radar – are more readily available to those who already enjoy a strong psychological and social grounding and least available to those who are already socially or psychologically vulnerable. Such is the ethical poverty of consumerism as a system for distributing justice.

In this light, it is interesting to note that an inadequate or unpalatable experience does not necessarily turn all clients away from intuitive medicine per se. While some may of course repudiate the system after a bad experience, others seek remediation from *within* it, much as someone might seek a medical second opinion. Most of my interviewees mentioned people who had come to them after they had had a bad experience elsewhere:

> Well, I do think it's a minefield out there. I've had people come to me who've been really harmed by having readings from people who are not picking up from the highest source or are giving information which comes from their own mind. So I've had to do, from time to time, correctional readings for people, for want of a better term, to settle them down and to help them rebalance.
>
> *(Mary)*

Clearly, the medical issue of the accuracy of the information provided slides into what I would consider to be the most significant ethical issue at stake in intuitive medicine – that of the power asymmetry between practitioner and client. Elsewhere, I have described in detail the dynamic of desire potentially at play in a clairvoyant reading; even though a client may remain sceptical or wary throughout, they are there because at least part of them actively *wants* to be 'seen through' by a licensed authority (Barcan 2011: 73). So the practitioner's power is precisely the point.

3 Private, individualized contexts

In traditional contexts, power relations are regulated to some extent through the prescriptions of ritual and the existence of communities of practice. This is also likely to be the case in contemporary diasporic healing practices, where participants in sacred medicine may perhaps be known to each other and where enmeshment in a local community may bring some form of protection or redress (although, conversely, it may also constrain participants). In the contemporary New Age/alternative context, clairvoyance has by and large been extracted from ongoing lineages and sometimes from communities of practice. For, despite the existence of informal networks of amateur practice, many experiences of medical clairvoyance or spiritual healing are commodified one-off transactions. Moreover, even though the New Age movement has accorded them a particular type of popular public visibility and an existence as commodified services, many occur in private locations, making them relatively unamenable to public scrutiny.

The professionalizing momentum that characterizes CAM in the contemporary moment may help to redress this problem. There already exist professional bodies for spiritual healers, some of them longstanding. (For example, in the UK, the National Federation of Spiritual Healers was founded in 1954.[9]) Part of their new role is to inform members about legal issues. For example, the Spiritual Workers Association in the UK describes its aims as 'raising standards, raising awareness, and driving change'.[10]

In Australia, intuitive spiritual practice takes place in a rather hazy legal and professional space. The people I interviewed were very aware that their practices could easily be ridiculed, but they viewed large-scale legitimation strategies as wasted effort. They were keen to be taken seriously and wary of being publically ridiculed (some having felt themselves to have been 'set up' by journalists or academics in the past). But they showed little knowledge of or interest in professional organizations as a means of legitimation or protection, despite the existence of such bodies in Australia (e.g. the National Federation of Healers). This is no doubt the result not only of the relatively marginal social status of their work but also of the belief in individual responsibility characteristic of New Age thought, whereby both the practitioner and the client are understood to be individuals exercising agency and responsibility within the therapeutic encounter.

IV Regulation: possible strategies

From the standpoint of scientific rationality, one logical response to the phenomenon of intuitive spiritual medicine is to argue that it should be banned, as a specious, potentially dangerous practice that dupes vulnerable individuals. But in a society in which freedom of choice is a core principle, this is untenable and, from the point of view of those who believe they have benefitted from these practices, clearly undesirable. Therefore, drawing on my interviews with practitioners, I discuss three broad strategies for improved practice: harm minimization through legal restrictions; ascertaining and improving practitioner quality, including via training; and the development of professional attitudes and strategies that enhance integration.

1 Harm minimization through legal restrictions

It is difficult to know what type of legislation should govern spiritual healing practices. They are simultaneously medical, spiritual, consumerist and recreational practices, and hence come under the ambit of not only health-care policy but also consumer protection legislation,[11] and they are supported by the fundamental rights and freedoms of belief and practice that characterize liberal democracies. Laws can really only address wilful fraudulence; the UK's Fraudulent Mediums Act 1951 (now repealed in 2008 and replaced by Consumer Protection from Unfair Trading Regulations 2008 (SI No 1277)), for example, addressed only attempts at gain via deliberate acts of deception. Deliberate fraud is difficult to prove; mutual participation in something one considers, even if naïvely, to be plausible and beneficial is a different question. As was pointed out in the UK in 2008, when the spiritual 'industry' faced new regulation under consumer protection legislation, limiting healing practices comes close to infringing on freedom of religious practice.

a Diagnosis

One starting point is to note that in most Australian states, CAM practitioners are not legally allowed to 'practise medicine', 'provide medical treatment' or give medical advice (Weir 2003: 303, 2005: 44).[12] My interviews with CAM practitioners of many types made it evident that this has become popularized as a general prohibition on 'diagnosing' (cf. Weir 2005: 108). All the healers and intuitives I interviewed told me that they were not allowed to diagnose, and they had all developed modes of working with or around this. Glen Margaret, for example, avoids diagnosing by consciously working with metaphor, using visual symbols to describe what she is perceiving and using creative visualization techniques as a healing mechanism. For her part, Mary suggests that intuitive medicine can provide a 'shortcut' to biomedical diagnosis. She does pass on quasi-diagnostic information to her clients, but sees her work as belonging to a separate epistemological register, so she encourages clients to have diagnoses biomedically confirmed.

But what, in any case, does 'diagnosis' mean? Does it refer only to the ascription of a medical label to a complaint, or can it include the battery of 'assessment and analysis tasks' (Grace et al. 2006: 695) performed by all CAM practitioners, whether by using Western techniques (e.g. taking blood pressure, palpation, postural assessment) and/or techniques specific to particular alternative practices, like iris diagnosis, tongue diagnosis or aura reading? Many CAM practitioners are formally trained in some of the former, and many of the latter techniques fall outside of biomedical recognition.

In the UK, the term 'complementary diagnosis' has arisen to suggest a diagnosis distinct from medical diagnosis that arises within the logic and context of a particular CAM practice. The British Register of Complementary Practitioners (BRCP) recognizes the right of accredited members to make such a diagnosis (Institute for Complementary and Natural Medicine n.d.). It is yet to be seen how widespread and effective this concept will become, the BRCP being just one of a plethora of voluntary registering bodies in the UK. In any case, the concept of a complementary diagnosis is precarious, raising the use of the medico-legal relation of a complementary diagnosis to a medical one, especially since one key reason many clients seek spiritual alternatives is because a biomedical diagnosis has not been forthcoming. In Australia, the problem of diagnosis is likely to become more pronounced, since the public are increasingly using CAM practices as their first point of contact (Grace *et al.* 2006: 695).

b Prescription of treatments

A second area for legal consideration is the prescription of treatments. It is not uncommon for Australian healers to suggest that clients augment their spiritual approach with some form of remedy, usually naturopathic, herbal or homeopathic. Such suggestions may be based on formal training (many healers are also trained homeopaths or naturopaths), on lay knowledge (the development of lay expertise being a feature of alternative health culture) or on information believed to be given purely intuitively.

So perhaps healers might be required to be formally trained in other disciplines if they want to suggest remedies or treatments. Healers might well point out, however, that most of these 'natural' remedies are available off the shelf to consumers anyway, their potential side-effects or contraindications notwithstanding. When does a recommendation become a prescription? And should recommendation be treated differently from sale? The practitioners I interviewed had no interest in the latter. Mary saw no ethical conflict of interest in her 'prescriptions', since she had nothing to gain from them:

> I don't myself sell minerals, vitamins, herbs. I say, 'Well, this is [the information] I'm getting – that [these herbs and vitamins] will help you'. And there's nothing that they can't buy over the counter so I send them off to the shop to buy these things.

2 Ascertaining and developing practitioner 'quality'

A second broad strategy is to ascertain and develop practitioner 'quality'. I have put 'quality' in inverted commas for two reasons: first, to signal my agreement with critiques of 'audit culture' (Power 1997), which note that the reification of quality in managerial discourse has led to a certain self-referentiality in auditing processes (i.e. auditing practices measure the ability of people to comply with auditing practice rather than capturing a pure empirical truth); and second, because of the very real possibility that many of the qualities, skills and talents of good healers may be relatively unamenable to capture via the mechanisms through which 'quality' is conventionally measured. The CAM literature frequently discusses factors that make the evaluation of the 'success' of spiritual medicine difficult (see, for example, Dossey 1993; Astin *et al.* 2000; Brown 2000).[13] This does not mean, however, that there is no place for professional development, only that I place more faith in, for example, the development of codes of professional behaviour and ethics than in the blunter mechanisms of 'quality control'. Still, I begin with an example of the latter, since to outsiders, sceptics and those tasked with bureaucratic regulation these may seem the most obvious starting point.

a Evidentiary testing

Some defenders of spiritual healing do believe that the scientific method is a good pathway for the legitimation of spiritual healing. Daniel Benor, a doctor and psychotherapist who has been a long-time advocate for spiritual healing, is one example. Out of his systematic meta-analysis of healing research (1993), he has developed a specialization in conducting and advising on studies for assessing the efficacy of spiritual healing using the scientific method, as well as evaluating the scientific rigour of existing studies (Wholistic Healing Research n.d.).

Scientific studies are useful in examining certain aspects of the healing process (such as recovery rates), but we might wonder how the interpretive practices I am describing fare under their terms. In other words, how scientifically accurate is the information practitioners 'pick up' and pass on? To a sceptic, this entire question is unreasonable and infuriating, since 'There is not a shred of evidence that any of this is real' (Shermer 2003, n.p.). Many who work in the great variety of CAM modalities see it differently, however, and characterize the problem as one of the fundamental unamenability of spiritual medicine to the evidence-based assessment that characterizes contemporary biomedical research. For those who believe that there are only two types of medicine – 'medicine that has been adequately tested and medicine that has not, medicine that works and medicine that may or may not work' (Angell and Kassirer 1998: 841) – submitting medical intuition to some form of evidentiary test seems a logical solution.

One of the often repeated stories about the origin of the longstanding collaboration between the US doctor Norman Shealy and the medical intuitive Carolyn Myss is that Shealy tested Myss's intuitive diagnoses and found she was 93 per cent accurate (Myss and Shealy 1993: 72), in contrast with what he estimated to be the average biomedical accuracy rate of around 80 per cent (1993: 59). This type of evidentiary test is rarely performed (Benor 1992: 47). Nor do pilot studies seem particularly promising (Benor 1992). For sceptics, this would seem to settle the matter. Interior to the logic of spiritual practice, however, things are muddier. As noted earlier, accuracy, while it is valued by clients, is not necessarily the whole point, and intuitive consultations can be appreciated regardless of their accuracy – sometimes even in spite of evident inaccuracies. From the sceptical standpoint, this preparedness to value the process even in the face of revelations of its fallibility 'shows just how vulnerable people are to these very effective nostrums' (Shermer 2003: n.p.). But there is, in fact, very little research on how clients respond to intuitive diagnosis – under what circumstances and in what ways they believe it (Jobst 1997: 2).

From a sympathetic standpoint, the therapeutic value that many clients find in intuitive medicine regardless of its truth status is not an annoying recalcitrance but potentially a useful criterion for evaluating the usefulness of a particular practice. Scientific rationality sees this form of efficacy as an example of the placebo effect. The holism of alternative medicine reframes the idea of placebo, since the process of producing beneficent effects by changing thoughts or feelings is, in fact, precisely the aim of healing. As medical doctor Karen Lawson notes, spiritual medicine actively seeks to promote the very processes that evidence-based medicine seeks to eliminate as interference: 'the placebo effect, mind-body interactions, self-healing, or the power of intention' (2002: 17).[14]

All in all, it seems that efforts to capitalize on this richness without compromising patient safety might be better focused on the enhancement of training, particularly in professional ethics, and in the encouragement of strategies of cooperation.

b Spiritual training

I have already noted how unamenable the idea of a perceptual gift is to regulatory protocols like mandatory accredited training. Interior to the logic of spiritual practice, however, debates about the varieties and effectiveness of spiritual training are possible. At the turn of the twentieth century, the British Theosophist Charles Webster Leadbeater, author of a book on clairvoyance, lamented the fact that the vast majority of European clairvoyants were untrained. He claimed that lack of training meant that they usually 'fall very far short' of what systematically learnt clairvoyance can achieve (Leadbeater 1918: 50). He pointed to shortfalls in the degree of clairvoyance, the variety of ways it can manifest, its permanence, and above all its precision (1918: 50).

Systematic training of subtle perception is at the heart of many non-Western spiritual traditions, yoga and meditation being two obvious examples. The New Age view on training is typically syncretic. The New Age's intellectual debt to Romanticism means that it places credence in the idea of an unteachable gift; on the other hand, its historical debt to the US metaphysical religions, in particular the pragmatism and belief in self-improvement that typified the Transcendentalism of Ralph Waldo Emerson (Melton 1988: 36–9), predisposes it towards the idea of teachability. The belief in self-improvement is evident in both the staple New Age genre – self-help – and its prime pedagogical genre – the workshop, and there exist examples of both books and workshops aimed at the cultivation of intuitive perception (for example, Susan Shumsky's book *Divine Revelation* [1996] and the Barbara Brennan School of Energetic Healing).

In the UK, there are numerous courses in spiritual healing techniques (e.g. courses run by the Healing Trust, formerly the National Federation of Spiritual Healers).[15] There exists an umbrella organization, UK Healers, which currently encompasses eighteen separate healing organizations.[16] It is a voluntary professional standards accreditation body, one of whose services is to accredit particular training courses in spiritual healing practices.

c Training in professional conduct

For those sceptical about the very existence of the types of healing energies and intuitive capacities presupposed within intuitive spiritual medicine, a more important part of the regulatory agenda is training not in healing per se, but in professional behaviour, legal parameters and professional ethics. The proliferation of, and frequent name changes of, professional bodies for training, accreditation and support indicates just how active a development this is, especially in the UK context where the EU adds impetus to other drivers of change.

Accreditation with UK Healers, for example, requires submission to a raft of professionalizing devices, such as its code of conduct and complaints mechanisms, as well as knowledge and acceptance of important legal restrictions and precepts (e.g. patient confidentiality). Its training standards document (UK Healers 2013b) stipulates a minimum two years'/100 hours' practice, and encompasses both training in the knowledge base of the healing modality in question (including anatomy and physiology) and other forms of professional training, such as patient care, risk assessment, communication, patient empowerment and the assessment of the suitability of one's own practice modality for a particular patient. Such stipulations aim at the codification of knowledge and they push towards its elaboration as 'technical' (and hence 'professional') rather than 'indeterminate' (and hence 'religious' or 'charismatic') (Jamous and Peloille, in Hirschkorn 2006: 537). In this light, it is interesting to note that UK Healers appear to consider that spiritual healing is more amenable to these procedures than is clairvoyance: its Code of Conduct document states that it covers healing, including distant or absent healing, but not clairvoyance or so-called 'psychic surgery' (UK Healers 2013a: 1).

d Professional ethics

A key plank of this type of professionalization is training in professional ethics. My interviews suggest that, when it comes to intuitive spiritual healing practices, the development of codes of ethics is of prime importance. In the relatively unstructured Australian environment in which my interviews took place – one, moreover, compounded by the individualist contexts that typify the New Age – it is unsurprising that the practitioners I interviewed had developed their own codes of ethics. They were well aware of some of the ethical dilemmas called up by their practice, but unevenly equipped to deal with them. Some, especially those who are trained in more recognized CAM therapies, had had some formal training in ethics and had access to professional support bodies. But the particular predicaments of intuitive spiritual medicine cannot always be addressed through the ethical frameworks used in other CAM therapies, derived, as these are, from mainstream medical ethics.

The reliance on a gifted individual situates intuitive practices within what Robert Veatch termed the 'priestly' model of doctor–patient relations, in which the doctor's technical expertise confers on him significant moral authority (1972: 6). But while in the biomedical context out of which this model arose the 'locus of decision-making' is transferred away from the patient (Veatch 1972: 6), in the New Age context, most practitioners and their clients bring an ethic of self-responsibility to the practice. Moreover, many clients visit with at least some scepticism, whether about the efficacy of the practice per se or about the skill of the particular practitioner. They are likely to actively negotiate their responses. Insofar as the practitioner and client are *jointly* engaged in a process socially marked as 'subversive' (whatever their individual attitudes towards it), they are also interpellated as co-conspirators. Such features draw these practices back closer again to the collaborative ethos that is one of the hallmarks of alternative medicine (Williams 1998) and indeed of progressive biomedicine (Chin 2002).

While the priestly model is thus complicated by the individualism of the New Age, it may still remain a potent operational force within the clairvoyant encounter. For it is one thing to ask questions of a clairvoyant, but quite another one to live with the answers. A clairvoyant reading may be quite destabilizing, especially given its commonly privatized nature (clients often don't tell their friends or family that they have undertaken this type of consultation). A welter of emotions and attitudes – hope, fear, desire, trust, scepticism, shame, anger – are likely to be at play, especially since in Western societies one is likely, almost by definition, to be consulting the practitioner with some degree of urgency, possibly after the failure of other more mainstream options. It is not hard to see how this might be emotionally and ethically fraught, especially for vulnerable people, like the mentally ill, the emotionally unstable, the socially isolated or the terminally ill.

It is not that spiritual practitioners remain unaware of or untroubled by ethical questions. But their ethics may come, at least in part, from experiences *interior* to the practice. Mary, for example, told me that she gets psychic warnings about when it is not appropriate to 'stir the pot': 'I kind of can tell if it's not wise to go to some places within the client so while I'm delivering information I'm also picking up other information.' Glen Margaret, for one, won't work with anyone she knows to be dependent on drugs or alcohol, and she is well aware of the psychological risks her work may pose for some clients:

> I won't take anyone who has a known mental illness. But generally, as a psychic if you get somebody in who has [these problems] [...], if my work would be dangerous or upsetting to the mind with them, then I can't work. I can't get a read; I just get a very clear 'no'. 'Thanks very much, but unfortunately at this stage I just can't work with you.' I won't go against a read of something being no.

In these examples, different logics produced similar results: a logic interior to the practice (Mary is psychically warned off or Glen Margaret can't 'get a read') coincides with an ethical precept born of, or compatible with, one of the core planks of biomedical ethics: the protection of vulnerable individuals. Indeed, Glen Margaret articulated it to me in terms of the Hippocratic Oath: 'I suppose it's the old thing of "first, do no harm".'

Nonetheless, it is an unalterable feature of clairvoyance that it involves asymmetrical power relations. This asymmetry is heightened both by intrinsic features (these practices are based on the figure of someone with special access to non-quotidian forms of knowledge) and by contingent ones, such as the way they are currently socially configured in the West, where their marginalized status may be a source of intrigue, delight or anxiety.

Of course, biomedical encounters are themselves never interpersonally pure – no clean transmission of information untainted by power imbalances. Doctors are the holders of authoritative knowledge and there is still no shortage of physicians and medical specialists who operate according to the priestly model, in spite of the prominent critiques of the practitioner-centredness of so-called paternalistic medicine (Chin 2002) and the rise of alternative models (the 'contractual', the 'collegial') of doctor–patient relations (Veatch 1972). Biomedical practitioners are, however, held accountable in ways that clairvoyants and healers are not.

It should be evident by now that the development of an ethical code appropriate to a spiritual logic and yet also adequate to the legal climate in which contemporary medical practice exists is not straightforward. After all, ethics are not transhistorical prescriptions of ideal behaviour, but rely on particular understandings of agency, telos, causation and even temporality,[17] and a particular view of the individual's place in the wider world (or cosmos). This difficulty is no doubt one of the reasons that the UK Healers Code of Conduct document (2013a) specifically excludes clairvoyance. There are, however, a number of principles from biomedical ethics that are sufficiently embedded in modern societies' ideas of correct behaviour that they might prove adaptable.

Biomedical ethics are based on rational principles like the impartial provision of accurate information and liberal values like freedom of choice. Core principles include informed consent; the protection of vulnerable subjects (children, the mentally ill); the recognition of structural asymmetries in power (e.g. in doctor–patient or teacher–student relations); the right to choose; and the provision of opportunities for redress. Such principles attempt to negate or sidestep the intensity of interpersonal relationships in emotionally charged and asymmetrical situations.

It is beyond the scope of this chapter to give a detailed account of the ethical conundrums arising in intuitive medicine and of my interviewees' ways of thinking about these (see Barcan 2009b and 2011). But my interviews have led me to conclude that training in ethics would be a good professionalizing strategy. In Britain, the British Clairvoyant Academy has a British Clairvoyants Registry that claims to promote ethical conduct via a voluntary code of conduct for internet services. They plan to lobby government to establish a recognized code of conduct for the psychic telephone industry (Hamilton-Parker, n.d.). Even in Australia, where it appears to me that intuitive healing practices are more marginal than in the UK, it is evident that the general climate of CAM professionalization has led some practitioners to adopt some ethico-legal principles and practices from biomedicine. These include the recognition of vulnerable individuals and the introduction of protocols for informed consent.

There are, of course, plenty of people for whom the whole idea of an ethical intuitive or spiritual medicine is nonsense:

> I ... do not believe that ESP, telepathy, clairvoyance, clairaudience, or any of the other forms of psi power have any basis whatsoever in fact ... I cannot imagine anything

more insulting to the dead, and more insidious to the living, than constructing a fantasy that they are hovering nearby in the psychic aether, awaiting some self-proclaimed psychic conduit to reveal to me breathtaking insights about scars on my knees, broken appliances, and unfulfilled desires. This is worse than wrong. It is wanton depravity.

(Shermer 2003, n.p.)

But like it or not, these forms of practice are unlikely to disappear in the medically pluralist, pluri-religious, socially liberal contexts of the modern West. For those who paddle about in muddier waters than the members of the Skeptics Society or the contributors to Quackwatch (where the above quotation was found), perhaps the strongest hope for a safe, enriched medicine lies in the promotion of strategies that encourage cooperation – that is, in the project of a truly integrative medicine.

e Integrative strategies

Given the fundamental and presumably unbridgeable gap between those who abhor intuitive spiritual practices and those who endorse them, it seems that the most realistic strategies to promote both patient safety and a richer cross-fertilization between different forms of care are those involving the development of cooperative attitudes and practices. Such cooperative and precautionary attitudes are espoused in the UK Healers' Code of Conduct (2013a), which requires practitioners to respect ethico-legal principles like patient confidentiality but also mandates more amorphous principles, such as respect for the medical profession and the recognition of one's own limits.

As it happens, the types of practices my interviewees had developed as individuals turn out to be of this kind. Mary, for example, espoused precautionary attitudes:

I'm also aware that whatever advice I give isn't something which would go against traditional medical advice. For example, if somebody's on medication from the doctor I always advise people that it's a good idea to work with your doctor and follow what the doctor says.

Glen Margaret has developed precautionary attitudes into quite formal protocols. She requires any client who is on medication to tell his/her doctor that they are doing emotional release work with her. She gave the example of someone on blood pressure tablets:

If they are on medicine they have to have their doctor's permission, because when you release emotions with a person then their medicine becomes stronger. So say if they are taking one tablet a day and you suddenly release all the emotions, you release all the reasons for them to have high blood pressure. Their blood pressure drops and they're still taking the tablets and their blood pressure drops even more, so they're in strife.

She requires them to take responsibility for monitoring their dosage with their doctor, even going so far as making them sign a form to say they have done this. Such cooperative practice cuts several ways: it protects the clairvoyant from accusations of medical meddling and shields patients from the excesses of naïve, overly zealous or dogmatic metaphysicians, while allowing scope for patients and indeed their doctors to be exposed to the benefits of perspectives that engage the interactions between different elements of the mind–body system. Glen Margaret is, I suspect, somewhat exceptional in the stringency of her professional principles and the clarity with which she articulates them. Her practice points to one possible mode of professionalizing that does not involve compromising the paradigmatic distinctiveness of her work.

Mary had a similar vision of her practice and conventional medicine working as two complementary and communicating spheres of action:

> MARY: You've got to work with the strictly scientific medical arena as well.
>
> RUTH: So spiritual practices should belong in separate spheres, like separating consulting rooms?
>
> MARY: Yes, but possibly working in harmony with each other. Like, if I break my leg I'm not going to rush off to a psychic for healing. I'm going to go to a doctor.... So there are areas [of expertise]. I think psychics can work well with emotions, as long as they're the *right* psychics. I think they can do a lot of healing with the emotional body and the mental body[18] and I also think that for lots of illnesses psychics can diagnose ... I had a client who happened to be a lawyer who had a son who was very ill so he rang me and asked me what could I see was the cause of the boy's problem. And I tuned in and I said, 'Look, he's got glandular fever'. So he went and asked for a test for glandular fever and it showed up that's what he had. So it can be something which can be very useful in speeding up the process of diagnosing.

Defenders of intuitive diagnosis agree that collaboration is the best pathway. Daniel Benor suggests that a panel of healers might work better than individuals, since the healers he has studied appear to have their own individual blind spots. He also suggests that some form of medical training for healers who wished to work with doctors 'would seem advisable' (1992: 60).

Numerous cooperative bodies have come into being, even some encompassing the rather more paradigmatically remote forms of CAM practice. The Doctor Healer Network,[19] for example, aims to facilitate the practice of and research into the incorporation of energetic healing techniques into mainstream medicine, and its membership comes from orthodox medicine as well as CAM therapies (Galbraith 2008).

Despite such signs, it would be naïve to believe that overt and mutual cooperation is an easily generalizable model of practice. While the existence of 'cross-over' practitioners, the burgeoning patient demand for CAM and the emergence of integrative medicine as a new paradigm all point in this direction, such developments can provoke harsh counter-reactions, especially from those who see even the more recognizable forms of CAM, let alone its outriders, as 'pernicious' (Donnelly *et al.* 1985: 539). In Australia, a number of recent examples point to the very real dangers of confiding to one's doctor that one is taking a less than conventional therapeutic approach.[20] Calls for more transparent cooperation between doctors and healers underestimate the entrenchment of power and overestimate the possibility of rational debate across radical, sometimes hostile, differences. Systematically asking clients of spiritual medicine to liaise with their doctors might be at best naïve and at worst foolhardy. It is not just patients and healers who might be put at risk, but also established doctors who are seen to countenance marginal practices. It is easier to imagine spiritual healers being forced by regulators to refer patients to general practitioners than it is to see GPs returning the favour. This is not only due to biomedical scepticism, but also because there are real professional risks for GPs prepared to entertain integration with spiritual or intuitive medicine. The spiritual healer Regina, for example, told me that she knew of a few GPs who refer clients to healers, but they do not tell their colleagues. Meanwhile, those on the less powerful side of the equation – the healers – may well find that their referrals to mainstream medicine are not reciprocated with any degree of symmetry and may even make them legal targets.

V Conclusion

To conclude, it is worth reiterating that, though a study of intuitive medicine may seem rather esoteric or marginal, the idea of intuition plays a central role in a great number of CAM practices, and the passing on of information believed to be picked up through spiritual or intuitive means may form a subterranean part of CAM practices even when that is not evident from the outside (e.g. in homeopathy, reiki, massage and so on). So these practices are worthy of exploration not only in and of themselves but because they are part of a larger phenomenon that will not go away or that cannot be understood, let alone managed, through ridicule.

Clearly, the pathway towards integrative medicine is much less straightforward when it comes to intuitive spiritual medicine than for those CAM practices with a more cognate epistemological base, for which scientific research can unequivocally provide an avenue for legitimation. Nonetheless, in a best case scenario it might work from both sides of the fence, promoting patient safety while addressing some of the well-documented limitations of classic medical practice.

But because of the evident difficulties, intuitive medical practices will undoubtedly continue to be practised in private or in particular communities of belief. Their mainstreaming is not everyone's goal nor, in any case, a fully realizable objective. But for those practitioners interested in the prospect of professionalization along the model of other CAM therapies, the development of trusting networks across the paradigmatic gulf seems the most appropriate pathway. True integration has to be a two-way street, and not just default to conventional practices 'plus' CAM (Caspi *et al.* 2003: 61). This requires more open attitudes, as well as the development of an appropriate research base, rather than the simple application of evidence-based biomedical studies, which are likely to prove inimical (Lawson 2002). Moreover, spiritual medicine can also have a proactive role, rather than being only the object of scrutiny. For example, it is indubitable that the science of mind–body medicine will continue to develop, through such fields as epigenetics, neuroscience and psychoneuroimmunology, and non-conventional medicine already plays a role in driving some of this science.

Certainly, some of my interviewees saw integration, and attendant processes like regulation, as the future of medicine. But currently, hopes for integration are undercut by a deep conundrum: that the safest and most ethical strategies – those promoting open dialogue and cooperation – are the most professionally risky for both healers and doctors. In the current climate of risk and hostility, the most likely strategy is that cooperative strategies will be limited, cautious and highly circumscribed, and that beneath the radar the 'two worlds' scenario will continue.

Notes

1 The study was conducted with ethics approval from the University of Sydney. My sincere thanks to my interviewees, who are referenced here using pseudonyms.

2 This commonsensical alignment of biomedicine with rationality does not mean, of course, that biomedicine is free of rationalism's 'others' – like emotion, intuition and tradition – but rather that their role is officially downplayed.

3 This plays out differently, of course, in different national contexts. In the US, research into the medical effects of religious belief on health and into faith-based practices like prayer-for-health has a more established place in biomedicine than it does in Australia.

4 As I will argue below, this is an oversimplification. The most common New Age view is that everyone has the potential to be intuitive, and that certain techniques can be learnt, but that, as with any skill, some people seem innately to have a greater capacity than others. Susan Shumsky (1996) has an evolutionary perspective on this. She claims that the era of the guru is drawing to a close and that the development of one's own intuition is more suited to contemporary times: 'You have within yourself all that you need. You do not need a guru or psychic adviser. You are the source of your own wisdom' (1996: 38).

5 Most practitioners reported the inhibiting effects of self-doubt, which for some were redoubled if a client appeared resistant or sceptical. It is inevitable that practitioners are aware of the social precariousness of their profession, and they are forced to manage, personally and socially, a somewhat marginalized professional identity (Barcan 2009b).

6 Michel Foucault coined the term 'heterotopia' to describe places or spaces that are somehow set outside the logic of the everyday, either because they combine a number of different logics within them or because they require particular entry rituals. His characterization of them as isolated but penetrable (Foucault 1986: 26) seems particularly apt for the clairvoyant's room.

7 I use the term 'she' rather than 's/he' because it points both to the cultural feminization of these practices and to the likely empirical dominance of women in this field.

8 The process cannot help but be interactive. Some interviewees stressed this dimension of their practice, describing how blockages might occur if there was no rapport between client and practitioner, or how their information relay was subject to interference from the emotions in the room. For a longer discussion of the intercorporeal dimensions of alternative therapies, see Barcan (2011), especially Chapter 5.

9 This Federation is now known as The Healing Trust. www.thehealingtrust.org.uk (accessed 15 March 2013).

10 www.theswa.org.uk (accessed 15 March 2013).

11 In the UK, the Fraudulent Mediums Act of 1951 was repealed in 2008, in favour of regulation under EU-directed consumer protection legislation (Consumer Protection from Unfair Trading Regulations 2008: SI No. 1277).

12 The exceptions are Queensland and Victoria (Weir 2003: 303).

13 Such problems are discussed in the emerging literature on the evaluation of spiritual medicine, which mentions the difficulty of accounting for intention methodologically (Brown 2000: 171); the incompatibility of the goal of healing with that of cure (Brown 2000: 171; Barcan and Johnston 2011); and particular problems with controls and placebos (Brown 2000: 173) and with defining outcomes (2000: 173).

14 CAM practitioners, including spiritual healers and intuitives, reject the idea that healing effects are *reducible* to placebo. As Regina put it in relation to homeopathy, 'For an adult you can say it's a placebo, but for a child – for a one-year-old or a two-year-old child or a dog – there's no way you can say that's placebo'.

15 www.thehealingtrust.org.uk (accessed 15 March 2013).

16 www.ukhealers.info (accessed 15 March 2013).

17 In a spiritual logic, truth is not linear: something might be temporarily true, or true in another lifetime or another plane of existence, or true not literally but symbolically, or true in the future.

18 Mary is using terminology drawn from a subtle body schema, in which the body is envisaged as comprised of multiple energetic bodies. For a detailed study of the subtle body model, see Johnston (2008).

19 www.doctorhealer.org (accessed 15 March 2013).

20 In a number of Australian states, children being treated naturopathically for chronic illnesses have been taken from their parents by welfare agencies in recent years (Whittaker 2012). In some of these cases, the naturopathic remedies (such as probiotics for gut conditions) had been prescribed by registered doctors. Medical anthropologist Helen Hayward-Brown (1999) sees this as one way of policing and punishing the new breed of educated middle-class women, the so-called 'PhD mothers' (Whittaker 2012: 16), who are threatening to established power because they bring a greater sense of entitlement, scrutiny and lay expertise to medical encounters. She has charted the use of the dubious psychiatric category of Munchausen Syndrome by Proxy to pathologize such women. The existence of such cases in relation to relatively mainstream treatment options such as naturopathy points to even greater risks with more marginal practices.

References

Angell, M. and Kassirer, J. P. (1998) 'Alternative Medicine – The Risks of Untested and Unregulated Remedies', *New England Journal of Medicine*, 339(12): 839–41.

Astin, J. A., Harkness, E. and Ernst, E. (2000) 'The Efficacy of "Distant Healing": A Systematic Review of Randomized Trials', *Annals of Internal Medicine*, 132(11): 903–10.

Barcan, R. (2009a) 'Intuition and Reason in the New Age: A Cultural Study of Medical Clairvoyance', in D. Howes (ed.), *The Sixth Sense Reader*, Oxford: Berg Publishers: 209–32.

Barcan, R. (2009b) 'Spiritual Boundary Work: How Spiritual Healers and Medical Clairvoyants Negotiate the Sacred', in E. B. Coleman and K. White (eds), *Medicine, Religion and the Body*, Leiden: Brill: 129–46.

Barcan, R. (2011) *Complementary and Alternative Medicine: Bodies, Therapies, Senses*, Oxford: Berg Publishers.

Barcan, R. and Johnston, J. (2011) 'Fixing the Self: Alternative Therapies and Spiritual Logics', in M. Bailey and G. Redden (eds), *Mediating Faiths: Religion and Socio-Cultural Change in the Twenty-First Century*, Farnham, UK: Ashgate Publishing: 75–87.

Benor, D. J. (1992) 'Intuitive Diagnosis', *Subtle Energies*, 3(2): 41–64.

Benor, D. J. (1993) *Healing Research*, Munich: Helix verlag GmbH.

Brown, C. K. (2000) 'Methodological Problems of Clinical Research into Spiritual Healing: The Healer's Perspective', *Journal of Alternative and Complementary Medicine*, 6(2): 171–6.

Carrette, J. and King, R. (2005) *Selling Spirituality: The Silent Takeover of Religion*, Abingdon: Routledge.

Caspi, O., Sechrest, L., Pitluk, H. C., Marshall, C. L., Bell, I. R. and Nichter, M. (2003) 'On the Definition of Complementary, Alternative, and Integrative Medicine: Societal Mega-Stereotypes vs. the Patients' Perspectives', *Alternative Therapies in Health and Medicine*, 9(6): 58–62.

Chauvet, L.-M. and Miklós, T. (eds) (1998) *Illness and Healing*, London: SCM Press.

Chin, J. J. (2002) 'Doctor-Patient Relationship: From Medical Paternalism to Enhanced Autonomy', *Singapore Medical Journal*, 43(3): 152–5.

Dawkins, R. (2006) *The God Delusion*, London: Bantam.

Donnelly, William J., Spykerboer, J. E. and Thong, Y. H. (1985) 'Are Patients who Use Alternative Medicine Dissatisfied with Orthodox Medicine?' *MJA*, 142(10): 539–41.

Dossey, L. (1993) *Healing Words: The Power of Prayer and the Practice of Medicine*, New York: Harper San Francisco.

Foucault, M. (1986) 'Of Other Spaces', *Diacritics*, 16(1): 22–7.

Frow, J. (1998). 'Is Elvis a God? Cult, Culture, Questions of Method', *International Journal of Cultural Studies*, 1(2): 197–210.

Galbraith, J. S. (2008) 'Update: News of the DHN UK, Dr Daniel Benor's Past Involvement, and the Current State of Healing in the UK', Wholistic Healing Research website, http://wholistichealingresearch.com/jgupdatemay08.html (accessed 4 March 2011).

Grace, S., Vemulpad, S. and Beirman, R. (2006) 'Training in and Use of Diagnostic Techniques among CAM Practitioners: An Australian Study', *Journal of Alternative and Complementary Medicine*, 12(7): 695–700.

Hamilton-Parker, C. (n.d.) 'The BCA Code of Conduct (Ethics)', http://psychics.co.uk/blog/code-of-conduct.html (accessed 8 December 2014).

Hay, L. L. (1987) *You Can Heal Your Life*, Concord, NSW: Specialist Printing.

Hayward-Brown, H. (1999) 'False and Highly Questionable Allegations of Munchausen Syndrome by Proxy', www.pnc.com.au/~heleneli/paper.htm (accessed 8 December 2014).

Heelas, P., Woodhead, L., Seel, B., Szerszynski, B. and Tusting, K. (2005) *The Spiritual Revolution: Why Religion is Giving Way to Spirituality*, Malden, MA: Blackwell Pub.

Hirschkorn, K. A. (2006) 'Exclusive Versus Everyday Forms of Professional Knowledge: Legitimacy Claims in Conventional and Alternative Medicine', *Sociology of Health & Illness*, 28(5): 533–7.

Hitchens, C. (2007) *God is not Great: How Religion Poisons Everything*, Crows Nest, NSW: Allen and Unwin.

Hodge, B. (1995) 'Monstrous Knowledge: Doing PhDs in the New Humanities', *Australian Universities' Review*, 2: 35–9.

Hume, L. (2007) *Portals: Opening Doorways to Other Realities Through the Senses*, Oxford: Berg Publishers.

Institute for Complementary and Natural Medicine (n.d.) 'FAQs'. http://icnm.org.uk/faqs#q30 (accessed 8 December 2014).

Jobst, K. A. (1997) 'One Man's Meat is Another Man's Poison: The Challenge of Psychic/Intuitive Diagnosis to the Diagnostic Paradigm of Orthodox Medical Science', *Journal of Alternative and Complementary Medicine*, 3(1): 1–3.

Johnston, J. (2008) *Angels of Desire: Esoteric Bodies, Aesthetics and Ethics*, London: Equinox.

Keller, C. (2008) 'Sight Unseen: Picturing the Invisible', in C. Keller (ed.), *Brought to Light: Photography and the Invisible 1840–1900*, New Haven: Yale University Press, in association with the San Francisco Museum of Modern Art: 19–35.

Lawson, K. (2002) 'Political and Economic Issues in CAM', in M. A. Herring and M. M. Roberts (eds), *Blackwell Complementary and Alternative Medicine: Fast Facts for Medical Practice*, Malden, MA: Blackwell Science, Inc: 14–19.

Leadbeater, C. W. (1918) *Clairvoyance*, 4th edn, London: Theosophical Publishing House.

Melton, J. G. (1988) 'A History of the New Age Movement', in R. Basil (ed.), *Not Necessarily the New Age: Critical Essays*, Buffalo: Prometheus: 35–53.

Myss, C. and Shealy, C. N. (1993) *The Creation of Health: The Emotional, Psychological, and Spiritual Responses that Promote Health and Healing*, New York: Three Rivers Press.

Power, M. (1997) *The Audit Society: Rituals of Verification*, Oxford: Oxford University Press.

de Rosny, E. (1998) 'The Longevity of the Practice of Traditional Care', in L.-M. Chauvet and T. Miklós (eds), *Illness and Healing*, London: SCM Press, 8–14.

Scruton, R. (1999) 'What Ever Happened to Reason?' *The City Journal* [New York], 9(2): 88–96.

Shermer, M. (2003) 'Psychic for a Day: How I Learned Tarot Cards, Palm Reading, Astrology, and Mediumship in 24 Hours', Quackwatch website, 1 May, www.quackwatch.com/01QuackeryRelatedTopics/psychic2.html (accessed 1 March 2011).

Shumsky, S. G. (1996) *Divine Revelation*, New York: Simon & Schuster.

UK Healers (2013a) 'Quality Criteria: Code of Conduct', www.ukhealers.info/index_htm_files/UKH%20Quality%20Criteria%20-%20Code%20of%20Conduct.pdf (accessed 8 December 2014).

UK Healers (2013b) 'Quality Criteria: Training', www.ukhealers.info/index_htm_files/UKH%20Quality%20Criteria%20-%20Training.pdf (accessed 8 December 2013).

Veatch, R. M. (1972) 'Models for Ethical Medicine in a Revolutionary Age', *The Hastings Center Report*, 2(3): 5–7.

Weir, M. (2003) 'Obligation to Advise of Options for Treatment – Medical Doctors and Complementary and Alternative Medicine Practitioners', *Journal of Law and Medicine*, 10(3): 296–307.

Weir, M. (2005) *Alternative Medicine: A New Regulatory Model*, Melbourne: Australian Scholarly Publishing.

Wheen, F. (2004) *How Mumbo-Jumbo Conquered the World: A Short History of Modern Delusions*, London: Harper Perennial.

Whittaker, M. (2012) 'Bitter Pills', *Sydney Morning Herald Good Weekend*, 13 October: 15–18.

Wholistic Healing Research (n.d.) 'Dr Daniel J. Benor, MD'. http://wholistichealingresearch.com/Daniel-Benor.html (accessed 4 March 2011).

Williams, A. (1998) 'Therapeutic Landscapes in Holistic Medicine', *Social Science and Medicine*, 46(9): 1193–203.

15

TRADITIONAL CHINESE MEDICINE AND ACUPUNCTURE PRACTITIONERS AND THE CANADIAN HEALTH CARE SYSTEM

The role of the state in creating the necessary vacancies

Sandy Welsh and Heather Boon

I Introduction

Responses to patients' demand for access to complementary and alternative medicine (CAM) health care services provide a unique opportunity to understand how health care systems evolve and change over time to accommodate new health care professions. Much of the research on the professional development of CAM practitioner groups focuses on the professional process, including what these groups are doing to attain professional status, especially regulation by the state (Adams, 2006; Boon *et al.*, 2004; Broom and Tovey, 2007; Cant and Sharma, 1996; Cant *et al.*, 2011; Kelner *et al.*, 2002; Saks, 1995; Shuval, 2006; Welsh *et al.*, 2004). The dominant theoretical perspective guiding this work is that of social closure (Collins, 1990; Hollengerg, 2006; Saks, 2001; Welsh *et al.*, 2004). Without denying the importance of social closure for understanding the professional development of CAM practitioner groups, we want to focus on a different aspect of this process. Using Abbott's system of professions model (1988), we use the case of traditional Chinese medicine/acupuncture (TCM/A) practitioners in Ontario to show how vacancies are created in the system of professions. It is through these vacancies that professional groups then gain entry into the system of professions and where social closure issues come into play. This focus allows us to discuss the role of the state in creating vacancies and how this has the potential to change the existing system of health care professions in Ontario. We also build on the work of Adams, who emphasizes the usefulness of examining professional processes and interprofessional conflict simultaneously (Adams, 2004). TCM/A practitioners are involved in a process whereby the state has opened up jurisdictions to the group, yet other groups are battling with TCM/A practitioners over these jurisdictions and TCM/A practitioners are battling within their own ranks to decide how best to capitalize on the newly opened jurisdiction.

Most analyses of the professionalization project of CAM occupations start with the assumption that there is potential space for these occupations if only they are organized and/or can obtain social closure and monopoly for their work. We take a step back to look at how vacancies are created for a particular CAM group: TCM/A practitioners. We want to look at the potential beginning of a "disturbance" in the system of health care professions in Ontario. Abbott's (1988) influential study of the system of professions uses vacancy models to illuminate how changes happen in the system of professions. Mobility within a system happens only when a jurisdiction over a set of professional work tasks is opened or closed. These openings and closings of jurisdictions are created by both internal and external forces, such as inter-professional conflict, technological change or social movements. These internal and external disturbances lead to vacancies; when there is a space or vacancy available, professional groups can move into these vacancies.

Our paper focuses on the role of the state as an external source opening up jurisdictions in the health care system in Ontario. Using the case of TCM/A practitioners in Ontario, we examine the lead-up to the Government of Ontario legislating the inclusion of this group under the Regulated Health Professions Act (RHPA), the same act that covers medical doctors, dentists and other health care providers in Ontario. It is often assumed that the state is moved to act due to intensive lobbying as the profession gains status and legitimacy with the public through the strength of their growing professional association and by demonstrating their willingness to shed practitioners deemed deviant or unsafe. Less discussed in the literature is when the state, due to their own interests, decides to grant self-regulatory status prior to an occupational group developing a cohesive professional project. It is this situation we make the focus of our chapter by asking, what happens when the state intervenes and decides to grant an occupational group the right to become a self-regulating profession?

II Vacancies and the Ontario regulatory framework for health care professions

In Canada, all health care professionals are regulated at the provincial level, meaning that who is regulated and what they are authorized to do varies from province to province. A review of the social context of the regulated health care professions in Ontario, Canada provides context for this study. The legislative review process begun in the 1980s and culminating in the 1991 Regulated Health Professions Act (RHPA) had the goal of "increasing the coordination and cooperation of the health professionals" (p. 199) (O'Reilly, 2000; see also Gilmour *et al.*, 2002). The new legislation was enacted to obtain greater public accountability, increase equity among the health care professions, increase direct-to-consumer access to a wider variety of professionals and provide a common framework for the regulation of all regulated health professions in the province of Ontario (Health Professions Legislation Review, 1989; O'Reilly, 2000). Rather than licensing practitioners per se, the Act focuses on licensing specific acts or procedures that are deemed potentially harmful. These "controlled" or "authorized" acts can legally be performed only by specific professional groups authorized by the statute to perform them. The same controlled act may be performed by more than one profession (thus effectively eliminating monopolies).

Groups that held monopolies are now doing much the same work that they did before the 1991 RHPA, but what has changed is that "space has now been created for others to perform a range of activities for which they used to risk prosecution" (p. 175) (O'Reilly, 2000). This "space" allows multiple tenancy of jurisdictions as discussed by Abbott (1988), thus creating vacancies for competing groups. The Ontario government explicitly opened the door for TCM/A practitioners when stating, in a 1996 discussion paper on the RHPA, "It is our view that the RHPA is flexible enough to include non-Western/non-allopathic medical systems and approaches.... The RHPA will be required to accommodate forms of health care practice that are not based on the Western medical model" (quoted in O'Reilly, 2000, p. 191). This was echoed in the formal review of the new legislation (Alder, 2001). However, our analysis of the challenges of the TCM/A group's attempt to gain inclusion in the RHPA suggests that this vision has been difficult to realize, due to both external and internal challenges.

III Moving into vacancies: inter-professional conflict and professionalization

Adams' analysis of dentists and dental hygienists in Ontario demonstrates the links between professionalization projects and inter-professional conflict. She shows that "professional projects quite often generate inter-professional conflict, and that inter-professional conflict is shaped by occupational groups' efforts to attain and/or maintain professional status and authority" (Adams, 2004, p. 2245). Within the TCM/A practitioners in our study, we see these two processes at work. TCM/A practitioners are engaged in professionalization projects that are designed to establish their authority to deliver their form of health care. At the same time, there are jurisdictional battles with existing health care professions, such as doctors and physiotherapists. Unlike dentists and dental hygienists in Adams' study, the TCM/A occupation is also rife with internal or intra-professional jurisdictional battles (Welsh *et al.*, 2004). For example, who is qualified to provide a TCM diagnosis or to practice acupuncture are contested areas. These internal battles are also linked to the professional projects of the group.

The purpose of this chapter is to analyze the process by which state intervention appears to be occurring and explore how the struggle to "fit" into the existing health care system may require changes in the groups that are striving to belong. This chapter focuses on the regulation of acupuncture and not on other health practices associated with TCM. In the early discussions around the regulation of TCM/A practitioners, much of the focus was on acupuncture as there are a range of CAM and allopathic practitioners providing this service. At the time of our study, the government was considering regulated acupuncture under the RHPA controlled act of "performing a procedure on tissue below the dermis".[1] Several regulated health professions, such as physicians, nurses, massage therapists and chiropractors, perform acupuncture as part of their practice. There were no plans by the government to limit the ability of these groups to engage in acupuncture. Instead, TCM/A would be sharing the authority to perform acupuncture with these other health professions. In Abbott's terms, the government deliberately set up a "multiple tenancy" situation for acupuncture whereby multiple groups would occupy the same jurisdictional space. Any hope on the part of TCM/A practitioners that regulation would create a monopoly on the procedure of acupuncture was certainly not part of the government's agenda. It is from this particular context that we derive the focus for our chapter: what happens when the state creates new vacancies that are designed to be shared by multiple groups?

1 Methods

Data for this chapter were derived from five sources. We conducted in-depth, personal interviews in 2001–2007 with eight senior TCM/A practitioner group leaders of schools and associations in Ontario (identified by convenience and snowball sampling), ten leaders of conventional health care practitioner groups currently considered "insiders" working within the existing health care system with real or perceived scopes of practice that had the potential to overlap with TCM/A practitioners (medicine, nursing, physiotherapy, clinical nutrition and public health) and ten government representatives with knowledge of, and in many cases responsibility for, policy decisions related to TCM/A and other CAM practitioner groups. In addition, we conducted a focus group with five frontline TCM/A practitioners and explored archival material (documents describing regulatory-related requests, recommendations or decisions related to TCM/A) up until 2012. Detailed descriptions of the methods used to collect these data are available elsewhere (Boon *et al.*, 2004; Welsh *et al.*, 2004; Kelner *et al.*, 2004a, 2004b). A key archive document was the HPRAC report on TCM/acupuncture (Health Professions Regulatory Advisory Council, 2001), published in 2001. All interviews and the focus group were audio-taped and transcribed verbatim.

All data were subjected to thematic analysis (Braun and Clarke, 2006). Constructs and concepts were identified independently by at least two members of the research team. Consensus on key themes was reached during regular coding meetings. The simultaneous data collection and analysis made it possible to explore and expand on themes from earlier interviews or data collection in later interviews with key informants. Although Abbot's *System of Professions* (1988) was known to us prior to data collection, it was only after the key themes emerged from data in the early analysis that its relevance for explaining our findings became clear.

2 Findings

Our analysis for this chapter focuses on three issues: the challenges of shared jurisdictional space for acupuncturists; external or interprofessional issues; and internal or intra-professional issues. First, we consider the challenges of shared jurisdictional space for acupuncturists. Government officials interviewed made the case for opening up space for TCM/A practitioners in the Ontario health care system. The following informant captures the sentiment acknowledged by others that the government needed to catch up with public demand for TCM/A.

> The system as a whole needs to reflect the reality of people's lives. We have to fit people's lives, as opposed to them fitting into the system ... I think that there is broad public support for it, political points to be made for governments.
>
> *(Government Key Informant 2)*

Despite reservations, especially regarding cost, this was perhaps the main driving force behind government involvement in this area and the provincial government's willingness to open up some areas for shared jurisdiction.

Even though the regulation of TCM/A practitioners was viewed as necessary, most government officials interviewed also recognized the challenges this group would face in a system of shared jurisdictions and competing interests from the other health care practitioners:

> It is harder for them [TCM/A practitioners] to squeeze in because it is musical chairs and 99 per cent of the chairs are taken.
>
> *(Government Key Informant 11)*

> I see the barriers from the medical associations across the country. They are totally opposed to anybody infringing on their territory. The battles that are going on are legion.
>
> *(Government Key Informant 1)*

Practitioners in our focus group also raised concerns about possible shared tenancy of jurisdictional areas. When discussing the HPRAC report (Health Professions Regulatory Advisory Council, 2001) recommending TCM/A practitioners' shared jurisdiction over the controlled act of "performing a procedure on tissue below the dermis" with medical doctors and other health care professionals, one participant explained:

> I am a bit confused about the whole situation. It sounds like there is a proposal that acupuncture is a treatment modality and that TCM is TCM. I don't know why we have to argue that acupuncture is a Chinese thing.... To me, acupuncture is a form of physical therapy just like giving an injection. In traditional Chinese medicine, when you practice acupuncture, you also use injections of whatever substance, and there are schools in North America using similar techniques but they developed differently from different roots than acupuncture, so, I must say, that acupuncture treatment ... belongs to Chinese medicine.
>
> *(TCM/A Focus Group Practitioner 1)*

The discussion above highlights both the external and the internal tensions the TCM/A profession faced as it moved towards self-regulatory status. These tensions are now briefly discussed.

From interviews with leaders and the focus group discussion with practitioners, interprofessional conflict emerged as a key issue. TCM/A practitioners were acutely aware of how shared tenancy of acupuncture means they will need to carve out their own "turf" in a health care system already overflowing with professions: "Competitors? I personally see the regular professions practicing acupuncture as competitors, for example, massage therapists" (TCM/A Focus Group Practitioner 2). For their part, other health care practitioners often expressed concern about the ability of TCM/A practitioners to credibly demonstrate evidence of the safety and efficacy of their practices (see also Kelner *et al.*, 2004b):

> If they progress to the point that they meet the standards that we have for our society – and show that they have something beneficial to add and that they are not harmful, then we would agree that they should be self-regulating professions.
>
> *(Allopathic Health Practitioner Leader 1)*

However, concerns about the safety and efficacy of the newcomers' practices often blended into concerns about overlapping scopes of practice, with conventional practitioners fighting to maintain control of their current jurisdiction:

> If the way that they gained that acceptance was based on science [we would accept it]. We would have qualms about the scope of practice of a group. We would certainly look at whether or not we felt that the scope requested by a group was really appropriate from our perspective.
>
> *(Allopathic Health Practitioner Leader 8)*

Overall, our findings show great reluctance on the part of established practitioners to support the government's plans to share authority to practice acupuncture with TCM/A practitioners. Yet, as discussed next, other health care professionals were not the only ones challenging this authority. Within the ranks of TCM/A practitioners, intra-professional conflict pointed to deep divides as to what type of TCM/A should be regulated.

Finally, we explore the intra-professional issues. A key concern among TCM/A practitioners was which TCM/A group or organization would set the standards for education and practice.

This is where the process of professionalization enters into our analysis. While Adams (2004) demonstrates the link between inter-professional battles and this process, the TCM/A practitioners' professionalization process was also affected by internal battles. Social closure strategies utilized as part of professional projects, such as setting educational or practice standards, can only be effective if the group can agree on the content and form of those standards. This appeared to be particularly problematic for the TCM/A practitioners who had a wide variety of training institutions and associations struggling for control of the profession in Ontario:

> The acupuncturists and different associations share different views on how they should be regulated. That is an internal friction which creates a hurtle.
>
> *(TCM/A Leader 63)*

> Right now, too many people are called acupuncturists. Who is qualified to do it? That should be our position point.
>
> *(TCM/A Focus Group Practitioner 3)*

The challenge posed by these divisions was also noted by government officials, aware of the impending difficulties of implementing regulation of TCM/A practitioners: "A problem is the controversy within the groups themselves.... They are not the easiest groups to deal with and that in itself is a challenge ... [T]hey are not willing to work together and they argue and argue" (Government Key Informant 9). Some of the fragmentation evident within the TCM/A group was a result of diverse practice styles and philosophies. Establishing standards was exceedingly difficult because practitioners adhered to different forms of TCM and/or acupuncture. As the TCM/A practitioners moved closer to gaining regulation, how internal groups mobilized was thought to determine who may "win" the internal jurisdictional battles – battles that had to be settled before statutory self-regulation could occur.

For their part, TCM/A practitioners often underplayed the need to unify the group. Instead, they tended to imbue regulation with the ability to overcome external and internal divisions.

> We want the profession to be recognized and standardized and put in legal status.... We need the medical doctors to recognize us.
>
> *(TCM/A Practitioner 63)*

> It [regulation] would help us to assimilate into the health care system. It would set standards of practice.... Right now anyone can do acupuncture and that is completely wrong. You need proper training.
>
> *(TCM/A Practitioner 67)*

> With this regulation we will have standards recognized by everyone and this has to be official regulation.... When you are a recognized profession, you are accepted.... If it is not regulated and there are not standards, who is going to think you are a profession? Recognition is the acceptance of the public. The public needs to be protected from unqualified practitioners.
>
> *(TCM/A Practitioner 64)*

Despite all the acknowledged obstacles, at the time of data collection, most TCM/A practitioners were excitedly (if perhaps unrealistically) looking forward to being regulated as a profession that was part of the Ontario health care system.

IV Discussion and conclusions

Since these data were collected, the state has passed legislation to formally regulate TCM/A practitioners, naturopathic practitioners and homeopaths under the RHPA. All three groups then entered the process of operationalizing this decision (the subject of an ongoing study). On April 1, 2013, TCM/A practitioners became the first of these three CAM groups to be formally regulated under the RHPA in Ontario – all practitioners must now be licensed with the College of Traditional Chinese Medicine Practitioners and Acupuncturists of Ontario (CTCMPAO) in order to practice (Traditional Chinese Medicine Act, 2006).

Our findings highlight the importance of exploring the role of the state in creating "room" for new professions like TCM/A within the system of professions. As several of our participants stressed, regulation of these groups is ultimately a political decision made for political reasons. Overall, the leaders of TCM/A expected that regulation would provide the necessary power to effect social closure around their jurisdictional expertise. It is interesting that the TCM/A practitioners who participated in our study looked to the state to force the currently regulated conventional health care practitioners to share their "turf", yet simultaneously expected that the state-sanctioned regulation would permit them to gain social closure around their jurisdiction. This appears to indicate a fundamental misunderstanding of the RHPA and the changes that had to occur now that they are included under this umbrella Act.

Even though the state created space for TCM/A practitioners within the Ontario health care system, there were inter- and intra-professional jurisdictional issues and professionalization process issues that continued to play out together. We agree with Adams (2004) about the need to examine these issues together. As she states, "It is not solely the possession of jurisdiction that groups fight for in the system of professions, but the *status, privilege and security that accompanies possession of specific jurisdictions*" (p. 2251). TCM/A practitioners believed that by gaining jurisdictional claims they would also gain a modicum of social closure and the privileges that come with that. However, their battles were far from over and the outcomes of those appeared far from clear when these data were collected.

Under the new legislation, the CAM groups are responsible for setting educational and practice standards, and given the divisions within the groups (especially TCM/acupuncture) this proved difficult (a story we are continuing to investigate in ongoing work). The Transitional Council of the College of Traditional Chinese Medicine Practitioners and Acupuncturists of Ontario (TC-CTCMPAO) appointed by the Provincial government developed regulations and standards for the profession (see www.ctcmpao.on.ca) which are currently being implemented as practitioners have required licenses to practice since April 1, 2013. Further study is needed to assess who is able to meet these standards (i.e. to become regulated) and how this changes the work of those that are licensed. Clearly, achieving internal cohesion is one of the key challenges facing CAM groups trying to professionalize. Another important challenge is whether CAM practitioners can maintain their distinct philosophies of care and unique practices within the regulatory framework that will be imposed upon them. Additional research in this area will be critical to enhance our understanding of the professionalization process.

The Ontario, Canada context for CAM professions shows both the usefulness and the limits of the social closure perspective which describes how occupational groups strive to monopolize key tasks or jurisdictions. First, the Ontario CAM regulation story is one of professional projects and internal strife, but it is also one of government intervention. The TCM/A community was not a cohesive lobbying group pushing forward a singular agenda of regulation and standards when the Ontario government passed legislation to regulate TCM/A practice. Second, due to the way regulation is structured in Ontario, monopolies over specific jurisdictions are no longer common. For example, other medical professions will still have the right to include some types of CAM work (e.g., acupuncture) in their practices. This is where an analysis that includes the complex system of professions is needed – in particular where more attention to the work of Andrew Abbott may shed light on the continuing jurisdictional battles between CAM groups themselves and between CAM and conventional medicine. In turn this highlights why it is imperative to move beyond the assumption that health care practitioners are regulated simply to protect the public from risk and to critically exam what is gained or lost (and by whom) when CAM practitioners such as TCM/A practitioners are regulated within the framework of a health care system.

Note

1 In 2006, when the legislation was passed, TCM/A practitioners were authorized to perform the following as part of the practice of traditional Chinese medicine: "performing a procedure on tissue below the dermis and below the surface of a mucous membrane for the purpose of performing acupuncture" (Traditional Chinese Medicine Act, 2006). Other health care groups, such as nurses, massage therapists and physiotherapists, can continue performing acupuncture but cannot refer to themselves as "acupuncturists". The term "acupuncturists" is now reserved for those registered with the TCM/A College created by the 2006 TCM Act.

References

Abbott, A. (1988) *The System of Professions. An Essay on the Division of Expert Labour.* Chicago: University of Chicago Press.

Adams, J. (2006) "An exploratory study of complementary and alternative medicine in hospital midwifery: Models of care and professional struggle", *Complementary Therapies in Clinical Practice*, 12: 40–47.

Adams, T. (2004) "Inter-professional conflict and professionalisation: Dentistry and dental hygiene in Ontario", *Social Science and Medicine*, 58: 2243–2252.

Alder, R. (2001) *Adjusting the Balance: A Review of the Regulated Health Professions Act.* Toronto, Ontario: Health Professions Regulatory Advisory Council.

Boon, H., Welsh, S., Kelner, M. J. and Wellman, B. (2004) "Complementary/alternative practitioners and the professionalisation process: A Canadian comparative case study". In P. Tovey, G. Easthope and J. Adams (Eds), *The Mainstreaming of Complementary and Alternative Medicine in Social Context: An International Perspective.* London: Routledge.

Braun, V. and Clarke, V. (2006) "Using thematic analysis in psychology", *Qualitative Research in Psychology*, 3: 77–101.

Broom, B. and Tovey, P. (2007) "Therapeutic pluralism? Evidence, power and legitimacy in UK cancer services", *Sociology of Health and Illness*, 29(4): 551–569.

Cant, S. and Sharma, U. (1996) "Demarcation and transformation within homeopathic knowledge: A strategy of professionalization", *Social Science and Medicine*, 42(4): 579–588.

Cant, S., Watt, P. and Rushton, A. (2011) "Negotiating competency, professionalism and risk: The integration of complementary and alternative medicine by nurses and midwives in NHS hospitals", *Social Science and Medicine*, 72(4): 529–536.

Collins, R. (1990) "Market closure and the conflict theory of professions". In M. Burrage and R. Torstendahl (Eds), *Professions in Theory and History: Rethinking the Study of the Professions.* London: Sage.

Gilmour, J., Kelner, M. J. and Wellman, B. (2002) "Opening the door to complementary and alternative medicine: Self-regulation in Ontario", *Law and Policy*, 24(2): 150–174.

Health Professions Legislation Review (HPLR) (1989) *Striking a New Balance: A Blueprint for the Regulation of Ontario's Health Professions.* Toronto, Ontario.

Health Professions Regulatory Advisory Council (2001) "Traditional Chinese medicine and acupuncture. Advice to the Minister of Health and Long Term Care", Toronto (available at: www.health.gov.on.ca/en/common/ministry/publications/reports/tc_med/tc_med_eng.pdf).

Hollengerg, D. (2006) "Uncharted ground: Patterns of professional interaction among complementary/alternative and biomedical practitioners in integrative health care settings", *Social Sciences and Medicine*, 62(3): 731–744.

Kelner, M., Boon, H., Wellman, B. and Welsh, S. (2002) "Complementary and alternative groups contemplate the need for effectiveness, safety and cost-effectiveness", *Complementary Therapies in Medicine*, 10: 235–239.

Kelner, M., Wellman, B., Boon, H. and Welsh, S. (2004a) "The role of the state in the social inclusion of complementary and alternative medical occupations", *Complementary Therapies in Medicine*, 12: 79–89.

Kelner, M. J., Wellman, B., Boon, H. and Welsh, S. (2004b) "Stakeholders' responses to the professionalisation of complementary and alternative medicine", *Social Science and Medicine*, 59: 915–930.

O'Reilly, P. (2000) *Health Care Practitioners. An Ontario Case Study in Policy Making*. Toronto: University of Toronto Press.

Saks, M. (1995) *Professions and the Public Interest. Medical Power, Altruism and Alternative Medicine*. London: Routledge.

Saks, M. (2001) "Alternative medicine and the health care division of labour: Present trends and future prospects", *Current Sociology*, 49(3): 119–134.

Shuval, J. (2006) "Nurses in alternative health care: Integrating medical paradigms", *Social Science and Medicine*, 63: 1784–1795.

Traditional Chinese Medicine Act, 2006, SO 2006, c 27.

Welsh, S., Kelner, M., Boon, H. and Wellman, B. (2004) "Moving forward? Complementary and alternative practitioners seeking self-regulation", *Sociology of Health & Illness*, 26(2): 2216–2241.

16

ASPIRATIONS, INTEGRATION AND THE POLITICS OF REGULATION IN THE UK, PAST AND FUTURE

Julie Stone

I Introduction

The regulatory status of CAM has been the subject of extensive debate (Saks 2002; Stone and Matthews 1996). Seen by many as an indicator of CAM's lack of recognition by the state, CAM's inability over the last twenty years to secure statutory regulation has been accompanied by failures to make inroads into state-funded health provision, despite usage and popularity of CAM remaining high, and successive governments' stated commitment to promoting patient choice.[1] This chapter will explore why the debate remains contested, how the broader regulatory environment has changed and how, despite signs of greater professionalism within parts of the CAM sector, the UK's National Health Service is unlikely to embrace CAM in the current climate. A key difficulty has been the failure of the disparate bodies and organisations within CAM to come together with a common purpose or sense of collegiality either across the sector, or even, necessarily, within single therapies. Comparing the far-reaching aspirations of CAM's more professionally organised and vocal groups with the modest inroads achieved, this chapter will argue that, in the last twenty years, CAM as a collective phenomenon has missed strategic opportunities, both politically and therapeutically, leaving little scope for creating a role for itself in a rapidly changing regulatory environment. As statutory regulation is now realistically beyond CAM's reach, the chapter will explore alternative forms of regulation open to CAM and question whether external validation is central to, or necessary for, CAM's longer term viability.

II Discerning CAM's aspirations in the UK

Trying to ascertain CAM's regulatory and broader ambitions, past or present, is not a straightforward matter. Attempting even to describe CAM as a single entity is problematic, save to the extent that professions which fall outside mainstream medicine have been lumped together, invariably in opposition to allopathic medicine (hence a politicised and contested nomenclature including 'alternative', 'non-traditional' and 'unconventional' [Stone and Matthews 1996]). In this regard, CAM is defined more easily by what it is not than what it might be. Historically, most therapies have been characterised by division and in-fighting, with the same therapy often having numerous competing registering bodies, sometimes based on a single tradition or teaching school. This fragmentation, together with the absence of a strong or credible voice within smaller therapies, has added to the difficulty of ascertaining political aspirations. Since external regulation depends, critically, on there being a discrete sphere of activity to be controlled, it is not surprising that each significant regulatory initiative to emerge over the last twenty years has required therapies to explore their commonalities and find sufficient common ground to be able to come together under a single professional registering organisation (see, for example, House of Lords 2000).[2] Yet, for many therapies, this still has not happened. Without a single (or, alternatively, credible) lead body, negotiating meaningfully in any political or healthcare arena is virtually impossible. The effect of multiple voices claiming to be authentic and representative is that none is seen as authoritative. This fragmentation has intensified the impression that CAM is professionally disunited, with the knock-on effect that, even in the more organised CAM therapies, there is an assumption that there are 'dissident' practitioners and splinter groups, and this has substantially undermined CAM's credibility. This has implications not only in terms of political advancement, but also affects who commissioning groups are prepared to enter into contracts with, and how patients are able to assess which practitioners are appropriately qualified.

Where therapies are well organised, and do have a professional body (albeit often serving as both a registering body and a trades union/representative body, despite the inherent tension in those two functions), it is easier to discern aspirations and regulatory ambitions. The explicit desire for statutory regulation on the part of acupuncture and herbal medicine (and, latterly traditional Chinese medicine [TCM]) has been repeatedly articulated (Department of Health 2009), if thwarted, since the publication of the influential House of Lords' Select Committee Science and Technology Report (House of Lords 2000). This recommended (at para. 5.53) that acupuncture and herbal medicine be statutorily regulated as a matter of public protection.[3] Successive governments have failed to implement this recommendation. The aspirations of other therapies are harder to ascertain, although a number of smaller therapies have now opted for voluntary regulation under the umbrella of the Complementary and Natural Healthcare Council (CNHC), the standing of which has been boosted by recent accredited status by the Professional Standards Authority.[4]

Much CAM activity takes place in the private sector and, because training routes into practice are so diverse, it would be hard to map even the numbers of practitioners working across CAM with any certainty. Formal regulation depends on both a critical mass of potential registrants and a delineated occupational sector, and it is hard to assess whether the numbers of practitioners practising more esoteric therapies fulfil these requirements.

Whilst practitioners who choose to become politically affiliated with a professional organisation are more visible and quantifiable, an unknown number of therapists may reject formal mechanisms altogether. If CAM therapists of the 1970s and 1980s were driven by a strong anti-establishment leaning, today's newly qualified practitioners are as likely to be politically disinterested, or are merely trying to generate a living in an economic downturn.

Anti-regulation therapists have long articulated fears that their therapeutic skill set could be constrained, altered or 'cherry picked' by other professions if they were to become more professionally visible (Saks 2002). It is fair to argue that statutory regulation does, in some ways, codify the nature of a therapeutic discipline and may attempt to identify a scope of practice, which itself may be anathema to practitioners who pride themselves as working in an intuitive, personalised way.

Whilst integrated care is a model gaining a strong foothold, particularly in the United States, it is notable that in areas such as integrative cancer care, these initiatives are very much being led by the medical profession, with potentially beneficial (and preferably evidence-based) CAM therapies being offered alongside mainstream care. Whether this constitutes colonisation or presents new opportunities to CAM depends, as does breaking into state-funded care generally, on therapies adducing a more robust research base, and therapists' preparedness to work within explicit clinical governance frameworks. Whilst many therapists claim to offer patient-centred care, the adoption, for example, of Patient Recorded Outcomes Measures (PROMs) is extremely patchy.[5] Within the NHS, there is now an express statutory duty to improve the quality of services, with explicit reference to the patient experience.[6]

In terms, too, of 'cherry picking', it is worth noting that clinical commissioners may have no problem with CAM therapeutic techniques being made available to patients per se. They may actively support their provision, for example, as part of hospice care. However, they are subject to intense financial constraints, so inevitably will be looking for cost-effective providers. Where, for example, physiotherapists may be able to be upskilled to offer manipulative techniques and/ or acupuncture, this may present a more attractive commissioning solution than contracting with unregulated, potentially uninsured CAM practitioners. There are obvious benefits for commissioners contracting with health workers who are already employed, already regulated, and who work within managed environments.

In short, if CAM's aspirations are directed towards working more closely as part of state-funded healthcare, there is an overwhelming need for the sector as a whole (and individual practitioners) to adopt more professionalised, up-to-date working methods characteristic of modern healthcare delivery, and to be prepared to be subject to far greater levels of accountability than currently. So too, the rhetoric of patient-centredness needs to be substantiated in CAM, not least of all as this is widely touted as CAM's 'unique selling point'. It is simply not possible to say whether CAM practitioners are up to that challenge, or even aspire to working in these sorts of ways.

III CAM's relationship with the state – an overview

The history and politics of CAM has been written about extensively, and several chapters in this volume trace the underpinnings of different CAM professions. For current purposes, it is helpful to discern some past and present aspects of CAM's vexed and longstanding relationship with the state. This shows that the battleground for what counts as 'proper' healthcare, and entitlement of who should provide it, has a long history. What this history shows is that CAM has, for centuries, had to look beyond external authorisation for either approval or a place in the market (Stone and Matthews 1996). Rather, CAM has responded to consumer-led demands for an alternative approach, with high estimated usage of various CAM therapies (Thomas *et al.* 2001). Reasons for seeking an alternative approach seem to be linked to a desire for a more holistic interpretation of health and illness, and a desire for non-institutionalised, personalised care. Whilst this chimes well with the rhetoric of the 'new NHS', with its greater emphasis on prevention and wellbeing, and individualised care,[7] there is little sign of CAM putting itself forward or being seen as having a significant part to play in delivery.[8] Individualised care, if still somewhat aspirational, is in the process of being mainstreamed and it is the NHS, rather than CAM, that seems to be making greater inroads into increased patient choice and personalisation of care, not least of all through its 'Any Qualified Provider' (AQP) scheme, which opens provision up to a wider range of service providers.[9]

1 Historical benign tolerance – no longer a given

Despite longstanding traditions of herbal and folk practices in the UK, there has been significant dominance of 'regulars' over 'irregulars', particularly since regulation of doctors by the state with the creation of the first Medical Act in 1858, reserving various privileges to registered medical practitioners. Despite this, a historical exemption existed for herbal practitioners to be able to make up remedies for individual clients following a one-to-one consultation. This remained part of UK law for centuries.[10] This, together with the funding of NHS homeopathic hospitals, and a permissive common law freedom to practise, characterised a political position from around the middle of the last century which has been described as 'benevolent neutrality' by the state towards CAM (Stone and Matthews 1996). During this time, CAM has flourished in the private sector, with minimal external interference. Access, however, is largely restricted to those who can afford to pay, which raises profound issues of equity.

More recently, however, this previously benign climate has been notably changing, and in certain quarters, given way to active hostility towards CAM. In an NHS committed to evidence-based rhetoric, much of the adverse comment is coming from pro-science groups, with particular hostility being demonstrated towards homeopathy. Parliamentary debates have called for the withdrawal of funding for NHS homeopathy, as being incompatible with an evidence-based NHS.[11] Whilst a lack of a credible scientific rationale is purported to underlie these calls, antipathy towards homeopathy far outstrips hostility, for example, towards traditional Chinese medicine (notably, the latter operates almost exclusively in the private sector, with a significant high street presence). Certainly, the level of recent antagonism should be a reminder to CAM that being part of mainstream health debates will require CAM, at the very least, to speak the language of the prevailing biomedical culture and organisational structures, if not to present itself as complementary to, and capable of being accommodated within, these structures. CAM's failure to appreciate this, whilst waiting for the world to change, has been somewhat naïve and accounts for a position which, in some respects, is even more marginalised than twenty years ago (Stone 2010).

2 CAM's regulatory relationship with the state

In the UK, CAM is largely absent from formal regulatory structures compared to other health professions. These are regulated either under single regulatory bodies, such as the General Medical Council (which regulates doctors), under a body which regulates the professional team, such as the General Dental Council (which regulates dentists and dental care practitioners), or under an umbrella regulator, such as the Health and Social Care Professionals Council (which regulates sixteen separate professions[12]). Whereas most CAM professions sit outside this framework, the two exceptions are osteopathy and chiropractic. For osteopaths, decades of lobbying eventually resulted in statutory regulation of osteopathy by the Osteopaths Act 1993, followed a year later by the Chiropractors Act 1994. Many hoped this would put these two professions on an equal footing with medicine and other regulated health professions.

Notably, in order to achieve statutory regulation, osteopathy and chiropractic had to allay establishment concerns that they had a scientific basis (King's Fund Institute 1991; Bingham 1992). At the time, osteopathy and chiropractic could adduce a plausible enough mechanism as to how the therapy might work in 'scientific terms' to pass muster. Adducing a 'scientific' explanation is simply not an option for those therapies grounded in different cosmologies and alternative belief systems. Whereas cultural plurality (or, variously, respect for equality and diversity, 'political correctness' and exoticism) may account for a more tolerant approach in the UK towards Eastern traditions such as traditional Chinese acupuncture, there is very little tolerance for theories such as the memory of water, which underpins homeopathy.

In 2000, the House of Lords Select Committee considered in depth the arguments for and against regulation and integration of CAM. Importantly, the report provided an early attempt to introduce 'risk-based regulation', a concept which is now a central tenet of proportionate, 'right-touch regulation' (Council for Healthcare Regulatory Excellence 2010). The House of Lords accepted evidence that the majority of CAMs did not require statutory regulation, on the basis that increased professionalisation, more formalised education and training and effective systems of voluntary self-regulation could provide many of the same safeguards for patients without imposing the burdens of a statutory scheme (Budd and Mills 2000). That report did, however, highlight the urgent need to regulate acupuncture and herbal medicine on the basis of patient safety. The government of the day accepted this recommendation. Fifteen years later, statutory regulation has not been forthcoming, despite subsequent commissioned working parties all arguing in its favour (Department of Health 2009). The failure to implement recommendations to regulate these professions, either singly or under an existing umbrella regulator, signals that the prospect of any CAM therapy achieving statutory regulation is highly unlikely.

The government has not been unaware of the need to find some workable regulatory solution for CAM, given its widespread usage in the UK. Its main approach has been supporting the creation of the Complementary and Natural Health Council[13] (CNHC), a body set up following a report commissioned by the Foundation for Integrated Health recommending a single federal voluntary regulator in CAM (the 'Stone Report'). CNHC currently holds registers for fifteen of the most popular CAM therapies in the UK (currently, Alexander technique teaching, aromatherapy, Bowen therapy, craniosacral therapy, healing, hypnotherapy, massage therapy, microsystems acupuncture, naturopathy, nutritional therapy, reflexology, reiki, shiatsu, sports therapy and yoga therapy). This created, for the first time in CAM, a government-sponsored voluntary register for CAM therapies which had achieved a certain level of professional organisation and had agreed educational standards. Further strengthening of this approach has been for CNHC being accredited, in 2013, by the regulatory oversight body, the Professional Standards Authority (previously the Council for Healthcare Regulatory Excellence), which now has powers to set standards for voluntary systems of accreditation.[14]

The CNHC provides a federal style of regulation similar to the Health and Care Professions Council, with a common code of conduct, complaints system and insurance requirement. Educational standards have been codified for those therapies seeking registration, and each aspirant therapy to the CNHC has had to come together to form a single lead body per profession. Whilst its uptake remains relatively modest (and other pan-profession bodies continue to register CAM practitioners), CNHC provides a level of 'brand recognition' which may be increasingly attractive to NHS commissioners and third-party payers, wishing to contract with 'recognised' practitioners.

Within conventional medicine, public protection and public reassurance is secured primarily through the regulation of professionals, but also through the regulation of any medicinal products (currently under the auspices of the Medicines and Healthcare Products Regulatory Agency [MHRA]). In this regard, CAM is less marginalised in so far as the MHRA now has mechanisms for regulating herbal and homeopathic products in the UK.[15] Controversially, the MHRA schemes accommodate traditional use of herbal medicines and homeopathic remedies without proof of effectiveness, but on the basis that they are safe and of consistent quality. This too, has come under criticism in recent years by critics who say that a government body should not be appearing to endorse products of unknown therapeutic value. Interestingly, the approach to continue regulating CAM products in this way is because people use these products regardless and it is better that they are subject to some formal scrutiny. This argument has not been felt to merit the regulation of CAM practitioners in the UK on the same basis, despite the high levels of access by consumers.

In addition to the regulation of health professionals and healthcare products, the last fifteen to twenty years has also seen the emergence of systems-based regulation, which is regulation of the environment in which healthcare is provided. This function is currently carried out in England by the Care Quality Commission (CQC), which inspects providers against a set of national standards.[16] Hospitals, GP surgeries and dental practices are all required to be registered annually with the CQC, but as CAM professionals fall outside the range of regulated health professionals for these purposes, CAM premises are not subject to CQC registration.[17] Many therapists in the UK work in unsupervised, private practice, often out of their own home, although it is also common to find groups of therapists hiring rooms in clinics offering a variety of therapies. Whilst offering a level of collegiality, and opportunities for inter-professional learning, peer review and audit, such arrangements tend to fall short of the governance hallmarks required of health professionals working in multi-disciplinary teams as understood within mainstream healthcare environments and which would be required as part of systems-based regulation and professional regulation. Working in this way also removes the regulatory oversight which could otherwise be provided by employers (as is the case for other unregulated occupational groups such as healthcare assistants).

The fact then that CAM therapists operate beyond the remit or interest of the CQC, as well as statutory regulation, indicates further the extent to which CAM is off the regulatory radar, at a time when the NHS is struggling to cope with a huge reorganisation and cost-saving agenda, and attempting to meet concerns highlighted in the recent Mid-Staffordshire Report (Francis 2013) that financial balance is not achieved at the cost of patient safety and dignity.

3 CAM provision and commissioning

There is no centralised provision of CAM within the NHS, except for the aforementioned limited provision of homeopathy (the longer term future of which seems extremely precarious). Beyond this, pockets of commissioning activity have occurred on an ad hoc basis. These have included, for example, NHS-funded acupuncture as part of pain-relieving services, packages of osteopathy or chiropractic as part of new musculo-skeletal pathways (including under the 'Any Qualified Provider' route) and therapies such as hypnotherapy, aromatherapy and reflexology as part of drug and alcohol addiction services. Despite patient satisfaction, many CAM services have been withdrawn once initial funding has ended, or because services are perceived as lacking an evidence base.[18] Since the move, in April 2013, away from commissioning by primary care trusts to clinical commissioning groups, there is little evidence of wider commissioning in this area. Any CAM services which are still being funded on the NHS are highly vulnerable to being cut at a time of significant cost-saving requirements. The absence of funding does not necessarily suggest hostility by doctors at a grass-roots level towards CAM. Many GPs recommend CAM therapies to their patients, but the absence of funding puts access beyond the reach of many patients.

For the reasons stated above, trying to discern whether more CAM practitioners wish to work within the NHS is not at all straightforward. As discussed, part of the increased competition within the NHS has been to open up provision to 'any qualified provider' (AQP).[19] Hypothetically, this has been a route for CAM practitioners to position themselves strategically to commissioners as being able to provide new pathways of care. To date, there is little evidence of the AQP route being a way in to the NHS for CAM providers, most of whom would baulk at the volume of paperwork, governance and costing requirements that such an approach would require.

In the same way as subsequent parts of this chapter will look at the changing requirements of statutory regulation, so too, the demands of working in a research-driven, clinical governance-based NHS sits at odds with how many CAM practitioners currently practise. Perhaps this is why, for the time being, much commissioned CAM activity operates in marginalised areas within the health system, such as hospice provision, drug and alcohol services and pain management, or as an adjunct to well-funded, highly respected clinical areas, where the benefits of CAM (e.g. in cancer care) are seen as add-ons to routine clinical management.

IV CAM regulation, patient protection and public reassurance

The question of how CAM ought to be regulated and whether, indeed, it is even amenable to regulation has been one of the most vexed questions surrounding CAM politics in the UK and elsewhere. Broadly, arguments against regulation are that it appears to confer legitimacy, which critics argue is unmerited. Others argue that every therapeutic relationship has the capacity to both benefit and cause harm. This latter view could be said to underpin the legislation in the Canadian state of Ontario. Its healthcare regulatory scheme adopts the view that, despite uncertainty as to explanatory models or efficacy, if members of the public are accessing these services, safeguards need to be put in place. Thus, Ontario's Regulated Health Professions Act 1991 regulates, for example, traditional Chinese medicine and kinesiology alongside medicine and other professions.[20] Where the Ontario scheme differs from a UK regulatory system based on protection of title is that Ontario regulates the competencies carried out by professionals. This allows for a diversity of providers, provided whoever is performing the regulated act has the requisite level of training and skill to do so. Such a scheme would prevent the situation, perceived by CAM therapists to be problematic in the UK, of regulated professionals, including doctors and physiotherapists, providing CAM therapies on the basis of a comparatively slim training (and able to do so because they are regulated therapists). However, a review of the UK's healthcare professions regulation, undertaken by the Law Commission,[21] does not recommend the adoption of such a model for the UK. (See McHale, in this volume.)

1 *Aspirations versus reality*

As noted, for many therapists in the UK, statutory regulation has been a major aspiration, precisely because it was achieved by osteopathy in 1993 and chiropractic in 1994. This undoubtedly created expectations that this route was possible for other therapies, and has given rise to a lot of frustration and disappointment among CAM practitioners, as the political landscape has changed whilst CAM has not necessarily moved in pace with the times.

So how far is statutory, or indeed any form of regulation necessary either to protect patients or to reassure the public, given many people seem to choose their therapist by word of mouth, preferring to rely on experiential recommendations from within their own communities and social networks? In terms of patient protection, CAM has tended to overplay the relative safety of the therapies themselves (although clearly there are some risks, particularly if the therapy is performed by poorly trained practitioners). Other risks, it has been argued, are inherent in all therapeutic relationships, and boundary violations and other inappropriate behaviours may be more likely in situations where practitioners operate in unsupervised, sole practice (Stone 2010). Quantifying the level of either of these risks in CAM is difficult, as the absence of complaints may be more a reflection of the inadequacy of current regulatory mechanisms than it is indicative of absence of harm. Nonetheless, the level of complaints appears to be low, whereas confidence in CAM practitioners is ostensibly high. This suggests significant levels of public reassurance *even in the absence of formal regulatory structures.*

This makes the pursuit, by some CAM groups, of statutory regulation in the UK an even more interesting phenomenon. CAM practitioners in the UK enjoy considerable latitude to practise their therapy (or indeed any profession which is not statutorily regulated) without fear of legal interference. Their scope of practice is not defined, meaning, for most therapists, that they decide what it is and is not legitimate to do under the guise of their practice, and it is common to find therapists who mix several modalities within a given treatment session. These 'add-ons' might be offered on the basis of a comprehensive or minimal training. The responsibility to work within limits of competence resides predominantly within the conscience of the individual practitioner, and is not externally policed. The regulatory regime in the UK is more permissive than in other countries, although statutory provisions vary from jurisdiction to jurisdiction (Dixon 2008).[22]

Despite fundamental philosophical concerns as to whether CAM is capable of being measured and regulated (Stone 2002), there persists a belief amongst holistic practitioners that in achieving statutory regulation, these therapies would achieve enhanced status and, consequently, entry into the health marketplace, rather than residing at the margins of healthcare (Stone 1996). This mindset is unhelpful as it is based on two false premises – the first, that the function of regulation is about enhancing the status of the profession rather than protecting patients and providing public reassurance, and the second, that statutory regulation is synonymous with NHS integration, despite osteopathy or chiropractic in the UK failing to make significant inroads into state-funded provision over the last twenty years.

2 Hallmarks of modern statutory regulatory schemes

For the sake of clarification, it is helpful to review the key functions of modern statutory regulation in health and to consider whether CAM as a sector, currently meets these requirements:

- A publicly accessible, single *register of practitioners*. This makes it possible for patients and the public, commissioners and employers to know who is and who is not regulated. Statutory registers increasingly indicate any fitness-to-practise findings against registrants, enabling better transparency and consumer choice. Currently CAM is characterised by multiple registers, and the emergence of the CNHC has not seen other registers ceasing to operate. Multiple qualifying bodies, awards and initials make it hard for CAM consumers to assess the quality or safety of any service they are accessing. The absence of a single lead body dilutes the legitimacy of more 'professional' registers.
- Access to register determined by successful achievement of a *registering qualification* – determined by the regulatory body, ensuring a set of learning outcomes achieved, with competence to practise autonomously and independently at the point of initial registration. Regulators employ a variety of mechanisms to quality assure 'registering qualifications' or those higher education institutes which provide them. Despite significant professionalisation in some therapies, awards in CAM range from a diploma for attending a weekend course, through to National Occupational Standards or degrees. Many awards are granted by private colleges, which sit outside the Higher Education remit and are not externally validated.
- Dissemination of *Codes of Ethics and Practice Standards, with or without Scope of Practice guidance.* These set out the standards of behaviour which are required of practitioners and which are

updated from time to time (see, for example, the 2012 Osteopathic Practice Standards). Many CAM registers purport to have a Code of Ethics, but these tend to be rather minimal, with little detailed guidance. Despite the existence of a range of National Occupational Standards (e.g. in aromatherapy, massage and hypnotherapy), it is rare for CAM bodies to identify a Scope of Practice, which makes it inherently difficult to regulate either what the therapy is, or what a consumer might reasonably assume the therapy involves.

- *Fitness to practise mechanisms.* These deal with allegations of impaired fitness to practise, whether by way of poor performance, misconduct or health issues. Committees comprised of professional and lay members may impose various sanctions on a practitioner, including, ultimately, the right to remove someone from a professional register. Currently, FtP mechanisms in CAM therapists are limited and lack the requirements of transparency, separation of investigation and adjudication functions, and commitment to natural justice/human rights which now characterise the mechanisms in place within statutory bodies. Specifically, outside of a statutory scheme, removal/erasure might result in being taken off a professional register, but would not stop an errant/incompetent practitioner immediately joining another register and continuing to practise. Arguably, FtP in CAM suffers from a fundamental problem, which is that, in the absence of clarity in CAM as to what the acceptable standard of care is, it may be a lot harder to know whether a practitioner has deviated from expected standards. Within mainstream medicine, clinical pathways, NICE guidelines and a research infrastructure provide structures for determining appropriate clinical courses of action.

- *Partnership working* is an intrinsic feature of 'stakeholder' or 'shared' regulation. Following the Shipman Inquiry (Shipman Inquiry 2004), which made recommendations in response to a mass-murdering GP who killed over 200 hundred of his patients, healthcare regulation in the UK has striven to move away from the self-regulation model. Modern regulators recognise the need to work closely with other organisations which exercise regulatory functions, and also with service users who help regulators to understand what the public expect from regulation. CAM regulators are often staffed and populated by politically active professionals from within that therapeutic discipline, and lack a substantial/any service user voice throughout their structures. Council/board appointments may still be based on election and representative function rather than possession of board-level competencies.

3 Voluntary regulatory systems and scope for enhancing professionalism

Current government thinking is that the form of regulation should be the least burdensome compatible with assuring public protection as the costs of regulation are ultimately passed on to the consumer. The 2011 White Paper *Enabling Excellence* states:

> the approach to professional regulation must be proportionate and effective, imposing the least cost and complexity consistent with securing safety and confidence for patients, service users, carers and the wider public. The current economic climate makes it all the more important to ensure that there are no unnecessary costs in the professional regulation system.
>
> *(Department of Health 2011)*

If it was not clear prior to the publication of this document, the regulatory direction of travel for CAM is now, assuredly, a voluntary route. *Enabling Excellence* further stated: 'Government will not support the health professions regulators in taking on any new responsibilities or roles which add to the costs to their existing registrants without providing robust evidence of significant additional protection or benefits to the public' (Department of Health 2011). As high-lighted eleven years previously by the House of Lords Report, most of the safeguards underpinning statutory regulation can be replicated within voluntary systems, albeit, now, with the option of underpinning voluntary schemes with a seal of approval from the Professional Standards Authority.[23] The main safeguard between statutory regulation and voluntary systems in CAM would be the ability of the former to enforce a protected title by statute (albeit at the cost of high registration fees). But the multiplicity of therapies and techniques which constitute CAM, and the similarities of different therapies, would make delineating titles highly problem-atic in this sector in any event.

Arguably, at this point in its development, the regulatory debate in CAM in the UK is a red herring. The unwillingness of the government to confer statutory regulation is no excuse not to continue to enhance the professionalisation of CAM, at an individual and a profession-wide level. Indeed, in many therapies, this is precisely what has occurred in the absence of state involvement or recognition. This is the approach taken by acupuncture in the UK, which, having been ear-marked then rejected for statutory regulation (and having sought Royal Charter status), has continued to professionalise and the register of its lead body, the British Acupuncture Council, has been approved by the Accredited Voluntary Register Scheme of the Professional Standards Authority (previously CHRE).[24]

V The evolving regulatory landscape

The pursuit of statutory regulation by some CAM professions has failed to take account of the tighter regulatory regime which characterises the post-Shipman environment. Other inquiries, including the most recent Francis Report, have found several gaps in public protection, which as a result have strengthened external systems of regulation in recent years.

Regulatory imperatives within central government have moved towards lighter touch, risk-based regulation, where therapies will be subject to the least burdensome form of regu-lation compatible with protecting patients and the public. Risk-based regulation broadly posits that different professions should be regulated according to the risk the profession poses to patients and the public. Thinking around risk-based regulation has been developing under the aegis of CHRE, now the Professional Standards Authority, the statutory body set up to oversee and improve excellence in healthcare in the UK. In its key 2010 document, 'Right Touch Regulation', in line with the recommendations set out by the Better Regulation Executive in 2000 (Better Regulation Executive 2000), healthcare regulation is expected to be proportionate, consistent, targeted, transparent and accountable (Council for Healthcare Regulatory Excellence 2010).

Originally, the focus of risk-based regulation attached to technical aspects of the profession, rather than risks posed to patients by unskilled or unscrupulous therapists, and within this frame-work, medicine, being highly invasive, is seen as highly risky, compared, for example, to arts therapy, and the safeguards and provisions to ensure initial and continued competence reflect this difference. More recently, however, thinking around risk-based/right-touch regulation is that account has to be taken of other systems of regulation in place which, together, create a web of protection and reassurance. This includes personal self-regulation on the part of the therapist, employer-based regulation, where this exists, and systems-wide regulation – for example, in the form of CQC registration. Practitioners who work in a managed clinical environment are less of a risk, potentially, than CAM practitioners operating in the unregulated private sector, even though the risks inherent in many CAM techniques may be low, relative, for example, to medicine.

Another key feature of regulatory reform has been improved governance of regulatory bodies themselves, in order to deliver more streamlined regulation (Department of Health 2007). Healthcare councils are expected to be smaller and more board like, with an even number of lay and practitioner members, and often a lay chair. Individuals are appointed against board-level competencies and are not representative of any professional group, school or sector. Regulation is viewed as a shared or stakeholder model, involving and accountable to all those with a key interest, as well as enhanced accountability to Parliament. Modern regulation has a very changed profile, and it is not obvious as to the extent to which CAM appreciates that some of its thinking around regulation is twenty years out of date. Regulation is first and foremost about patient protection and public confidence. Whilst enhanced professional status may be a fact of professional regulation, it is not the primary function of regulation and is important only to the extent that this raises visibility of the regulated nature of the profession and enhances professional standards (as opposed to professional standing). Should any regulator fail to deliver its statutory functions, there is power to remove their regulatory functions and hand the regulation of that profession over to another regulator.

Ensuring that regulated professionals remain fit for practise has been another significant development, with doctors being the first profession required to introduce 'revalidation', which is essentially a periodic process for ensuring that registered practitioners remain fit for purpose. Although revalidation has been formally rolled out in medicine, non-medical professions have also been required to explore mechanisms for ensuring ongoing competence. For most health professions, and especially those whose practitioners work in sole private practice, this has involved revisiting requirements for continuing professional development (CPD) and building on these, together with any existing systems for revalidation. Systems for demonstrating reflective practice and self-development have been formalised so that there will be a greater link, increasingly, between an individual's CPD activities and public expectations of what professionals need to be able to demonstrate (for example, ability to gain consent and effective communication skills). CAM's current commitment to lifelong learning falls considerably short of what would be required by statute. This is not to say that many individual CAM professionals are not committed to their professional development, but again, here, the sector as a whole lacks formalised and enforceable requirements.

VI Other relevant considerations: threats and opportunities

After a period of investment, the NHS is facing unprecedented cutbacks at the same time as a significant reorganisation. Commissioning has ostensibly been placed in the hands of clinicians, although strong levels of centralised and regional bureaucracy are retained to NHS England, formerly the National Commissioning Board. Significantly, the new Health and Social Care Act 2012 removes the Secretary of State's duty to provide a comprehensive health service. Forms of prioritisation, if not rationing, are emerging and this is not a good climate for any 'add-ons' to get commissioned. Whereas integrative approaches seem to be making far more of an impact in the US (potentially, as they tend to be under the auspices of medical facilities, and could be described as a classic example of cherry picking/colonisation), CAM is likely to remain very much at the margins of state-funded healthcare, although this is unlikely to impact on its popularity.

There are, however, opportunities which remain to be exploited by CAM, if it positions itself accordingly. There is now an unprecedented emphasis on public health and prevention and, as part of that, a national system of Health and Wellbeing Boards, designed to ensure that the focus of healthcare commissioning is more holistic (hence the siting of public health within local authorities). This could present a real opportunity for CAM, sitting well with its wider understandings of health and illness and self-care emphasis, but will require CAM to be fully versed in NHS commissioning and seeking out opportunities for providing services to new market opportunities by way of commissioners' freedom to contract with 'any qualified providers'. To date, however, there is little systematic evidence of CAM practitioners accessing such contracts. An alternative route for CAM practitioners to pursue is working with health insurers. Private sector/third-party payers may look favourably at CAM's potential role (e.g. in musculo-skeletal/long-term conditions) if these can be provided cheaply, safely and effectively.

Finally, personalised budgets are being rolled out in health and social care to give patients with long-term conditions direct control over the services they want to buy, allowing them to do so in the open market. For many patients with long-term conditions, including mental health, obesity and musculo-skeletal conditions, CAM therapies might, with some restructuring, be sought out as part of healthcare plans. Again, there is little evidence whether this is happening but, hypothetically, opportunities could exist.

VII Conclusion

The regulatory climate towards CAM has cooled considerably over the last twenty years. Frustrating as this has been, CAM has been naïve in failing to appreciate the extent to which the regulatory debate is about politics, not therapeutics, whilst simultaneously failing to capitalise on new opportunities arising, for example, out of the shift towards personalised care, self-care and prevention and health and wellbeing.

CAM's regulatory position is unlikely to change significantly, given the government's lack of interest in regulating these groups, given the more pressing issue of fundamental restructuring of the NHS. For professional groups which have actively campaigned for statutory regulation (including acupuncture, herbal medicine and traditional Chinese medicine), this is seen as a significant blow. On the whole, however, absence of statutory regulation does not seem to have dented CAM's popular appeal. This suggests that CAM's appeal transcends its regulatory form, and the absence of formal structures is not necessarily a bar to consumers making an active choice to seek CAM out in a plural health market. If CAM wants greater interface with the NHS, it will certainly have to make changes at the level of individual practitioner and profession. The sorts of requirements imposed by the CNHC show that alternative regulatory models may yet be helpful in securing NHS employment. For some practitioners, this will be an attractive route, whereas others will continue to reject any formalism which they see as fettering their choice to treat patients as they see fit.

Ultimately, professionalism comes from within, whatever the external demands chosen by or placed on practitioners. In terms of ethical practice, developing a sense of professionalism includes keeping up to date, working within limits of competence and any scope of practice if this exists, being suitably trained if offering multiple therapies, ensuring patients have adequate information to make informed choices and speaking out if poor practice on the part of others is encountered. These should be the aspiration of all working therapists – political tides will ebb and flow, but true professionalism should be what every therapist aspires to regardless.

Notes

1 Patient choice is now enshrined in the NHS Constitution for England, 26 March 2013.
2 See, for example, the recommendation of the House of Lords' Select Committee Report (2000) at para. 5.12, which stated: 'We recommend that, in order to protect the public, professions with more

than one regulatory body make a concerted effort to bring their various bodies together and to develop a clear professional structure.'

3 HL at para. 5.54:

> Our main criterion for determining the need for statutory regulation is whether the therapy poses significant risk to the public from its practice. We believe that both acupuncture and herbal medicine do carry inherent risk, beyond the extrinsic risk that all CAMs pose, which is the risk of omission of conventional medical treatment.

4 www.professionalstandards.org.uk/voluntary-registers/about-accreditation.

5 Patient Reported Outcome Measures (PROMs) assess the quality of care delivered to NHS patients from the patient perspective. See: www.hscic.gov.uk/proms (accessed 18 October 2013).

6 Section 2 Health and Social Care Act 2012.

7 All key government plans for the NHS starting with the NHS Plan (Department of Health 2000) have stressed the importance of building services around the needs of individuals, prevention and self-care. The influential Wanless Report, *Securing our Future Health*, was highly influential and highlighted the need for UK health services to concentrate on improving public health and prevention in order to reduce health inequalities.

8 Despite the inclusion of musculo-skeletal services as a relevant area for greater patient choice, provision of CAM via the 'Any Qualified Provider' scheme is small scale and ad hoc, in the same way that provision via GP fund-holding was in previous years.

9 See *Operational Guidance to the NHS. Extending Patient Choice of Provider*: www.gov.uk/government/uploads/system/uploads/attachment_data/file/216137/dh_128462.pdf (accessed 18 October 2013).

10 Section 12 Medicines Act 1968 (as amended). This exemption currently contained in Regulation 3(6) of The Human Medicines Regulations 2012 (SI 1916) grants a person (rather than a qualified herbalist) the right to manufacture or assemble herbal medicines at the request of individual patients. UK herbalists fear that failing to create statutory regulation will threaten this right.

11 See House of Commons Science and Technology Committee Evidence Check 2: Homeopathy. Fourth Report of 2009.

12 Currently, arts therapists, biomedical scientists, chiropodists/podiatrists, clinical scientists, dieticians, hearing aid dispensers, occupational therapists, operating department practitioners, orthoptists, paramedics, physiotherapists, practitioner psychologists, prosthetists/orthotists, radiographers, social workers in England and speech and language therapists.

13 www.cnhc.org.uk.

14 Notably, having failed to secure statutory regulation, the British Acupuncture Council, the main UK registering body for acupuncture, has also sought and been granted voluntary accredited status via this route.

15 For regulation of herbal medicines, see: www.mhra.gov.uk/Howweregulate/Medicines/Herbalmedicinesregulation/RegisteredTraditionalHerbalMedicines. For regulation of homeopathic products, see: www.mhra.gov.uk/Howweregulate/Medicines/Homeopathicmedicines. See also McHale, this volume.

16 See: www.cqc.org.uk.

17 Albeit regulated health professionals providing CAM therapies may require regulation. Current guidance on registration can be found at: www.cqc.org.uk/content/revisions-our-scope-registration-guidance (accessed 7 January 2015).

18 For example, a Scottish health board has recently withdrawn a £250,000 homeopathy service for want of scientific evidence: www.scotsman.com/news/health/nhs-lothian-axes-250k-homeopathy-funding-1-2976923.

19 Previously, 'any willing provider'. For resources on the AQP system, see: www.supply2health.nhs.uk/aqpresourcecentre/Pages/AQPHome.aspx.

20 www.e-laws.gov.on.ca/html/statutes/english/elaws_statutes_91r18_e.htm (accessed 18 October 2013).

21 For the Law Commission's review of the UK law relating to regulation of health and social care professionals, see: http://lawcommission.justice.gov.uk/areas/Healthcare_professions.htm.

22 Portugal, for example, has recently regulated osteopathy, traditional Chinese medicine and homeopathy. See: Diário da República, 1.ª série – N.º 168 – 2 September 2013.

23 See too, *Enabling Excellence*, which introduced the scheme for PSA/CHRE voluntary assured registers.

24 See www.acupuncture.org.uk/public-content/public-pr-press-releases/independent-quality-mark-for-the-british-acupuncture-council-bacc.html.

References

Better Regulation Executive (2000) *Five Principles of Good Regulation*. London: Better Regulation Executive.

Bingham, T. (1992) *Report of a Working Party on Osteopathy chaired by Sir Thomas Bingham*. London: King Edward's Hospital Fund for London.

Budd, S. and Mills, S. (2000) *Regulatory Prospects for Complementary and Alternative Medicine: Information Pack*. University of Exeter, on behalf of the Department of Health.

Council for Healthcare Regulatory Excellence (2010) (now Professional Standards Authority). 'Right-touch regulation', August 2010. www.professionalstandards.org.uk/docs/psa-library/right-touch-regulation.pdf.

Department of Health (2000) *NHS Plan. A Plan for Investment. A Plan for Reform*. Cm 4818-I. Department of Health. http://webarchive.nationalarchives.gov.uk/20130107105354/www.dh.gov.uk/prod_consum_dh/groups/dh_digitalassets/@dh/@en/@ps/documents/digitalasset/dh_118522.pdf.

Department of Health (2007) *Trust, Assurance and Safety – The Regulation of Health Professionals in the 21st Century*. www.official-documents.gov.uk/document/cm70/7013/7013.pdf.

Department of Health (2009) 'A joint consultation on the Report to Ministers from the DH Steering Group on the Statutory Regulation of Practitioners of Acupuncture, Herbal Medicine, Traditional Chinese Medicine and other Traditional Medicine Systems Practised in the UK', London: Department of Health.

Department of Health (2011) *Enabling Excellence. Autonomy and Accountability for Healthcare Workers, Social Workers and Social Care Workers*. Cm 8008. HMSO.

Dixon, A. (2008) *Regulating Complementary Medicine Practitioners*. London: King's Fund. www.kingsfund.org.uk/sites/files/kf/regulating-complementary-medical-practitioners-case-studies-anna-dixon-mar08.pdf (accessed 18 October 2013).

Francis, Robert QC (2013) *The Mid Staffordshire NHS Foundation Trust Public Inquiry Chaired by Robert Francis QC*. HC 898. London: The Stationery Office.

House of Lords (2000) *Complementary and Alternative Medicine: House of Lords Science and Technology Select Committee Sixth Report*. www.publications.parliament.uk/pa/ld199900/ldselect/ldsctech/123/12301.htm.

King's Fund Institute (1991) *Reports of the Working Party on Osteopathy*. London: King's Fund.

Saks, M. (2002) 'Professionalization, regulation and alternative medicine'. In Saks, M. and Allsop, J. (eds), *The Health Professions. New Approaches to Regulation*. London: Sage.

Shipman Inquiry, Fifth Report (2004) *Safeguarding Patients: Lessons from the Past, Proposals for the Future*, 9 December, Cm 6394.

Stone, J. (1996) 'Regulating complementary medicine: standards not status', *BMJ*, 312: 1492.

Stone, J. (2002) *An Ethical Framework for Complementary and Alternative Therapists*. London: Routledge.

Stone, J. (2010) 'Risk, regulation and the growing marginalisation of CAM', *Complementary Therapies in Clinical Practice*, 16: 1–2.

Stone, J. and Matthews, J. (1996) *Complementary Medicine and the Law*. Oxford: Oxford University Press.

Thomas, K. J., Nicholl, J. P. and Coleman, P. (2001) 'Use and expenditure on complementary medicine in England: a population-based survey', *Complementary Therapies in Medicine*, 9: 2–11.

Wanless, D. (2002) *Securing Our Future Health: Taking a Long-term View. Final Report*. London: HM Treasury.

PART 4

Critical perspectives on knowledge in CAM

17

CAM AND CONVENTIONAL MEDICINE IN SWITZERLAND

Divided in theory, united in practice

Hélène Martin and Jérôme Debons[1]

I Introduction

Between 1999 and 2005 in Switzerland, coverage for five types of "*médecines complémentaires*" (the French term for complementary medicine) was temporarily integrated into compulsory public health insurance (CHI): these included anthroposophic medicine, homeopathy, neural therapy, herbal medicine and traditional Chinese medicine. During that time, these specific kinds of medical care were covered for all insured patients, as long as treatments were prescribed and carried out by physicians recognized by the Swiss Federation of Physicians (FMH). At the end of the period, these approaches were deemed unable to meet the three criteria set in the law permitting reimbursement by CHI (article 32 of the LAMal or health insurance federal law) – that is, efficacy, appropriateness and economic efficiency; they were thus no longer to be covered by public insurance. However, the decision to terminate public coverage was contested and a renewed temporary integration into CHI of these five treatment approaches is being tested for a new period extending from January 1, 2012 to the end of 2017.

The study we conducted examined the impact of the inclusion of these *médecines complémentaires* into CHI from 1999 to 2005. Theoretically, the effects of the legislative change might have been significant: persons who held private insurance contracts to cover these five types of treatments could have cancelled, them whilst people who were not previously covered for these types of medical care could have seized the opportunity to try them out. However, as our study shows, this change had very little actual impact on health consumers.[2] We therefore attempted to understand this apparent lack of connection between legal entitlement and consumer behaviour through an analysis of the ways patients using these five types of *médecines complémentaires* were situated within the field of Swiss health insurance as well as within the realm of health care reimbursed by various types of insurance schemes (public and/or private).

Let us end this introduction with a brief caveat about a specific terminological issue. Except when we are referring to particular official terminologies (such as *médecines complémentaires*, in Swiss law), we will use the acronym CAM, commonly used in current English language research. Used to refer to "complementary and alternative medicine", this acronym combines two concepts corresponding to two types of uses of these medicines (Tovey *et al.* 2004). The use of this terminology helps to preserve an open definition of these medicines and their usage. In accordance with a constructivist approach, we hold the view that CAMs are socially defined as different from mainstream medicine (Saks 2003), the latter being legitimized by the Swiss state and covered by compulsory public health insurance; in contrast we shall call the latter "conventional medicine".

II Literature review: causes and characteristics of CAM use

For the past four decades in contemporary Western societies, CAM use has grown and practitioners have become more professionalized. Medical pluralism has become the norm rather than the exception (Cant and Sharma 1999). Epidemiological studies of CAM use carried out in various national contexts, including Switzerland, show a constant and massive increase of CAM use since the 1970s (Eisenberg et al. 1993, Ernst 2000, Sommer et al. 1996, Bizig et al. 2004). The emergence of an interest – both popular and scientific – for CAM has given rise to a range of explanations.

Furnham and Vincent (2000) have conducted an analysis of the first socio-anthropological studies of the increasing popularity of CAM. According to these authors, these studies put forth two main hypotheses. The first states that patients' dissatisfaction with biomedical health care leads them to turn to CAM: the lack of results of some treatments, their side-effects, especially in cases of chronic conditions, but also the characteristics of the doctor–patient relationship seen as inadequate (insufficient time and attention paid to patients and strong asymmetry between professionals and users) are viewed as factors feeding into various forms of distrust or disillusionment with regard to biomedicine (Williams and Calnan 1996). The second hypothesis emphasizes the innovative and original character of CAM, viewed as the main cause of their success (Bakx 1991): CAMs are seen as having seduced the public by deeply drawing upon the realm of nature (natural-seeming treatments described as mild and devoid of side-effects), by presenting themselves as holistic and promoting a view of health as a general state of well-being (taking into account not only physical but psychological and spiritual dimensions), or by referring to the individual responsibility of patients and claiming to found their practices on a partnership between therapist and patient (Aakster 1986, Goldstein 1999). In both types of hypotheses, the popularity of CAM is thus seen as linked to a context of scepticism about the promises of scientific progress, to which CAM offers an alternative to the methods of conventional medicine viewed as narrowly focused, authoritarian and dehumanizing (McKee 1988).

Research conducted in the 1990s in Canada (Kelner and Wellman 1997), in the USA (Astin 1998, Ernst et al. 1995) or in England (Sharma 1992) show that dissatisfaction with conventional medical treatments and a pull towards alternative practices are dimensions that are frequently combined in individuals' health care "careers". Sharma's studies clearly show the complex process that underlies therapeutic choices: CAM use must be viewed as a *pragmatic* response containing elements related to the nature of the health problem (chronic illness, failure of conventional treatments) and ideological reasons (need for personalized attention, dissatisfaction with the side-effects of conventional treatments). In most cases, these motives are combined within the course of one person's trajectory and may vary in importance over time (Sharma 1992).

In fact, as more recent empirical studies have continued to show, complete rejection of conventional medicine remains a minority opinion, the more commonly held stance favouring combined use of conventional medicine and CAM (Kelner et al. 2000, Hildreth and Elman 2007, Tovey et al. 2004). Such an observation is in line with the principles of therapeutic pluralism, and implies that patients are becoming better informed and more ready to reflect upon their options (Cant and Sharma 1999); health care users thus may resort to conventional medicine for acute care, because of its high level of expertise and ability to provide diagnoses, while also turning to CAM for other reasons (Marcellini et al. 2000, Hammer 2010). The failure of conventional treatments to cure chronic health problems, as well as the undesirable side-effects of long-term conventional drug use, may contribute to users seeking therapies viewed as less harsh and more natural, such as treatments based on homeopathy or on the healing properties of plants to complement their conventional treatment. Studies that focused on the use of complementary or alternative treatments by people with cancer, who are often high users of CAM, are illustrative of the pragmatic approaches at play in patients' care pathways (Hök et al. 2007, Broom 2009, Begot 2010, Cohen and Rossi 2011).

As well as the diversity of trajectories, a few other global elements emerge from the international as well as the Swiss literature about the reasons for CAM use. Research has shown that predictive factors of CAM use include gender as well as socio-economic status; women with a higher level of education and comfortable incomes represent a majority of CAM users (Kersnik 2000, Astin 1998, Bizig et al. 2004, Eisenberg et al. 1998). Moreover, studies show that most CAM users state that they suffer from chronic health problems such as allergies, back and joint pain, emotional problems, gynaecological or digestive problems (Busato et al. 2006, Astin 2000, Kelner et al. 2000, Sommer et al. 1996, Tovey et al. 2004).

The literature also shows that a holistic approach to the patients' physical and mental health is not – or is no longer – associated solely with CAM practitioners: such an ethos is also found in many conventional physicians' stance, notably GPs (Kelner 2000). On the other hand, the degree of patient participation in the therapeutic process does seem to distinguish care provided by CAM practitioners from conventional treatment plans, although this may also be showing signs of changing with an increasing emphasis on patient choice and involvement in health care in international policy (Fotaki et al. 2008, Coulter 2009). As Kelner emphasizes, "the physician relationship is based primarily on trust in expertise, while the CAM relationship is based principally on partnership in healing" (2000: 94). Studies of the CAM consultation have often construed it as an exploration process in which patient and therapist are mutually involved (Hughes 2004). This is particularly exemplified by the high degree of importance placed upon *body work* (Gale 2010). By straddling the border between health and well-being, CAM practices could be leading users towards an inner quest, a path of discovery of their own agency in the health field (Sointu 2006). In many CAMs, the self becomes the primary source of knowledge and understanding; reflexivity, narration and (inter)subjective experience are strongly emphasized (O'Connor 2000, Barcan 2006). As a result, the therapeutic partnership, central to care provided by CAM practitioners, may have an impact not only in physical or physiological terms, but also in terms of perception and identity (Baarts and Pedersen 2009, McClean 2005). A critical perspective focused on these dimensions of CAM reveals that the emphasis placed on expertise and partnership in the care relationship echoes a more general social tendency clearly at play in the public health field that promotes responsibility and the empowerment of patients (Hughes 2004, Goldner 2004). More broadly, some authors point out that, far from existing on the margins, CAM, or at least some alternative or complementary medicines, actively contribute to the normative production of the contemporary individual, who is "not only capable, but obliged to be responsible and productive in terms of personal health" (Sointu 2006: 339).

This critical perspective informs our own analysis. Our examination of the motives put forth by CAM users we interviewed to explain their health care choices show that they are "good" patients in terms of an ideology of individual responsibility; indeed they are so "responsible" that their care choices display a priority put on health issues rather than economic rationality. In a recent article, Hildreth and Elman (2007) indicated that having insurance coverage, among other enabling factors, was not a determining factor for CAM use:

> However, none of the enabling factors that encourage conventional use predict "Any CAM use". Health insurance does not generally cover CAM, and having or not having insurance does not appear to influence its use. Perceived financial status does not shape the use of CAM, nor does income. Education may be picking up this enabling aspect

of socioeconomic status effects: the odds of CAM use increase monotonically with higher education [...]. But the odds of CAM use does not significantly decline with lower income.

(Hildreth and Elman 2007: 92–93)

As we shall see, our study's results mirror the findings of quantitative research, whilst opening up new avenues of understanding about the types of motives underlying users' choices. Conducted on the basis of qualitative methods through interviews with persons who had purchased complementary health insurance (with different profiles in terms of education, age, gender and chronicity), our research shows that coverage provided by these insurance plans is not put forth as a justification for CAM use; rather, what CAM users share first is a value system that organizes the respective characteristics of conventional medicine and CAM. Our participants framed conventional medicine and CAM as antagonists and ascribed distinct qualities to them; yet these views tended to lead them to thoughtful conjoined recourse to both types of approaches and treatments. These beliefs and representations, rather than economic considerations, thus seemed to shape their choices.

In order to develop and support this thesis, we will first present the context of medical pluralism in Switzerland and, second, try to understand the sense given by participants to their use of different medicines. In the last part, we shall discuss our results.

III Methodology

To set the context for our empirical study, we have summarized below, drawing on official documents,[3] the changing debate on medical pluralism from the 1970s in Switzerland (specifically its definition as a range of various practices and viewpoints about health, body and care [Cant and Sharma 1999], as well as its increasingly politicized character in the 1990s) and the organization of health insurance in Switzerland. Our empirical study focuses on the social ranking of different health care approaches in terms of qualities that are attributed to them. Social judgment, itself founded upon structured social relations in a specific societal context, are in fact the basis upon which some types of medical practices remain largely outside the realm of official legitimacy whilst others seek and obtain recognition from the state. As we view the object of our research as a product of historical and social forces, we adopt a realist constructivist stance (Olivier de Sardan 2008). This stance leads us to conduct our research on the basis of

> discursive data produced within interactions between researchers and the social actors they are studying, collected in the form of a "corpus" (register of the expressed) as well as that of the "representations of the subjects" [...]. These are notions, concepts and views that are commonly present in a social group, i.e. sets, configuration or schemes of knowledge and interpretation that are largely shared (register of the potentially expressed).
>
> (Olivier de Sardan, 2008: 116)

Our research object is thus not founded upon a primary, or essential, reality; it emerges as the result of a "double" construction process, social and scientific.

1 Sampling

We conducted 21 semi-structured interviews with 22 participants (one of the interviews involved a couple), living in the French-speaking part of Switzerland, who had been users of one of the five types of CAM reimbursed by compulsory health insurance between 1999 and

2005 when provided by a recognized physician. Four other selection criteria were added to this first central one. Because of the characteristics of CAM users highlighted by the literature, we oversampled female respondents (17 women and five men were interviewed). Women, as managers of the health practices of members of the family, in particular where children are concerned, are the main users of medical care – whether conventional or CAM. Yet, because of their broad investment in domestic tasks, they are more frequently without professional status or hold jobs that do not correspond to the level of education and training they achieved. For that reason, and more generally because studies show that CAM users are more frequently found in the middle and upper reaches of the social hierarchy, we classified the social status of sample members using a three-level scale – primary, secondary and tertiary educational achievement – using the categories of the Federal Statistical Office. In keeping with proportions observed in other studies, out of the 22 interviewees, two people had completed primary school education only, 11 has completed secondary school and nine had a tertiary-level education. Third, we wanted to include persons who had chronic health problems. In order to identify them, we used the self-definition of persons interviewed: 12 interviewees stated that they were suffering from chronic problems such as asthma, allergies, joint pain, migraines or fatigue. Finally, we tried to broaden the age distribution of our sample, as we surmised that practices and discourse may vary on a generational basis: the youngest person we interviewed was 26 and the oldest was 76 at the time of the interview (see Table 17.1).

Table 17.1 Summary of persons interviewed

Name[1]	Sex	Age[1]	Chronic illness	Education level
Annie	F	33	Yes	2
Bernard	M	73	Yes	2
Christophe	M	47	No	3
Didier	M	45	Yes	3
Eliane	F	49	No	2
Elise	F	26	No	3
Françoise	F	44	Yes	3
Gaëlle	F	28	Yes	1
Henri	M	42	No	3
Jacques	M	68	No	2
Laurence	F	30	No	3
Line	F	71	No	2
Marianne	F	76	Yes	2
Maude	F	53	No	2
Nathalie	F	54	Yes	2
Patricia	F	43	Yes	3
Pauline	F	67	No	2
Pierrette	F	71	Yes	1
Sophie	F	45	Yes	3
Sylvie	F	54	No	3
Véronique	F	31	Yes	2
Yvette	F	66	Yes	2

Note
1 Names have been changed and ages are approximate.

2 Access and recruitment

In order to obtain access to our participants, we first enlisted the help of physicians whom we were also interviewing; they agreed to pass along our request for interviewees to one or two of their patients who fit into our selection criteria and whom they thought might be interested in being interviewed. We also asked two pharmacies specializing in homeopathic remedies to make a presentation of our research available to their clients, who were then able to contact us if they so wished. We thus initiated a "network-based study" making use of our own contacts and seizing new opportunities to recruit persons to interview during the study, with reference to the specific field study methodology conceptualized by Beaud and Weber (2003).

3 Data collection and analysis

The interviews were conducted by JD, in French, mostly in the participant's home. The interviews lasted between 60 and 90 minutes; they were audio recorded and transcribed. We designed a topic guide on the basis of existing literature on CAM users, with an emphasis on the most recently published materials. The first part of the interview focused on the conceptions of health and of health care held by participants in the study: how did they take care of their health? How did they explain their use of conventional medicine and of CAM? Did they suffer from chronic pain or chronic health problems requiring continuing care? The second part of the interview explored their relationship to various types of health insurance: what kind of insurance coverage had they chosen and what were the reasons for their decisions? Did they make a choice solely based on what kind of medical care was covered? Were they aware of the details of different types of contracts? In the last part of the interview, we focused on the type of health practices and the kind of coverage they had chosen during the 1999–2005 period. As a conclusion, we asked a few factual questions about health budgets and sought our participants' opinions on the current functioning of the Swiss health system. Two questions were asked in order to place the interviewee on our social status scale – namely their level of education and their age – gender having been coded by the interviewer. We also asked our participants whether they wanted to receive the transcript of their interviews, and if they wished to be kept informed of the research results. We analysed the interview data using the thematic saturation method of qualitative content analysis (Bardin 1991). Our research design was accepted by Lausanne University through its Ethics Committee for Clinical Research.

IV The Swiss system of health insurance

1 Context: medical pluralism in Switzerland

Our analysis of the literature published in Switzerland on CAM during the last 40 years shows us that two distinct periods can be identified. The first period, from the end of the 1970s to the beginning of the 1990s, is characterized by the emergence of an interest in CAM within the broader discourse on medical pluralism. Although medical pluralism has probably always existed, it became visible – according to international literature – in the early 1970s; in this regard, Switzerland is no exception. Between 1970 and 1990, our corpus shows a limited number of actors engaged in discussion on medical pluralism. For the most part, these actors are researchers or associations created to promote CAM. CAMs are mostly termed "alternative" or "parallel" until the 1990s, when the word "complementary" first appears.

During this first period, the literature published on CAM in Switzerland is mostly exploratory. Attempts are made to characterize who chooses to use CAM and for what type of reasons.
Findings reported are of the same kind as those set forth in the international literature presented
above: salient results include a critique of authority and positivism within conventional medicine (Cuendet 1984, Feuardent 1986, Choffat 1986) that would incite patients to seek in CAM
a more collaborative therapeutic setting and a holistic view of illness (Meier and Grau 1992,
Scheder 1986). Modalities of CAM studied during this first phase are very heterogeneous (e.g.
lay healers, bonesetters, homeopathy), so that their results are difficult to compare. From the
second half of the 1980s, physicians – mostly younger doctors – describe themselves as affiliated
to some complementary and alternative approaches.

Our second period starts at the beginning of the 1990s; it is characterized by an increasing
politicization of the CAM issue. This shift is part of a general change taking place all over
Europe: whilst CAM had been viewed by conventional medicine as illegitimate or even illegal
for most of the twentieth century, by the end of the century some modalities are being examined in terms of their efficacy with a view to endowing them with a form of legitimacy (Debons
2011, Wahlberg 2007).

In Switzerland, this politicization is observed mostly in debates and national programmes
accompanying the implementation of the new federal legislation on compulsory health insurance (LAMal). More and more actors come into play in the 1990s: the political realm takes an
important place with debates in Parliament about health insurance issues but also in some
cantons, with issues about the integrating optional courses on CAM in the university curricula
of medical schools. Two oversight associations for the CAM field, financially supported by
health insurers, are set up during this period (ASCA and RME). The terminology used to refer
to CAM is illustrative of a change in how some of them are viewed; the term *médecines complémentaires* tends to become official, with the support of the Executive Board of the Swiss Federation of Physicians (FMH), who formally proposed, in 1992, the use of this terminology to
replace the term "alternative medicine". In this regard again, Switzerland does not differ from
several other Western countries.

Two large research programmes were launched by the state during the 1990s: the National
Research Programme 34 (between 1992 and 1998), called "*Médecines complémentaires*"[4] and the
"Evaluation programme of complementary medicine",[5] which started in 1999 and ended in
2005. A range of specific issues were raised: the potentials and implications of medical pluralism
were investigated (Baumann and Von Berlepsch 2000, Bonard 1993), the cost and efficacy of
CAM were examined (Kessler *et al.* 1999, Sommer 2000, Melchart *et al.* 2005); on each issue,
varied and sometimes contradictory answers were provided. In the wake of the previous era,
questions were still being asked about the characteristics of CAM users (Sommer *et al.* 1996,
Allaz *et al.* 1992, Busato *et al.* 2006, Wapf and Busato 2007, Inglin *et al.* 2008, Melchart *et al.*
2005, Jenny *et al.* 2002, Kranz and Rosenmund 1998, Messerli-Rohrbach and Schär 1999b), the
frequency of their use of complementary and alternative treatments, as well as users' motivations
for choosing CAM (Sommer *et al.* 1996, Bizig *et al.* 2004, Melchart *et al.* 2005, Calmonte *et al.*
2000, Spuhler *et al.* 1998). Again, studies were yielding results that are difficult to compare as
the foci of investigation differ. The number of users of CAM thus varied, depending on the
sources considered, between 10 per cent and 40 per cent of the population (Martin and Debons
2014).

As far as user profiles are concerned, Swiss studies have shown that the proportion of CAM
users is strongly and positively related to level of education, that the user population contains
more women than men and that members of middle or higher socio-economic classes are over-
represented (Messerli-Rohrbach and Schär 1999a, Sommer *et al.* 1996, Schär *et al.* 1994).

The results of Swiss studies carried out from the 1990s onwards are thus largely consistent with findings reported in the international literature. These results also show that the highly individual-focused approach propounded by some CAM practitioners is favoured mainly by persons who have time and resources to envisage putting life-style recommendations into practice – for instance, by modifying some of their daily habits (Sommer *et al.* 1996) or by adopting a preventative stance with regard to their own health (Kranz and Rosenmund 1998, Melchart *et al.* 2005).

2 Swiss health insurance – straddling the private and public realms

In Switzerland, the first non-compulsory public health insurance was introduced in 1911. On March 18, 1994, a new health insurance law was adopted (LAMal). It came into force on January 1, 1996 and was revised in 2007.[6] Under legislative arrangements before 1996, public health insurance was not compulsory (even if specific cantonal legislation made it compulsory for some groups – for instance, children, the elderly or foreign nationals residing in Switzerland), insurance contracts were not standardized and the costs depended on age and sex.

Since 1996, basic public health insurance has been compulsory for any person who resides in Switzerland. People may choose their insurer from an official list of approved health insurance providers, who are required to admit all persons who request it. All insurance providers must cover the same items (no less, no more), yet monthly premiums vary widely between insurers.[7] Everybody can switch their insurance provider each year, when premiums for the following year are announced. Politicians and the authorities present this opportunity as a means of heightening the "personal responsibility" of insured persons and a way to better stabilize or increase mastery over public insurance cost increases. The market-based idea is that people, as consumers, will choose the cheapest public insurance providers. People can also take higher optional deductibles in order to decrease their premiums, or choose an "alternative" model to the free choice of their physician, such as an HMO (Health Maintenance Organization) model; choosing an HMO insurance model restricts the choice of care providers available to insured persons as they must first consult with a medical team or primary physician approved by the insurer.

Legal provisions make a clear distinction between compulsory health insurance, governed by public legislation, and private insurance contracts, governed by private contract law (LCA),[8] so that the "Swiss health insurance system is situated half-way between social insurance and private insurance" (Bolgiani *et al.* 2006: 242). Providers of CHI can indeed propose almost any types of private insurance to their clients; private insurance may cover such benefits as a private room in public hospitals or care in private clinics; they may also – and this is of particular interest here – offer coverage for CAM and other types of measures viewed as promoting good health (e.g. passes for a health club or spa). In order to choose the CAM practitioners they will cover in their private insurances, health insurers rely on one or other oversight associations mentioned above (ASCA and RME). These bodies give a certification to CAM practitioners based on the type of training they have followed as well as their years of experience as CAM therapists. The registers produced by these associations are updated on a regular basis (Despland 2007).

3 A complex system – befuddled clients

Having briefly examined the main features of the social, historical and legal backdrop of medical pluralism in Switzerland, we now turn to our first main finding from the interview study: users are confused by the Swiss system of health insurance and most of our participants were unclear about the political shift that had taken place between 1999 and 2005 in terms of CAM coverage. This lack of detailed understanding of relatively subtle changes goes some way towards explaining the fact that user behaviour has largely remained stable during the 1999 to 2005 period (Melchart *et al.* 2005, Sommer 2000).

This lack of changes in users' practices may indeed be due to the complex character of the Swiss health insurance system. As a matter of fact, insured patients, questioned in 2008, had trouble remembering legal changes, in terms of time frame as well as in terms of content. When asked whether they knew that five types of CAM had been integrated into CHI coverage in 1999, they gave answers such as: "They were integrated, so they weren't part of it beforehand?" (Sylvie); or: "I had no idea and it did not make any difference to my life" (Laurence).

More generally, insured clients do not have a clear idea of what their insurance contracts actually cover: "Last year they reimbursed me money twice, and I have no idea why" (Françoise). This is easily understandable: CAMs were only covered for six years by public insurance, and in the case of private insurance contracts, insurers draw upon lists of reimbursed therapies or practitioners; such lists are not always sent along with contracts, and they are frequently modified; insurance clients thus have difficulty knowing whether their visit to a CAM therapist or the CAM treatment prescribed will be covered. All of this becomes even more complicated when one takes into consideration the fact that coverage and reimbursement rates are highly variable depending on the type of private contract, that some insurance companies cover some practitioners while others do not and that practitioners themselves thus cannot meaningfully advise their clients on likely coverage. Finally, some insurers offer different levels of deductibles for LCA contracts, others write coverage maxima into contracts, and even reimbursement mechanisms vary. For instance, some insurers (for private and public insurance) require clients to send in bills to be reimbursed only after the deductible requirement has been fulfilled, a practice which leads to omissions: "Typically my doctor, well that particular natural healer I mean, my insurer covers him partially but I have a bit of a tendency to forget to send those bills in" (Henri).

A dissociation between care chosen by patients and its reimbursement by health insurers is obvious, since coverage cannot really function as a rational criterion for decisions to be made: "It was never a criterion, to be reimbursed or not. If it happens to be covered, well, that's good" (Didier). Whilst other insurance users pay closer attention to their insurance contract, they do not necessarily master all its details, even when their income is not particularly high:

> I would say the only thing of interest I get from the insurance company is the insurance contract, to see by how much premiums have gone up. After that, I just glance through. How they work out all this stuff, I don't really understand it all too well, the terms they use – they are real ball-breakers! I don't waste my time with all that, I figure if it is covered, good; if it isn't, never mind.
>
> *(Annie)*

In this context of generalized bewilderment, some people view the pressure to make use of competitive mechanisms within CHI primarily as a way to "hassle" insurance clients:

> Some politician in charge of health does tell us to change insurers, but honestly I find it to be such a drag, this health insurance business. I feel like, well, they just want to hassle us, and you know what? It works. They really do cause us hassles.
>
> *(Sylvie)*

Others may become fatalistic, or even somewhat paranoid:

> Me, I'm not in favour of switching insurers. I figure, it's six of one and half a dozen of another; they're all the same. One time you gain something, but then premiums go back up again, I figure in the end it all comes to the same thing.
>
> *(Pierrette)*

Switching CHI insurer does mean, as we stated earlier, obtaining potentially cheaper premiums for the exact same coverage; such a switch is a risk-free operation since CHI insurers legally have to accept since 1996 any person who requests basic coverage. However, insurance users if ill or too old can be refused a private insurance contract, or be expelled from coverage by an LCA insurer. As insurance users usually have public and private contracts with the same insurer, for both ideological and pragmatic reasons, they tend to remain loyal to their current insurer. This finding about our participants' reluctance to switch insurance carriers seems to be widely shared; according to a nationwide survey (Frei 2009), 250,000 CHI clients in Switzerland switched insurer each year between 2007 and 2009, and most of them were younger, comparatively healthy clients, which is only about 3 per cent of the population of Switzerland (total population at the time of the study was 7.7 million).

Using the same insurer for all types of health coverage does facilitate the management of administrative tasks – especially when submitting bills for reimbursement:

> I don't know how they cook it up to decide what is complementary and what is conventional medicine. I don't look too closely at how they do their business. [...] So my bills, well I keep them for a year and after that I send them in to the insurance company and they reimburse me for what part they figure they can cover.
>
> *(Pierrette)*

Remaining loyal to the same insurance company is the norm for our participants, and switching remains exceptional: only two of our interviewees attempted to change insurer between 1999 and 2005. While switching to another CHI insurer is always possible, attempts to move to another company for private insurance often does not work out:

> When things started to get bad with this insurance, they weren't reimbursing us, it was a catastrophe. So then we started to look into changing. Because of our age, we had to hurry. And at that point, all private insurers were turning us away.
>
> *(Line)*

Insurance companies do not have to justify turning away new LCA clients; as private, for-profit businesses they have an explicit policy of excluding bad risks. As well as older people, people who seek private insurance who suffer from chronic health problems or might present with such problems in the near future are excluded. These experiences are well known, clearly understood and feared by insurance clients: "If you have a serious claim once, after that they don't want to insure you anymore" (Christophe). Although they are aware of how insurers behave, patients often still mistakenly believe that they will be better protected if they remain loyal to their long-time insurer, whereas in fact CHI insurers can change or terminate an LCA policy whenever they want. Insurance clients thus enter into the Swiss health insurance system sometimes with exaggerated optimism:

To be truthful I didn't look around too much because my insurance offers pretty good private coverage: they don't make a fuss and they reimburse you promptly, whereas some private insurers don't cover things or they make it difficult to get reimbursed. [...] There is a health questionnaire to fill out and they are allowed to ask all kinds of questions. Now I'm sure there are cheaper insurers but I figure: if I leave this insurance, another insurer might not take me. You can't be sure. So I'd say I'm satisfied.

(Elise)

Whilst clients remain relatively faithful to the same insurers and policies, this does not mean that they do not try to calculate potential usage and cost in order to make what they view as rational decisions about their insurance contracts. However, these calculations are not founded upon comparisons between insurers, but rather on trying to balance deductible and other out-of pocket expenses with level of coverage. Some insurance clients thus take into account their private policies to make decisions about the characteristics of their CHI coverage:

Because as it is then, for compulsory coverage I take the highest optional deductible, because I'm hardly ever sick; if I am, then I use natural medicines. For the private policy, I can pick an annual ceiling of 1000 francs or 2000 francs; I chose 1000 francs. That means I can have 1000 francs worth of natural medicine treatments covered and reimbursed right from the start. There is no deductible. I only pay 10 per cent of the bill.

(Elise)

This interviewee thus bases her calculations on the expectation that her medical bills will not exceed 1000 francs a year and that she will not have to use her CHI coverage. In other words, she thinks she will not become gravely ill and she does not intend to consult any conventional medicine specialist practitioners for tests or check-ups.

On the other hand, some insurance clients are primarily worried about not being able to cover the out-of-pocket costs should they become ill or have an accident. They consequently sign up for the lowest optional deductible and attempt to minimize unplanned out-of-pocket expenses; as a result they pay high monthly premiums:

I always had the lowest optional deductible: my mother already had it that way and I didn't change it. [...] It's a 300 francs deductible. Of course then I pay a big monthly premium – about 450 francs a month. [...] In there, there's also 6 francs[9] for the private insurance, it's included.

(Annie)

These hypotheses and calculations do not truly help insurance clients actually sign up for the most suitable type of policies for their financial and health circumstances; neither does that mean that patients are aware of specific conditions included in their contracts. Rather, the strategies our interviewees show that the supposed market competition brought into social health insurance by current policies clash with other types of rationales; most insurance clients tend to keep their policy with the same CHI insurer; switching remains the exception. These behaviours are rooted in deep beliefs about health. For our interviewees, as was the case for Hildreth and Elman's participants (2007), insurance coverage was not a determining factor for CAM use. We shall now examine these beliefs more closely and attempt to better understand, within the context of our study, how this dissociation between recourse to various treatment approaches and insurance coverage arises and plays itself out.

V Deeply rooted beliefs about health care

Our second major finding was that, whilst conventional medicine and CAM are often structured on the basis of opposing positions, they are in fact constitutive elements of the same system.

1 Nature-focused beliefs

Much of the discourse we heard in interviews carried the opposition between conventional medicine and CAM, and ordered them in a moral hierarchy – giving high value to one and devaluing others. In keeping with the results of Swiss and international studies presented above, CAMs are described positively through references to "nature" viewed as a positive, generative entity, calling on concepts such as "truth", "purity" or "authenticity"; CAMs are thought of as "natural" and "non-chemical". Conversely, conventional medicine is described as chemically based, "polluting" and blamed for causing "side-effects". Exhibiting a line of thought recalling the universal dichotomy between purity and impurity (Douglas 2001), one of our interviewees thus states: "Using natural medicines, it does not pollute your body nearly as much as conventional, allopathic treatments, I mean the kind of drugs you buy at the pharmacy" (Maude).

The moral opposition put forward between the good that comes of nature and the ill effects of chemistry is linked to another dichotomy, between "depth", referring to ideas of origins and of truth, and "superficiality" – that would characterize more easily accessible, less profound or even misleading approaches. In this view, conventional medicine focuses on treating the surface (e.g. "symptoms"), whereas CAMs are able to reach the depths of the body – that is, the true "causes" of the problem or illness:

> The medicine we all know deals with symptoms, treats an illness, but it does not look at all at what the cause of the illness might be, it does not look for its origin or try to correct the evil from its beginning ... or at least to go back to the start, while taking the personal condition of each patient into consideration, that is the person who is sick.
>
> *(Bernard)*

2 Person-focused beliefs

Another finding, which reinforces previous research, is founded upon the notion put forward by participants that CAMs, as their in-depth approach claims to be concerned with the origin of the problem or imbalance, treat "the whole person": "What I liked about homeopathy, it's that the sick person is being treated and not just the illness. And that means something to me" (Eliane).

For care to reach the person, it should thus go beyond symptoms, because symptoms are viewed as signs by which "the body tries to express something: an overflow, a need to evacuate toxins" (Elise). Whereas conventional medicine, intent on treating the symptoms, would erase them, CAM would listen to them and try to understand them through taking individuals and their life world into account.

Actively involved in their own healing processes, ready to explain that they are prepared to change their habits in order to be healthier, the interviewees view themselves as actors of their recovery: "So, later on, one feels better; one doesn't get sick as often and then one learns to function different" (Nathalie). The central role our interviewees attribute to themselves for their recovery explains the emphasis they place on being heard, understood and able to express their opinions to the therapist; they also describe the relationship with the physician as one between team members, a view that echoes the attention they pay to their own body and the "signals" it sends: "It's true that this kind of approach suits me better, in the sense that I'd say I find that one communicates adult to adult" (Sylvie). This highly engaged and prevention-oriented use of CAM goes along with a promotion, or even an injunction to individual responsibility towards one's own health. Illness not only can but should be avoided by a preventative attitude:

> I am not against classical medicine you see. I think it is well adapted to situations where intervention comes later than it should. [...] But before one gets to that point I'd say there have been many stages at which if one had been a bit more conscious of certain things, one would not have gone to that place.
>
> *(Christophe)*

While for some people the preventive use of CAM is just a way of staying in good health or "preparing for one's own old age" (Sylvie), for others, CAMs have potential benefits for the whole society: "There are less hospitalisations because people are perhaps more conscious of their own health, they don't panic as much, maybe there is another way to approach things..." (Maude). All these quotes illustrating the value placed on approaches taking into account the whole person are founded on a critique of conventional medicine: it is described as paying selective attention to parts rather than the whole and as relying excessively on science and on technical means of intervention. Some complementary and alternative approaches are also thought of as promoting the view that dissociation between soma and psyche is impossible (Goldstein 1999, Cant and Sharma 1999, Rossi 1994). We also find in our participants' discourse the high value placed on a therapeutic model viewing practitioners and patients as equals and functioning as partners; patients are also described as depositories of specific knowledge, as was found in CAM previously studied in Switzerland and elsewhere.

Finally, participants strongly emphasize personal responsibility, a principle also identified as underlying recourse to CAM by Hildreth and Elman (2007). Personal responsibility is the focus of active welfare state policies and is now built into a range of social security contexts (Martin 2009, Martin and Debons 2010, Valli *et al.* 2002). In the realm of health, this principle of responsibility carries, more or less explicitly, the notion that individuals must manage their health – that is, maintain it and even strengthen it (Martin 2011). The ideology of individual responsibility is at the heart of the neoliberal ideology that underpins the discourse on private insurance (Harley *et al.* 2011, Natalier and Willis 2008). As we have seen, this ideology is also prominent in the discourse of CAM practitioners, leading to a highly individualized conception of health problems and of the ways to deal with them (Sointu 2006, McClean 2005, Hughes 2004). The notion of individual responsibility thus plays a part in masking inequalities between social groups, which have been emphasized by social scientists for decades. About 40 years ago, Luc Boltanski (1971) and Pierre Bourdieu (1977) analysed health inequalities as well as unequal access to medical care in terms of socio-economic status: members of lower socio-economic classes are more frequently ill but seek treatment more rarely than members of higher socio-economic groups; this difference is due in part to use and perception both of the body and of illness. Other studies showed that, unlike other types of domination that impact negatively on the health of dominated groups, male domination is a disadvantage in terms of health; this is due, for example, to the very socialization of men into dominant behaviours that include stamina, risk taking, strategies to attain and maintain status etc. and lead to lower life expectancy coupled with lower morbidity, men seeking treatment less frequently and belatedly (Aïach *et al.* 2001). Social inequalities in terms of health have also been shown to be associated with other social determinants, such as risks linked to certain types of work (Dejours 1999, Messing 1999, Gollac and Volkoff 2002) and to work organization – for example, the policy of migration assigning some types of foreign workers to dangerous professions (Fassin 1997, Tabin *et al.* 2008). The combination of these various social determinants and relationships gives rise to a range of conditions that can be analysed in terms of their specificity and socially based characteristics; yet the dominant discourse focused on individual responsibility masks these structural issues.

Our interviewees are carriers of this discourse, and take it on board by conforming to social pressures to preserve one's own health. In this sense – and we shall come back to this point in the discussion section – neither recourse to CAM nor the way its use is explained and justified by our interviewees represent a transgression of dominant norms. On the contrary, they can be viewed as reinforcing these norms. As Caspi *et al.* show, users never make decisions regarding their health "in a vacuum but in a social context with varying degrees and types of social influence" (2004: 77). As members of the middle and upper classes, the CAM and conventional medicine users we met behave in keeping with dominant views of health: as carriers of the contemporary critique of the ideology of continuous progress, they are somewhat critical of conventional medicine, though they do not reject it outright. This view leads them to see themselves as valid partners in their exchanges with doctors; along the lines of neoliberal health policies. These users take it upon themselves to manage their own health, using CAM to achieve objectives of risk reduction and maximization of the positive impacts of allopathic treatments, as we will show in the next section.

3 Conventional medicine and CAM: opposed poles of the same system

Despite criticisms addressed to it, conventional medicine actually remains the central reference point for most people we interviewed. Thus, for instance, one of our interviewees states that: "I am viscerally opposed to allopathic medicine because of the side-effects of drug treatments" and yet says a few seconds later: "I do use allopathic remedies because I'm not a fundamentalist. I use paracetamol and other types of substances like that for myself and my children because those things are OK and there's no point having pain when remedies exist" (Elise). Here, our interviewees echo Caspi *et al.*'s "complementary group": they felt responsible and confident enough to go "out of their way to gather information before making a decision", they give "the most sway to scientific evidence", especially for "severe pain and disability", whilst considering "the alternatives [...] as 1 or 2 options when making health care decisions, and evidence of effectiveness was considered paramount to any decision being made" (2004: 73).

Conventional medicine and CAM thus are constituted by, and through, their binary relationship; for instance, the fact that one approach is viewed as dangerous implies that the other is viewed as softer, but it also means that the first is apt to treat diseases viewed as serious and the second used on a day-to-day, ordinary basis. The integrated use of both approaches built into their discursively constructed opposition becomes wholly meaningful when their characteristics and attributed roles are analysed. Whatever the way in which conventional medicine and CAM are integrated, the latter are always analysed and described in comparison with conventional medicine. In that sense, conventional medicine remains the central reference.

First of all, CAM can be used in the period that precedes the illness episode, their regular use being viewed as preventing its occurrence and thus avoiding resorting to conventional medicine. Yet if illness occurs nonetheless and/or if resorting to conventional medicine seems necessary, CAM may serve to attenuate the side-effects of a medical treatment viewed as (potentially) dangerous and thus particularly effective. For instance the practice of "draining" antibiotics or vaccines through the use of homeopathy: "My two daughters go to a doctor and have the required vaccinations but they also have a GP that practices some homeopathy and gives them granules to neutralize the vaccine" (Yvette). In that sense, one might say that CAM supports the use of conventional medicine as it is thought to be able to mitigate its negative effects. This use of CAM as support and complement is also underlined in cases where CAM serves to ameliorate the comfort of patients going through aggressive treatments such as cancer therapies prescribed by conventional medicine, as our participants point out: "Homeopathy can support allopathy. Sometimes it will give you strength, strength also to be able to fight the effects of allopathy" (Jacques). The idea that CAMs are able to treat health problems in an in-depth manner while conventional medicine only addresses them superficially is also prevalent; CAMs are thus seen as preventative therapeutic measures to be used after an episode of ill health:

> If I really had a problem, if I have a heart problem and then an actual heart attack I hope somebody sends me straight to the emergency room to get shocked and then to see whether I need a bypass or something surgical like that, typically Western. But the thing is I would say to myself: "Wait a minute … what was that all about, how come it happened to me now? What do I have to change so it doesn't happen again in six months?"
>
> *(Sophie)*

Finally, CAM may replace conventional medicine when the latter turns out to be ineffective, particularly in cases of recurring health problems such as sinusitis, bronchitis, allergies, etc. that are viewed as requiring treatment implying global changes in the person's habits and lifestyle:

> I think medicine these days is very technical. It knows how to give drug treatments. I think that when you have an infection and you have to take antibiotics for a bit it's fine; but when you have more chronic or more tricky problems that can't easily be treated with drugs, such as things linked to posture or to movements, then conventional medicine is often not very effective.
>
> *(Françoise)*

VI Discussion

If the Swiss health insurance system is founded upon market-type economic rationality, our interviewees make choices that are rational to them from the standpoint of their own conceptions of health and illness, a topic well documented in the field of anthropology both in Western (see Schmitz 2006) and in non-Western contexts (see Benoist 1996; Massé and Benoist 2002). They anchor their health practices in moral convictions and in lifestyle choices; when they choose treatment options, economic motivations are secondary, or even non-existent.

In that sense, our interviewees are similar to those studied by Sharma (1992) and by other social scientists working on the topic of integrative medicine, especially in the field of CAM use by cancer patients (see Begot 2010, Broom 2009, Hök *et al.* 2007); cancer patients often combine CAM and conventional medicine for pragmatic, efficacy reasons, because of their own priorities and circumstances, or because of their representations of the characteristics of different types of medicine. Besides, our results are also in keeping with those of Natalier and Willis who, in the context of a study of the reasons for subscribing to a private health insurance contract in Australia, also found that decisions are not strictly governed by cost-benefit analysis – that is, by "the reasoning expected of neo-liberal citizens" (2008: 399).

Our analysis shows that qualities attributed to CAM are far from referring to a form of ideological rupture or of transgression of dominant social norms. CAM actually represents a way to support and further existing norms, putting a high value on nature, individualism and personal responsibility (Coward 1989). As far as a discursive dichotomy between CAM and conventional medicine is concerned, and in terms of a clear preference affirmed for the latter, it does not lead to an actual rejection of conventional medicine; neither does it imply requiring it to change, since patients actually draw from the various approaches by making careful choices. The combined use of different types of medicine, not only by patients but also by some medical practitioners, leads us to believe that several types of medicine cohabit while enjoying varying degrees of power and legitimacy in a context of medical pluralism.

Our interviewees conform with the ideology of individual responsibility in terms of health: they talk about preventing diseases through a healthier lifestyle; when they are sick, they tend to describe themselves as partly responsible for the health problems that affect them and try to find solutions to regain their health. They behave "responsibly" when they venture outside the realm of conventional treatments and pay for their own care, showing that they are active consumers within the health system (Goldner 2002, Hildreth and Elman 2007, Hughes 2004, Kelner and Wellman 1997).

Moreover, as insurance clients, CAM users are ideal customers: not only do they remain faithful to public and private insurance contracts that are not necessarily favourable to them, but they accept the partial reimbursement they receive without complaints. The economic debate concerning coverage for CAM within CHI actually remained on the margins of these patients' preoccupations, since their financial calculations mostly focus on premiums and optional deductibles. Even when they attempt to implement strategies to reduce their health insurance costs, these do not necessarily pay off since CAM users do not master all aspects of the complex field of health insurance. They also sometimes reason and act in ways that no longer correspond to current rules, where reimbursement regulations have changed; they tend to stick with their existing insurer, fearing to lose conditions they consider as relatively favourable, and hope against hope that their loyalty will be rewarded.

Since it makes a strict distinction between coverage by public insurance, reserved to conventional medicine, and coverage by private health insurance for some complementary and alternative modalities, the Swiss health insurance system is the cause of marked discriminations. On the one hand, as long as some CAMs are only covered by private insurance contracts, they are not widely accessible to persons who lack financial resources. We did not attempt, in the context of this study, to meet users who had given up private complementary health insurance coverage for financial reasons, yet discrimination clearly does exist; even when clients have subscribed to some private coverage, conditions for reimbursement are often highly restrictive.[10] Clearly, discriminations stemming from the distinction between conventional medicine and CAM do feature in the calculations subscribers make when choosing their insurance contract. We have seen that some clients "gamble" in order to make sure they continue to afford paying for CAM: they opt for a very high deductible and a lower premium for their basic compulsory contract and hope not to have to use conventional medicine in the coming year. Yet even partial and conditional reimbursement for complementary and alternative treatments is not available to persons who are already in poor health or seen as bad risks by insurers, who systematically turn them down for private insurance; Swiss legislation, which places complementary insurance in the realm of private contract law, allows them to exclude clients for pre-existing conditions or for any other reason.

Finally, we wish to outline some of the limitations of our study and to propose new avenues for further research. Our results can probably be viewed as generalizable to CAM users whose sociological profiles resemble that of our interviewees (middle and upper income women for the most part). For this population, we feel we have identified coherent and credible modes of thought and rationales for action. These motives and behaviour patterns are probably also found, in varying proportion and under various forms, in other social groupings, since they stem from widespread ideologies in contemporary Western contexts. We must, however, also hypothesize that other views and rationales should be found among people who are not endowed with the relative financial security characteristic typical of our interviewees; unlike our interviewees, they may not have the "luxury" of choosing among different types of considerations, particularly putting values and preferences ahead of economic issues. It therefore seems crucial to us to promote future studies to be conducted with persons living in more difficult financial situations and/or suffering from chronic health problems and who consequently have to make difficult choices between equally necessary vital purchases on a daily basis.

VII Conclusion

After having provided a historical context for medical pluralism in Switzerland and shown how it has become a political issue from the 1990s onwards, we have attempted to demonstrate that the Swiss health insurance system, straddling as it does the social security and private insurance realms, is very difficult for clients to decipher. A lack of transparency of the system itself is compounded by modes of thought and behaviour on the part of insurance clients that clearly stray from the principles of economic rationality that underpin current arrangements. These motives and actions are deeply rooted into material and symbolic conditions and are founded upon symmetrically opposed views of conventional medicine and CAM. Previous studies have shown that, just like the discourse of our participants indicated, conventional medicine and CAM are qualified differently: the former being associated with science, danger, symptoms and to the body "surface", to authority and to scientific positivism, while the latter are seen as natural, mild and deep-acting as they call upon the individual expertise of the patient. The very dichotomous construction between CAM and conventional medicine actually represents the poles of an integrated system, symbolically as well as practically. Moreover, within this constructed opposition constituting a system, CAM allows and even supports conventional medicine, regarded as being able to prevent disease, limit conventional medicine's ill effects and optimize healing. Patients choose different therapeutic measures on the basis of their beliefs and the attributes they confer to, respectively, conventional medicine and CAM. Their choices are guided by their view of the health problem at hand rather than by economic reasoning. They do echo dominant views set forth in the public health field in the form of neoliberal promotion of individual responsibility and "empowerment". It is, however, worth noting that such a stance is nowadays, and perhaps paradoxically, very poorly rewarded by current health insurance legislation and coverage.

Notes

1 The analysis we put forward is based upon a study funded by the University of Applied Sciences and Arts Western Switzerland. Main applicant: Hélène Martin; Researcher: Jérôme Debons. We thank Elisabeth Hirsch Dürret for her translating expertise.
2 In Switzerland, stable CAM use, despite changes in coverage, has also been shown in Melchart *et al.* (2005) and Sommer (2000).
3 Document issued by the Federal Department of the Interior and parliamentary debates.
4 http://nfp.snf.ch/F/recherorientee/pnr/acheves/Pages/_xc_nfp34.aspx (accessed on December 6, 2014).

5 www.bag.admin.ch/themen/krankenversicherung/00263/00264/04102/index.html (accessed on November 21, 2012).

6 Official website: www.admin.ch/ch/f/rs/832_10/ (accessed on November 6, 2012).

7 Each CHI insurer must offer lower premiums for minors (under 18). CHI insurers may also propose reduced premiums for young people (19–25).

8 Official website: www.admin.ch/ch/f/rs/c221_229_1.html (accessed on November 6, 2012).

9 This very cheap complementary insurance was proposed to clients only a few weeks after removing the five CAM from the compulsory public health insurance.

10 If this problem is somewhat alleviated when doctors who practise CAM adapt their billing to the personal circumstances of their patients, it is a problem to leave resolving health care inequalities up to individual practitioners.

References

Aakster, C. 1986. Concepts in alternative medicine. *Social Science and Medicine*, 22, 265–273.

Aïach, P., Cèbe, D., Cresson, G. and Phillippe, C. eds. 2001. *Femmes et hommes dans le champ de la santé. Approches sociologiques*. Paris: Editions ENSP.

Allaz, A.-F., Robert, A. and Dayer, P. 1992. Recours aux soins médicaux conventionnels et complémentaires chez les patients souffrant de douleurs chroniques non cancéreuses. *Schweizerische Medizinische Wochenschrift*, 122, 1954–1956.

Astin, J. A. 1998. Why patients use alternative medicine. *JAMA*, 279, 1548–1553.

Astin, J. A. 2000. The characteristics of CAM users: a complex picture. In: Kelner, M., Wellman, B., Pescosolido, B. and Saks, M. eds. *Complementary and alternative medicine: challenge and change*. Amsterdam: Harwood Academic, 101–114.

Baarts, C. and Kryger Pedersen, I. 2009. Derivative benefits: exploring the body through complementary and alternative medicine. *Sociology of Health & Illness*, 31(5), 719–733.

Bakx, K. 1991. The "eclipse" of folk medicine in Western society. *Sociology of Health & Illness*, 13(1), 20–35.

Barcan, R. 2006. Subtle transformations. Imagining the body in alternative health practices. *International Journal of Cultural Studies*, 19(1), 24–44.

Bardin, L. 1991. *L'analyse de contenu*. Paris: PUF.

Baumann, P. H. and Von Berlepsch, K. eds. 2000. *Médecines complémentaires. Point de vue de la science. Rapport du groupe d'experts du PNR 34, Médecines complémentaires, 1992–1998*. Genève: Médecine et Hygiène.

Beaud, S. and Weber, F. 2003. *Guide de l'enquête de terrain*. Paris: La Découverte.

Begot, A.-C. 2010. *Médecines parallèles et cancer: une étude sociologique*. Paris: L'Harmattan.

Benoist, J. 1996. *Soigner au pluriel. Essais sur le pluralisme médical*. Paris: Karthala.

Bizig, B., Wietlisbach, V. and Gutzwiller, F. 2004. Inanspruchnahme von Behandlungen der Komplementärmedizin nach sozio-demographischen, kulturellen und regionalen Indikatoren. In: Bizig, B. and Gutzwiller, F. eds. *Gesundheitswesen Schweiz: gibt es unter-oder Ueberversorgung? Gesamtübersicht*. Zurich/Chur: Rügger, Band 1 und 2, 191–215.

Bolgiani, I., Crivelli, L. and Domenighetti, G. 2006. Le rôle de l'assurance maladie dans la régulation du système de santé en Suisse. *Revue française des affaires sociales*, 2/3, 239–262.

Boltanski, L. 1971. Les usages sociaux du corps. *Annales ESC*, 26, 205–233.

Bonard, E. C. 1993. Médecines parallèles ou complémentaires? *Revue Médicale de la Suisse Romande*, 113, 329–330.

Bourdieu, P. 1977. Remarques provisoires sur la perception sociale du corps. *Actes de la recherche en sciences sociales*, 14, 51–54.

Broom, A. 2009. Intuition, subjectivity, and the bricoleur: cancer patients' accounts of negotiating a plurality of therapeutic options. *Qualitative Health Research*, 19, 1050–1059.

Busato, A., Dönges, A., Herren, S., Widmer, M. and Marian, F. 2006. Health status and health care utilisation of patients in complementary and conventional primary care in Switzerland – an observational study. *Family Practice*, 23, 116–124.

Calmonte, R., Koller, C. and Weiss, W. 2000. *Santé et comportement vis-à-vis de la santé en Suisse 1997: enquête suisse sur la santé*. Neuchâtel: OFS.

Cant, S. and Sharma, U. 1999. *A new medical pluralism? Alternative medicine: doctors, patients and the state*. London: Routledge.

Caspi, O., Koithan, M. and Criddle, M. W. 2004. Alternative medicine or "alternative" patients: a qualitative study of patient-oriented decision-making processes with respect to complementary and alternative medicine. *Medical Decision Making*, 24, 64–79.

Choffat, F. 1986. L'homéopathie vue par un généraliste. *Revue Médicale de Suisse romande*, 106, 131–135.

Cohen, P. and Rossi, I. 2011. Le pluralisme thérapeutique en mouvement. Introduction du numéro thématique "Anthropologie des soins non-conventionnels du cancer". *Anthropologie & Santé*, 2, 2–7.

Coulter, A. 2009. What's happening around the world? In: Edwards A. and Glyn E. eds. *Shared decision-making in health care: achieving evidence-based patient choice*. Oxford: Oxford University Press, 159–163.

Coward, R. 1989. *The whole truth: the myth of alternative health*. London: Faber Stationery Office.

Cuendet, C. 1984. *Importance des médecines parallèles*. Lausanne: Université de Lausanne.

Debons, J. 2011. Aspects de l'institutionnalisation de l'homéopathie en Suisse. *Studia Philosophica (revue annuelle de la Société suisse de philosophie) ["Aux limites de la condition humaine. Santé, justice, pouvoir"]*, 70, 27–33.

Dejours, C. 1999. Violence ou domination. *Travailler*, 3, 11–31.

Despland, B. 2007. Les médecines complémentaires dans le système d'assurance-maladie suisse. In: Durisch Gauthier, N., Rossi, I. and Stolz, J. eds. *Quêtes de santé. Entre soins médicaux et guérisons spirituelles*. Genève: Labor et Fides, 111–121.

Douglas, M. 2001. *De la Souillure*. Paris: la Découverte.

Eisenberg, D. M., Davis, R. B., Ettner, S. L., Appel, S., Wilkey, S., Van Rompay, M. and Kessler, R. C. 1998. Trends in alternative medicine use in the United States, 1990–1997: results of a follow-up national survey. *The Journal of the American Medical Association*, 280, 1569–1575.

Eisenberg, D. M., Kessler, R. C., Foster, C., Norlock, F. E., Calkins, D. R. and Delbanco, T. L. 1993. Unconventional medicine in the United States. Prevalence, costs and patterns of use. *New England Journal of Medicine*, 328(4), 246–252.

Ernst, E. 2000. Prevalence of use of complementary/alternative medicine: a systematic review. *Bulletin of the World Health Organisation*, 78(2), 252–257.

Ernst, E., Willoughby, M. and Weihmayr, T. 1995. Nine possible reasons for choosing complementary medicine. *Perfusion*, 8, 356–359.

Fassin, D. 1997. La santé en souffrance. In: Fassin, D., Morice, A. and Quiminal, C. eds. *Les lois de l'inhospitalité. Les politiques de l'immigration à l'épreuve des sans-papiers*. Paris: La Découverte, 107–123.

Feuardent, R. 1986. Qu'entend-on par médecines alternatives? *Revue Médicale de Suisse romande*, 106, 93–95.

Frei, Walter. 2009. Assureurs-maladie. In: Kocher, G. and Oggier, W. eds. *Système de santé suisse 2007–2009. Survol de la situation actuelle*. Berne: Huber, 83–94.

Fotaki, M., Roland, M., Boyd, A., McDonald, R., Sceaff, R. and Smith, L. 2008. What benefits will choice bring to patients? Literature review and assessment of implications. *Journal of Health Services Research & Policy*, 13(3), 178–184.

Furnham, A. and Vincent, C. 2000. Reasons for using CAM. In: Kelner, M., Wellman, B., Pescosolido, B. and Saks, M. eds. *Complementary and alternative medicine: challenge and change*. Amsterdam: Harwood Academic, 61–78.

Gale, N. K. 2010. From body-talk to body-stories: body work in complementary and alternative medicine. *Sociology of Health & Illness*, 33(2), 237–251.

Goldner, M. 2002. The dynamic interplay between Western medicine and the complementary and alternative medicine movement: how activitsts perceive a range of responses from physicians and hospitals. *Sociology of Health and Illness*, 26(6), 710–736.

Goldner, M. 2004. Consumption as activism. An examination of CAM as part of the consumer movement in health. In: Tovey, P., Easthope, G. and Adams, J. eds. *The mainstream of complementary and alternative medicine*. London/New York: Routledge, 11–24.

Goldstein, S. M. 1999. *Alternative health care. Medicine, miracle or mirage?* Philadelphia: Temple University Press.

Gollac, M. and Volkoff, S. 2002. La mise au travail des stéréotypes de genre. Les conditions de travail des ouvrières. *Travail, genre et sociétés*, (8), 25–53.

Hammer, R. 2010. *Expériences ordinaires de la médecine. Confiances, croyances et critiques profanes*. Zürich: Seismo.

Harley, K., Willis, K., Gabe, J., Short, S., Collyer, F., Natalier, K. and Calnan, M. 2011. Constructing health consumers: private health insurance discourses in Australia and the United Kingdom. *Health Sociology Review*, 20(3), 306–320.

Hildreth, K. D. and Elman, C. 2007. Alternative worldviews and the utilization of conventional and complementary medicine. *Sociological Inquiry*, 77(1), 76–103.

Hök, J., Wachtler, C., Falkenberg, T. and Tishelman, C. 2007. Using narrative analysis to understand the combined use of complementary therapies and bio-medically oriented health care. *Social Science & Medicine*, 65, 1642–1653.

Hughes, K. 2004. Health as individual responsibility. Possibilities and personal struggle. In: Tovey, P., Easthope, G. and Adams, J. eds. *The mainstream of complementary and alternative medicine*. London/New York: Routledge, 25–46.

Inglin, S., Amsler, S., Burton Jeangros, C., Arigoni, F., Pargoux-Vallade, C. and Sappino, A. P. 2008. Evaluation du recours aux médecines complémentaires chez les patients en suivi oncologique. *Revue médicale suisse*, 4, 1264–1269.

Jenny, S., Simon, M. and Meier, B. 2002. Haltung der Bevölkerung gegenüber der Komplementärmedizin. Eine repräsentative Befragung in der Schweiz im Auftrag der Forschungsstiftung Komplementärmedizin. *Schweizerische Zeitschrift für GanzheitsMedizin*, 14(6), 340–347.

Kelner, M. 2000. The therapeutic relationship under fire. In: Kelner, M., Wellman, B., Pescosolido, B. and Saks, M. eds. *Complementary and alternative medicine: challenge and change*. Amsterdam: Harwood Academic, 79–97.

Kelner, M. and Wellman, B. 1997. Health care and consumer choice: medical and alternative therapies. *Social Science and Medicine*, 45(2), 203–212.

Kelner, M., Wellman, B., Pescosolido, B. and Saks, M. eds. 2000. *Complementary and alternative medicine: challenge and change*. Amsterdam: Harwood Academic.

Kersnik, J. 2000. Predictive characteristics of users of alternative medicine. *Schweizerische Medizinische Wochenschrift*, 130, 390–394.

Kessler, D., Hatz, C. and Schär, A. 1999. Parallel use of medical services? Patterns of using complementary medicine and biomedecine. *Schweizerische Rundschau für Medizin (PRAXIS)*, 88, 113–119.

Kranz, R. and Rosenmund, A. 1998. Über die motivation zur Verwendung komplementärmedizinischer Heilmethoden. *Schweizerische Medizinische Wochenschrift*, 128, 616–622.

Marcellini, A., Turpin, J. P., Rolland, Y. and Ruffie, S. 2000. Itinéraires thérapeutiques dans la société contemporaine: le recours aux thérapies alternatives, une éducation à un autre corps? *Corps et Culture* [online], 5, http://corpsetculture.revues.org/710 (accessed December 7, 2014).

Martin, H. 2009. Le marché parodié? Regard sur les dispositifs de l'assurance-chômage et de l'aide sociale publique. In: Donzé, P.-Y. and Fior, M. eds. *Transitions historiques et construction des marchés*. Neuchâtel: Editons Alhil, Presses universitaires suisses, 111–132.

Martin, H. 2011. Écouter son corps. *Studia Philosophica (revue annuelle de la Société suisse de philosophie) ["Aux limites de la condition humaine. Santé, justice, pouvoir"]*, 70, 69–74.

Martin, H. and Debons, J. 2010. Virevoltes de l'assurance maladie, constance des pratiques de soins des assuré·e·s. *Tsantsa. Revue suisse d'ethnologie*, 15, 11–16.

Martin, H. and Debons, J. 2014. *Le soin et la politique. Cinq médecines non conventionnelles et la LaMal.* Lausanne: Les cahiers de l'EESP.

Massé, R. and Benoist, J. eds. 2002. *Convocations thérapeutiques du sacré*. Paris, Karthala.

McClean, S. 2005. "The illness is part of the person": discourses of blame, individual responsibility and individuation at a centre for spiritual healing in the north of England. *Sociological of Health and Illness*, 27(5), 628–648.

McKee, J. 1988. Holistic health and the critique of Western medicine. *Social Science and Medicine*, 26, 775–785.

Meier, V. and Grau, P. 1992. Alternativmedizin – ihre Denkweisen und AnwenderInnen. *Perspektiven*, 3.

Melchart, D., Mitscherlich, F., Amiet, M., Eichenberger, R. and Koch, P. 2005. *PEK – Programm für Komplementärmedizin. Schlussbericht.* Berne: OFS.

Messerli-Rohrbach, V. and Schär, A. 1999a. Beweggründe für die Wahl von Komplementär- und Schulmedizin. Patientenverhalten in einem pluralistischen Medizinsystem. *Forschende Komplementärmedizin*, Suppl. 1, 10–13.

Messerli-Rohrbach, V. and Schär, A. 1999b. Komplementär- und Schulmedizin: Vorurteile sowie Ansprüche an die Natur- bzw. die Hausärztin. *Schweizerische Medizinische Wochenschrift*, Suppl. 129, 1535–1544.

Messing, K. 1999. *Comprendre le travail des femmes pour le transformer.* Bruxelles: Institut syndical européen pour la recherche, la formation et la santé-sécurité.

Natalier, K. and Willis, K. 2008. Taking responsability or averting risk? A socio-culutral approach to risk and trust in private health insurance decisions. *Health, Risk & Society*, 10(4), 399–411.

O'Connor, B. B. 2000. The conceptions of the body in complementary and alternative medicine. In: Kelner, M., Wellman, B., Pescosolido, B. and Saks, M. eds. *Complementary and alternative medicine: challenge and change*. Amsterdam: Harwood Academic, 27–39.

Olivier de Sardan, J.-P. 2008. *La rigueur du qualitatif. Les contraintes empiriques de l'interprétation socioanthropologique*. Louvains-La-Neuve: Bruylant-Academia.

Rossi, I. 1994. Corps-sujet et miroirs culturels. Santé et maladie: une diagonale anthropologique. *Ethnologica Helvetica*, 17/18, 47–64.

Saks, M., 2003. *Orthodox and alternative medecine: politics, professionalization and health care*. London: SAGE Publications Ltd.

Schär, A., Messerli-Rohrbach, V. and Schubarth, P. 1994. Schulmedizin oder Komplementärmedizin: nach welchen Kriterien entscheiden sich die Patientinnen une Patienten? *Schweizerische Medizinische Wochenschrift*, Suppl. 62, 18–27.

Scheder, P.-A. 1986. Le recours aux médecines alternatives en Suisse. Résultats de recherches récentes. *Revue Médicale de Suisse romande*, 106, 97–104.

Schmitz, O. ed. 2006. *Les médecines en parallèle. Multiplicité des recours au soin en Occident*. Paris: Karthala.

Sharma, U. 1992. *Complementary medicine today: practitioners and patients*. London/New York: Routledge.

Sointu, E. 2006. The search for wellbeing in alternative and complementary health practices. *Sociology of Health & Illness*, 28(3), 330–349.

Sommer, J. 2000. Analyse de l'incidence économique de l'offre de prestations thérapeutiques complémentaires par les caisses-maladies. In: Baumann, P. H. and Von Berlepsch, K. eds. *Médecines complémentaires. Point de vue de la science. Rapport du groupe d'experts du PNR 34, Médecines complémentaires, 1992–1998*. Genève: Médecine et Hygiène, 17–21.

Sommer, J., Bürgi, M. and Theiss, R. 1996. *Alternative Heilmethoden, Verbreitungsmuster in der Schweiz*. Chur: Rüegger.

Spuhler, T., Koller, C., Herren, B. and Calmonte, R. 1998. *Santé et comportement vis-à-vis de la santé en Suisse: enquête suisse sur la santé. Résultats détaillés de la première enquête suisse sur la santé 1992/93*. Neuchâtel: OFS.

Tabin, J.-P., Probst, I. and Waardenburg, G. 2008. Accidents du travail: la régularité de l'improbable. *Interrogations: revue pluridisciplinaire de l'homme et de la société*, 6, 131–159.

Tovey, P., Easthope, G. and Adams, J. eds. 2004. *The mainstream of complementary and alternative medicine*. London/New York: Routledge.

Valli, M., Martin, H. and Hertz, E. 2002. Le "feeling" des agents de l'État providence. *Ethnologie française*, 2, 221–231.

Wahlberg, A. 2007. A quackery with a difference – new medical pluralism and the problem of "dangerous practitioners" in the United Kingdom. *Social Science and Medicine*, 65, 2307–2316.

Wapf, V. and Busato, A. 2007. Patient's motives for choosing a physician: comparison between conventional and complementary medicine in Swiss primary care. *BMC Complementary and Alternative Medicine*, 7, 7–41.

Williams, S. and Calnan, M. 1996. The "limits" of medicalization? Modern medicine and the lay populace on "late" modernity. *Social Science and Medecine*, 42, 1609–1620.

18

PATIENT CHOICE AND PROFESSIONAL REGULATION

How patients choose CAM practitioners

Felicity L. Bishop

I Introduction

Policy makers in the UK and elsewhere emphasise the importance of patient choice in health care. The King's Fund has identified four particular health care choices in which patients can be involved: choice of provider, appointment, treatment, and individual health professional (Dixon *et al.*, 2010). Within mainstream settings, initiatives such as "Choose and Book" and "NHS Choices" have been developed to empower and facilitate patients to make these choices. In complementary and alternative medicine (CAM) settings, patient choice is the norm: in the UK, most CAM is provided and accessed in the private sector (Thomas, Nicholl, & Coleman, 2001) where patients typically experience greater choice and control than in the public sector (Bishop, Barlow, Coghlan, Lee, & Lewith, 2011). This chapter explores patients' perspectives on one particular health care choice in CAM: the choice of individual CAM practitioner. After a brief introduction, I will focus on a series of three mixed methods studies in which my team investigated how UK patients choose acupuncturists (Bishop, Massey, Yardley, & Lewith, 2011), osteopaths (Bishop, Bradbury, Jeludin, Massey, & Lewith, 2012), and chiropractors (Bishop, Smith, & Lewith, 2013). I will use these studies to illustrate how patients choose CAM practitioners, the factors that they take into account, and the sources they consult. Finally, I will consider the implications of these findings for professional and regulatory bodies.

II Patient choices in CAM

A substantial proportion of the general public in the UK and elsewhere use CAM (Thomas *et al.*, 2001; Harris, Cooper, Relton, & Thomas, 2012). Their reasons for choosing CAM are varied and can be conceptualised using existing theoretical frameworks. According to Anderson's socio-behavioural model, we can see CAM use as a consequence of certain predisposing factors, enabling resources, and perceived medical need (Andersen & Newman, 1973; Andersen, 1995). While reasons for using and pathways into CAM can differ for different CAM modalities, a number of studies have now found evidence supporting the application of the socio-behavioural model to CAM use (Upchurch *et al.*, 2008; Kelner & Wellman, 1997; Sirois & Gick, 2002; Bishop, Lim, Leydon, & Lewith, 2009; Lorenc, Ilan-Clarke, Robinson, & Blair,

2009; Robinson, Lorenc, & Blair, 2009). Specific predisposing factors associated with CAM use include demographic factors (e.g. female, middle-aged; Bishop & Lewith, 2010) and psychological factors (e.g. holding pro-CAM beliefs and values; Furnham & Kirkaldy, 1996; Sirois & Gick, 2002; Bishop, Yardley, & Lewith, 2007). Enabling resources include insurance, income and education, local availability and geographies of CAM, and knowing others who use CAM (Astin, 1998; Andrews, 2003). In terms of perceived need, patients often turn to CAM when they have more than one health problem, when they are dissatisfied with side-effects or lack of effect from conventional medicine, or because they seek a positive sense of wellness which is not emphasised in conventional medicine (Bishop & Lewith, 2010). Inductively derived qualitative analyses emphasise the dynamic nature of decisions to use CAM and demonstrate how patients revisit and review decisions iteratively over time as they gain experience of treatment (Bishop, Yardley, & Lewith, 2010; Balneaves, Bottorff, Hislop, & Herbert, 2006; Balneaves, Truant, Kelly, Verhoef, & Davison, 2007).

Studies have also investigated the information or evidence that patients seek out to inform their decisions about CAM. Unlike health care providers, patients are not always particularly interested in high-quality scientific evidence about the specific efficacy of CAM therapies, they may not have the necessary scientific literacy to understand such evidence, and they often have priorities that differ from those of their doctors (Tasaki, Maskarinec, Shumay, Tatsumura, & Kakai, 2002; Verhoef, Mulkins, Carlson, Hilsden, & Kania, 2007; Evans et al., 2007a). Instead of abstract "facts" about CAM, patients seem to value more concrete experiential evidence. For example, Danish users of acupuncture and reflexology valued the experiential evidence that comes from personal experience of a hands-on therapy and see the expertise of such practitioners as embodied, rather than based in abstract knowledge (Pedersen & Baarts, 2010). As a precursor to direct personal experience, vicarious experiences are valued and trusted – that is, advice, anecdotes, "lay" referrals and recommendations from patients' social networks (Kelner & Wellman, 1997; Verhoef et al., 2007; Evans et al., 2007a). Patients also seek out information online, in books, and in other media, but these sources may be less ubiquitous than the experiences and views of trusted co-workers, acquaintances, friends, and family members (Kelner & Wellman, 1997). Health care professionals including pharmacists, doctors, and nurses, can have a role in informing decisions to try CAM (Verhoef et al., 2007) but, at least in the UK, referrals from conventional medicine practitioners remain rare and very much patient-driven (Brien, Howells, Leydon, & Lewith, 2008).

The patient–practitioner relationship appears to have a very important role throughout CAM choices. In an age of increasingly technical specialist interventions in conventional medicine, CAM is valued as offering a more personal form of healing involving a partnership between therapist and patient. In particular, there is evidence that CAM patients value empathic therapeutic relationships which make them feel cared for and understood by their CAM practitioner; new ways of making sense of their illness that their CAM practitioners discuss with them; and the way in which CAM practitioners work collaboratively with patients, sharing control and decision-making about treatments (Canales & Geller, 2003; Luff & Thomas, 2000; Paterson & Britten, 2004; Cartwright & Torr, 2005). CAM practitioners also have an influential role in patients' decisions to keep attending therapy (Bishop, Yardley, & Lewith, 2008b; Bishop et al., 2010). Furthermore, it has been suggested that CAM therapies are particularly good at providing therapeutic relationships which a) have a large direct effect on patients' health outcomes (Kaptchuk, 2002) and/or b) help to maximise the effectiveness of the therapy itself (Paterson & Dieppe, 2005). Enhanced therapeutic relationships have indeed been shown to predict clinical outcomes in CAM (Kaptchuk et al., 2008; Brien, Lachance, Prescott, McDermott, & Lewith, 2011). The choice of individual CAM practitioner thus forms the start of a therapeutic relationship that will probably be characterised by continued patient involvement in decision-making and will likely have a powerful influence on patient satisfaction and health outcomes.

Despite the importance of the patient–practitioner relationship in CAM, few studies have explored how patients select an individual CAM practitioner to consult. Consistent with the literature on lay referral networks in general (Young, 2004), there is evidence that CAM users value personal recommendations/referrals from trusted friends and family members when choosing an individual practitioner (Kelner & Wellman, 1997; Eng et al., 2003; Balneaves et al., 2007; Evans et al., 2007a; Caspi, Koithan, & Criddle, 2004). An early Canadian study provides a rare detailed analysis of how patients choose individual practitioners, having asked CAM users for the primary reason why they chose a specific practitioner (Kelner & Wellman, 1997). The most popular reason by far (endorsed by 50 per cent of 240 participants) was having a personal referral from a social contact; Kelner and Wellman interpreted these personal referrals as serving both a practical function of alerting patients to the existence of a local practitioner and a more psychological function of validating patients' choices. Other common reasons for choosing a practitioner were reputation (endorsed by 25 per cent, and based on public resources such as alternative publications) and referrals from alternative medicine practitioners (12 per cent). Very few patients based their choice of practitioner primarily on convenience (5 per cent) or referrals from a GP (4 per cent). More recently, two studies have examined the impact of traditional Korean medicine doctors' attire and appearance on patients' preferences. In one, patients' preferences for different doctors' faces were not associated with perceptions of the doctor's levels of empathy (Lee et al., 2012); in the other, patients preferred the doctor to be dressed in a white coat or traditional dress (compared to suit or casual clothes), perceiving him to be more empathic and more competent (Chung et al., 2012).

To summarise, we have an increasingly good understanding of how and why patients make decisions to use CAM. However, few studies have focused on how patients choose an individual CAM practitioner to consult. We therefore conducted three studies in the UK to address this gap, exploring how patients choose acupuncturists, osteopaths, and chiropractors.

III How patients choose acupuncturists, osteopaths, and chiropractors

1 Acupuncture, chiropractic, and osteopathy

In the UK, acupuncture, chiropractic, and osteopathy are all considered major forms of CAM. For example, they were all listed as professionally organised alternative therapies in the House of Lords report on CAM (House of Lords, 2000). Acupuncture involves the insertion of fine needles into particular points on the body and can be practised within diverse theoretical frameworks including traditional Chinese medicine and Western medicine (Vickers & Zollman, 1999). Osteopathy is a holistic, patient-centred manipulative therapy with an emphasis on preventative care (Licciardone, 2004; Howel, 1999; Licciardone, Brimhall, & King, 2005). Chiropractic is concerned with the diagnosis, manual treatment, and prevention of musculoskeletal disorders (World Federation of Chiropractic, 1999). All three are particularly popular among patients with musculoskeletal problems such as back pain (Ong, Doll, Bodeker, & Stewart-Brown, 2004; Xue et al., 2008; Foltz et al., 2005; MacPherson, Sinclair-Lian, & Thomas, 2006).

All three therapies are predominantly provided in the private sector, where patients will typically pay out-of-pocket for treatment and some will have private insurance that covers all or part of the cost (Peters, Davies, & Pietroni, 1994; General Osteopathic Council, 2011; MacPherson et al., 2006; General Chiropractic Council, 2004). All three therapies also have some presence in the public sector National Health Service (NHS), and are recommended in national frameworks and guidelines (Department of Health, 2006; Savigny *et al.*, 2009). This is important for widening access as some patients cannot afford private sector CAM therapy (Cartwright, 2007), some see the NHS as a safe environment to try CAM (Shaw, Thompson, & Sharp, 2006; Evans *et al.*, 2007b, 2007a), and some use it as a stepping-stone to subsequent use in the private sector (Bishop, Barlow *et al.*, 2011). Local availability of services is, however, highly dependent on local commissioning decisions.

There are important differences in regulation between acupuncture, osteopathy, and chiropractic. Acupuncture is practised by different professionals, including acupuncturists, traditional Chinese medicine doctors, Western medicine doctors (GPs, orthopaedic specialists), nurses, and physiotherapists (Bishop, Zaman, & Lewith, 2011). Some of these groups are currently subject to statutory regulation while others are not. For example, GPs, nurses, and physiotherapists are regulated (by the General Medical Council, the Nursing and Midwifery Council, and the Health and Care Profession Council) and often when they use acupuncture they do so to supplement other practices. Acupuncturists who do not have Western medicine qualifications are not currently regulated by statute but they do have a voluntary regulation system and are working towards statutory regulation (Walker & Budd, 2002; Department of Health, 2004). Overall this creates a potentially confusing situation for patients seeking acupuncture. Not only can patients choose between acupuncturists with very different backgrounds but also they have very many individual practitioners to choose from: more than 10,000 UK registered acupuncturists provided over three million treatments in 1998 (Thomas *et al.*, 2001). Perhaps most important, however, is that the lack of statutory regulation means that at the moment in the UK anyone can, legally, call themselves an acupuncturist. The situation for patients choosing an osteopath or chiropractor is somewhat more straight-forward as osteopaths and chiropractors are already subject to statutory regulation and have been since 1993 (osteopathy) and 1994 (chiropractic) after lengthy endeavours to achieve this status (Walker & Budd, 2002). Other practitioners (e.g. physiotherapists) might occasionally incorporate osteopathic or chiropractic techniques into their practice, but this is less pronounced than it is for acupuncture and such practitioners are not allowed by law to call themselves osteopaths or chiropractors (unless they are also registered with the General Osteopathic Council or the General Chiropractic Council).

2 Methods

In each of the three studies that I draw on in this chapter, we used mixed methods to investigate how UK patients choose acupuncturists (Bishop, Massey *et al.*, 2011), osteopaths (Bishop *et al.*, 2012), and chiropractors (Bishop *et al.*, 2013). In brief, all three studies involved a quantitative component and a qualitative component. The quantitative components were designed to test which factors influence people's preferences for individual practitioners. The qualitative components were designed to explore how patients go about choosing an individual CAM practitioner to consult.

The quantitative component of all three studies comprised a questionnaire which required participants to imagine they wanted to consult a new CAM practitioner. Box 18.1 shows the basic scenario that was adapted for use in each study. Following the scenario, patients were shown descriptions of a series of fictional CAM practitioners and were asked to rate them. These fictional practitioners' characteristics were manipulated to investigate their impact on patients' preferences. Characteristics were chosen for manipulation based partly on a review of patient choices in CAM and partly on the extensive literature on patients' preferences for GPs and other conventional medicine practitioners (for example, see: Kerssens, Bensing, & Andela, 1997; Jung,

---

Box 18.1 Fictional scenario adapted for use in each study

Imagine that you have been suffering back pain recently. Despite several visits to your general practitioner, there seems to be no conventional treatment that works for you. Both your doctor and a good friend recommend trying [therapy]. You decide to have [therapy].

Your doctor recommends [a/two] local [therapy] centre[s]. Eight [therapists] work at the centre[s]. Each [therapist] is British, and was born and raised in the United Kingdom. They all speak English as their first language.

On the following page are the names of all eight [therapists]. They are all registered members of the [professional body]. All practitioner members of [professional body] are fully qualified and observe strict Codes of Ethics and Practice.

Box 18.2 Descriptions of fictional osteopaths rated by participants

The Hampshire NHS Osteopathic Centre

- All osteopaths are members of the General Osteopathic Council.
- All osteopaths are fully qualified in osteopathy.
- Appointments available from 7 a.m. to 9 p.m.
- Appointments are free.

	1 Never	2	3	4	5	6	7	8	9	10 Certainly
DR GEORGE SHEPHERD. Also medically trained as a doctor. How likely are you to book Dr Shepherd?	O	O	O	O	O	O	O	O	O	O
MS JULIA BROWN. How likely are you to book Ms Brown?	O	O	O	O	O	O	O	O	O	O
MR ALAN HARPER. How likely are you to book Mr Harper?	O	O	O	O	O	O	O	O	O	O
DR KATIE DAVIES. Also medically trained as a doctor. How likely are you to book Dr Davies?	O	O	O	O	O	O	O	O	O	O

The Elite Osteopathic Centre of Hampshire

- All osteopaths are members of the General Osteopathic Council.
- All osteopaths are fully qualified in osteopathy.
- Appointments available from 7 a.m. to 9 p.m.
- Appointments cost £40.

	1 Never	2	3	4	5	6	7	8	9	10 Certainly
MS OLIVIA JONES. How likely are you to book Ms Jones?	O	O	O	O	O	O	O	O	O	O
DR DANIEL WILLIAMS. Also medically trained as a doctor. How likely are you to book Dr Williams?	O	O	O	O	O	O	O	O	O	O
DR SAMANTHA COLE. Also medically trained as a doctor. How likely are you to book Dr Cole?	O	O	O	O	O	O	O	O	O	O
MR ROBERT FIELD. How likely are you to book Mr Field?	O	O	O	O	O	O	O	O	O	O

Baerveldt, Olesen, Grol, & Wensing, 2003; Fang, McCarthy, & Singer, 2004). In the acupuncture study, the fictional CAM practitioners varied systematically in terms of gender (male/female), qualifications (biomedical/not) and where they had trained (UK/China). Each participant rated their likelihood of consulting eight different fictional acupuncturists representing every combination of these factors (e.g. male, biomedically qualified, trained in the UK). In the osteopathy study, the fictional osteopaths varied systematically in terms of gender (male/female), health care sector (NHS/private sector) and qualifications (biomedical/not). In the chiropractic study, the fictional chiropractors systematically varied in terms of gender (male/female) and reputation (for good technical skills/for good interpersonal skills).[1] As an illustration, Box 18.2 shows the fictional therapists that participants rated in the osteopathy study. Mixed ANOVAs were used to test the effect of each factor on participants' preferences (the within-subjects factors were those which were varied in the descriptions of the fictional therapists; the between-subjects factor was the participant's gender).

The qualitative component of each study varied slightly. In the acupuncture and osteopathy studies, semi-structured interviews were analysed that had been conducted as part of broader qualitative studies of patients' experiences of acupuncture and osteopathy. Inductive and deductive thematic analyses (Braun & Clarke, 2006) focused on the processes involved in choosing an individual practitioner. In the chiropractic study, qualitative data were collected through open-ended questions on the questionnaire and qualitative content analysis was carried out (Joffe & Yardley, 2004).

Table 18.1 Participants in the studies

	Quantitative component	Qualitative component
Acupuncture	73 members of the general public recruited from the university and a local church (mean age = 44; 59% female).	Purposive maximum-variation sample of 35 acupuncture patients (median age = 53; 83% female).
Osteopathy	176 former or current patients at a large CAM clinic (mean age = 53; 84% female).	Purposive maximum-variation sample of 19 osteopathy patients (median age = 41; 63% female).
Chiropractic	Random sample of 653 members of the general public (mean age = 51; 64% female).	

Participants in the studies were recruited from the general public and through CAM clinics. Table 18.1 describes the people who took part in each component of each study.

3 Results: the influence of CAM practitioners' personal and professional characteristics on patients' preferences

The influence of practitioner gender on patients' preferences was tested in all three studies, and the results showed small but significant preferences for female CAM practitioners. Participants rated themselves as both more likely to consult female than male acupuncturists and more likely to consult female than male chiropractors. This preference for female practitioners seemed to be strongest among female patients (in what is known as a gender-concordance effect): in the chiropractic study, the preference for female practitioners was statistically most pronounced for female respondents while in the acupuncture study the majority of participants were female. In comparison, gender did not have an effect on participants' preferences for osteopaths.

Practitioners' qualifications influenced people's preferences for acupuncturists and osteopaths. Across both studies, people rated themselves as more likely to consult those practitioners described as having additional qualifications in biomedicine than those described as having qualifications in acupuncture or osteopathy only.

The influence of other practitioner characteristics was tested in only one study each. The practitioner's training location (in China or in the UK) had no effect on participants' preferences for acupuncturists. The health care sector (private, fee-charging clinic or public, free clinic) had no effect on participants' preferences for osteopaths. Finally, the practitioner's reputation (as being particularly good at technical or interpersonal aspects of care) had a very strong effect on participants' preferences for chiropractors. Participants rated themselves as more likely to consult chiropractors with a reputation for excellent technical skills than to consult those with a reputation for excellent interpersonal skills.

Overall then, when patients are forced to imagine that they have a personal recommendation for a particular therapy but *not* for a specific therapist it seems that they are influenced by gender (with female patients showing a slight preference for female practitioners), qualifications (preferring practitioners with additional biomedical qualifications) and reputation (preferring technical excellence to excellence in interpersonal skills). A female gender-concordance effect is also found in studies of conventional medicine and appears to be a relatively robust, if ultimately small, effect (Kerssens *et al.*, 1997; Fang *et al.*, 2004). Preferences for CAM practitioners with additional biomedical qualifications and reputed technical skills do not seem to have been reported (or indeed tested for) in other samples. It may be that, given no other differences between them, a practitioner with an additional qualification (of any sort) will be preferred to one without that qualification. The preference for technical over interpersonal skills may be specific to chiropractic or may generalise to forms of CAM which are seen as technical specialties (Bishop, Yardley, & Lewith, 2008a). The next section provides additional insight into why these factors are relevant and how patients go about choosing CAM practitioners.

4 Results: how patients choose CAM practitioners

Table 18.2 presents a synthesis of the original themes identified in the qualitative analyses from the three studies. As can be seen, there is a good deal of consistency across the studies and patients appear to go through similar processes and value similar sources of evidence when choosing acupuncturists, osteopaths, and chiropractors. Throughout the data there was evidence that patients do orient to the challenges of choosing an individual CAM practitioner. However, this only emerged as an explicit theme in the acupuncture study, where participants reflected that "you have to be very careful who you go to" and clearly communicated a sense of vulnerability and risk involved in selecting a practitioner:

> Where do you go to find out where you should go? Ah, yeah, you go on the web and, you know, you look them all up and you find ones in your area and you look at their qualifications and all this sort of thing. And it's exactly the same with people who do sports massages and everything else. You don't know whether you're safe in their hands.

Table 18.2 Themes identified in the qualitative analyses

Synthesis	Acupuncture	Osteopathy	Chiropractic*
Importance of the decision	The importance of the decision		
Wanting a qualified, skilled practitioner	Relevant characteristics – technical competence	An osteopath's qualifications and skills; first impressions and loyalty – perceived competence; first impressions and loyalty – immediate treatment effect	
Wanting a personable, trustworthy practitioner	Relevant characteristics – personal attributes	First impressions and loyalty – interpersonal fit	Communication
Personal recommendations and anticipated trust	How participants found acupuncturists – direct personal recommendations	Personal recommendations and anticipated trust	Personal recommendations
Practicalities	How participants found acupuncturists – other means	Health care sector and practicalities	Practicalities
Demographic characteristics		Gender	Ethnicity

Note

* Qualitative content analysis of responses to open-ended questionnaire items conducted for this chapter, not included in original publication.

Those few acupuncture patients who did not orient to the risks of finding a practitioner tried acupuncture within the context of an existing therapeutic relationship – for example, during a course of physiotherapy when acupuncture was offered and introduced as an adjunctive modality.

The importance of lay referral networks for guiding patient choice of CAM practitioner was striking throughout the data, and can be conceptualised more broadly in terms of personal recommendations and anticipated trust. Indeed, personal recommendations seemed to be by far the most highly valued source of information to patients seeking an individual practitioner. Personal recommendations were so highly valued by some participants that a number of questionnaires were returned without being completed because participants were unwilling to enter into the scenario in which their friend or doctor was unable to recommend a specific individual practitioner. A typical example is this comment written on one of the questionnaires from the osteopathy study: "I would not see any complementary practitioner unless via personal recommendation, no matter whether they are NHS/private/medical doctor/male or female." Having a personal recommendation from a trusted friend, family member, or even a friend-of-a-friend helped participants to have confidence in a practitioner before meeting them. As one participant in the acupuncture study explained, "It's nice to know other people have tried and tested a person. You feel a little more confident about it then, especially if it's a new treatment that you've never had before." Personal recommendations helped participants to trust a practitioner would be suitably skilled, would not take advantage of them (of particular concern in the private sector), and would probably not cause them harm (through poor application of what are all physical, hands-on treatments). Interestingly, recommendations from biomedical doctors were not universally wanted or trusted, with some participants expressing concern that doctors would receive financial "kick backs" for referrals to private sector CAM practitioners. Ultimately, patients valued personal recommendations from "satisfied customers", people who had been helped by the practitioner in the past: "Other people's recommendations [are important] based on their experiences and treatments and obviously the final outcome."

In the absence of personal recommendations, the clinic at which a practitioner worked provided some patients with a sense of reassurance and helped them to have some confidence and anticipated trust in an individual practitioner. For some patients, the NHS as a public institution was able to fulfil this function: patients felt that practitioners working in the NHS would be subject to strict standards and would therefore be suitably qualified to provide a therapy safely. For others, a private sector CAM clinic provided similar reassurance. For example, one participant in the acupuncture study explained how she felt safe choosing to consult the acupuncturist at a particular clinic because "I trusted her [the clinic owner] sufficiently to know that she wouldn't have anybody on the premises that was not properly qualified." Professional regulatory bodies were not spontaneously mentioned as providing this kind of safeguarding.

Patients talked about considering two sets of characteristics of a potential practitioner: they wanted a qualified technically skilful practitioner (who would help them to get better and not cause more damage or pain) and a personable practitioner (with whom they felt comfortable, could talk openly with, and could trust). Different indicators were used by different patients to try to ascertain whether a practitioner would be technically skilful or not. Participants rarely talked explicitly about considering an osteopath's qualifications before booking an appointment and instead talked in more general terms about wanting a practitioner who "knows what they are doing". In the acupuncture study, patients were more likely to talk about wanting to know about an acupuncturist's qualifications and training. Some concerns were based on awareness that biomedical doctors can practice acupuncture with very little training:

I knew of two people and they just go to their doctors who've been on a short course, enough to be able to push a needle into you. But do they know, learn, enough on a short course? I rather compare them with [my acupuncturist] who did seven years' training.

Other concerns were based on a belief that biomedical qualifications in addition to acupuncture training can provide a "safety net" allowing practitioners to provide more comprehensive care and diagnostic skills:

I was particularly pleased that [acupuncturist] is dual qualified. As with a number of other alternative treatments, I do like the person to have a strong background in conventional Western medicine in case there's something there that they were to spot which wears the Western hat.

Consistent with the quantitative findings, some participants valued technical skills above all else and were not particularly interested in trying to find a practitioner who they would be able to talk to easily or develop a good therapeutic relationship with. For example, in the chiropractic study, one participant commented that they did not "want a friend" for a chiropractor. However, others felt it was vital that a practitioner would listen to them carefully, would respect them as people (and not just as "bad backs", for example), would put them at ease, and would make them feel comfortable both physically and emotionally (for example, in relation to disrobing for treatments). As one participant in the acupuncture study explained, interpersonal "soft" skills can be vital elements of health care:

They've all got the qualifications, but like the medics it still doesn't make them a good doctor. And you know if you go to a multi-doctor practice that you'll always say, oh there's no way even if I'm dying I'm going to see him.

While participants found it difficult to predict whether they would get on with a practitioner before consulting them for the first time, first impressions were seen as sufficient to make this judgement. One participant in the osteopathy study described this succinctly: "I saw one osteopath that I didn't feel I clicked with, didn't get on particularly well with. I didn't go back." Some patients mentioned (and valued) very early opportunities to interact with a practitioner – for example, on the telephone or via email – which helped to create positive first impressions even before a first consultation.

In all three studies, practicalities and personal demographic characteristics of practitioners appeared to be less important to patients than the other factors already discussed. Some patients talked about preferring to see a practitioner based in the NHS, while others preferred to choose a practitioner based in the private sector. Often this was based purely on financial considerations but some participants described being willing to "go private" in order to avoid waiting lists in the NHS, to get more choice of appointment times, or as a means of accessing what was perceived to be better quality treatment: "I am prepared to pay for first class [osteopathy] treatments." Some patients placed more emphasis on practical or structural issues such as a clinic's location, parking, financial cost, opening hours, and speed of getting appointments. These factors seemed to be more important when participants did not have personal recommendations to guide them and instead relied on the limited information available in directories and other similar sources: "I went onto the 'net and the British Acupuncture Society or whatever it was, and I just chose somebody really, looking at the different profiles, but somebody who was near to me." Patients very rarely mentioned taking into account or even considering a practitioner's gender, age, or ethnicity.

The relative importance of different types of factors is nicely illustrated by data from the chiropractic study, in which participants were given a checklist and ticked all items on it that they felt were important in choosing a practitioner. The three most commonly endorsed items related to technical skills (experience, endorsed by 85 per cent of participants; good technical skills, 85 per cent; qualifications, 77 per cent); similar to the main quantitative analysis from this study, participants did not value interpersonal skills as highly, with only 34 per cent endorsing good listening skills as important when choosing a chiropractor. Waiting times were important (endorsed by 76 per cent), followed by safety record (67 per cent), and convenient appointment times (65 per cent). A smaller majority of participants agreed that they considered travel issues to be important (ease of travel to clinic, 57 per cent; distance to clinic, 54 per cent). Finally, a practitioner's demographic characteristics were only endorsed as important by a small minority of participants (age, 10 per cent; ethnicity, 7 per cent; gender, 6 per cent). Similar priorities are found in the context of conventional primary care, where being able to choose an individual doctor is more important to patients than practical factors such as appointment time and speed of access (Gerard, Salisbury, Street, Pope, & Baxter, 2008; Rubin, Bate, George, Shackley, & Hall, 2006).

IV Patient choice and professional and regulatory bodies

Personal recommendations are highly valued by patients choosing acupuncturists, osteopaths, and chiropractors. Personal recommendations from trusted individuals help people to have confidence in a practitioner's technical skills and to anticipate trusting them; institutions can have a similar but apparently less powerful effect. These findings confirm and extend previous observations about the role of lay referral networks in CAM use (Kelner & Wellman, 1997; Eng *et al.*, 2003; Balneaves *et al.*, 2007; Evans *et al.*, 2007a; Caspi *et al.*, 2004). In the absence of personal recommendations, it seems that technical skills are the most important consideration to most patients but that some also highly value a practitioner's interpersonal skills. While patients do consider a future therapeutic relationship when selecting a CAM practitioner, final judgements about the interpersonal aspects of care appear to be made after a first consultation rather than before: some participants described deciding not to return to a practitioner who made a poor first impression and whom they did not "get on with" on an interpersonal level at a first meeting. Patients will also take into account practicalities around clinic location and appointments, and the demographic characteristics of practitioners, but such considerations are rarely of prime importance.

So how might professional and regulatory bodies fit into this picture? On one level, patients value technical and interpersonal skills. It is therefore important for professional and regulatory bodies to continue to develop, monitor, and police minimum standards around practitioner's technical skills (encompassing effectiveness and safety) and interpersonal skills (encompassing communication skills and ability to create therapeutic relationships). At a more fine-grained level, one can think about how professional and regulatory bodies might contribute to the process of choosing an individual CAM practitioner.

In relation to patients' interest in a practitioner's technical skills, professional bodies could usefully provide patients with the necessary frameworks to judge a practitioner's qualifications. They could explain the training that is required of their members and the meaning of supplementary or advanced specialist qualifications in very clear, accessible terms. This task is comparatively straightforward for osteopaths and chiropractors, with their single dedicated professional bodies who can provide authoritative educational materials for patients to enable them to make informed decisions. However, the situation is currently more confusing for patients seeking an acupuncturist; they can consult a number of organisations all claiming to regulate the practice of acupuncture (albeit as delivered by different professional groups) and all providing different information about the training and qualifications of practitioners who provide acupuncture. A single statutory regulator and umbrella professional body for all practitioners of acupuncture could provide a much-needed authoritative sign-posting function for patients seeking to understand the different types of acupuncture and make an informed choice.

Information about the minimum communication standards a patient should expect from a practitioner can also be provided by professional bodies. Practitioners' communication skills are already key components of the required standards of proficiency and codes of conduct for osteopaths (General Osteopathic Council, 2012), chiropractors (General Chiropractic Council, 2010), and acupuncturists (e.g. British Acupuncture Council, 2012), and this could be communicated clearly to patients. While professional standards are publicly available, they are ultimately quite technical documents, which could be somewhat daunting for a lay person; such official documents could be usefully supplemented with materials developed specifically for patients with lower levels of health literacy. Moving beyond communication skills in general, it is inherently challenging for professional bodies to inform patients' decisions about the personal character of a practitioner, given the subjective and interpersonal nature of such judgements. Individual practitioners themselves often do provide prospective patients with basic information about their communication skills (e.g. fluency in different languages, training in communication skills). Practitioners could consider making more use of technologies such as video-blogging to provide potential patients with additional insight before booking a first consultation. More opportunities could be provided to interact directly with a practitioner before a first consultation (e.g. via email, telephone) as these could enable patients to feel more confident that they would feel comfortable entering into a therapeutic relationship.

While patients primarily want to know about a practitioner's qualifications, technical skills, and communication skills/personality, they also want to know about the financial cost of treatment, the location/ease of access, and the availability of appointments (immediacy and timings). Some of this information is already provided on websites and marketing materials at the level of individual clinics and practitioners. Professional bodies already provide searchable databases of practitioners which include geographical location; they might consider providing additional practical information (e.g. financial cost, opening hours) to facilitate patients comparing such details across different practitioners.

While there is relevant information that could be communicated by professional bodies to patients attempting to choose an individual practitioner, it is interesting to note that professional bodies and regulators were rarely mentioned by participants in the three studies discussed in detail above. Indeed, levels of awareness about statutory regulation and professional bodies appeared to be very low even among survey respondents and interviewees who were using acupuncture, osteopathy, and/or chiropractic. It certainly appears that, among the participants in the qualitative studies, professional bodies and regulators were consulted very rarely for information about practitioners. On the one occasion when an acupuncture patient mentioned consulting a professional body's website, the website was only used to identify a practitioner in geographical proximity and not to provide any further information, either about a specific practitioner or about the standards and skills of acupuncturists in general. Campaigns to raise awareness of the professional and regulatory bodies could encourage patients to use their resources more. However, information from trusted members of a patient's social network might be more highly valued and acted upon than information from a disembodied institution, which might be perceived as having its own agenda. Professional bodies might be able to address this issue by providing transparent, reliable information summarising previous patients' experiences, in a similar way to the patient-satisfaction ratings that are available for NHS services on NHS Choices (www.nhs.uk). Financial resources would be needed to fund regular independent patient satisfaction audits and then to report the findings through sophisticated accessible and searchable databases. Extensive pilot work would of course be required to test whether such information would indeed be valued by potential patients. Overall, the evidence at present suggests that professional bodies are unlikely to be able to position themselves successfully as the only source of useful information about CAM practitioners. They might do better to focus on maintaining *and communicating* professional standards and on guiding patients through the process of choosing a practitioner, by providing relevant and accessible information but acknowledging that patients will also be seeking anecdotal and experiential evidence from personal contacts.

V Conclusions

There is a growing multi-disciplinary knowledge base around CAM use. Many studies have focused on who uses CAM and why, finding that while CAM use is not restricted to certain groups it is more common among women, middle-aged adults, those with the educational and financial resources to investigate and fund CAM, and people whose values and beliefs about health are consistent with CAM. Knowing other people who use CAM also seems to facilitate CAM use, and might be particularly important in helping new patients to choose a specific CAM practitioner. These observations appear to be robust across many studies and thus offer a reliable knowledge base to inform policy.

The three studies presented in this chapter provide new insights into other factors and processes involved when patients choose an individual CAM practitioner to consult. From these studies, it appears that patients value recommendations and advice from trusted social contacts and this helps them to develop anticipated trust in a CAM practitioner, from whom they want an excellent standard of technical skill and good interpersonal care. Practicalities and demographic characteristics are less important to patients but can still influence their choices, particularly in the absence of personal recommendations. However, these studies were all carried out in the UK and the findings must be viewed within that context, including, for example, the distinction between the NHS and private sector and the current regulatory situation for acupuncture, osteopathy, and chiropractic. Within the UK, professional bodies could have a greater role in providing patient-centred, relevant, and accessible information about their standards and individual practitioners, to complement patients' preferences for lay referrals. Future studies should examine choice of individual CAM practitioners in other countries and as changes occur to the professionalisation and regulation of CAM. For example, it would be interesting to explore if and how the role of lay referral networks changes as both the professionalisation and regulation of CAM evolve. To date, researchers have focused on understanding why patients choose CAM. A complementary focus on how and why patients choose specific CAM practitioners is needed to extend our understanding of social practices around CAM.

Note

1 In the chiropractic study, participants also rated fictional physiotherapists, but in this chapter I discuss the ratings of the chiropractors only.

References

Andersen, R. (1995). Revisiting the behavioral model and access to medical care: does it matter? *Journal of Health and Social Behavior, 36*, 1–10.

Andersen, R. & Newman, J. F. (1973). Societal and individual determinants of medical care utilization in the United States. *Milbank Memorial Fund Quarterly, 51*, 95–124.

Andrews, G. J. (2003). Placing the consumption of private complementary medicine: everyday geographies of older people's use. *Health & Place, 9*, 337–349.

Astin, J. A. (1998). Why patients use alternative medicine. Results of a national study. *Journal of the American Medical Association, 279*, 1548–1553.

Balneaves, L. G., Bottorff, J. L., Hislop, T. G., & Herbert, C. (2006). Levels of commitment: exploring complementary therapy use by women with breast cancer. *Journal of Alternative and Complementary Medicine, 12*, 459–466.

Balneaves, L. G., Truant, T. L. O., Kelly, M., Verhoef, M. J., & Davison, B. J. (2007). Bridging the gap: decision-making processes of women with breast cancer using complementary and alternative medicine (CAM). *Supportive Care in Cancer, 15*, 973–983.

Bishop, F. L., Barlow, F., Coghlan, B., Lee, P., & Lewith, G. T. (2011). Patients as healthcare consumers in the public and private sectors: a qualitative study of acupuncture in the UK. *BMC Health Services Research, 11*, www.biomedcentral.com/1472-6963/11/129.

Bishop, F. L., Bradbury, K., Jeludin, N. N. H., Massey, Y., & Lewith, G. T. (2012). How patients choose osteopaths: a mixed methods study. *Complementary Therapies in Medicine, 21*, 50–57.

Bishop, F. L. & Lewith, G. T. (2010). Who uses CAM? A narrative review of demographic characteristics and health factors associated with CAM use. *Evidence-based Complementary and Alternative Medicine, 7*, 11–28.

Bishop, F. L., Lim, C. Y., Leydon, G. M., & Lewith, G. T. (2009). Overseas Chinese students in the UK: patterns and correlates of their use of Western and traditional Chinese medicine. *Complementary Therapies in Clinical Practice, 15*, 8–13.

Bishop, F. L., Massey, Y., Yardley, L., & Lewith, G. T. (2011). How patients choose acupuncturists: a mixed-methods project. *Journal of Alternative and Complementary Medicine, 17*, 19–25.

Bishop, F. L., Smith, R., & Lewith, G. T. (2013). Patient preferences for technical skills versus interpersonal skills in chiropractors and physiotherapists treating low back pain. *Family Practice, 30*, 197–203.

Bishop, F. L., Yardley, L., & Lewith, G. T. (2007). A systematic review of beliefs involved in the use of complementary and alternative medicine. *Journal of Health Psychology, 12*, 851–867.

Bishop, F. L., Yardley, L., & Lewith, G. T. (2008a). Treat or treatment: a qualitative study conceptualising patients' use of complementary and alternative medicine (CAM). *American Journal of Public Health, 98*, 1700–1705.

Bishop, F. L., Yardley, L., & Lewith, G. T. (2008b). Treatment appraisals and beliefs predict adherence to complementary therapies: a prospective study using a dynamic extended self-regulation model. *British Journal of Health Psychology, 13*, 701–718.

Bishop, F. L., Yardley, L., & Lewith, G. T. (2010). Why consumers maintain complementary and alternative medicine use: a qualitative study. *Journal of Alternative and Complementary Medicine, 16*, 175–182.

Bishop, F. L., Zaman, S., & Lewith, G. T. (2011). Acupuncture for low back pain: a survey of clinical practice in the UK. *Complementary Therapies in Medicine, 19*, 144–148.

Braun, V. & Clarke, V. (2006). Using thematic analysis in psychology. *Qualitative Research in Psychology, 3*, 77–101.

Brien, S., Howells, E., Leydon, G. M., & Lewith, G. (2008). Why GPs refer patients to complementary medicine via the NHS: a qualitative exploration. *Primary Health Care Research & Development, 9*, 205–215.

Brien, S., Lachance, L., Prescott, P., McDermott, C., & Lewith, G. (2011). Homeopathy has clinical benefits in rheumatoid arthritis patients that are attributable to the consultation process but not the homeopathic remedy: a randomized controlled clinical trial. *Rheumatology, 50*, 1070–1082.

British Acupuncture Council. (2012). *Code of Professional Conduct*. London: British Acupuncture Council.

Canales, M. K. & Geller, B. M. (2003). Surviving breast cancer. The role of complementary therapies. *Family & Community Health, 26*, 11–24.

Cartwright, T. (2007). "Getting on with life": the experiences of older people using complementary health care. *Social Science & Medicine, 64*, 1692–1703.

Cartwright, T. & Torr, R. (2005). Making sense of illness: the experiences of users of complementary medicine. *Journal of Health Psychology, 10*, 559–572.

Caspi, O., Koithan, M., & Criddle, M. W. (2004). Alternative medicine or "alternative" patients: a qualitative study of patient-oriented decision-making processes with respect to complementary and alternative medicine. *Medical Decision Making, 24,* 64–79.

Chung, H., Lee, H., Chang, D. S., Kim, H. S., Lee, H., Park, H. J. *et al.* (2012). Doctor's attire influences perceived empathy in the patient-doctor relationship. *Patient Education and Counseling, 89,* 387–391.

Department of Health. (2004). *Regulation of Herbal Medicine and Acupuncture. Proposals for Statutory Regulation.* Leeds: Department of Health.

Department of Health. (2006). *Musculoskeletal Services Framework.* London: Department of Health.

Dixon, A., Robertson, R., Appleby, J., Burge, P., Devlin, N., & Magee, H. (2010). *Patient Choice. How Patients Choose and How Providers Respond.* London: The King's Fund.

Eng, J., Ramsum, D., Verhoef, M., Guns, E., Davison, J., & Gallagher, R. (2003). A population-based survey of complementary and alternative medicine use in men recently diagnosed with prostate cancer. *Integrative Cancer Therapies, 2,* 212–216.

Evans, M., Shaw, A., Thompson, E. A., Falk, S., Turton, P., Thompson, T. *et al.* (2007a). Decisions to use complementary and alternative medicine (CAM) by male cancer patients: information-seeking roles and types of evidence used. *BMC Complementary and Alternative Medicine, 7,* 25.

Evans, M. A., Shaw, A. R. G., Sharp, D. J., Thompson, E. A., Falk, S., Turton, P. *et al.* (2007b). Men with cancer: is their use of complementary and alternative medicine a response to needs unmet by conventional care? *European Journal of Cancer Care, 16,* 517–525.

Fang, M. C., McCarthy, E. P., & Singer, D. E. (2004). Are patients more likely to see physicians of the same sex? Recent national trends in primary care medicine. *The American Journal of Medicine, 117,* 575–581.

Foltz, V., St Pierre, Y., Rozenberg, S., Rossignol, M., Bourgeois, P., Joseph, L. *et al.* (2005). Use of complementary and alternative therapies by patients with self-reported chronic back pain: a nationwide survey in Canada. *Joint Bone Spine, 72,* 571–577.

Furnham, A. & Kirkaldy, B. (1996). The health beliefs and behaviours of orthodox and complementary medicine clients. *British Journal of Clinical Psychology, 35,* 49–61.

General Chiropractic Council. (2004). *Consulting the Profession: A Survey of UK Chiropractors, 2004.* London: General Chiropractic Council.

General Chiropractic Council. (2010). *Code of Practice and Standard of Proficiency.* London: General Chiropractic Council.

General Osteopathic Council. (2011). "Osteopathy in practice". www.osteopathy.org.uk/practice/ (last accessed on 27 April 2011).

General Osteopathic Council. (2012). *Osteopathic Practice Standards.* London: General Osteopathic Council.

Gerard, K., Salisbury, C., Street, D., Pope, C., & Baxter, H. (2008). Is fast access to general practice all that should matter? A discrete choice experiment of patients' preferences. *Journal of Health Services Research & Policy, 13,* 3–10.

Harris, P. E., Cooper, K. L., Relton, C., & Thomas, K. J. (2012). Prevalence of complementary and alternative medicine (CAM) use by the general population: a systematic review and update. *International Journal of Clinical Practice, 66,* 924–939.

House of Lords (2000). *Complementary and Alternative Medicine. Select Committee on Science and Technology – 6th Report, Session 1999–2000.* London: HMSO.

Howel, J. D. (1999). The paradox of osteopathy. *The New England Journal of Medicine, 341,* 1465–1468.

Joffe, H. & Yardley, L. (2004). Content and thematic analysis. In D. F. Marks (Ed.), *Research Methods for Clinical and Health Psychology* (pp. 56–68). London: Sage.

Jung, H. P., Baerveldt, C., Olesen, F., Grol, R., & Wensing, M. (2003). Patient characteristics as predictors of primary health care preferences: a systematic literature analysis. *Health Expectations, 6,* 160–181.

Kaptchuk, T. J. (2002). The placebo effect in alternative medicine: can the performance of a healing ritual have clinical significance? *Annals of Internal Medicine, 136,* 817–825.

Kaptchuk, T. J., Kelley, J. M., Conboy, L. A., Davis, R. B., Kerr, C. E., Jacobson, E. E. *et al.* (2008). Components of placebo effect: randomised controlled trial in patients with irritable bowel syndrome. *British Medical Journal, 336,* 999–1003.

Kelner, M. & Wellman, B. (1997). Health care and consumer choice: medical and alternative therapies. *Social Science & Medicine, 45,* 203–212.

Kerssens, J. J., Bensing, J. M., & Andela, M. G. (1997). Patient preference for genders of health professionals. *Social Science & Medicine, 44,* 1531–1540.

Lee, S.-H., Chang, D.-S., Kang, O.-S., Kim, H.-H., Kim, H., Lee, H. *et al.* (2012). Do not judge according to appearance: patients' preference of a doctor's face does not influence their assessment of the patient-doctor relationship. *Acupuncture in Medicine, 30,* 261–265.

Licciardone, J. C. (2004). The unique role of osteopathic physicians in treating patients with low back pain. *The Journal of the American Osteopathic Association, 104,* 13–18.

Licciardone, J. C., Brimhall, A. K., & King, L. N. (2005). Osteopathic manipulative treatment for low back pain: a systemic review and meta analysis of randomized controlled trials. *BMC Musculoskeletal Disorders, 6,* 43.

Lorenc, A., Ilan-Clarke, Y., Robinson, N., & Blair, M. (2009). How parents choose to use CAM: a systematic review of theoretical models. *BMC Complementary and Alternative Medicine, 9,* 9.

Luff, D. & Thomas, K. J. (2000). "Getting somewhere", feeling cared for: patients' perspectives on complementary therapies in the NHS. *Complementary Therapies in Medicine, 8,* 253–259.

MacPherson, H., Sinclair-Lian, N., & Thomas, K. (2006). Patients seeking care from acupuncture practitioners in the UK: a national survey. *Complementary Therapies in Medicine, 14,* 20–30.

Ong, C. K., Doll, H., Bodeker, G., & Stewart-Brown, S. (2004). Use of osteopathic or chiropractic services among people with back pain: a UK population survey. *Health & Social Care in the Community, 12,* 265–273.

Paterson, C. & Britten, N. (2004). Acupuncture as a complex intervention: a holistic model. *Journal of Alternative and Complementary Medicine, 10,* 791–801.

Paterson, C. & Dieppe, P. (2005). Characteristic and incidental (placebo) effects in complex interventions such as acupuncture. *British Medical Journal, 330,* 1202–1205.

Pedersen, I. K. & Baarts, C. (2010). "Fantastic hands" – but no evidence: the construction of expertise by users of CAM. *Social Science & Medicine, 71,* 1068–1075.

Peters, D., Davies, P., & Pietroni, P. (1994). Musculoskeletal clinic in general practice: study of one year's referrals. *British Journal of General Practice, 44,* 25–29.

Robinson, N., Lorenc, A., & Blair, M. (2009). Developing a decision-making model on traditional and complementary medicine use for children. *European Journal of Integrative Medicine, 1,* 43–50.

Rubin, G., Bate, A., George, A., Shackley, P., & Hall, N. (2006). Preferences for access to the GP: a discrete choice experiment. *British Journal of General Practice, 56,* 743–748.

Savigny, P., Kuntze, S., Watson, P., Underwood, M., Ritchie, G., Cotterell, M. *et al.* (2009). *Low Back Pain. Early Management of Persistent Non-specific Low Back Pain* (Rep. No. NICE clinical guideline 88). London: National Collaborating Centre for Primary Care and Royal College of General Practitioners.

Shaw, A., Thompson, E. A., & Sharp, D. (2006). Expectations of patients and parents of children with asthma regarding access to complementary therapy information and services via the NHS: a qualitative study. *Health Expectations, 9,* 343–358.

Sirois, F. M. & Gick, M. L. (2002). An investigation of the health beliefs and motivations of complementary medicine clients. *Social Science & Medicine, 55,* 1025–1037.

Tasaki, K., Maskarinec, G., Shumay, D. M., Tatsumura, Y., & Kakai, H. (2002). Communication between physicians and cancer patients about complementary and alternative medicine: exploring patients' perspectives. *Psycho-Oncology, 11,* 212–220.

Thomas, K. J., Nicholl, J. P., & Coleman, P. (2001). Use and expenditure on complementary medicine in England: a population based survey. *Complementary Therapies in Medicine, 9,* 2–11.

Upchurch, D. M., Burke, A., Dye, C., Chyu, L., Kusunoki, Y., & Greendale, G. A. (2008). A sociobehavioral model of acupuncture use, patterns, and satisfaction among women in the United States, 2002. *Women's Health Issues, 18,* 62–71.

Verhoef, M. J., Mulkins, A., Carlson, L. E., Hilsden, R. J., & Kania, A. (2007). Assessing the role of evidence in patients' evaluation of complementary therapies: a quality study. *Integrative Cancer Therapies, 6,* 345–353.

Vickers, A. & Zollman, C. (1999). ABC of complementary medicine. Acupuncture. *British Medical Journal, 319,* 973.

Walker, L. A. & Budd, S. (2002). UK: the current state of regulation of complementary and alternative medicine. *Complementary Therapies in Medicine, 10,* 8–13.

World Federation of Chiropractic. (1999). *A General Dictionary Definition of Chiropractic.* Approved by the World Federation of Chiropractic, Auckland, 19 May. www.wfc.org/website/docs/992003143231.PDF.

Xue, C. C., Zhang, A. L., Lin, V., Myers, R., Polus, B., & Story, D. F. (2008). Acupuncture, chiropractic and osteopathy use in Australia: a national population survey. *BMC Public Health, 8,* 105.

Young, J. T. (2004). Illness behaviour: a selective review and synthesis. *Sociology of Health and Illness, 26,* 1–31.

19

(RE)ARTICULATING IDENTITIES THROUGH LEARNING SPACE

Training for massage and reflexology

Emma Wainwright and Elodie Marandet

I Introduction

This chapter examines the processes of learning professionalism and regulation in CAM by offering a geographical reading of training for massage and reflexology. As two types of CAM, massage and reflexology have become more widely practised and consumed over the past 20 years (Andrews, 2003). In particular, moving beyond a specialist medical intervention, their place in mainstream health and wellbeing service consumption has grown significantly. With a 'rediscovery of the senses' in consumer culture, a 'new pleasure in the body' has been validated (Jutte, 2005: 238, in Paterson, 2007), binding the embodied and the affective. The growth, use and practice of massage and reflexology are just two examples of this sensual commodification.

The conceptual territory of this paper lies first and foremost in the literature relating to the pervasive gendering of body work and emotional labour and the recursive relationship between the spaces and experiences of learning bodily and emotional skills for transfer to paid employment. While not wishing to repeat arguments already established (see Wainwright *et al.*, 2010a, 2011b), body work, as elucidated by Wolkowitz (2002, 2006) and defined as work involving interaction between bodies, has been conceptualised through a highly gendered and maternalised discourse of motherhood, care and familial responsibility. Through essentialist and performed (self)constructions of women's abilities, it is 'intimately linked with women's bodily lives through motherhood and nurturance. Because women do this work for babies and children, these activities are generalised as female' (Twigg, 2000a: 407). Drawing on Hochschild's formative writings (1983), body work has also been explicitly related to the emotional labour that it more than frequently requires (Gimlin, 2007). For example, Twigg (2000a, 2000b) and Milligan (2000, 2003) have drawn attention to both the physicality and the emotionality of the caring dimensions of body work, pointing to how care is implicitly entangled in gendered meanings of home and identity. Put simply, the more intimate the contact and handling of bodies in a range of settings, the more necessary the sensitive handling of emotions.

In the next section, this initial conceptual grounding is tallied with an appraisal of the therapeutic landscapes literature and subsequent limited research looking at the geographies of CAM. Then, with an empirical focus on training for massage and reflexology, we outline the research project which, through a focus on mothers' participation in training for body work, sought, in part, to explore the (re)articulation of trainee-practitioner identities through the spatial tactics implicit in the training process and learning environment. This empirical attention is primarily based on focus groups and interviews with mothers participating in reflexology and massage training courses in London further education colleges, and interviews with training providers and tutors in these fields, as detailed below.

This interest in training is, we suggest, an important one. At a conceptual level, the *processes* of training have been largely absent in now numerous appraisals of body work (see Gale, 2007 for a detailed exception). And, we argue here as elsewhere (Wainwright *et al.*, 2010b), a focus on *spaces* of training enables much insight to be yielded into how bodily and emotional 'skills' are learned and practised and how practitioner identity is created and defined. At the empirical level, such an appraisal is politically current given the relentlessness of neo-liberal welfare-to-work rhetoric in the UK and beyond, that is actively encouraging training for work. This has been especially the case for mothers, the focus of our research, where an expectation of 'good' mothering is now implicitly bound to being economically active (Wainwright *et al.*, 2011a).

What is termed the 'classroom-salon' lies at the centre of our substantive arguments, and the regulatory and often iterative relationship produced between bodies and space in the learning of professionalism. In particular, the paper moves on to explore some of the tensions brought to bear on trainee-practitioner identity; that is, the need to re-articulate aspects of normative gender and maternal identity whilst simultaneously articulating a new 'professional' identity. By tracing some of the dimensions of this learning process, we argue for a more spatially attuned understanding of the work of CAM trainees and practitioners.

II Therapeutic landscapes and the geographies of CAM

The concept of therapeutic landscapes was first introduced by Will Gesler over 30 years ago (Gesler, 1992) and since this time has become central to health-place studies and health geographies (Laws, 2009; Smyth, 2005; Williams 1999, 2007). Stemming from the humanistic tradition of geographic thinking and grounded in qualitative study, at its simplest, the concept of therapeutic landscapes is used to refer to the positive associations of health and wellbeing people ascribe to certain places and spaces. Such landscapes are socially constructed and have achieved lasting reputations for providing physical, mental and spiritual healing. As Gatrell (2002: 10) observes:

> reputations may be built on the qualities of the physical environment, such as a source of water or a distinctive piece of topography. Or they may rest on the qualities of buildings, such as temples. But such places are built on reputations and in this sense their therapeutic properties are socially and culturally constructed. People will seek out such places in order to be 'cured' of a chronic disease, perhaps, or to hope for an improvement in well-being.

What is clear here is that geography matters. Gatrell talks about landscape in a physical and often natural sense, whether in terms of experiencing a specific topography, location or material environment. Such research initially focused on traditional landscapes and 'big' places such as hot springs, open wilderness and holiday destinations, but everyday 'ordinary' and more mundane spaces can also be viewed as offering important therapeutic qualities, such as gardens, hospitals, community organisations and sites and spaces of home (see Andrews *et al.*, 2004; Andrews, 2004; Williams, 2007 for useful overviews). Moreover, informal, unconventional and more 'alternative' spaces have also recently courted interest, such as Laws' (2009) research on the use of urban park spaces for psychiatric self-help groups (see also Parr, 1999).

With this approach to therapeutic landscapes, the co-presence of physical locations and physical bodies has been considered essential. Yet, this is somewhat limiting and the term has been extended to the importance of imagined places in the therapeutic process or what can be termed 'landscapes of the mind' (Williams, 1998). Some research, drawing on psychoanalysis and psychoanalytic geographies recognises that therapeutic places 'may not necessarily exist in "real" (linear) time and in physical space. Rather, they could exist as spaces and places created by, and located in, the mind' (Andrews, 2004: 309). For example, Bondi's (2003 and 2005) attention to psychotherapy suggests how, by exploring the inner worlds of their clients, counsellors work with and through geographical imaginaries and this hinges on the emotional relatedness of therapist and client. This has also been extended to CAM practices, with Andrews (2003), for example, exploring how the mental imagery of places plays a central role in aiding calm and relaxation or for expressing feelings. Images of place are constructed and manipulated by both therapist and client:

> The places imagined may be real, in the sense that they exist physically in other times and places, whilst they may also be created by the therapist and client. Therapeutic images of places are not always remote from physical settings of clinics, and they may be initially facilitated and assisted by the therapeutic encounter of the clinic, its design and decoration. However, this physical aspect is often superseded, as clients drift off to places 'elsewhere', aided by therapists and created in patients' minds.
>
> *(Andrews, 2003: 315)*

Imagined places can effectively be fashioned and manipulated through contrived spatial constructions and arrangements of bodies and/or objects and their relatedness in the therapeutic encounter. Following this, and writing about psychological therapies from beyond the discipline of geography, Fenner (2011) notes that the role of the actual physical setting within which therapy takes place has attracted little research attention to date and what we think of as the practitioner–client relationship needs to be expanded to include the material environment and place in the ways suggested.

These examples, with their emphasis on real and imagined place, demonstrate the potential resonance of the therapeutic landscapes concept for considering CAM, and allow us to think of the geographies and spatialities implicit in its training, practice and experience. Indeed, as substantive research on therapeutic landscapes has grown, there has been attendant interest in CAM. In geography, this has been coupled with the rise of cultural and feminist enquiry and specific interest in the spatialities of body/bodies, emotions and affect which are central to any immediate CAM encounter.

In an article written specifically for CAM researchers and as an 'exploration of, and invitation to, geographic enquiry', Andrews *et al.* (2004) effectively argue for CAM issues to be researched through a geographic lens. In particular, and moving beyond mere quantitative mapping and spatial distribution, they argue that geographic perspectives help better understand the *relationship* between patient/consumer and provider/practitioner. This dynamic can be explored at the macro-level in relation to the geographies of CAM consumption and the influence of political, economic and cultural contexts (Andrews, 2003; Wiles and Rosenberg, 2001). But it is also useful at the micro-scale and for thinking through the dynamics between bodies and bodies/objects in the immediate CAM environment and encounter. However, though writing a decade ago, this call from Andrews *et al.* (2004) has been given only limited consideration.

There are a wide range of settings in which CAM is provided and consumed, including conventional hospitals, community-based health services, private clinics, homes and workplaces.

All of these shape the CAM encounter and the way in which CAM is practised and consumed, with specific routines, practices, professionals and power relations. Moreover, and what we argue here, is that rather than reflecting on CAM in the final site of consumption, the sites and spaces of training for CAM are worth exploring as it is at this point that the techniques of the therapeutic encounter can be teased out – the spatial tactics of routines, professional identities and power relations are taught and learnt. So rather than focus on the experiences of those receiving treatment/therapy, we explore the training process and training environment, and the reworking of space and identity in producing CAM skills in the learning of massage and reflexology.

III Researching 'body training' in massage and reflexology

The research from which this paper originates, together with previous research (Wainwright *et al.*, 2010a, 2010b), has found that the choice of 'body training' courses that focus on the embodied, emotional and, by extension, the care of others are popular among mothers for reasons linked to expectation and performativity of a feminised and very often presumed 'natural' maternal identity, and linking home, family, leisure and work. Though training choices are not the focus here, this indicates strong and persistent gendered understandings of skills and interests held by women, particularly mothers, and that have been perpetuated by tutors, training advisors and government policy (Osgood, 2005; Skeggs, 1997; Smith *et al.*, 2008).

Here we draw on research examining training experiences and the training environment and, as a starting point, use Wolkowitz's (2002, 2006) body work categories of 'pleasuring' and 'curing' to look at massage courses (Indian head massage, full body massage and aromatherapy massage) and a reflexology course. This research was part of a wider 30-month ESRC-funded project on the 'body-training choices, expectations and experiences of mothers' and covered a range of body work subject areas.[1] The research was located in West London, which is comprised of six of the 33 London boroughs: Harrow, Hillingdon, Brent, Ealing, Hammersmith and Fulham, and Hounslow.

As a qualitatively based project, we draw here on four classroom observations in two West London colleges, interviews of approximately 30 minutes in length with each of the three tutors teaching these classes, two two-hour scoping focus groups with mothers taking the courses and two waves of one-to-one and paired-depth interviews with nine enrolled mothers, which lasted from 30 minutes to one hour. Following Wolkowitz's categorisation, the scoping groups are designated here under the headings 'curing' (involving students taking reflexology and aromatherapy massage) and 'pleasuring' (involving students taking Indian head and full body massage)[2] and interview data are presented under pseudonyms (mothers) and numbers (tutors) to protect participant identity.

Courses to observe and recruit from were chosen on the advice of tutors as being popular with mothers. The sample chosen was opportunistic and dependent on participant availability and willingness. The interviewed students varied in age, from their early 20s to late 40s and, reflecting the West London area, were racially and ethnically diverse (using census categorisation, interviewees self-identified as White British, White 'other' (Polish), Black/Black British African, Caribbean and 'other' and Asian Indian).

In the absence of access to data on the student body, we cannot say how far our interviewees are representative of all those taking these CAM courses at FE colleges. Instead, what we offer is insight into the learning experiences and environment of one group that makes up a large contingent of the student body in these areas of training as confirmed by further education college tutors and section managers. And, in so doing, we point to the (re)articulation of gender and maternal identity as bound up with the processes of professionalism and regulation in learning space.

Here, learning space takes on two related meanings. First, we explore the making of what we term the 'classroom-salon', the locus of the practice-training process, and the role of the physical setting – its objects, ambience and embodied presences – for creating a place for CAM practice. And second, we discuss the learning *of* space within the classroom-salon – the spacings and spatial tactics – necessary for body-to-body/object encounters and embodied intersubjectivity.

IV The learning space

College, as a site of learning academic and professional skills, is marked by partitioning. For massage and reflexology, along with other CAM and beauty therapy courses, the 'classroom-salon' is the locus of training activity.[3] Classroom-salons have their own particular geography, marked off from other learning spaces and placed in their own designated wing and with their own reception and waiting areas. The waiting areas replicate, at least to some extent, that which could be found in related CAM workplaces, with magazines for waiting clients, the sale of therapeutic products and the aroma of numerous treatments being taught, learnt and practised. Leading off from this space are rooms that double up as both conventional classrooms and salons. Here we focus on the classroom-salon – its particular physical design and layout, placing of bodies and objects, and its sensual alterations, which ensure it becomes a suitable site for practising therapies.

The classroom-salon is a hybrid space, carrying particular meanings and identities for those inside, which are produced through the interaction of bodies, objects and senses. It is a transformative space as the learner moves from trainee to practitioner, and the space changes from more typical site of learning, with desks, chairs, white board, textbooks and tutor, to a site for practising body work and CAM techniques, with benches, cubicles and clients. As one tutor explains, the ability to create a realistic environment is central to the training process:

> The salon is made to be a realistic working environment, so that once they're ready, you know, they've done their practice and we've done a mock assessment, and we feel that they're ready to do the public, then we turn it into a salon, where we book appointments, the public books in and they come in for a treatment, and that's how they get assessed, by doing the treatment on someone they don't know.
>
> *(Tutor 2)*

For the practice-based sessions, students have to recreate a precise salon environment: removing discarded chairs, turning on work lights 'at a certain shade' and turning off the main fluorescent lights, drawing the curtain round individual work benches, laying tissues over benches and collecting head cushions (massage). Creating this aesthetic of space needs to be coupled with sensual alterations: temperature is checked – 'it mustn't be too hot, mustn't be too cold' (Nina) – to make comfortable exposed bodies, and sound – soft music or bird song – is played to create a calming soundscape: 'we set the environment, we have soft music playing, the lights are dimmed, you know … it's all very nice' (Tutor 2). As a means of marking the 'purity' of this new space (Oerton, 2004), these tactics point to the oft-cited role and manipulation of nature in creating therapeutic environments (see Parr, 1999; Gesler, 2003; Lea, 2008) with 'naturalness' fashioned in highly contrived spatial and sensual form. Moreover, following the literature on therapeutic landscapes, these changes in ambience are a means of encouraging personal geographical imaginaries to aid the relaxation and therapy process (Andrews, 2003). Recognising that clients 'come in for lots of different reasons and relaxation is always one of them' (Nina), the newly created salon environment has to become a place of calm and tranquillity and an affective sensuousness needs to pervade: 'the body massage and even the reflexology you want the client to RELAX' (Tutor 3). These changes are aimed at creating a particular sense of place in the classroom-salon; a sense of place that moves beyond the materiality of the immediate environment to evoke a landscape in the mind that facilitates relaxation and enables the body to relax.

The right atmosphere is perceived as necessary to aid the healing process as the body relaxes into the calming environment. This reiterates Parr's (1999: 192) findings in relation to the use of therapeutic massage in the treatment of people with mental health problems, highlighting that 'the locations (in physical and body space) where therapies take place are of crucial import- ance, and are linked to the personal and the emotional'. Thus the sensual experience of the classroom-salon relies not only on embodied knowledge present in the treatment encounter, but on the spatiality of bodies, objects and ambience within a therapeutic setting.

In addition to the correct objects and appropriate ambience, the 'right' practitioner body also needs to be present in this therapeutic space, and uniform, as the first marker of embod- ied practice, has a fundamental role in bringing this learning space and new learner identity into being. As one of the first aspects students are taught, presentation is a chief aid to learn- ing the bodily and emotional skills of the therapeutic encounter. Used to mark the profes- sionalism, uniforms are perceived to mirror the 'cleanness' and purity – in a conceptual and material sense – of the practice to be learned: 'If the uniform is clean and ironed and you behave in a confident and well-mannered way, people will put their trust in you. ... And they are quite happy for you to do treatments on them' (Vera). Students stress how uniform is a social marker, linking appearance, professionalism, knowledge, seriousness and confidence-building:

> It makes you look more professional. It makes you look like you're serious about what you do. And it makes the client have more confidence in you because they can see that you are serious, you're portraying that image so it's very important.
>
> *(Nina)*

As Twigg (2000a: 391) points out in relation to the dematerialising tendency within body work, 'status in a profession is marked by distance from the bodily'. With the corporeal processes of touch and the learning and practice of embodied knowledge central to massage and reflexology, uniforms and presentation of the body are hugely important for professionalising and, paradoxi- cally, moving beyond the bodily by indicating professional skills.

Uniforms mark the partitioning of the classroom-salon from the outside: marking the new identity of trainee-practitioner. As one student explained, 'you feel better because you look professional' (Krysia) and another pointed out that it helps you 'get into that image ... a char- acter' (Nina). This homogenising exercise for the students is deemed an essential part of training: the right body is necessary in this salon space: 'For this sort of field, you've got to look the part, you know, so you've got to look sort of smart and clean, you know, clean and everything tidy, or someone will come in and think, oh...' (Tutor 2). Students are assessed on their 'image', requiring compliance of this particular professional embodiment and regulation of bodyspace, before being allowed to progress to practice-based sessions.

Uniform also promotes conformity, erasing individual styles and promoting an homogenous professional identity: 'it's good because everybody looks the same' (Krysia). But this new image also represents a calculated adjustment of trainee-practitioners' embodied gendered identities. It is especially for female students that this is current as interviewees noted changes they needed to make to particular 'feminine' aspects of their appearance: keeping makeup to a minimum, tying hair back, shortening nails and keeping artificial nails and nail polish 'for the weekends': 'I would love to grow my nails. That's something I missed from the beginning, because I used to love having long nails. You can't even wear nail polish' (Nina). Certain aspects of femininity have to be tamed, tempered and kept out of the salon, with interviewees showing a clear awareness of the gendered nature of self-presentation.

This particular articulation of a defeminised gender identity is explained through the language of professionalism:

> You have to have your hair off your face, obviously because if you were doing a massage, or if you are leaning over someone's face they don't want your hair ... it's not very hygienic you know. No your hair must be back. All earrings must be out.... You shouldn't wear any jewellery.
>
> *(Vera)*

This is also linked to a determined desexualisation given the common elision between massage and sex work (Nicholls and Holmes, 2012) and was indicated by one student who explained: 'you can wear a little bit of makeup but obviously don't overdo it' (Nina). As Oerton (2004) suggests, women therapeutic workers have to work hard to mark out their professional distance from clients by deploying professional identification and using boundary-setting devices or techniques. As society has become more sexualised, steps are taken in therapeutic work to remove from this sexualisation, with 'professional' appearance and bodyspace through uniform closely regulated and constantly re-enforced.

V The learning *of* space

While the creation of a very specific learning space in which to practise massage and reflexology is a key component of the skilling process and the move towards 'professionalism', the learning *of* space in the corporeal encounter – between bodies and the objects for practice and between the bodies of practitioner and client – is also vital. Students need to learn to be in, and be a part of, this space.

'Proper' bodily comportment and organisation in relation to the objects of learning and practice are essential from the outset. This helps ensure that the smooth choreography of professional treatment unfolds without disruption:

> to be organised really, you know, so that everything's in its place.
>
> *(Tutor 2)*

> [You need to] make sure that your section – you've got everything you need for the treatment before you do the treatment, before you bring the client in, because you don't want to be running off, because that's not very professional either. It's all part of that look basically.
>
> *(Vera)*

For example, in the observed aromatherapy massage class, which was entirely practice-based, the tutor reprimanded students for sitting on massage tables. The need to learn how to *use* the space is reiterated throughout the training experience.

Beyond the body of the practitioner, students need to work with their clients in this space. They need to alter the treatment space to create an environment conducive to a professional encounter. When clients arrive in the classroom-salon, there is a clear spatial dimension to verbal communication in the initial consultation. Curtains are drawn round each cubicle, creating a private space for personal details and feelings. This intersubjective space works through close spatial proximity, allowing care and empathy to be communicated (Bondi, 2003).

Verbal communication is one of the key skills for any practitioner in establishing and negotiating therapeutic spaces. Creating an impression of care can be viewed as a process of learning 'surface acting' (Hochschild, 1983):

> Making them feel confident in you. You know greeting them with a smile you know making them, a friendly manner, giving them a very friendly manner and polite.

> It's making them feel special.

> *(Focus group, curing)*

Though tutors reflect on the importance of learning appropriate communication through role play and practice, many mothers feel it is something you either 'have' or 'don't have': 'I was born that way' (Focus group, pleasuring). As seen in this paired-interview section, this is often considered an inherent skill:

> BHARTI: But we are better than men.
> INTERVIEWER: In what ways are you better than men?
> BHARTI: We have more patience, just naturally.
> NICOLE: Better at multi-tasking.
> BHARTI: Don't pretend, we are what we are.

This was closely linked not only to femininity, as noted by a tutor who insisted that women are better than men at caring (Tutor 3), but by mothers to their experiences of mothering. The necessary communication and interpersonal skills required were not so much taught but seen as 'common parenting skills' (Focus group, pleasuring) produced out of familiar maternal and feminine subject positions. Elements of being professional were perceived as capitalising on prior female experience (Skeggs, 1997), with skills naturalised through 'performativity' (Butler, 1990). Listening to mothers and tutors speaking in this way, there were clear contradictions between these assertions of innately possessing or developing these skills from being a woman and/or mother, and claims of academic rigour, hence simultaneously supporting and undermining claims to professional knowledge.

The setting of bodily boundaries in the body-to-body encounter is based on touch and proximity and, conversely, avoidance and distance, which are couched through a discourse of professionalism requiring a self-reflexive process by the trainee-practitioner (Gale, 2009). The negotiation of this 'dialectic of distance and intimacy' (Churchill and Churchill, 1982) is essential and it is the role of the trainee-practitioner – working with the co-presence of bodies and objects – to control what is and is not seen:

> when they have to turn from their back onto their stomach, there's a certain way of holding the towels in the position they do, so that nothing shows, they have to learn how to do that properly, so that nothing exposes any parts of the body.

> *(Tutor 2)*

Students learn a set of tactics to ensure privacy in this semi-public domain. The towel is the first of a number of shielding devices – creating a sense of privacy and security but also confidence in the practitioner. The second shield is the curtain that separates the cubicle – the immediate site of relaxation and wellbeing – from the outside. Yet, though an intimate space, the cubicle needs to be open enough to enable both escape from difficult situations and clients, and suitably exposed to ensure the tutor can watch, teach, regulate and reprimand.

This curtained space becomes *the* therapeutic space (Paterson, 2007) and is primarily about the relationship between the client and the trainee-practitioner through the process of touch. Tutors speak of the need to learn quickly how and where touch can be inappropriate. This was easier for reflexology than for body massage: 'Reflexology is the foot. So the foot is ... it's intimate but is different from the body massage ... it's only up to half the calf so that is okay' (Tutor 3). For full body massage, this was relayed in relation to the sensitivities of dealing with male clients:

> And we teach them with a man, how to approach the man because certain areas in a man can be stimulated more easily than a woman so we teach them all those things.
>
> *(Tutor 3)*

> They explain to us about all of that, the professional Code of Conduct and you have to be careful how you lean over the client, you've got to behave in a professional manner.
>
> *(Vicky)*

Bodily displays of sexuality are considered an incursion into this therapeutic space. Students need to learn quickly the balance between closeness and distance (Nicholls and Holmes, 2012).

For one pregnant mother, this issue of closeness and distance came to the fore through changes to her own body:

> A couple of weeks before we stopped and then [Tutor 3] says 'you're not massaging' and I thought 'oi, I can stand up, just'. And she goes 'no your belly is getting in the way'. I goes 'it's not getting in the way yet'.
>
> *(Annie)*

The touch of her stomach with the body of her client disrupts the prescribed bodily boundaries. The pregnant body – through inappropriate touch – literally becomes matter out of place in the training environment (Longhurst, 2000). Moreover, as her pregnant body grew, the student could no longer fit into her uniform, exceeding the bounds of professionalism, marking her as 'other' and further distancing her from the appropriate embodied practice of the classroom-salon.

Reflexology and massage are based on gleaning knowledge on the body – its physiology and anatomy – and learning and following techniques of touch and pressure. Their learning is a form of embodied knowledge acquired through and lodged in practices of the body. Learning embodied knowledge requires a spatial ordering of one body in relation to another (Lea, 2009) as the body is mapped, manipulated and impressed through fleshy encounter. Though in the classroom-salon textbooks are present, the main process of learning this spatial ordering comes through embodied demonstrations between tutor and trainee and between trainees:

Obviously, how to do the movements. I'll do a demonstration on an arm, and they all practice on the arm. Types of movements, the pressure that you use, you know, how to do it, so you know to be safe.

(Tutor 2)

In the full body massage observation, the tutor reiterates embodied knowledge by talking through the different techniques of touch, emphasising the need to work with strength and apply pressure.

Embodied knowledge is not simply about remembering and then doing, but 'considering the (inter-personal and inter-corporeal) relation set up between the massage practitioner and recipient' (Lea, 2009: 473). Students speak about the learning process in stages, moving from the space of the textbook, a necessary object for learning, to the bodyspace of their classmates and eventually paying client until reaching a point of embodied knowledge:

That was what I found really hard when you've got a book there and you have to keep doing this and looking and you're trying to remember and trying to keep contact with the client because you can't lose touch … especially as most of the time my book fell on the floor and it was like, 'aargh'.

(Amy)

Since I've started this course … my movements and the pressure I'm doing is completely different to what I used to do it. I can see the change in how I'm doing it.

(Focus group, pleasuring)

In reaching a point where the academic and bodily are inseparable in touching, students speak of 'feeling' the course:

At the beginning I couldn't get into it. But then once I started to know about the anatomy and it's all in your head and it stays there, it all sort of makes sense and now I actually feel the course, if you know what I mean. I actually understand it better and know what I'm doing, and it's more meaningful to me now I understand everything.

(Nina)

This process of 'feeling' is an accumulative one, reached through constant learning and doing (Butler, 1990). It is a process of skill, discipline and reiteration, of training the mind and body to work together, creating an ambient and therapeutic space, and working with the objects of learning/practice and the body of another.

VI Conclusions

In this chapter, with a focus on training for massage and reflexology, we have argued that research on CAM practices could benefit from more thoroughly attending to what we term 'learning space'. Drawing on the concept of therapeutic landscapes – in both real and imagined senses – we have traced some of the processes of learning space; in other words, the manipulation of the physical setting (its objects, ambience and embodied presences) and the role of spacings and spatial tactics (of body-to-body/object encounters and embodied intersubjectivity) that the training process necessitates. Through these tracings, the initial physical design and layout of the therapeutic environment has a vital role in situating, contextualising and ordering the

317

embodied social relations of practice that are then played out. In terms of both practitioners and clients, these serve to regulate and normalise certain kinds of behaviour and to include as well as exclude from this space (see Smyth, 2005).

Discourses of professionalism are inscribed in and through the processes and spaces of learning in the classroom-salon, and these work through both articulating and negating aspects of identity. A focus on the learning space and the learning of space has shown how the management of spaces, bodies and objects is used to facilitate and reinforce the display of well-chosen and controlled gendered identities. And, for our research here, these resonate strongly given our focus on training for massage and reflexology among mothers. For example, the intimacy provided by the curtained treatment space is conducive to caring qualities and inter-personal skills, highlighting the tension between a performed caring self and recourse to professional distance, while uniform, corporeal presentation and careful body handling participate in bringing out a pure, clean, unadorned and de-sexualised version of femininity. There is a clear yet contested dialogue and negotiation between space and the creation of a professional but gendered therapeutic identity.

We have focused here on a very particular institutional space, that of further education colleges in West London. These are sites of training and learning that are bound by and work out of specific cultural, social and structural processes shaped by professional and educational systems, knowledges and identities. The classroom-salon, as one particular location within these college environments, is a specifically constructed space for the learning and practice of therapy. Yet the skills learned and practised inside will travel and move beyond these physical institutional confines to be replicated elsewhere. They will either be spatially 'deinstitutionalised', to be practised in, for example, private homes and sites of 'leisure', or will shift institution to, for example, hospitals, clinics and care homes. There is an inevitable process of skill relocation. As new 'professionals', practitioners need to carry the marks of their professional identity and knowledge beyond the gaze of college tutors and relocate their skills within new contexts and spaces, and in relation to new clients/customers and bodies. How identities and skills are then reproduced in and with new spaces, contexts and bodies is worth attention.

Finally, this chapter makes a play for an explicitly geographical reading of CAM practices and a more spatially attuned understanding of the work of CAM trainees and practitioners. In recent years, space has begun to '[spin] out of geography through the intellectual curiosities and investments of many other disciplines' (Thrift and Whatmore, 2004: 2). Research on CAM emanates from a range of different disciplinary traditions and is now a thoroughly trans-disciplinary substantive issue of critical enquiry. Yet a full engagement with the role of space in CAM practice is wanting. In talking about a geographical reading, it is not places and spaces as mere settings or backdrops for training, but recognition that they are an integral and active component of the learning process. Space is an active and dynamic force in creating the treatment encounter and articulating practitioner identity and expertise. While educators have prioritised learning processes over learning spaces, it is not a matter of simply reversing this order, but recognising that spaces and processes cannot be separated out. There is then a need to reposition research and debates on CAM to think through the co-construction of space, identity and professionalism. The geographic literature on real and imagined therapeutic landscapes and a geographic reading of body work and emotional labour are useful and productive points for further enquiry.

Notes

1 The research was funded by the ESRC (First grants scheme no. RES–061–23–0106). Further details can be found at www.esrc.ac.uk/my-esrc/grants/RES-061-23-0106/read.

2 We use these terms merely as a means of initial categorisation and an aid to the research process. We therefore acknowledge that the subject areas they include are overlapping and entangled.

3 Though in some research (for example, research on beauty work by Furman, 1997, and Gimlin, 1996, and training in osteopathy and homeopathy, by Gale, 2007) the term 'clinic' is employed, we adopt the term salon as that is what research participants here – both students and staff – used, and hence best marks college culture.

References

Andrews, G. (2003) Placing the consumption of private complementary medicine: everyday geographies of older people's use, *Health and Place* 9: 337–349.

Andrews, G. (2004) (Re)thinking the dynamic between healthcare and place: therapeutic geographies in treatment and care practices, *Area* 36: 307–318.

Andrews, G., Wiles, J. and Miller, K.-L. (2004) The geography of complementary medicine: perspectives and prospects, *Complementary Therapies in Nursing and Midwifery* 10: 175–185.

Bondi, L. (2003) A situated practice for (re)situating selves: trainee counsellors and the promise of counselling, *Environment and Planning* A 35: 853–870.

Bondi, L. (2005) Making connections and thinking through emotions: between geography and psychotherapy, *Transactions of the Institute of British Geographers* 30: 433–448.

Butler, J. (1990) *Gender trouble: feminism and the subversion of identity*. London: Routledge.

Churchill, L. and Churchill, S. (1982) Storytelling in medical arenas: the art of self-determination, *Literature and Medicine* 1: 73–79.

Fenner, P. (2011) Place, matter and meaning: extending the relationship in psychological therapies, *Health and Place* 17: 851–857.

Furman, F. (1997) *Facing the mirror: older women and beauty shop culture*. New York: Routledge.

Gale, N. (2007) *Knowing the body and embodying knowledge: an ethnography of student practitioner experiences in osteopathy and homeopathy*. Warwick: Unpublished PhD thesis, University of Warwick.

Gale, N. (2009) Promoting patient-practitioner partnership in clinical training, *Learning in Health and Social Care* 8: 13–21.

Gatrell, A. (2002) *Geographies of health: an introduction*. Oxford: Blackwell.

Gesler, W. (1992) Therapeutic landscapes: medical issues in the light of the new cultural geography, *Social Science and Medicine* 34: 735–746.

Gesler, W. (2003) *Healing places*. Maryland: Rowman and Littlefield.

Gimlin, D. (1996) Pamela's place: power and negotiation in the hair salon, *Gender and Society* 10(5): 505–526.

Gimlin, D. (2007) What is body work? A review of literature, *Sociology Compass* 1: 353–370.

Hochschild, A. (1983) *The managed heart: commercialisation of human feeling*. Los Angeles: University of California Press.

Laws, J. (2009) Reworking therapeutic landscapes: the spatiality on an 'alternative' self-help group, *Social Science and Medicine* 69: 1827–1833.

Lea, J. (2008) Retreating to nature: rethinking 'therapeutic landscapes', *Area* 40: 90–98

Lea, J. (2009) Bridging skills: the geographies of teaching and learning embodied knowledges, *Geoforum* 40: 465–474.

Longhurst, R. (2000) Corporeographies of pregnancy: 'bikini babes', *Environment and Planning D* 18: 453–472.

Milligan, C. (2000) Bearing the burden: towards a restructured geography of caring, *Area* 32: 49–58.

Milligan, C. (2003) Location or dis-location: from community to long-term care – the caring experience, *Social & Cultural Geography* 4: 455–470.

Nicholls, D. and Holmes, D. (2012) Discipline, desire and transgression in physiotherapy practice, *Physiotherapy Theory and Practice* 28: 454–465.

Oerton, S. (2004) Bodywork boundaries: power, politics and professionalism in therapeutic spaces, *Gender, Work and Organization* 11: 544–565.

Osgood, J. (2005) Who cares? The classed nature of childcare, *Gender and Education* 17: 289–303.

Parr, H. (1999) Bodies and psychiatric medicine: interpreting different geographies of mental health. In Butler, R. and Parr, H. (eds) *Mind and body spaces: geographies of illness, impairment and disability*. London: Routledge.

Paterson, M. (2007) *The senses of touch: haptics, affects and technologies*. Oxford: Berg.

Skeggs, B. (1997) *Formations of class and gender*. London: Sage.

Smith, F., Barker, J., Wainwright, E., Marandet, E. and Buckingham, S. (2008) A new deal for lone parents? Training lone parents for work in West London, *Area* 40: 237–244.

Smyth, F. (2005) Medical geography: therapeutic places, spaces and networks, *Progress in Human Geography* 29: 488–495.

Thrift, N. and Whatmore, S. (2004) *Cultural geography*. London: Routledge.

Twigg, J. (2000a) Carework as a form of bodywork. *Ageing and Society* 20: 389–411.

Twigg, J. (2000b) *Bathing: the body and community care*. London: Routledge.

Wainwright, E., Buckingham, S., Marandet, E. and Smith, F. (2010a) 'Body training': investigating the embodied training choices of/for mothers in West London, *Geoforum* 41: 489–497.

Wainwright, E., Marandet, E., Smith, F. and Rizvi, S. (2010b) The microgeographies of learning bodies and emotions in the 'classroom-salon', *Emotion, Space and Society* 3: 80–89.

Wainwright, E., Marandet, E. and Rizvi, S. (2011a) The means of correct training: embodied regulation in training for body work among mothers, *Sociology of Health and Illness* 33: 220–236.

Wainwright, E., Marandet, E., Buckingham, S. and Smith, F. (2011b) The training-to-work trajectory: pressures for and subversions to participation in the neoliberal learning market in the UK, *Gender, Place and Culture* 18: 635–654.

Wiles, J. and Rosenberg, M. (2001) 'Gentle caring experience'. Seeking alternative health care in Canada, *Health and Place* 7: 209–224.

Williams, A. (1998) Therapeutic landscapes in holistic medicine, *Social Science and Medicine* 5: 83–97.

Williams, A. (ed.) (1999) *Therapeutic landscapes: the dynamic between wellness and place*. Lanham: University Press of America.

Williams, A. (2007) Introduction: the continuing maturation of the therapeutic landscape concept. In Williams, A. (ed.) *Therapeutic Landscapes*. Aldershot: Ashgate.

Wolkowitz, C. (2002) The social relations of body work, *Work, Employment and Society* 16: 497–510.

Wolkowitz, C. (2006) *Bodies at work*. London: Sage.

20

RESEARCH, EVIDENCE AND CLINICAL PRACTICE IN HOMEOPATHY

Morag Heirs

I Introduction

This chapter outlines the current status of evidence-based practice within homeopathy in the UK and touches on some of the key issues around concepts such as research and evidence. It draws on data collected as part of a grounded theory study of the practice of professional UK homeopaths when treating Attention Deficit Hyperactivity Disorder (ADHD) in children. The full grounded theory "getting to the heart of the case" can be found in (Heirs 2012), while this chapter focuses on the issue of research and the use of evidence in practice.

This chapter presents the key ways in which homeopaths made use of research and evidence as concepts in relation to their personal practice. These findings are discussed within a broader context of the rise of evidence-based practice in many areas of health and social care. Finally, reflections on both the practice and the teaching of homeopathy are offered, while remaining mindful of the changing territory.

In the following section, an overview of homeopathy and its current status within the UK healthcare system is provided, followed by a brief discussion on evidence, evidence-based practice and research, both generally and within complementary medicine.

II Overview of homeopathy

Homeopathy originated 200 years ago with the German physician and pharmacologist Samuel Hahnemann (1755–1843). It has numerous features to distinguish it from botanical and allopathic approaches to diagnosis and treatment (Hahnemann 1913). The fundamental principle is the treatment of "like with like": any natural or man-made substance capable of causing specific disease states and symptoms in healthy individuals may be used to treat the same symptoms when they occur as part of sickness. The *materia medica* of homeopathy is based on three main forms of evidence: "provings" (notes and observations of healthy individuals' symptoms in response to being given a homeopathic "remedy", i.e. medicine), clinical observations and toxicology reports.

During homeopathic diagnosis, the symptoms of each patient are considered primarily as an expression of a unique personal state of dis-ease or illness (Gale 2011, Heirs 2012). Qualitative aspects of the patient's experience of illness (for instance, emotions such as "feeling forsaken" or symptom modalities such as "restlessness increased after 1800 hours") are of particular relevance in determining treatment. Concomitant symptoms and co-morbid conditions are also included in the analysis as part of a "symptom complex".

Although homeopaths do take into account allopathic diagnoses and the "Repertory" (systematised list of symptoms and the remedies that can be used to treat them) contains these diagnoses to aid remedy selection, within homeopathic treatment, according to strict Hahnemanian principles, there are no uniform medicines to be given for particular conditions. The remedy for each patient is chosen based on the closest match of a remedy picture to the patients' symptom picture and unique characteristics. Homeopathic pharmacy involves a unique process in which the source material is serially diluted, with violent "succussion" (shaking) at each stage. Called dynamisation or potentisation, the process may be repeated many times until no molecules of the starting substance theoretically remain. During treatment, remedies, potency (level of dilution), dosage and repetition may be changed in response to changes in the patient's condition.

Different homeopathic approaches have been tested in clinical trials and categorised as classical, clinical, complex and isopathic subtypes (Linde *et al.* 1997). Classical homeopathy is the complex intervention described above, involving an in-depth consultation and individualised analysis regardless of the condition being treated (Chapman *et al.* 1999). Clinical homeopathy provides a standardised prescription for a predefined condition, based either on traditional recommendations or on new analysis of symptoms (Clark and Percivall 2000). Complex homeopathy combines several clinical medicines into a single formula (Weiser *et al.* 1998). Isopathic medicines are prepared from known or presumed aetiological agents (Taylor *et al.* 2000). Classical homeopathy can potentially include the other modalities, as part of an individualised course of treatment. It is difficult to define homeopathy as such, but it is worth noting that, when the term classical homeopathy is used in the literature, this usually refers to the Kentian tradition.

III Homeopathy in the UK

In the UK, the majority of homeopathic consultations take place outside of the National Health Service (NHS) and are paid for by patients directly. There are three homeopathic hospitals within the NHS in the UK (correct at time of writing), around 400 homeopathically qualified general practitioners (GPs) practising in the NHS and some small NHS outpatient clinics, in contrast to over 2,000 non-medically qualified (NMQ) or professional homeopaths.[1] Non-medically qualified homeopaths are not statutorily regulated in the UK at present and there are no minimum training requirements, although they have been encouraged to explore voluntary regulation by the House of Lords report and various initiatives by the Foundation for Integrated Health (FIH) (Select Committee on Science and Technology 2000). A promising collaborative initiative between organisations representing professional homeopaths was set up under the name Council of Organisations Registering Homeopaths (CORH); however, this process stalled and was disbanded in 2007. A compromise was reached a few years later with the main registering bodies setting up a single register (www.findahomeopath.org.uk), and the individual organisations, including the largest registering body, the Society of Homeopaths, are continuing with their own approaches to voluntary regulation.

Homeopathy courses for non-medical practitioners are provided by private colleges (some of which were affiliated to universities between 2004 and 2010) and universities, resulting in diplomas, certificates or degrees. Training usually lasts around three years on a part-time or full-time basis and is likely to include supervised practice before and after qualification (Alliance of Registered Homeopaths 2004). The Faculty of Homeopathy provides recognised training courses for qualified healthcare professionals: doctors, nurses, dentists, pharmacists and veterinary surgeons. These are postgraduate modular courses which take 2–3 years to complete.

1 Research and evidence-based practice

Evidence-based medicine (EBM) as an approach is generally associated with the writings of Archie Cochrane, the establishment of the Cochrane Collaboration and extensive work carried out at McMaster University (Lambert 2006). The concepts of EBM and evidence-based practice have begun to spread into most areas of medicine and healthcare, and more recently into education, crime, justice and social welfare (e.g. the Campbell Collaboration), though this has not been without controversy (Kristiansen and Mooney 2004).

Although EBM is by most definitions concerned with synthesising research evidence, clinical expertise and patient values, commentators have highlighted the overwhelming focus on the results of research such as randomised controlled trials. EBM handbooks tend to focus on the location and synthesising of trial evidence, rather than clinical decision-making or elicitation of patient preferences (for example, see Sackett *et al.* 2000). Studies have demonstrated that clinicians and health professionals tend, as do lay people, to make decisions on the basis of heuristics and partial information rather than consistent use of evidence (Elstein and Schwarz 2002). There is therefore a tension between the evidence produced by clinical trials and the actual implementation of the results. The slow pace of research influencing actual clinical practice within conventional medicine is an area of ongoing research (Hanbury *et al.* 2010). The issue of what constitutes evidence has been discussed in detail in numerous papers (for example, Rycroft Malone *et al.* 2004, Glasby *et al.* 2007). There tends to be a contrast between those who argue that "evidence" should be a restricted term used only for research findings, and those who suggest a broader definition that recognises the use of observational, experiential information in decision-making. Researchers from the traditions of anthropology and ethnography have highlighted the narrow definition of what is usually accepted as evidence within EBM – quantitative and usually epidemiological (Lambert 2006), a definition which by its nature appears to exclude patient voices and narratives. These non-statistical research findings have not as yet been formally incorporated into the EBM framework, although systematic reviews have begun to take account of both quantitative and qualitative studies – for example, Kate Flemming's work on palliative care and pain relief, and the work of the EPPI Centre in London (Flemming 2010).

2 Homeopathy, CAM and evidence-based medicine

Complementary and alternative medicine (CAM) has engaged with the development of evidence-based practice in a number of different ways and for various reasons. In general, CAM practitioners operate out-with the conventional medical systems regardless of country, and patients often fund the costs of such treatments from their own pocket rather than being covered by the national health system/insurance schemes. CAM is a heterogeneous group of therapies and systems and it may not always be helpful to think of them as a block.

Some CAM professions have actively encouraged a process of professionalisation within their practitioners – for example, medical herbalists, acupuncturists, chiropractors and osteopaths. The reasons behind such a move may relate to the apparent imbalance in power between the accepted and fringe medicines, lack of access to patients and desire to provide integrated healthcare. For example, by claiming an EBM basis for a therapy or treatment system, practitioners have a clearer case for arguing in favour of insurance coverage or health service provision. As

Barry wrote: "increasing integration requires alternative therapists to start to play the 'evidence' game" (Barry 2006, p. 47).

Homeopathy is an interesting example of CAM and continues to provoke strong feelings within the orthodox medical profession, as evidenced by the ongoing debate about placebo effects and mechanisms of action (e.g. Kleijnen *et al.* 1991, Linde *et al.* 1997, Cucherat *et al.* 2000, Linde and Jobst 2000, Ernst 2002, Dean 2004, Shang, Huwiler-Muntener *et al.* 2005, Shang, Juni *et al.* 2005, Ludtke 2007, Ludtke and Rutten 2008, Rutten and Stolper 2008, Wilson 2009, *Homeopathy* 2006, 2008).

This has implications in terms of adopting an EBM approach and subscribing to the underlying values. As Evans (2008) has reported, the main Australian professional organisation (National Herbalists Association of Australia, NHAA) has been lobbying for increased professionalism and recognition alongside using the discourse of science to explain herbal medicine effects. In a similar vein, Kelner *et al.* (2006) have described how the curriculum for homeopathic training in Canada now includes basic medical sciences, yet research is not seen as particularly relevant to the profession as a whole. These two examples indicate that CAM practitioner training courses and promotional materials are increasingly incorporating elements of conventional science, even though practitioners themselves may not adhere to these beliefs or find research to be relevant to their individual practice.

The use of evidence-based discourse has not been a move greeted with universal approval across the CAM community. For example, there appears to be an emerging division between herbalists who embrace "scientism" versus those who prefer a more traditional approach that incorporates vitalism (the belief that living organisms contain a unique vital spark) and holism (Jagtenberg *et al.* 2006). A similar situation can be seen within the chiropractic profession in the USA as the distance between those practitioners espousing the philosophy of vitalism and those advocating the specific techniques of adjustment has increased. As a result, three quite different chiropractic practice guidelines have been developed and the internal debate continues (Villanueva-Russell 2005).

The tension between scientific and other forms of knowledge is not limited to CAM practitioners. Adams (2000) examined the attitudes and perspectives of UK GPs who used both complementary and conventional medicine within their NHS practices. These doctors described their style of practice as a mixture of scientifically based principles combined with the intuitive application of knowledge to individual patient situations – much as most conventional doctors might identify with. Of the practitioners who contributed data to Adams' study, a small number stressed that EBM was a useful approach when combined with their clinical expertise, but the majority felt EBM was both restrictive and a threat to their style of practice. The GPs' desire for clinical freedom included the ability to practise CAM, which was seen as a clear example of individualised treatment (Adams 2000).

The evidence-based approach may offer valuable opportunities for CAM practitioners both in terms of evaluating and refining their treatments, and in potentially allowing access to NHS patients. However, the suggestion from the research described earlier is that practitioners may have to adjust their practice to accommodate these changes.

The evidence-based movement within most healthcare professions has promoted research from lab-based through to clinical trials as a way to investigate tentative theories of disease and treatment, using research to promote understanding and produce effective treatments. Although there is evidence that the dissemination and implementation of best practice can be patchy within conventional medicine, the healthcare community as a whole is clearly involved with the evolving idea of evidence-based practice (Moulding *et al.* 1999, Grimshaw *et al.* 2004, Sheldon *et al.* 2004, Wigmore *et al.* 2007, National Prospective Tonsillectomy Audit 2008).

III Context to the current research

Initially, a pragmatic pilot randomised controlled trial (RCT) of homeopathy for children and young people (CYPs) with ADHD had been planned to be carried out in North Yorkshire with the aim of trialling recruitment procedures, outcome measures and exploring the CYPs' experiences of homeopathic treatment. This project was part of a funding initiative by the Research Capacity Development programme sponsored by the Department of Health. As part of the preparation for this trial, a systematic review of the existing evidence was carried out (Heirs and Dean 2007). At this point, two key facts emerged; first, due to external circumstances, it would be extremely difficult to continue with the planned pilot RCT and, second, the significant differences in treatment approach used in the published research versus that of the practitioners who would treat the children in the trial cast real doubts on the validity of the proposed trial.

Therefore, a research project which used mixed methods to achieve comprehensiveness and development of the controversial topic area was developed.

IV Aims

This chapter examines how professional homeopaths thought about and made use of research and research evidence within their clinical practice both generally and within the context of treating children and young people. The extent to which homeopaths might be willing or interested in adapting their practice as a result of formal research was unclear from an initial literature review and formed one of the questions addressed in this piece of work.

V Overview of the methods

A mixed methods approach was adopted to achieve comprehensiveness and development across the broader research programme (O'Cathain *et al.* 2007). The specific context (homeopathy for children with ADHD) is both controversial and poorly understood, indicating a need to explore and chart details of the homeopathic treatment of children. As a result of scarce previous work in this area, it was unclear if one research method would be sufficient to provide a detailed picture; therefore, several methods were considered. Each individual method was used to develop and refine the other methods, and this is reflected in the data which form this chapter.

Ethical approval was obtained from the relevant departmental ethics committee (no NHS approval was required) and multiple approaches were made as the project developed and new data were required to be collected.

1 Grounded theory and mixed methods

A grounded theory approach was adopted throughout this project from design, through data collection, to analysis (Glaser and Strauss 1967, Glaser 1999, 2008). While grounded theory is generally used within purely qualitative research traditions, it was originally conceived of as an approach to data collection and analysis that emphasised working from the original data and remained open to emerging concepts, without limiting the methods themselves.

The following key elements of grounded theory were adopted in this piece of research: theoretical sensitivity; purposive and theoretical sampling; constant comparison; and memo writing. Strauss and Corbin's writings were used along with Charmaz's practical guide to grounded theory when applying the coding stages (incident, open and axial) (Strauss and Corbin 1998, Charmaz 2005, 2006). Throughout the project, attention was paid to the roots of grounded theory while bearing in mind the more recent awareness of constructivism introduced by Charmaz, among others, and the ongoing development of the methodology itself (Charmaz 2005, 2006, Clarke 2007, White et al. 2012). Data were collected using interviews with key informants, a written survey, documentary analysis, practitioner interviews and participant observations (see later sections for more details).

Only modest claims are offered within the analysis, attempting to avoid over-generalisation and maintaining an awareness of a constructivist viewpoint (Charmaz 2005, Clarke 2007) – the resultant theory is therefore presented as a "located and limited story" (Daly 1997, p. 360). This allows a researcher to develop a solid grounded theory that is transparently based on the collected data and offers clear areas for further developmental research without the risk of overstating the findings.

The constructivist approach to grounded theory clearly foregrounds the importance of considering the impact and identity of the researcher themselves (Hall and Callery 2001, Mruck and Mey 2007). A deliberate effort was made to consider how I would present myself at the outset of the project. The focus was on coming across as a well-informed researcher who was interested in homeopathy, but without any strong beliefs around effectiveness. This position of an open-minded, relatively agnostic but homeopathy-sensitive researcher was an accurate reflection of my personal position. I had a reasonable understanding of homeopathy at the outset of the project due to previous work as a researcher with the Glasgow Homeopathic Hospital. I also taught modules on complementary medicine to medical students for Glasgow and Hull York Medical Schools, and provided advice to several students studying for BScs in homeopathy. Throughout the project, I used bracketing and discussion of my prior beliefs with supervisors and mentors to create awareness of my impact on the collection and analysis of the data.

2 Data collection

a Key informants

The key informants comprised four experienced homeopaths based within both academia and clinical practice; they provided specialist knowledge and balanced views across different styles of homeopathy, and contributed to various stages of the project. They were involved in the development of this research and informed the survey, participant observation and interview contents.

b Survey of practitioners

The targeted self-completion survey included a mixture of structured and semi-structured items and covered demographic information, details on the respondents' training and current practice, practical considerations around working with CYPs and opinions of the homeopathy evaluated in trials around ADHD. The second section used short vignettes describing the treatment approach adopted in each of the published trials of homeopathy for ADHD, and asked respondents to rate similarity to their own practice on a range of Likert scales.

The survey was administered at the Society of Homeopaths' 2007 annual conference. Thirty-eight completed questionnaires were returned at the research desk or by post, giving a response rate of 19 per cent for the survey. Survey respondents were 8 per cent students and 92 per cent qualified practitioners, which mirrored the conference attendance overall (10 per cent students, 90 per cent qualified practitioners; information supplied by the event organisers). The majority of respondents were female (31 out of 38) and the mean age was 52 years (min = 38 yrs, max = 66 yrs, SD 6.51). Respondents had been in practice for between 0 and 25 years, with a mean of 9.5 years (SD 7.14). Most of the survey respondents practised in England (84 per cent), covering nine regions, with three respondents attending from Scotland. Survey respondents were drawn from over 15 different training colleges covering a variety of styles, mainly classical but also including practical homeopathy. Three practitioners had studied with more than one college for their basic certificate and three gave only the duration of their course rather than the provider.

c Documentary analysis

Information on how homeopaths treat children is relatively scarce and tends to be found in specialist booklets, occasional textbooks and case reports. The documentary evidence was gathered from the systematic review search results (producing case reports and seminar descriptions), suggested references mentioned by the key informants and further sources/references given by the survey respondents (see Table 20.1).

Table 20.1 Documentary evidence sources

Type	n	Notes
Theoretical articles	14	These papers presented treatment strategies, remedy lists or case taking suggestions relating to working with children in particular and ADHD in most cases. Three of the fourteen papers also presented brief case studies. However, the main focus was on the treatment details and theory of ADHD according to homeopathy. Three articles discussed novel prescribing methods used in the Frei cross-over trial.
		(Frei *et al.* 2006; Frei *et al.* 2007; Frei 2009b; Glass 1994; Guess 1995; Goodman-Herrick 1997; Reichenberg-Ullman and Ullman 2000a, 1999; Diamond 1995; Ball 1997; Reichenberg-Ullman and Ullman 1993; Schulz 2005; Reichenberg-Ullman and Ullman 1990; Jordan 2000)
Dissertations	2	Philippa Fibert's undergraduate dissertation summarised trials and compiled remedy lists (Fibert 2009).
		Nancy Kelly's undergraduate dissertation presented case summaries, not all of which had been published elsewhere, and discussed the homeopathic approach to ADHD (Kelly 1995)
General textbooks	10	These sources comprised a mixture of classic texts as recommended by key informant 1 and those given as essential reading on homeopathy training courses between 2005 and 2007 (Watson 1991; Dudgeon 1994 [1854]; Hahnemann 1913 [1810]; Kurz 2005; Dhawale 1985; Roberts 2005; Campbell 1984; Owen 2007; Hughes 1994 [1902]; Sankaran 1999)
Child/ADHD specific homeopathic texts	9 booklets, texts and chapters	Textbooks, booklets and chapters found through literature searches suggested by survey responses and browsing homeopathic book stands at CPD events (Foubister 1954 [1994]; Herscu 1991, 1996; Kaplan 2002; Jain 2004; Borland 1929, unknown; Rousseau and Fortier-Bernoville 1988 [1976]; Reichenberg-Ullman and Ullman 2000b)

d Practitioner interviews

There were three main phases of interview schedule used in this project; the initial exploratory schedule which was used with the first three participants; a revised interview schedule which was used with the remainder; and a follow-up schedule that was used with those participants who were interviewed more than once.

The key topics covered were: practitioner background and style of homeopathy; experience with children and ADHD; first and follow-up appointments for CYP patients; homeopathy as practised in the published trials; research and homeopathy.

The main differences between the initial and revised interview schedule was the removal of questions about particular outcome measures. It was clear both from the initial interviews and the survey data that these questions were difficult for practitioners to answer and failed to generate useful data.

The vignettes constructed for the survey were incorporated into the interview and broadly similar questions were asked. Ten further interviews were carried out using this revised schedule and format. A total of 14 homeopaths were interviewed, with 19 formal interviews being recorded and transcribed. Some homeopaths were interviewed more than once to clarify responses, to follow up issues that arose during research and to explore emergent themes during the analysis. The three participants who were also key informants contributed more informally during discussions and email correspondence, with such data being incorporated into field notes and a research journal. The majority (79 per cent) of the interviewees were female ($n = 11$) and the mean age of the sample was 51 years (38–61 yrs, SD 6.24). Interviews were deliberately conducted over a range of experience levels as is reflected in the data on years in practice. Practitioners had been in practice for an average of 9.6 years at the time of interview (SD 7.9), and this ranged from six months to over 30 years. All participants have been anonymised. As with respondents to the survey, the majority of those interviewed trained at a college which followed a classical approach at least in the early years. Two homeopaths were introduced to practical homeopathy in the early stages of their career, and a further two underwent an apprenticeship-style training – an approach which is now largely extinct.

e Participant observation

Participant observation was undertaken at four events: a workshop on homeopathy for CYPs run by a leading practitioner, a continuing professional development (CPD) workshop on a particular method of prescribing, a seminar on evidence and research in homeopathy and a conference devoted to homeopathy for CYPs (see Table 20.2).

VI Analysis overview

Analysis was ongoing during data collection, as is usual within any grounded theory project, and crossed over between data types. For example, the initial interviews were analysed concurrently with some of the survey responses, while later interviews were analysed without specific reference to the survey. Participant observation during the workshop on research for homeopaths generated ideas which informed both the conduct and the analysis of the final few interviews. The initial models were generated from the interview data and information from the clinical trials. The categories established at this stage were then explicitly explored using data from observations, the survey and textbooks/published papers. These additional sources of information provided angles to interrogate and challenge the developing model.

Table 20.2 Participant observation settings

	Children and Homeopathy Workshop	Sankaran and Sensation Prescribing CPD	Children and Homeopathy Conference	Research and Homeopathy CPD
Event details	Part of a series of CPD workshops organised by the Society of Homeopaths. This workshop focused on working with children and adolescents, including techniques and ethical issues.	A regional workshop to explore and demonstrate the Sankaran style of homeopathy. Included case studies, videoed consultations and group discussions.	Society of Homeopaths' annual conference devoted to CYPs and homeopathy. Included expert speakers on various conditions, approaches and methods.	Part of a series of CPD workshops organised by the Society of Homeopaths. This workshop was advertised as suitable for new and experienced practitioners who wished to be able to deal with those who questioned the research on homeopathy.
Location	London, UK 2007	North-East England 2006	Leicester, UK, 2007	North-West England 2008
Delegate details	36 delegates. Most were new to working with children and had come for advice and recommendations. Most had qualified in the previous three years and included homeopaths from across the UK.	24 delegates. All were practising homeopaths with a range of familiarity in the topic.	200 delegates from across the UK and Europe.	36 delegates, including final-year students, newly qualified and experienced practitioners.

Grounded theory advocates using both broad and focused coding styles simultaneously and/ or cyclically. Throughout the coding process, Strauss and Corbin's guidelines on open and axial coding proved to be the most fruitful, alongside Charmaz's incident-to-incident coding (Strauss and Corbin 1998, Charmaz 2006).

This chapter focuses on homeopaths' attitudes to and use of research evidence within their personal practice, the data for which were analysed within a broader category of "what shapes and changes practice" within the full grounded theory "getting to the heart of the case" (Heirs 2012).

VI Findings

Figure 20.1 illustrates the components of the key concept that research and evidence-based practice were poorly understood and strategically used by homeopaths. Interest and willingness to alter clinical practice based on research varied. The following themes contributed: the impact

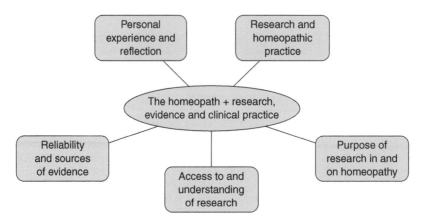

Figure 20.1 Research, evidence-based practice and homeopaths.

of personal experience and reflection, the reliability of sources of evidence, practitioner access to and understanding of research, the purpose of homeopathic research and its relation to homeopathic practice.

1 Impact of personal experience and reflection

When homeopaths were asked about what had shaped their clinical practice or might change it in the future, there was a strong theme around learning and adapting from personal experience or from the experience of other practitioners. Key factors ranged from an encounter with a particular patient, to knowledge gained from attending practitioner seminars and the discussion of case studies. An interviewee (a long-term practitioner) described her experiences of attending seminars in novel or unusual methods of prescribing, adapting the ideas by integrating them into her practice where appropriate and continuing to evaluate their usefulness. One key informant suggested that personal experience may be the thing most likely to influence or change a homeopath's practice, simply because of the nature of the profession:

> BETH: Homeopaths are very individual, like working on their own, they don't like being told what to do. There are lots of ways of doing homeopathy which work, it's really down to personal preference which you adopt.

When discussing the example of one particular trial of homeopathy for ADHD with Beth (the trial used LMs[2] and polarity analysis, which Beth does not currently use in her practice), Beth made it clear that she felt that very little would change her practice. She uses her individual way of working, which is borne out by the results seen in her patients.

In contrast to this, several practitioners categorically stated that they would consider changing their practice if offered "evidence" that their methods were not the most effective, or there might be a quicker solution. During follow-up interviews, a scenario was posed where a good-quality trial directly contradicted the homeopath's clinical experience. This provoked a mixed response. Some practitioners felt they would want to re-examine their own practice and carefully compare their methods with those tested in trials, which points to an openness to reflecting on one's practice; however, others felt that trials were by their design too different from real practice and therefore not relevant. Those practitioners who were open to the idea of changing or adapting their practice also referred to seeing persuasive case studies or attending workshops as being previous triggers for change. There was considerable emphasis placed on the patient's responses: if it could be shown that patients were improving, then the homeopaths felt they would at least explore the treatment.

> GLORIA: If there was a way of coming to a homeopathic remedy to treat eczema that made a big difference to eczema, to people suffering from eczema, I would change my practice and work that way. Certainly I would, because I would want the best for that patient. But to change my whole practice (to this new way of working), I would want to know that it worked well for everything and not just eczema.

One key informant described her experience of prescribing within a clinical trial for patients with fibromyalgia. She mentioned that when reviewing the notes and prescriptions it appeared that nosodes (a particular type of remedy) had been a turning point for many of the patients.

> MARY: It was interesting because there was two of us working, so it made us a lot more classical actually because we had to really justify our every prescription and decisions.... It made us very much more conscientious and grounded and justified. Less off the cuff, gut feeling and more justified.

This careful reflection on one's own results was part of the trial procedure rather than part of normal practice, although Mary commented that she felt they had obtained better results because of this rigour.

This theme suggests that at least some practitioners display an open-minded, empirical style of working. It could be argued that this pragmatic approach reflects the original development of homeopathy based on directly observable patient improvement as a form of useful evidence to inform clinical practice. However, this was not true for all participants, some of whom felt their current practice was sufficiently effective.

2 *Sources of evidence*

Practitioners detailed a range of sources of evidence in the survey responses, and again in the interviews. These included case studies, practice guidelines, textbooks and seminar notes, along-side personal experience. Published trials were rarely mentioned as sources of information to inform clinical practice. The topic of reliability or trustworthiness of these sources was mentioned in three interviews with experienced practitioners.

For example, when talking about her understanding of homeopathy and research, Violet brought up the idea of differing reliability. Case studies and personal guidelines are often reported in the homeopathic literature and are then adopted by other practitioners. In contrast, Violet adopted a critical attitude to these sources, suggesting that you need lots of information to actually progress, and that following new sets of rigid rules would not necessarily make practitioners more methodical. She appeared to be particularly critical where "different principles were getting mixed up". Violet was one of only two practitioners who mentioned being wary of relying on dramatic case studies in particular, while most other participants indicated such evidence was very persuasive.

This theme introduces the idea of multiple types of evidence being acceptable to homeopaths, although trials were not usually included in this body of information. There was limited evidence of critical appraisal when practitioners discussed the various sources.

3 Access to and understanding research

This theme was directly addressed within much of the interview and participant-observation data, and more broadly through survey and documentary sources. Key elements included awareness and access to research, understanding of terminology and critical appraisal skills.

Respondents in the interviews talked about reading journals, such as the *Society of Homeopaths Journal* and *Homeopathic Links*, both of which focus heavily on case studies and similar descriptive accounts of practice, rather than comparative studies as you might expect in conventional medical publications. These participants had limited access to scientific papers, journals and research-oriented conferences, with professional publications focusing on individual case studies, provings and discursive pieces.

During the research workshop, there was a display and introduction to some of the typical CAM journals – it was clear from the comments that most of the participants had never seen or read these. Many practitioners are not connected to a university so will have little access to these publications. The day itself consisted of overview lectures on research methods in homeopathy, summaries of some systematic reviews and introductions to some of the apparent challenges for homeopathy research.

Analysis of the interview and research workshop observation data in particular suggested that homeopaths were not particularly comfortable with the terminology around research. Concepts such as randomisation and the purpose of comparative studies were unfamiliar to most of the participants. My observations suggested there were several occasions during the day where the audience appeared to be confused.

Medicine has been historically taught as a large, complex subject best learned through lectures and one-way provision of information. The newer approach to teaching, such as that exemplified by the Hull York Medical School, is problem-based learning with a strong patient focus (General Medical Council 2009). Rather than expecting students to learn large quantities of information by rote, critical thinking and information-finding skills are emphasised during sessions which help future doctors learn how to identify and appraise the available evidence when making clinical decisions. In contrast, my experience of providing advice and supervision to several Homeopathy BSc-level students suggests that the main teaching is still carried out in the direct information provision style with relatively little critique of the sources themselves.

These data suggest that these homeopathic practitioners had relatively little exposure to the range of formal research within and on homeopathy. They may lack the understanding of the various research methods or have yet to develop critical appraisal skills. Such research is less likely therefore to impact directly on homeopaths' clinical practice.

4 Research and homeopathic practice

Research within homeopathy may be characterised as falling into three camps: provings and case studies carried out by and reported for other homeopaths (e.g. Anwer 2007); lab-based research trying to show an effect of homeopathic remedies at a cellular or animal level (e.g. Bellavite *et al.* 2009); observational studies and trials trying to show the effectiveness or efficacy of homeopathy in named conditions (e.g. Frei *et al.* 2005). The latter two categories are most often published in mainstream medical journals that practitioners find difficult to access, with relatively few papers about how the findings might be implemented. For one unusual example of a trial leading to the evolution of a refined prescribing approach, see Frei (2009a).

According to a key informant and many of the delegates at the workshop on homeopathy research, the purpose of research for practising homeopaths fell under three main headings, none of which related directly to treatment per se but indicated strategic use:

- We need research for the public: "we know it works but we need to show them".
- We need research "for quotes/back-up in our own writing and articles".
- We need research for communicating with organisations like local government/NHS.

Practitioners seemed to be referring to trials and similar publications when they talked about "research". It was referred to frequently as a way of providing answers to sceptics and the public, since practitioners knew homeopathy works anyway. "I know it works, I've seen it working and I want to have the information to convince other people it works" (new graduate at the Research in Homeopathy workshop). Observational data from the workshop on research for practitioners illustrated the use of research as a strategic tool by focusing on the problems of the classic placebo-controlled RCT, which appeared to be set up for criticism rather than explored in detail. The evidence was presented as lists of studies with favourable results (lacking in critical evaluation) and de-constructing those trials which had less positive outcomes. The focus was explicitly on helping practitioners answer common criticisms, with little discussion of the implications of research findings for clinical practice. There was a strong emphasis on the positive findings of trials and systematic reviews both at a basic mechanistic level and at a clinical level. Where there were negative studies, these were often dismissed as having used inappropriate methods (workshop presenter) or as irrelevant where practitioners knew treatment was effective based on their own experience (practitioner).

> RUTH: maybe the lab methods don't work for testing homeopathy? Fundamentally if my patients get better then we know it works.

Reflecting this attitude, I noted in December 2007 that the Society of Homeopaths' web page on research made the following strong claim, which was followed by a list of positive trials and systematic reviews (without an accompanying quality appraisal) and a list of conditions where there was "sufficient evidence" to support homeopathic treatment, again without quality appraisal: "Although more research is needed, the balance of evidence already shows that treatment by a homeopath is clinically effective, cost-effective and safe" (www.homeopathy-soh.org/research/, December 2007). The page was edited to read as follows in February 2014, although there was still no clear appraisal as to the quality or reliability of the evidence: "Although more research is needed, the balance of evidence so far suggests that homeopathy can be a clinically effective and safe treatment option." Subsequently (December 2014), the research pages have been updated and display more measured summaries of homeopathic research, including discussion of trial design and quality.

Drawing on the documentary data, a published case study by the Reichenberg-Ullmans from 1999 provides a further exemplar of the uncritical use of published research (Reichenberg-Ullman and Ullman 1999). The article briefly mentioned a piece of previous research (Lamont 1997) as corroborating their experience as practitioners with success in treating ADHD. The Lamont study was referred to as a supportive source without particular details or any critique, despite the research being fundamentally flawed and unreliable for a number of reasons (Heirs and Dean 2007, Heirs 2009).

The idea of needing "evidence" when communicating with health professionals came through very strongly during the research workshop for homeopaths. A substantial proportion of delegates were new or final year graduates looking to start their practice or make connections in the local healthcare setting. The following extracts from my field-notes are illustrative of the statements which were repeated throughout the introductions from both new and experienced practitioners:

> HOMEOPATH (Wales and Nigeria clinics): felt "quite knocked" by scientific community, difficult to find answers to friends who are scientific. Wanted answers.
>
> NEW GRADUATE: Gave talk to Women's Institute but a GP in the audience asked about research – felt thrown because had no answers. Want answers and to monitor own practice.

This theme provides evidence that most participants conceptualised research in terms of trials and published studies that were useful when providing proof to sceptics, potential clients and healthcare commissioners. There were indications that research was being strategically used by individual practitioners, organisations and other researchers.

Research was never directly mentioned as being a source of ideas for changing practice for these homeopaths. "Research" appeared to be conceptualised as something that was most often done to homeopathy with the purpose of proving or disproving efficacy.

While there was some evidence of increased awareness of the evidence-based medicine movement generally and within the NHS in particular, this was mostly couched in terms of defending homeopathy and justifying its availability. There seemed to be little recognition that research itself could be a useful learning tool for practitioners.

VII Summary

This chapter has outlined a piece of grounded theory research which proposes that research and evidence-based practice was poorly understood, and strategically used by some homeopathic practitioners. Practitioner interest and willingness to alter clinical practice based on research evidence varied considerably. Homeopaths in this study were more likely to refer to clinical experiences, case studies from the literature and workshops as significant influences on their practice than formally published research, such as observational or experimental studies. The findings from these data suggest that homeopaths are much less engaged with the evidence-based practice/research movement than healthcare professionals in the conventional healthcare sector.

There are clear discrepancies between the types of research being conducted in the scientific homeopathic community and the relevance of this research for homeopathic practitioners. This is likely to contribute to the current lack of engagement with the evidence-based movement. The situation has strong echoes of the Cooksey report of 2006, which reviewed the design and funding arrangements of the public funding of conventional health research in the UK (Cooksey 2006). Cooksey highlighted two "gaps in translation": the first gap referred to the lack of follow-through between basic level research and clinical trials; the second gap referred to where evidence exists but there is a lack of implementation in practice (see Figure 20.2).

Within the homeopathic research world, laboratory-based research on molecular-level action does not appear linked to clinical trials (for example, see Lahnstein et al. 2009); and results of clinical trials do not routinely seem to be disseminated to practitioners or implemented in daily practice. For example, a feasibility trial looking at treating childhood asthma within an NHS homeopathic hospital concluded that, although this condition represented one of the most common reasons for referral, the results showed insufficient benefit and any future trial should

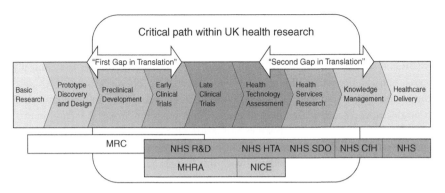

Figure 20.2 Cooksey's "gaps in translation" in healthcare research.

concentrate on primary care level referrals (Thompson *et al.* 2011). Interestingly, despite the lack of a cost-effective or clinically useful improvement in symptoms, the paper did not address the issue of whether children with severe asthma should continue to be referred to NHS homeopathic hospitals or other secondary care facilities.

The ongoing resistance to evidence-based medicine in conventional healthcare has been characterised as a reaction from professionals who feel threatened, and who fear losing their clinical autonomy to formulaic approaches. Some of these responses were clearly echoed in the data from the homeopaths, where practitioners felt research was distant from their experience and could not adequately reflect their interests. There was a strong sense that "research" findings were thought of as strategic tools to gain service funding, or to answer critics, rather than as a way to inform clinical practice.

It is suggested that the reactions to, understanding of and use of "research" in these contexts reflects an ongoing struggle faced by practising homeopaths between the desire to professionalise and the desire to continue practising in their own unique and individualised styles.

VIII Implications

The findings from this project suggest there are a number of ways that homeopathic research and teaching may develop in the future. The teaching of homeopathy has moved in recent years from private colleges towards further and higher education establishments; however, this has taken the form of a physical movement/application for accreditation rather than a wholesale embracing of critical thinking and evidence-based teaching.

At present, there is a lack of good-quality research that progresses from case studies/series, through observational to clinical comparative trials. The homeopathic community is relatively new to the idea of a research culture, and to date has focused on the strategic use of results to shore up their position rather than reflecting on their own practice. In contrast, data from two homeopaths who were involved in pragmatic trials suggested that the process of in-depth case discussion and reaching prescribing decisions helped to clarify the decision-making processes, highlighted similarities across patients and may have increased consistency. Research itself has the potential to be a useful learning tool for individual practitioners as well as the wider homeopathic community.

Homeopathy has long prided itself on a strong foundation of observed data from the original writings of Samuel Hahnemann; the application of critical appraisal and modern research methods could be a natural evolution of homeopathy. Research around cognitive biases have helped to inform current research practices in medicine by highlighting the need to do more than rely on retrospective reports of health improvements or deterioration. Indeed, two small studies have previously suggested that homeopathic prescribing may not be reproducible across practitioners (Brien *et al.* 2004, Burch *et al.* 2008). Clearly, there is an interesting and clinically valuable research opportunity within this area.

Homeopathic teaching could take account of this increasing body of knowledge when dealing with original sources rather than present the information as definitive. It seems essential that modern homeopaths understand the benefits and shortcomings of clinical research methods, rather than focusing on the placebo controlled RCT as being the only face of research. Ultimately, researchers need to acknowledge their own prior beliefs, and remain open to the possibility that the research data may require a change in attitude, beliefs and practice.

Notes

1 Based on membership figures and registrations with the main accrediting and professional bodies in the UK: Society of Homeopaths, Alliance of Registered Homeopaths, Faculty of Homeopathy and the British Homeopathic Association.
2 LM refers to a particular potency sometimes used in homeopathic remedies, distinct from the centesimal scale.

References

Adams, J. (2000). "General practitioners, complementary therapies and evidence-based medicine: the defence of clinical autonomy". *Complementary Therapies in Medicine* 8(4): 248–252.

Alliance of Registered Homeopaths (2004). *Which Homeopathy Course? Second Edition*. Nutley, East Sussex: Alliance of Registered Homeopaths.

Anwer, B. M. (2007). "The proving of OPV-num in infantile dementia". *National Journal of Homoeopathy* 9(9): 31–33.

Ball, N. (1997). "Anti-social behaviour, hyperactivity and poor concentration in children, or attention deficit hyperactive disorder". *Homeopathy International* 11(1): 29–30.

Barry, C. A. (2006). "The role of evidence in alternative medicine: contrasting biomedical and anthropological approaches". *Social Science & Medicine* 62(11): 2646–2657.

Bellavite, P., P. Magnani, M. Marzotto and A. Conforti (2009). "Assays of homeopathic remedies in rodent behavioural and psychopathological models". *Homeopathy: the Journal of the Faculty of Homeopathy* 98(4): 208–227.

Borland, D. M. (unknown). *Children's Types*. London: British Homeopathic Association.

Borland, D. M. (1929). *Homeopathy for Mother and Infant*. New Delhi: B. Jain.

Brien, S., P. Prescott, D. Owen and G. Lewith (2004). "How do homeopaths make decisions? An exploratory study of inter-rater reliability and intuition in the decision making process". *Homeopathy* 93(3): 125–131.

Burch, A. L., B. Dibb and S. B. Brien (2008). "Understanding homeopathic decision-making: a qualitative study". *Forschende Komplementarmedizin* 15(4): 218–225.

Campbell, A. (1984). *The Two Faces of Homeopathy*. New Delhi: Robert Hale.

Chapman, E. H., R. J. Weintraub, M. A. Milburn, T. O. Pirozzi and E. Woo (1999). "Homeopathic treatment of mild traumatic brain injury: a randomized, double-blind, placebo-controlled clinical trial". *Journal of Head Trauma Rehabilitation* 14(6): 521–542.

Charmaz, K. (2005). "Grounded theory: objectivist and constructivist methods". *Handbook of Qualitative Research*. N. Denzin and Y. Lincoln. Thousand Oaks, CA: Sage.

Charmaz, K. (2006). *Constructing Grounded Theory: A Practical Guide Through Qualitative Analysis*. London: Sage.

Clark, J. and A. Percivall (2000). "A preliminary investigation into the effectiveness of the homeopathic remedy, Ruta graveolens, in the treatment of pain in plantar fasciitis". *British Journal of Podiatry* 3(3): 8185.

Clarke, A. E. (2007). "Grounded theory: critiques, debates and situational analysis". *The Sage Handbook of Social Science Methodology*. W. Outhwaite and S. P. Turner. London: Sage Publications.

Cooksey, D. (2006). *A Review of UK Health Research Funding*, London: HM Treasury.

Cucherat, M., M. C. Haugh, M. Gooch and J. P. Boissel (2000). "Evidence of clinical efficacy of home-opathy. A meta-analysis of clinical trials. HMRAG. Homeopathic Medicines Research Advisory Group". *European Journal of Clinical Pharmacology* 56(1): 27–33.

Daly, K. (1997). "Replacing theory in ethnography: a postmodern view". *Qualitative Enquiry* 3(3): 343–365.

Dean, M. E. (2004). *The Trials of Homeopathy: Origins, Structure and Development*. Essen, Germany: KVC-Verlag.

Dhawale, M. L. (1985). *Principles and Practice of Homeopathy (Part I)*. Bombay: Institute of Clinical Research.

Diamond, W. J. (1995). "The homeopathic treatment of attention deficit disorder and behavior problems in children". *Biological Therapies* 13(2): 38–41.

Dudgeon, R. E. (1994 [1854]). *Lectures on the Theory and Practice of Homeopathy*. New Delhi: DEL, India.

Elstein, A. S. and A. Schwarz (2002). "Clinical problem solving and diagnostic decision making: selective review of the cognitive literature". *BMJ* 324(7339): 729–732.

Ernst, E. (2002). "A systematic review of systematic reviews of homeopathy". *British Journal of Clinical Pharmacology* 54(6): 577–582.

Evans, S. (2008). "Changing the knowledge base in Western herbal medicine". *Social Science & Medicine* 67(12): 2098–2106.

Fibert, P. (2009). *What Is an Appropriate Method for the Homoepathic Treatment of and Research Into ADHD*. BSc, Purton House School of Homeopathy/Thames Valley University.

Flemming, K. (2010). "The use of morphine to treat cancer-related pain: a synthesis of quantitative and qualitative research". *Journal of Pain and Symptom Management* 39: 139–154.

Foubister, D. M. (1954). *Homeopathy and Paediatrics*, pamphlet, New Delhi: B. Jain.

Frei, H. (2009a). "Polarity analysis, a new approach to increase the precision of homeopathic prescriptions". *Homeopathy: the Journal of the Faculty of Homeopathy* 98(1): 49–55.

Frei, H. (2009b). "Homeopathic treatment of children with attention deficit hyperactivity disorder: results of a long-term study over 5 years, including a randomized double-blind placebo controlled crossover trial". *Attention Deficit Hyperactivity Disorder (ADHD)*. M. Gordon and E. Michell. New York: Nova Biomedical Books.

Frei, H., R. Everts, K. von Ammon, F. Kaufmann, D. Walther, S. F. Hsu-Schmitz, M. Collenberg, K. Fuhrer, R. Hassink, M. Steinlin and A. Thurneysen (2005). "Homeopathic treatment of children with attention deficit hyperactivity disorder: a randomised, double blind, placebo controlled crossover trial". *European Journal of Pediatrics* 164(12): 758–767.

Frei, H., R. Everts, K. von Ammon, F. Kaufmann, D. Walther, S. F. Schmitz, M. Collenberg, M. Steinlin, C. Lim and A. Thurneysen (2007). "Randomised controlled trials of homeopathy in hyperactive children: treatment procedure leads to an unconventional study design. Experience with open-label homeopathic treatment preceding the Swiss ADHD placebo controlled, randomised, double-blind, cross-over trial". *Homeopathy* 96(1): 35–41.

Frei, H., K. von Ammon and A. Thurneysen (2006). "Treatment of hyperactive children: increased efficiency through modifications of homeopathic diagnostic procedure". *Homeopathy* 95(3): 163–170.

Gale, N. K. (2011). "From body-talk to body-stories: educating for body work in complementary and alternative medicine". *Sociology of Health and Illness Special Edition/Monograph, Body Work in Health and Social Care: Critical Themes, Future Agendas* 33(2): 237–251.

General Medical Council (2009). *Tomorrow's Doctors*. London: GMC.

Glasby, J., K. Walshe and G. Harvey (2007). "What counts as 'evidence' in evidence-based practice?" *Evidence and Policy* 3(3): 325–327.

Glaser, B. G. (1999). "The future of grounded theory". *Qualitative Health Research* 9(6): 836–845.

Glaser, B. G. (2008). *Doing Quantitative Grounded Theory*. Mill Valley, CA: Sociology Press.

Glaser, B. G. and A. Strauss (1967). *Discovery of Grounded Theory: Strategies for Qualitative Research*. Chicago: Aldine.

Glass, M. (1994). "Hyperactive children and attention deficit disorder". *Journal of the American Institute of Homeopathy* 87(4): 234–236.

Goodman-Herrick, P. (1997). "Children with pervasive development delay or attention deficit disorder/hyperactivity: working with their parents". *New England Journal of Homoeopathy* 6(2–3): 31–35.

Grimshaw, J. M., R. E. Thomas and G. MacLennan (2004). "Effectiveness and efficiency of guideline dissemination and implementation strategies". *Health Technology Assessment* 8(6).

Guess, G. (1995). "Rethinking attention deficit disorder: seminar presented by Paul Herscu". *Homoeopathic Links* 8(3): 46–47.

Hahnemann, S. (1913). *Organon of the Rational Healing Art*. London: J. M. Dent, Everyman's Library.

Hall, W. A. and P. Callery (2001). "Enhancing the rigor of grounded theory: incorporating reflexivity and relationality". *Qualitative Health Research* 11(2): 257–272.

Hanbury, A., C. Thompson, P. Wilson, K. Farley, D. Chambers, E. Warren, J. Bibby, R. Mannion, I. Watt and S. Gilbody (2010). "Translating research into practice in Leeds and Bradford (TRiPLaB): a protocol for a programme of research". *Implementation Science* 5(1): 37.

Heirs, M. (2009). " 'Further research required' ". *Homoeopath* 28(1): 9–12.

Heirs, M. and M. E. Dean (2007). "Homeopathy for attention deficit/hyperactivity disorder or hyper-kinetic disorder". *Cochrane Database of Systematic Reviews* 4.

Heirs, M. K. (2012). *A Mixed Methods Exploration of Homeopathy for Attention Deficit Hyperactivity Disorder: Comparing Research Evidence and Clinical Practice*. PhD, University of York.

Herscu, P. (1991). *The Homeopathic Treatment of Children; Pediatric Constitutional Types*. Berkeley, CA: North Atlantic Books.

Herscu, P. (1996). *Stramonium: With an Introduction to Analysis Using Cycles and Segments*. Amherst, MA: New England School of Homeopathy Press.

Homeopathy (2006). "Special issue reporting on the Shang *et al.* meta-analysis". *Homeopathy: the Journal of the Faculty of Homeopathy* 95(1): 1–64.

Homeopathy (2008). "The 2005 meta-analysis of homeopathy: the importance of post-publication data". *Homeopathy: the Journal of the Faculty of Homeopathy* 97(4): 169–177.

Hughes, R. (1994 [1902]). *The Principles and Practice of Homeopathy*. New Delhi: B. Jain.

Jagtenberg, T., S. Evans, A. Grant, I. Howden, M. Lewis and J. Singer (2006). "Evidence-based medicine and naturopathy". *Journal of Alternative and Complementary Medicine* 12(3): 323–328.

Jain, P. B. (2004). *Essentials of Pediatrics*. Mumbai: Nitya Publications.

Jordan, L. (2000). "Homeopathic treatment of challenging children". *Journal of the Australian Traditional-Medicine Society* 6(3): 97–99.

Kaplan, B. (2002). *The Homeopathic Conversation: The Art of Taking the Case*. London, Natural Medicine Press.

Kelly, N. A. (1995). *Standard of Care: A Critical Comparison of Pharmacological and Homeoapthic Treatment of Childhood Attention Deficit Disorders*. BSc, Prescott College AZ.

Kelner, M., B. Wellman, S. Welsh and H. Boon (2006). "How far can complementary and alternative medicine go? The case of chiropractic and homeopathy". *Social Science & Medicine* 63(10): 2617–2627.

Kleijnen, J., P. Knipschild and G. Ter Riet (1991). "Clinical trials of homoeopathy". *British Medical Journal* 302(6772): 316–323.

Kristiansen, I. S. and G. H. Mooney (2004). *Evidence-Based Medicine: In Its Place*. London; New York: Routledge.

Kurz, C. (2005). *Imagine Homeopathy: A Book of Experiments, Images and Metaphors*. Harrogate, N. Yorks: Thieme.

Lahnstein, L., M. Binder, A. Thurneysen, M. Frei-Erb, L. Betti, M. Peruzzi, P. Heusser and S. Baum-gartner (2009). "Isopathic treatment effects of Arsenicum album 45x on wheat seedling growth–further reproduction trials". *Homeopathy: the Journal of the Faculty of Homeopathy* 98(4): 198–207.

Lambert, H. (2006). "Accounting for EBM: notions of evidence in medicine". *Social Science & Medicine* 62(11): 2633–2645.

Lamont, J. (1997). "Homoeopathic treatment of attention deficit hyperactivity disorder: a controlled study". *British Homeopathic Journal* 86(10): 196–200.

Linde, K. and K. A. Jobst (2000). "Homeopathy for chronic asthma". *Cochrane Database of Systematic Reviews* 2: CD000353.

Linde, K., N. Clausius, G. Ramirez, D. Melchart, F. Eitel, L. V. Hedges and W. B. Jonas (1997). "Are the clinical effects of homeopathy placebo effects? A meta-analysis of placebo-controlled trials". *Lancet* 350(9081): 834–843.

Ludtke, R. (2007). "Confessions of a researcher: are we guilty of reviewing homeopathy to the point of irrelevance?" *Complementary Therapies in Medicine* 15(3): 155–156.

Ludtke, R. and A. L. B. Rutten (2008). "The conclusions on the effectiveness of homeopathy highly depend on the set of analyzed trials". *Journal of Clinical Epidemiology* 61(12): 1197–1204.

Moulding, N. T., C. A. Silagy and D. P. Weller (1999). "A framework for effective management of change in clinical practice: dissemination and implementation of clinical practice guidelines". *Qualitative Health Care* 8(3): 177–183.

Mruck, K. and G. Mey (2007). "Grounded theory and reflexivity". *The SAGE Handbook of Grounded Theory*. A. Bryant and K. Charmaz. London: Sage Publications: 515–538.

National Prospective Tonsillectomy Audit (2008). "Impact of NICE guidance on rates of haemorrhage after tonsillectomy: an evaluation of guidance issued during an ongoing national tonsillectomy audit". *Quality & Safety in Health Care* 17(4): 264–268.

O'Cathain, A., E. Murphy and J. Nicholl (2007). "Why, and how, mixed methods research is undertaken in health services research in England: a mixed methods study". *BMC Health Services Research* 7: 85.

Owen, D. (2007). *Principles and Practice of Homeopathy: The Therapeutic and Healing Process*. Pennsylvania: Churchill Livingston Elsevier.

Reichenberg-Ullman, J. and R. Ullman (1990). "Healing through homeopathy: a case of hyperactivity". *Townsend Letter for Doctors and Patients* 81: 186–190.

Reichenberg-Ullman, J. and R. Ullman (1993). "The homeopathic treatment of attention deficit disorder". *Townsend Letter for Doctors and Patients* 123: 928–932.

Reichenberg-Ullman, J. and R. Ullman (1999). "Homeopathic treatment of children with ADHD and other behavioral and learning problems". *Journal of Naturopathic Medicine* 8(2): 49–52.

Reichenberg-Ullman, J. and R. Ullman (2000a). "The ADHD pressure cooker: kids, teachers, parents, and doctors, all feel the heat". *Townsend Letter for Doctors and Patients* 206: 144–147.

Reichenberg-Ullman, J. and R. Ullman (2000b). *Ritalin-free Kids: Safe and Effective Homeopathic Medicine for ADHD and Other Behavioral and Learning Problems*. Roseville, CA: Prima Health.

Roberts, E. (2005). *Homeopathy: Principles and Practice*. West Wickham, UK: Winter Press.

Rousseau, L. and D. Fortier-Bernoville (1988). *Diseases of the Respiratory and Digestive System of Children*. New Delhi: B. Jain.

Rutten, A. L. B. and C. F. Stolper (2008). "The 2005 meta-analysis of homeopathy: the importance of post-publication data". *Homeopathy: the Journal of the Faculty of Homeopathy* 97(4): 169–177.

Rycroft Malone, J., K. Seers, A. Titchen, G. Harvey, A. Kitson and B. McCormack (2004). "What counts as evidence in evidence-based practice?" *Journal of Advanced Nursing* 47(1): 81–90.

Sackett, D. L., S. E. Straus, W. S. Richardson, W. Rosenberg and R. B. Haynes (2000). *Evidence-Based Medicine: How to Practice and Teach EBM*. London: Churchill Livingstone.

Sankaran, R. (1999). *The Spirit of Homeopathy*. India: Homeopathic Educational Services.

Schulz, E. (2005). "Can you not hear what I cannot tell you? Accompanying children in crisis with homeopathy". *Homeopathic Links* 18: 92–97.

Select Committee on Science and Technology (2000). *6th Report: Complementary and Alternative Medicine*. London: The Stationery Office.

Shang, A., K. Huwiler-Muntener, L. Nartey, P. Juni, S. Dorig, J. A. Sterne, D. Pewsner and M. Egger (2005). "Are the clinical effects of homoeopathy placebo effects? Comparative study of placebo-controlled trials of homoeopathy and allopathy". *Lancet* 366(9487): 726–732.

Shang, A. J., P. Juni, J. A. C. Sterne, K. Huwiler-Muntener and M. Egger (2005). "Are the clinical effects of homoeopathy placebo effects? Reply". *Lancet* 366(9503): 2083–2085.

Sheldon, T. A., N. Cullum, D. Dawson, A. Lankshear, K. Lowson, I. Watt, P. West, D. Wright and J. Wright (2004). "What's the evidence that NICE guidance has been implemented? Results from a national evaluation using time series analysis, audit of patients' notes, and interviews". *BMJ* 329(7473): 999.

Strauss, A. and J. Corbin (1998). *Basics of Qualitative Research: Second Edition: Techniques and Procedures for Developing Grounded Theory*. London: Sage.

Taylor, M. A., D. Reilly, R. H. Llewellyn-Jones, C. McSharry and T. C. Aitchison (2000). "Randomised controlled trial of homoeopathy versus placebo in perennial allergic rhinitis with overview of four trial series". *British Medical Journal* 321(7259): 471–476.

Thompson, E. A., A. Shaw, J. Nichol, S. Hollinghurst, A. J. Henderson, T. Thompson and D. Sharp (2011). "The feasibility of a pragmatic randomised controlled trial to compare usual care with usual care plus individualised homeopathy, in children requiring secondary care for asthma". *Homeopathy* 100: 122–130.

Villanueva-Russell, Y. (2005). "Evidence-based medicine and its implications for the profession of chiropractic". *Social Science & Medicine* 60(3): 545–561.

Watson, I. (1991). *A Guide to the Methodologies of Homeopathy*. Cumbria: Cutting Edge Publications.

Weiser, M., W. Strosser and P. Klein (1998). "Homeopathic vs conventional treatment of vertigo: a randomized double-blind controlled clinical study". *Archives of Otolaryngology Head Neck Surgery* 124(8): 879–885.

White, P., F. L. Bishop, P. Prescott, C. Scott, P. Little and G. Lewith (2012). "Practice, practitioner, or placebo? A multifactorial, mixed-methods randomized controlled trial of acupuncture". *PAIN* 153(2): 455–462.

Wigmore, T. J., J. F. Smythe, M. B. Hacking, R. Raobaikady and N. S. MacCallum (2007). "Effect of the implementation of NICE guidelines for ultrasound guidance on the complication rates associated with central venous catheter placement in patients presenting for routine surgery in a tertiary referral centre". *British Journal of Anaesthesia* 99(5): 662–665.

Wilson, P. (2009). "Analysis of a re-analysis of a meta-analysis: in defence of Shang *et al.*". *Homeopathy: the Journal of the Faculty of Homeopathy* 98(2): 127–128; author reply 129.

21

TOWARDS A LEARNING PROFESSION?

Adapting clinical governance for complementary and alternative medicine

Jane Wilkinson and Nicola K. Gale

I Introduction

In many areas of the world, the CAM sector is growing and becoming increasingly professionalised and integrated within conventional healthcare systems. In the UK, three of the major challenges for integration into the National Health Service (NHS) have been: the failure to create a regulatory framework that adequately encompasses professions with varying degrees of professionalisation and training; the early stage of development of the evidence base partly due to the lack of research investment by the government and professional bodies; and a lack of inter-professional communication and collaboration regarding the implementation of standards and guidelines developed for the sector.

Clinical governance (CG) is a comprehensive framework for assuring the quality and safety of healthcare services. It was introduced in the UK in the late 1990s via a series of White Papers (Department of Health 1997, 1998, 1999) and culminated in the Health Act 1999, which made accountability for clinical quality and performance a legal requirement for all NHS organisations. The fundamental role of CG in safeguarding patients has been highlighted in several investigations into serious failings within the NHS, including the recent Francis Report (2013) and Keogh Review (2013). However, there is also a focus within CG on improving the quality of patient care through innovative service redesign. Although many different terms have been used to describe systematic approaches to assurance and improvement, the central aim is to create services that are 'learning organisations' that continually monitor the quality and safety of services and learn from mistakes so as to continuously improve patient care (Davies and Nutley 2000, de Burca 2000, Garside 1999). Whilst commitment to quality and safety seems like a self-evident professional value that any healthcare practitioner should hold, to date, clinical governance approaches seem to have had relatively little impact on the CAM sector.

In this chapter, we first explore what clinical governance is and why it is relevant to the CAM sector. We then briefly explore the UK context of CAM and why there has been little adoption of CG approaches. We then argue that, as medical and social science research on CAM continues to expand and regulation of the sector evolves, CG is a useful way forward in raising levels of understanding and trust in CAM practice. We propose that the adaption and adoption of a framework for CG within the sector would not only provide a means for assuring the quality and safety of patient care but also support individual practitioners in their own professional development.

There are important differences between the position of CAM practitioners and employees of large NHS and private healthcare organisations which mean that it is not straightforward to map CG processes from a hospital, for instance, onto the practice of an independent CAM practitioner. However, parallels can be drawn between the organisational position of CAM practitioners and other independent healthcare professionals, such as dentists or psychotherapists: many of whom operate solely in the private sector, but also act as professionals delivering NHS care where they have to comply with clinical governance systems. Our argument, therefore, has three main components: first, if CAM wishes to continue professionalising, it requires more systematic engagement with quality and safety monitoring and improvement; second, it is possible to adapt the principles of CG to CAM; and third, whilst the way CAM professions are currently organised and practised is not particularly conducive to the development of a learning organisation, the potential to create a 'learning profession' is a worthwhile and necessary goal for CAM practitioners and their professional organisations.

II What is clinical governance and why is it important for CAM?

Clinical governance (CG) formed the cornerstone of the 'modernisation agenda', the term introduced by the New Labour government to describe a ten-year radical overhaul of and investment in the NHS (Department of Health 1997). 'It is a framework through which NHS organisations are accountable for continually improving the quality of their services and safeguarding high standards of care by creating an environment in which excellence in clinical care will flourish' (Scally and Donaldson 1998) CG incorporates systems and processes for both monitoring and improving services and was introduced as a means of systemising several interrelated activities at both strategic and operational levels of service delivery. In 2004, CG was incorporated into a comprehensive Integrated Governance framework for NHS organisations that included financial and corporate governance (Stanton 2004).

The concept of a systematic approach to monitoring and improving the quality and safety of healthcare services has been subject to a great deal of reinterpretation over the years, including ideas such as total quality management (TQI), continuous quality improvement (CQI), business process reengineering (BPR), rapid cycle change, lean thinking and six sigma (Powell *et al.* 2009), with greater or lesser emphasis on cost reduction. Some have referred to these many approaches as 'pseudoinnovation' (Walshe 2009) because most of them rely on broadly similar principles. Certainly most are aiming for something akin to a 'learning organisation' where safety and quality improvement are embedded in such a way that it becomes 'the norm'.

Over the past 15 years, there has also been a steady increase in the monitoring and regulation of standards within NHS organisations. The Care Quality Commission (CQC) regulates and monitors the performance of NHS and private healthcare providers based on a clinical governance framework and the organisational strategic capacity for implementing it.[1] To date, however, CAM services have not been subject to reviews by this Commission or any of its predecessors.

The Department of Health and the King's Fund funded a study in the early 2000s which found that the following 'core operational' activities relating to the day-to-day activities involved in service design and provision were a priority for the integration of CAM within NHS primary care (Wilkinson *et al.* 2004):

- clinical effectiveness and research
- clinical audit
- risk management and patient safety
- education and training
- patient and public involvement and experience
- effective information management
- staffing and staff management.

There are clear reasons why more systematic engagement with quality and safety monitoring and improvement might be important for CAM: first, to improve the safety of services; second, to continually develop and improve services; and third, to increase trust and confidence in 'the professions' as well as individual practitioners. The increased trust could apply both to individual consumers of CAM in the private sector and, potentially, to commissioners of NHS services.

1 Safety

The broad term 'patient safety' has increasingly been pushed to the forefront of regulatory reform in the UK (Department of Health 1998, 2000, 2001a, 2001b, 2006a, 2007, 2010b, 2012, Donaldson 2000, National Patient Safety Agency 2004, CQC 2010), including in the recent Health and Social Care Act (2012).[2] Many CAM practitioners argue that their treatments are safe, usually drawing on language such as 'natural', 'holistic' or 'gentle' to describe them. However, there are some real risks that are not just related to one profession. For instance, there are straightforward 'accidents', such as needle stick injuries, errors, which can be related to diagnosis, treatment, prevention, communication or equipment (Leape *et al.* 1993), and also more generic, interactional risks associated with therapeutic relationships, such as professional boundary transgressions (e.g. intimate relationships with clients). In their study of risk management in CAM, Gale *et al.* (2008) collected examples of real-life errors in CAM practice from their stakeholder group. Table 21.1 provides a summary of errors that could occur in the CAM sector (adapted from Gale *et al.* 2008).

Table 21.1 Examples of types of errors relating to CAM

Type of error	Example
Diagnosis	Failure to refer a patient with a 'red flag' symptom for a medical diagnosis.
Treatment	Injury during treatment; prescribing a herb that interacts with a drug the patient is taking.
Prevention	Failure to advise about potential worsening of a condition that would require a patient to go to A&E.
Communication	Failure to warn a patient about side effects of treatment (such as pain or discomfort after massage); miscommunication in referrals between GPs and CAM practitioners.
Equipment	Failure to ensure all equipment is maintained and meets regulatory health and safety standards, e.g. a broken treatment table that means that a patient is unable to get on or off safely.

Table 21.2 Five stages in developing a culture of safety

1 **Pathological culture** where practitioners believe there is no need for thinking about safety issues, whistleblowers are marginalised or punished, and information required to evaluate risks is hidden or not recorded.

2 **Reactive culture** where risk begins to be taken seriously and individual incidents are monitored and responded to.

3 **Calculative culture** where new systems are introduced to think more holistically about risk and the conditions that might promote unsafe practice (rather than blaming individuals), but these systems tend to result in overload of paperwork and data.

4 **Proactive culture** where people start to think about potential risks rather than just responding to problems.

5 **Generative culture** where risk management is an integral part of everything that happens in the profession or organisation, responsibilities are shared and new ideas for improving practice are welcomed.

Developing a culture of safety

Between 2001 and 2012, the National Patient Safety Agency (NPSA) served to provide training and resources for improving patient safety and risk management within the NHS.[3] Their work highlighted the critical importance of creating a culture which values and prioritises patient safety. Morath and Turnbull (2005) identify five stages of development in relation to this (Table 21.2). Realistically, most CAM professions are at stage one or two, either denying that there are any risks or just beginning to introduce some form of monitoring, including those that are already statutorily regulated. The British Acupuncture Council took an early lead in the UK sector with the introduction of a risk audit tool in 2009,[4] although currently registrants are not required to demonstrate that they use it. The commitment of this profession to the safeguarding of patients was further confirmed through prioritising the safety of acupuncture treatments as a focus for research (MacPherson *et al.* 2001). The National Council for Osteopathic Research has also begun to undertake similar work on behalf of registered osteopaths; however, there has been relatively little work undertaken across the sector to develop adequate systems and processes to monitor patient safety and risk management.

2 *Quality*

Quality must be everybody's business.

(Department of Health 2000)

Clinical governance provides a set of tools around improving the quality of care –in terms of both quality assurance and service improvement referred to as the 'twin foci' of assurance and transformation. CG therefore offers a framework for CAM in relation to innovation in service redesign and improvement:

Transformation is about reconfiguring current patterns of care and governance is the process which should guide and inform the development. The emerging CAM field must begin to recognise the twin foci of governance and be prepared to embrace both sides of this important concept. It is not just sufficient to review how current CAM provision may reflect governance requirements but perhaps more importantly CAM practitioners should be concerned with their role in transformation and choice and be clear on what this may mean for the delivery of their services.

(Wilkinson et al. *2004)*

Adopting clinical governance systems and processes includes the development of protocols, performance indicators and integrated care pathways for specific patient groups. The rationale for developing such 'tools' is to improve the quality of patient care and increase choice by addressing identified gaps in provision and coordinating services in service redesign. The scale of these transformations and their implementation across a large health system may not be appropriate for CAM but many of the tools and techniques are. For instance, audit cycles enable the monitoring and adaption of services to tailor services to meet patients' needs. These kinds of activities can be enhanced by the active engagement of patients and potential patients in the design of services as well as providing feedback on quality and satisfaction and the use of patient recorded outcome measures (PROMs).

3 Trust

The introduction of CG was considered a fundamental tool in promoting 'trust' in the medical profession in the wake of various 'crises'. In 1998, the GP Harold Shipman (Shipman Inquiry 2002) was arrested for the murder of at least 236 patients. A year later, it came to light that organs and other human tissue were removed, stored or disposed of without consent from families of the deceased in UK hospitals (Redfern *et al.* 2001 [Royal Liverpool Children's Inquiry Report], Bristol Royal Infirmary Inquiry 2001). Trust has also been perceived to be a serious problem in CAM, from historical concerns with 'quackery' to more recent criticisms of the limited evidence base for CAM and variable regulation and hence differing levels of protection for patients against bad or ineffective practice (Wahlberg 2007).

Brown (2008) argues that there are two types of trust: instrumental and communicative. Healthcare practitioners have to negotiate striking a fine line between an independent professional model of intuitive and embodied knowledge based on empathy, compassion and care and a large systems/organisation model in which codified forms of knowledge are articulated, evidenced and abstracted. While formal governance systems promote instrumental trust, patients tend to value communicative trust in their relationships with medical professionals. This argument certainly resonates with the observation that many CAM practitioners build their practice through word-of-mouth recommendations.

We are not arguing that formal methods exclusively are preferable. Indeed, despite increasing levels of professional accountability within mainstream medicine in the UK, the recent cases involving Mid Staffordshire NHS Hospital Trust, (Francis 2013), Winterbourne View (an NHS-funded private hospital) and the Morecambe Bay NHS Foundation Trust have demonstrated a need for a more balanced approach in the NHS. As a result of these incidences, there have been increased calls for a greater emphasis on clinical skills and compassion to form part of the integration agenda.[5] This may be an opportunity for the CAM sector to bring appropriate skills and perspectives that could enhance mainstream healthcare provision and reinvigorate NHS services (Russell 2014). The exponential growth of mindfulness training being offered to patients and carers by various NHS trusts across the UK[6] reflects the fact that this intervention is primarily delivered by mainstream practitioners, delivered within a framework of clinical governance, and is evidence based. Mindfulness based stress reduction (MBSR) and mindfulness based cognitive therapy (MBCT) are included in the National Institute for Health and Clinical Excellence guidelines (NICE 2009). Mindfulness is also being delivered to leaders and professionals in health and social care (King's Fund 2014, Happier@work 2013, Russell and Tatton-Ramos 2014), civil servants working for the Department of Health (Breathworks 2013) and even Members of Parliament and the House of Lords (Oxford Mindfulness Foundation 2013). In summary, while CAM prides itself on its ability to develop communicative trust, we argue that ideally a balance of formal and communicative approaches to building trust in CAM (and other) therapeutic relationships needs to be struck.

III UK policy context relating to NHS access to CAM services

In the UK, the majority of CAM services are paid out-of-pocket by patients or through private healthcare insurance. Mintel (2009) reported a steady growth in this sector in terms of both products and therapeutic services. Recent systematic reviews suggest that CAM usage amongst the general population has remained stable over the past decades; however, these reviews do not differentiate between NHS and private access (Harris *et al.* 2012, Cooper *et al.* 2013). Many potential users of CAM are unable to pay privately for treatments or insurance in addition to paying significant contributions towards the NHS via taxes and National Insurance contributions. Access to these services within the NHS over the past decades has been limited and highly variable. The 'postcode lottery' of access to CAM modalities reflects the fact that services are commissioned at a local level. A 2004 survey (Wilkinson *et al.* 2004) estimated that 43 per cent of primary care trusts (the bodies responsible for commissioning local services at that point in time) were providing some form of access to CAM, but with significant regional variations, with more affluent areas of the UK having greater access. This work has not been updated but anecdotally many of the CAM services included in this survey were vulnerable to cuts and were decommissioned over the past several years during a time of severe financial austerity, targeted anti-CAM (social) media campaigns and the prominence of evidence-based commissioning.

At a policy level, the 2006 command paper *Our Health, Our Care, Our Say* explicitly encouraged commissioners to consider using CAM as an option for innovation in service redesign and a means for widening patient choice: 'PCTs will be expected to support practices that are innovative and entrepreneurial; working with them to redesign clinical pathways and secure the services that are needed locally, for example ... exploring opportunities to develop complementary and alternative health therapies' (Department of Health 2006a, p. 165). The Department of Health also, up until 2006, had a dedicated department working to support the development of CAM, which included the jointly funded project with the King's Fund to develop guidance on CG in the sector in the acknowledgement that this would increase the likelihood of integration within mainstream healthcare (Wilkinson *et al.* 2004).

Throughout the 'modernisation era', policy changes presented a number of opportunities for NHS CAM provision, such as a drive for innovation and increased patient choice; the prevention, personalisation and self-management agendas; a focus on compassion, spirituality, patient engagement and experience; and opening up of the NHS 'market' to 'any qualified provider' – that is, private and 'third sector' organisations. The contractual conditions for 'qualified providers' include the capacity to implement a clinical governance infrastructure and provide assurances on the quality and safety of services. These developments are, on the face of it, in line with many of the aims of CAM approaches, but there does not seem to have been an associated growth of the sector within the NHS. Whether this is the result of purposeful exclusion, a case of missed opportunities by the CAM sector or simply a result of growing financial pressure on the system is unclear but it is probably a combination of all three.

At a local strategic level, the sector struggles to make significant inroads with local commissioners. Despite support for CAM by general practitioners (evidenced during the days of GP fundholding in the 1980s), very few GPs who are supportive of CAM have held much sway on the boards of local commissioning organisations and thus had a relatively weak influence in ensuring the integration of these services into local care pathways. Also, some CAM practitioners keen to engage in the NHS have also struggled in dealing with local commissioners suspicious of CAM and reluctant to introduce interventions with a limited evidence base and variable regulation.

There are still opportunities available to this sector. The recent Health and Social Care Act (2012) reflects and builds on the legislation introduced during the 'modernisation agenda' and current thinking in mainstream medicine reflects the values held by most CAM practitioners – that is, personalised care, 'upstream' preventative healthcare, self-management, compassionate care, spirituality, self-efficacy and patient activation (McSherry 2006, McSherry and Ross 2010, Mooney 2009, Narayanasamy 2001, Janki Foundation 2004, Parliamentary and Health Service Ombudsman 2011, The Patients Association 2009, 2011, Dixon 2013). Demand is now outstripping supply in terms of many of the major public health areas – for example, mental health, diabetes, obesity and musculoskeletal problems – and these are all areas where CAM practitioners have provided services and sought to develop an evidence base.

Services will continue to be commissioned locally through the clinical commissioning groups,[7] and commissioners have to balance the arguments for and against providing CAM services. The emphasis now, more than ever, is to introduce interventions that are supported by high-quality evidence of efficacy, cost-effectiveness and safety and this argument is regularly cited as a reason why these interventions should not be offered on the NHS (Derkatch 2008, Goldenberg 2006; Villanueva-Russell 2005). Others counter this by arguing that many treatments currently offered on the NHS are not proven effective through trial evidence but through experiential and other forms of evidence, and that patient preferences are an important component in selecting appropriate treatment (Davies and Cleary 2005). However, unless the CAM sector adopts adequate systems and processes that meet legal requirements, it is extremely unlikely that CAM will make inroads within the NHS.

IV What are the challenges of adopting CG in CAM?

Unlike the NHS, there is no healthcare organisation within which to build an appropriate culture of safety and assurance. Few CAM practitioners operate in an organisational context and many of the central elements of effective CG, such as committed leadership and an engaged workforce (Department of Health 2006c), are not relevant for independent practitioners, usually practising in small private clinics, at home, at spas or in gyms, without formal career structures or mentoring/line management arrangements.

In mainstream medicine, CG was driven by policy and supported through a range of arm's-length bodies. Without any similar legislation, individual practitioners, educational institutions and professional representative bodies have not had the same impetus to change. However, there have been some examples of support offered to CAM in this area, even if not legally binding. The Commission for Health Improvement[8] seconded a member of staff to support the clinical governance for CAM project (Wilkinson *et al.* 2004), which also had significant input from representatives of the Modernisation Agency, the National Patient Safety Agency, the Commission for Health Improvement, NHS Alliance, the National Association of Primary

Care, NHS Primary Care Commissioning and leads within the mainstream health and social care sector, including patient and public involvement specialists. These individuals were engaged in events at the House of Commons, various university-based debates and workshops, as well as consensus building on guidelines, events and workshops. The range and profile of the stakeholders that were engaged in this process indicated that there was genuine support for the sector from a broad range of stakeholders – that is, policy makers, commissioners, consultants, GPs, arm's-length bodies, practitioners and patient representatives.

Throughout this time, there has been significant resistance to engagement with the NHS from more anti-establishment parts of the CAM sector, who have remained distrustful of mainstream medicine. There are concerns that increased professional accountability would dilute the traditional values held by the sector (Schneirov and Geczik 2002). Whilst some CAM practitioners remain resistant to working with the NHS and some patients prefer to access their CAM care outside of the NHS, some CAM practitioner groups have successfully engaged with the NHS in several areas across the UK. There are indeed numerous examples of CAM services that have developed CG systems and managed to build productive and well-evaluated collaborations with the public sector (e.g. Penny Brohn Cancer Care, Freshwinds, Impact Integrated Medicine Partnership, Blackthorn Medical Trust, Culm Valley Integrated Centre for Health, Bromley-by-Bow Health Centre). We would argue that these examples show that it is possible to adapt the principles of CG to CAM without threatening the holistic principles that many practitioners hold.

Whatever the opportunities and constraints faced, it is clear that many CAM practitioners are still unfamiliar with the language of CG and for some it is perceived as incompatible with their individualised practice. In fact, the majority of practitioners incorporate some aspects of CG into their practice without associating it with that terminology as their practice is based on professional values and genuine care and concern for others. However, there is a need to increase their awareness and improve and/or formalise the systems that support them in their daily practice and we argue below that it is the responsibility of the professions to take a lead on this and work collaboratively to support their members.

V How can clinical governance be applied to CAM?

The possibility of adapting appropriate indicators of quality and safety employed in mainstream care to the CAM sector has been demonstrated (Wilkinson *et al.* 2004). If these were to be embraced fully by the sector, it would serve to develop greater trust amongst politicians, healthcare commissioners and practitioners, reporters and not least the general public. However, given the absence of organisational structures and the relatively small size of the professions, it is appropriate for professional organisations to take the lead in the drive for greater professionalism in the sector through CG. The ideal then might be to create a 'learning profession', rather than a learning organisation. Communication and collaboration between representative bodies and regulators could be productive in ensuring consistency with the standards set for registrants, and in promoting CG as a priority topic for continuing professional development and lifelong learning.[9]

If, within the current policy environment, the sector wants to move towards greater integration and the ideal of a 'learning profession', then a concerted effort needs to be made across the professions to strike a balance between the formal and intuitive, the instrumental and the communicative. There is much to learn from the work already undertaken in the mainstream sector over the past decade as well as consensus-based guidelines developed for the CAM sector (Wilkinson *et al.* 2004).[10] The core operational/service level components of CG have been identified as the most relevant aspects that could be adapted to facilitate greater integration within NHS primary care. Given the fact that most CAM practitioners operate as individuals or in small groups, attention needs to be focused on the practical day-to-day tasks that will enable them to work within different employment structures and importantly ensure they are 'NHS ready' (Wilkinson *et al.* 2004, Wye *et al.* 2008).

Groups such as herbal medicine, acupuncture, osteopathy and chiropractic have made a great deal of improvements in professional standards and codes of conduct.[11,12,13] The Osteopathic Development Group has already initiated work to develop standards for service delivery.[14] However, the important role that CG systems and processes play has not been fully realised more broadly across the sector. Table 21.3 illustrates the kinds of activities that could be undertaken by both individual practitioners and their representative bodies in developing a CG framework that is relevant for the sector. There are massive disciplinary crossovers but work does need to be undertaken on how CG themes could be applied appropriately to the level of risk that any particular intervention poses.

The most significant challenge perhaps for this sector is generating a culture that values and generates formal/systems-based approaches and capitalises on the communicative/intuitive strengths of the sector (Baker and Lakhani 2004, de Burca 2000). This would be a model that does not involve excessive paperwork and box ticking, but rather one that focuses on the quality of care, and works to co-create health and wellbeing, and has care and compassion at its very core.

Whilst currently the focus for most professions should be to ensure that their members are appropriately regulated (e.g. by registering with the Complementary and Natural Healthcare Council [CNHC]), parallel work could be undertaken as an interdisciplinary collaboration to develop a 'community of practitioners' who are dedicated to ensuring the best possible care for patients. This could be supported at both national and local levels, with collaboration at an international level so as to avoid reinventing the wheel.

VI Conclusions

We propose that clinical governance systems and processes developed within the UK NHS can be usefully adapted to the CAM sector and provide a means to improve quality of care and increase understanding and trust of the professions. Those NHS CAM services that have managed to survive during a climate of austerity measures are those that have successfully implemented CG systems and process at a service level. Similarly, healthcare insurers are now beginning to approve those therapies that are registered with the CNHC.

The NHS is in a period of unprecedented change, with national commissioning strategies up for further review and opportunities for personalisation emerging (The Commissioning Review, 2014). At this critical juncture, CAM once again has an opportunity to demonstrate that it can have a role in promoting health and helping address some of the most pertinent contemporary issues being debated in mainstream care (i.e. compassion, spirituality, patient experience, engagement and activation). It is more likely to do so if it can demonstrate a commitment to ongoing development of quality and safety.

In line with the House of Lords recommendations, most CAMs have been entrusted to voluntary regulation as proportionate to the level of risk. Although a regulator, like CNHC, would ensure that individual practitioners have acquired sufficient basic skills as part of their preregistration training, the bottom line is that all practitioners willing to work within an NHS organisation, or have their services commissioned by the NHS or by individual patients directly through personal care budgets, will be required to engage with a range of clinical

Table 21.3 Examples of CG activities relevant to individuals and CAM professions

CG activity	Professional bodies	Individual practitioners
Clinical audit	Adapt existing audit tools so that they are relevant to each profession. Encourage members to participate in annual audit cycles.	Learn how to complete audit tools, understand how audit cycles work and participate in regular auditing activity.
Clinical effectiveness and research	Develop a research infrastructure and prioritise areas of importance, e.g. safety or good outcomes for specific patient groups. Encourage the use of Patient Recorded Outcome Measures (PROMs). Provide support for dedicated R&D activity.	Gain an understanding of research methodologies and become 'research ready', i.e. learn how to participate in research projects, e.g. completing questionnaires and undertaking service evaluations.
Patient safety and risk management	Support generic PSRM strategies. Develop generic consent forms that can be adapted where appropriate. Encourage members to focus on safety as a priority for CPD. Promote awareness of legal issues.	Undertake training and engage in appropriate monitoring activity. Report any incidences appropriately. Refresh learning on red and yellow flags. Ensure patients are fully informed and gain consent. Gain an understanding of legal issues.
Education and training	Indicate priority areas for CPD. Audit the type of CPD being undertaken by members and identify high-quality training programmes.	Undertake regular CPD, reflective practice and commit to lifelong learning. Prioritise aspects of CG missing from basic training.
Patient and public involvement and experience	Produce patient information leaflets, generic satisfaction and complaints forms, engage patient representative groups.	Engage with local Health and Wellbeing Boards and local patient representative groups. Lay membership within practice leadership (where relevant). Encourage patients to complete satisfaction/complaints surveys, PROMs and their participation in audit, evaluation and research.
Effective information management	Develop data capture and management systems for the sector. Encourage practitioners to move to a paperless environment.	Collate relevant information and keep accurate patient notes. Learn how to use IT, ensure patient confidentiality. With patient consent, communicate with mainstream providers, e.g. GPs.
Staffing and staff management	Provide opportunities for inter- and intra-professional communication and collaboration.	Participate in activities that involve other professions so as to facilitate multidisciplinary teamwork.

Source: Health Academix 2013: www.healthacademix.co.uk.

governance activities. As CAM provision is predominantly within the private sector and thus outside of an organisational healthcare infrastructure that supports professionalisation at a service delivery level, we would recommend that CAM professional representative bodies work towards supporting their members in developing a 'learning profession', with due systems of accountability. In developing appropriate CG systems and processes, CAM professions may be able to balance their high levels of communicative trust with equivalent levels of instrumental trust.

Notes

1 The Health and Social Care Act (2008) established the Care Quality Commission (www.cqc.org.uk) as the regulator of all health and adult social care services.
2 The Health and Social Care Act 2012 ([Consequential Amendments] [No. 2] Order 2013 No. 2341) gives effect to the policies that were set out in the White Paper *Equity and Excellence* (Department of Health 2010a), bringing about an extensive reorganisation of the NHS. Changes made include the abolition of the National Patient Safety Agency (NPSA) and the formation of the NHS Commissioning Board Special Health Authority (NHS CBA). From June 2012, NHS CBA took on the functions of the NPSA with Imperial College Healthcare NHS Trust (ICHT) responsible for the operational delivery of the National Reporting and Learning System (NRLS).
3 In 2012, these key functions were transferred to the NHS Commissioning Board Special Health Authority.
4 British Acupuncture Council. Code of Safe Practice Clinical Self Audit Tool (CoSPCAT). www. acupuncture.org.uk/images/stories/old_site_pdfs/cospcat.pdf.
5 As highlighted in the Integrated Commissioning Reports prepared by Clinical Commissioning Groups, e.g. http://stockportccg.org/wp-content/uploads/2012/01/Integrated-Commissioning-Plan.pdf (Commissioning Board Chief Nursing Officer and DH Chief Nursing Adviser 2012).
6 Mindfulness based stress reduction and mindfulness based cognitive therapy, Russell and Tatton-Ramos (2014), Avon & Wiltshire NHS, County Durham and Darlington NHS, Dorset NHS, Gloucestershire Foundation Trust NHS, Lanarkshire NHS, Norfolk and Waveney PCT and Plymouth NHS are just a handful of examples.
7 Clinical commissioning groups replaced primary care trusts in 2012 via the Health and Social Care Act.
8 The Commission was abolished on 31 March 2009 and its responsibilities in England broadly subsumed by the Care Quality Commission.
9 As is being demonstrated by the work of the Osteopathic Development Group, www.osteopathy.org. uk/about/our-work/Developing-the-profession/.
10 This continues to be supported via a small-social enterprise, Health Academix Ltd, established in 2009 by Jane Wilkinson to provide research and development support for the sector.
11 http://ehtpa.eu/standards/national_professional_standards/index.html.
12 www.acupuncture.org.uk/public-content/public-pr-press-releases/independent-quality-mark-for-the-british-acupuncture-council-bacc.html or www.acupuncture.org.uk/public-content/effective-practice/bacc-professional-codes.html; www.osteopathy.org.uk/uploads/osteopathic_practice_standards_public.pdf.
13 www.gcc-uk.org/good-practice/.
14 www.osteopathy.org.uk/about/our-work/Developing-the-profession/.

References

Baker, R. and Lakhani, M. (2004) *Quality Improvement Processes. In Clinical Governance in Primary Care.* Second Edition. Edited by Tim van Zwanenberg and Jamie Harrison. Oxford: Radcliffe Medical Press.

Breathworks (2013) *Department of Health – Staff Wellbeing Pilot.* www.breathworks-mindfulness.org.uk/blog/entry/department-of-health-staff-wellbeing-pilot.

Bristol Royal Infirmary Inquiry (2001) *Learning from Bristol. The Report of the Public Inquiry into Children's Heart Surgery at the Bristol Royal Infirmary 1984–1995.* London: The Stationery Office.

Brown, P. R. (2008) 'Trusting in the New NHS: instrumental versus communicative action', *Sociology of Health and Illness*, 30(3), 349–363.

Care Quality Commission (2010) *Essential Standards of Quality and Safety*. London: CQC/. Available at www.cqc.org.uk/file/4471.

Commissioning Board Chief Nursing Officer and DH Chief Nursing Adviser (2012) *Compassion in Practice*. DH Policy Document, London: Department of Health.

Commissioning Review (2014) '"Right to ask" for personal health budget now in place', 2 April. www.thecommissioningreview.com/article/right-ask-personal-health-budget-now-place.

Cooper, K. L., Harris, P. E., Relton, C. and Thomas, K. J. (2013) 'Prevalence of visits to five types of complementary and alternative medicine practitioners by the general population: a systematic review', *Complementary Therapies in Clinical Practice*, 19(4), 214–220.

Davies, H. T. O. and Nutley, S. M. (2000) 'Developing learning organisations in the new NHS', *BMJ*, 320, 998.

Davies, E. and Cleary, P. D. (2005) 'Hearing the patient's voice? Factors affecting the use of patient survey data in quality improvement', *Quality and Safety in Health Care*, 14(6), 428–432

De Burca, S. (2000) 'Editorial: The learning health care organisation', *International Journal for Quality in Health Care*, 12(6), 457–458.

Department of Health (1997) *The New NHS: Modern, Dependable*. London: The Stationery Office.

Department of Health (1998) *A First Class Service: Quality in the New NHS*. London: The Stationery Office.

Department of Health (1999) *Clinical Governance: Quality in the New NHS*. London: The Stationery Office.

Department of Health (2000) *An Organisation with a Memory*. London: The Stationery Office.

Department of Health (2001a) *Building a Safer NHS: Improving Medication Safety*. London: The Stationery Office.

Department of Health (2001b) *The Report of the Public Inquiry into Children's Heart Surgery at the Bristol Royal Infirmary 1984–1995: Learning from Bristol*. Cm 5207 (Redfern Inquiry). London: The Stationery Office.

Department of Health (2006a) *Safety First: A Report for Patients, Clinicians and Healthcare Managers*. London: The Stationery Office.

Department of Health (2006b) *Our Health, Our Care, Our Say*. London: The Stationery Office.

Department of Health (2006c) *Integrated Governance Handbook: A Handbook for Executives and Non-executives in Healthcare Organisations*. London: The Stationery Office. www.dh.gov.uk/en/Publicationsandstatistics/Publications/PublicationsPolicyAndGuidance/DH_4128739.

Department of Health (2007) *The White Paper Trust, Assurance and Safety: The Regulation of Health Professionals*. London: The Stationery Office.

Department of Health (2008) *The Health and Social Care Act*. London: The Stationery Office.

Department of Health (2010a) *Equity and Excellence: Liberating the NHS*. London: The Stationery Office.

Department of Health (2010b) *Independent Inquiry into the Care Provided by Mid Staffordshire NHS Foundation Trust, January 2005–March 2009* (Chairman R. Francis). London: The Stationery Office.

Department of Health (2012) *The 'Never Events' List 2012/13: Policy Framework for Use in the NHS*. London: The Stationery Office.

Derkatch, C. (2008) 'Method as argument: boundary work in evidence-based medicine', *Social Epistemology*, 22(4), 371–388.

Dixon, A. (2013) 'Building a culture of compassionate care', *King's Fund blog*, 6 February. www.kingsfund.org.uk/blog/2013/02/building-culture-compassionate-care-nhs.

Donaldson, L. (2000) *An Organisation with a Memory: Report of an Expert Group on Learning from Adverse Events in the NHS*. London: The Stationery Office.

Francis, R. (2013) *Report of the Mid Staffordshire NHS Foundation Trust Public Inquiry: Executive Summary*, 6 February. London: Stationery Office.

Gale, N. K., Bark, P., Stone J. and Wilkinson, J. (2008) *Safety in Practice: A Guide on Patient Safety and Risk Management for Complementary and Alternative Medical Practitioners*. London: iCAM, University of Westminster.

Garside, P. (1999) 'The learning organisation: a necessary setting for improving care?', *Quality in Health Care*, 8, 211.

Goldenberg, M. J. (2006) 'On evidence and evidence-based medicine: lessons from the philosophy of science', *Social Science and Medicine*, 62(11), 2621–2632.

Happier@work (2013) 'Staff development programme delivered to staff across King's Health Partnership', *SLaM News*, Winter edition, p. 30. www.slam.nhs.uk/media/50375/slam%20news%20winter%20 2012%2013.pdf.

Harris, P. E., Cooper, K. L., Relton, C. and Thomas, K. J. (2012) 'Prevalence of complementary and alternative medicine (CAM) use by the general population: a systematic review and update', *International Journal of Clinical Practice*, 66(10), 924–939.

Janki Foundation for Global Health Care (2004) *Values in Healthcare: A Spiritual Approach. A Personal and Team Development Programme for the Well-being of Healthcare Practitioners.* London, The Janki Foundation.

Keogh, B. (2013) *Review into the Quality of Care and Treatment Provided by 14 Hospital Trusts in England: Overview Report.* www.nhs.uk/NHSEngland/bruce-keogh-review/Documents/outcomes/keogh-review-final-report.pdf.

King's Fund (2014) *Developing Compassionate Leadership Through Mindfulness. Training Programme for Leaders in Health and Social Care.* London: King's Fund. www.kingsfund.org.uk/leadership/developing-compassionate-leadership-through-mindfulness.

Leape, L. L., Lawthers, A. G., Brennan, T. A. and Johnson, W. G. (1993) 'Preventing medical injury', *Quality Review Bulletin*, 19(5): 144–149.

MacPherson, H., Thomas, K. J., Walters, S. and Fitter, M. (2001) 'The York Safety Study: a prospective survey of 34,000 treatments by traditional acupuncturists', *BMJ*, 323(7311), 486–487.

McSherry, W. (2006) *Making Sense of Spirituality in Nursing and Health Care Practice.* London: Jessica Kingsley Publishers.

McSherry, W. and Ross, L. (eds) (2010) *Spiritual Assessment in Healthcare Practice.* Keswick: M&K Publishing.

Mintel (2009) *Complementary Medicines – UK – December 2009.* London: Mintel Oxygen.

Mooney, H. (2009) 'Can the NHS cope with God?' *Nursing Times*, 105(7), 8–10.

Morath, J. and Turnbull, J. E. (2005) *To Do No Harm: Ensuring Patient Safety in Healthcare Organizations.* California: Jossey-Bass.

Narayanasamy, A. (2001) *Spiritual Care: A Practical Guide for Nurses and Health Care Practitioners.* London: Quay.

National Institute for Health and Clinical Excellence (2009) *Clinical Guideline 90. Depression: The Treatment and Management of Depression in Adults.* London: NICE.

National Patient Safety Agency (2004) *Seven Steps to Patient Safety.* London: NPSA. www.npsa.nhs.uk/patientsafety/improvingpatientsafety/7steps/.

Oxford Mindfulness Foundation (2013) *Annual Report and Financial Statements for the Year Ended 21 March 2012*, p. 6. http://oxfordmindfulness.org/wp-content/uploads/financial-report-2012-13.pdf.

Parliamentary and Health Service Ombudsman (2011) *Care and Compassion? Report of the Health Service Ombudsman on Ten Investigations into NHS Care of Older People.* London: The Stationery Office.

Patients Association (2009) *Patients, Not Numbers, People, Not Statistics.* London: TPA.

Patients Association (2011) *Listen to Patients, Speak up for Change.* London: TPA.

Powell, A. E., Rushmer, R. K. and Davies, H. T. O. (2009) *A Systematic Narrative Review of Quality Improvement Models in Health Care.* Edinburgh: NHS Quality Improvement Scotland.

Redfern, M., Keeling, J. W. and Powell, E. (2001) *The Royal Liverpool Children's Inquiry Report.* London: The Stationery Office.

Russell, T. (2014) 'Body in mind? The need for an integrative approach to compassion in the NHS', *Journal of Holistic Healthcare*, 11(1), 7–11.

Russell, Tamara A. and Tatton-Ramos, Tiago P. (2014) 'Body in mind training: mindful movement for the clinical setting', *Neuro-Disability and Psychotherapy: A Forum for the Practice and Development of Psychological Therapies for Neurological Conditions*, 2(1),108–136.

Scally, D. and Donaldson, J. (1998) 'Clinical governance and the drive for quality improvement in the new NHS in England', *BMJ*, 317, 61–65.

Schneirov, M. and Geczik, J. D. (2002) 'Alternative health and the challenges of institutionalization', *Health: An Interdisciplinary Journal for the Social Study of Health, Illness and Medicine*, 6, 201–220.

Shipman Inquiry (2002) *Death Disguised*, First Report, Volume One. Chairman: Dame Janet Smith. Manchester: The Shipman Inquiry.

Stanton, P. (2004) *The Strategic Leadership of Clinical Governance in PCTs*, 2nd edn. NHS Modernisation Agency, Clinical Governance Support Team, National Primary Care Trust Development Programme, March.

Villanueva-Russell, Y. (2005) 'Evidence-based medicine and its implications for the profession of chiro-practic', *Social Science and Medicine*, 60(3), 545–561.

Wahlberg, A. (2007) 'A quackery with a difference – new medical pluralism and the problem of "danger-ous practitioners" in the United Kingdom', *Social Science and Medicine*, 65, 2307–2316.

Walshe, K. (2009) 'Pseudoinnovation: the development and spread of healthcare quality improvement methodologies', *International Journal for Quality in Health Care*, 21(3), 153–159.

Wilkinson, J., Peters, D. and Donaldson, J. (2004) *Clinical Governance for Complementary and Alternative Medicine in Primary Care. Final Report to the Department of Health and the King's Fund*. London: University of Westminster.

Wye, L., Shaw, A. and Sharp, D. (2008) 'Designing a "NHS friendly" complementary therapy service: a qualitative case study', *BMC Health Services Research*, 8(1), 173.

22

THE RELATIONSHIP BETWEEN THE ADVANCEMENT OF CAM KNOWLEDGE AND THE REGULATION OF BIOMEDICAL RESEARCH

Marie-Andrée Jacob[1]

em·pir·ic

n.

1 a person who relies on empirical methods

2 (Medicine) a medical quack; charlatan

adj.

empirical.

(Collins English Dictionary, HarperCollins, 2003)

I Introduction

Knowledge, law, and the state are intimately connected. The advancement of knowledge through research and development is never completely lawless (Stokes 2012, Golan 2004); instead, it often emerges with the support of an array of regulatory apparatuses, audit practices, and public subsidies. In turn, policies, and legislative and judicial decisions are increasingly developed under the influence of experts in various bodies of knowledge (Fischer 1990, Irwin 2008).

However, the state is not neutral *vis-à-vis* all 'forms of knowledge' as taken in their broadest sense (de Camargo 2002, Casey and Picherack 2001). In fact, it simply could not be. State recognition and support rather tend to be geared towards formal knowledge, understood as a 'cognitive content acquired from formal education, professional practice or technoscientific literature' (de Camargo 2002: 828). The type of knowledge that the state is interested and invested in is actually even more restricted than that: more often than not it refers to bodies of knowledge that live up to what are commonly recognized as 'scientific standards'. This is particularly patent in the context of health care, where policymakers increasingly use evidence-based medicine (EBM) as a basis for decision-making. In order to receive the state imprimatur, diagnostic methods and therapies ought to prove efficient according to conventional medicine's scientific standards, especially the randomized clinical trial (RCT) method. Legal scholar Ireh

Iyioha thus aptly speaks of a 'nexus between statutory legitimacy and scientific validation of health systems' (2011: 1; see also Polich *et al.* 2010).

It might not come as a surprise, then, that in the eyes of the public, scientists, like politicians, bureaucrats, and businessmen, are under increased scrutiny. The public now demands integrity, accountability, and transparency from all spheres of public life. Hence the science–law–state nexus is itself up for grabs. This is part of the context in which complementary and alternative medicine (CAM) researchers currently work.

In this chapter, I am interested in CAM as a mode of knowledge production, and in how CAM and the 'state law's espousal of science' (Santos 2002, Iyohia 2011) negotiate each other. The chapter aims to explain the way the state–knowledge–law nexus operates in the context of CAM, to identify tensions and potential in that operation, and finally to point towards an alternative pathway that might allow the alternative knowledge base (or disciplinary ecology) of CAM to have a greater impact on its own patterns of governance. I hope the chapter will invite a reflection on how CAM mimics and resists mainstream biomedicine in the context of research, and about the way legitimation can iron out distinctiveness.

I come to CAM research's engagement to regulation from the perspectives of socio-legal studies. To be brief, socio-legal scholarship is an interdisciplinary field that has long assumed an outsider's perspective on law (Riles 1994) as well as an interest in 'law in action' as much as in 'law in the books'. Socio-legal scholars have examined the way law (mainly positive law, see Constable 2008) is experienced in its 'trenches', that is, from below, or from an outlaw's perspectives. More recently, socio-legal scholars have also began to study law's 'ivory towers' – that is, they have approached law by self-consciously describing it from the top down by paying attention to the actors that craft law's legitimacy and power. Some socio-legal scholars have employed their empirical, theoretical, doctrinal, and critical tools to examine the relationship between law and other privileged professions, such as medicine (Feldman 2000, Jacob 2012, Cloatre 2013). The field of socio-legal studies also increasingly converses with science and technology studies (Valverde 2003, Faulkner *et al.* 2012, Cloatre and Pickersgill 2014).

This chapter is based on a literature review on the topic and does not make empirical claims, although it is inspired by fieldwork begun in 2010 in the milieu of research governance (Jacob 2014).[2] With respect to the concept of *knowledge* of biomedical and CAM research, I try to adopt a middle-ground approach: I aim to surpass the rehearsed distinctions found in legislation and policies about scientific vs. non-scientific knowledge, and to encompass less formal and official modes of knowing, but I do not aim to discuss high-level epistemological debates as to what counts or should count as 'knowledge'. I hope readers will forgive the loose ways with which I engage with that division. In fact, if you are reading this handbook you are probably accustomed to this problem and struggle with it, as it seems endemic to any conversation about CAM. So, what indeed does constitute CAM knowledge?

II CAM knowledge and CAM rhetoric

Historian Roberta Bivins suggests that to have medical systems, theories, and practices that can 'be regarded as "alternative" one must have a recognized, definable, and at least relatively stable orthodoxy to which they oppose themselves' (Bivins 2010: 171). In other words, the world of CAM itself would be founded on a binary, as discussed in the introduction to this handbook. This is illustrated at several junctures in this chapter. In practice, Bivins' observation means that 'boundary-work' constitutes, unavoidably, an important part of the self-fashioning of CAM knowledge. Initially, 'boundary-work' (Gieryn 1983) referred to the discursive practices of scientists as they stress their difference and superiority over less 'authoritative' forms of non-scientific knowledge. Since then, it has been interpreted more broadly, as a strategy taken up by a group, an institution, or profession (Gieryn 1983, Thomson 2013), to assert its epistemic authority, or perhaps even more generally its distinction, by working out boundaries around its expertise. Gieryn calls the resulting boundaries 'lines in the sand', hence highlighting how strategic and volatile they are. CAM proponents have shown up their distinct contribution in such ways.

For instance, the entire venture of CAM could not exist without a mode of opposition. Seventeenth-century 'empiricism', which was an alternative to the mainstream medicine of the time, explicitly showcased 'the promise of freedom, the bolster against tyranny, and the endorsement of individual ambition', and was associated with subversiveness against dogmas (Benedict 2001: 26–7). One interpretation of the genealogy of CAM knowledge (in the Western world) is that it emerged in the nineteenth century out of the holistic movement from within medicine, based on alternate models in medicine, including the biopsychosocial model. The tone of the proponents was resolutely oppositional. Holist thinkers also rapidly distanced themselves not only from orthodox, reductionist medicine, but from notions of 'medical progress' and modern technological civilization. They also criticized what they saw as the dehumanization of society (Weisz 1998: 75). Rosenberg notes that, throughout the twentieth century, well-known 'jeremiads against fragmentation, alienation, against reductionism of market-oriented social relations' (1998: 337) have at once paralleled and supported different forms of medical holism, such as the one put forward by some CAM approaches.

In addition, scholars of CAM have marshalled distinctions and binaries coming from within the field of CAM itself. Historian Roy Porter (1989) has provided the very useful distinction between the rhetoric and the practice of CAM. Self-fashioning is critical in the field. The very term 'alternative' carries positive baggage and can almost immunise CAM to critique in some ways. Who can be against a medicine that does things differently, is more informal, humane, context based?[3] The term 'natural', which is often associated with CAM, carries its own normative load (Anderson 2010). CAM researchers have described themselves as being 'on the edge' (Polich *et al.* 2010: 112). Note that in the context of this chapter, we should be wary not to associate CAM with necessarily progressive views and cutting-edge critiques of research and regulation, as CAM is also likely to produce romantic, conservative approaches to research which are suspicious of the mainstream for regressive, back-to-nature kinds of reasons.

Those who study CAM ought to pay attention to its alignment with the powerful rhetoric of alternativeness, and analyse them against CAM practices that can be rather conformist, mainstream, and mercantile (Porter 1989). CAM researchers have been agile at negotiating the boundaries between CAM and biomedicine, and position their CAM research on the spectrum of CAM therapies (Polich *et al.* 2010, Wolffram 2010). To do this, CAM researchers use 'scientific terminology', de-emphasize certain aspects of their work, highlight their 'conventionality' (Polich *et al.* 2010: 113), and compare themselves to the less mainstream, that is, distance themselves from alternative medicine and see themselves as closer to norms of biomedical research. Note that the boundary-work is also mobilized in opposite ways, in order to emphasize the dividends of the 'difference' that CAM offers (Micollier 2011: 59). These positionings, as we will see, extend to the engagement of CAM researchers with research regulation, and hence they are at the centre of this chapter.

The science-culture is another binary that is critical to the self-making rhetoric of CAM research. CAM researchers confront the assumption, particularly tenacious, that science is culture-free. Interestingly science and technology studies scholars have used the metaphor of magic to describe how science has managed to remain cut off from culture: 'laboratory science … still moves around the globe like a fetish, with its social relations conveniently erased. It seems to arrive with capitalism, "like a ship," then magically arrive elsewhere, just as powerful, packaged, and intact' (Anderson and Adams 2008: 182). This particular account might be over-stating the point, but it rightfully directs to the problems faced by knowledge that stands outside the 'intactness' of science. CAM knowledge, in contrast to science, is perceived as belonging to the sticky realm of culture, of religion and magic (Langford 1999). As mentioned above, CAM researchers often use boundary-work to distance themselves from culture and align themselves with science.

However, again, we ought to remain careful not to caricature the difference between bio-medicine and CAM. Science is increasingly aware of its cultural specificity and attuned to post-modernism (see Saks 1998). As an illustration, the Cochrane Collaboration defines CAM as a domain of healing resources 'other than those intrinsic to the politically dominant health system of a particular society or culture in a given historical period' (Zollman and Vickers 1999: 693). 'Boundaries', as it reads in this *British Medical Journal* article, 'between the CAM domain and that of the dominant system are not always sharp or fixed' (Zollman and Vickers 1999: 693).

In the next sections, I will discuss the connection, and possible mismatch, between CAM research and the regulatory benchmarks of science – in particular, the randomized controlled trial. This dissonance is illustrated, but also modulated, when looking at state-sanctioned hierar-chies of evidence. Next, I will contextualize the discussion within the larger issue of the state's commitment towards science. I will conclude that. contrary to common wisdom, the norms and practices of CAM research make it more similar in form and technique to biomedical research than we might think. The puzzle for CAM, then, may well lie in how to translate the alterna-tiveness of its knowledge into genuinely alternative research practices. CAM knowledge-makers might ask themselves whether they can and should contribute to further defining what it means to produce trustworthy knowledge, or enacting alternative research regulation.

III The regulation of non-CAM research and the scienticization of CAM

Let me turn to an overview of how non-CAM and CAM research is regulated. Mike Saks points out how the increase in scandals and misconduct in orthodox medicine (and arguably, medical research) has benefited CAM by keeping the spotlight on the deficiencies of the ethics and methods of orthodox medicine (Saks 2003; and see Porter 1989).[4] However, in the current climate of rising scrutiny from the public towards science, and of growing demands for account-ability and transparency in all public spheres, there are higher expectations about regulation and scrutiny in CAM research as well (Mills 2001).

Let us note at the outset that various commentators have highlighted that contemporary Western biomedicine is increasingly standardized (Timmermans and Berg 2003). The standards in question vary greatly; they can be mandated by state law, but can also be the product of private governance (Faulkner et al. 2012). The diversity in standards means that highly standard-ized medicine is not necessarily a more standard or universal medicine (Timmermans and Epstein 2010). The concept of 'regulatory objectivity' was crafted to refer to this currently dominant model of medicine (Cambrosio et al. 2006, Lewis and Atkinson 2011). 'Regulatory objectivity' is a new form of objectivity in biomedicine that generates conventions and norms through con-certed programmes of action based on the use of a variety of systems for the collective produc-tion of evidence (Cambrosio et al. 2009: 651). In line with the insights of science and technology studies, the theorists of 'regulatory objectivity' alert us to ensuing changes to biomedicine itself, not only to its so-called external regulatory environment. In other words, the regulatory frame-works on safety, human subjects, and so on (to which I turn to next) that may seem external to and imposed on biomedicine are in fact more and more *built-in* biomedicine. So-called external regulation from the field of law and ethics gets enmeshed with layers of intrinsic categorizations, classifications, and measurement regimes (Lezaun 2012), and thus co-produce biomedical knowledge itself (Jasanoff 2008). Today, research is governed *ex ante* through state, research councils, and sponsor guidelines, but also *ex post*, through state, non-state, and self-regulatory responses to scientific misconduct, as outlined below (EMRC 2011, ESF 2010).

1 Ex ante

The *Declaration of Helsinki*, drawn in 1964 but revised several times since 2008, is the first international instrument setting out principles governing research with human participants, whether mainstream biomedical or CAM research. The principles of the Declaration derive from the Nuremberg Code, drafted by judges in the Nuremberg Trial of Nazi war criminals.

Since then, the regulation of medical research, at the international, regional, and national level, has become a 'growth industry' whose voluminous documentation ironically comes in the way of good research practice (Mason and Laurie 2013: 648; see also Jacob and Riles 2007). The internationalization of research has complicated matters further (Anderson and Steneck 2011) by expanding even more the number and levels of regulation. It is beyond the scope of this chapter to offer a comprehensive précis of all the regulatory requirements that apply to modern research.

In Europe, the Additional Protocol to the Convention of Human Rights and Biomedicine Concerning Biomedical Research (2005) sets principles governing research with human participants. The Forum for National Ethics Council attempts to coordinate ethical reflection and to raise and maintain regulatory standards in medical research. The European Directive of 2001 relating to the implementation of good clinical practice in the conduct of clinical trials on medicinal products for human use has been implemented by member states. It has been criticized by professional bodies for causing a drop in clinical trials in Europe (Mason and Laurie 2013: 650, and see further below). In July 2012, the European Commission's proposal for a new European Clinical Trials Regulation replacing the Directive has been adopted. This new Regulation is expected to come into effect in 2016.

The UK regulatory framework of clinical research in the UK is not a coherent, across-the-board set of regulations (Dixon-Woods 2010). The main concerns of the UK legal framework and 'research governance culture' (Mason and Laurie 2013: 656) involve responsibility and accountability, as well as consent of participants. Since 1968, following the recommendation of the Medical Research Council, the regulation of medical research consisted of ethics committees (Boden *et al.* 2009, citing Committee of Privy Council for Medical Research 1964). The constitution of these local research ethics committees was sporadic and uneven until the first piece of formal guidance from the Department of Health in 1991 (Brazier and Cave 2011). The first UK piece of legislation consisted of the *Medicines for Human Use (Clinical Trials) Regulations 2004* (amended since) implementing the European Directive. The Department of Health published its Research Governance Framework for Health and Social Care in 2001, with an update in 2005. The Framework establishes the principle of good research governance and clarifies the arrangements for research ethics committees, in line with the legacy of the *Declaration of Helsinki*. An annex published in 2008 provides detailed guidance for areas of research that activate the application of the Mental Capacity Act 2005 or the Human Tissue Act 2004.

Another body of 'legislation, guidance and policy' (MHRA website 2012) is applied by the Inspection, Enforcement and Standards Division of the Medicine and Healthcare Products Regulatory Agency. The MHRA provides oversight over research in the form of trials on medicinal products, including herbal and homeopathic medicines. This set of regulation is thus relevant for CAM research and responds to three main stated policy concerns: first, the protection of subjects who participate in this research; second, the public interest in the safety of research; and third, the promotion of the research industry. The first two concerns are translated in licensing authorities that oversee research (Hervey and McHale 2004). However, the MHRA does not have oversight over research ethics committees. The third policy concern about the importance of promoting research industry is translated in regulatory requirements of speediness in the licensing and approval processes. The Good Clinical Research Practice Inspectorate is responsible for inspections of research practices (MHRA website 2012).

Recently, criticisms of the over-regulation of research have been voiced and, in 2010, the UK government mandated the Academy of Medical Sciences (AMS) to review the regulation of research with a view of radically simplifying the oversight process. Approximately at the same time though, the National Institute for Health Research published a new standards framework for local NHS research management. The stated objectives related to: 'Bureaucracy – cut red tape and gold-plating of regulation; Accountability – enable the public to hold public bodies to account; Efficiency – cut the costs of administration; and Autonomy – enable front line staff to use their professional judgment'.

In December 2011, the NHS launched a new organization with special authority, the Health Research Authority (HRA), whose purpose is to protect and promote the interests of patients and the public in health research. The HRA intends to work closely with the MHRA to 'create a unified approval process and to promote proportionate standards for compliance and inspection within a consistent national system of research governance' (HRA website 2012) The work of the National Research Ethics Service and of the National Information Governance Board's Ethics and Confidentiality Committee has now transferred to the new HRA.

Another body of rules that concerns both CAM and non-CAM research constitutes legislation regarding the transparency of public bodies (including publicly funded activities) and the handling of personal data. The remit of these legislations (Freedom of Information Act 2000, the Environmental Information Regulations[5] and the Data Protection Act 1998) far extends the domain of scientific research, and their importance was highlighted recently (House of Commons Science and Technology Committee 2011, Russell 2010). Research using personal data (for instance, patient data or samples obtained previously for another purposes) also needs to comply with the laws concerning privacy and confidentiality, as well as with relevant sections of the Human Tissue Act 2004 and its Codes of Practice, and related cases (Lowrance 2012, Mason and Laurie 2013). These legislative instruments all have the consent of the research participant as their 'primary policy device' (Mason and Laurie 2013: 679), while regulators such as the Health Research Authority's Confidentiality Advisory Group in the UK work to strike a balance between consent and the public interest value of research.

The Medicines Act 1968 sets its own requirements as to the quality, safety, and efficacy of medicines before they can be manufactured and put on the market. These regulatory requirements are significant to the ways researchers and their sponsors ought to conduct research on medicinal products. Herbal remedies and homeopathic products can be treated as ordinary medicinal products, but they also have access to a different scheme, the Traditional Herbal Medicine Registration Scheme (THMRS), which only requires proof of quality and safety, but not efficacy. Instead of efficacy (itself a contested term, which I will discuss below), other indicators are used, such as proof of traditional use for various lengths of time (Jackson 2012: 8–18). Such distinct product recognition thresholds signal different, somewhat 'weaker' (Jackson 2012: 12) legal expectations for researchers, sponsors, and manufacturers of complementary and alternative medicines than for biomedical researchers working on conventional medicines.

The industry and other prominent research funders (the Medical Research Council and the Wellcome Trust in the UK, and the National Institutes of Health in the US) have enacted their own guidelines for the good conduct of research. In addition, the work of the researchers who are registered medics is governed by the General Medical Council (GMC), via its Guidance *Good Practice in Research* (2010) and *Consent to Research* (2010). Irrespective of the disciplines used in their research, researchers who are also registered professionals are bound by their regulatory bodies. Thus, in an analogous manner to medical researchers being regulated by the GMC, CAM researchers who are, say, licensed nurses, chiropractors, or osteopaths have their professional work regulated by their respective professional self-regulatory bodies (see McHale, this volume, Saks, this volume). In addition, complementary health care practitioners are represented as well as regulated by various groups, including the national voluntary regulator Complementary and Natural Healthcare Council, and others like the British Acupuncture Council or the Society of Homeopaths.

Last but not least is the requirement for clinical trials registration as a measure to maintain the integrity and transparency of research (Horton and Smith 1999, Abbasi 2004). In 2004, a consortium of medical journals, the International Committee of Medical Journal Editors (ICMJE), announced that all trials must register in a public trials registry as soon as it starts patient enrolment, in order to be considered for publication in those journals. It is increasingly recognized that underreporting of research can also be a form of research misconduct (Chalmers 1990). There are public trials registries, such as www.clinicaltrials.gov, which is sponsored by the US National Library of Medicine. In the UK, policy for mandatory registration and reporting of all clinical trials has been implemented via the National Institute for Health Research Clinical Research Network (NIHR CRN) Portfolio, a database of high-quality clinical research studies that are eligible for support from the NIHR Clinical Research Network in England in the UK. These public registries have entry criteria that are often not met by many clinical trials conducted worldwide. This in turn affects greatly the comprehensiveness and reliability of public registries. There are also private trials registries, such as the International Standard Randomised Controlled Trial Number (ISRCTN) registry, hosted by the commercial company Current Controlled Trials (www.controlled-trials.com). These are freely available to the public.

2 Ex post

The UK does not have state regulations overseeing publication, authenticity, and conflicts of interests in research practice. However, different advisory bodies have attempted to define research integrity (Jacob 2013) and to apply definitions to real-life cases. For instance, an international charity which started as a local group in London, the Committee on Publication Ethics (COPE), is providing advice to editors about good practice and research integrity in publishing. Many national or regional agencies, such as the UK Research Integrity Office (UKRIO), act as advisory bodies for researchers and the researchers' institutions, whereas their US, Danish, and Norwegian counterparts[6] have regulatory as well as advisory powers (ENRIO 2014). Research funders also publish guidance about research integrity. Various possible regulatory and non-regulatory responses to occurrences of research misconduct are increasingly debated in the UK,[7] as well as internationally.

The three-prong definition of research misconduct was initially comprised of fabrication, falsification, and plagiarism (LaFollette 1992), but it has since expanded to include: ghostwriting, gift authorship, non-disclosure of conflict of interests, and data editing (Edmond 2008). It has been argued that biotechnologies themselves have prompted novel regulatory and ethical problems (Oliver and Montgomery 2009). For instance, technological breakthroughs generate new ethical questions about genetic engineering, cloning, reproductive rights, and informed consent; industry–university joint ventures pose problems of conflict of interests and disclosure of financial agreements; advances in electronic publication prompt questions about proprietary knowledge and authorship claims. According to this view, the traditional and 'natural' aspects of CAM would make it less vulnerable to certain newer forms of research misconduct. But note that research misconduct is not in itself a new issue: for instance, the falsification of data is an old problem which can now be expressed in new forms – for example, via image or gels manipulation. In this sense, there is no reason to think that CAM research is immune to basic forms of research misconduct.

In the US context, it has been argued that there is a lack of regulatory oversight of CAM therapies (e.g. chiropractic, acupuncture, traditional oriental medicine, and massage therapy) with respect to the protection of human subjects and of animal populations (Cohen and Schachter 2004). From a scoping overview of the field thus far, it is notable from the outset that CAM researchers have in general created little infrastructure for implementing research integrity and dealing with research misconduct.

In the field of publication ethics, a recent study on journals retractions published in Medline (Wager and Williams 2011) found no retraction coming from CAM journals during 1998–2008 (although it is important to note that not all CAM journals are published on Medline). Between 1997 and 2011, amongst the hundreds of reported cases discussed by the Committee on Publication Ethics (COPE),[8] only one relates to CAM: a case of homeopathy research on AIDS.

Despite the Complementary and Natural Healthcare Council's own statement that decisions made by the investigations committee on conduct and competence will be made available on its website, as of January 2015, only one conduct and competence case had been reported (let alone research conduct cases) on the online database.[9] As US research integrity experts Rennie and Gunsalus (2008: 30) suggest, in the context of research misconduct, an absence of reported cases is more likely to signal a lack of oversight than the absence of misconduct. There is, however, some evidence of infrastructure – for instance, at the National Council for Osteopathic Research, which has published a Research Governance Framework in 2007. The Health Professions Council (which is not a specifically CAM regulator, but regulates, amongst others, art and music therapists) has an easily accessible database of all fitness-to-practice cases, including those related to research activities.

The engagement of CAM research with regulation that we have reviewed so far indicates a one-way, top-down regulator–regulatee relationship, one in which a body of knowledge and knowledge-makers is under regulatory oversight. What kinds of regulatory conversations are taking place between CAM researchers and state and non-state regulators of research?

IV Regulatory engagements

The chapter now turns to exploring how CAM research fares in a highly standardized world, and in the face of biomedicine tailored by 'regulatory objectivity' as referred to earlier. Critical questions to be addressed include: Does the claimed 'alternativeness' of the knowledge base of CAM demand alternative definitions of research conduct and of research governance? In CAM and non-CAM contexts, how do people innovate by crafting alternative and complementary regulatory frameworks? Is the field of CAM not an ideal place to *begin* to rethink the way trustworthy knowledge is produced? Can CAM contribute to thinking about the ways in which research should get regulated by state and non-state actors? Indeed, the idea of an alternative way to do medicine that could positively inspire an alternative way to regulate is not new. This idea developed nearly two decades ago, when pioneering legal scholars of CAM, Julie Stone and Joan Matthews, pointed out the need for a 'holistic regulation' (1996: 291) and 'spectrum approach to regulation' (215) as a way to govern complementary medicine. Despite all this, in the context of CAM, the idea of an alternative mode of caring and doing research has not yet triggered a profound rethinking of the idea of research governance and research conduct. Interestingly, the term 'holistic research governance' was used recently in a leading medical law textbook (Mason and Laurie 2013: 679) in reference to new approaches to regulating research that emphasize a broader engagement with ethical, legal, and social implications (ELSI) of biomedicine and to a *reflexive* governance approach that sees research as a partnership between researchers and participants.[10]

The CAM literature is divided as to whether CAM research should follow the same standards as Western biomedical research: some highlight the 'mismatch' between CAM knowledge and the randomized control trial, as mentioned above, and some, to the contrary, go to great lengths to explain the need for robust RCT to provide a research base for CAM knowledge. The 2008 Report of the Department of Health Steering Group on the Statutory Regulation of Practitioners of Acupuncture, Herbal Medicine, Traditional Chinese Medicine and Other Traditional Medicine Systems Practised in the UK (the 'DH Steering Group') illustrates the ambivalence of CAM proponents towards the 'regulatory' force (Cambrosio *et al.* 2006, Micollier 2011) of the RCT. In its discussion of the need for a 'robust evidence base' for these practices, the Steering Group interestingly refers specifically to the European Directive on Traditional Herbal Medicinal Products, which notes that: 'The long tradition of the medicinal product makes it possible to reduce the need for clinical trials insofar as the efficacy of the medicinal product is plausible on the basis of long-standing use and experience.'[11] Yet, when the 'hard' evidence of randomized clinical trials is available and shows the internal and external validity of a technique (for example, for Chinese herbal medicine and acupuncture), the Steering Group seems to uncritically embrace this RCT evidence, and finds it 'essential' in order 'to establish further the safety and effectiveness of these forms of intervention' (DH Steering Group 2008: 25). Whilst RCT could be thought essential for the *further* establishment of safety and effectiveness without being thought essential for establishing the efficacy of a CAM product, reducing the need for RCTs and then claiming that they are essential for establishing effectiveness sounds contradictory.

In addition, looking at what CAM researchers had to say about complementary and alternative ways of knowing and researching, there appears to be a high degree of methodological and theoretical conservatism in the writings on research ethics (Ernst 1994, 1996, Van Haselen 2006, Tilburt and Kaptchuk 2008), including, for instance, a straightforward application of the four bioethical principles of Beauchamp and Childress (autonomy, justice, beneficence, non-maleficence) as a basis for research ethics (Ernst 1996).[12] Social scientific and in particular science and technology studies work on CAM seem by far more critical of how knowledge is researched, regulated, and marketed both in RCT and in CAM contexts (Adams 2002, Kim 2007). In other words, whilst there could be a window of opportunity for more critical distancing from the mainstream model of building and governing research, in academic CAM journals, for instance, what one finds is rather a repeating of the well-rehearsed axioms of mainstream biomedical and bioethical thinking (Cohen and Schacter 2004, Mills 2001). As often is the case in legitimation through regulation, when one might expect to see alternative regulatory principles and ethical frameworks, what one gets is rather the reinforcing of mainstream norms.

V Resistance or compliance? Randomized controlled trials and their ir/relevance to CAM

In 2000, the House of Lords Select Committee on Science and Technology stated:

> Very little high-quality CAM research exists; reasons for this may include: a lack of training in the principles and methods of research; inadequate research funding and a poor research infrastructure within the CAM sector. Another contributing factor may

be methodological issues, with many CAM practitioners believing that conventional research methods are not suitable tools with which to investigate CAM.

A major implication of the 'regulatory objectivity' referred to above is medicine's normative commitment to the RCT as gold standard for both conventional biomedicine and CAM (Cambrosio *et al.* 2006, Moreira and Will 2010).

Still CAM researchers and practitioners have long highlighted the differences between biomedical and CAM knowledge, and complained about the limits and inadequacy of biomedical 'evidence base' methods to evaluate CAM therapies. At the outset, CAM researchers and practitioners sometimes use 'terms and ideas that are not easily translated into Western scientific language' (Zollman and Vickers 1999: 695). They have advocated a 'methodological pluralism' (Callahan 2004, Cohen 2003) to account for the epistemological diversity that characterizes medical knowledge broadly understood, including different forms of CAM. To them, biomedical research methods – including their gold standard, the randomized controlled trial – despite adequately testing biomedical treatments and drugs, are ill suited to properly assess many CAM therapies.

In order to prove its efficacy and effectiveness under the terms of modern scientific standards, research in CAM must often stay in synch with the dominant scientific paradigms of the time, and science's own theoretical conservatism. To fit within the scientific paradigm, researchers in CAM often have to proceed against hierarchies of evidence, and literally reverse the normative order of biomedical testing. Let us use as an example the biomedical investigation of a drug, which usually proceeds from chemical and animal experiments first, and then moves on to clinical experiments. In order to align themselves with these biomedical conventions, some researchers in Korean medicine and Chinese medicine, for example, have translated their observations and anecdotes, in other words their clinical evidence, into chemical and animal experiments (Kim 2007: 871, Lei 1999). By doing so, these CAM researchers attempt to show the scientific relevance of their alternative, so-called 'cultural' knowledge capital to the biomedical community, whilst at the same time building on that biomedical community's own cultural tradition.

The RCT gold standard also shows its epistemological limitations if we further problematize the binary that posits CAM's personalization of medicine in opposition to the standardization of Western biomedicine. For instance, if we look at what CAM and mainstream medicine have in common, rather than at what sets them apart, we can clearly see a misalignment between the RCT and what it is cut to measure in *both* CAM and mainstream medicine. It may not be possible to translate faithfully the long-term clinical and experiential evidence developed in traditional and indigenous forms of medicine into scientific knowledge through a short-term RCT. But the RCT is not limited solely with respect to assessing CAM. Analogies have been drawn in this sense between CAM and the medical specialization of surgery. To assess the validity of surgery, it is not advisable to rely on clinical trials; instead, it needs to be experienced, that is, done again and again, hands-on, as well as taught and observed by peers over many years (Institute of Medicine 2005). In surgery, medical value and knowledge is attributed to a specific person, healer or professional, who performs the therapeutic act in question. In the field of surgery, the same procedure done by an experienced surgeon is not the same as by any other surgeon (Institute of Medicine 2005: 126). A given procedure, which can be scientifically proven as efficacious, might be effective only if a specific, experienced surgeon performs it. This is likely to also be the case with many CAM therapies. The CAM–surgery analogy further shows the slipperiness of the binary between CAM and science as they are ordinarily understood.

At this point, it is worth having a look at state-sanctioned hierarchies of evidence, which highlight the difficulties of differentiating biomedical knowledge from CAM knowledge, and the limits of evidence methods to trace such boundaries. The hierarchies of evidence can also offer a point of entry for opening a larger debate on the relevance of finding a scientific basis for CAM.

State-sanctioned hierarchies 'rate the strength of a body of published data on a specific test or treatment', for the purpose of providing 'recommendations' for the use of 'preventive interventions in office-based clinical practice' (Institute of Medicine 2005: 94–5). Clinic practitioners, health organizations, and 'patients' or 'payers' tend to pay close attention to them. In *CAM in the United States* (2005), the Institute of Medicine (IOM) discussed how these state-sanctioned hierarchies of knowledge get negotiated and used. In the UK, according to the National Health Service's Centre for Evidence-Based Medicine, the hierarchy of evidence depends on 'the study design, the number of studies in the body of evidence, and the consistency of study results' (Institute of Medicine 2005: 96). The UK hierarchy of study designs suggests the following descending order:

> the combined results of several randomized controlled clinical trials (RCTs) receive the greatest weight in evaluating treatment effectiveness. The results of a single, well-designed RCT is given the next greatest weight. The combined results of observational studies or other non-RCT study designs comes next, followed by case series or anecdotal reports, and professional judgment or consensus.
>
> *(Institute of Medicine 2005: 96)*

By contrast to the UK hierarchy, the US Preventive Services Task Force (under the Agency for Healthcare Research and Quality, Department of Health and Human Services) does not hierarchize methods per se: 'it does not use a hierarchy of study designs ranging from the most powerful (randomized clinical trials) to the weakest (case series)'. Instead, it uses the generic characteristics of a study (e.g. 'well designed') (Institute of Medicine 2005: 94–5). In theory, this would means that a rigorous, 'well designed' case, if suited to evaluate a given treatment, could rank high in the hierarchy. In addition, the hierarchy is described as a 'hierarchy of rating of the strengths of recommendations' rather than of evidence.

In another report, the Institute of Medicine (2001) explained how the distinction between treatment effectiveness and treatment efficacy can affect levels of evidence. Whereas efficacy refers to the ability to produce measurable desired medical results in 'experts' hands' – that is, in laboratories or in controlled contexts like the RCT – effectiveness refers to this ability in the daily routine practice of medicine, with unselected clinicians and patients. In other words, efficacy is about what a treatment *can* do in ideal circumstances, and effectiveness is what it actually *does* in daily use.[13] In the milieu, it parallels the distinction between explanatory studies (focused on efficacy) and pragmatic studies (focused on effectiveness). Namely, the IOM states that, if evaluating treatment effectiveness, 'the results of a single well-designed outcomes study should be considered to be as compelling as the results of a single well-controlled randomized trial' (Institute of Medicine 2001). This modulation by the IOM on levels of evidence, induced by the efficacy vs. effectiveness distinction, highlights the methodological need to examine the practical and subjective aspects of treatment. This could be read, in principle, as an approach more sympathetic to CAM. However, efficacy and effectiveness are understood as not exclusive of each other, but cumulative. Hence proving *both* efficiency and effectiveness can constitute a high threshold for CAM therapies to meet. For instance, a narrow study of physiological value (efficacy) of a CAM technique or treatment would say little about its effectiveness in real practice, although it could still produce a body of evidence that would give it credit (see Weisz 2011). It has been noted that, because of the placebo effect, any non-efficacious technique or treatment could be found to be effective in certain situations (UK Select Committee on Science and Technology 2010). I cannot provide here a full account of the power, complexity, and mystery of the placebo effect (Harrington 1999), but the fact that it applies to both CAM and mainstream medicine further erodes the strict binary between the two.

The state-sanctioned hierarchies of evidence also shed light on the limitations of the gold standard of biomedical knowledge as a measuring instrument for *both* biomedical and CAM therapies and treatments. Read carefully, state-sanctioned hierarchies support a moderate form of 'methodological pluralism' (Callahan 2004, Cohen 2002–3; see also Welsh *et al.* 2004). They back *measuring* tools and *measureable* therapies that stand outside of the highly controlled contexts of laboratory science. In addition, they show how under the normative conditions of evidence-based medicine (Weisz 2005, Cambrosio *et al.* 2006, Moreira and Will 2010), even mainstream medicine can be, as we saw in the case of surgery, closer to CAM than we might think. In this sense, the hierarchies contain built-in openness to CAM, throughout explicit and implicit analogies with non-CAM knowledge.

Seen in the context of the state–law–science nexus, they indicate that the state is, in principle, less directly hostile to CAM knowledge than some accounts might suggest, and they even highlight potential ammunition for those who wish to push a regulatory and scientific agenda for CAM. This is especially true given that the nexus is itself contestable and contested.

VI Avenues for recognition? CAM research and its nexus with the state

In the UK in 2000, the House of Lords Select Committee on Science and Technology emphasized the need for a stronger scientific research base in CAM, especially in relation to efficacy and safety of CAM. Further, the Committee had explicitly stated that:

> [m]any CAM therapies are based on theories about their modes of action that are not congruent with current scientific knowledge. That is not to say that new scientific knowledge may not emerge in the future. Nevertheless as a Select Committee on Science and Technology we must make it clear from the outset that while we accept that some CAM therapies, notably osteopathy, chiropractic and herbal medicine, have established efficacy in the treatment of a limited range of ailments, we remain sceptical about the modes of action of most of the others.

Ties with the state can be institutional: state funding for research; education training within recognized state institutions; 'legislative recognition, incorporation in various health policies, insurance coverage' (Iyioha 2009). They can also be less immediately tangible and more directly related to the knowledge base: informing state policies, being recognized as experts by tribunals, and slowly attracting the attention of public and private research funders and sponsors (cf. Pressman 1998).

The historian of medicine George Weisz is interested in understanding what exactly makes a 'therapy convincing in one national context and not in another' (2001: 451). In his work on the therapeutic use of thermal waters in twentieth-century France, he notes that students of regulation and professionalization of health practices often see, with good reason, power relationships and the market as the main drivers for regulation and professionalization. However, he pointedly warns that we should not forget the critical impact of medical and scientific validation itself; that is, not necessarily scientific validity itself (Iyioha 2011, Casey and Picherack 2001), but debates *on* scientific validity. 'Battles over the infusion of scientific medicine' in CAM is thus part of the fight for their legitimacy (Welsh *et al.* 2004: 217).

Further, Weisz (2001) highlights the usefulness of 'specialization' in national debates on the legitimacy of a field of knowledge. In the context of French debates over the legitimacy of hydrology, and over whether spa and thermal waters treatment should be covered by national health insurance, for example, Weisz points out that specialization broke down broad claims and categorized them into different expert claims. In this case, specialization, by reducing the scope of claims, made them more convincing for clinicians, who tended to be sceptical towards general, grand statements: 'It is perhaps the very excess of these successes that awakens our mistrust to some degree', a doctor was reported to write about hydrology in 1911 (Weisz 2001). In other words, claims that are carefully tailored, toned down, modulated, and coming from a restricted specialist field would be more convincing.

'State law's espousal of science' (Santos 2002, Iyioha 2011) is, to many, critical to the history of exclusion of alternative knowledge systems, whether within or outside the health care domain (Iyioha 2009; see also Polich *et al.* 2010): 'Historically, state law has been known to espouse the dictates of science, and science, bolstered by the force of law, has been deployed as a tool of exclusion of nonwestern medical norms', writes Iyioha (2011: 8; see also Cohen 2004). The emergence and current domination of evidence-based medicine (EBM) further consolidated an epistemological commonality between law and science which goes back as far as the seventeenth century: a 'concern with degrees of certainty or, in more modern terminology, probability' (Shapiro 1983: 168), manifest in 'emphasis on the grading of evidence on scales of reliability and probable truth' (168). As an enveloping, encompassing paradigm, EBM is more controversial than biomedicine: its goal is to trim down as much as possible what it calls 'biases', that is, any knowledge that is intuitive and unsystematic (EBM Working Group 1992, as cited in Micollier 2011; see also Timmermans and Berg 2003). Further drawing on Iyioha, these current conditions mean that science 'sits at the root of the efficacy, safety and regulation debate on CAM' (2011: 8), and that state validation of CAM – via political, economic, statutory, and judicial recognition – and scientific validation go hand in hand. Those who pursue CAM research and work at situating CAM within the large domain of scientific research are at the forefront of this problem.

There are, however, ongoing debates about whether CAM therapies can be recognized unless they can demonstrate that their knowledge passes scientific evidential tests. Willis and White (2004) on their part, rather speak of 'clinical legitimacy'; to them, the patronage of therapy (like that of Prince Charles for alternative therapies) and the loyalty of consumers willing to pay for CAM could outweigh scientific legitimacy as a basis for 'politico-legal legitimacy' (58).

In a positivist fashion, Casey and Picherack acknowledge that 'formal bureaucratic organizational status' clearly fosters 'credibility with the dominant structures of the day' (2001: 69). CAM research generally tends to lack such infrastructures. Building such institutional arrangements, and skilful handling of the legalistic language of guidelines, flowcharts, codes of conducts and the like, constitute powerful tools of legitimation. With its mimicking of the state's language and audits, the pharmaceutical sector offers a particularly telling illustration of this form of legitimation (Petryna 2007, Jacob and Riles 2007). In addition, and although it has been somewhat overlooked, what makes a certain type of medicine (or any type of discipline for that matter) flourish and look successful in a particular state is also its main proponents' flair and agility at institutional and bureaucratic politics and their ability 'to schmooze and negotiate with government bureaucrats' (see Riles 2012). This last point makes explicit that CAM is, like other bodies of knowledge, shaped by institutional and bureaucratic logics. Its knowledge is purportedly alternative and distinct. However, as we saw above, its approach to regulation tends to mimic that of mainstream biomedicine. Why is that so? Could it be different?

VII Concluding thoughts: alternative regulation?

As highlighted above, recent calls by medical law academics for a more 'holistic' governance of research (Mason and Laurie 2013: 679) resonate with Stone and Matthews' proposal for holistic regulation of CAM (1996: 291). In the conclusion, I would like to explore what an alternative regulation of research could look like.

Recent works on knowledge practices by science and technology studies scholars and anthropologists (e.g. Timmermans and Berg 2003, Gusterson 2003, and Blum 2009) have documented a refreshing willingness to critically revisit current scientific research governance and research integrity frameworks. As I have discussed elsewhere (Jacob 2011), these accounts provide open-minded engagement with other modes of producing and regulating knowledge that do not fit with the current research governance frameworks.

To take one example, historian of science Mario Biagioli (2003) has discussed a practical alternative to current research governance norms stemming from his work not on CAM but on mainstream science. This radical departure from the current normative framework of research governance in the area of authorship comes from the field of particle physics. Biagioli explains how, in 1998, the Collider Detector at Fermilab (CDF) Collaboration[14] members appointed their own committee to draft bylaws that would regulate the CDF research project with respect to authorship, responsibility, and credit. The CDF regulated on the basis of a 'labor mentality' that accumulates work credit, and is in stark contrast with the 'originality mentality' that prevails in IP and in biomedical science (ICMJE 1997). Think, for example, of the impact on authorship of the following rule on parental and sick leave policies: for up to a year, a member can have his or her name appear on all publications produced, 'based on research they may or may not have directly contributed to' (Biagioli 2003: 270). CDF also puts forward corporate, rather than individual, definitions of authorship, credit, and responsibility. Biagioli conceived of the possibility to redefine these regulatory concepts as a product of the specific 'disciplinary ecology' (2003: 273) of particle physics: for example, highly bureaucratic internal structure, small size, people working together in the same site (in contrast to clinical trials in biomedicine, where co-authors may never meet each other).

I find the example of the CDF useful for thinking about CAM research regulation because of the boldness with which particle physics researchers and research administrators rewrote mainstream regulatory concepts, establishing their discipline as a genuine alternative. The example is also useful because CDF shows that research governance norms – in this case, norms of authorship – can hardly be universal, and ought to be linked to the 'disciplinary ecologies' of fields and practices. Although much CAM research derives out of insights from mainstream scientific research, I suspect some forms of CAM research have many distinct features it could build upon while thinking about its own norms of research governance.

Hence the importance of recalling Porter's (1989) critical point, on the value of examining the self-representation of CAM, in light of CAM practices. There is currently very little CAM-ness with respect to research governance per se. Explanations for this could be that CAM research is under-funded and barely surviving, and that in this context, proposing a radical, transformative alternative is a luxury the CAM research community cannot afford. At the CAM conference *Regulation and Professionalization in Complementary and Alternative Medicine* in May 2011, I asked the question: Why do CAM researchers not take a more radical, alternative approach to research and, for example, rewrite codes of conduct for research like the CDF particle physicists did? The retort I received was that CAM researchers were less interested in creating new ways of thinking about research and regulation than about getting standard EBM to recognize them. This of course resonated with the 'old' problem of negotiating the tension between innovation, recognition, and regulation. Nevertheless, one cannot help but wonder whether in the future we will witness more ethical–legal audacity on the part of those who practise and research alternative ways of caring and knowing.

Notes

1 I wish to thank the *Handbook* editors, Jean McHale and Nicola Gale, as well as Ruth Fletcher, Tsachi Keren-Paz and Michael Thomson for helpful comments. Part of the research was supported by AHRC grant no. AH/J008338/1 and by the Centre for Law Ethics and Society at Keele University.
2 Since 2010, I have been conducting ethnographic fieldwork for the quarterly Forum meetings of the Committee on Publication Ethics, and doing legal and archival research of General Medical Council research misconduct cases.
3 For an interesting analogy, see the discussion of Riles (2002) on alternative dispute resolution and its immunity to critique.
4 Already in the nineteenth century, the move towards alternative to regular medicine ('fringe medicine') was motivated by disappointment that orthodox medicine caused. Roy Porter (1989) describes how CAM in Europe were perceived as a radical dissent and presented themselves as 'the antithesis of an orthodoxy that could be accused of being no less therapeutically foolish then ethically and professional corrupt'.
5 2004/3391, pursuant to the European Communities Act 1972.
6 The US Office of Research Integrity, the Danish Committee on Scientific Dishonesty, and the Norway National Commission for the Investigation of Research Misconduct.
7 For instance, the joint conference on misconduct in 1999 in Edinburgh, the Research Integrity Futures Working Group (2010) and the Research Integrity Concordat (2012).
8 COPE is an international, London-based advisory body for editors as to how to handle cases of research and publication misconduct, including a forum for editors and publishers of peer-reviewed journals to discuss all aspects of publication ethics: http://publicationethics.org.
9 A Five-year Report of the CNHC covering the years 2008–2013 mentions that out of 86 complaints made to the CNHC, 'Two complaints were made by patients/clients of practitioners. One of these was resolved informally. The other complaint did not meet the threshold for referral.' (CNHC 2013)
10 Also known in the sociology of science as Mode 2 knowledge (Nowotny *et al.* 2001).
11 Directive 2004/24/EC.
12 Interestingly, in an editorial on the issue of research misconduct, the editor of the journal *Complementary Therapies in Medicine* committed to deal with the problem 'on a synergetic basis', a surprising, if not alternative, turn of phrase, admittedly rarely found in mainstream writings on research misconduct (Van Haselen 2006).
13 The IOM considered the importance of looking at how evidence fares in practice, and thus described the components of what an 'effectiveness RCT' study would include:

- light patient exclusion criteria;
- conducted in a range of treatment settings;
- treatment provided by the kinds of providers who would provide treatment in non-study settings;
- no elaborate data collection (e.g. extra lab test or imaging studies);
- analysis done on 'intention to treat' basis; and
- random assignment with one or more control groups.

(Institute of Medicine 2005: 96)

14 CDF is a consortium of institutions that provide staff and support the Fermilab laboratory. Potential members of CDF are selected by their home institutions to work at Fermilab for a specific period.

References

Abbasi, K. (2004) 'Compulsory Registration of Clinical Trials' 329 *BMJ* 637.
Adams, V. (2002) 'Randomized Controlled Crime: Postcolonial Sciences in Alternative Medicine Research' 32 *Social Studies of Science* 659–90.
Anderson, K. T. (2010) 'Holistic Medicine is not "Torture": Performing Acupuncture in Galway, Ireland' 29(3) *Medical Anthropology* 253–77.

Anderson, W. and Adams, V. (2008) 'Pramoedya's Chicken: Postcolonial Studies of Medicine', in: E. J. Hackett, O. Amsterdamska, M. Lynch, and J. Wajcman (eds) *Handbook of Science and Technology Studies*, Boston: MIT Press.

Anderson, M. and Steneck, N. (eds) (2012) *International Research Collaborations: Much to be Gained, Many Ways to Get in Trouble*, New York: Routledge.

Benedict, B.M. (2001) *Curiosity: A Cultural History of Early Modern Inquiry*, Chicago: Chicago University Press.

Biagioli, M. (2003) 'Rights of Rewards? Changing Frameworks of Scientific Authorship', in: M. Biagioli and P. Galison (eds) *Scientific Authorship*, New York: Routledge.

Bivins, R. (2010) *Alternative Medicine? A History*, Oxford: OUP.

Blum, S. (2009) *My Word! Plagiarism and College Culture*, Ithaca: Cornell University Press.

Boden, R., Epstein, D., and Latimer, J. (2009) 'Accounting for Ethos or Programmes for Conduct? The Brave New World of Research Ethics Committees' 57(4) *Sociological Review* 727–49.

Brazier, M. and Cave, E. (2011) *Medicine Patients and the Law*, 5th edn, London, New York: Penguin.

Callahan D. (ed.) (2004) *The Role of Complementary and Alternative Medicine: Accommodating Pluralism*, Washington: Georgetown University Press.

de Camargo, K. R (2002) 'The Thought *Style* of Physicians: Strategies for Keeping up with Medical Knowledge' 32 *Social Studies of Science* 827–55.

Cambrosio, A., Keating, P., Schlich, T., and Weisz, G. (2006) 'Regulatory Objectivity and the Generation and Management of Evidence in Medicine' 63(1) *Social Science and Medicine* 189–99.

Casey, J. and Picherack, F. (2001) 'The Regulation of Alternative and Complementary Health Care Practitioners: Policy Considerations', in: *Perspectives on Complementary and Alternative Healthcare: A Collection of Papers Prepared for Health Canada*, Ottawa: Public Works and Government Services Canada.

Chalmers, I. (1990) 'Under Reporting Research Is Research Misconduct' 263(10) *Journal of the American Medical Association (JAMA)* 1405–8.

Cloatre, E. (2013) *Pills for the Poorest, An Exploration of TRIPS and Access to Medication in Sub-Saharan Africa*, Basingstoke: Palgrave Macmillan.

Cloatre, E. and Pickersgill, M. (eds) (2014) *Knowledge, Technology and Law*, London: Routledge.

Cohen, M. H. (2002–3) 'Of Rogues and *Regulation*: A Review of *The Roles of Complementary and Alternative Medicine: Accommodating Pluralism*' 27 *Vermont Law Review* 801–15.

Cohen, M. H. (2003) 'Of Rogues and Regulation: A Review of the Role of Complementary and Alternative Medicine: Accommodating Pluralism' 27 *Vermont Law Review* 801–15.

Cohen, M. H. (2004) 'Regulating "Healing": Notes on the Ecology of Awareness and the Awareness of Ecology' 78 *St. John's Law Review* 1167–92.

Cohen M. H. and Schacter, S. (2004) 'Facilitating IRB Consideration of Protocols Involving Complementary and Alternative Medicines' 4(3) *Clinical Researcher* 12–16.

Complementary and Natural Healthcare Council (2013) *The First Five Years*, London, CNHC.

Constable, M. (2008) 'On the (Legal) Study *Methods* of our Time: Vico Redux' 83 *Chicago-Kent Law Review* 1303–32.

Department of Health Steering Group on the Statutory Regulation of Practitioners of Acupuncture, Herbal Medicine, Traditional Chinese Medicine and Other Traditional Medicine Systems Practised in the UK (2008) *Report to Ministers from The Department of Health Steering Group on the Statutory Regulation of Practitioners of Acupuncture, Herbal Medicine, Traditional Chinese Medicine and Other Traditional Medicine Systems Practised in the UK* (Chairman: Professor R. Michael Pittilo), Aberdeen, Robert Gordon University.

Dixon-Woods, M. (2010) 'Regulating Research, Regulating Professionals' 103(4) *Journal of the Royal Society of Medicine* 125–6.

Edmond, G. (2008) 'Judging the Scientific and Medical Literature: Some Legal Implications of Changes to Biomedical Research and Publication' 28 *Oxford Journal of Legal Studies* 523–61.

ENRIO (2014) *Members 2014*, map available at: www.enrio.eu.

Ernst, E. (1994) 'Research. Complementary Medicine: Changing Attitudes' 2 *Complementary Therapies in Medicine* 121–2.

Ernst, E. (1996) 'The Ethics of Complementary Medicine' 22 *Journal of Medical Ethics* 197–8.

European Medical Research Councils (EMRC) (2011) *White Paper II: A Stronger Biomedical Research for a Better European Future*, Strasbourg: European Science Foundation.

European Science Foundation (ESF) (2010) *Fostering Research Integrity in Europe*, www.esf.org/fileadmin/Public_documents/Publications/research_integrity_exreport.pdf (accessed 3 December 2014).

Faulkner, A., Lange, B., and Lawless, C. (2012) 'Introduction: Material Worlds' 39(1) *Journal of Law and Society* 1–19.

Feldman, E. (2000) *The Ritual of Rights in Japan: Law, Society, and Health Policy*, Cambridge: Cambridge University Press.

Fischer, F. (1990) *Technocracy and the Politics of Expertise*, Newbury Park, CA: Sage.

Gieryn, T. F. (1983) 'Boundary-Work and the Demarcation of Science from Non-Science: Strains and Interests in Professional Ideologies of Scientists' 48(6) *American Sociological Review* 781–95.

Golan, T. (2004) 'The Emergence of the Silent Witness: The Legal and Medical Reception of X-rays in the USA' 34 *Social Studies of Science* 469–99.

Gusterson, H. (2003) 'The Death of the Authors of Death: Prestige and Creativity among Nuclear Weapons Scientists', in: M. Biagioli and P. Galison (eds) *Scientific Authorship: Credit and Intellectual Property in Science*, London: Routledge.

Harrington, A. (ed.) (1999) *The Placebo Effect: An Interdisciplinary Exploration*, Cambridge, MA: Harvard University Press.

Hervey, T. and McHale, J. (2004) *Health Law and the European Union*, Cambridge: Cambridge University Press.

Horton, R. and Smith, R. (1999) 'Time to Register Randomised Trials' 319 *BMJ* 865–6.

House of Commons Science and Technology Committee (2011) *The Disclosure of Climate Data from the Climatic Research Unit at the University of East Anglia*, London: The Stationery Office Limited.

House of Lords Select Committee on Science and Technology (2000) *Sixth Report, Complementary and Alternative Medicine*, 21 November.

Institute of Medicine (IOM) (2001) *Gulf War Veterans: Treating Symptoms and Syndromes*, Washington, DC: National Academy Press.

Institute of Medicine (IOM) (2005) *Complementary Medicine in the United States*, Washington, DC: National Academy Press.

International Committee of Medical Journal Editors (ICMJE) (1997) 'Uniform Requirements for Manuscripts Submitted to Biomedical Journals' 277 *JAMA* 927–34.

Irwin, A. (2008) 'STS Perspectives on Scientific Governance', in: E. J. Hackett, O. Amsterdamska, M. Lynch, and J. Wajcman (eds) *The Handbook of Science and Technology Studies*, 3rd edition, Cambridge, MA: MIT Press.

Iyioha, I. (2009) 'In Search of Law's Residence: Towards the Creation of a Mosaic Healthcare State' 24(2) *Canadian Journal of Law and Society* 251–76.

Iyioha, I. (2011) 'Law's Dilemma: Validating Complementary and Alternative Medicine and the Clash of Evidential Paradigm', *Evidence-Based Complementary and Alternative Medicine* 2011, Article 389518.

Jackson, E. (2012) *Law and the Regulation of Medicines*, Oxford: Hart.

Jacob, M. A. (2011) 'But What Does Authorship Mean, Indeed? Open Peer Commentary' 11(10) *American Journal of Bioethics* 28–30.

Jacob, M. A. (2012) *Matching Organs with Donors: Legality and Kinship in Transplants*, Philadelphia: University of Pennsylvania Press.

Jacob, M. A. (2013) *Scientific Research Integrity: Background Paper*, London: Nuffield Council on Bioethics.

Jacob, M. A. (2014) 'Misconduct Hunting: Research Integrity via Law, Science and Technology', in: M. Pickersgill (ed.) *Knowledge, Technology and Law*, London: Routledge.

Jacob, M. A. and Riles, A. (2007) 'The New Bureaucracies of Virtue: Introduction' 30(2) *Political and Legal Anthropology Review* 181–91.

Jasanoff, S. (2008) 'Making Order: Law and Science in Action', in E. J. Hackett, O. Amsterdamska, M. Lynch, and J. Wajcman (eds) *The Handbook of Science and Technology Studies*, 3rd edition, Cambridge, MA: MIT Press.

Kim, Jongyoung (2007) 'Alternative Medicine's Encounter with Laboratory Science: The Scientific Construction of Korean Medicine in a Global Age' 37(6) *Social Studies of Science* 855–80.

LaFollette, M. (1992) *Stealing into Print: Fraud, Plagiarism and Misconduct in Scientific Publishing*, Berkeley: University of California Press.

Langford, J. M. (1999) 'Medical Mimesis: Healing Signs of a Cosmopolitan Quack' 26(1) *American Ethnologist* 24–46.

Lei, Sean Hsiang-lin (1999) 'From Changsan to a New Anti-Malarial Drug: Re-Networking Chinese Drugs and Excluding Chinese Doctors' 29(3) *Social Studies of Science* 323–58.

Lewis, J. and Atkinson, P. (2011) 'The Surveillance of Cellular Scientists' Practice' 6 *BioSocieties* 381–400.

Lezaun, J. (2012) 'The Pragmatic Sanction of Materials: Notes for an Ethnography of Legal Substances' 39(1) *Journal of Law & Society* 20–38.

Lowrance, W. (2012) *Privacy, Confidentiality, and Health Research*, Cambridge: Cambridge University Press.

Mason, K. and Laurie, G. (2013) *McCall and Smith's Law and Medical Ethics*, 9th edition, Oxford: Oxford University Press.

Micollier, E. (2011) 'Un savoir thérapeutique hybride et mobile: éclairage sur la recherche médicale en medicine chinoise en Chine d'aujourd'hui' 5(1) *Revue d'anthropologie des connaissances* 41–70.

Mills, S. Y. (2001) 'Regulation in Complementary and Alternative Medicine' 322 *British Medical Journal* 158–60.

Moreira, T. and Will, C. (2010) 'Introduction: Medical Proofs, Social Experiments: Clinical Trials in Shifting Contexts', in: T. Moreira and C. Will (eds) *Medical Proofs, Social Experiments: Clinical Trials in Shifting Contexts*, Aldershot: Ashgate.

Nowotny, H., Scott, P., and Gibbons, M. (2001) *Re-thinking Science: Knowledge and the Public in an Age of Uncertainty*, London: Polity Press.

Oliver, A. and Montgomery, K. (2009) 'Shifts in Guidelines for Ethical Scientific Conduct: How Public and Private Organizations Create and Change Norms of Research Integrity' 39 *Social Studies of Science* 137–55.

Petryna, A. (2007) 'Experimentality: On the Global Mobility and Regulation of Human Subjects Research' 30(2) *Political and Legal Anthropology Review* 288–304.

Polich, G., Dole, C., and Kaptchuk, T. (2010) 'The Need to Act a Little More "Scientific": Biomedical Researchers Investigating Complementary and Alternative Medicine' 32(1) *Sociology of Health and Illness* 106–22.

Porter, R. (1989) *Health for Sale: Quackery in England, 1660–1850*, Manchester: Manchester University Press.

Pressman, J. D. (1998) 'Human Understanding: Psychosomatic Medicine and the Mission of the Rockefeller Foundation', in: Christopher Lawrence and George Weisz (eds) *Greater Than The Parts: Holism in Biomedicine 1920–1950*, New York: Oxford University Press.

Rennie, D. and Gunsalus, K. (2008) 'What Is Research Misconduct?', in: Frank Wells and Michael Farthing (eds) *Fraud and Misconduct in Biomedical Research*, 4th edition, London: The Royal Society of Medicine Press.

Riles, A. (1994) 'Representing In-between: Law, Anthropology and the Rhetoric of Interdisciplinarity" 3 *University of Illinois Law Review* 597–650.

Riles, A. (2002) 'User Friendly: Informality and Expertise' 32 *Law and Social Inquiry* 613–19.

Riles, A. (2012) 'Is This Capitalism? If Not, Then What Is It?' *Cultural Anthropology*, May.

Rosenberg, C. (1998) 'Holism in Twentieth-Century Medicine', in: Christopher Lawrence and George Weisz (eds) *Greater Than The Parts: Holism in Biomedicine 1920–1950*, New York: Oxford University Press.

Russell, M. (2010) *The Independent Climate Change Emails Review*, available at: www.cce-review.org.

Saks, M. (1998) 'Medicine and Complementary Medicine: Challenge and Change', in: G. Scambler and P. Higgs (eds) *Modernity Medicine and Health: Medical Sociology Toward 2000*, London: Routledge.

Saks, M. (2003) *Orthodox and Alternative Medicine: Politics, Professionalization and Health Care*, London: Continuum.

Santos, B. S. (2002) *Toward a New Legal Common Sense: Law, Globalization and Emancipation*, 2nd edition, London: Butterworths.

Shapiro, B. J. (1983) *Probability and Certainty in Seventeenth Century England: A Study of the Relationships Between Natural Science, Religion, History, Law and Literature*, Princeton, NJ: Princeton University Press.

Stokes, E. (2012) 'Nanotechnology and the Products of Inherited Regulation' 39 *Journal of Law and Society* 93–112.

Stone, J. and Matthews, J. (1996) *Complementary Medicine and the Law*, Oxford: Oxford University Press.

Thomson, M. (2013) 'Abortion Law and Professional Boundaries' 22 *Social and Legal Studies* 191–210.

Tilburt, J. C. and. Kaptchuk, T. J.(2008) 'Herbal Medicine Research and Global Health: An Ethical Analysis' 86(8) *Bulletin of the World Health Organization* 594–99.

Timmermans, S. and Berg, M. (2003) *The Gold Standard: The Challenge of Evidence-Based Medicine and the Standardization of Healthcare*, Philadelphia: Temple University Press.

Timmermans, S. and Epstein, X. (2010) 'A World of Standards but not a Standard World: Toward a Sociology of Standards and Standardization' 36 *Annual Review of Sociology* 69–89.

UK Select Committee on Science and Technology (2010) *Fourth Report. Evidence Check 2: Homeopathy*, Science and Technology Committee Publications, House of Commons, 2009–10.

Valverde, M. (2003) *Law's Dream of a Common Knowledge*, Chicago: University of Chicago Press.

Van Haselen, R. (2006) 'Misconduct in CAM Research: Does it Occur?' 14 *Complementary Therapies in Medicine* 89–90.

Wager, L. and Williams, P. (2011) 'Why and How Do Journals Retract Articles? An Analysis of Medline Retractions 1988–2008' 37(9) *Journal of Medical Ethics* 567–70.

Weisz, G. (1998) 'A Moment of Synthesis: Medical Holism in France Between the Wars', in: Christopher Lawrence and George Weisz (eds) *Greater than the Parts: Holism in Biomedicine 1920–1950*, New York: Oxford University Press.

Weisz, G. (2001) 'Spa, Mineral Waters and Hydrological Science in Twentieth Century France' 92 *Isis* 451–83.

Weisz, G. (2005) 'From Clinical Counting to Evidence-Based Medicine', in: Gérard Jorland, Annick Opinel, and George Weisz (eds) *Body Counts: Medical Quantification in Historical and Sociological Perspective*, Montreal and Kingston: McGill-Queen's University Press.

Weisz, G. (2011) 'Historical Reflections on Medical Travel' 18(1) *Anthropology & Medicine* 137–44.

Welsh, S., Kelner, M., Wellman, B., and Boon, H. (2004) 'Moving Forward? Complementary and Alternative Practitioners Seeking Self-regulation' 26 *Sociology of Health and Illness* 216–41.

Willis, E. and White, K. (2004) 'Evidence-based Medicine and CAM', in: P. Tovey, G. Easthope, and J. Adams (eds) *The Mainstreaming of Complementary and Alternative Medicine: Studies in Social Context*, New York: Routledge.

Wolffram, H. (2010) 'An Object of Vulgar Curiosity: Legitimizing Medical Hypnosis in Imperial Germany' 67(1) *Journal of the History of Medicine and Allied Sciences* 149–76.

Zollman, C. and Vickers, A. (1999) 'What is Complementary Medicine?' 319 *British Medical Journal* 693–6.

CONCLUDING CHAPTER

Jean V. McHale and Nicola K. Gale

I Introduction

As we saw in the introduction to this handbook, the first hurdle with the topic of complementary and alternative medicine (CAM) is terminology. Stone reiterated this in her chapter:

> Attempting even to describe CAM as a single entity is problematic, save to the extent that professions which fall outside mainstream medicine have been lumped together, invariably in opposition to allopathic medicine (hence a politicised and contested nomenclature including 'alternative', 'non-traditional' and 'unconventional'). [...] CAM is defined more easily by what it is not than what it might be.
>
> *(Stone, at page 255)*

Nonetheless, the terms CAM and traditional medicines (TM) have currency in both the popular and policy arenas, and the legal and social science scholarship in this field has grown a great deal since the turn of the century. It was our intention to make the case for the importance of this scholarship because of its ability to challenge the current popular and policy debates, which have remained 'stuck' in a polarized and largely asocial discourse. It is our view, which has been illustrated by the contributions in the handbook, that introducing nuance and theorizing diversity in the field will provide a much more robust interdisciplinary evidence base for policy and practice in the field. In short, it is our hope, and intention, that we can help with this contribution to re/position the debates on practice, professions and the law, using interdisciplinary perspectives.

In this volume, we cannot claim nor indeed have we attempted to provide a comprehensive analysis of all the debates which arise in relation to CAM across jurisdictions, something which would clearly be impossible to effectively achieve. Moreover, each of the chapters themselves are necessarily shaped through the perspective of the individual authors. What the volume rather seeks to do is examine legal, sociological and historical perspectives which arise in relation to this area and in doing so start to unpick some of the complexity that characterizes the social and legal picture of CAM.

In this concluding chapter, we reflect upon the preceding parts of the book and explore some of the cross-cutting themes which have emerged from the volume, and we discuss what these may add to scholarship in this area, how they might shape future scholarship, and to the dialogue

374

between academia and policy. We have grouped these into: first, 'professions and regulation'; second, 'risk' and third, 'the CAM user as consumer'. Finally, we return to the issue of polarized debates in CAM and conventional medicine and summarize the contribution of the volume in breaking these down.

II CAM professions and regulation

Regulation in CAM has been one of the most vociferously debated issues in the policy arena, and as a topic it cuts across the parts of the handbook because it is closely linked to the question of what constitutes a 'profession' and how that varies in different parts of the world. This includes both the issue of what the knowledge claims are of that profession and the issues of what counts as a risk in the practice that might need to be regulated for. In terms of the literature, the professionalization of CAM has one of the most developed parts of the social science literature on CAM (Saks, this volume) and the chapters here move these debates forward by exploring and comparing legal and regulatory challenges posed by CAM in a range of different jurisdictions. What is striking is that, despite coming from different jurisdictional perspectives, there is notable commonality.

The drive to regulate has been driven both from the public and from CAM professionals themselves. Methods for the public to assess the competence of practitioners and to be assured of the safety of their practice – in short, public protection – underlies many of the demands for regulation. However, there are critics of this from within and outside of CAM. From within, some CAM practitioners argue that this sets up CAM practice as 'dangerous' or 'risky' when they argue that the risks are low, or that it threatens the counter cultural or 'alternative' nature of the practice by bringing it under conventional regulation mechanisms. From outside, those who doubt the effectiveness of CAM argue that regulation brings a false degree of legitimacy to the practice. This latter point leads on to the drivers from CAM professionals for regulation. Regulation is closely linked to professional identity because it shapes identity and perceived status and role through the structures it imposes. The process of professionalization and perceptions of professionalism are inevitably underpinned by debates concerning power and the societal structures of power (see Saks, and Wahlberg, this volume).

The debates concerning the regulation of CAM practice mirror the debates concerning the regulation of other areas of health care. The idea that 'caring' practitioners need to be regulated to facilitate competence and safety is reflected, for example, in the recent discussion in the UK concerning the role of health care assistants in hospitals following the Francis Inquiry into the failures of Mid Staffordshire Foundation Trust (Mid Staffordshire 2013). The need to go beyond self-regulation of professions, towards more formal and independent oversight is seen in the debates concerning the role of the General Medical Council (see McHale, this volume and the Shipman Inquiry 2004). Nonetheless, movement towards regulatory oversight in the context of CAM has been slow. We have seen that in relation to CAM there is a spectrum of regulatory possibilities (Saks, Stone, and McHale chapters, this volume). Regulation may impose formal statutory structures that, although emanating from the state, may have been developed in conjunction with the professional body itself. Alternatively, regulation may be of a more fluid nature, providing regulatory oversight but of a permissive rather than compulsory regulatory nature. Whatever the form, regulation by itself does not finally determine and resolve the characteristics of a profession.

The complexity of the interface between professions and the state through regulation has been explored in the volume in new ways. Welsh and Boon, for instance, have documented that, in the context of traditional Chinese medicine and acupuncture in Canada, legislative change by itself does not constitute social closure (Welsh and Boon, this volume). McHale has highlighted that, even where CAM professionals eschew formal regulatory structures (compulsory or permissive), they are still inevitably subject to some regulation. These regulations include the first accepted norms of practice within a professional group, and explicit regulation through common legal and regulatory principles which apply generically across a particular jurisdiction and which are not specific to a particular group. For example, principles of civil liability for harm or consequent criminal offences (McHale, this volume, pp. 52–54) still apply to CAM practitioners without professional regulation.

Chapters by Wainwright and Marandet, and Wilkinson and Gale have problematized the idea in much current health care policy debate that professionalism is necessarily dependent on regulation. The form and development of professional identity and professionalism in practice is first and clearly related to the learning environment, which is brought out by Wainwright and Marandet in their chapter on the geographies of learning spaces in massage and reflexology. They argue that the spatial awareness of the practitioner can facilitate and delineate the professional role, in both explicit and implicit ways that are structured by gender and class norms (Wainwright and Marandet, this volume). Wilkinson and Gale argue that professionalism in the form of robust clinical governance can be taught and implemented without presupposing formal regulation. This has implications for both professional ethics and the social organization and social closure of health care professions Wilkinson and Gale, this volume.

Finally, the boundaries between professional and other spaces, and the regulatory implications of these, are destabilized and challenged in the way that CAM is organized and practised, often in private clinics or in private homes. Interestingly, this is now not so unique to CAM; increasingly, with the growth of long-term conditions and the advent of new technologies, such as telehealth, a patient, consumer or client's home may in turn itself become a 'professional' space in both conventional and CAM approaches (Gale and Sultan 2013). While the 'place' and 'space' where conventional medical practitioners operate is increasingly the subject of regulation, in contrast, the regulation of practitioners themselves, as Stone suggests in the context of the discussion of the UK CQC, seems to be somewhat 'off the radar' (Stone, this volume, p. 60).

For future research, it is worth asking whether the delineation of professional identity and its relationship to regulation is truly different from the debates which arise in relation to lawyers and to accountants or indeed the accreditation of engineers and plumbers. It will be important to understand how the answers vary by jurisdiction or within different types of health space within jurisdictions. These kinds of research questions could be usefully addressed for CAM in collaboration with scholars working in other areas of the regulation of the professions.

III Risk

Alongside issues of professional identity, legitimation and regulation, the risk, or lack of risk, of CAM practices has long driven the debates about the appropriateness of statutory or voluntary forms of regulation. Key to this is whether CAM treatments are 'safe' and 'effective'. Safety is growing as an issue in conventional medicine and some of these concerns have also been raised about CAM, either through the direct risks of treatment or through the indirect risk of not receiving timely conventional treatment (Wilkinson and Gale, this volume). Effectiveness is highly controversial and it has been regularly argued that CAM treatments and medicines need to be subject to clinical trials to ensure that practice is based on evidence of efficacy and effectiveness.

The issue of safety is complex. While the level of complaints in relation to CAM practitioners seems low, there are risks, whether in relation to therapies themselves in specific contexts or potential harms caused by poorly trained or unethical practitioners (Stone, this volume, pp. 261–262; Alich, this volume). Here again issues in CAM practice can be seen as similar to those faced in relation to conventional medicine, albeit some years behind in their development. Alongside the growing dominance of a 'risk society', there has been, as Ayo Wahlberg noted in his chapter, a consequent growth of the audit culture in conventional medicine generally. This has been driven by a need to be seen to be putting their house in order. In the UK, this was largely the consequence of notable scandals in relation to conventional medical practice, from unsafe clinical trials, as in the case of Northwick Park, where a trial concerning medicinal products went disastrously wrong (The Expert Group on Phase One Clinical Trials 2006), to unsafe hospitals and poor standards of practice, as graphically illustrated in the UK in relation to, for example, the events of Bristol Royal Infirmary and Mid Staffordshire NHS Trust (Kennedy 2001; Francis 2013). It has taken many years for a culture of audit, accountability and transparency to be permeated through conventional medicine.

It was thus perhaps inevitable that these cultural changes are finding their way across to CAM practice (Wahlberg, this volume). It may be something which patients can come to expect as being a standard mode of practice and these mechanisms of assurance themselves are by no means the sole preserve of medical practice. Indeed, an audit and validation culture is something inherent in relation to other areas of 'professional' practice, from gas service engineers to builders. Ensuring effective governance is likely critical if CAM practitioners want to be further integrated into conventional health care systems that have already undergone this change, as Wilkinson and Gale (this volume) illustrate using the UK NHS as an example.

The dialogue in relation to risk and audit does not mean that CAM standards and those of conventional medical practice are yet aligned. As discussed above, the move towards such alignment of regulation and audit could be seen as an acceptance that a practice is 'risky', a position not universally supported because of the paradoxical notion that, while risk may be seen as a reason to limit practice, it is also the very fact that a practice is risky that may confer legitimacy. Monique Lewis argued in her chapter that the very fact that some medicines have potency (i.e. can have an effect) means they could be dangerous, and this has resulted in 'new-found medical meaningfulness' (Lewis, this volume, p. 174), which may contribute to the ultimate mainstreaming of herbal medicines in Australia. This has many parallels with the approach taken at European Union level in relation to herbal medicine. Bringing herbal medicine within the EU pharmaceutical regulation system and establishing an EU-level permanent committee to scrutinize this speaks to the dialogue of risk but equally to that of legitimacy, legitimation and continuity of therapies. Acceptability may also come from practitioners who experiment with new forms of practice not being held to be liable for malpractice, as we saw in relation to Ireh Iyioha's chapter in the context of the health freedom laws in the US and Canada and in relation to English medical negligence law as discussed by Jean McHale.

IV The CAM user as consumer

A prominent theme that cuts across the chapters is the notion of the CAM user as a consumer of health care services. Whether we frame the user of CAM as a patient, a consumer, a client or another term has social and legal implications. Contributions to this handbook have demonstrated that users have at once both a position of relative power (because of their ability to exercise choice in their purchase of health care services) and a position of embodied vulnerability (because of their need for care), although both vary considerably depending on the type of condition and the socio-political context.

Addressing first the issue that CAM is part of a medical marketplace and the 'consumer' can choose to exercise their spending power as they see fit: this may seem to be in tension with the counter-cultural aspirations of some users and practitioners of CAM (Gale 2014). While CAM may, by some, be seen in terms of a counterpoint to conventional medicine, in fact a holistic non-market ethos may in some circumstances be seen as illusory upon closer examination. As John Harrington has highlighted in the context of Kenya:

> contrary to the idealization of traditional medicine as a holistic non-market alternative to commodified biomedicine, it is clear that there is a stratified market for both forms of medicine in Kenya [...]. As one expert put it, in 'the urban areas healers compete with medical doctors as well as unlicensed for-profit clinics, in the rural areas they compete with poverty'.
>
> *(Harrington, this volume, p. 185)*

CAM must be seen as a business to the extent that, whatever the context, both complementary health treatments (CAM) and traditional and indigenous medicines (TM) are often only available in the context of the private sector. This may not necessarily be that different from conventional health care, which is increasingly being viewed in business terms as well (Collyer 2004). Indeed, the notion of health care as a public good rather than a commercial entity or provided through charity is in fact a comparatively recent historical development and limited to certain jurisdictions. Although there are clearly tensions, it should not be assumed that medical practitioners cannot equally be seen as pursuing a vocation *and* running a business. However, this does not mean that it is necessarily accurate to characterize the CAM user as a consumer, which implies a high level of autonomous decision making.

The capacity of patients to make such autonomous choices in relation to CAM has long been questioned (see Bivins, this volume). But such characterization can mean that we fail to properly engage with the characteristic of the consumer and of consumer choice and how real this is in practice. Several authors in this volume highlighted the vulnerability of CAM 'patients' as 'consumers'. So, for example, as Willis and Rayner note in their chapter, 'the context of infertility means that this group is most vulnerable to claims made by those who are offering services, and a market-based approach using, in particular, web-based advertising can prey on the vulnerability of this group' (Willis and Rayner, p. 120). This applies equally in the context of CAM therapies and in the context of those seeking conventional infertility treatment. Communication skills is something which has been highlighted by Bishop as something which is important and valuable for CAM patients and where much more can be done by CAM regulatory bodies and other areas where CAM is provided in relation to such things as 'patient-centered, relevant and accessible information about their standards and individual practitioners' (Bishop, p. 304). The type of consumer that the CAM user is is fundamentally context dependent and CAM users are both patients and consumers, in many ways similar to those of conventional medical treatments.

CAM users may be empowered to make broader choices concerning their care but equally they may be vulnerable. Vulnerability in relation to ill health and disability is something which is a common theme across conventional medical care and CAM therapies. There are innate tensions here with the dialogue of consumerism. We have seen in various chapters of this volume how across health care patients are being framed as 'consumers'. Patients are being encouraged to make choices; in the UK context, literally, to 'choose and book' services (Bishop, p. 292). What is notable is that, as Felicity Bishop's chapter suggests, many characteristics in choosing practitioners are aligned with those in relation to conventional medical care, gender, qualifications and reputation (Bishop, this volume).

The role and power of the health care user, whether of conventional or complementary and alternative medicines, is an area of great significance in legal and social studies and has already demonstrated its potential for disrupting the dominance of biomedicine – both because users have voted with their feet in terms of their use of CAM and because policy makers have been supporting a drive for greater patient involvement in the design of health care and in the genera-tion of evidence itself through involvement in health research (Ives *et al.* 2013). Research itself may provide an individual with the opportunity of care – but equally may contribute to the withdrawal of choices for care when treatments are not proven effective. Research involves, at times, unknown risks and research itself is an activity undertaken with the aim which goes beyond the individual and looks at the broader public who may benefit in the future. CAM itself, as Jacob illustrates in this volume, has an opportunity to engage with models of research and the research participant and to determine whether and to what extent new research govern-ance models may be appropriate, and this could include public involvement in research.

V Challenging the notion that CAM and conventional medicine are polar opposites

The idea that CAM and conventional medicine are in opposition to each other is of course a crude stereotype:

> As far as a discursive dichotomy between CAM and conventional medicine is concerned, and in terms of a clear preference affirmed for the latter, it does not lead to an actual rejection of conventional medicine; neither does it imply requiring it to change, since patients actually draw from the various approaches by making careful choices. The combined use of different types of medicine, not only by patients but also by some medical practitioners, leads us to believe that several types of medicine cohabit while enjoying varying degrees of power and legitimacy in a context of medical pluralism.
>
> *(Martin and Debons, this volume, p. 286)*

However, these concepts of 'opposition' are still regularly used in public and policy debates.

We argue that we may not be ready for a fundamental reconstitution of terminology and that, indeed while polar opposites may be problematic, being able to distinguish between medi-cines that operate in different spaces with different positions of power is still helpful. We believe that in order to move on, we must consistently challenge and interrogate the assumptions that underlie many debates and discussions. Their continued use and political currency means that they still have value as an object of study (hence the title of this handbook); however, the bin-aries seem to be more accurate socially, politically and economically than they are in terms of the actual content of the treatments themselves, or the legal frameworks that guide them, where there are few clear lines of distinction between different medical approaches. Furthermore, the variation of use and practice so dramatically over time and space makes essentialist definitions hard to sustain when bringing social scientific critique to this topic. For instance, the common assumption of the political dominance of conventional medicine is an assumption of time and of place, as has been highlighted by Harrington in his chapter on traditional medicine in Kenya. Cant and Watts' chapter on the use of CAM by the established health professional groups of nurses and midwives shows that it was, perhaps counter-intuitively, used as a means of enhanc-ing their own roles. Some nurses saw CAM as taking them back to a caring holistic approach to practice, to in effect the essence of nursing, rather than the nurse operating simply in a quasi-medical model as a technician (Cant and Watts, this volume).

Finally, the conception of CAM and conventional medicine as opposites masks the potential for both to change. CAM, like conventional medicine, can innovate and evolve. Changes may derive from the practitioner, from the place or from external considerations. The drives for 'integration' in the West have shown the potential for change on both 'sides' of the debate, although in practice have been 'more likely to maintain modernist and colonial structures and perpetuate social inequalities rather than challenge them' (Gale 2014, p. 812). Some forms of CAM practice if transplanted to a new jurisdiction then evolve in such a way as to be perceived as being 'hyphenated' or 'hybrids' of their original form, as Romila Santosh suggests in her chapter on the practice of Ayurveda in the UK. The very nature of a practice may evolve due to legal constraints or due to practical difficulties, such as obtaining herbal materials. In the context of Ayurveda, rather than stopping the practice, the legal regulation of herbal medicines led to practitioners taking different approaches (Santosh, this volume).

What remains uncertain is whether CAM practice itself will diversify in this way or whether, if increased legitimacy is sought, homogenized 'gold' standards backed by more formal regulatory structures inevitably become the norm. This will clearly vary across the world, and be affected not only by the goals and actions of practitioners, but the increased awareness of practice and treatments which the internet provides to the consumer. Movements to drive international standards and processes, through the World Health Organization and other cross-national bodies, may ultimately filter down to state level. Regulation of herbal medicines in the EU is one example (see McHale, this volume). Another example, as posed by Harrington, is the use of a very different area of law – that of intellectual property to preserve traditional approaches to medicines and treatments (see Harrington, this volume, p. 189). Stone and Matthews suggested almost two decades ago that there is a need for 'holistic regulation' (1996: 291) and Jacob in this volume has questioned whether alternative models for the governance of knowledge generation are needed. In practice, what has happened is that, where regulatory models have been developed, these can be seen very much as identikit models adopted from standard biomedical models of professional or research regulation. No alternative models have yet emerged. A future question for researchers is whether what we are dealing with is a gradual and inevitable evolution to a single definition of 'professionalism' and model of regulation that incorporates standard norms common across a range of professional groups, whether the regulation of professional services is different if it is 'health' or whether indeed it is different if it is CAM.

VI Concluding remarks

The image in Bivins' chapter of four physicians fighting over a patient is an evocative symbol of many of the social and legal issues raised in this handbook. With more changes afoot across the medical marketplace globally in the form of drives for regulation, governance, evidence-based practice, new financial management and patient involvement, the boundaries between 'complementary', 'alternative' and 'conventional' medicines are likely to become blurred in new ways. Dialogue across disciplines and a willingness to be open and to engage with these practices will give us a much more robust basis on which to make sense of these changes and develop both responsive and strategic laws and policies. Although this role for the state was noted at the turn of the century (Cant and Sharma 1999), the ways in which this challenge has been taken up has been severely limited due to the overreliance on biomedical evidence. In this volume, we demonstrate that a much richer tapestry of evidence, including from historical, social science and legal scholarship, can bring useful insights for policy makers about how risks are formed, then regulated, then used and embodied by patients/consumers who then go out and take decisions about their own bodies and health care.

References

Cant, S. and U. Sharma (1999). *A New Medical Pluralism?* London: UCL Press.

Collyer, F. (2004). 'The corporatisation and commercialization of CAM', in P. Tovey, G. Easthope and J. Adams (eds) *The Mainstreaming of Complementary and Alternative Medicine: Studies in a Social Context.* London: Routledge.

The Expert Group on Phase One Clinical Trials (2006) *Final Report.* London: The Stationery Office.

Francis, R. (2013). *Report of the Mid Staffordshire NHS Foundation Trust Public Inquiry*, HC 898–1.

Gale, N. (2014). 'The sociology of traditional, complementary and alternative medicine', *Sociology Compass* 8(6): 805–822.

Gale, N. and H. Sultan (2013). 'Telehealth as "peace of mind": embodiment, emotions and the home as the primary health space for people with chronic obstructive pulmonary disorder', *Health & Place* 21: 140–147.

Ives, J., S. Damery and S. Redwood (2013). 'PPI, paradoxes and Plato: who's sailing the ship?' *Journal of Medical Ethics* 39(3): 181–185.

Kennedy, I. (2001). *The Report of the Public Inquiry into Children's Heart Surgery at the Bristol Royal Infirmary 1984–1995: Learning from Bristol*, Cond. 5207 (I) 2001.

Shipman Inquiry (2004) *Fifth Report, Safeguarding Patients: Lessons from the Past, Proposals for the Future*, 9 December, Cm 6394.

Stone, J. and J. Matthews (1996). *Complementary Medicine and the Law.* Oxford: Oxford University Press.

INDEX

Page references to Figures will be in **bold**, while those for Tables will be *italics*. CAM stands for 'complementary and alternative medicine', while TM represents 'traditional medicine'. Page references to notes will contain the letter 'n' and relevant note number following.

conventional medicine and CAM 284–5; data collection and analysis 276; health insurance 276–81; LAMal (Swiss federal legislation on compulsory health insurance) 277, 278; literature review 272–4; medical pluralism 276–8; methodology 274–6; sampling 274–5
symptoms, as disease 17

Tataryn, D. J. 157n54
TCM *see* traditional Chinese medicine (TCM)
Temple, Sir William 15
TGA *see* Therapeutic Goods Administration (TGA), Australia
Thairu, Kihumbu 195n10
Thalidomide disaster (1960s) 23, 54
Therapeutic Goods Act (1966), Australia 212
Therapeutic Goods Act (1989), Australia 162, 174, 202, 203, 212
Therapeutic Goods Administration (TGA), Australia 162, 164, 208; and regulation of CAM 202, 204–5, 211, 212, 217, 218
Therapeutic Goods Advertising Code (TGAC), Australia 213, 221n2
Therapeutic Goods Advertising Code Council (TGACC), Australia 205, 211, 213
Therapeutic Goods Committee (TGC), Australia 205
Therapeutic Goods Regulations (1990), Australia 202, 203–4
therapeutic landscapes 309–11, 312, 317
therapeutic nihilism 17, 23
therapeutic potency 17
Thomson, James 66, 67, 68, 69, 71
Thomson, Jessie 67
time factors 6
TM *see* traditional medicine (TM)
Trade Related Intellectual Property Agreement (TRIPS) 190
trade restrictions, historical perspective 21–3
traditional Chinese medicine (TCM) 36, 37, 82, 83, 134, 163, 187; *see also* acupuncture; acupuncture and TCM, Canada
traditional herbal registration (THR) 75
traditional medicine (TM) 1, 229; defining 181–2; growth in academic study 3–4; in Kenya 7, 180–201; problematizing 191–5
Traditional Medicines Evaluation Committee (TMEC) 212
training and education: professional conduct 237; professionalization of CAM 35; shamanism 95–6; spiritual training 236–7
trait approach to professions 31
trance 89
Transitional Council of the College of Traditional Chinese Medicine Practitioners and Acupuncturists of Ontario (TC-CTCMPAO) 252

transparency 49
Trans-Tasman Mutual Recognition Arrangement (TTMRA), Australia 207–8
Trust, Assurance and Safety – The Regulation of Health Professionals in the 21st Century (Department of Health 2007) 37
trust issues 345–6
tuberculosis 65
Turnbull, J. 96, 344
Tuskegee Syphilis Study 24
Twigg, J. 313

UK Healers 237; Code of Conduct 239, 240
UK Research Integrity Office (UKRIO) 361
uniforms 313–14
United Kingdom 4, 41–60; as audit society 137; Ayurvedic medicine 74, 75, 76, 78, 82, 84, 85n9, 380; CAM provision and commissioning 260–1; clinical governance in 107n1; discerning CAM's aspirations in 255–7; historical perspectives 19–20, 21, 23, 24, 25, 32, 33; homeopathy in 322–5; Law Commission proposals 42, 48–52, 56, 58, 267n21; Medical Act (1858) 19–20, 32, 33, 64, 258; naturopathy in interwar Britain, status 63–73; NHS access to CAM services 346–7; nurses' and midwives' integration of CAM, in NHS hospitals 98–109; osteopaths and chiropractors 44–7; policy context 346–7; professionalization of CAM 34–7; relationship of CAM with state 257–61; research, nexus with the state 366–7; responsibility, accountability and courts 52–4; spiritual healing 233, 237; thalidomide disaster (1960s) 23; *see also* Care Quality Commission (CQC); Department of Health, UK; Medicines and Healthcare Products Regulatory Agency (MHRA), UK; Mid Staffordshire NHS Foundation Trust; professionalization of CAM; regulation of CAM in United Kingdom; Shipman, Harold/Shipman Inquiry (2004)
United States: Acts regulating medical practice 145; Army Medical Corps 20; Federal Drug Administration 163; and Germany 65–6; healthcare pluralism 144; historical perspectives 18, 20–1, 23, 24, 25, 33; lack of regulatory oversight 362; National Center for Complementary and Alternative Medicine 2; naturopathy 65, 66; Preventive Services Task Force 365; regulation of CAM 38; shamanism, First Nations communities 87, 88, 91–2; "Spiritual Warrior" retreat, Sedona (Arizona), 2009 93–4; *see also* health freedom laws, comparative analysis of Canada and US

vaccine therapy 18, 65
vaidyas 75, 84n7
Veatch, Robert 238